T0214784

Lecture Notes in Computer Science   10202

Commenced Publication in 1973
Founding and Former Series Editors:
Gerhard Goos, Juris Hartmanis, and Jan van Leeuwen

Advanced Research in Computing and Software Science
Subline of Lecture Notes in Computer Science

More information about this series at http://www.springer.com/series/7407

Marieke Huisman · Julia Rubin (Eds.)

Fundamental Approaches to Software Engineering

20th International Conference, FASE 2017
Held as Part of the European Joint Conferences
on Theory and Practice of Software, ETAPS 2017
Uppsala, Sweden, April 22–29, 2017
Proceedings

 Springer

Editors
Marieke Huisman
University of Twente
Enschede
The Netherlands

· Julia Rubin
University of British Columbia
Vancouver, BC
Canada

ISSN 0302-9743   ISSN 1611-3349   (electronic)
Lecture Notes in Computer Science
ISBN 978-3-662-54493-8   ISBN 978-3-662-54494-5   (eBook)
DOI 10.1007/978-3-662-54494-5

Library of Congress Control Number: 2017934067

LNCS Sublibrary: SL1 – Theoretical Computer Science and General Issues

Printed on acid-free paper

This Springer imprint is published by Springer Nature
The registered company is Springer-Verlag GmbH Germany
The registered company address is: Heidelberger Platz 3, 14197 Berlin, Germany

ETAPS Foreword

Welcome to the proceedings of ETAPS 2017, which was held in Uppsala! It was the first time ever that ETAPS took place in Scandinavia.

ETAPS 2017 was the 20th instance of the European Joint Conferences on Theory and Practice of Software. ETAPS is an annual federated conference established in 1998, and consists of five conferences: ESOP, FASE, FoSSaCS, TACAS, and POST. Each conference has its own Program Committee (PC) and its own Steering Committee. The conferences cover various aspects of software systems, ranging from theoretical computer science to foundations to programming language developments, analysis tools, formal approaches to software engineering, and security. Organizing these conferences in a coherent, highly synchronized conference program enables participation in an exciting event, offering the possibility to meet many researchers working in different directions in the field and to easily attend talks of different conferences. Before and after the main conference, numerous satellite workshops take place and attract many researchers from all over the globe.

ETAPS 2017 received 531 submissions in total, 159 of which were accepted, yielding an overall acceptance rate of 30%. I thank all authors for their interest in ETAPS, all reviewers for their peer reviewing efforts, the PC members for their contributions, and in particular the PC (co-)chairs for their hard work in running this entire intensive process. Last but not least, my congratulations to all authors of the accepted papers!

ETAPS 2017 was enriched by the unifying invited speakers Kim G. Larsen (Aalborg University, Denmark) and Michael Ernst (University of Washington, USA), as well as the conference-specific invited speakers (FoSSaCS) Joel Ouaknine (MPI-SWS, Germany, and University of Oxford, UK) and (TACAS) Dino Distefano (Facebook and Queen Mary University of London, UK). In addition, ETAPS 2017 featured a public lecture by Serge Abiteboul (Inria and ENS Cachan, France). Invited tutorials were offered by Véronique Cortier (CNRS research director at Loria, Nancy, France) on security and Ken McMillan (Microsoft Research Redmond, USA) on compositional testing. My sincere thanks to all these speakers for their inspiring and interesting talks!

ETAPS 2017 took place in Uppsala, Sweden, and was organized by the Department of Information Technology of Uppsala University. It was further supported by the following associations and societies: ETAPS e.V., EATCS (European Association for Theoretical Computer Science), EAPLS (European Association for Programming Languages and Systems), and EASST (European Association of Software Science and Technology). Facebook, Microsoft, Amazon, and the city of Uppsala financially supported ETAPS 2017. The local organization team consisted of Parosh Aziz Abdulla (general chair), Wang Yi, Björn Victor, Konstantinos Sagonas, Mohamed Faouzi Atig, Andreina Francisco, Kaj Lampka, Tjark Weber, Yunyun Zhu, and Philipp Rümmer.

The overall planning for ETAPS is the main responsibility of the Steering Committee, and in particular of its executive board. The ETAPS Steering Committee consists of an executive board, and representatives of the individual ETAPS conferences, as well as representatives of EATCS, EAPLS, and EASST. The executive board consists of Gilles Barthe (Madrid), Holger Hermanns (Saarbrücken), Joost-Pieter Katoen (chair, Aachen and Twente), Gerald Lüttgen (Bamberg), Vladimiro Sassone (Southampton), Tarmo Uustalu (Tallinn), and Lenore Zuck (Chicago). Other members of the Steering Committee are: Parosh Abdulla (Uppsala), Amal Ahmed (Boston), Christel Baier (Dresden), David Basin (Zurich), Lujo Bauer (Pittsburgh), Dirk Beyer (Munich), Giuseppe Castagna (Paris), Tom Crick (Cardiff), Javier Esparza (Munich), Jan Friso Groote (Eindhoven), Jurriaan Hage (Utrecht), Reiko Heckel (Leicester), Marieke Huisman (Twente), Panagotios Katsaros (Thessaloniki), Ralf Küsters (Trier), Ugo del Lago (Bologna), Kim G. Larsen (Aalborg), Axel Legay (Rennes), Matteo Maffei (Saarbrücken), Tiziana Margaria (Limerick), Andrzej Murawski (Warwick), Catuscia Palamidessi (Palaiseau), Julia Rubin (Vancouver), Alessandra Russo (London), Mark Ryan (Birmingham), Don Sannella (Edinburgh), Andy Schürr (Darmstadt), Gabriele Taentzer (Marburg), Igor Walukiewicz (Bordeaux), and Hongseok Yang (Oxford).

I would like to take this opportunity to thank all speakers, attendees, organizers of the satellite workshops, and Springer for their support. Finally, a big thanks to Parosh and his local organization team for all their enormous efforts enabling a fantastic ETAPS in Uppsala!

January 2017   Joost-Pieter Katoen

Preface

This book contains the proceedings of FASE 2017, the 20th International Conference on Fundamental Approaches to Software Engineering, held in Uppsala, Sweden in April 2017, as part of the annual European Joint Conferences on Theory and Practice of Software (ETAPS 2017).

As usual for FASE, the contributions combine the development of conceptual and methodological advances with their formal foundations, tool support, and evaluation on realistic or pragmatic cases. As a result the volume contains regular research papers, long tool papers, and short tool demo papers. The papers in this volume cover a wide range of topics, such as program and system analysis, model transformations, configuration and synthesis, graph modeling and transformation, software product lines, test selection, and learning and inference. We hope that the community will find this volume engaging and worth reading.

The contributions included have been carefully selected. For the second time, FASE used a double-blind review process, as last year's experiment was considered valuable by authors and worth the additional effort of anonymizing the papers. We received 114 abstract submissions from 33 different countries, from which 91 full-paper submissions materialized. All papers were reviewed by three experts in the field, and after intense discussion, only 25 were accepted, giving an acceptance rate of 27%.

We thank the ETAPS 2017 organizers, Parosh Aziz Abdulla and his team, the ETAPS publicity chair, Tarmo Uustala, and the ETAPS SC chair, Joost-Pieter Katoen, for their support during the whole process. We thank all the authors for their hard work and willingness to contribute. Last but not least, we thank all the Program Committee members and external reviewers who invested time and effort in the selection process to ensure the scientific quality of the program.

January 2017

Marieke Huisman
Julia Rubin

Organization

Program Committee

Jordi Cabot	ICREA, Spain
Yuanfang Cai	Drexel University, USA
Sagar Chaki	Carnegie Mellon University, USA
Hana Chockler	King's College London, UK
Ewen Denney	SGT/NASA Ames, USA
Bernd Fischer	Stellenbosch University, South Africa
Milos Gligoric	University of Texas at Austin, USA
Stefania Gnesi	ISTI-CNR, Italy
Dilian Gurov	KTH Royal Institute of Technology, Sweden
Mark Harman	University College London, UK
Reiko Heckel	University of Leicester, UK
Marieke Huisman	University of Twente, The Netherlands
Valérie Issarny	Inria Paris – Rocquencourt, France
Einar Broch Johnsen	University of Oslo, Norway
Martin Leucker	University of Lübeck, Germany
Antónia Lopes	University of Lisbon, Portugal
Shiva Nejati	University of Luxembourg, Luxembourg
Fabrizio Pastore	University of Milano-Bicocca, Italy
Julia Rubin	University of British Columbia, Canada
Bernhard Rumpe	RWTH Aachen, Germany
Alessandra Russo	Imperial College London, UK
Rick Salay	University of Toronto, Canada
Ina Schaefer	Technische Universität Braunschweig, Germany
Andy Schürr	TU Darmstadt, Germany
Perdita Stevens	University of Edinburgh, UK
Gabriele Taentzer	Philipps-Universität Marburg, Germany
Dániel Varró	McGill University, Canada, and Budapest University of Technology and Economics, Hungary
Andrzej Wasowski	IT University of Copenhagen, Denmark
Virginie Wiels	ONERA, France

Additional Reviewers

Adam, Kai	Baumann, Christoph	Bürdek, Johannes
Al-Sibahi, Ahmad Salim	Bergmann, Gábor	Canovas Izquierdo,
Angarita, Rafael	Boniol, Frédéric	Javier Luis
Balliu, Musard	Bruce, Bobby	Carnevali, Laura
Basile, Davide	Butting, Arvid	Chemouil, David

Ciccozzi, Federico
Clarisó, Robert
D'Ausbourg, Bruno
Daniel, Gwendal
De Vink, Erik
Debreceni, Csaba
Decker, Normann
Dimovski, Aleksandar S.
Din, Crystal Chang
Eikermann, Robert
Enea, Constantin
Fantechi, Alessandro
Ferrari, Alessio
Franco, Juliana
Greene, Gillian
Greifenberg, Timo
Guanciale, Roberto
Gómez, Abel
Heim, Robert
Janota, Mikolas
Kautz, Oliver
Kluge, Roland
Knüppel, Alexander
Kulcsár, Géza
Kusmenko, Evgeny
Kästner, Christian
Lachmann, Remo

Lamo, Yngve
Leblebici, Erhan
Lity, Sascha
Luthmann, Lars
Mao, Ke
Markin, Grigory
Markov, Minko
Martins, Francisco
Martínez, Salvador
Mauro, Jacopo
Melgratti, Hernan
Melo, Jean
Nagy, András Szabolcs
Nassar, Nebras
Nemati, Hamed
Nesic, Damir
Nieke, Michael
Picazo-Sanchez, Pablo
Planas, Elena
Proenca, Jose
Pun, Ka I.
Raco, Deni
Roth, Alexander
Roux, Pierre
Santos, André
Scheffel, Torben
Schlatte, Rudolf

Schlie, Alexander
Schmitz, Malte
Schwarz, Oliver
Semeráth, Oszkár
Semini, Laura
Stanciulescu, Stefan
Stolz, Volker
Stümpel, Annette
Szárnyas, Gábor
T. Vasconcelos, Vasco
Tapia Tarifa, Silvia Lizeth
Ter Beek, Maurice H.
Thoma, Daniel
Thorn, Johannes
Tomaszek, Stefan
Tribastone, Mirco
van der Berg, Freark
Varro, Gergely
Vaupel, Steffen
von Wenckstern, Michael
Weckesser, Markus
Westman, Jonas
Whiteside, Iain
Wong, Peter
Xiao, Lu

Contents

Model Transformations

Configuration and Synthesis

Software Product Lines

Learning and Inference

Should We Learn Probabilistic Models for Model Checking? A New Approach and An Empirical Study

Jingyi Wang[1(✉)], Jun Sun[1], Qixia Yuan[2], and Jun Pang[2]

[1] Singapore University of Technology and Design, Singapore, Singapore
jingyi_wang@mymail.sutd.edu.sg, sunjun@sutd.edu.sg
[2] University of Luxembourg, Luxembourg City, Luxembourg
{qixia.yuan,jun.pang}@uni.lu

Abstract. Many automated system analysis techniques (e.g., model checking, model-based testing) rely on first obtaining a model of the system under analysis. System modeling is often done manually, which is often considered as a hindrance to adopt model-based system analysis and development techniques. To overcome this problem, researchers have proposed to automatically "learn" models based on sample system executions and shown that the learned models can be useful sometimes. There are however many questions to be answered. For instance, how much shall we generalize from the observed samples and how fast would learning converge? Or, would the analysis result based on the learned model be more accurate than the estimation we could have obtained by sampling many system executions within the same amount of time? In this work, we investigate existing algorithms for learning probabilistic models for model checking, propose an evolution-based approach for better controlling the degree of generalization and conduct an empirical study in order to answer the questions. One of our findings is that the effectiveness of learning may sometimes be limited.

Keywords: Probabilistic model checking · Model learning · Genetic algorithm

1 Introduction

Many system analysis techniques rely on first obtaining a system model. The model should be accurate and often is required to be at a proper level of abstraction. For instance, model checking [3,10] works effectively if the user-provided model captures all the relevant behavior of the system and abstracts away the irrelevant details. With such a model as well as a given property, a model checker would automatically verify the property or falsify it with a counterexample. Alternatively, in the setting of probabilistic model checking

This work was supported by NRF Award No. NRF2014NCR-NCR001-40.

M. Huisman and J. Rubin (Eds.): FASE 2017, LNCS 10202, pp. 3–21, 2017.
DOI: 10.1007/978-3-662-54494-5_1

(PMC, see Sect. 2) [3,5], the model checker would calculate the probability of satisfying the property.

Model checking is perhaps not as popular as it ought to be due to the fact that a good model is required beforehand. For instance, a model which is too general would introduce spurious counterexamples, whereas the checking result based on a model which under-approximates the relevant system behavior is untrustworthy. In the setting of PMC, users are required to provide a probabilistic model (e.g., a Markov chain [3]) with accurate probabilistic distributions, which is often challenging.

In practice, system modeling is often done manually, which is both time-consuming and error-prone. Worse, it could be infeasible if the system is a black box or it is so complicated that no accurate model is known (e.g., the chemical reaction in a water treatment system [35]). This is often considered by industry as one hindrance to adopt otherwise powerful techniques like model checking. Alternative approaches which would rely less on manual modeling have been explored in different settings. One example is statistical model checking (SMC, see Sect. 2) [33,41]. The main idea is to provide a statistical measure on the likelihood of satisfying a property, by observing sample system executions and applying standard techniques like hypothesis testing [4,13,41]. SMC is considered useful partly because it can be applied to black-box or complex systems when system models are not available.

Another approach for avoiding manual modeling is to automatically learn models. A variety of learning algorithms have been proposed to learn a variety of models, e.g., [7,17,31,32]. It has been showed that the learned models can be useful for subsequent system analysis in certain settings, especially so when having a model is a must. Recently, the idea of model learning has been extended to system analysis through model checking. In [9,23,24], it is proposed to learn a probabilistic model first and then apply techniques like PMC to calculate the probability of satisfying a property based on the learned model. On one hand, learning is beneficial, and it solves some known drawbacks of SMC or even simulation-based system analysis methods in general. For instance, since SMC relies on sampling *finite* system executions, it is challenging to verify un-bounded properties [29,39], whereas we can verify un-bounded properties based on the learned model through PMC. Furthermore, the learned model can be used to facilitate other system analysis tasks like model-based testing and software simulation for complicated systems. On the other hand, learning essentially is a way of generalizing the sample executions and there are often many variables. It is thus worth investigating how the sample executions are generalized and whether indeed such learning-based approaches are justified.

In particular, we would like to investigate the following research questions. Firstly, how can we control the degree of generalization for the best learning outcome, since it is known that both over-fitting or under-fitting would cause problems in subsequent analysis? Secondly, often it is promised that the learned model would converge to an accurate model of the original system, if the number of sample executions is sufficiently large. In practice, there could be only a limited number of sample executions and thus it is valid to question how fast the learning algorithms converge. Furthermore, do learning-based approaches offer better analysis results if alternative approaches which do not require a learned model, like SMC, are available?

In order to answer the above questions, we mainly make the following contributions. Firstly, we propose a new approach (Sect. 4) to better control the degree of generalization than existing approaches (Sect. 3) in model learning. The approach is inspired by our observations on the limitations of existing learning approaches. Experiment results show that our approach converges faster than existing approaches while providing better or similar analysis results. Secondly, we develop a software toolkit ZIQIAN, realizing previously proposed learning approaches for PMC as well as our approach so as to systematically study and compare them in a fair way. Lastly, we conduct an empirical study on comparing different model learning approaches against a suite of benchmark systems, two real world systems, as well as randomly generated models (Sect. 5). One of our findings suggests that learning models for model checking might not be as effective compared to SMC given the same time limit. However, the learned models may be useful when manual modeling is impossible. From a broader point of view, our work is a first step towards investigating the recent trend on adopting machine learning techniques to solve software engineering problems. We remark there are extensive existing research on learning non-probabilistic models (e.g., [1]), which is often designed for different usage and is thus beyond the scope of this work. We review related work and conclude this paper in Sect. 6.

2 Preliminary

In this work, the model that we focus on is discrete-time Markov chains (DTMC) [3]. The reason is that most existing learning algorithms generate DTMC and it is still ongoing research on how to learn other probabilistic models like Markov Decision Processes [6,9,23,24,32]. Furthermore, the learned DTMC is aimed for probabilistic analysis by methods like PMC, among others. In the following, we briefly introduce DTMC, PMC as well as SMC so that we can better understand the context.

Markov Chain. A DTMC $\mathcal{D}$ is a triple tuple (S, ι_{init}, Tr), where S is a countable, nonempty set of states; $\iota_{init} : S \to [0,1]$ is the initial distribution s.t. $\sum_{s \in S} \iota_{init}(s) = 1$; and $Tr : S \times S \to [0,1]$ is the transition probability assigned to every pair of states which satisfies the following condition: $\sum_{s' \in S} Tr(s, s') = 1$. $\mathcal{D}$ is *finite* if S is finite. For instance, an example DTMC modelling the *egl* protocol [21] is shown in Fig. 1.

A DTMC induces an underlying digraph where states are vertices and there is an edge

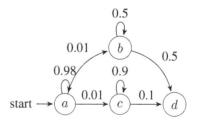

Fig. 1. DTMC of *egl* protocol.

from s to s' if and only if $Tr(s, s') > 0$. *Paths* of DTMCs are maximal paths in the underlying digraph, defined as infinite state sequences $\pi = s_0 s_1 s_2 \cdots \in S^\omega$ such that $Tr(s_i, s_{i+1}) > 0$ for all $i \geq 0$. We write $Path^\mathcal{D}(s)$ to denote the set of all infinite paths of $\mathcal{D}$ starting from state s.

Probabilistic Model Checking. PMC [3,5] is a formal analysis technique for stochastic systems including DTMCs. Given a DTMC $\mathcal{D} = (S, \imath_{init}, Tr)$ and a set of propositions Σ, we can define a function $L : S \rightarrow \Sigma$ which assigns valuation of the propositions in Σ to each state in S. Once each state is labeled, given a path in $Path^\mathcal{D}(s)$, we can obtain a corresponding sequence of propositions labeling the states.

Let $\Sigma^\star$ and Σ^ω be the set of all finite and infinite strings over Σ respectively. A property of the DTMC can be specified in temporal logic. Without loss of generality, we focus on Linear Time Temporal logic (LTL) and probabilistic LTL in this work. An LTL formula φ over Σ is defined by the syntax:

$$\varphi ::= true \mid \sigma \mid \varphi_1 \wedge \varphi_2 \mid \neg\varphi \mid \mathbf{X}\varphi \mid \varphi_1 \mathbf{U} \varphi_2$$

where $\sigma \in \Sigma$ is a proposition; $\mathbf{X}$ is intuitively read as 'next' and $\mathbf{U}$ is read as 'until'. We remark commonly used temporal operators like $\mathbf{F}$ (which reads 'eventually') and $\mathbf{G}$ (which reads 'always') can be defined using the above syntax, e.g., $\mathbf{F}\varphi$ is defined as $true\mathbf{U}\varphi$. Given a string π in $\Sigma^\star$ or Σ^ω, we define whether π satisfies a given LTL formula φ in the standard way [3].

Given a path π of a DTMC, we write $\pi \models \varphi$ to denote that the sequence of propositions obtained from π satisfies φ and $\pi \not\models \varphi$ otherwise. Furthermore, a probabilistic LTL formula ϕ of the form $Pr_{\bowtie r}(\varphi)$ can be used to quantify the probability of a system satisfying the LTL formula φ, where $\bowtie \in \{\geq, \leq, =\}$ and $r \in [0, 1]$ is a probability threshold. A DTMC $\mathcal{D}$ satisfies $Pr_{\bowtie r}(\varphi)$ if and only if the accumulated probability of all paths obtained from the initial state of $\mathcal{D}$ which satisfy φ satisfies the condition $\bowtie r$. Given a DTMC $\mathcal{D}$ and a probabilistic LTL property $Pr_{\bowtie r}(\varphi)$, the PMC problem can be solved using methods like the automata-theoretic approach [3]. We skip the details of the approach and instead remark that the complexity of PMC is doubly exponential in the size of φ and polynomial in the size of $\mathcal{D}$.

Statistical Model Checking. SMC is a Monte Carlo method to solve the probabilistic verification problem based on system simulations. Its biggest advantage is perhaps that it does not require the availability of system models [11]. SMC works by sampling system behaviors randomly (according to certain underlying probabilistic distribution) and observing how often a given property φ is satisfied. The idea is to provide a statistical measure on the likelihood of satisfying φ based on the observations, by applying techniques like hypothesis testing [4,13,41]. We refer readers to [3,41] for details.

3   Probabilistic Model Learning

Learning models from sample system executions for the purpose of PMC has been explored extensively in recent years [7,9,17,23,24,31,32]. In this section, we briefly present existing model learning algorithms for two different settings.

3.1   Learn from Multiple Executions

In the setting that the system can be reset and restarted multiple times, a set of independent executions of the system can be collected as input for learning. Learning algorithms in this category make the following assumptions [23]. First, the underlying system can be modeled as a DTMC. Second, the sampled system executions are mutually independent. Third, the length of each simulation is independent.

Let Σ denote the alphabet of the system observations such that each letter $e \in \Sigma$ is an observation of the system state. A system execution is then a finite string over Σ. The input in this setting is a finite set of strings $\Pi \subseteq \Sigma^*$. For any string $\pi \in \Sigma^*$, let $prefix(\pi)$ be the set of all prefixes of π including the empty string $\langle\rangle$. Let $prefix(\Pi)$ be the set of all prefixes of any string $\pi \in \Pi$. The set of strings Π can be naturally organized into a tree $tree(\Pi) = (N, root, E)$ where each node in N is a member of $prefix(\Pi)$; the root is the empty string $\langle\rangle$; and $E \subseteq N \times N$ is a set of edges such that (π, π') is in E if and only if there exists $e \in \Sigma$ such that $\pi \cdot \langle e \rangle = \pi'$ where $\cdot$ is the sequence concatenation operator.

The idea of the learning algorithms is to generalize $tree(\Pi)$ by merging the nodes according to certain criteria in certain fixed order. Intuitively, two nodes should be merged if they are likely to represent the same state in the underlying DTMC. Since we do not know the underlying DTMC, whether two states should be merged is decided through a procedure called *compatibility test*. We remark the compatibility test effectively controls the degree of generalization. Different types of compatibility test have been studied [7,20,30]. We present in detail the compatibility test adopted in the AALERGIA algorithm [23] as a representative. First, each node π in $tree(\Pi)$ is labeled with the number of strings str in Π such that π is a prefix of str. Let $L(\pi)$ denote its label. Two nodes π_1 and π_2 in $tree(\Pi)$ are considered compatible if and only if they satisfy two conditions. The first condition is $last(\pi_1) = last(\pi_2)$ where $last(\pi)$ is the last letter in a string π, i.e., if the two nodes are to be merged, they must agree on the last observation (of the system state). The second condition is that the future behaviors from π_1 and π_2 must be sufficiently similar (i.e., within Angluin's bound [2]). Formally, given a node π in $tree(\Pi)$, we can obtain a probabilistic distribution of the next observation by *normalizing* the labels of the node and its children. In particular, for any event $e \in \Sigma$, the probability of going from node π to $\pi \cdot \langle e \rangle$ is defined as: $Pr(\pi, \langle e \rangle) = \frac{L(\pi \cdot \langle e \rangle)}{L(\pi)}$. We remark the probability of going from node π to itself is $Pr(\pi, \langle\rangle) = 1 - \sum_{e \in \Sigma} Pr(\pi, \langle e \rangle)$, i.e., the probability of not making any more observation. The multi-step probability from node π to $\pi \cdot \pi'$ where $\pi' = \langle e_1, e_2, \cdots, e_k \rangle$, written as $Pr(\pi, \pi')$, is the product of the one-step probabilities:

$$Pr(\pi, \pi') = Pr(\pi, \langle e_1 \rangle) \times Pr(\pi \cdot \langle e_1 \rangle, \langle e_2 \rangle) \times \cdots \times Pr(\pi \cdot \langle e_1, e_2, \cdots, e_{k-1} \rangle, \langle e_k \rangle) \tag{1}$$

Two nodes π_1 and π_2 are compatible if the following is satisfied:

$$|Pr(\pi_1, \pi) - Pr(\pi_2, \pi)| < \sqrt{6\epsilon \log(L(\pi_1))/L(\pi_1)} + \sqrt{6\epsilon \log(L(\pi_2))/L(\pi_2)} \tag{2}$$

for all $\pi \in \Sigma^\star$. We highlight that ϵ used in the above condition is a parameter which effectively controls the degree of state merging. Intuitively, a larger ϵ leads to more state merging, thus fewer states in the learned model.

If π_1 and π_2 are compatible, the two nodes are merged, i.e., the tree is transformed such that the incoming edge of π_2 is directed to π_1. Next, for any $\pi \in \Sigma^*$, $L(\pi_1 \cdot \pi)$ is incremented by $L(\pi_2 \cdot \pi)$. The algorithm works by iteratively identifying nodes which are compatible and merging them until there are no more compatible nodes. After merging all compatible nodes, the last phase of the learning algorithms in this category is to normalize the tree so that it becomes a DTMC.

3.2 Learn from a Single Execution

In the setting that the system cannot be easily restarted, e.g., real-world cyber-physical systems. We are limited to observe the system for a long time and collect a single, long execution as input. Thus, the goal is to learn a model describing the long-run, stationary behavior of a system, in which system behaviors are decided by their finite variable length memory of the past behaviors.

In the following, we fix α to be the single system execution. Given a string $\pi = \langle e_0, e_1, \cdots, e_k \rangle$, we write $suffix(\pi)$ to be the set of all suffixes of π, i.e., $suffix(\pi) = \{\langle e_i, \cdots, e_k \rangle | 0 \leq i \leq k\} \cup \{\langle \rangle\}$. Learning algorithms in this category [9,31] similarly construct a tree $tree(\alpha) = (N, root, E)$ where N is the set of suffixes of α; $root = \langle \rangle$; and there is an edge $(\pi_1, \pi_2) \in E$ if and only if $\pi_2 = \langle e \rangle \cdot \pi_1$. For any string π, let $\#(\pi, \alpha)$ be the number of times π appears as a substring in α. A node π in $tree(\alpha)$ is associated with a function Pr_π such that $Pr_\pi(e) = \frac{\#(\pi \cdot \langle e \rangle, \alpha)}{\#(\pi, \alpha)}$ for every $e \in \Sigma$, which is the likelihood of observing e next given the previous observations π. Effectively, function Pr_π defines a probabilistic distribution of the next observation.

Based on different suffixes of the execution, different probabilistic distributions of the next observation will be formed. For instance, the probabilistic distribution from the node $\langle e \rangle$ where e is the last observation would predict the distribution only based on the last observation, whereas the node corresponding to the sequence of all previous observations would have a prediction based the entire history. The central question is how far we should look into the past in order to predict the future. As we observe more history, we will make a better prediction of the next observation. Nonetheless, constructing the tree completely (no generalization) is infeasible and the goal of the learning algorithms is thus to grow a part of the tree which would give a "good enough" prediction by looking at a small amount of history. The questions are then: what is considered "good enough" and how much history is necessary. The answers control the degree of generalization in the learned model.

Algorithm 1. *Learn PST*

1: Initialize T to be a single root node representing $\langle\rangle$;
2: Let $S = \{\sigma | fre(\sigma, \alpha) > \epsilon\}$ be the candidate suffix set;
3: **while** S is not empty **do**
4:     Take any π from S; Let π' be the longest suffix of π in T;
5:     (B) If $fre(\pi, \alpha) \cdot \sum_{\sigma \in \Sigma} Pr(\pi, \sigma) \cdot \log \frac{Pr(\pi, \sigma)}{Pr(\pi', \sigma)} \geq \epsilon$
        add π and all its suffixes which are not in T to T;
6:     (C) If $fre(\pi, \alpha) > \epsilon$, add $\langle e \rangle \cdot \pi$ to S for every $e \in \Sigma$ if $fre(\langle e \rangle \cdot \pi, \alpha) > 0$;
7: **end while**

In the following, we present the approach in [9] as a representative of algorithms proposed in the setting. Let $fre(\pi, \alpha) = \frac{\#(\pi, \alpha)}{|\alpha| - |\pi| - 1}$ where $|\pi|$ is the length of π be the relative frequency of having substring π in α. Algorithm 1 shows the algorithm for identifying the right tree by growing it on-the-fly. Initially, at line 1, the tree T contains only the root $\langle\rangle$. Given a threshold ϵ, we identify the set $S = \{\pi | fre(\pi, \alpha) > \epsilon\}$ at line 2, which are substrings appearing often enough in α and are candidate nodes to grow in the tree. The loop from line 3 to 7 keeps growing T. In particular, given a candidate node π, we find the longest suffix π' in T at line 4 and if we find that adding π would improve the prediction of the next observations by at least ϵ, π is added, along with all of its suffixes if they are currently missing from the tree (so that we maintain all suffixes of all nodes in the tree all the time). Whether we add node π into tree T or not, we update the set of candidate S to include longer substrings of α at line 6. When Algorithm 1 terminates, the tree contains all nodes which would make a *good enough* prediction. Afterwards, the tree is transformed into a DTMC where the leafs of $tree(\alpha)$ are turned into states in the DTMC (refer to [31] for details).

4 Learning Through Evolution

Model learning essentially works by generalizing the sample executions. The central question is thus how to control the degree of generalization. To find the best degree of generalization, both [9,23] proposed to select the 'optimal' ϵ value using the golden section search of the highest Bayesian Information Criterion (BIC) score. For instance, in [23], the BIC score of a learned model M, given the sample executions Π, is computed as follows: $log(Pr_M(\Pi)) - \mu \times |M| \times log(|\Pi|)$ where $|M|$ is the number of states in M; Π is the total number of observations and μ is a constant (set to be 0.5 in [23]) which controls the relative importance of the size of the learned model. This kind of approach to optimize BIC is based on the assumption that the BIC score is a concave function of the parameter ϵ. Our empirical study (refer to details in Sect. 5), however, shows that this assumption is flawed and the BIC score can fluctuate with ϵ.

In the following, we propose an alternative method for learning models based on genetic algorithms (GA) [18]. The method is designed to select the best degree of generalization without the assumption of BIC's concaveness. The idea is that instead of using a predefined ϵ value to control the degree of generalization, we systematically generate candidate models and select the ones using the principle of natural selection so that the "fittest" model is selected eventually. In the following, we first briefly introduce the relevant background on GA and then present our approach in detail.

4.1   Genetic Algorithms

GA [18] are a set of optimization algorithms inspired by the "survival of the fittest" principle of Darwinian theory of natural selection. Given a specific problem whose solution can be encoded as a chromosome, a genetic algorithm typically works in the following steps [12]. First, an initial population (i.e., candidate solutions) is created either randomly or hand-picked based on certain criteria. Second, each candidate is evaluated using a pre-defined fitness function to see how good it is. Third, those candidates with higher fitness scores are selected as the parents of the next generation. Fourth, a new generation is generated by genetic operators, which either randomly alter (a.k.a. mutation) or combine fragments of their parent candidates (a.k.a. cross-over). Lastly, step 2–4 are repeated until a satisfactory solution is found or some other termination condition (e.g., timeout) is satisfied. GA are especially useful in providing approximate 'optimal' solutions when other optimization techniques do not apply or are too expensive, or the problem space is too large or complex.

GA are suitable for solving our problem of learning DTMC because we view the problem as finding an optimal DTMC model which not only maximizes the likelihood of the observed system executions but also satisfies additional constrains like having a small number of states. To apply GA to solve our problem, we need to develop a way of encoding candidate models in the form of chromosomes, define operators such as mutation and crossover to generate new candidate models, and define the fitness function to selection better models. In the following, we present the details of the steps in our approach.

4.2   Learn from Multiple Executions

We first consider the setting where multiple system executions are available. Recall that in this setting, we are given a set of strings Π, from which we can build a tree representation $tree(\Pi)$. Furthermore, a model is learned through merging the nodes in $tree(\Pi)$. The space of different ways of merging the nodes thus corresponds to the potential models to learn. Our goal is to apply GA to search for the best model in this space. In the following, we first show how to encode different ways of merging the nodes as chromosomes.

Let the size of $tree(\Pi)$ (i.e., the number of nodes) be X and let Z be the number of states in the learned model. A way of merging the nodes is a function which maps each node in $tree(\Pi)$ to a state in the learned model. That is, it can be encoded as a chromosome in the form of a sequence of integers $\langle I_1, I_2, \cdots, I_X \rangle$ where $1 \leq I_i \leq Z$ for all i such that $1 \leq i \leq X$. Intuitively, the number I_i means that node i in $tree(\Pi)$ is mapped into state I_i in the learned model. Besides, the

---

Algorithm 2. Model learning by GA from multiple executions

---

input: $tree(\Pi)$ and the alphabet Σ
output: A chromosome encoding a DTMC $\mathcal{D}$
1: Let Z be $|\Sigma|$; Let $Best$ be $null$;
2: **repeat**
3:    Let $population$ be an initial population with Z states;
4:    Let $generation$ be 1;
5:    **repeat**
6:       Let $newBest$ be the fittest in $population$;
7:       **if** $newBest$ is fitter than $Best$ **then**
8:          Set $Best$ to be $newBest$;
9:       **end if**
10:       **for all** fit pairs (p_1, p_2) in $population$ **do**
11:          Crossover (p_1, p_2) to get children C_1 and C_2;
12:          Mutate C_1 and C_2;
13:          Add C_1 and C_2 into $population$;
14:          Remove (p_1, p_2) from $population$;
15:       **end for**
16:       $generation \leftarrow generation + 1$;
17:    **until** $generation > someThreshold$
18:    $Z \leftarrow Z + 1$;
19: **until** $Best$ is not improved
20: **return** $Best$

---

encoding is done such that infeasible models are always avoided. Recall that two nodes π_1 and π_2 can be merged only if $last(\pi_1) = last(\pi_2)$, which means that two nodes with different last observation should not be mapped into the same state in the learned model. Thus, we first partition the nodes into $|\Sigma|$ groups so that all nodes sharing the same last observation are mapped to the same group of integers. A chromosome is then generated such that only nodes in the same group can possibly be mapped into the same state. The initial population is generated by randomly generating a set of chromosomes this way. *We remark that in this way all generated chromosomes represent a valid DTMC model.*

Formally, the chromosome $\langle I_1, I_2, \cdots, I_X \rangle$ represents a DTMC $M = (S, \iota_{init}, Tr)$ where S is a set of Z states. Each state s in S corresponds to a set of nodes in $tree(\Pi)$. Let $nodes(s)$ denote that set. Tr is defined such that for all states s and s' in M,

$$Tr(s, s') = \frac{\sum_{x \in nodes(s)} \sum_{e \in \Sigma | \langle s, e \rangle \in nodes(s')} L(x \cdot \langle e \rangle)}{\sum_{x \in nodes(s)} L(x)} \tag{3}$$

The initial distributions ι_{init} is defined such that for any state $s \in S$, $\iota_{init}(s) = \sum_{x \in nodes(s)} L(x)/L(\langle \rangle)$.

Next, we define the fitness function. Intuitively, a chromosome is good if the corresponding DTMC model M maximizes the probability of the observed sample executions and the number of states in M is small. We thus define the fitness function of a chromosome as: $log(Pr_M(\Pi)) - \mu \times |M| \times log|\Pi|$ where

$|M|$ is the number of states in M and $|\Pi|$ is the total number of letters in the observations and μ is a constant which represents how much we favor a smaller model size. The fitness function, in particular, the value of μ, controls the degree of generalization. If μ is 0, $tree(\Pi)$ would be the resultant model; whereas if μ is infinity, a model with one state would be generated. We remark that this fitness function is the same as the formula for computing the BIC score in [23]. Compared to existing learning algorithms, controlling the degree of generalization in our approach is more intuitive (i.e., different value of μ has a direct effect on the learned model). In particular, a single parameter μ is used in our approach, whereas in existing algorithms [9,23], a parameter μ is used to select the value of ϵ (based on a false assumption of the BIC being concave), which in turn controls the degree of generalization. From a user point of view, it is hard to see the effect of having a different ϵ value since it controls whether two nodes are merged in the intermediate steps of the learning process.

Next, we discuss how candidate models with better fitness score are selected. Selection directs evolution towards better models by keeping good chromosomes and weeding out bad ones based on their fitness. Two standard selection strategies are applied. One is *roulette wheel selection*. Suppose f is the average fitness of a population. For each individual M in the population, we select f_M / f copies of M. The other is *tournament selection*. Two individuals are chosen randomly from the population and a tournament is staged to determine which one gets selected. The tournament is done by generating a random number r between zero and comparing it to a pre-defined number p (which is larger than 0.5). If r is smaller than p, the individual with a higher fitness score is kept. We refer the readers to [18] for discussion on the effectiveness of these selection strategies.

After selection, genetic operators like mutation and crossover are applied to the selected candidates. Mutation works by mapping a random node to a new number from the same group, i.e., merging the node with other nodes with the same last observation. For crossover, chromosomes in the current generation are randomly paired and two children are generated to replace them. Following standard approaches [18], we adopt three crossover strategies.

- *One-point Crossover.* A crossover point is randomly chosen, one child gets its prefix from the father and suffix from the mother. Reversely for the other child.
- *Two-point Crossover.* Two crossover points are randomly chosen, which results in two crossover segments in the parent chromosomes. The parents exchange their crossover segments to generate two children.
- *Uniform Crossover.* One child gets its odd bit from father and even bit from mother. Reversely for the other child.

We remark that during mutation or crossover, we guarantee that only chromosomes representing valid DTMC models are generated, i.e., only two nodes with the same last observations are mapped to the same number (i.e., a state in the learned model).

The details of our GA-based algorithm is shown as Algorithm 2. Variable Z is the number of states in the learned model. We remark that the number of states in the learned model M is unknown in advance. However, it is at least the number of letters in alphabet Σ, i.e., when all nodes in $tree(\Pi)$ sharing the same last observation are merged. Since a smaller model is often preferred, the initial population is generated such that each of the candidate models is of size $|\Sigma|$. The size of the model is incremented by 1 after each round of evolution. Variable $Best$ records the fittest chromosome generated so far, which is initially set to be $null$ (i.e., the least fit one). At line 3, an initial population of chromosome with Z states are generated as discussed above. The loop from line 5 to 17 then lets the population evolve through a number of generations, during which crossover and mutations take place. At line 18, we then increase the number of states in the model in order to see whether we can generate a fitter chromosome. We stop the loop from line 2 to 19 when the best chromosome is not improved after increasing the number of states. Lastly, the fittest chromosome $Best$ is decoded to a DTMC and presented as the learned model.

Example. We use an example to illustrate how the above approach works. For simplicity, assume we have the following collection of executions $\Pi = \{\langle aacd \rangle, \langle abd \rangle, \langle acd \rangle\}$ from the model shown in Fig. 1. There are in total 10 prefixes of these execution (including the empty string). As a result, the tree $tree(\Pi)$ contains 10 nodes. Since the alphabet $\{a, b, c, d\}$ has size 4, the nodes (except the root) are partitioned into 4 groups so that all nodes in the same group have the same last observation. The initial population contains a single model with 4 states, where all nodes in the same groups are mapped into the same state. After one round of evolution, models with 5 states are generated (by essentially splitting the nodes in one group to two states) and evaluated with the fitness function. The evolution continues until the fittest score does not improve anymore when we add more states.

4.3   Learn from Single Execution

In the following, we describe our GA-based learning if there is only one system execution. Recall that we are given a single long system observation α in this setting. The goal is to identify the *shortest dependent history memory* that yields the most precise probability distribution of the system's next observation. That is, we aim to construct a part of $tree(\alpha)$ which transforms to a "good" DTMC. A model thus can be defined as an assignment of each node in $tree(\alpha)$ to either true or false. Intuitively, a node is assigned true if and only if it is selected to predict the next observation, i.e., the corresponding suffix is kept in the tree which later is used to construct the DTMC model. A chromosome (which encodes a model) is thus in the form of a sequence of boolean variable $\langle B_1, B_2, \cdots, B_m \rangle$ where B_i represents whether the i-th node is to be kept or not. We remark that not every valuation of the boolean variables is considered a valid chromosome. By definition, if a suffix π is selected to predict the next observation, all suffixes of π are not selected (since using a longer memory as in π predicts better) and therefore their corresponding value must be false. During mutation and crossover, we only generate those chromosomes satisfying this condition so that only valid chromosomes are generated.

A chromosome defined above encodes a part of $tree(\alpha)$, which can be transformed into a DTMC following the approach in [31]. Let M be the corresponding DTMC. The fitness function is defined similarly as in Sect. 4.2. We define the fitness function of a chromosome as $log(Pr_M(\alpha)) - \mu \times |M| \times log(|\alpha|)$ where $Pr_M(\alpha)$ is the probability of exhibiting α in M, μ is a constant that controls the weight of model size, and $|\alpha|$ is the size of the input execution. Mutation is done by randomly selecting one boolean variable from the chromosome and flip its value. Notice that afterwards, we might have to flip the values of other boolean values so that the chromosome is valid. We skip the discussion on selection and crossover as they are the same as described in Sect. 4.2.

We remark that, compared to existing algorithms in learning models [9,23, 24], it is straightforward to argue that the GA-based approaches for model learning do not rely on the assumption needed for BIC. Furthermore, the learned model improves monotonically through generations.

5 Empirical Study

The above mentioned learning algorithms are implemented in a self-contained tool called ZIQIAN (available at [37], approximately 6 K lines of Java code). In this work, since the primary goal of learning the models is to verify properties over the systems, we evaluate the learning algorithms by checking whether we can reliably verify properties based on the learned model, by comparing verification results based on the learned models and those based on the actual models (if available). All results are obtained using PRISM [22] on a 2.6 GHz Intel Core i7 PC running OSX with 8 GB memory. The constant μ in the fitness function of learning by GA is set to 0.5.

Our test objects can be categorized in two groups. The first group contains all systems (*brp*, *lse*, *egl*, *crowds*, *nand*, and *rsp*) from the PRISM benchmark suite for DTMCs [21] and a set of randomly generated DTMC models (*rmc*) using an approach similar to the approach in [36]. We refer the readers to [21] for details on the PRISM models as well as the properties to be verified. For these models, we collect multiple executions. The second group contains two real-world systems, from which we collect a single long execution. One is the probabilistic boolean networks (*PBN*), which is a modeling framework widely used to model gene regulatory networks (GRNs) [34]. In *PBN*, a gene is modeled with a binary valued node and the interactions between genes are expressed by Boolean functions. For the evaluation, we generate random PBNs with 5, 8 and 10 nodes respectively using the tool ASSA-PBN [25]. The other is a real-world raw water purification system called the Secure Water Testbed (*SWaT*) [35]. *SWaT* is a complicated system which involves a series of water treatments like ultrafiltration, chemical dosing, dechlorination through an ultraviolet system, etc. We regard *SWaT* as a representative complex system for which learning is the only way to construct a model. Our evaluation consists of the following parts (all models as well as the detailed results are available at [38]).

We first show that assumptions required by existing learning algorithms may not hold, which motivates our proposal of GA-based algorithms. Existing learning algorithms [9,23] require that the BIC score is a concave function of ϵ in order to select the best ϵ value which controls the degree of generalization. Figure 2 shows how the absolute value of BIC scores ($|BIC|$) of representative models change with ϵ. It can be observed that this assumption is not satisfied and ϵ is not controlling the degree of generalization nicely. For example, the $|BIC|$ (e.g., for *brp*, *PBN* and *egl*) fluctuate with ϵ. Besides, we observe climbings of $|BIC|$ for *lse* when ϵ increases, but droppings for *crowds*, *nand* and *rsp*. What's worse, in the case (e.g., *PBN*) of learning from a single execution, if the range of ϵ is selected improperly, it is very likely that an empty model (a tree only with root $\langle\rangle$) is learned.

Second, how fast does learning converge? In the rest of the section, we adopt absolute relative difference (ARD) as a measure of accuracy of different approaches. The ARD is defined as $|P_{est} - P_{act}|/P_{act}$ between the precise result P_{act} and the estimated results P_{est}, which can be obtained by AA, GA as well as SMC. A smaller ARD implies a better estimation of the true probability. Figure 3 shows how the ARD of different systems change when we gradually increase the time cost from 30 seconds to 30 min by increasing the

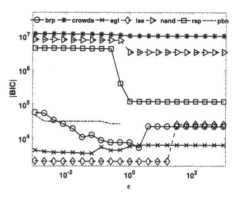

Fig. 2. How the absolute values of BIC score change over ϵ.

size of training data. We remark that some systems (*brp*, *egl*, *lse*) are not applicable due to different reasons. We can observe that GA converges faster and better than AA. In general, both AA and GA converges to relatively accurate results when we are given sufficient time. But there are also cases of fluctuation of ARD, which is problematic, as in such cases, we would not know which result to trust (given the different verification results obtained with different number of sampled executions), and it is hard to decide whether we have gathered enough system executions for reliable verification results.

Third, how accurate can learning achieve? We compare the accuracy of AA, GA, and SMC for benchmark systems given the same amount of time in Fig. 4. We remark that due to the discrimination of system complexity (state space, variable number/type, etc.), different systems can converge in different speed. For SMC, we adopt the statistical model checking engine of PRISM and select the confidence interval method. We fix confidence to 0.001 and adjust the number of samples to adjust time cost. We have the following observations based on Fig. 4. Firstly, for most systems, GA results in more accurate results than AA given same amount of time. This is especially true if sufficient time (20 m or 30 m) are given. *However, it should be noticed that SMC produces significantly*

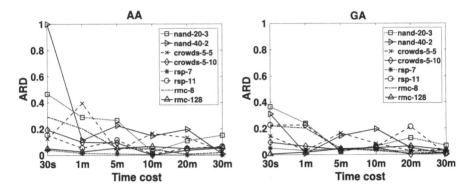

Fig. 3. Convergence of AA and GA over time. The numbers after the system of legends are one kind of system configuration.

more accurate results. Secondly, we observe that model learning works well if the actual model contains a small number of states. Cases like random models with 8 states (rmc-8) are good examples. For systems with more states, the verification results could deviate significantly (like nand-20-3, rsp-11).

Among our test subjects, *PBN* and *SWaT* are representative systems for which manual modelling is extremely challenging. Furthermore, SMC is not applicable as it is infeasible to sample the executions many times for these systems. We evaluate whether we can learn precise models in such a scenario. Note that since we do not have the actual model, we must define the preciseness of the learned model without referring to the actual model. For *PBN*, following [34], we use mean squared error (MSE) to measure how precise the learned models are. MSE is computed as follows: $MSE = \frac{1}{n} \sum_{i=1}^{n} (\hat{Y_i} - Y_i)^2$ where n is the number of states in *PBN* and Y_i is the steady-state probabilities of the original model and $\hat{Y_i}$ is the corresponding steady-state probabilities of the learned model. We remark that the smaller its value is, the more precise the learned model is. Table 1 shows the MSE of the learned models with for *PBN* with 5, 8, and 10 nodes respectively. Note that AA and GA learn the same models and thus have the same MSE, while GA always consumes less time. We can observe the MSEs are very small, which means the learned models of *PBN* are reasonably precise.

For the *SWaT* system, we evaluate the accuracy of the learned models by comparing the predicted observations against a set of test data collected from the actual system. In particular, we apply steady-state learning proposed in [9] (hereafter SL) and GA to learn from executions of different length and observe the trends over time. We select 3 critical sensors in the system (out of 50), named *ait*502, *ait*504 and *pit*501, and learn models on how the sensor readings evolve over time. During the experiments, we find it very difficult to identify an appropriate ϵ for SL in order to learn a non-empty useable model. Our GA-based approach however does not have such problem. Eventually we managed to identify an optimal ϵ value and both SL and GA learn the same models given the same training data. A closer look at the learned models reveals that they are all

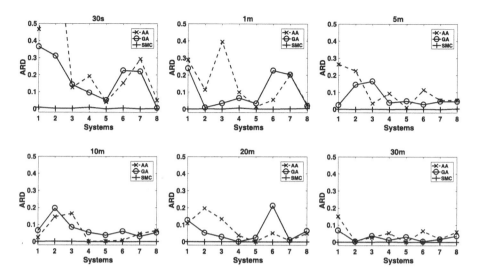

Fig. 4. The comparison of accuracy of AA, GA, and SMC given same amount of time, which varies from 30 s to 30 min. The horizontal-axis point represents a benchmark system with certain configuration in Fig. 3.

first-order Markov chains. This makes sense in the way that sensor readings in the real $SWaT$ system vary slowly and smoothly. Applying the learned models to predict the probability of the test data (from another day with length 7000), we observe a very good prediction accuracy. We use the average prediction accuracy for each observation $\bar{P}_{obs} = P_{td}^{1/|td|}$, where td is the test data and $|td|$ is its length, to evaluate how good the models are. In our experiment, the average accuracy of prediction for $ait502$ and $pit501$ is over 0.97, and the number is 0.99 for $ait504$, which are reasonably precise.

Last, there are some potential problems that may render learning ineffective. One of them is the known problem of rare-events. For *brp* system, the probability of satisfying the given properties are very small. As a result, a system execution satisfying the property is unlikely to be observed and learned from. Consequently, the verification results based on the learned models are 0. It is known that SMC is also ineffective for these properties since it is also based on random sampling. Besides, learning doesn't work when the state space of underlying system is too large or even infinite. If there are too many variables to observe (or when float/double typed variables exist), which induces a very large state space, learning will become infeasible. For example, to verify the fairness property of *egl* protocol, we need to observe dozens of integer variables. Our experiment suggests that AA and GA take unreasonable long time to learn a model, e.g., more than days. In order to apply learning in this scenario, we thus have to apply abstraction on the sampled system executions and learn from the abstract traces. Only by doing so, we are able to reduce the learning time significantly (in seconds) and successfully verified the *egl* protocol by learning.

Table 1. Results of *PBN* steady-state learning.

# nodes	# states	trajectory size ($\times 10^3$)	time cost(s)		MSE ($\times 10^{-7}$)	# nodes	# states	trajectory size ($\times 10^3$)	time cost(s)		MSE ($\times 10^{-7}$)
			SL	GA					SL	GA	
5	32	5	37.28	6.37	36.53	8	256	5	29.76	2.36	1.07
		15	161.57	53.49	15.21			15	105.87	26.4	0.03
		25	285.52	182.97				25	197.54	73.92	0.37
					6.04						
		35	426.26	348.5				35	310.87	122.61	0.94
					7.75						
		45	591.83	605.1				45	438.09	429.81	0.78
					5.74						
		50	673.55	767.7				50	509.59	285.66	0.34
					4.28						
10	1024	5	902.69	266.74		10	1024	15	5340.54	2132.68	0.61
					1.78						
		10	2772.56	1010.16				20	8477.24	3544.82	0.47
					1.01						

However, how to identify the right level of abstraction is highly non-trivial in general and is to be investigated in the future. What's more, there are other complications which might make model learning ineffective. For the *lse* protocol, the verification results based on the learned models may deviate from actual result for properties that show the probability of electing a leader in L rounds, with a different value for L. While the actual result 'jumps' as L increases, the result based on the learned model is smooth and deviates from actual results significantly when L is 3, 4 or 5, while results based on SMC are consistent with the actual results.

6   Conclusion and Related Work

In this work, we investigate the validity of model learning for the purpose of PMC. We propose a novel GA-based approach to overcome limitations of existing model learning algorithms and conducted an empirical study to systematically evaluate the effectiveness and efficiency of all these model learning approaches compared to statistical model checking over a variety of systems. We report their respective advantages and disadvantages, potential applications and future direction to improve.

This work is inspired by the work on comparing the effectiveness of PMC and SMC [40] and the line of work on adopting machine learning to learn a variety of system models (e.g., DTMC, stationary models and MDPs) for system model checking, in order to avoid manual model construction [9,23,24]. Existing learning algorithms are often based on algorithms designed for learning (probabilistic) automata, as evidenced in [1,7,8,17,30,31]. Besides the work in [9,23,24] which have been explained in detail, this work is also related to the work in [32], which learns continuous time Markov chains. In addition, in [6], learning algorithms are applied in order to verify Markov decision processes, without constructing explicit models. Our proposal on adopting genetic algorithms is related to work on applications of evolutionary algorithms for system analysis. In [14], evolutionary algorithm is integrated to abstraction refinement for model checking. This work is remotely related to work on SMC [33,41], some recent work on extending SMC to unbounded properties [29,39]. Lastly, our work uses the PRSIM model checker as the verification engine [22] and the case studies are taken from various practical systems and protocols including [15,16,19,25–28].

References

1. Angluin, D.: Learning regular sets from queries and counterexamples. Inf. Comput. **75**(2), 87–106 (1987)
2. Angluin, D.: Identifying languages from stochastic examples (1988)
3. Baier, C., Katoen, J.P., et al.: Principles of Model Checking. MIT press, Cambridge (2008). vol. 26202649
4. Bauer, A., Leucker, M., Schallhart, C.: Monitoring of real-time properties. In: Arun-Kumar, S., Garg, N. (eds.) FSTTCS 2006. LNCS, vol. 4337, pp. 260–272. Springer, Heidelberg (2006). doi:10.1007/11944836_25
5. Bianco, A., Alfaro, L.: Model checking of probabilistic and nondeterministic systems. In: Thiagarajan, P.S. (ed.) FSTTCS 1995. LNCS, vol. 1026, pp. 499–513. Springer, Heidelberg (1995). doi:10.1007/3-540-60692-0_70
6. Brázdil, T., Chatterjee, K., Chmelík, M., Forejt, V., Křetínský, J., Kwiatkowska, M., Parker, D., Ujma, M.: Verification of markov decision processes using learning algorithms. In: Cassez, F., Raskin, J.-F. (eds.) ATVA 2014. LNCS, vol. 8837, pp. 98–114. Springer, Cham (2014). doi:10.1007/978-3-319-11936-6_8
7. Carrasco, R.C., Oncina, J.: Learning stochastic regular grammars by means of a state merging method. In: Carrasco, R.C., Oncina, J. (eds.) ICGI 1994. LNCS, vol. 862, pp. 139–152. Springer, Heidelberg (1994). doi:10.1007/3-540-58473-0_144
8. Carrasco, R.C., Oncina, J.: Learning deterministic regular grammars from stochastic samples in polynomial time. Informatique théorique et applications **33**(1), 1–19 (1999)
9. Chen, Y., Mao, H., Jaeger, M., Nielsen, T.D., Guldstrand Larsen, K., Nielsen, B.: Learning Markov models for stationary system behaviors. In: Goodloe, A.E., Person, S. (eds.) NFM 2012. LNCS, vol. 7226, pp. 216–230. Springer, Heidelberg (2012). doi:10.1007/978-3-642-28891-3_22
10. Clarke, E.M., Grumberg, O., Peled, D.: Model Checking. MIT press, Cambridge (1999)
11. Clarke, E.M., Zuliani, P.: Statistical model checking for cyber-physical systems. In: Bultan, T., Hsiung, P.-A. (eds.) ATVA 2011. LNCS, vol. 6996, pp. 1–12. Springer, Heidelberg (2011). doi:10.1007/978-3-642-24372-1_1
12. Dyer, D.W.: Watchmaker framework for evolutionary computation. http://watchmaker.uncommons.org
13. Havelund, K., Roşu, G.: Synthesizing monitors for safety properties. In: Katoen, J.-P., Stevens, P. (eds.) TACAS 2002. LNCS, vol. 2280, pp. 342–356. Springer, Heidelberg (2002). doi:10.1007/3-540-46002-0_24
14. He, F., Song, X., Hung, W.N., Gu, M., Sun, J.: Integrating evolutionary computation with abstraction refinement for model checking. IEEE Trans. Comput. **59**(1), 116–126 (2010)

15. Helmink, L., Sellink, M.P.A., Vaandrager, F.W.: Proof-checking a data link protocol. In: Barendregt, H., Nipkow, T. (eds.) TYPES 1993. LNCS, vol. 806, pp. 127–165. Springer, Heidelberg (1994). doi:10.1007/3-540-58085-9_75

16. Herman, T.: Probabilistic self-stabilization. Inf. Process. Lett. **35**(2), 63–67 (1990)

17. De la Higuera, C.: Grammatical Inference, vol. 96. Cambridge University Press, Cambridge (2010)

18. Holland, J.H.: Adaptation in Natural and Artificial Systems. MIT Press, Cambridge (1992)

19. Itai, A., Rodeh, M.: Symmetry breaking in distributed networks. Inf. Comput. **88**(1), 60–87 (1990)

20. Kermorvant, C., Dupont, P.: Stochastic grammatical inference with multinomial tests. In: Adriaans, P., Fernau, H., Zaanen, M. (eds.) ICGI 2002. LNCS (LNAI), vol. 2484, pp. 149–160. Springer, Heidelberg (2002). doi:10.1007/3-540-45790-9_12

21. Kwiatkowska, M., Norman, G., Parker, D.: The PRISM benchmark suite. In: Proceedings of 9th International Conference on Quantitative Evaluation of SysTems (QEST 2012), pp. 203–204. IEEE CS Press (2012)

22. Kwiatkowska, M., Norman, G., Parker, D.: PRISM: probabilistic symbolic model checker. In: Field, T., Harrison, P.G., Bradley, J., Harder, U. (eds.) TOOLS 2002. LNCS, vol. 2324, pp. 200–204. Springer, Heidelberg (2002). doi:10.1007/3-540-46029-2_13

23. Mao, H., Chen, Y., Jaeger, M., Nielsen, T.D., Larsen, K.G., Nielsen, B.: Learning probabilistic automata for model checking. In: 2011 Eighth International Conference on Quantitative Evaluation of Systems (QEST), pp. 111–120. IEEE (2011)

24. Mao, H., Chen, Y., Jaeger, M., Nielsen, T.D., Larsen, K.G., Nielsen, B.: Learning markov decision processes for model checking. arXiv preprint (2012). arXiv:1212.3873

25. Mizera, A., Pang, J., Yuan, Q.: ASSA-PBN: an approximate steady-state analyser of probabilistic boolean networks. In: Finkbeiner, B., Pu, G., Zhang, L. (eds.) ATVA 2015. LNCS, vol. 9364, pp. 214–220. Springer, Cham (2015). doi:10.1007/978-3-319-24953-7_16

26. Norman, G., Parker, D., Kwiatkowska, M., Shukla, S.: Evaluating the reliability of nand multiplexing with prism. IEEE Trans. Comput. Aided Des. Integr. Circ. Syst. **24**(10), 1629–1637 (2005)

27. Norman, G., Shmatikov, V.: Analysis of probabilistic contract signing. J. Comput. Secur. **14**(6), 561–589 (2006)

28. Reiter, M.K., Rubin, A.D.: Crowds: anonymity for web transactions. ACM Trans. Inf. Syst. Secur. (TISSEC) **1**(1), 66–92 (1998)

29. Rohr, C.: Simulative model checking of steady state and time-unbounded temporal operators. In: Koutny, M., Aalst, W.M.P., Yakovlev, A. (eds.) Transactions on Petri Nets and Other Models of Concurrency VIII. LNCS, vol. 8100, pp. 142–158. Springer, Heidelberg (2013). doi:10.1007/978-3-642-40465-8_8

30. Ron, D., Singer, Y., Tishby, N.: On the learnability and usage of acyclic probabilistic finite automata. In: Proceedings of the Eighth Annual Conference on Computational Learning Theory, pp. 31–40. ACM (1995)

31. Ron, D., Singer, Y., Tishby, N.: The power of amnesia: learning probabilistic automata with variable memory length. Mach. Learn. **25**(2–3), 117–149 (1996)

32. Sen, K., Viswanathan, M., Agha, G.: Learning continuous time markov chains from sample executions. In: Proceedings of First International Conference on the Quantitative Evaluation of Systems, QEST 2004, pp. 146–155. IEEE (2004)

33. Sen, K., Viswanathan, M., Agha, G.: Statistical model checking of black-box probabilistic systems. In: Alur, R., Peled, D.A. (eds.) CAV 2004. LNCS, vol. 3114, pp. 202–215. Springer, Heidelberg (2004). doi:10.1007/978-3-540-27813-9_16

34. Shmulevich, I., Dougherty, E., Zhang, W.: From boolean to probabilistic boolean networks as models of genetic regulatory networks. Proc. IEEE **90**(11), 1778–1792 (2002)

35. SUTD: Secure water treatment testbed. http://itrust.sutd.edu.sg/research/testbeds/secure-water-treatment-swat/

36. Tabakov, D., Vardi, M.Y.: Experimental evaluation of classical automata constructions. In: Sutcliffe, G., Voronkov, A. (eds.) LPAR 2005. LNCS (LNAI), vol. 3835, pp. 396–411. Springer, Heidelberg (2005). doi:10.1007/11591191_28

37. Wang, J.: ZIQIAN. https://bitbucket.org/jingyi_wang/ziqian_develop

38. Wang, J.: ZIQIAN evaluation. https://bitbucket.org/jingyi_wang/ziqian_evaluation

39. Younes, H.L.S., Clarke, E.M., Zuliani, P.: Statistical verification of probabilistic properties with unbounded until. In: Davies, J., Silva, L., Simao, A. (eds.) SBMF 2010. LNCS, vol. 6527, pp. 144–160. Springer, Heidelberg (2011). doi:10.1007/978-3-642-19829-8_10

40. Younes, H.L., Kwiatkowska, M., Norman, G., Parker, D.: Numerical vs. statistical probabilistic model checking. Int. J. Softw. Tools Technol. Transf. **8**(3), 216–228 (2006)

41. Younes, H.L.S., Simmons, R.G.: Probabilistic verification of discrete event systems using acceptance sampling. In: Brinksma, E., Larsen, K.G. (eds.) CAV 2002. LNCS, vol. 2404, pp. 223–235. Springer, Heidelberg (2002). doi:10.1007/3-540-45657-0_17

Bordeaux: A Tool for Thinking Outside the Box

Vajih Montaghami$^{(\boxtimes)}$ and Derek Rayside

Electrical & Computer Engineering, University of Waterloo, Waterloo, Canada
{vmontagh,drayside}@uwaterloo.ca

Abstract. One of the great features of the Alloy Analyzer is that it can produce examples illustrating the meaning of the user's model. These *inside-the-box* examples, which are formally permissible but (potentially) undesirable, help the user understand underconstraint bugs in the model. To get similar help with overconstraint bugs in the model the user needs to see examples that are desirable but formally excluded: that is, they need to see *outside-the-box* (near-miss) examples. We have developed a prototype extension of the Alloy Analyzer, named Bordeaux, that can find these examples that are near the border of what is permitted, and hence might be desirable. More generally, Bordeaux finds a pair of examples, a, c, at a minimum distance to each other, and where a satisfies model A and c satisfies model C. The primary use case described is when model C is the negation of model A, but there are also other uses for this *relative minimization*. Previous works, such as Aluminum, have focused on finding inside-the-box examples that are absolutely minimal.

1 Introduction

Examples can help people understand abstractions [1,6,22,23] such as models. One of the great features of the Alloy Analyzer is that it can mechanically generate examples of the user's model (formula). These examples are *inside-the-box*, meaning that they are consistent with the model. If the user deems the generated example desirable then it affirms that the model is a true expression of the user's intent. If the user deems the generated example undesirable, then it is a concrete representation of an *underconstraint* problem in the model: the model needs to be tightened to exclude the undesirable example. The Alloy Analyzer generates examples arbitrarily, without specifically targeting towards either desirable or undesirable examples.

If the model has a *partial overconstraint* bug, then Alloy's example generation facility is of limited assistance. A partial overconstraint bug means that the model unintentionally excludes some examples that should be included. Total overconstraint means that there are no examples that are consistent with the model. Alloy's *unsatisfiable core* feature highlights a subset of the model that causes the total overconstraint. Partial overconstraint bugs are tricky to detect [14], and currently have no explicit tool support in Alloy.

A facility for generating *near-miss examples* (*i.e.*, outside-the-box examples) might help the user diagnose partial overconstraint bugs. What the user might

M. Huisman and J. Rubin (Eds.): FASE 2017, LNCS 10202, pp. 22–39, 2017.
DOI: 10.1007/978-3-662-54494-5_2

like to see is an example that is formally excluded by the model but which she actually intends the model to include (*i.e.*, is desirable). Cognitive psychologists have found that near-miss examples revealing contrast are effective for human learning [6].

A simple, if inconvenient, technique for generating outside-the-box examples is to manually negate the model and use Alloy's existing example generation facility. But the chances of this technique generating examples that are desirable is slim, since there are typically so many more examples outside the box than inside the box. The chances of a near-miss example being desirable are higher, because a near-miss example is similar to examples that are desirable.

We have developed a technique and prototype tool, named Bordeaux, for doing *relative minimization* of examples. Given mutually inconsistent constraints, A and C, it will search for examples a and c, respectively, that are at a minimum distance to each other (measured by the number of tuples added or removed).

To find a near-miss example for A, simply set C to be the negation of A and commence the relative minimization procedure. We say that a is a *near-hit* example and that c is a *near-miss* example (both of A with respect to C). The space between the near-hit and the near-miss is the *border*: there are, by definition, no examples of either A or C on the border. Examples consistent with either A or C must be within A or C and hence are not on the border. Therefore, the distance of an example to the border cannot be assessed directly: only the distance between the near-hit and the near-miss examples can be measured.

To further guide the search towards desirable near-miss examples, the Bordeaux tool has an affordance for the user to specify which relations are permitted to differ. Bordeaux uses Alloy* [9], which is an extension of Alloy Analyzer, to solve formulas with higher-order quantifiers.

The experiments in Sect. 5 compare Bordeaux with Aluminum [13] and the Alloy Analyzer version 4.2. Bordeaux does a better job of producing pairs of near-hit and near-miss examples that are close to each other, with some computational cost. In some cases the absolute minimization technique of Aluminum produces results similar to the relative minimization technique of Bordeaux, but in other cases the results differ significantly.

Based on observations of the experiments, we design and implement two optimizations for Bordeaux in Sect. 6: scope tightening and parallelization. The key observation is that, in practice, the near-hit and near-miss are usually very close to each other. The optimizations reduce the computational cost of Bordeaux by over an order of magnitude.

In the next section, we review related works and discuss how Bordeaux differs from similar tools. Section 3 sketches an illustrative example. In Sect. 4, we define the concepts and formulas for finding near-hit and near-miss examples, and discuss some other special cases of these formulas that might be interesting for users. Section 5 demonstrates the experimental evaluation of Bordeaux and its comparison with the state-of-the-art Alloy analysis tools. Two approaches to optimize the prototype are described in Sect. 6. Section 7 concludes.

2   Related Work

Both Nelson et al. [13] and Cunha et al. [4] have proposed techniques to guide Alloy Analyzer's example generation facility towards more interesting inside examples. The stock Alloy Analyzer generates arbitrary inside examples, which might or might not be interesting, and might or might not help the user discover underconstraint bugs.

The Nelson et al. [13] extension of Alloy, called Aluminum, generates *minimal* inside examples. We say that this approach produces *absolute minimum* examples, because it finds the smallest examples that satisfy a given model. By contrast, our technique looks for *relatively minimum* pairs of examples: one inside (near-hit) and the other outside (near-miss) that are at a minimum distance from each other; they might not be absolutely minimal from Aluminum's perspective. Aluminum also has a facility for growing the minimal example, called *scenario exploration*.

Cunha et al. [4] used PMax-SAT [3] to enhance Kodkod [21] to find examples that are close to a target example. They discussed applications in data structure repair and model transformation. Perhaps this technique could be modified to replace our usage of Alloy* in Bordeaux.

When the model is completely overconstrained (*i.e.*, inconsistent), then no inside examples are possible. Shlyakhter et al. [19] enhanced Alloy to highlight the *unsatisfiable core* of such models; Torlak et al. [20] further enhanced this functionality. This tells the user a subset of the model (*i.e.*, formula) that needs to be changed, but does not give an example (because none are possible inside).

Browsing desirable outside examples might help the user understand what is wrong with the model [1]. In an empirical user study, Zayan et al. [23] evaluated the effects of using inside and outside examples in model comprehension and domain knowledge transfer. The study demonstrated evidence of the usefulness of outside in understanding the models, but did not state any preferences for particular examples. Browsing (desirable) outside examples might also help the user understand partially overconstrained models (in which some, but not all, desirable instances are possible).

Batot [2] designed a tool for automating MDE tasks. The tool generates examples from partial or complete metamodels to be evaluated or corrected by an expert. The minimality and coverage of examples are two major criteria for generating useful examples. Mottu et al. [12] proposed a mutation analysis technique to improve model transformation testing. Their technique mutates the model w.r.t. four abstract model transformation operators and generates mutants for evaluating test-suites. Macedo and Cunha [7] proposed a tool for analyzing bidirectional model transformations based on least changes using Alloy. The tool tries different number of changes to find the least number. Selecting proper scopes for Alloy Analyzer is a major obstacles to scaling the tool.

In his seminal work Winston [22], introduced using near-miss examples in learning classification procedures as well as explaining failures in learning unusual cases. Gick and Paterson [6] studied the value of near-miss examples for human learning. They found that contrasting near-miss examples were the most effective examples for learning. Popelínsky [15] used near-miss examples for synthesizing normal logic programs from a small set of examples. Seater [18] employed the concepts of near-miss and near-hit examples to explain the role, *i.e.*, restricting or relaxing, of a constraint in a given model. Modeling By Example [8] is an unimplemented technique used to synthesize an Alloy model using near-miss and near-hit examples. The technique synthesizes an initial model from a set of examples; it learns the boundaries by generating near-miss and near-hit examples to be reviewed by the user. The near-hit and near-miss examples are from a slightly modified model.

ParAlloy [16] and Ranger [17] realize parallel analysis of models written in Alloy. Both tools partition a given Alloy model and make multiple calls to the underlying SAT-solver. The idea of parallelization in Bordeaux relies on selecting proper scopes as opposed to partitioning the model.

3   Illustrative Example

Consider a model that describes an undergraduate degree in computer engineering, as in Fig. 1. In this illustrative model, a student must take two courses to graduate, and she must have taken all necessary prerequisites for each course.

One can ask Alloy Analyzer to generate an inside example consistent with the model, the analyzer generates an example similar to Fig. 2a. Everything looks OK: this example corresponds with the user's intentions. But this model harbours a partial overconstraint bug: there are examples that the user intends, but which are not consistent with the model.

Bordeaux generates two near-miss examples (Figs. 2b and c). These are outside examples at a minimum distance from the example in Fig. 2a, adding one tuple to relations courses and reqs, respectively. The first near-miss example reveals the partial overconstraint: a student is prevented from graduating if they take an extra course. The user rectifies this by changing the equality predicate (eq[]) on Line 6 of Fig. 1 to a less-than-or-equal-to (leq[]). The second near-miss example is not interesting to the user because it just involves a perturbation of the pre-requisites. Subsequent searches can be set to exclude the reqs relation.

Alloy can be used to generate an arbitrary outside example (*e.g.*, Fig. 2d) if the user manually negates the model. This unfocused outside example is unlikely to be meaningful for the user, as it might be too divergent from her intention.

```
1  abstract sig Course{reqs: set Course}
2  one sig ECE155, ECE240, ECE250, ECE351 extends Course{}
3  one sig Program{courses: set Course}
4  pred prerequisites{ reqs = ECE240→ECE155 + ECE250→ECE155 + ECE351→ECE250 }
5  fun graduationPlan[]: Program{ {p: Program| eq[#p.courses, 2] and
6      all c: p.courses| some c.reqs implies c.reqs in p.courses} }
7  pred showSuccesfulPlan[]{  prerequisites and some graduationPlan }
8  run showSuccesfulPlan
```

Fig. 1. Model of requirements for undergraduate Computer Engineering degree

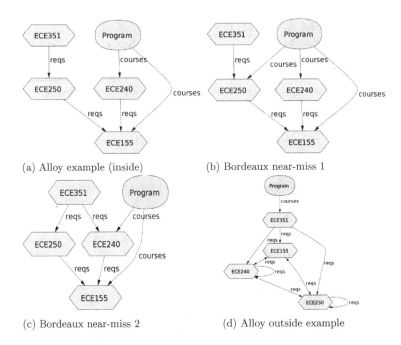

(a) Alloy example (inside)   (b) Bordeaux near-miss 1

(c) Bordeaux near-miss 2   (d) Alloy outside example

Fig. 2. Examples revealing an overconstraint issue in the model of Fig. 1

4 Proximate Pair-Finder Formula

We first define the basic concepts and formulas required to understand the formulas that Bordeaux synthesizes for producing near-hit and near-miss examples.

Definition 1 (Model). *We define an Alloy model as triple $\langle R, C, B \rangle$ comprising an ordered set of relations R, a set of constraints (formulas) on those relations C, and finite bounds B for those relations.*

Definition 2 (Valuation). *A valuation V of model M is a sequence of sets of tuples, where each entry in the sequence corresponds to a relation in M, and is within M's bounds B. Let $\mathcal{V}$ name the set of all possible valuations of M.*

The size (#) of a valuation is the number of tuples: $\#V \triangleq \sum_{i=1}^{|R|} |V_i|$

Definition 3 (Instance). *An instance I of model M is a type-correct valuation of M, according to Alloy's type system [5]. Briefly, every atom contained in the instance will be in exactly one unary relation, and the columns of each non-unary relation will be defined in terms of the unary relations.*

Suppose that I and J are two instances of model M.

The difference of I and J $(I - J)$ is a valuation of model M that, for each relation, contains the tuples from I that are not in J.

We say that J is a subset ($\subset$) of I if there is at least one relation for which J's tuples are a strict subset of I's tuples, and no relation for which I's tuples are not included in J's tuples; formally: $J \subset I \triangleq \wedge_{i=1}^{|R|}(J_i \subseteq I_i) \wedge \exists i | J_i \subset I_i$
The distance from I to J is $\#(I - J)$.
Let $\mathcal{I}$ name the set of all instances M.

Definition 4 (Inside-the-box Example). *Instance I is an inside example of model M if I satisfies M's constraints C.*

Definition 5 (Outside-the-box Example). *Instance O is an outside example of model M if O does not satisfy M's constraints C.*

4.1 Proximate Pair-Finder Formula

The core of Bordeaux generates variants of the *Proximate Pair-Finder Formula* (PPFF), which it gives to Alloy* to solve. The input to the PPFF generation is two mutually inconsistent sets of constraints, C_1 and C_2, over the same set of relations, R. A solution to the PPFF is a pair of examples, one of which (e_1) is inside C_1, and the other of which (e_2) is inside C_2. The key property of these two examples is that they are a minimum distance to each other. In the special case where C_2 is the negation of C_1, which the narrative of this paper focuses on, then e_1 is a *near-hit* example of C_1 and e_2 is a *near-miss* example of C_1.

The PPFF is expressed as a set-comprehension that returns a pair of examples e_1 and e_2. The PPFF contains two higher-order quantifiers: they are higher-order because they quantify over valuations (sets of sets). The formula effectively says that there is no other pair of examples that are closer to each other than are e_1 and e_2. Valuation v in the PPFF is the difference $e_2 - e_1$. Valuation w in the PPFF is the difference $e_2' - e_1'$. The relative minimization condition is that the size of w is not smaller than the size of v: $\#v \leq \#w$.

In the degenerate case where C_1 and C_2 are not mutually inconsistent, then the PPFF will always return $e_1 = e_2$, because any arbitrary example is at distance zero to itself. The PPFF is not designed to be meaningful when the constraints are not mutually inconsistent.

$$\{e_1, e_2 : \mathcal{I} \mid C_1[e_1] \wedge C_2[e_2] \wedge$$
$$\exists v : \mathcal{V} \mid (v = e_2 - e_1 \wedge e_1 \subset e_2) \wedge$$
$$\forall e_1' : \mathcal{I} - e_1, \ e_2' : \mathcal{I} - e_2, \ w : \mathcal{V} \mid$$
$$(C_1[e_1'] \wedge C_2[e_2'] \wedge w = e_2' - e_1' \wedge e_1' \subset e_2') \Rightarrow \#v \leq \#w\}$$

Fig. 3. Proximate Pair-Finder Formula (PPFF). The first line defines e_1 and e_2 as examples of C_1 and C_2, respectively. The second line defines v as the difference $e_2 - e_1$. The third line introduces alternative examples e_1' and e_2', and their difference w. The fourth line says that w is not less than v: *i.e.*, there is no pair of alternative examples that are closer to each other than are e_1 and e_2.

The examples e_1 and e_2 are not necessarily absolutely minimal with respect to C_1 and C_2, respectively. These two examples are *relatively* minimal with respect to each other: that is, the distance between them is small.

4.2   Encoding the PPFF for Alloy*

Alloy* supports higher-order quantifiers: *i.e.*, quantifiers over relations, which is required to solve PPFF. The user's model must be written in regular Alloy, with no higher-order quantifiers. Bordeaux transforms the user's Alloy model into an Alloy* model and adds a variant of the PPFF synthesized for the user's desired search. Bordeaux then transforms the Alloy* solution back into the terms of the user's original model.

While the Alloy* language is syntactically a superset of the regular Alloy language, so the user's model is a legal Alloy* model, simply taking the user's model as-is will not work for the PPFF. This paper focuses on the special case where C_2 is the negation of C_1, and C_1 is all of the constraints of the model. So the transformation to prepare for solving the PPFF must bundle up all of the constraints of the original model (fact blocks, multiplicity constraints, *etc.*) into a single predicate.

In actuality, the PPFF is generated using existential quantifiers rather than a set comprehension, and the skolemization gives the examples e_1 and e_2.

4.3   Special Cases of Potential User Interest

The user might be interested in some of the following special cases, which can all be easily accommodated by generating the PPFF with specific settings for C_1 and C_2 (some of these are not yet implemented in the current prototype [10]):

1. **Find a near-miss example and a near-hit example:** Set C_2 to be the negation of C_1 (as discussed above).
2. **Find a near-miss example close to an inside example:** Set C_1 to be a predicate that defines the inside example, and set C_2 to be the negation of the model's constraints.
3. **Find a near-hit example close to an outside example:** Set C_1 to be a predicate that defines the outside example, and set C_2 to be the model's constraints.
4. **Restrict the difference between the examples to certain relations:** The difference operation can easily be generated over a user-specified subset of the relations, rather than all of them.
5. **Smaller near-miss examples:** In PPFF, e_2 is bigger than e_1. If C_2 is the negation of the model's constraints, this will result in a near-miss example that is larger than the near-hit. To get a smaller near-miss example, simply set C_1 to be the negation of the model's constraints, and C_2 to be the model's constraints.

6. **Find a near-miss example for an inconsistent model:** If the original model is inconsistent, then it has no inside examples. A workaround for this situation is to set C_1 to be an empty example (no tuples), and set C_2 to be the negation of the model.

5   Experiments

To study the idea of browsing near-hit and near-miss examples, we have developed Bordeaux, a prototype that extends Alloy Analyzer. This study includes the experiments carried out to compare Bordeaux with other tools. From this study, we also show paths that optimize the performance of Bordeaux in finding near-miss examples. In this section, we explore the experiments revealing the position of Bordeaux among other similar tools. The next section discusses our ideas to optimize the prototype.

Given an example, Bordeaux can find a near-miss example. Users can browse more near-miss examples or ask for a near-hit example. To support this way of browsing, Bordeaux performs a relative minimization; namely, minimizing a distance between an inside example and an outside example. Although users cannot browse near-hit and near-miss examples with Alloy Analyzer, they can manually modify models to produce inside example and outside examples. Using Aluminum, the users can find minimal examples, and if they manually negate the model, they can browse minimal outside examples, too. Aluminum's concept of a minimal example, which we call *absolute* minimal, is an example with the smallest number of tuples.

The experiment includes five models that are shown in Table 1. We have used an Intel i7-2600K CPU at 3.40 GHz with 16 GB memory. All experiments are done with MiniSat. In what follows, we explain the experiments and discuss their contribution to answer the following research questions:

RQ-1 What is the extra cost for the relative minimums?
RQ-2 How many near-miss examples can Bordeaux find in one minute?
RQ-3a How far are arbitrary outside examples from the near-miss?
RQ-3b How far are absolute minimum outside examples from the near-miss?

To study the extra cost for finding near-miss examples with Bordeaux, we used Alloy Analyzer to find arbitrary inside examples and outside examples and compared their costs to using Bordeaux to find near-hit/near-miss example pairs (Table 1). To find the outside examples, we manually negated the studied models, *i.e.*, if C is a model's constraint, then $\neg C$ gives the negation of the model. In these experiments, for Bordeaux, we set C_1 to be equal to the arbitrary example returned by Alloy.

In Table 1, it can be seen that Bordeaux does not incur much additional cost for small models, but once the model gets larger the costs get significant (Item RQ-1). The small Binary Tree model is an exception where Bordeaux appears to run faster than the stock Alloy Analyzer. Occasional anomalies such as this are common with technology based on SAT solvers.

Table 1. Comparing Bordeaux (B) and Alloy Analyzer (A) to find outside examples

	Number of relations	Size of example	# SAT variables			# SAT clauses			Translation time(ms)			Execution time(ms)		
			B	A	B/A	B	A	B/A	B	A	B/A	B	A	B/A
Singly-linked List	2	1	846	492	1.72	2,518	757	3.33	15	26	0.58	29	20	1.45
Doubly-linked List	3	7	20,531	1,909	10.75	56,358	4,580	12.31	39,700	141	281.56	121,664	111	1,096.07
Binary Tree	3	1	1,088	710	1.53	3,295	1,440	2.29	12	438	0.03	44	166	0.27
Graduation Plan	5	8	5,934	734	8.08	17,846	1,276	13.99	381	336	1.13	439	74	5.93
File System	10	8	8,154	2,605	3.13	27,672	4,690	5.90	3,883	571	6.80	13,366	308	43.40

For answering Item RQ-2, we have done another experiment to count the number of distinct near-miss examples that Bordeaux generates in one minute. The results show how the prototype's performance degrades for the Alloy models with more relations or larger formula size. Given examples, Bordeaux produces *27*, *4*, *31*, *15*, and *9* distinct near-miss examples respectively for Singly-linked List, Doubly-linked List, Binary Tree, Graduation Plan, and File System models in one minute. The performance descends because Bordeaux reformulates and resolves the model per each distinct inside example and outside example. Bordeaux returns more near-miss examples for Singly-linked List and Binary Tree models, as the given examples of both models are fairly simpler than the others. Therefore, the near-miss examples will have relatively fewer tuples. That is, smaller near-miss examples lead to smaller and relatively simpler formulas for excluding redundant near-miss examples.

To answer Item RQ-3a and Item RQ-3b, we have performed another experiment to demonstrate how near-miss examples that Bordeaux systematically produces differ from outside examples that other tools produce from manually modified models. To do so, using various sizes of examples of different models, we evaluated their distances to outside examples that each instance-finder produces. We have selected Alloy Analyzer and Aluminum for comparing with Bordeaux. Although Alloy Analyzer and Aluminum do not provide capabilities for browsing outside examples, we have manually transformed the models and synthesized required statements.

For comparing relative minimal, absolute minimal, and arbitrary outside examples, we have used the aforementioned tools to find outside examples given arbitrary, small, medium, and large size examples. In the case of arbitrary examples, each tool finds a pair of inside example and outside example without any extra constraints on the size of examples. With restricted-size examples, all the tools have to first generate the same size examples, then generate outside examples for them. Depending on the models, the size of the examples varies from *two* to *five* tuples in small size examples and *nine* to *thirteen* tuples for the large size examples. We have recorded the size of inside examples and outside examples that each tool produces, as well as the number of tuples that should be added or removed from an example to make an example identical with its paired outside example.

As Fig. 4 shows, Aluminum generates absolute minimal inside examples and outside examples once the example size is arbitrary. It also always produces minimal outside examples regardless of the size of given examples. Alloy Analyzer generates arbitrary examples close to absolute minimal size, but the sizes of outside examples do not follow any particular pattern. Although Bordeaux produces examples in arbitrary sizes, it produces outside examples with one more tuple in all the models.

Depicted in Fig. 4, Bordeaux produces an outside example in a minimum distance from a given example. Answering Item RQ-3a, Alloy Analyzer behaves arbitrarily to produce outside examples close to the examples. The distances from examples to outside examples increase for larger examples. Answering RQ-3b,

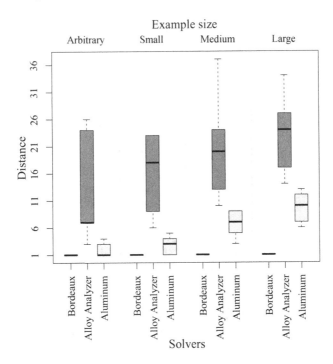

Fig. 4. Comparing Bordeaux, Alloy Analyzer, and Aluminum with respect to the number of tuples that differ between an example and an outside-the-box example.

for arbitrary and small examples, Aluminum produces outside examples that are fairly close to the examples. Given medium and large examples, Aluminum finds outside examples with larger distances from the given examples. Although the distances between inside examples and outside examples, generated by Aluminum, do not fluctuate like the distances between inside examples and outside examples produced by Alloy Analyzer, they show relative minimum distance similar to those found by Bordeaux.

Moreover, finding an outside example by negating the model provides no direction for adding or removing tuples. Although we expected to see a near-miss example with extra tuples, as generated by Bordeaux, Aluminum produced an outside example with fewer tuples for the Singly Linked-list model. Unlike Bordeaux, Alloy Analyzer and Aluminum do not directly produce outside examples of a model. Simulating a model's negation does not necessarily cause that Alloy Analyzer and Aluminum produce outside examples in a minimum distance from given examples of the studied models.

6   Optimization

By reviewing the experiment results, we have observed a trend in distances between inside examples and outside examples returned by Bordeaux. In the studied models, with the addition of a single tuple, all inside examples and outside examples become identical. In the other words, the examples are already near-hit examples, and they can be pushed to be outside examples with the minimum number of changes, *i.e.*, a single tuple. This observation assists us to select tighter scopes and parallelize searches for inside examples and outside examples. Without choosing tight scopes, the analysis becomes infeasible. Using parallelization, the time to find near-miss examples improves to *2.2* s on average from several minutes without parallelization.

6.1   Selecting Tighter Scopes

If most examples are near-hit examples, as the case studies show, Bordeaux can approximate the scope of each unary relation to be one more than the number of its tuples in the example when Alloy* is used for the underlying solver. As depicted in Table 2, we have rerun our experimental models by selecting scopes of *one* (+1), *two* (+2), and *three* (+3) more than the number of tuples of the example for each unary relation in the models. Note that these scopes limit the number of tuples only for unary relations. Non-unary relations still can have any tuples in difference between inside example and an outside example.

When the scopes of unary relations increase by *one*, Bordeaux can find a near-miss example for a studied model within *7.5* min on average. Provided the scopes increase by two, the time to find a near-miss example is inflated by the ratio of *8.43* on average. If the scopes increase by three, the time to find a near-miss example is *fifteen* times longer than the scopes with one more unary tuple. Moreover, except for one model, Bordeaux did not terminate within *90* min if the example size is large, and the scopes increase by two. Such a lack of results within the time-limit is more frequent once the scope increases by three. Selecting the tightest scope increase can make the problem tractable for Bordeaux. If Bordeaux cannot find a near-miss example with the least scope increase, it can increase the scopes and search in a larger universe of discourse.

6.2   Parallelization

Increasing the number of atoms exponentially elevates the size of the SAT-formula, the translation time to generate it, and its solving time. In some cases, such as the Binary Tree model with a large size example, if the scope is not properly selected, Alloy* cannot find a near-miss example within several hours. Another factor that influences on the magnitude of the SAT-formula is the number of integer atoms that Bordeaux incorporates into the formula to prevent the integer overflow that might occur for distance calculations.

Observing that most examples are near-hit examples and can become near-miss examples by adding or removing a single tuple, we make new formulas so that each one applies PPFF on individual relations. Solving each formula, Bordeaux may find a near-miss example for a given example regarding a particular relation of the model.

Table 2. Showing how selecting different scopes affects the cost of analysis performed by Alloy*. The notations '+1', '+2', and '+3' show the records when the scopes of all unary relations in the studied models are set to one, two, and three more tuples than the number of tuples in the same relations of examples. The columns with '+1' in their headers contain the actual records. The other columns contain the increase ratios.

		SAT variables			SAT clauses			Translation time(ms)			Execution time(ms)			Total time(ms)		
		+1	+2/+1	+3/+2	+1	+2/+1	+3/+2	+1	+2/+1	+3/+2	+1	+2/+1	+3/+2	+1	+2/+1	+3/+2
Arbitrary	Singly-linked List	846	1.8842	1.5558	2,518	1.9682	1.5672	15	1.0667	1.2500	29	0.828	1.458	44	0.9091	1.3750
	Doubly-linked List	20,531	2.4871	T/O	56,358	2.7368	T/O	39,700	11.8532	T/O	121,664	1.172	T/O	161,364	3.7998	T/O
	Binary Tree	1,088	1.9743	1.6294	3,295	2.0859	1.6770	12	1.1667	1.2857	4	3.500	1.429	16	1.7500	1.3571
	Graduation Plan	5,934	1.9821	1.4840	17,846	2.0284	1.5026	381	7.4436	1.7585	439	3.146	1.547	820	5.1427	1.6891
	File System	8,154	2.1634	T/O	27,672	2.2664	T/O	3,883	12.4074	T/O	13,366	15.239	T/O	17,249	14.6013	T/O
Small	Singly-linked List	1,862	1.5397	1.6993	5,858	1.5683	1.7648	12	1.4167	1.4118	19	0.947	2.222	31	1.1290	1.8286
	Doubly-linked List	3,204	1.8121	2.0541	10,922	1.9736	2.2635	31	1.7742	2.8364	174	0.632	2.036	205	0.8049	2.3030
	Binary Tree	5,371	2.0646	2.2615	17,404	2.1485	2.3097	105	5.5429	7.3849	141	13.652	3.484	246	10.1911	4.3893
	Graduation Plan	4,342	1.7725	1.5654	13,244	1.7882	1.5503	292	7.7671	1.7637	503	5.865	2.271	795	6.5635	2.0502
	File System	2,890	1.8218	1.5470	8,910	1.9274	1.5852	60	1.0500	1.2540	138	3.732	1.450	198	2.9192	1.4291
Medium	Singly-linked List	3,537	1.8476	1.3770	10,887	1.9555	1.4716	66	4.3030	0.7007	49	3.490	2.146	115	3.9565	1.2440
	Doubly-linked List	6,175	1.9869	2.1946	20,109	2.1358	2.3287	178	5.8427	7.6663	388	1.284	57.504	566	2.7173	23.8036
	Binary Tree	13,153	2.4004	T/O	44,972	2.4702	T/O	20,804	14.7966	T/O	9,873	11.299	T/O	30,677	13.6711	T/O
	Graduation Plan	4,862	1.8375	1.5640	14,838	1.8684	1.5456	291	8.0584	1.7693	155	23.587	0.963	446	13.4552	1.2781
	File System	6,946	2.2469	T/O	21,008	2.2076	T/O	12,256	15.8204	T/O	13,174	59.415	T/O	25,430	38.4043	T/O
Large	Singly-linked List	45,668	T/O	T/O	91,495	T/O	T/O	1,040,121	T/O	T/O	260	T/O	T/O	1,040,381	T/O	T/O
	Doubly-linked List	20,549	2.4846	T/O	56,436	2.7332	T/O	35,275	14.9564	T/O	163	1.227	T/O	35,438	14.8932	T/O
	Binary Tree	24,149	T/O	T/O	79,127	T/O	T/O	1,860,944	T/O	T/O	924,176	T/O	T/O	2,785,120	T/O	T/O
	Graduation Plan	16,528	T/O	T/O	34,806	T/O	T/O	7,814	T/O	T/O	35	T/O	T/O	7,849	T/O	T/O
	File System	14,215	T/O	T/O	41,246	T/O	T/O	2,839,697	T/O	T/O	2,018,781	T/O	T/O	4,858,478	T/O	T/O

Table 3. Parallelizing PPFF can improve the efficiency of Bordeaux. Columns show the ratio of metrics measured from solving without breaking PPFF, recorded in columns labeled by '+1' in Table 2, to different approaches solving PPFF for each relation. The columns Min-R and Max-R show the improvement ratio for using parallelization. For Min-R, the first process finds a near-miss example, and for Max-R, all processes finish their searches. Columns Seq-R shows the differences while all processes run sequentially.

		SAT variables			SAT clauses			Translation time			Execution time			Total time		
		Min-R	Max-R	Seq-R	Min-R	Max-R	Seq-R	Min-R	Max-R	Seq-R	Min-R	Max-R	Seq-R	Min-R	Max-R	Seq-R
Arbitrary	Singly-linked List	4.43	1.25	0.55	5.07	0.74	0.60	1.67	1.50	0.52	5.80	4.83	1.81	3.14	2.75	0.98
	Doubly-linked List	3.24	1.89	0.45	3.81	0.48	0.51	72.58	45.74	10.79	10,138.67	322.72	170.40	288.67	129.61	36.72
	Binary Tree	5.04	1.27	0.84	5.84	0.74	0.92	1.33	1.20	0.43	1.00	1.00	0.33	1.23	1.14	0.40
	Graduation Plan	2.05	1.49	0.28	2.11	0.65	0.28	2.01	1.37	0.26	54.88	36.58	13.30	4.14	2.83	0.55
	File System	2.98	2.22	0.27	3.28	0.41	0.30	23.25	14.93	1.96	1,336.60	636.48	230.45	97.45	61.38	8.44
Small	Singly-linked List	2.25	1.32	0.51	2.44	0.71	0.55	1.33	1.20	0.43	4.75	3.17	1.27	2.38	1.94	0.72
	Doubly-linked List	1.45	1.45	0.34	1.57	0.64	0.37	1.15	1.07	0.24	2.68	2.38	1.23	2.23	2.01	0.76
	Binary Tree	1.49	1.38	0.47	1.57	0.70	0.49	2.76	2.39	0.88	20.14	4.15	2.82	5.47	3.15	1.45
	Graduation Plan	2.36	1.67	0.31	2.48	0.57	0.33	2.25	1.36	0.29	83.83	71.86	22.86	5.85	3.58	0.77
	File System	5.49	2.30	0.34	6.27	0.40	0.38	1.25	1.11	0.12	1.05	1.02	0.15	1.10	1.05	0.14
Medium	Singly-linked List	1.95	1.18	0.46	2.07	0.80	0.48	4.40	1.53	0.70	9.80	6.13	2.45	5.75	2.25	1.01
	Doubly-linked List	2.19	1.49	0.34	2.42	0.62	0.37	3.71	2.66	0.60	5.54	4.04	0.92	4.80	3.47	0.79
	Binary Tree	3.07	2.07	0.88	3.34	0.46	0.94	73.25	44.45	19.87	580.76	46.79	38.72	101.92	45.18	23.56
	Graduation Plan	2.27	1.60	0.30	2.35	0.61	0.31	2.22	1.21	0.29	19.38	3.30	2.25	3.21	1.55	0.41
	File System	2.80	1.93	0.23	2.73	0.53	0.23	3.44	2.11	0.27	823.38	268.86	75.71	7.11	4.35	0.55
Large	Singly-linked List	2.52	1.31	0.52	3.19	0.62	0.64	98.98	19.26	13.85	8.67	4.56	1.90	98.73	19.24	13.83
	Doubly-linked List	3.23	1.88	0.45	3.78	0.48	0.51	69.71	37.89	9.72	7.76	0.40	0.20	67.24	26.45	7.96
	Binary Tree	2.81	1.75	0.78	3.16	0.55	0.84	312.76	182.68	83.34	3,513.98	337.54	168.55	448.27	215.48	100.14
	Graduation Plan	2.55	1.91	0.35	2.31	0.51	0.32	2.26	1.42	0.31	1.84	1.59	0.51	2.26	1.42	0.31
	File System	3.94	2.79	0.32	4.03	0.34	0.34	155.98	54.37	9.71	112,154.50	151.16	149.89	266.60	74.08	15.88

Finding near-miss examples for each relation has the benefit of avoiding additional integers in the universe of discourse. Depending on how many relations a model has, Bordeaux can solve a PPFF per each relation that leads to a relatively smaller universe of discourse. As Bordeaux can independently find near-miss examples per each relation, one approach is to parallelize the search so that each process searches for a near-miss example per each relation.

The parallelization applies to all relations in the model. The parallelization has no particular restriction on the scopes of the model's relations. However, selecting proper scopes increases the performance. If a process tries to find a minimum distance with respect to a unary relation, increasing the scope of the relation by one causes a found instance to be in the distance of one, provided adding tuples is requested. Since Alloy only allows restricting scope for unary relations, no increase is the tightest scopes for a process that tries to find a minimum distance with respect to a non-unary relation; more than one tuple of a non-unary relation can also change.

In this approach, if a process finds a near-miss example first that is at a distance of one from the given example, then all other processes can stop their searches. Otherwise, all processes should continue. In the end, either (a) the last process returns a near-miss example with the distance of one from the given example, (b) all processes return nothing, (c) some processes return near-miss examples with a distance of two, or (d) some processes return near-miss examples with a distance of three or more.

If PPFF can find a near-miss example in distance one from the given example, then one of the processes must be able to find it too. Clearly, the near-border examples finder formula found the example because only one relation gets or loses a tuple, so running the formula over that relation will get the same result. If such a near-miss example exists, one process has to return it. In case (a), the last finished process returns such a near-miss example.

If no process returns a near-miss example, $i.e.$, case (b), either such an instance does not exist at any distance from the given example or adding or removing more than one tuple from two or more relations turns the given example into an outside example. In the first situation, PPFF also returns no near-miss example; however, PPFF returns a near-miss example once tuples of more than a single relation need to be changed.

In case (c), some processes return near-miss examples with distance two from the given example. Then two is the true minimum distance. If there were a closer near-miss, it would be at distance one, and one of the other processes would have found it. Since that didn't happen, two is the minimum distance.

If a process returns a near-miss example with a distance of three from a given example and all other processes return no shorter distances, the PPFF might find a near-miss example in a closer distance which is exactly two. The distance might be two if simultaneously altering tuples of two relations makes a near-miss example; therefore, the individual processes cannot find such a near-miss example. If there was a near-miss example with distance one, processes should have returned it. In this case, distance three might be a local minimum. The same argument is valid for a distance of four or more in case (d).

As the case studies show, distances between an example and its paired near-miss example is highly likely to be one; therefore, parallelizing Bordeaux would often give the near-miss examples. As discussed, the process could also provide a good approximation of the minimum distance. In our practiced cases, all near-miss examples are found in distance one from given examples.

As Table 3 shows, parallelization improves the search for near-miss examples. In all studied models, regardless of the sizes of the given examples, parallelization decreases the size of the SAT-formula, the translation time to generate it, and the solving time. We have measured this improvement by recording the time and resources taken to find the first near-miss example, as well as the time and resources taken to finish all parallel processes. Compared to using non-broken PPFF with the least scope increase, the time to concurrently find the first near-miss example decreases by the ratio of 70.9 on average. Waiting for the termination of all processes' results changes the ratio to 30.2.

If there are not enough resources available for parallelization, sequentially running the decomposed processes still has value. The studied models show that the sum of the process times is often less than the general time when the size of an example is large. Since most of the Alloy statements synthesized for each process are the same, the translation time might be saved by reusing some parts that have already been translated for the formula of another relation. Full assessment of this idea is left for future work.

7   Conclusion

Bordeaux is a tool for finding near-hit and near-miss example pairs that are close to each other. The near-hit example is inside-the-box: it is an example of the model the user wrote. The near-miss example is outside-the-box: it is almost consistent with the user's model except for one or two crucial details. Others have found near-miss examples to be useful [1,6,22,23]. In particular, Gick and Paterson [6] found that pairing a near-miss example with a similar near-hit example increased human comprehension of the model. We posit that such pairs might be particularly helpful for discovering and diagnosing partial over-constraints in the model. Tool support for this task is currently limited.

The Bordeaux prototype has been built to work with ordinary Alloy models. It works by transforming the user's Alloy model and synthesizing a query with higher-order quantifiers that can be solved by Alloy* [9]. Through experiments we have observed that near-hit and near-miss examples often differ in no more than one tuple. We have based two optimizations on this observation: scope tightening and parallelization. Together, they significantly reduce the cost of searching. The formalization of the idea, the PPFF (Fig. 3), is more general than the specific use-case that our narrative has centred on. The formalization works from a pair of inconsistent constraints. The use-case narrative in this paper has focused on the specific circumstance when one constraint is the negation of the other, and sometimes even more narrowly on when the first constraint is a specific example. We intend to make use of the more general facility in our forthcoming implementation of a pattern-based model debugger [11].

Acknowledgements. We thank Vijay Ganesh, Krzysztof Czarnecki, and Marsha Chechik for their helpful discussions. This work was funded in part by NSERC (National Science and Engineering Research Council of Canada).

References

1. Bak, K., Zayan, D., Czarnecki, K., Antkiewicz, M., Diskin, Z., Wasowski, A., Rayside, D.: Example-driven modeling: model = abstractions + examples. In: Proceedings of the 2013 International Conference on Software Engineering, ICSE 2013, pp. 1273–1276. IEEE Press (2013)
2. Batot, E.: Generating examples for knowledge abstraction in MDE: a multi-objective framework. In: Balaban, M., Gogolla, M. (eds.) Proceedings of the ACM Student Research Competition at MODELS 2015 co-located with the ACM/IEEE 18th International Conference MODELS 2015, Ottawa, Canada, 29 September, 2015. CEUR Workshop Proceedings, vol. 1503, pp. 1–6 (2015). CEUR-WS.org
3. Cha, B., Iwama, K., Kambayashi, Y., Miyazaki, S.: Local search algorithms for partial maxsat. AAAI/IAAI 263268 (1997)
4. Cunha, A., Macedo, N., Guimarães, T.: Target oriented relational model finding. In: Gnesi, S., Rensink, A. (eds.) FASE 2014. LNCS, vol. 8411, pp. 17–31. Springer, Heidelberg (2014). doi:10.1007/978-3-642-54804-8_2
5. Edwards, J., Jackson, D., Torlak, E.: A type system for object models. In: Taylor, R.N., Dwyer, M.B. (eds.) Proceedings of the 12th ACM/SIGSOFT International Symposium on the Foundations of Software Engineering (FSE). Newport Beach, CA, USA, November 2004
6. Gick, M.L., Paterson, K.: Do contrasting examples facilitate schema acquisition and analogical transfer? Can. J. Psychol./Rev. Can. Psychol. 46(4), 539 (1992)
7. Macedo, N., Cunha, A.: Implementing QVT-R bidirectional model transformations using Alloy. In: Cortellessa, V., Varró, D. (eds.) FASE 2013. LNCS, vol. 7793, pp. 297–311. Springer, Heidelberg (2013). doi:10.1007/978-3-642-37057-1_22
8. Mendel, L.: Modeling by example. Master's thesis, Massachusetts Institute of Technology, September 2007
9. Milicevic, A., Near, J.P., Kang, E., Jackson, D.: Alloy*: a general-purpose higher-order relational constraint solver. In: Proceedings of the 37th International Conference on Software Engineering - vol. 1, pp. 609–619. ICSE 2015, IEEE Press (2015)
10. Montaghami, V., Odunayo, O., Guntoori, B., Rayside, D.: Bordeaux prototype (2016). https://github.com/drayside/bordeaux
11. Montaghami, V., Rayside, D.: Pattern-based debugging of declarative models. In: 2015 ACM/IEEE 18th International Conference on Model Driven Engineering Languages and Systems (MODELS), pp. 322–327. IEEE (2015)
12. Mottu, J.-M., Baudry, B., Traon, Y.: Mutation analysis testing for model transformations. In: Rensink, A., Warmer, J. (eds.) ECMDA-FA 2006. LNCS, vol. 4066, pp. 376–390. Springer, Heidelberg (2006). doi:10.1007/11787044_28

13. Nelson, T., Saghafi, S., Dougherty, D.J., Fisler, K., Krishnamurthi, S.: Aluminum: principled scenario exploration through minimality. In: Cheng, B., Pohl, K. (eds.) Proceedings of the 35th ACM/IEEE International Conference on Software Engineering (ICSE), San Francisco, CA, pp. 232–241 (2013)

14. Newcombe, C.: Debugging designs using exhaustively testable pseudo-code. Amazon Web Services (2011). Presentation Slides http://hpts.ws/papers/2011/sessions_2011/Debugging.pdf

15. Popelínský, L.: Efficient relational learning from sparse data. In: Scott, D. (ed.) AIMSA 2002. LNCS (LNAI), vol. 2443, pp. 11–20. Springer, Heidelberg (2002). doi:10.1007/3-540-46148-5_2

16. Rosner, N., Galeotti, J.P., Lopez Pombo, C.G., Frias, M.F.: ParAlloy: towards a framework for efficient parallel analysis of alloy models. In: Frappier, M., Glässer, U., Khurshid, S., Laleau, R., Reeves, S. (eds.) ABZ 2010. LNCS, vol. 5977, pp. 396–397. Springer, Heidelberg (2010). doi:10.1007/978-3-642-11811-1_33

17. Rosner, N., Siddiqui, J.H., Aguirre, N., Khurshid, S., Frias, M.F.: Ranger: parallel analysis of alloy models by range partitioning. In: 2013 IEEE/ACM 28th International Conference on Automated Software Engineering (ASE), pp. 147–157. IEEE (2013)

18. Seater, R.M.: Core extraction and non-example generation: debugging and understanding logical models. Master's thesis, Massachusetts Institute of Technology (2004)

19. Shlyakhter, I., Seater, R., Jackson, D., Sridharan, M., Taghdiri, M.: Debugging overconstrained declarative models using unsatisfiable cores. In: Proceedings of the 18th IEEE International Conference on Automated Software Engineering, pp. 94–105. IEEE (2003)

20. Torlak, E., Chang, F.S.-H., Jackson, D.: Finding minimal unsatisfiable cores of declarative specifications. In: Cuellar, J., Maibaum, T., Sere, K. (eds.) FM 2008. LNCS, vol. 5014, pp. 326–341. Springer, Heidelberg (2008). doi:10.1007/978-3-540-68237-0_23

21. Torlak, E., Jackson, D.: Kodkod: a relational model finder. In: Grumberg, O., Huth, M. (eds.) TACAS 2007. LNCS, vol. 4424, pp. 632–647. Springer, Heidelberg (2007). doi:10.1007/978-3-540-71209-1_49

22. Winston, P.H.: Artificial Intelligence, 3rd edn, pp. 150–356. Addison-Wesley, Reading (1992)

23. Zayan, D., Antkiewicz, M., Czarnecki, K.: Effects of using examples on structural model comprehension: a controlled experiment. In: Proceedings of the 36th International Conference on Software Engineering, pp. 955–966. ACM (2014)

Test Selection

Bucketing Failing Tests via Symbolic Analysis

Van-Thuan Pham[1(✉)], Sakaar Khurana[2], Subhajit Roy[2],
and Abhik Roychoudhury[1]

[1] National University of Singapore, Singapore, Singapore
{thuanpv,abhik}@comp.nus.edu.sg
[2] Indian Institute of Technology Kanpur, Kanpur, India
sakaark@gmail.com, subhajit@iitk.ac.in

Abstract. A common problem encountered while debugging programs is the overwhelming number of test cases generated by automated test generation tools, where many of the tests are likely to fail due to same bug. Some coarse-grained clustering techniques based on point of failure (PFB) and stack hash (CSB) have been proposed to address the problem. In this work, we propose a new symbolic analysis-based clustering algorithm that uses the *semantic reason* behind failures to group failing tests into more "meaningful" clusters. We implement our algorithm within the KLEE symbolic execution engine; our experiments on 21 programs drawn from multiple benchmark-suites show that our technique is effective at producing more fine grained clusters as compared to the FSB and CSB clustering schemes. As a side-effect, our technique also provides a semantic characterization of the fault represented by each cluster—a precious hint to guide debugging. A user study conducted among senior undergraduates and masters students further confirms the utility of our test clustering method.

1 Introduction

Software debugging is a time consuming activity. Several studies [4,6,8,9,18] have proposed clustering techniques for failing tests and proven their effectiveness in large-scale real-world software products. The Windows Error Reporting System (WER) [8] and its improvements such as ReBucket [6] try to arrange error reports into various "buckets" or clusters. WER employs a host of heuristics involving module names, function offset and other attributes. The Rebucket approach (proposed as an improvement to WER) uses specific attributes such as the call stack in an error report.

Although the techniques have been applied widely in industry, there are three common problems that they can suffer from (as mentioned in [8]). The first problem is *"over-condensing"* in which the failing tests caused by multiple bugs are placed into a single bucket. The second problem is *"second bucket"* in which failing tests caused by one bug are clustered into different buckets. The third one, *"long tail"* problem, happens if there are many small size buckets with just one or a few tests. For example, using failure type and location (as used in KLEE [4]) for clustering tests are more likely to suffer from both *over-condensing* and *second bucket* problems as they would group all tests that fail

© Springer-Verlag GmbH Germany 2017
M. Huisman and J. Rubin (Eds.): FASE 2017, LNCS 10202, pp. 43–59, 2017.
DOI: 10.1007/978-3-662-54494-5_3

at the same location, completely insensitive to the branch sequence and the call-chain leading to the error. Call stack similarity for clustering tests also suffers from the "over-condensing" and "second bucket" problems because it is insensitive to the intraprocedural program paths (i.e. the conditional statements within functions). One of the main reasons why techniques in [4,6,8,9,18] suffer from these problems is that they do not take program *semantics* into account.

In this work, we propose a novel technique to cluster failing tests via symbolic analysis. Unlike previous work that drive bucketing directly from error reports, we adapt symbolic path exploration techniques (like KLEE [4]) to cluster (or bucket) the failing tests on-the-fly. We drive bucketing in a manner such that tests in each group fail due to the same *reason*. Since we use symbolic analysis for clustering, our technique leads to more accurate bucketing; that is (a) tests for two different bugs are less likely to appear in the same bucket, and (b) tests showing the same bug are less likely to appear in different buckets. We experimentally evaluate our semantics-based bucketing technique on a set of 21 programs drawn from five repositories: IntroClass, Coreutils, SIR, BugBench and exploit-db. Our results demonstrate that our symbolic analysis based bucketing technique is effective at clustering tests: for instance, the **ptx** program (in our set of benchmarks) generated **3095** failing tests which were grouped into 3 clusters by our technique. Similarly, our tool clustered **4510** failing tests of the **paste** program into 3 clusters.

In addition to bucketing failures, our tool provides a *semantic characterization* of the reason of failure for the failures in each cluster. This characterization can assist the developers better understand the nature of the failures and, thus, guide their debugging efforts. The existing approaches are not capable of defining such an accurate characterization of their clusters (other than saying that all tests fail at a certain location or with a certain stack configuration).

While our algorithm is capable of bucketing tests as they are generated via a symbolic execution engine, it is also capable of clustering failures in existing test-suites by a post-mortem analysis on the set of failures.

The contributions of this paper are as follows:

- We propose an algorithm to efficiently cluster failing test cases, both for the tests generated automatically by symbolic execution as well as tests available in existing test-suites. Our algorithm is based on deriving a *culprit* for a failure by comparing the failing path to the nearest correct path. As we use semantic information from the program to drive our bucketing, we are also able to derive a *characterization* of the reason of failure of the tests grouped in a cluster. The existing approaches are not capable of defining such characterization for the clusters they produce.
- We implement a prototype of the clustering approach on top of the symbolic execution engine KLEE [4]. Our experiments on 21 programs show that our approach is effective at producing more meaningful clusters as compared to existing solutions like the point of failure and stack hash based clustering.

2   Overview

We illustrate our technique using a motivating example in Fig. 1. In the `main()` function, the code at line 27 manages to calculate the value of $(2^x + x! + \sum_{i=0}^{y} i)$ in which x and y are non-negative integers. It calls three functions, `power()`, `factorial()` and `sum()`, to calculate 2^x, $x!$ and sum of all integer numbers from 0 to y. While `sum()` is a correct implementation, both `power()` and `factorial()` are buggy.

In the `power()` function, the programmer attempts an optimization of saving a multiplication: she initializes the result (the integer variable `pow()`) to 2 (line 2) and skips the multiplication at line 5 if n equals 1. However, the optimization does not handle the special case in which n is zero. When n is zero, the loop is not entered and the function returns 2: it is a wrong value since 2^0 must be 1. Meanwhile, in the `factorial()` function the programmer uses a wrong condition for executing the loop at line 13. The correct condition should be $i \leq n$ instead of $i < n$. The incorrect loop condition causes the function to compute factorial of $n - 1$ so the output of the function will be wrong if $n \geq 2$.

```
1   unsigned int power(unsigned int n) {
2       unsigned int i, pow = 2;
3   /* Missing code: if (n == 0) return 1; */
4       for(i=1; i<=n; i++) {
5           if(i==1) continue;
6           pow = 2*pow;
7       }
8       return pow;
9   }
10  unsigned int factorial(unsigned int n) {
11      unsigned int i,result = 1;
12  /* Incorrect operator: < should be <= */
13      for(i=1;i<n;i++)
14          result = result*i;
15      return result;
16  }
17  unsigned int sum(unsigned int n) {
18      unsigned int result = 0, i;
19      for (i=0; i<=n; i++)
20          result += i;
21      return result;
22  }
23  int main() {
24      unsigned int, x, y, val, val_golden;
25      make_symbolic(x, y);
26      assume(x<=2 && y<=2);
27      val = power(x)+factorial(x)+sum(y);
28      assert(val == golden_output(x, y));
29      return 0;
30  }
```

Fig. 1. Motivating example

We can use a symbolic execution engine (like KLEE) to generate test cases that expose the bugs. In order to do that, we first mark the variables x and y as symbolic (line 25) and add an assert statement at line 28. The assertion is used to check whether the calculated value for $2^x + x! + \sum_{i=0}^{y}$ (as stored in val) is different from the expected value which is fetched from `golden_output()`.

The specification *oracle* `golden_output()` can be interpreted in many ways depending on the debugging task: for example, it can be the previous version of the implementation when debugging regression errors, or the expected result of each test when run over a test-suite. For the sake of simplicity, we add an `assume()` statements at line 26 to bound the values of symbolic variables x and y.

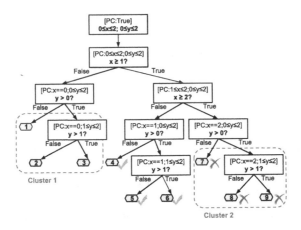

Fig. 2. Symbolic execution tree for motivating example

Figure 2 shows the symbolic execution tree that KLEE would explore when provided with this example. In this paper, we use the term **failing path** to indicate program paths that terminate in error. The error can be assertion violation or run-time error detected by symbolic execution engine such as divide-by-zero or memory access violation (as supported in KLEE). In contrast, the term **passing path** indicates paths that successfully reach the end of the program (or the *return* statement in the intraprocedural setting) with no errors.

As shown in Fig. 2, KLEE explores 9 feasible executions and detects 6 failing paths; the paths are labeled from 1 to 9 in the order tests are generated while following the Depth-First-Search (DFS) search strategy. If we apply failure location based or call-stack based bucketing techniques, *both of them will place all 6 failing tests in a single cluster* as there is only one failure location at line 28, and the call stacks are identical when the failure is triggered. Hence, both the techniques suffer from the "over-condensing" problem as the failures are due to two different bugs (in the `power()` and `factorial()` functions).

Let us now present our approach informally: given a failing test t encountered during symbolic exploration, our algorithm compares the path condition of t with the path condition of a successful test t' that has the *longest common prefix* with t. The branch b at which the execution of t and t' differ is identified as the *culprit branch* and the branch condition at b which leads to the failing path is identified as the *culprit constraint*—the "reason" behind the failure of t. Intuitively, the reason behind blaming this branch for the failure is that the failing path t could have run into the passing execution t'—only if this branch b had not misbehaved!

Table 1 presents the result produced by our clustering algorithm (refer to Fig. 2 for the symbolic execution tree). The failing tests 1–3 fail due to the bug in the `power()` function. The *culprit constraint* or "reason" for these failures is attributed as $x < 1$, since it is the condition on the branch where these failing tests diverge from their nearest passing test (Test 4), after sharing the *longest common prefix* $((0 \leq x \leq 2) \wedge (0 \leq y \leq 2))$. Hence, we create the first cluster

Table 1. Clustering result: Symbolic analysis

Path ID	Test Case	Path Condition	Culprit Constraint	Clus. ID
1	x=0, y=0	$(0 \leq x, y \leq 2) \wedge (x < 1) \wedge (y \leq 0)$	$(x < 1)$	1
2	x=0, y=1	$(0 \leq x, y \leq 2) \wedge (x < 1) \wedge (y > 0) \wedge (y \leq 1)$	$(x < 1)$	1
3	x=0, y=2	$(0 \leq x, y \leq 2) \wedge (x < 1) \wedge (y > 0) \wedge (y > 1) \wedge (y \leq 2)$	$(x < 1)$	1
4	x=1, y=0	$(0 \leq x, y \leq 2) \wedge (x \geq 1) \wedge (\boldsymbol{x} < \boldsymbol{2}) \wedge (y \leq 0)$	NA	NA
5	x=1, y=1	$(0 \leq x, y \leq 2) \wedge (x \geq 1) \wedge (\boldsymbol{x} < \boldsymbol{2}) \wedge (y > 0) \wedge (y \leq 1)$	NA	NA
6	x=1, y=2	$(0 \leq x, y \leq 2) \wedge (x \geq 1) \wedge (\boldsymbol{x} < \boldsymbol{2}) \wedge (y > 0) \wedge (y > 1) \wedge (y \leq 2)$	NA	NA
7	x=2, y=0	$(0 \leq x, y \leq 2) \wedge (x \geq 1) \wedge (x \geq 2) \wedge (y \leq 0)$	$(x \geq 2)$	2
8	x=2, y=1	$(0 \leq x, y \leq 2) \wedge (x \geq 1) \wedge (x \geq 2) \wedge (y > 0) \wedge (y \leq 1)$	$(x \geq 2)$	2
9	x=2, y=2	$(0 \leq x, y \leq 2) \wedge (x \geq 1) \wedge (x \geq 2) \wedge (y > 0) \wedge (y > 1) \wedge (y \leq 2)$	$(x \geq 2)$	2

(Cluster 1) and place tests 1–3 in it, with the characterization of the cluster as $(x < 1)$. Similarly, the failing tests 7–9 (failing due to the bug in `factorial()`) share the longest common prefix $((0 \leq x \leq 2) \wedge (0 \leq y \leq 2) \wedge (x \geq 1))$ with Test 4; thus, the culprit constraint for tests 7–9 is inferred as $(x \geq 2)$. Hence, these tests are placed in Cluster 2 with the *characterization* $(x \geq 2)$. Note that the culprit constraints $(x < 1)$ and $(x \geq 2)$ form a neat *semantic characterization* of the failures in these two clusters.

Summary. In this example, our semantic-based bucketing approach correctly places 6 failing tests into 2 different clusters. Unlike the two compared techniques, it does not suffer from the "over-condensing" problem, and therefore, yields a more *meaningful* clustering of failures. Moreover, we provide a *semantic characterization* for each cluster that can assist developers in their debugging efforts. In fact, the characterization for `Cluster1` $(x < 1)$ exactly points out the bug in `power()` (as x is non-negative integer, $x < 1$ essentially implies that x equals zero). Likewise, the characterization for `Cluster2` $(x \geq 2)$ hints the developer to the wrong loop condition in the `factorial()` function (as the loop is only entered for $x \geq 2$). We, however, emphasize that our primary objective is **not** to provide root-causes for bugs, but rather to enable a good bucketing of failures.

3   Reasons of Failure

The *path condition* ψ_p of a program path p is a logical formula that captures the set of inputs that exercise the path p; i.e. ψ_p is true for a test input t if and only if t exercises p. We say that a path p is *feasible* if its path condition ψ_p is satisfiable; otherwise p is *infeasible*.

We record the *path condition* ψ_p for a path p as a list of conjuncts l_p. Hence, the *size* of a path condition $(|\psi_p|)$ is simply the cardinality of the list l_p. We also assume that as symbolic execution progresses, the branch constraints (encountered during the symbolic execution) are recorded in the path condition *in order*. This enables us to define *prefix(i, ψ_p)* as the prefix of length i of the list l_p that represents the path condition ψ_p. Hence, when we say that two paths p and q have a *common prefix* of length i, it means that $prefix(i, \psi_p) = prefix(i, \psi_q)$.

Definition 1 (Culprit Constraint). *Given a failing path π_f with a path condition ψ_f (as a conjunct $b_1 \wedge b_2 \wedge \cdots \wedge b_i \wedge \ldots b_n$) and an exhaustive set of all feasible passing paths Π, we attribute b_i (the i-th constraint where i ranges from 1 to n) as the culprit constraint if and only if $i - 1$ is the maximum value of j $(0 \leq j < n)$ such that $prefix(j, \psi_f) = prefix(j, \psi_p)$ among all passing paths $p \in \Pi$.*

We use the *culprit constraint* (as a symbolic expression) as the reason why the error path "missed" out on following the passing path; in other words, the failing path could have run into a passing path, only if the branch corresponding to the culprit constraint had not *misbehaved*.

Our heuristic of choosing the culprit constraint in the manner described above is primarily designed to achieve the following objectives:

- **Minimum change to Symbolic Execution Tree**: Our technique targets well-tested production-quality programs that are "almost" correct; so, our heuristic of choosing the latest possible branch as the "culprit" essentially tries to capture the intuition that the symbolic execution tree of the *correct* program must be similar to the symbolic execution tree of the faulty program. *Choosing the latest such branch as the culprit is a greedy attempt at encouraging the developer to find a fix that makes the minimum change to the current symbolic execution tree of the program.*

- **Handle "burst" faults**: In Fig. 2, all paths on one side of the node with $[PC : 1 \leq x \leq 2; 0 \leq y \leq 2]$ fail. So, the branching predicate for this node, $x \geq 2$, looks "suspicious". Our heuristic of identifying the latest branch as the culprit is directed at handling such scenarios of "burst" failures on one side of a branch.

4   Clustering Framework

4.1   Clustering Algorithm

Algorithm 1 shows the core steps in dynamic symbolic execution with additional statements (highlighted in grey) for driving test clustering. The algorithm operates on a representative imperative language with assignments, assertions and conditional jumps (adapted from [3, 13]). A symbolic executor maintains a state (l, pc, s) where l is the address of the current instruction, pc is the path condition, and s is a symbolic store that maps each variable to either a concrete value or an expression over input variables. At line 3, the algorithm initializes the worklist with an initial state pointing to the start of the program $(l_0, true, \emptyset)$: the first instruction is at l_0, the path condition is initialized as $true$ and the initial store map is empty.

The symbolic execution runs in a loop until the worklist W becomes empty. In each iteration, based on a search heuristic, a state is picked for execution (line 7). Note that to support failing test bucketing, the search strategy must be DFS

Algorithm 1. Symbolic Exploration with Test Clustering

1: **procedure** SYMBOLICEXPLORATION(l_0, W)
2:     $C \leftarrow \{\}$; $passList \leftarrow [\,]$; $failList \leftarrow [\,]$ ▷ initialization for bucketing
3:     $W \leftarrow \{(l_0, true, \emptyset)\}$ ▷ initial worklist
4:     **while** $W \neq \emptyset$ **do**
5:         $(l, pc, s) \leftarrow pickNext(W)$
6:         $S \leftarrow \emptyset$
7:         **switch** $instrAt(l)$ **do**   ▷ execute instruction
8:             **case** $v := e$ ▷ assignment instruction
9:                 $S \leftarrow \{(succ(l), pc, s[v \rightarrow eval(s, e)])\}$
10:             **case** $if\ (e)\ goto\ l'$ ▷ branch instruction
11:                 $e \leftarrow eval(s, e)$
12:                 **if** $(isSat(pc \wedge e) \wedge isSat(pc \wedge \neg e))$ **then**
13:                     $S \leftarrow \{(l', pc \wedge e, s), (succ(l), pc \wedge \neg e, s)\}$
14:                 **else if** $(isSat(pc \wedge e)$ **then**
15:                     $S \leftarrow \{(l', pc \wedge e, s)\}$
16:                 **else**
17:                     $S \leftarrow \{(succ(l), pc \wedge \neg e, s)\}$
18:                 **end if**
19:             **case** $assert(e)$ ▷ assertion
20:                 $e \leftarrow eval(s, e)$
21:                 **if** $(isSat(pc \wedge \neg e))$ **then**
22:                     $testID \leftarrow$ GENERATETEST($\mathbf{l}, pc \wedge \neg e, \mathbf{s}$)
23:                     $pc' \leftarrow ConvertPC(pc \wedge \neg e)$
24:                     ADDTOLIST(**failList**, (**testID**, pc'))
25:                     **continue**
26:                 **else**
27:                     $S \leftarrow \{(succ(l), pc \wedge e, s)\}$
28:                 **end if**
29:             **case** halt   ▷ end of path
30:                 $testID \leftarrow$ GENERATETEST($\mathbf{l}$,**pc**,**s**)
31:                 $pc' \leftarrow ConvertPC(pc)$
32:                 ADDTOLIST(**passList**, (**testID**, pc'))
33:                 **if** $failList \neq [\,]$ **then**
34:                     CLUSTERTESTS(**C**,**passList**,**failList**)
35:                     $failList \leftarrow [\,]$ ▷ empty failing list
36:                 **end if**
37:                 **continue**
38:         $W \leftarrow W \cup S$ ▷ update worklist
39:     **end while**
40:     **if** $failList \neq [\,]$ **then**
41:         CLUSTERTESTS(**C**,**passList**,**failList**)
42:     **end if**
43: **end procedure**

---

or an instance of our clustering-aware strategy (*clustering-aware search strategy* discussed in Sect. 4.2). A worklist S (initialized as empty) keeps all the states created/forked during symbolic exploration.

If the current instruction is an assignment instruction, the symbolic store s is updated and a new state pointing to the next instruction is inserted into S (lines $8 - 9$). A conditional branch instruction is processed (line 10) via a constraint solver that checks the satisfiability of the branch condition; if both its branches are satisfiable, two new states are created and inserted into S. If only one of the branches is satisfiable, the respective state is added to S. For *assert* instructions, the symbolic execution checks the assert condition, and if it holds, a new program state is created and the state is added to S. If the condition does not hold, it triggers an assertion failure, thereby, generating a failing test case (we call the respective test case a **"failing test"**). Some symbolic execution engines (like KLEE [4]) perform run-time checks to detect failures like divide-by-zero and memory access violations; in this algorithm, the *assert* instruction is used to represent the failures detected by such checks as well. On encountering a halt instruction, the symbolic execution engine generates a test-case for the path (we refer to such a test case as a **"passing test"**). The *halt* instruction represents a normal termination of the program.

To support clustering of tests, we define two new variables, *passList* and *failList*, to store information about all explored passing and failing tests (respectively). For each test, we keep a pair ($testID$, $pathCondition$), where $testID$ is the identifier of the test generated by symbolic execution, and $pathCondition$ is a list of branch conditions (explained in Sect. 3). We also introduce a variable C that keeps track of all clusters generated so far; C is a map from a culprit constraint (cluster reason) to a list of identifiers of failing tests. The bucketing functionality operates in two phases:

Algorithm 2. Clustering failing tests

```
 1: procedure CLUSTERTESTS(Clusters,passList,failList)
 2:     for (failID, failPC) ∈ failList do
 3:         maxPrefixLength ← 0
 4:         for (passID, passPC) ∈ passList do
 5:             curPrefixLength ← LCP(failPC, passPC)
 6:             if curPrefixLength > maxPrefixLength then
 7:                 maxPrefixLength ← curPrefixLength
 8:             end if
 9:         end for
10:         reason ← failPC[maxPrefixLength+1]
11:         UPDATE(Clusters,failID,reason)
12:     end for
13: end procedure
14: ────────────────────────────────────────
15: procedure UPDATE(Clusters,failID,reason)
16:     for r ∈ Clusters.Reasons do
17:         if ISVALID(reason ⇒ r) then
18:             Clusters[r].ADD(failID)
19:             return
20:         else if ISVALID(r ⇒ reason) then
21:             UPDATEREASON(Clusters[r], reason)
22:             Clusters[reason].ADD(failID)
23:             return
24:         end if
25:     end for
26:     ADDCLUSTER(Clusters, reason, failID)
27: end procedure
```

Phase 1: Searching for failing and passing tests. The selected search strategy guides the symbolic execution engine through several program paths, generating test cases when a path is terminated. We handle the cases where tests are generated, and update the respective list (*passList* or *failList*) accordingly. In particular, when a failing test case is generated, the path condition (*pc*) is converted to a list of branch conditions (pc'). The pair comprising of the list pc' and the identifier of the failing test case form a representation of the failing path; the pair is recorded in *failList* (lines 23–24). The *passList* is handled in a similar manner (lines 31–32).

Phase 2: Clustering discovered failing tests. Once a passing test is found (lines 35–37) or the symbolic execution engine completes its exploration (lines 42–43), the clustering function *ClusterTests* will be invoked. The procedure *ClusterTests* (Algorithm 2) takes three arguments: (1) all clusters generated so far (*Clusters*), (2) all explored passing tests (*passList*) and (3) all failing tests that have not been clustered (*failList*). In this function, the culprit constraints of all failing tests in *failList* is computed (lines 2–9) and, then, the function *Update* is called (line 10) to cluster the failing tests accordingly.

The *Update* function (Algorithm 2) can place a failing test into an existing cluster or create a new one depending on the culprit constraint (reason) of the test. We base our clustering heuristic on the intuition that the reason of failure of each test within a cluster should be *subsumed* by a core reason (r_c) represented by the cluster. Hence, for a given failing test f (with a reason of failure r_f) being clustered and a set of all clusters *Clusters*, the following three cases can arise:

– **There exists $c \in C$ such that r_c subsumes r_f**: in this case, we add the test f to the cluster c (line 18);
– **There exists $c \in C$ such that r_f subsumes r_c**: in this case, we *generalize* the core reason for cluster c by resetting r_f as the general reason for failure for tests in cluster c (lines 21–22);
– **No cluster reason subsumes r_f, and r_f subsumes no cluster reason**: in this case, we *create* a new cluster c' with the sole failing test f and attribute r_f as the core reason of failure for tests in this cluster (line 26).

4.2 Clustering-Aware Search Strategy

It is easy to see that Algorithm 1 will yield the correct *culprit constraints* if the search strategy followed is DFS: once a failing path f_i is encountered, the passing path that shares the maximum common prefix with f_i is either the last *passing* path encountered before the failure, or is the next *passing* path after f_i (i.e. ignoring all failures in the interim). Hence, a depth-first traversal of the symbolic execution tree will always find the culprit constraints by constructing the *largest common prefix* of the failing paths with at most two passing paths (the passing executions just before and just after encountering the failures).

However, DFS has a very poor coverage when used with a time-budget. Hence, we require search strategies different than DFS (like the Random and CoverNewCode strategies in KLEE) to achieve a good coverage. In fact, during our experiments, we could not trigger most of the failures in our benchmarks with DFS within reasonable timeouts.

We design a new *clustering-aware search strategy* (CLS) that is capable of discovering the precise culprit constraint while achieving a high coverage at the same time. CLS is built on a crucial observation that we *only* require DFS on a failing test to guide the search to its nearest passing test; on a passing test, the next test can be generated as per any search heuristic. Hence, one can implement any combination of suitable search strategies (to achieve high code coverage) while maintaining the use of DFS on encountering a failure (to identify the culprit constraint precisely).

We leverage a so-called *branching tree*, a data structure maintained by many symbolic execution engines (like KLEE) to record the symbolic execution tree traversed in terms of the branching/forking history (KLEE refers to it as the *process tree*). Let us illustrate as to how we combine an arbitrary search strategy (*SS*) with DFS exploration to implement an instance of CLS using the branching tree in Fig. 3. In the tree,

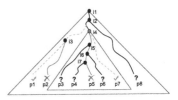

Fig. 3. A branching tree

$i1$–$i7$ are internal nodes while $p1$–$p8$ are leaf nodes. Note that in the following paragraphs, we will use the term (leaf) node and path interchangeably. Basically, CLS works in two phases:

Phase 1: *SS* searches for a failing test. The search heuristic *SS* searches for a failure using its own algorithm. Suppose *SS* first detects a failing path $p5$, it returns control to CLS that now switches to the DFS heuristic (to locate the "nearest" passing test, i.e. the one that has the longest common prefix with $p5$).

Phase 2: DFS looks for "nearest" passing test. Continuing with our example (Fig. 3), by the time *SS* detects the failing path $p5$, assume that we have explored three paths $p1$, $p2$, $p7$ and successfully put the failing path $p2$ into its correct cluster. So, now only four active paths remain: $p3$, $p4$, $p6$ and $p8$. At this point, our CLS search strategy uses another crucial observation: since $p7$ is a passing path and $i4$ is the closest common ancestor node of $p5$ and $p7$, the nearest passing path for $p5$ must be $p7$ or another passing path spawned from intermediate nodes $i5$, $i6$ or $i7$. Hence, we can reduce the search space for finding the nearest passing path for $p5$ from the space represented by outer blue triangle to the inner (smaller) triangle (as $p7$ is a passing path, it must be the nearest passing path if no "nearer" passing path is discovered in the subtree rooted at $i4$). We omit the details of how it is achieved for want of space.

If the symbolic execution is run with a timeout setting, the timeout can potentially fire while CLS is searching for the nearest passing path to a failing execution. In this case, we simply pick the nearest passing path to the failing execution among the paths explored so far to compute the culprit constraint.

Our technique is potent enough to cluster an existing test-suite by running the symbolic execution engine needs to run in a mode that the exploration of a path that is controlled by the failing test (like the "seed" mode in KLEE [4]). During path exploration, the first passing test encountered in a depth-first traversal seeded from the failing test t would necessarily be the passing test that has the longest common prefix with t. Thus, we can compute the *culprit constraint* accordingly, and use it to form a new cluster or update an existing cluster.

4.3 Generalize Reasons for Failure

Consider Fig. 4: the program checks if the absolute value of each element in the array is greater than 0. The buggy assertion contains $>$ comparison instead of $\geq$), which would cause 10 failing test cases $\forall\ i \in \{0..9\}$. Since each array element is modeled as a different symbolic variable, all 10 cases are clustered separately.

```
1  int main() {
2    int arr[10], int i;
3    make_input(arr, sizeof(arr));
4    for (i = 0; i < 10; i++) {
5      if (a[i] < 0) a[i] = -a[i];
6      assert(a[i] > 0); // a[i] >= 0
7    }
8  }
```

Fig. 4. Generalization for arrays

In such cases, we need to *generalize* errors that occur on different indices but due to the same core reason. For example, if the reason is: $arr[4] > 0 \wedge arr[4] < 10$, we change this formula to $\exists x\ (arr[x] > 0 \wedge arr[x] < 10)$. Note that this is only a heuristic, and our implementation allows the user to disable this feature.

5 Experimental Evaluation

We evaluated our algorithm on a set of 21 programs: three programs from *Intro-Class* [10] (a micro benchmark for program repair tools) and the remaining eighteen real-world programs taken from four benchmarks-suites: eleven programs from Coreutils [1] version 6.10, three from SIR [7], one from BugBench [16] and three from exploit-db [2]. The three subject programs from exploit-db (downloaded them from the project's website) were used in [11]. The bugs in IntroClass, Coreutils, exploit-db and BugBench programs are real bugs, whereas the ones in SIR are seeded.

We manually inserted **assert** statements in the programs taken from the Intro-Class benchmark to specify the test oracle, while all remaining 18 real-world programs were kept unchanged. During symbolic execution, the failing test cases are generated due to the violation of embedded assertions or triggering of run-time errors (captured by KLEE) like divide-by-zero and invalid memory accesses.

We compared our symbolic-analysis based (SAB) test clustering method to two baseline techniques: call-stack based (CSB) and point-of-failure based (PFB) clustering. While SAB refers to the implementation of our algorithm within KLEE, we implemented CSB and PFB on top of KLEE to evaluate our implementation against these techniques. Specifically, our implementation first post-processes the information of test cases generated by KLEE to compute the stack hash (on function call stack) and extract failure locations. Based on the computed and extracted data, they cluster the failing tests.

We conducted all of the experiments on a virtual machine created on a host computer with a 3.6 GHz Intel Core i7-4790 CPU and 16 GB of RAM. The virtual machine was allocated 4 GB of RAM and its OS is Ubuntu 12.04 32-bit. For our experiments, we use the clustering-aware search strategy (CLS), enable array generalization and use a timeout of one hour for each subject program. KLEE is run with the `--emit-all-errors` flag to enumerate all failures.

5.1   Results and Analysis

Table 2 shows the results from our experiments on selected programs. Size provides the size of the program in terms of the number of LLVM bytecode instructions. #Fail Tests provides the number of failing tests. The rest of the columns provide the number of clusters (#C) for Point-of-failure (PFB), Stack Hash (CSB) and our Symbolic Analysis (SAB) based methods. Note that #C(PFB) doubles up to also record the number of failing locations. As KLEE symbolically executes the LLVM [14] bitcode, we show the size of the program in terms of the total lines of the LLVM bitcode instructions.

In several programs (like **ptx**, **paste**, **grep**) SAB places thousands of failing tests into manageable number of clusters. Compared to CSB, in 12 out of 21 subjects (∼57%), our method produces more fine-grained clustering results. Compared to PFB, our technique expands the number of clusters to get a more fine-grained set in 10/21 subjects. However, our method also collapses the clusters in case the program has failures that are likely to be caused by the same bug but the failures occur at several different locations (like **ptx** and **paste**) (Table 2).

RQ1. Does our technique produce more fine-grained clusters? In the experiments, we manually debugged and checked the root causes of failures in all subject programs. Based on that, we confirm that our SAB approach does

Table 2. Test clustering: num. of clusters   **Table 3.** Test clustering: overhead

Program	Repository	Size (kLOC)	#Fail Tests	#C PFB	#C CSB	#C SAB
median	IntroClass	1	7	1	1	5
smallest	IntroClass	1	13	1	1	3
syllables	IntroClass	1	870	1	1	5
mkfifo	Coreutils	38	2	1	1	1
mkdir	Coreutils	40	2	1	1	1
mknod	Coreutils	39	2	1	1	1
md5sum	Coreutils	43	48	1	1	1
pr	Coreutils	54	6	2	2	4
ptx	Coreutils	62	3095	16	1	3
seq	Coreutils	39	72	1	1	18
paste	Coreutils	38	4510	10	1	3
touch	Coreutils	18	406	2	3	14
du	Coreutils	41	100	2	2	8
cut	Coreutils	43	5	1	1	1
grep	SIR	61	7122	1	1	11
gzip	SIR	44	265	1	1	1
sed	SIR	57	31	1	1	1
polymorph	BugBench	25	67	1	1	2
xmail	Exploit-db	30	129	1	1	1
exim	Exploit-db	253	16	1	1	6
gpg	Exploit-db	218	2	1	1	1

Program	#Pass paths	#Fail paths	Time (sec)	Ovrhd (%)
median	4	7	5	∼0
smallest	9	13	5	∼0
syllables	71	870	1800	4.35
mkfifo	291	2	3600	∼0
mkdir	326	2	3600	∼0
mknod	72	2	3600	∼0
md5sum	62449	48	3600	0.42
pr	540	6	3600	∼0
ptx	9	3095	3600	2.04
seq	445	72	1800	0.73
paste	3501	4510	3600	16.17
touch	210	406	3600	0.84
du	44	100	3600	0.81
cut	38	5	3600	∼0
grep	169	7122	3600	34.13
gzip	5675	265	3600	0.7
sed	3	31	3600	0.03
polymorph	3	67	3600	14.36
xmail	1	129	3600	0.06
exim	178	16	3600	0.03
gpg	10	2	3600	∼0

```
1   int a, b, c, d, smallest;
2   make_symbolic(a, b, c, d);
3   assume(a>=-10 && a<=10);
4   assume(b>=-10 && b<=10);
5   assume(c>=-10 && c<=10);
6   assume(d>=-10 && d<=10);
7   if (a < b && a < c && a < d)
8       smallest = a;
9   if (b < a && b < c && b < d)
10      smallest = b;
11  if (c < b && c < a && c < d)
12      smallest = c;
13  if (d < b && d < c && d < a)
14      smallest = d;
15  assert(smallest ==
16      golden_smallest(a,b,c,d));
```

Fig. 5. Code snippet from 'smallest'

```
1   case 'e':
2   if (optarg)
3       getoptarg (optarg, 'e', ...);
4   //...
5   break;
6   //other cases
7   case 'i':
8   if (optarg)
9       getoptarg (optarg, 'i', ...);
10  //...
11  break;
12  //other cases
13  case 'n':
14  if (optarg)
15      getoptarg (optarg, 'n', ...);
16  break;
```

Fig. 6. Code snippet from 'pr'

effectively produce more fine-grained clusters. For instance, as shown in Fig. 5, the buggy **smallest** program, which computes the smallest number among four integer values, does not adequately handle the case in which at least two of the smallest integer variables are equal. For example, if d equals b, none of the four conditional statements (at lines 7, 9, 11 and 13) take the true branch; the result is incorrect as the variable **smallest** then takes an arbitrary value.

As shown in Fig. 5, we instrumented the program to make it work with KLEE. During path exploration, KLEE generated 13 failing tests for this program and the CSB technique placed all of them into one cluster as they share the same call stack. However, our SAB approach created three clusters with the following reasons: (Cluster 1) $d \geq b$, (Cluster 2) $d \geq c$ and (Cluster 3) $d \geq a$. The reasons indeed show the corner cases that can trigger the bugs in the program. We observed similar cases in **median** and **syllables** programs (see Table 2).

In the subject program **pr** (a Coreutils utility), we found that 6 failing tests due to two different bugs are placed in two clusters on using stack hash similarity. Meanwhile, our approach placed these 6 failing tests into 4 different clusters: one cluster contained 3 failing tests corresponding to one bug, and the other three clusters contain three failing tests of the second bug. Figure 6 shows a code snippet from **pr** that shows three call sites for the buggy function *getoptarg()* (at lines 3, 9 and 15). In this case, because all of the three call sites are in one function, so the stack hash based technique placed the three different failing paths in the same cluster. Similar cases exist in the **exim** and **du** applications.

RQ2. Can our clustering reasons (culprit constraints) help users to look for root causes of failures? One advantage of our bucketing method compared to CSB and PFB approaches is its ability to provide a *semantic characterization* of the failures that are grouped together (based on the culprit constraint). The existing techniques are only capable of capturing syntactic information like the line number in the program or the state of the call-stack when the failure is triggered.

Table 4. Sample culprit constraints

Program	Culprit constraint
mkfifo	`(= (select arg0 #x00000001) #x5a)`
pr	`(= (select stdin #x00000009) #x09)`

Table 4 shows a few examples of the culprit constraints that our technique used to cluster failing tests for **mkfifo** and **pr**. In **mkfifo**, the culprit constraint can be interpreted as: *the second character in the first argument is the character 'Z'*. This is, in fact, the correct characterization of this bug in **mkfifo** as the tests in this cluster fail for the "-Z" option. In case of **pr**, the culprit constraint indicates that: *the tenth character of the standard input is a horizontal tab (TAB)*. The root cause of this failure is due to incorrect handling of the backspace and horizontal tab characters.

RQ3. What is the time overhead introduced by our bucketing technique over vanilla symbolic execution? Overall, in most of the subject programs the time overhead is negligible (from 0% to 5%), except in some programs where the overhead is dominated by the constraint solving time (Table 3).

5.2 User Study

A user study was carried out with 18 students enrolled in a Software Security course (CS4239) in the National University of Singapore (NUS) to receive feedback on the usability and effectiveness of our bucketing method. Among the students, there were 14 senior undergraduate and 4 masters students. Before attending the course, they had no experience on applying bucketing techniques. The students were required to run the three bucketing techniques (our method and two others based on call-stack and point of failure information) to cluster the found failing tests, and (primarily) answer the following questions:

Q1. Rate the level of difficulty in using the three techniques for bucketing failing tests.
Q2. To what extent do the bucketing techniques support debugging of program error?
Q3. Are the numbers of clusters generated by the bucketing techniques manageable?

Table 5. Responses from the user study. Q1 enquires about the difficulty of using a technique: Easy (E), Moderate (M), Difficult (D) and Very Difficult (VD). Q2 responses are about the usefulness of a method: Not Useful (N), Useful (U) and Very Useful (VU).

Bucketing technique	Difficult(Q1)				Useful(Q2)		
	E	M	D	VD	N	U	VU
Point of failure (PFB)	8	8	2	0	0	7	11
Stack hash (CSB)	3	13	2	0	3	8	7
Symbolic analysis (SAB)	1	9	7	1	2	4	12

The users' responses for Q1 & Q2 are summarized in Table 5; for example, the first cell of Table 5 shows that 8 of the 18 respondents found the PFB technique "Easy" for bucketing. In response to Q3, 14 out of the 18 respondents voted that the number of clusters generated by our technique is manageable.

In terms of usefulness as a debugging aid, our technique is ranked "Very Useful" by 12 of the 18 respondents. It gains a high rating for its usefulness as it provides a *semantic characterization* for each bucket (in terms of the culprit constraint), that can help users locate the root cause of failure. At the same time, we found that the main reason that they found our technique harder to use was that this characterization was shown in the form of logical formula in the SMT-LIB format—a format to which the students did not have enough exposure. We list some of the encouraging feedback we got:

- "I believe it is the most powerful of the three techniques, letting me understand which assert are causing the crash or how it is formed."
- "It is very fine grain and will allow us to check the path condition to see variables that causes the error."

6   Related Work

One related line of research involves clustering crash reports or bug reports [6,8, 12,17,20]. Crash Graph [12] uses graph theory (in particular, similarity between graphs), to detect duplicate reports. In terms of duplicate bug report detection, Runeson [20] proposed a technique based on natural language processing to check similarity of bug reports.

Another relevant work involves clustering program failing traces. Liu and Han [15] proposed the technique to use results of fault localization methods for clustering failing traces. Given two set of failing and passing traces which are collected from instrumented predicates of software program, they statistically localize the faults and two failing traces are considered to be similar if the pointed fault locations in the two traces are the same. Podelski et al. [19] cluster failure traces by building symbolic models of their execution (using model checking tools) and use interpolants as signatures for clustering tests. Due to the cost of symbolic model-checking, their technique seems to suffer from scalability issues as in their experiments, even their intraprocedural analysis times out (or the interpolant generator crashes) on a large number of methods.

Although the above-mentioned lines of research are relevant to our work, we target our research on clustering *failing tests* — instead of crash reports, bug reports or failing traces. The other lines of research do not assume they have concrete test inputs to trigger the bugs, so they build the techniques on exploring run-time information collected in the field (i.e.,where the software systems are deployed). In our case, we work on failing tests obtained during symbolic exploration of software programs or provided by test teams.

To the best of our knowledge, all popular symbolic execution engines only borrow and slightly change the techniques that have been proposed for clustering crash reports to cluster their generated failing tests. The clustering approach can be as simple as using point of failure in KLEE [4] or using call stack information in SAGE [9] and MergePoint [3].

7   Conclusions

We leverage the symbolic execution tree built by a symbolic execution engine to cluster failing tests found by symbolic path exploration. Our approach can also be implemented on symbolic execution engines like S2E [5] for clustering tests for stripped program binaries (when source code is not available). Unlike many other prior techniques, our technique should be able to handle changing of addresses when Address Space Layout Randomization (ASLR) is enabled as symbolic expressions are unlikely to be sensitive to address changes.

Acknowledgment. This research is supported in part by the National Research Foundation, Prime Minister's Office, Singapore under its National Cybersecurity R&D Program (TSUNAMi project, Award No. NRF2014NCR-NCR001-21) and administered by the National Cybersecurity R&D Directorate.

References

1. Coreutil benchmarks: http://www.gnu.org/software/coreutils/coreutils.html
2. Exploit-db benchmarks. https://www.exploit-db.com/
3. Avgerinos, T., Rebert, A., Cha, S.K., Brumley, D.: Enhancing symbolic execution with veritesting. In: Proceedings of the 36th International Conference on Software Engineering, ICSE 2014, pp. 1083–1094. ACM, New York (2014)
4. Cadar, C., Dunbar, D., Engler, D.: KLEE: Unassisted and automatic generation of high-coverage tests for complex systems programs. In: Proceedings of the 8th USENIX Conference on Operating Systems Design and Implementation, OSDI 2008, pp. 209–224. USENIX Association, Berkeley (2008)
5. Chipounov, V., Kuznetsov, V., Candea, G.: S2E: A platform for in-vivo multi-path analysis of software systems. SIGPLAN Not. **47**(4), 265–278 (2011)
6. Dang, Y., Wu, R., Zhang, H., Zhang, D., Nobel, P.: Rebucket: A method for clustering duplicate crash reports based on call stack similarity. In: Proceedings of the 34th International Conference on Software Engineering, ICSE 2012, pp. 1084–1093. IEEE Press, Piscataway (2012)
7. Do, H., Elbaum, S., Rothermel, G.: Supporting controlled experimentation with testing techniques: An infrastructure and its potential impact. Empirical Softw. Engg. **10**(4), 405–435 (2005)
8. Glerum, K., Kinshumann, K., Greenberg, S., Aul, G., Orgovan, V., Nichols, G., Grant, D., Loihle, G., Hunt, G.: Debugging in the (very) large: Ten years of implementation and experience. In: Proceedings of the ACM SIGOPS 22Nd Symposium on Operating Systems Principles, SOSP 2009, pp. 103–116. ACM, New York (2009)
9. Godefroid, P., Levin, M.Y., Molnar, D.: SAGE: Whitebox fuzzing for security testing. Commun. ACM **55**(3), 40–44 (2012)
10. Goues, C.L., Holtschulte, N., Smith, E.K., Brun, Y., Devanbu, P., Forrest, S., Weimer, W.: The manybugs and introclass benchmarks for automated repair of C programs. IEEE Trans. Softw. Eng. **41**(12), 1236–1256 (2015)
11. Jin, W., Orso, A.: F3: Fault localization for field failures. In: Proceedings of the 2013 International Symposium on Software Testing and Analysis, ISSTA 2013, pp. 213–223. ACM, New York (2013)
12. Kim, S., Zimmermann, T., Nagappan, N.: Crash graphs: An aggregated view of multiple crashes to improve crash triage. In: Proceedings of the 2011 IEEE/IFIP 41st International Conference on Dependable Systems & Networks, DSN 2011, pp. 486–493. IEEE Computer Society, Washington, DC (2011)

13. Kuznetsov, V., Kinder, J., Bucur, S., Candea, G.: Efficient state merging in symbolic execution. In: Proceedings of the 33rd ACM SIGPLAN Conference on Programming Language Design and Implementation, PLDI 2012, pp. 193–204. ACM, New York (2012)

14. Lattner, C., Adve, V.: LLVM: A compilation framework for lifelong program analysis & transformation. In: Proceedings of the International Symposium on Code Generation and Optimization: Feedback-directed and Runtime Optimization, CGO 2004, p. 75, . IEEE Computer Society, Washington, DC (2004)

15. Liu, C., Han, J.: Failure proximity: A fault localization-based approach. In: Proceedings of the 14th ACM SIGSOFT International Symposium on Foundations of Software Engineering, SIGSOFT 2006/FSE-14, pp. 46–56. ACM, New York (2006)

16. Lu, S., Li, Z., Qin, F., Tan, L., Zhou, P., Zhou, Y.: Bugbench: Benchmarks for evaluating bug detection tools. In: Workshop on the Evaluation of Software Defect Detection Tools (2005)

17. Modani, N., Gupta, R., Lohman, G., Syeda-Mahmood, T., Mignet, L.: Automatically identifying known software problems. In: Proceedings of the 2007 IEEE 23rd International Conference on Data Engineering Workshop, ICDEW 2007, pp. 433–441. IEEE Computer Society, Washington, DC (2007)

18. Molnar, D., Li, X.C., Wagner, D.A.: Dynamic test generation to find integer bugs in x86 binary linux programs. In: Proceedings of the 18th Conference on USENIX Security Symposium, SSYM 2009, pp. 67–82. USENIX Association, Berkeley (2009)

19. Podelski, A., Schäf, M., Wies, T.: Classifying bugs with interpolants. In: Aichernig, B.K.K., Furia, C.A.A. (eds.) TAP 2016. LNCS, vol. 9762, pp. 151–168. Springer, Cham (2016). doi:10.1007/978-3-319-41135-4_9

20. Runeson, P., Alexandersson, M., Nyholm, O.: Detection of duplicate defect reports using natural language processing. In: Proceedings of the 29th International Conference on Software Engineering, ICSE 2007, pp. 499–510. IEEE Computer Society, Washington, DC (2007)

Selective Bisection Debugging

Ripon Saha[1]([⊠]) and Milos Gligoric[2]

[1] Fujitsu Laboratories of America, Sunnyvale, CA 94085, USA
rsaha@us.fujitsu.com
[2] The University of Texas at Austin, Austin, TX 78712, USA
gligoric@utexas.edu

Abstract. Bisection debugging, which is based on binary search over software version history, is widely used in practice to identify the bug introducing commit. However, this process can be expensive because it requires costly compilation and test execution at many commits. We introduce a novel technique—selective bisection (consisting of test selection and commit selection)— reduce the number of bisection steps, the number of compiler invocations, and the number of executed tests. We evaluated selective bisection on 10 popular open-source projects by performing 25,690 debugging sessions and measuring: (1) savings in number of compiler invocations obtained by commit selection, (2) savings in number of executed tests obtained by test selection, and (3) savings in overall debugging time by selective bisection. Our results show that, in 65% of debugging sessions, commit selection saves between 14% and 71% compiler invocations. Test selection saves 74% of testing effort on average (ranging from 42% to 95%) compared to when developers do not use any test selection. Finally, we demonstrate that one can save substantial time using selective bisection for large projects.

1 Introduction

In large software systems, where many developers work together making hundreds of commits per day [14,36,37], coping with regression bugs is one of the most challenging problems. According to Linux Kernel developers, 80% of the release cycle time is dedicated to fixing regression bugs [3]. Identifying the *bug introducing commit* is very important to isolate and understand regression bugs. *Bisection debugging* is a well known technique that performs a binary search over software version history to identify the bug introducing commit. The popular version control systems, such as Git and Mercurial, have in-built commands (`git bisect` and `hg bisect`) to help developers perform bisection debugging [7,15]. Since these commands are integrated with the version control systems, they are frequently used by developers. For example, a well known Linux developer, Ingo Molnar says about his use of Git bisect [3]:

Most of this work was completed when Ripon Saha was a Ph.D. Student at The University of Texas at Austin.

© Springer-Verlag GmbH Germany 2017
M. Huisman and J. Rubin (Eds.): FASE 2017, LNCS 10202, pp. 60–77, 2017.
DOI: 10.1007/978-3-662-54494-5_4

"I most actively use it during the merge window (when a lot of trees get merged upstream and when the influx of bugs is the highest) - and yes, there have been cases that I used it multiple times a day. My average is roughly once a day."

Although bisection debugging can isolate the bug introducing commit quickly in terms of number of bisection steps, the whole process could be still expensive if the program takes a long time (even a couple of minutes) to compile and the tests take a long time to run, which is the case for most large systems [2,8].

This paper presents a novel technique called *selective bisection* that frequently reduces the cost of bisection debugging by minimizing (1) the number of compiler invocations using *commit selection* and (2) the number of tests to execute using *test selection* . Test selection [10,14,19,20,23,30,31,35–39,42] is a well known technique to select tests that are affected by a particular change. Therefore, test selection is used to speed up regression testing [39]. Our key insight is that a significant amount of compilation and testing effort could be reduced during debugging by selecting only relevant commits and running only those tests that are relevant to the buggy changes. To this end, we have proposed a commit selection technique and leveraged an existing test selection technique for bisection debugging. In order to evaluate the effectiveness of our idea, we performed 25,690 bisection debugging sessions in 10 open-source projects. Our empirical evaluation shows that commit selection saves between 14% and 71% compiler invocations across all projects in 65% of debugging sessions. Additionally, test selection saves 74% of testing effort on average (ranging from 42% to 95%) compared to when developers do not use any test selection. This paper makes the following key contributions:

- To the best of our knowledge, we are the first to introduce the notion of commit selection and test selection in bisection debugging.
- We present a commit selection approach to save the number of compilations. We also present various testing strategies used in bisection debugging, and show how an existing test selection technique can be integrated with various strategies to substantially reduce the testing effort.
- We present an extensive evaluation to demonstrate the effectiveness of commit selection and test selection.

2   Background

This section introduces the basic terminology used in this paper and briefly describes bisection debugging and test selection.

2.1   Commit and Version

In this paper, by a *commit* we mean a set of changes that developers include one at a time in a version control system. By a *version,* we mean the snapshot of the code base at a given commit.

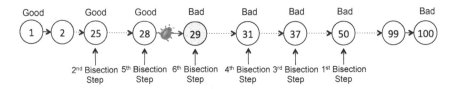

Fig. 1. Process of bisection debugging

2.2   Bisection Debugging

In large projects, commits happen so frequently that a bug introducing commit, even after a few days of introduction, can be hundreds of commits away from the current version [2]. Certainly, going through all the commits in software history from the latest known good version is not feasible. Bisection debugging performs a binary search through the commit history to help developers quickly identify the bug introducing commit. `git bisect` is a popular tool for bisection debugging [7]. Given a range of commits where the version (ν_{good}) at the first commit is good and the version (ν_{bad}) at the last commit is bad, `git bisect` checks out the version (ν_{bisect}) at the middle commit. Then ν_{bisect} is tested (manually or automatically) to determine whether it is good or bad, and marked as ν_{good} or ν_{bad} for the next step depending on the test results. The whole process is repeated until a ν_{good} followed by a ν_{bad} is found. Figure 1 illustrates a debugging scenario where a developer starts bisection debugging with 100 commits and finally discover that 29th commit introduced the bug.

Although bisection debugging is based on the binary search, the number of steps in bisection debugging to isolate a bug introducing commit and that of binary search to search a value in a list is not the same. In a list of n values, a binary search can terminate even at the first step if the value is found there. Therefore, the best case performance of binary search is $\mathcal{O}(1)$. On the other hand, in the worst case when the desired value is not in the list, the complexity is $\mathcal{O}(\log_2 n)$. However, the number of steps in bisection debugging is always $\lfloor \log_2 n + 1 \rfloor$, since we do not know which commit actually introduced the bug. Even if the version at first bisection step introduced the bug, we cannot terminate the search until we find two consecutive versions such that a good version is followed by a bad version.

2.3   Test Selection

Given a set of changes in a project, a test selection technique [10,14,19,20,23, 30,31,35–37,39,42] seeks to select a subset of tests that are sufficient to test the new version of the program. A test selection technique is *safe* if it selects all tests affected by changes. Among many test selection techniques, we have chosen Ekstazi [9,10] for our work, since our goal was to improve bisection debugging of projects written in JVM languages (e.g., Java, Scala, etc.). Additionally, Ekstazi is publicly available. Ekstazi collects *coverage* for each test class, i.e., dynamically accessed files. It then selects, at a new version, all tests that depend on at least one modified file. Ekstazi collects both the executable and data files (e.g., property files) that are used during the execution of the test class; in the reminder of the text, we denote a test class with test. Ekstazi is considered safe under certain assumptions [29,32], e.g., that test cases are deterministic and that the environments used in testing remains unchanged. Prior work showed Ekstazi's effectiveness (selects a small number of tests and provides speedup compared to running all the tests) on a number of open-source projects [4,10]. Recently, Ekstazi has been adopted by several open-source projects and companies.

In the default configuration, which we use in Sect. 4, Ekstazi collects a checksum for each dependency used by tests; the checksum is used later to find the tests that should be run after code changes. Ekstazi computes the checksum of executable files (i.e., classfiles) by ignoring the content that is commonly not observed by tests (e.g., debug information). Ekstazi smoothly integrates with popular testing frameworks (e.g., JUnit) and build systems (e.g., Maven) [5], which simplified our study.

3   Selective Bisection

This section describes selective bisection that comprises of two techniques: commit selection and test selection.

3.1   Commit Selection

In bisection debugging, at each bisection step, first the current version is compiled and then tests are executed. However, compiling a large project is costly [12,40]. *Commit selection* predicts if a certain commit in a bisection step is likely irrelevant to failing tests. If it predicts that a commit is irrelevant to the failing tests, it skips compiling that version, and moves to the next bisection step. Predicting if a given commit ν_{bisect} is relevant or irrelevant to the failing tests is always performed with respect to a reference version ν_{ref}, for which we already have the test results. Our key insight is that for a given pair of versions (ν_{ref} and ν_{bisect}), if we have the test coverage for ν_{ref} and we know all the source code changes between ν_{ref} and ν_{bisect}, we can predict whether the failing tests are affected due to changes between ν_{ref} and ν_{bisect} without compiling ν_{bisect}. If failing tests are not affected by the changes, the test results of ν_{ref} and ν_{bisect} are the same, i.e., if ν_{ref} is good, ν_{bisect} is good; if ν_{ref} is bad, ν_{bisect} is also bad.

Note that this is a prediction, not a determination, because it detects differences between source files, but test selection technique that we used collects tests coverage on compiled code (i.e., classfiles). For example, if two classes are defined in a single source file, they are compiled to two classfiles (and a test can depend on either of those classfiles or both of them), however, by looking at differences between source files, we can detect changes only in the classfile that matches the name of the source file. However, we can make the whole approach

Table 1. An example of commit selection for Jackrabbit for the failing test `OakSolrNodeStateConfigurationTest`. Result: Number of compilations with and without commit selection is 2 and 7 respectively. Savings: 71%.

G = Good, B = Bad, C = Current, LAG = Last Actual Good, LAB = Last Actual Bad

Step	G	B	C	Affected (G, C)	Affected (B, C)	Compile	LAG	LAB
1	1	100	50	Yes	No	No	1	100
2	1	50	25	No	Yes	No	1	100
3	25	50	37	Yes	No	No	1	100
4	25	37	31	Yes	No	No	1	100
5	25	31	28	Yes	Yes	Yes&Run	1	28
6	25	28	26	No	Yes	No	1	28
7	26	28	27	No	Yes	No	1	28
8	27	28	–	–	–	Yes&Run	27	28

correct by automatically detecting inconsistencies due to any inaccurate prediction, and then switching back to traditional bisection debugging. On the other hand, if prediction is accurate, we may save substantial amount of compile time.

Prediction. This section describes our technique to predict if the failing tests are affected by the change between ν_{ref} and ν_{bisect}. The following steps describe the way we predict if a test should execute:

1. For a given version ν_{bisect}, and a reference version ν_{ref}, we extract the source code differences between (ν_{bisect} and ν_{ref}) = Δ_{ref} only for Java source files.
2. We extract the file names of each added, deleted, and modified Java files from Δ_{ref}, and store them in a list, $F_{ref} = \{F_1, F_2, .., F_k\}$.
3. We extract the coverage information from ν_{ref}, which contains the information of all tests and the name of source code classes that each test class executes. We convert class names to file names. For most classes, class name is the same as the file name. However, if a class is an inner class then file name does not directly match the class name. For example, for an inner class B in file A, the fully qualified name would be $A\$B$. We will discard the later part of the fully qualified name to get the file name A.
4. Then we search if the failing tests access any of the files in F_{ref}. If yes, then we conclude that we have to run that test for ν_{bisect}.

Commit selection in action. A developer generally starts bisection debugging with a known good version ν_{good} and a known bad version ν_{bad}.

1. We instrument both versions using Ekstazi to collect test coverage matrix at file level for a negligible cost [10].
2. In each bisection step, we predict if failing tests are affected by the changes between (i) ν_{bisect} and ν_{good}, and (ii) ν_{bisect} and ν_{bad}.

(a) If both reference versions tell that the failing tests are affected at ν_{bisect}, then we compile ν_{bisect}, run the tests, and mark ν_{bisect} as ν_{good} or ν_{bad} depending on the results.

(b) If one of the reference versions (ν_{good} or ν_{bad}) tells that the failing tests are not affected, we would simply transfer the corresponding test result of ν_{ref} (ν_{good} or ν_{bad}) to ν_{bisect}, and thus would not compile ν_{bisect}.

3. We keep track of versions where the test results are updated using prediction, and where the results are updated after actual test run. Therefore, we always know the last *actual* good version ($\nu_{lastActualGood}$) and the *actual* bad version ($\nu_{lastActualBad}$) where the good or bad was decided after running tests.

Detecting inconsistencies and switching back. After we get a buggy version ($\nu_{probableBuggy}$) at the end of a debugging session, we check the consistency of our result. For a valid bug introducing version, the version before the bug introducing changes ($\nu_{probableBuggy-1}$) should be good. Therefore, we test $\nu_{probableBuggy-1}$. If that is a good version, then we conclude that $\nu_{probableBuggy}$ is actually buggy. Otherwise, we perform traditional bisect (without prediction) between $\nu_{lastActualGood}$ and $\nu_{lastActualBad}$. Table 1 illustrate commit selection on an open-source project, Jackrabbit, when its 28th commit is buggy.

3.2 Test Selection

During a bisection debugging session, at each step, (some) tests are executed to determine if the current version is good or bad. To this end, developers may follow one of the three testing strategies:[1]

1. **All Tests** (*AT*): In the safest form, developers run all the tests to determine if a given version is good or bad.
2. **Failing Tests** (*FT*): In the most optimistic form, developers only run the failing tests to determine if a given version is good or bad.
3. **All Tests After Failing Tests** (*ST*): A middle ground may be that developers first run the failing tests. If they keep failing, the version is marked as bad. However, if the failing tests pass, developers run other tests to make sure that the version is good indeed.

At a first glance, the second strategy may be tempting but it may not always give the expected result, since even if the failing test passes, it is not guaranteed that the version is good since other affected tests may fail. To get developers' feedback, we asked a question on Stack Overflow[2]. As we expected, we got mixed answers. One developer prefers the second strategy but another developer disagrees. By combining the first and the second strategy, we introduced *ST*, which we believe is the optimal strategy that gives the expected result.

---

[1] It should be noted that we have not found any study on the use of bisection debugging; the identified methodologies are inspired by reading blogs and posts on GitHub related to bisection debugging [7,8].

[2] http://goo.gl/oHyX2g.

Our key insight is that developers could safely use a test selection tool such as Ekstazi to select only the tests that are affected by the changes between ν_{bad}/ν_{good} and ν_{bisect} in each debugging step. In traditional test selection, generally a subset of tests are selected with respect to a single (often the previous) version. However, for bisection debugging, we can take advantage of both ν_{good} and ν_{bad} to reduce the number of tests further. The idea is that only intersection of two selected subsets for ν_{bisect} with respect to ν_{good} and ν_{bad} are enough to test ν_{bisect} safely [11].

Let us discuss a debugging scenario with a hypothetical example, as presented in Fig. 2. Assume that Alice is debugging with seven versions of a program (ν_1 and ν_7) to identify a bug introducing commit (which are changes introduced in ν_2 in our example). Let us assume that there are n source files $\{C_1, C_2, \ldots, C_n\}$ and m tests $\{T_1, T_2, \ldots, T_m\}$ in the project. In Fig. 2, the label between two consecutive versions represents the program difference between those two versions in terms of Java files. For instance, $\delta(\nu_1, \nu_2) = C_1$, which means that the file C_1 has been changed between ν_1 to ν_2. The level of granularity in our example is at the file level, which is also the level of granularity of Ekstazi (Sect. 2). Table 2 represents a hypothetical test coverage matrix. In this example, we assume that the matrix remains constant, but our approach works even if the matrix changes due to changes in code.

Table 2. A hypothetical test coverage matrix

	C1	C2	C3	C4	C5	C6	$\cdots$	Cn
T_1	✓			✓			$\cdots$	
T_2		✓		✓			$\cdots$	
T_3	✓		✓				$\cdots$	
T_4				✓			$\cdots$	
T_5					✓		$\cdots$	
T_6		✓					$\cdots$	✓
$\cdots$	$\cdots$	$\cdots$	$\cdots$	$\cdots$	$\cdots$	$\cdots$	$\cdots$	$\cdots$
T_m							$\cdots$	✓

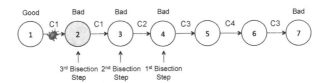

Fig. 2. Some hypothetical change scenarios in a git repository

Savings when running all tests (AT). Now let us simulate the number of tests Alice has to run without test selection during this debugging session. First, Alice marked ν_1 as good and ν_7 as bad. At this step bisection debugging moves to ν_4. Alice runs all m tests to test ν_4. In this case, ν_4 would be buggy since the bug was introduced in ν_2. So Alice marks ν_4 as bad. The next bisection step is at ν_3. Alice runs the tests again, marks ν_3 as buggy. Finally Alice does the same thing for ν_2, and identifies that ν_2 is the bug introducing commit. So Alice executed all tests 3 times, which is $3 \times m$ tests in total.

Now we simulate the same scenario when Alice integrates Ekstazi in the project and then starts debugging. In the first step at ν_4, Ekstazi first uses ν_1 and then ν_7 as a reference version to select tests for ν_4. When ν_7 is the reference version, $\delta(\nu_4, \nu_7) = \{C_3, C_4\}$. From the coverage matrix in Table 2 (which is generated by Ekstazi) we see that only T_1, T_2, T_3, T_4, and T_6 are affected by the changes. When ν_1 is the reference version, the affected tests are T_1, T_2, T_3 since the change set is $\{C_1, C_2\}$. Therefore, Alice runs only the tests in the intersection, i.e., $T_1, T_2, and\ T_3$, to test ν_4. The results for the other tests can be transferred from the corresponding reference versions. In the second bisection step, Alice need not run any tests in ν_3 since no test is affected by both changes in C_1 and C_2. Finally, Alice runs T_1 and T_3 to test ν_2 due to the change in C_1. Therefore, in total Alice runs only five tests using test selection instead of $3 \times m$ tests.

Savings when running only failing tests (FT). Now we consider the scenario where Alice plans to run only failing tests. Even in this scenario, Ekstazi can save testing effort by not running the failing tests at all, if they are not affected by the changes. Since in this scenario Alice would run only the failing tests, she knows the failing tests in advance. To simplify the discussion, let us assume that Alice got only one failing test, T_1. Now while testing at the first bisection step ν_4, we can see that the changes between ν_4 and ν_7 are $\{C_3, C_4\}$. From the coverage matrix we observe that test T_1 is affected by the change in C_3 and C_4. Therefore, Ekstazi would run T_1. Since at ν_4 the result of T_1 should be a failure, ν_4 would be bad. Now for the second bisection step, ν_3, Ekstazi sees that only C_2 changed. From the coverage matrix we observe that T_1 is not affected by this change. Therefore, Ekstazi would not run the test at all, and would transfer the results of T_1, which is a "failure" from ν_4 to ν_3. Therefore, ν_3 would be bad. Further, Ekstazi would run T_1 for ν_2 since it is affected. So Ekstazi would save running the failing test one out of three times for this example.

Savings when running all tests after failing tests (ST). Since ST is a combination of AT and FT, we do not describe it step by step.

4   Empirical Evaluation

To investigate the effectiveness of selective bisection, we performed an empirical evaluation in terms of three research questions.

RQ1: How much compilation effort is saved through commit selection?
RQ2: How much testing effort is saved through test selection for different testing strategies (*AT*, *FT*, and *ST*)?
RQ3: How much overall time is saved through selective bisection?

4.1 Projects

We used 10 open-source projects in our evaluation. We followed several criteria, similar to prior studies on regression testing [10,34], to select these projects. Specifically, the projects (i) use Git as a version control system, (ii) use Maven as a build system, (iii) have at least 100 commits, and (iv) build without any error. These projects are from diverse application domains and have been widely used in software testing research. The first requirement is necessary since we are investigating git bisect as bisection debugging. The requirements of Maven and JUnit tests were set to make our experiments fully automatic. Finally, the requirement of 100 commits helps ensure that the projects are non trivial. For each selected project, Table 3 shows its name, the start and end version SHA (which we consider to be a starting pair of a good and a bad version in each debugging session), the code size in terms of lines of code (LOC), the number of source files and test classes, and their build time and test execution time (on the latest version). From the table, we can see that the sizes of the projects vary from small (Codec) to fairly large (Jetty) in terms of LOC. Their build times (without test execution) vary from few seconds to several minutes, and test execution times vary from few seconds to 44 minutes (Jackrabbit). The last two rows show the total and average values computed across all projects.

Table 3. Projects used in the evaluation

Project	Start SHA	End SHA	KLOC	#Source files	#Test classes	Time [mm:ss] build	test
CCompiler	14a9e6fe	a8a53e83	239.2	630	262	01:08	02:20
Codec	5af6d236	535bd812	17.6	67	48	00:29	00:18
Collections	45a0337e	c87eeaa4	60.3	357	160	00:24	00:42
Lang	9e575c4d	17a6d163	69.0	159	134	00:30	00:33
Math	ff4ec1a3	471e6b07	174.8	841	479	00:30	02:35
Net	17ecff74	4450add7	26.9	224	42	00:26	01:13
GraphHopper	d1a0fd81	c0a328f8	43.6	254	100	00:35	00:45
Guava	67695cce	e9a23fe5	274.2	1,372	364	01:09	08:15
Jackrabbit	4a309b76	222b4cda	253.1	1,654	539	02:12	44:18
Jetty	f645e186	f630a841	301.1	1,929	550	07:05	30:29
$\sum$	N/A	N/A	1,459.8	7,487	2,678	14:28	91:28
Average	N/A	N/A	146.0	749	268	01:27	09:08

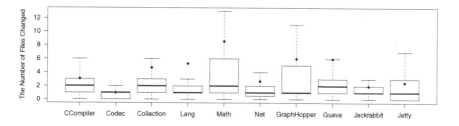

Fig. 3. Distribution of number of files changed in each commit

We also present the distribution of changes per commit in Fig. 3 in terms of the number of files added, deleted or modified. We presented the changes at file level, since all of our analysis is at that level. From the figure we observe that in all projects the number of files changed was one or two (median values). This statistics further motivated us to propose selective bisection debugging since it is highly likely that a small number of tests would be selected due to small changes.

4.2   Experimental Setup

For an extensive evaluation, we designed our experiment based on simulation to replicate the steps in bisection debugging. More specifically, in order to answer **RQ1** we took 100 versions $[\nu_i, \nu_{i+99}]$ for each project, and considered that any of the intermediate versions $[\nu_{i+1}, \nu_{i+98}]$ can be the one with a bug introducing commit. Then for each intermediate version ν_j where $(i + 1) \leq j \leq (i + 98)$, we set the test results w.r.t. the bug introducing commit. For example, if for a given debugging session we assume that ν_5 is the bug introducing commit, all the commits after (and including) ν_5 would be bad, and all the commits before ν_5 would be good. Then for each bisection step, we have used Ekstazi to select tests for the version under test based on the real changes between that version and good/bad version and test coverage information.

To answer **RQ2**, in addition to assuming a buggy version, we also had to assume the fault-revealing tests. For a change set between two versions, literally any test, which is affected by the changes, can be the failing test. For example, when we assume that ν_j is buggy, we first check which tests are affected by the changes between ν_{j-1} and ν_j. If there are m tests that are affected by the bug introducing change, any subset of them can be failing. If we assume that there is only one failing test, we have to simulate our experiment m times for the buggy version ν_j. For two failing tests, we have to simulate for $\binom{m}{2}$ times, and so on. In order to keep the experiment cost affordable, we assumed there is only one failing test due to the bug. Even for a single test failure, we have simulated our experiment 25,690 times in 10 projects.

4.3   Results

This section presents the experimental results for our research questions.

RQ1: Savings due to commit selection. We present the savings in compilation effort in terms of the proportion of compilations skipped. More specifically, for a given bisection debugging session, if we need to compile nc times without commit selection and mc times with commit selection, the savings is computed as $\frac{nc-mc}{nc}$. It should be noted that a negative saving indicates the case where commit selection actually increases the cost. This may happen when commit selection predicts an irrelevant commit inaccurately, and our technique moves some steps back to perform traditional bisection (Sect. 3). Therefore, to present the complete results, we provide the number of simulations where we decreased or increased the number of compilations in Table 4, and complete distribution of savings, both positive and negative, in Fig. 4.

From the results, we observe that commit selection frequently reduces compilation cost. The "Total" row in Table 4 shows that commit selection helped saving compilation cost in 65% of simulations, whereas it increased the cost in only 6% of simulations. Interestingly, most of the cost increase came from Jetty. For other projects, the cost increase happened in only 1% of simulations. Commit selection did not change any effort in compilation in 29% of simulations. From Fig. 4, we observe that the improvement (in 65% of simulations) varied between 14% and 71% across projects. Although cost increase can be also high in some cases (up to 67% for Jetty; this cannot be seen in Fig. 4 as we do not show the outliers), our results show that this happens rarely.

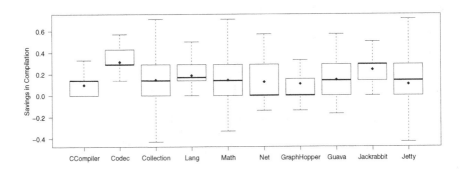

Fig. 4. Savings in the number of compiler invocations via commit selection

RQ2: Savings Due to Test Selection. We present the savings in testing effort in terms of the proportion of tests that one can skip with test selection. More specifically, for a given bisection debugging, we compute the savings as:

$$PT_{ts} = \frac{\sum_{for-each-bisection-step} n(T_{ts})}{\sum_{for-each-bisection-step} n(T)} \tag{1}$$

$$savings = 1 - PT_{ts} \tag{2}$$

Table 4. Number of simulations when the compilation cost decreased, remained the same, or increased due to commit selection

Projects	#Simulations	#Decreased	#Same	#Increased	%Decreased
CCompiler	6,171	3,615	2,556	0	59
Codec	91	87	4	0	96
Collection	975	657	212	106	67
Lang	678	548	125	5	81
Math	5,275	3,411	1,856	8	65
Net	204	96	104	4	47
GraphHopper	1,247	613	612	22	49
Guava	1,347	997	346	4	74
Jackrabbit	3,436	3,034	313	89	88
Jetty	6,266	3,667	1,404	1195	59
All projects	25,690	16,725	7,532	1,433	65

where $n(T_{ts})$ is the number of tests to run selected by Ekstazi and $n(T)$ is the number of tests to run without Ekstazi. Therefore, the savings may vary between 0 and 1, which can be translated to percentages as well.

Figure 5 presents the distribution of savings, computed by Eq. 2, for AT, FT, and ST strategies. Our results show that, regardless of a testing strategy, test selection is very effective to reduce the number of tests in bisection debugging. For AT (the first/orange box in each group), the median savings varied from 43% (CCompiler) to 95% (Codec). Considering that there are hundreds of tests in projects and a number of steps in bisection debugging, the savings are significant. For example, Jetty has 550 test classes. In our simulation for 100 commits, it takes 6 or 7 steps to complete a bisection debugging. Therefore, we may need to run 3,850 tests to test Jetty in a single debugging session if all tests are executed.

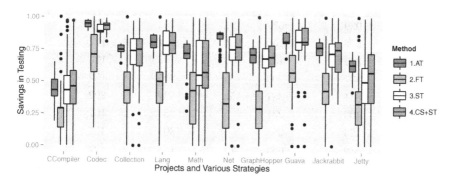

Fig. 5. Savings in the number of tests during bisection debugging via test selection (Color figure online)

From Fig. 5, we see that the median savings in Jetty is 63%. So test selection may skip running 2,425 tests to debug Jetty. For majority of the projects, the savings in AT is 70% or more. Even in FT (the second/gray box in each group), where only the failing tests are run, test selection can reduce the number of executed tests by 29%–71% (median values). Like AT, we also observe a similar savings in ST, which we consider to be the optimal strategy. The median savings (the third/white box in each group) varied from 42% to 91% across projects. For majority of projects, the median savings are more than 70%. Finally, the fourth/blue box in each group shows the savings for ST when we also apply commit selection. Results show that the savings of ST is further increased (up to 7%) by commit selection. Interestingly, although in some cases commit selection increases the number of compilation, it does not increase the number of tests to run.

RQ3: Overall time savings. Since ST is the optimal strategy with respect to the testing effort and correctness, we calculate the end-to-end time savings for ST. It should be also noted that we considered the median compilation and testing savings for each project. Table 5 presents the total time required for traditional bisection and selective bisection including the time required for program instrumentation and test coverage collection by Ekstazi. From the results, we observe that, on average, we achieved 24% to 60% of time savings across projects. Even for small projects like Codec, we achieved more than 2 min of savings, which is 44% of time using traditional bisection. The savings can be as big as 1 h and 23 min (Jackrabbit). It also should be noted that this saving is for ST, which is already considered optimal for traditional bisection. If developers follow AT, the savings would be even more.

Table 5. Time savings (in seconds) using selective bisection for ST

Projects	Traditional bisection	CS + TS	Ekstazi over-head	Selective bisection	Total time savings	Savings [%]
CCompiler	1,029	672	81	753	276	27
Codec	276	150	4	154	122	44
Collection	329	187	6	193	136	41
Lang	337	200	5	205	132	39
Math	831	387	152	539	292	35
Net	403	231	5	236	167	41
GraphHopper	423	295	6	301	122	29
Guava	1,880	683	75	758	1,122	60
Jackrabbit	8,873	3,299	544	3,843	5,030	57
Jetty	8,462	5,515	908	6,423	2,039	24

5 Discussion

Effect of simulation based evaluation. Our evaluation is based on simulation. However, in the context of measuring savings using selective bisection debugging, there is no difference between a real bug reproducing experiment and a simulation. For example, in our evaluation, when we assume that ν_i is buggy and T_j is the failing test, we followed exactly the same steps to isolate the bug what any bisection debugging technique (e.g., git bisect) would take if there is a real bug in ν_i and T_j is the real failing test. And since, we have used real tests in each version and the real commits, we got exact number of tests in simulation that developers need to run with and without test selection. Furthermore, due to simulation our advantage is that we were able to conduct massive number of experiments for many combination of buggy version and failing tests, that would have never been possible with real bugs.

Effect of number of commits. In our simulation, we have isolated each bug by considering only 100 commits. Our rational is that developers use bisection debugging like git bisect for a reasonable number of commits since linear search for a bug introducing commit is not effective [2]. Therefore, we believe that the evaluation with 100 commits shows the effectiveness of our technique but in a wider range of commits, our technique would provide additional savings.

6 Threats to Validity

External. The projects used in our evaluation may not be the representative of the general projects population. To mitigate the threat, we performed our experiments on a diverse set of projects in terms of size, number of tests, and applications. However, we do not generalize our results to other projects. Furthermore, we performed our experiments with 100 commits in each project. For a different set or length of commits, we may have different savings. We discussed the rationale and effect of this choice in the previous section. We have used only projects that are written in the Java programming language. In the future, it will be interesting to explore if the results differ for projects written in other programming languages.

We have used Ekstazi as the test selection tool. A different tool, which tracks test dependencies on methods or statements, would likely produce different results (and select even small number of tests). Future work should evaluate various test selection techniques with selective bisection.

Internal. The implementation of Ekstazi or our scripts for bisection debugging may have bugs which may impact our conclusion. However, Ekstazi is, to the best of our knowledge, the only available tool for regression test selection (for Java). Furthermore, it has been adopted in a number of open-source projects, which increases our confidence in its correctness. We have also performed many small experiments and code reviews to validate our scripts. Therefore, the effect of this threat should be minimal.

We have assumed that there is only one bug introducing commit in the versions under investigation. Furthermore, we assume that the monotonicity property holds, i.e., once a change introduces a bug, any subsequent version manifests the bug as well.

Construct. Our experiment is based on simulation. We have already discussed the effect of this threat in detail.

7   Related Work

Automated debugging has been an active research area over the past few decades. To date, researchers proposed many approaches for localizing and isolating the root causes of bugs automatically. Test selection is also an active research area for a long time. Therefore, related work in these fields are enormous. In this section, we focus on the representative work in each area.

Bug localization. Researchers proposed many automated bug localization approaches to aid debugging. Existing techniques can be broadly categorized into two categories: dynamic [1] and static [16]. Spectrum based bug localization [1,17,21] and dynamic slicing [43] are some of the well known techniques in this category. Spectrum based techniques generally monitor the program execution of passing and failing tests. Then based on the execution traces, these tools present developers a ranked list of suspicious lines. Pastore et al.'s [27] and Zuddas et al.'s [46] techniques do not only provide the suspicious lines but also provide explanations to help developers understand the bug.

Static approaches, on the other hand, do not require any program tests or execution traces. In most cases, they need only program source code and/or bug reports. The static approaches can be also divided into two categories: (i) program analysis based approaches, and (ii) information retrieval based approaches. FindBug [16] and Error Prone [6] are two popular bug localization tools based on static program analysis that can detect bugs by identifying buggy patterns that frequently happen in practice. On the other hand, IR based approaches utilize the contents of bug reports. In these approaches [22,25,28,33,45], each bug report is treated as a *query*, and all the source files in the project comprise the *document collection*. IR techniques then rank the documents by predicted relevance, returning a ranked list of candidate source code files that may contain the bug. Recently, researchers also combined the spectrum based and IR-based bug localization to get advantages from both approaches [18]. Unlike the foregoing techniques, selective bisection localizes the bug introducing commit rather than suspicious lines.

Isolating buggy changes. Ness and Ngo [24] first proposed a linear approach to isolate buggy changes. In their approach, when a bug is discovered in a particular version, they consider a set of ordered changes to investigate, and apply one after another until they find first buggy version. Gross first introduced the notion of bisection debugging [13]. However, his context was a little different from `git` bisect. Given two versions of a program, Gross applied binary search by partitioning program source code until the bug is isolated in minimum changed lines. Delta debugging is a well known technique to isolate a buggy change between two versions [41].

Recently Ziftci and Ramavajjala [2] proposed an algorithm to rank all the commits based on a suspiciousness score to find the bug introducing commit as early as possible. They calculated the suspicious score using metrics such as the change size, and the distance between changed files and the project under investigation. However, all these prior approaches run all tests once a version is selected for testing. In this paper, we use dynamic test dependencies to select commits and then we reduce the number of executed tests at each version.

Test selection. To date, researchers have proposed quite a few approaches for test section [10,14,19,20,23,30,31,35–37,39,42]. These approaches vary in terms of strategies such as static program analysis based [44] vs. dynamic test coverage based [10], and/or granularity of tests e.g., class [10,26] vs. method [29]. In this paper, we have used Ekstazi, which is a dynamic tool and works at the class granularity. In this work, our objective is not to introduce any new test selection technique. Rather, we introduce an application of test selection in automated debugging to improve debugging effectiveness.

8 Conclusion

In a large software project, it frequently happens that a bug is detected many commits after it was actually introduced. In this case, bisection debugging such as git bisect is frequently used to isolate the bug introducing commit. However, for large projects even bisection debugging may be expensive. In this paper, we introduced selective bisection debugging, which comprises of commit selection and test selection. We investigated the savings through selective bisection debugging for various testing strategies, where developers execute all tests, only failing tests, and execute passing tests if and only if the failing tests pass. Our evaluation shows that commit selection can save compilation time in 65% of debugging scenarios. The savings (in number of compiler invocations) may vary from 14% to 71%. Test selection can skip up to 95% tests during debugging, where developers follow safe approach, i.e., execute all tests. The saving is also very similar if a developer first execute the failing tests, and then execute the passing tests if and only if failing tests pass. Finally, we demonstrate that the overall time savings can be substantial using selective bisection for large projects. We believe our results will encourage developers to use selective bisection debugging, and researchers to investigate commit selection and test selection in more detail.

Acknowledgments. We thank Ahmet Celik, Julia Lawall, and Darko Marinov for their feedback on a draft of this paper. This research was partially supported by the NSF Grant No. CCF-1566363 and a Google Research Faculty Award.

References

1. Abreu, R., Zoeteweij, P., Golsteijn, R., Van Gemund, A.J.C.: A practical evaluation of spectrum-based fault localization. JSS **82**(11), 1780–1792 (2009)
2. Finding culprits automatically in failing builds - i.e. who broke the build? GTAC (2013). https://www.youtube.com/watch?v=SZLuBYlq3OM
3. Couder, C.: Fighting regressions with git bisect. https://www.kernel.org/pub/software/scm/git/docs/git-bisect-lk2009.html
4. Dini, N., Sullivan, A., Gligoric, M., Rothermel, G.: The effect of test suite type on regression test selection. In: ISSRE, pp. 47–58 (2016)
5. Ekstazi. http://www.ekstazi.org
6. Error Prone. http://errorprone.info/
7. Git bisect. https://git-scm.com/docs/git-bisect
8. OrientDB. https://github.com/orientechnologies/orientdb/issues/2581
9. Gligoric, M., Eloussi, L., Marinov, D.: Ekstazi: lightweight test selection. In: ICSE Tool Demonstration Track, pp. 713–716 (2015)
10. Gligoric, M., Eloussi, L., Marinov, D.: Practical regression test selection with dynamic file dependencies. In: ISSTA, pp. 211–222 (2015)
11. Gligoric, M., Majumdar, R., Sharma, R., Eloussi, L., Marinov, D.: Regression test selection for distributed software histories. In: Biere, A., Bloem, R. (eds.) CAV 2014. LNCS, vol. 8559, pp. 293–309. Springer, Cham (2014). doi:10.1007/978-3-319-08867-9_19
12. Gligoric, M., Schulte, W., Prasad, C., van Velzen, D., Narasamdya, I., Livshits, B.: Automated migration of build scripts using dynamic analysis and search-based refactoring. In: OOPSLA, pp. 599–616 (2014)
13. Gross, T.R.: Bisection debugging. In: AADEBUG, pp. 185–191 (1997)
14. Herzig, K., Greiler, M., Czerwonka, J., Murphy, B.: The art of testing less without sacrificing quality. In: ICSE, pp. 483–493 (2015)
15. Hg bisect. https://www.mercurial-scm.org/repo/hg/help/bisect
16. Hovemeyer, D., Pugh, W.: Finding bugs is easy. SIGPLAN Note **39**(12), 92–106 (2004)
17. Jones, J.A., Harrold, M.J.: Empirical evaluation of the Tarantula automatic fault-localization technique. In: ASE, pp. 273–282 (2005)
18. Le, T.-DB., Oentaryo, R.J., Lo, D.: Information retrieval and spectrum based bug localization: better together. In: FSE, pp. 579–590 (2015)
19. Leung, H., White, L.: A cost model to compare regression test strategies. In: ICSM, pp. 201–208 (1991)
20. Leung, H.K.N., White, L.: Insights into regression testing. In: ICSM, pp. 60–69 (1989)
21. Liblit, B., Naik, M., Zheng, A.X., Aiken, A., Jordan, M.I.: Scalable statistical bug isolation. In: PLDI, pp. 15–26 (2005)
22. Lukins, S., Kraft, N., Etzkorn, L.: Bug localization using latent Dirichlet allocation. IST **52**(9), 972–990 (2010)
23. Nanda, A., Mani, S., Sinha, S., Harrold, M.J., Orso, A.: Regression testing in the presence of non-code changes. In: ICST, pp. 21–30 (2011)
24. Ness, B., Ngo, V.: Regression containment through source change isolation. In: COMPSAC, pp. 616–621 (1997)
25. Nguyen, A.T., Nguyen, T.T., Al-Kofahi, J., Nguyen, H.V., Nguyen, T.: A topic-based approach for narrowing the search space of buggy files from a bug report. In: ASE, pp. 263–272 (2011)

26. Orso, A., Shi, N., Harrold, M.J.: Scaling regression testing to large software systems. ACM SIGSOFT Softw. Eng. Notes **29**(6), 241–251 (2004)
27. Pastore, F., Mariani, L., Goffi, A.: Radar: a tool for debugging regression problems in C/C++ software. In: ICSE Tool Demonstration Track, pp. 1335–1338 (2013)
28. Rao, S., Kak, A.: Retrieval from software libraries for bug localization: a comparative study of generic and composite text models. In: MSR, pp. 43–52 (2011)
29. Rothermel, G., Harrold, M.: A safe, efficient regression test selection technique. TOSEM **6**(2), 173–210 (1997)
30. Rothermel, G., Harrold, M.J.: A safe, efficient algorithm for regression test selection. In: ICSM, pp. 358–367 (1993)
31. Rothermel, G., Harrold, M.J.: A framework for evaluating regression test selection techniques. In: ICSE, pp. 201–210 (1994)
32. Rothermel, G., Harrold, M.J.: Analyzing regression test selection techniques. TSE **22**(8), 529–551 (1996)
33. Saha, R.K., Lease, M., Khurshid, S., Perry, D.E.: Improving bug localization using structured information retrieval. In: ASE, pp. 345–355 (2013)
34. Shi, A., Gyori, A., Gligoric, M., Zaytsev, A., Marinov, D.: Balancing trade-offs in test-suite reduction. In: FSE, pp. 246–256 (2014)
35. Streamline testing process with test impact analysis. http://msdn.microsoft.com/en-us/library/ff576128%28v=vs.100%29.aspx
36. Testing at the speed and scale of Google. http://google-engtools.blogspot.com/2011/06/testing-at-speed-and-scale-of-google.html
37. Tools for continuous integration at Google scale. http://www.youtube.com/watch?v=b52aXZ2yi08
38. Yoo, S., Harman, M.: Pareto efficient multi-objective test case selection. In: ISSTA, pp. 140–150 (2007)
39. Yoo, S., Harman, M.: Regression testing minimization, selection and prioritization: a survey. STVR **22**(2), 67–120 (2012)
40. Yu, Y., Dayani-Fard, H., Mylopoulos, J.: Removing false code dependencies to speedup software build processes. In: CASCON, pp. 343–352 (2003)
41. Zeller, A.: Yesterday, my program worked. Today, it does not. Why? In: Nierstrasz, O., Lemoine, M. (eds.) ESEC/SIGSOFT FSE -1999. LNCS, vol. 1687, pp. 253–267. Springer, Heidelberg (1999). doi:10.1007/3-540-48166-4_16
42. Zhang, L., Kim, M., Khurshid, S.: Localizing failure-inducing program edits based on spectrum information. In: ICSM, pp. 23–32 (2011)
43. Zhang, X., He, H., Gupta, N., Gupta, R.: Experimental evaluation of using dynamic slices for fault location. In: AADEBUG, pp. 33–42 (2005)
44. Zheng, J., Robinson, B., Williams, L., Smiley, K.: An initial study of a lightweight process for change identification and regression test selection when source code is not available. In: ISSRE, pp. 225–234 (2005)
45. Zhou, J., Zhang, H., Lo, D.: Where should the bugs be fixed? More accurate information retrieval based bug localization based on bug reports. In: ICSE, pp. 14–24 (2012)
46. Zuddas, D., Jin, W., Pastore, F., Mariani, L., Orso, A.: Mimic: locating and understanding bugs by analyzing mimicked executions. In: ASE, pp. 815–826 (2014)

On the Effectiveness of Bug Predictors with Procedural Systems: A Quantitative Study

Cristiano Werner Araújo[1(✉)], Ingrid Nunes[1,2], and Daltro Nunes[1]

[1] Instituto de Informática, Universidade Federal do Rio Grande do Sul (UFRGS),
Porto Alegre, Brazil
{cwaraujo,ingridnunes,daltro}@inf.ufrgs.br
[2] TU Dortmund, Dortmund, Germany

Abstract. Many bug predictors have been proposed, and their main target is object-oriented systems. Although object-orientation is currently the choice for most of the software applications, the procedural paradigm is still being used in many—sometimes crucial—applications, such as operating systems and embedded systems. Consequently, they also deserve attention. We present a study in which we investigated the effectiveness of existing bug prediction approaches with procedural systems. Such approaches use as input static code metrics. We evaluated to what extent they are applicable to our context, and compared their effectiveness using standard metrics, with adaptations when needed. We assessed five approaches, using eight procedural software systems, including open-source and industrial projects. We concluded that lines of code is the metric that plays the key role in our context, and approaches that use of a large set of metrics can introduce noise in the prediction model. In addition, the best results were obtained with open-source systems.

Keywords: Bug prediction · Procedural programming · Static code metrics

1 Introduction

Software testing is a crucial task to improve software quality, as it identifies software defects (or bugs) to be fixed. This task can be complemented by automated approaches that identify fault prone software components, potentially decreasing verification time, and thus improving software maintenance and reducing costs. By learning which components are fault prone, it is possible to prioritize system modules or components to be verified, thus allowing defects to be identified earlier. Given these potential benefits, many *bug prediction* approaches [7,14,16,18,22,28,34] have been proposed, investigating the use of different types of information in order to improve precision and recall when predicting defects.

Examples of inputs used by bug prediction approaches are static code metrics, change metrics, and previous defects [6]. Such approaches were individually evaluated by their authors using different software projects, or compared using

© Springer-Verlag GmbH Germany 2017
M. Huisman and J. Rubin (Eds.): FASE 2017, LNCS 10202, pp. 78–95, 2017.
DOI: 10.1007/978-3-662-54494-5_5

the same set of projects. These evaluations involved mostly, if not only, object-oriented (OO) systems. Object orientation is the choice for many software systems, such as web and mobile applications. However, the procedural paradigm is still being used in many—sometimes crucial—software systems, such as operating systems, embedded systems, and scientific computing applications. These applications deserve attention not only because they must be maintained, but also because they are often long-lived systems and procedural languages lack some mechanisms (e.g. inheritance and polymorphism) that improve code quality. These factors may cause the maintenance and evolution of those systems to be even harder. A previous study, performed by Khoshgoftaar and Allen [15], focused specifically on embedded systems. Nevertheless, they used information collected at runtime, which requires many scenarios of system execution to obtain data.

Approaches that rely on change metrics, e.g. number of changes, which often come from version control systems (VCSs), can also be adopted in the context of procedural systems, because they are paradigm- and language-independent. However, this is not the case of approaches that use static code metrics. Although there are metrics that can be measured in procedural systems, such as lines of code or cyclomatic complexity [21], most of the approaches also use OO-specific metrics, such as depth of inheritance tree or coupling between object classes [5]. Consequently, such approaches must be adapted and evaluated to be used with procedural software systems. There is evidence that change metrics can outperform static code metrics, but: (i) the former may not always be available, because of the need for the existence and access to VCSs, and (ii) information provided by static code metrics and change metrics are complementary [22].

We thus in this paper present a study conducted to evaluate approaches that rely on static code metrics [28] in the context of procedural software systems. Approaches were evaluated from two perspectives: (i) *degree of applicability*, by measuring the amount of OO-specific information they use; and (ii) *effectiveness*, by measuring their precision, recall and F-measure with a set of procedural software systems. Effectiveness was evaluated with the subset of metrics applicable to procedural systems, and with this subset together with metrics adapted to the procedural paradigm. For building our dataset, we selected a range of procedural software systems from many application domains, both open-source and proprietary, including operating systems and tools, bare-metal environments (software that does not require the support of a host operating system), and embedded commercial applications. Static code metrics and defects were extracted from each target system. Prediction was performed using learning techniques applied by the evaluated approaches. As result, we concluded that lines of code is the metric that plays the key role in our context, and approaches that use of a large set of metrics can introduce noise in the prediction model. In addition, the best results were obtained with open-source systems.

We next discuss existing bug prediction approaches. Then, we present our study settings and target systems in Sect. 3. Results and discussions are detailed in Sects. 4 and 5, respectively. Finally, we conclude in Sect. 6.

2   Related Work

As said in the introduction, bug prediction approaches make predictions based on different kinds of information. We classify such approaches into three groups. The first group of approaches [4, 7, 14, 18, 25, 26, 34] is based on static code metrics. They use only a snapshot of the source code, using information such as number of lines, in order to extract static code metrics. Such approaches are founded by prior studies, which concluded that there is a correlation between static code metrics and defects [4]. The second group of approaches [9, 10, 13, 17, 19, 23, 24, 31] requires another type of information, change metrics, which is usually obtained from VCSs. Such systems allow extraction of metrics associated with changes made during the software project evolution. Examples of typical metrics of this type are number of changes and change size. Some approaches use the frequency and recency of file change [10, 24], using caching concepts to indicate the most fault prone components. In addition to change metrics, Li et al. [19] used information collected from e-mails to predict a release quality. Approaches [6, 16, 22, 33] in the last group mixed different types of metrics, and some evaluated different proposed approaches.

Given that change metrics do not depend on the language or paradigm of the analyzed project, they can be used both for OO and procedural systems. In fact, some approaches included in their evaluation procedural systems [9] or used multiple versions of a single procedural system [19]. Nevertheless, approaches based on static code metrics typically rely on a metric set that includes OO-specific metrics. Koru and Liu [18], in particular, included two procedural systems in their evaluation, ignoring the OO-specific metrics for these systems. However, none of the approaches focused solely on procedural systems or contrasted results obtained with OO and procedural systems.

In Table 1, we detail a set of recent approaches that proposed bug predictors based on static code metrics—approaches that simply evaluated the correlation between metrics and defects rather than proposed predictors were excluded. They vary mainly in two aspects: (i) used metrics (this table overviews used metric suites); and (ii) investigated learning techniques. These approaches are those evaluated in this paper, and hereafter they are referred to as the acronyms introduced in Table 1. We included in the study approaches that *also* use change metrics [16], but only static metrics were taken into account. Moser et al. [22]'s approach extended that proposed by Zimmermann et al. [34], by including change metrics and exploring other learning techniques. In our evaluation, we use the static code metrics as well as learning techniques used by Moser et al. They used a subset of metrics from Zimmermann et al.'s dataset because all code metrics would *"involve overly complex models and not yield better performance as most of the measures are highly correlated with each other."*

3   Study Settings

Given the lack of provision of bug predictors dedicated to procedural software systems, we performed a study to fulfill this gap. We used existing bug prediction

Table 1. Summary of investigated approaches.

Approach	Acronym	Metric suites	Learning techniques
Gyimothy et al. [7]	GY	CK [5]	Decision Trees Linear Regression Neural Networks
Jureczko and Madeyski [14]	JU	CK [5], QMOOD [2], Tang et al. [29], Martin [20], Henderson-Sellers [11]	Linear Regression
Kim et al. [16]	KI	Metrics provided by the Understand [1] tool	SVM
Koru and Liu [18]	KO	Halstead [8], McCabe [21]	Decision Tree K-Star Random Forests
Moser et al. [22]	MO	CK [5], traditional OO metrics	Decision Trees Logistic Regression Naive Bayes

approaches with procedural software systems, also making required adaptations in this process, and evaluated and compared the obtained performance. We next provide details of our study.

3.1 Goal and Research Questions

In order to design our study, we followed the GQM (*goal-question-metric*) paradigm proposed by Basili et al. [3]. According to it, the first step is to specify the goal of the study, which is the following according to the GQM template: *to assess the effectiveness of existing bug prediction approaches in the context of procedural software systems, evaluate existing bug prediction approaches based on static code metrics from the perspective of the researcher in the context of 8 open source and proprietary software projects.* Based on our goal, we derived two research questions presented as follows.

RQ-1: *How bug prediction approaches based on static code metrics can be applied to procedural software systems?* Given that some approaches consider OO-specific metrics, we investigate the amount of metrics that can be used with procedural software systems and, from metrics that cannot be used, which can be adapted to our context.

RQ-2: *What is the effectiveness of bug prediction approaches based on static code metrics, possibly adapted, with procedural software systems?* Considering the investigated approaches and the set of metrics that can be extracted from procedural software, possibly with adaptations, we measure and compare the effectiveness of each approach. We evaluate both the set of metrics that can be extracted *as-is*, and also a set including adapted metrics.

The metrics used to answer these research questions are detailed in the next section together with our study procedure.

3.2   Procedure

Our study procedure is composed of three main steps. We first analyzed each investigated approach in order to verify whether their metrics can be used in our study. In the second step, we prepared our dataset, by performing two activities: (i) extraction of defects; and (ii) extraction of static code metrics. Last, we executed all the approaches with our target systems and measured their performance. We next provide details regarding our procedure.

Metric Adaptations. In order to answer our RQ1, we identified all metrics used by each approach, and verified whether they can be extracted from procedural systems. In the cases that they cannot, we adapted the metric calculation using the following mapping between OO concepts and procedural structures. In OO systems, there are classes with attributes and methods, with visibility modifiers. In procedural systems, there are source files (in C, files *.c), which contain global variables and functions, and header files (in C, files *.h), which contain function declarations and possibly global variables. In order to adapt metrics, we map: (i) classes to a combination of header and source files; (ii) public attributes and methods to variables and functions, respectively, declared in header files; and (iii) private attributes and methods to variables and functions, respectively, declared only in source files. Header files are thus considered similar to public interfaces of classes. Inheritance is not mapped, given that there is no similar concept in procedural languages, like C.

For evaluating the applicability of each approach to procedural systems, we measured the following scores.

Applicability with No Adaptations Ratio (A-score$_{NA}$) is the fraction of metrics that can be extracted from procedural systems with no adaptations. It is calculated as follows:

$$\text{A-Score}_{NA} = \frac{|M_P|}{|M|}$$

where M_P is the set of metrics that can be extracted from procedural systems with no adaptations, and M is the set of all metrics used by the approach.

Applicability with Adaptations Ratio (A-score$_{WA}$) is the fraction of metrics that can be extracted from procedural systems with or without adaptations. It is calculated as follows:

$$\text{A-Score}_{WA} = \frac{|M_P \cup M_A|}{|M|}$$

where M_P is the set of metrics that can be extracted from procedural systems with no adaptations, M_A is the set of metrics that can be extracted from procedural systems with adaptations, and M is the set of all metrics used by the approach.

Defect and Metric Extraction. We used commits indicated as *fixes* to identify defects in our target systems, which is an approach typically used in similar work. When a certain file is modified in a fix, it counts as one defect in that file. In order to mine commits, we used two approaches, depending on the tools available (only VCS, or VCS and issue tracker). For projects in which an *issue tracker* was available, we searched for commit messages that contained the issue id of issues that are bugs (and not features). Therefore, the issue category was used to identify commits that are fixes. For projects in which we had no access to an issue tracker, we searched for commit messages that matched a regular expression, which is a method adopted in previous work [14,16,32]. Regular expressions were selected for *each project* according to *message patterns* adopted by developers, e.g. in Linux, the regular expression includes *"fix"* and its variants.

Extraction of static source code metrics was performed using the Understand [1] static code analysis tool. Metrics for pure C not available in the Understand, or those we adapted, were extracted using: (i) implemented and available scripts[1]; and (ii) open-source tools, namely Cflow, CTags, and CCCC[2]. Cflow provides a call-graph for a C file, which can be parsed and used for extracting the fan-in and fan-out metrics. Complementary, CTags provides the functions and variables available both in header and source files, used for computing the public and private attributes and methods. CCCC, in turn, is a tool for metric measurement for C and C++.

Prediction and Evaluation. The evaluation of the effectiveness of each approach was made by building a predictor for our dataset using machine learning algorithms adopted by each investigated approach. Details of how these algorithms were executed are available elsewhere[3], as well as the used dataset. We then measured results with common machine learning scores, also used by most of the evaluated approaches (thus being used as a baseline), and used 10-fold cross-validation. The Scikit-Learn Framework [27] was used for prediction and score calculation. The following scores were used.

Precision is the fraction of all classified files that are classified as defective. It is calculated as follows: Precision $= TP/(TP + FP)$, where TP is the correctly classified defective files and FP is non-defective files classified as defective.

Recall is the fraction of all files that should be classified as defective that are classified as defective. It is calculated as follows: Recall $= TP/(TP + FN)$, where TP is the correctly classified defective files and FN is the defective files classified as non-defective.

F-measure is a score that combines recall and precision. It is the harmonic mean between them, calculated as follows: F-measure $= (2 \cdot Precision \cdot Recall)/(Precision + Recall)$.

---

[1] https://github.com/dborowiec/commentedCodeDetector.

[2] Available at http://www.gnu.org/software/cflow/, http://ctags.sourceforge.net/, and http://cccc.sourceforge.net/, respectively.

[3] http://www.inf.ufrgs.br/prosoft/resources/bug-prediction-procedural/.

All presented scores are in $[0,1]$, were the closer to one, the better the classification. Now that we have described our procedure, we proceed to the presentation of the target procedural systems of our study.

3.3 Target Systems

In order to build our dataset, we selected known open-source procedural systems as well as proprietary systems to which we have access. The latter have the advantage of having an accessible issue tracker, from which we can extract reported bugs and associated commits. Some open-source systems have available issue trackers, but we could not trace bug fixes to the files that changed in commits. In total, our study involved eight target systems, as listed in Table 2, from which three are proprietary. In order to be selected, systems had to satisfy two requirements. The first is that selected systems must be implemented in the C language. This is mainly due to two reasons: (i) it simplifies the process of extracting metrics; and (ii) C is the most popular and used procedural language. The second requirement is that information regarding bug fixes should be available, either through commit messages or an issue tracker. Selected applications are from different domains and have multiple sizes, as can be seen in Table 2.

Table 2. Target systems.

System	Description	LOC	#Files	#Commits	Bugs (%)
Linux	Operating system	9,434,808–9,529,552	30,058–30, 252	560,519	16–22%
Commercial system A	Telecom embedded application	407,660–509,856	1027–1148	1,027–1148	4–10%
Commercial system B	Telecom embedded application	337,203–351,923	939–949	2,211	6–12%
Commercial system C	Telecom embedded application	279,325	394	109	5%
BusyBox	Operating system applications	153,448	624	13,891	19%
Git	Version control system	153,855–157,193	500–507	41,356	16–29%
Light weight IP	Network stack for microcontrollers	18,510–32579	89–132	3,658	14–49%
CpuMiner	Bitcoin mining application	4,455–6,927	20	339	20%

Our target systems include Linux, which is an established operating system and a well documented project. Much work has been developed specifically on bug prediction for Linux [13,31], but all used change metrics. It is the largest project used in our study. BusyBox, in turn, provides operating system tools for embedded systems, being associated with Linux. Git is a widely used multi-platform VCS, with a consolidated development process, while Light Weight IP is a bare-metal network stack, thus being a low-level microcontroller environment, with restricted resources. CpuMiner is the smallest investigated system, but with a complex domain. It consists of a Bitcoin calculator, performing cryptographic calculations. Finally, the commercial applications included in our study consist of logic controllers for network devices containing hardware configuration, network protocols, configuration management and user interface.

To investigate a larger dataset, we used more than one system version when possible—some versions were not available and we excluded versions that diverged from the master branch. For each system, we analyzed bug fixes of a release i, extracting metrics from the source code of this release and bugs using commits made before the release $i + 1$. Therefore, if we had N releases available, we managed to evaluate $N - 1$ releases. Consequently, for applications with just one analyzed release, e.g. Commercial System C, we had, in fact, two available releases. Releases were determined using VCS tags for all systems. We investigated only two Linux versions due to the computational time needed for metric extraction. Moreover, only one version was investigated from the Commercial System C, because it was mostly developed by a third-party company, and the company that gave us access to it is responsible only for evolving it. Therefore, we had no access to the source code repository used during this initial application development. This explains the low number of commits presented in Table 2. In Table 2, we also present the percentage of files containing bugs for each system. In next section, we present how the investigated bug prediction approaches performed using these introduced systems.

4   Results and Analysis

In this section, we report obtained results, after performing the procedure described above. Results are presented and discussed according to our research questions.

RQ1: How bug prediction approaches based on static code metrics can be applied to procedural software systems? Each of the five investigated approaches was analyzed, and we assessed how applicable they are to our context. In Table 3, we list all static code metrics used by the selected approaches. We grouped some sets of metrics, due to space restrictions. The number in parenthesis indicate the number of metrics in each group. Based on Table 3, it is possible to observe that all but one of the approaches use metrics that rely on OO concepts. Therefore, we adapted such metrics in order to extract them from procedural systems to build bug predictors—they are described in the last column of Table 3. Adaptations follow the overall mapping rule described in our study procedure.

Considering this information, we classified metrics used by each approach in three classes (column *Class*): (i) those that *can* be extracted from procedural systems, labeled with Y; (ii) those that *cannot* be extracted from procedural systems, labeled with N; and (iii) those that can be extracted from procedural systems only *with adaptations*, labeled with A. Based on this classification, we verified how much applicable each approach is, using the measurements described in the previous section. We present results in Table 4, which shows the applicability ratios (without and with adaptations) of each approach. Note that, although

Table 3. Static code metrics used by bug prediction approaches.

Suite	Metric	GY	JU	KI	KO	MO	Class	Adaptation
	Lines of Code (LOC)	✓	✓	✓	✓	✓	Y	
	Line count			✓	✓		Y	
	Lines of comment			✓	✓		Y	
	Lines of code with comments				✓		Y	
	Blank lines			✓	✓		Y	
	Fan-in/fan-out (2)					✓	Y	
	Branch count				✓		Y	
McCabe	Cyclomatic complexity (avg)	✓	✓				Y	
McCabe	Cyclomatic complexity (max)	✓	✓	✓			Y	
McCabe	Essential complexity			✓	✓		Y	
McCabe	Design complexity			✓	✓		Y	
Halstead	Standard and derived metrics (12)				✓		Y	
	Understand metrics (29)		✓				Y	
	Understand metrics - OO (18)						N	
OO	Number of inherited attributes					✓	N	
OO	Number of inherited methods					✓	N	
OO	Number of attributes					✓	A	Number of global variables
OO	Number of methods					✓	A	Number of functions
OO	Number of private attributes					✓	A	Number of global variables not declared in the header file
OO	Number of public attributes					✓	A	Number of global variables declared in the header file
OO	Number of private methods					✓	A	Number of functions not declared in the header file
QMOOD	Number of public methods (NPM)		✓			✓	A	Number of functions declared in the header file
QMOOD	Data Access Metrics (DAM)		✓				Y	
QMOOD	Measure of Aggregation (MOA)		✓				Y	
QMOOD	Measure of Functional Abstraction (MFA)		✓				N	
QMOOD	Cohesion among Methods of Class (CAM)		✓				A	Use of types of function parameters instead of method parameters

Table 3. *(Continued)*

Suite	Metric	GY	JU	KI	KO	MO	Class	Adaptation
CK	Depth of Inheritance Tree (DIT)	✓	✓	✓		✓	N	
CK	Number of Children (NOC)	✓	✓	✓		✓	N	
CK	Coupling between Object Classes (CBO)	✓	✓	✓		✓	A	Functions or global variables from other files used in a target file
CK	Response for a Class (RFC)	✓	✓	✓		✓	A	Number of distinct functions from other files called by a target file
CK	Weighted Methods per Class (WMC)	✓	✓	✓		✓	A	Weighted functions per file
CK	Lack of Cohesion in Methods (LCOM)	✓	✓	✓		✓	A	Global variables count as attributes and functions count as methods
HS	Lack of Cohesion in Methods (LOCM3)		✓				Y	Same as LCOM
	Lack of Cohesion on Methods allowing Negative value (LCOMN)	✓					Y	Same as LCOM
Tang et al.	Inheritance Coupling (IC)		✓				Y	
Tang et al.	Coupling between Methods (CBM)		✓				N	
Tang et al.	Average Method Complexity (AMC)		✓				A	Average complexity of functions in file
Martin	Afferent Couplings (Ca)		✓				A	Number of files that use a pair of header and source file
Martin	Efferent Couplings (Ce)		✓				A	Number of referenced header files

Legend: Y-Yes; N-No; A-Adaptations Required.

MO approach, in theory, uses 31 static code metrics from Zimmermann et al.'s [34] dataset, its provided dataset contains only 17 metrics extractable from source code. Other metrics in the dataset are target metrics, e.g. *TrivialBugs*, or rely on CVS information, e.g. *CvsEntropy*, which is not our focus.

Results indicate that the GY, JU, and MO approaches largely rely on OO metrics, while KO uses only metrics that do not rely on OO concepts. With our

Table 4. Approach applicability to procedural software systems.

	GY	JU	KI	KO	MO
Extractable metrics	1	5	37	21	3
Metrics extractable with adaptations	5	11	4	0	10
Not extractable metrics	2	4	20	0	4
Total	8	20	61	21	17
A-Score$_{NA}$	0.12	0.25	0.60	1.00	0.17
A-Score$_{WA}$	0.75	0.80	0.67	1.00	0.76

adaptations, it is possible to use at least 67% (KI has the minimum A-Score$_{WA}$) of proposed metrics of each approach. Given this analysis, we proceed to the evaluation of the effectiveness of each approach.

RQ2: What is the effectiveness of bug prediction approaches based on static code metrics, possibly adapted, with procedural software systems? We executed each investigated approach, considering different learning techniques, with all target systems (and their different versions). As result, we obtained the precision, recall and F-measure values presented in Fig. 1 and Table 5. On the left hand side charts of Fig. 1, we show results using only the metrics that can be extracted from procedural systems, while those on the right hand side also include adapted metrics. Table 5 reports the mean and standard deviation of the values obtained with our different target systems. For a comparison, we show in the baseline row the results reported by each approach's authors, if they were provided.

Comparing results obtained with and without adaptations, we observed that they are similar to each other—all measurements vary ±0.05. The differences are so small that they could be due to the randomness of the 10-fold cross validation. This can be seen in the KO approach (A-Score$_{NA}$ = 1.00), which uses no OO metrics, thus both evaluations use the same set of metrics. Consequently, there is evidence that the OO-inspired metrics bring little information associated with defect presence in procedural software systems and increase model complexity. Therefore, they can be discarded. Note that, for some approaches, the number of adapted metrics is not small, as discussed in the previous research question.

The best results were obtained with KO RF (which is based only on no OO metrics), considering F-measure, which combines precision and recall. Two approaches presented the worst results. The first, KI, relies on a large set of metrics. The second, GY, presented worse results only with NN, but results obtained with the other algorithms (DT and LR) are much better, providing evidence of the importance of the selected algorithm. Considering precision and recall individually, it is possible to observe that two other approaches (GY LR and MO LR) have higher precision than KO, at the cost of compromising recall.

With respect to the GY approach, the approach that with DT obtained the second best results, it is interesting to highlight that it has only one metric used without adaptations: LOC. Other approaches with best results also use this metric.

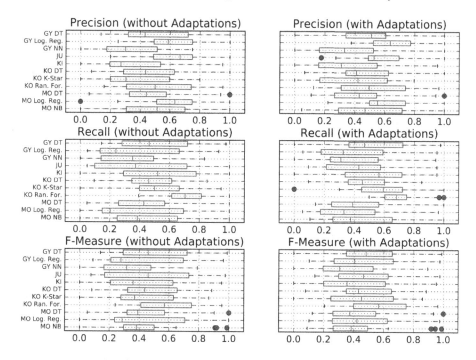

Fig. 1. Effectiveness measurements by each approach.

Table 5. Summary of effectiveness evaluation of each approach.

	GY DT	GY LR	GY NN	JU	KI	KO DT	KO KS	KO RF	MO DT	MO LR	MO NB
Precision											
Without adaptations	0.52 (0.27)	**0.64** **(0.21)**	0.34 (0.21)	0.62 (0.22)	0.36 (0.30)	0.49 (0.28)	0.39 (0.26)	0.52 (0.26)	0.48 (0.25)	**0.64** **(0.25)**	0.53 (0.30)
With adaptations	0.52 (0.28)	**0.66** **(0.20)**	0.38 (0.27)	0.59 (0.21)	0.38 (0.30)	0.49 (0.28)	0.40 (0.26)	0.53 (0.26)	0.46 (0.25)	0.61 (0.21)	0.53 (0.30)
Baseline	0.68		0.68	0.82	0.72	0.62				0.65	
Recall											
Without adaptations	0.51 (0.25)	0.37 (0.30)	0.35 (0.25)	0.42 (0.33)	0.52 (0.35)	0.47 (0.23)	0.55 (0.25)	**0.72** **(0.18)**	0.45 (0.25)	0.39 (0.34)	0.44 (0.29)
With adaptations	0.51 (0.26)	0.40 (0.29)	0.40 (0.25)	0.44 (0.27)	0.50 (0.30)	0.47 (0.22)	0.57 (0.28)	**0.71** **(0.15)**	0.44 (0.24)	0.41 (0.29)	0.47 (0.28)
Baseline	0.67		0.64	0.89	0.68	0.68			0.42	0.33	0.40
F-Measure											
Without adaptations	0.51 (0.26)	0.44 (0.29)	0.33 (0.22)	0.47 (0.31)	0.40 (0.31)	0.48 (0.24)	0.44 (0.26)	**0.59** **(0.23)**	0.46 (0.25)	0.45 (0.32)	0.42 (0.26)
With adaptations	0.51 (0.26)	0.48 (0.28)	0.37 (0.25)	0.49 (0.25)	0.40 (0.30)	0.47 (0.24)	0.45 (0.27)	**0.58** **(0.23)**	0.45 (0.24)	0.46 (0.27)	0.43 (0.25)
Baseline	0.67		0.65	0.85	0.69	0.65				0.36	

Legend: DT-Decision Trees; KS-K-Star; LR-Logistic Regression; NB-Naive Bayes; NN-Neural Networks; RF-Random Forest.

However, the other metrics used by GY slightly improved both precision and recall for LR and NN but for DT, which obtained the best results for GY, they remained the same. Therefore, there is evidence that LOC plays a key role in our context. Although KI also uses LOC, the other used metrics might have introduced noise in the model used for prediction.

In addition to comparing results across different approaches, we also investigated how our measurements vary across different target systems, as presented in Fig. 2. We observed that commercial applications presented worse results in comparison with open source systems. This observation holds even for the Commercial System C, which has a low number of commits as described in Sect. 3.3. Analyzing results, we considered two hypotheses: (1) there are differences in the

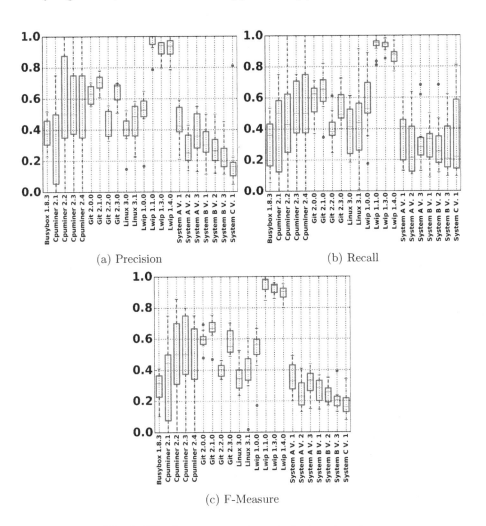

(a) Precision

(b) Recall

(c) F-Measure

Fig. 2. Effectiveness measurements by target system.

system datasets that has impact in the construction of the prediction model; and (2) coding standards and practices adopted by developers of our commercial applications are less suitable for bug prediction. The number of investigated systems is not large enough to allow us to reach a conclusion regarding this and, therefore, further studies could help clarify this issue. However, it is possible to observe in Table 2 that the percentage of files with bugs is much lower in commercial applications. Consequently, the highly unbalanced classes in these datasets make the prediction model construction more difficult. Moreover, although our proprietary applications are maintained by the same company, they were originally developed outside this company (not by the same provider). Consequently, hypothesis (2) is less likely to be true.

With LWIP, an open source system, results obtained were impressively high, for three of its four analyzed versions. Based on an analysis of LWIP's commits and release information, our hypothesis is that, again, the balance between the dataset classes is the reason for these results. In the version in which LWIP performed significantly well, the number of files with bugs are similar to that of files with no bugs. Therefore, this facilitates the machine learning process.

5   Discussion

We now discuss relevant issues that emerged from the analysis of our results. These issues are related to the differences of results obtained using different sets of metrics or systems.

Use of Adapted Object-Oriented Metrics. Based on our results, we observed that all metrics adapted from OO metrics were not helpful to predict defects in procedural systems. On the one hand, this was expected given that programming practices are different in procedural and OO systems. Moreover, metrics that are associated with inheritance could not be adapted, because this concept does not exist in procedural systems, and such metrics may be relevant to be used in combination with other OO metrics to build predictors. On the other hand, some of the metrics, such as CBO, capture coupling and cohesion in classes, while our adapted metrics capture them in source files. Therefore, they could have been helpful. Although coupling is useful in predictors for OO systems, we could not observe this in our study. Possibly, this metric alone may be not enough for the predictor, and it should be combined with other metrics that cannot be adapted, e.g. those related with inheritance, so that a proper correlation with bugs is found.

Open-Source vs. Proprietary Systems. As discussed before, the results obtained with open-source and proprietary systems are different. This can be seen in Fig. 2. As discussed before, a potential explanation is that these differences are due to the unbalanced classes (i.e. number of files with bugs and with no bugs) in the proprietary systems' datasets. Because of the low number of instances of files with bugs, it is difficult to the learning technique to build a model that distinguishes these two classes. This is actually a general problem of bug prediction because, typically, the number of files with bugs is relatively small. Moreover, datasets usually contain noise, because the bugs are not those that exist, but those that were identified. Therefore, techniques that address these issues are essential and should be explored in the context of bug prediction.

Another possible explanation for the differences between results is the development process adopted in open-source and proprietary systems. In the former, developers have their own agenda (most of them are volunteers or employers of different companies), while in the latter changes can be limited to a set of files in each software release, because it may be focused on a particular system feature.

Effectiveness with Object-Oriented vs. Procedural Systems. In Table 5, we presented previously reported results for us to have as a baseline. Note that the results reported by the KI approach include change metrics, and KO's evaluation included procedural and OO systems, made available by NASA. As can be seen, for all approaches but MO, our results are worse. The only approach that presented results similar to ours is KO but with a different learning technique (our results with RF is similar to the baseline performance, which used DT). All approaches performed better with the original set, indicating that obtained results may not generalizable to systems other than those obtained with the dataset used for evaluation. Moreover, the differences between results can also be explained using the arguments we presented above, when we compared results using adapted OO metrics—use of a subset of metrics and different meanings of the relationships between the metrics and defects.

In addition to these issues that might explain difference between results, the typical application domains of procedural systems may also be an issue. Such domains often involve low level details or complex calculations. Consequently, complexity metrics may be more correlated with defects than metrics associated with aspects more relevant to OO systems, such as response for a class or number of children. In fact, previous work indicates that there is a correlation between code complexity and defects [30]. Moreover, variability is often present in such application domains, which results in the inclusion of macro definitions from the C language. This may compromise code legibility and make it more fault-prone.

A relevant observation from the results of the GY approach is the importance of the lines of code (LOC) metric for building a bug predictor for procedural systems. Using only LOC for identifying fault-prone files is almost as good as using other metrics, confirming the correlation between LOC and defects [12,25]. This may be an indication that approaches are overfitting their models with large amounts of metrics, which do not bring useful information. Therefore, studies that identify which metrics are in fact responsible for good prediction results, both for OO and procedural systems, are needed. This also helps reduce the cost of metric extraction.

Threats to Validity. We performed an empirical evaluation of existing bug predictors, and we mitigated identified threats that could invalidate our results. An external threat is the number of projects used for evaluation. In order to address this, we selected systems from different domains, with difference sizes, and both open-source and proprietary.

A construction threat is the procedure adopted to extract defects. To mitigate this, we followed a procedure similar to that adopted by existing approaches, when issue trackers were not available. Based on the analysis of our systems, we observed that we would not be able to detect defects introduced and fixed during the development of a single release—we are not aware how or if prior work has addressed this issue, given that this was not reported. It would be inadequate to count them as bugs, because they were not present in the code from which metrics were extracted. Therefore, we added an additional step in the defect extraction, which verified if the fix commit changed code present in the code baseline. Another construction validity is that we implemented ourselves the investigated approaches. Although most approaches require only to execute learning techniques, parameters used in previous studies were not published. Consequently, we calibrated the models. For mitigating this threat, we replicated published studies using datasets that were made available by the authors, before performing our study.

6 Conclusion

In this paper, we presented a study in which we investigated how existing bug prediction approaches perform in the context of procedural software systems, using static code metrics. Although object orientation is currently the most used paradigm, procedural languages are still largely used for many fundamental applications, such as operating systems and scientific computing applications. The only investigated approach that relies solely on metrics that can be extracted from procedural systems is that proposed by Koru and Liu [18]. This approach presented one of the best results, followed by the approach proposed by Gyimothy et al. [7]. Note that such results were obtained with a subset of metrics used by these authors, given that some metrics rely on object-oriented concepts. In fact, the second best approach uses only one metric that can be extracted, namely lines of code. Therefore, we concluded that this metric plays a key role to build bug predictors in our context. We also adapted object-oriented metrics to be extracted from procedural systems. Our conclusion is that they do not improve the bug prediction for these systems.

Our results showed that bug predictors that have good performance with object-oriented systems do not necessarily are the best with procedural systems. Therefore, our future work includes the exploration of particularities of procedural systems and exploitation of metrics based on these particularities to build prediction models. Moreover, based on the analyzed systems, there is evidence that it is difficult to obtain good results with systems associated with datasets that have a low number of files with bugs. Therefore, it is important to explore techniques in the context of machine learning that deal with the issue of unbalanced classes.

Acknowledgments. The authors are very grateful to the Parks S/A (http://www. parks.com.br) Company that allowed analyzing three of their proprietary projects. Ingrid Nunes would like to thank for research grants CNPq ref. 303232/2015-3, CAPES ref. 7619-15-4, and Alexander von Humboldt, ref. BRA 1184533 HFSTCAPES-P.

References

1. Understand static code analysis tool. https://scitools.com/. Accessed 01 June 2016
2. Bansiya, J., Davis, C.G.: A hierarchical model for object-oriented design quality assessment. IEEE Trans. Softw. Eng. **28**(1), 4–17 (2002)
3. Basili, V.R., Selby, R.W., Hutchens, D.H.: Experimentation in software engineering. IEEE Trans. Softw. Eng. **12**(7), 733–743 (1986)
4. Basili, V.R., Briand, L.C., Melo, W.L.: A validation of object-oriented design metrics as quality indicators. IEEE Trans. Softw. Eng. **22**(10), 751–761 (1996)
5. Chidamber, S.R., Kemerer, C.F.: A metrics suite for object oriented design. IEEE Trans. Softw. Eng. **20**(6), 476–493 (1994)
6. D'Ambros, M., Lanza, M., Robbes, R.: An extensive comparison of bug prediction approaches. MSR **2010**, 31–41 (2010)
7. Gyimothy, T., Ferenc, R., Siket, I.: Empirical validation of object-oriented metrics on open source software for fault prediction. IEEE Trans. Softw. Eng. **31**(10), 897–910 (2005)
8. Halstead, M.H.: Elements of Software Science (Operating and Programming Systems Series). Elsevier Science Inc., New York (1977)
9. Hassan, A.E.: Predicting faults using the complexity of code changes. In: ICSE 2009, pp. 78–88. IEEE Computer Society, USA (2009)
10. Hassan, A.E., Holt, R.C.: The top ten list: dynamic fault prediction. In: ICSM 2005, pp. 263–272. IEEE Computer Society, USA (2005)
11. Henderson-Sellers, B.: Object-Oriented Metrics: Measures of Complexity. Prentice-Hall Inc., Upper Saddle River (1996)
12. Jay, G., Hale, J.E., Smith, R.K., Hale, D., Kraft, N.A., Ward, C.: Cyclomatic complexity and lines of code: empirical evidence of a stable linear relationship. J. Softw. Eng. Appl. **2**(3), 137–143 (2009)
13. Jiang, T., Tan, L., Kim, S.: Personalized defect prediction. In: 2013 IEEE/ACM 28th International Conference on Automated Software Engineering (ASE), pp. 279–289, November 2013
14. Jureczko, M., Madeyski, L.: Towards identifying software project clusters with regard to defect prediction. In: PROMISE 2010, pp. 9:1–9:10. ACM, USA (2010)
15. Khoshgoftaar, T.M., Allen, E.B.: Predicting fault-prone software modules in embedded systems with classification trees. In: The 4th IEEE International Symposium on High-Assurance Systems Engineering (HASE 1999), p. 105. IEEE Computer Society, Washington, DC (1999)
16. Kim, S., Whitehead, E.J., Zhang, Y.: Classifying software changes: clean or buggy? IEEE Trans. Softw. Eng. **34**(2), 181–196 (2008)
17. Kim, S., Zimmermann, T., Whitehead Jr., E.J., Zeller, A.: Predicting faults from cached history. In: ICSE 2008, pp. 15–16. ACM, USA (2008)
18. Koru, A.G., Liu, H.: Building effective defect prediction models in practice. IEEE Softw. **22**(6), 23–29 (2005)
19. Li, P.L., Herbsleb, J., Shaw, M.: Finding predictors of field defects for open source software systems in commonly available data sources: a case study of openBSD. In: METRICS 2005, pp. 10–32, September 2005

20. Martin, R.: OO design quality metrics: an analysis of dependencies. In: OOPSLA 1994 (1994)
21. McCabe, T.: A complexity measure. IEEE Trans. Softw. Eng. SE **2**(4), 308–320 (1976)
22. Moser, R., Pedrycz, W., Succi, G.: A comparative analysis of the efficiency of change metrics and static code attributes for defect prediction. In: ICSE 2008, pp. 181–190. ACM, USA (2008)
23. Munson, J.C., Elbaum, S.G.: Code churn: a measure for estimating the impact of code change. In: ICSM 1998, pp. 24–31. IEEE Computer Society, USA (1998)
24. Nagappan, N., Ball, T.: Use of relative code churn measures to predict system defect density. In: ICSE 2005, pp. 284–292. ACM, USA (2005)
25. Nagappan, N., Ball, T., Zeller, A.: Mining metrics to predict component failures. In: Proceedings of the 28th International Conference on Software Engineering (ICSE 2006), pp. 452–461. ACM, New York (2006)
26. Olague, H.M., Etzkorn, L.H., Gholston, S., Quattlebaum, S.: Empirical validation of three software metrics suites to predict fault-proneness of object-oriented classes developed using highly iterative or agile software development processes. IEEE Trans. Softw. Eng. **33**(6), 402–419 (2007)
27. Pedregosa, F., Varoquaux, G., Gramfort, A., Michel, V., Thirion, B., Grisel, O., Blondel, M., Prettenhofer, P., Weiss, R., Dubourg, V., Vanderplas, J., Passos, A., Cournapeau, D., Brucher, M., Perrot, M., Duchesnay, E.: Scikit-learn: machine learning in Python. J. Mach. Learn. Res. **12**, 2825–2830 (2011)
28. Radjenović, D., Heričko, M., Torkar, R., Živkovič, A.: Software fault prediction metrics. Inf. Softw. Technol. **55**(8), 1397–1418 (2013)
29. Tang, M.H., Kao, M.H., Chen, M.H.: An empirical study on object-oriented metrics. In: METRICS 1999, p. 242. IEEE Computer Society, USA (1999)
30. Tashtoush, Y., Al-maolegi, M., Arkok, B.: The correlation among software complexity metrics with case study. Int. J. Adv. Comput. Res. **4**(2), 414–419 (2014)
31. Tian, Y., Lawall, J., Lo, D.: Identifying linux bug fixing patches. In: 2012 34th International Conference on Software Engineering (ICSE), pp. 386–396, June 2012
32. Zhang, F., Mockus, A., Keivanloo, I., Zou, Y.: Towards building a universal defect prediction model. In: MSR 2014, pp. 182–191. ACM, USA (2014)
33. Zimmermann, T., Nagappan, N., Zeller, A.: Predicting bugs from history. In: Mens, T., Demeyer, S. (eds.) Software Evolution, pp. 69–88. Springer, Heidelberg (2008)
34. Zimmermann, T., Premraj, R., Zeller, A.: Predicting defects for eclipse. In: PROMISE 2007, p. 9. IEEE Computer Society, USA (2007)

Program and System Analysis

Inference and Evolution of TypeScript Declaration Files

Erik Krogh Kristensen and Anders Møller[(✉)]

Aarhus University, Aarhus, Denmark
{erik,amoeller}@cs.au.dk

Abstract. TypeScript is a typed extension of JavaScript that has become widely used. More than 2000 JavaScript libraries now have publicly available TypeScript declaration files, which allows the libraries to be used when programming TypeScript applications. Such declaration files are written manually, however, and they are often lagging behind the continuous development of the libraries, thereby hindering their usability. The existing tool TSCHECK is capable of detecting mismatches between the libraries and their declaration files, but it is less suitable when creating and evolving declaration files.

In this work we present the tools TSINFER and TSEVOLVE that are designed to assist the construction of new TypeScript declaration files and support the co-evolution of the declaration files as the underlying JavaScript libraries evolve. Our experimental results involving major libraries demonstrate that TSINFER and TSEVOLVE are superior to TSCHECK regarding these tasks and that the tools are sufficiently fast and precise for practical use.

1 Introduction

The TypeScript [13] programming language has become a widely used alternative to JavaScript for developing web applications. TypeScript is a superset of JavaScript adding language features that are important when developing and maintaining larger applications. Most notably, TypeScript provides optional types, which not only allows many type errors to be detected statically, but also enables powerful IDE support for code navigation, auto-completion, and refactoring. To allow TypeScript applications to use existing JavaScript libraries, the typed APIs of such libraries can be described in separate *declaration files*. A public repository exists containing declaration files for more than 2000 libraries, and they are a critical component of the TypeScript software ecosystem.[1]

Unfortunately, the declaration files are written and maintained manually, which is tedious and error prone. Mismatches between declaration files and the corresponding JavaScript implementations of libraries affect the TypeScript application programmers. The type checker produces incorrect type error messages, and code navigation and auto-completion are misguided, which may cause

---

[1] https://github.com/DefinitelyTyped/DefinitelyTyped

© Springer-Verlag GmbH Germany 2017
M. Huisman and J. Rubin (Eds.): FASE 2017, LNCS 10202, pp. 99–115, 2017.
DOI: 10.1007/978-3-662-54494-5_6

programming errors and increase development costs. The tool TSCHECK [8] has been designed to detect such mismatches, but three central challenges remain. First, the process of constructing the initial version of a declaration file is still manual. Although TypeScript has become popular, many new libraries are still being written in JavaScript, so the need for constructing new declaration files is not diminishing. We need tool support not only for checking correctness of declaration files, but also for assisting the programmers creating them from the JavaScript implementations. Second, JavaScript libraries evolve, as other software, and when their APIs change, the declaration files must be updated. We observe that the evolution of many declaration files lag considerably behind the libraries, which causes the same problems with unreliable type checking and IDE support as with erroneous declaration files, and it may make application programmers reluctant or unable to use the newest versions of the libraries. With the increasing adaptation of TypeScript and the profusion of libraries, this problem will likely grow in the future. For these reasons, we need tools to support the programmers in this co-evolution of libraries and declaration files. Third, TSCHECK is not sufficiently scalable to handle modern JavaScript libraries, which are often significantly larger than a couple of years ago.

The contributions of this paper are as follows.

- To further motivate our work, we demonstrate why the state-of-the-art tool TSCHECK is inadequate for inference and evolution of declaration files, and we describe a small study that uncovers to what extent the evolution of TypeScript declaration files typically lag behind the evolution of the underlying JavaScript libraries (Sect. 2).
- We present the tool TSINFER, which is based on TSCHECK but specifically designed to address the challenge of supporting programmers when writing new TypeScript declaration files for JavaScript libraries, and to scale to even the largest libraries (Sect. 3).
- Next, we present the tool TSEVOLVE, which builds on top of TSINFER to support the task of co-evolving TypeScript declaration files as the underlying JavaScript libraries evolve (Sect. 4).
- We report on an experimental evaluation, which shows that TSINFER is better suited than TSCHECK for assisting the developer in creating the initial versions of declaration files, and that TSEVOLVE is superior to both TSCHECK and TSINFER for supporting the co-evolution of declaration files (Sect. 5).

2   Motivating Examples

The PixiJS Library. PixiJS[2] is a powerful JavaScript library for 2D rendering that has been under development since 2013. A TypeScript declaration file[3] was written manually for version 2.2 (after some incomplete attempts), and the authors have since then made numerous changes to try to keep up-to-date with

---

[2] http://www.pixijs.com/
[3] https://github.com/pixijs/pixi-typescript

```
1  export class Sprite extends PIXI.DisplayObjectContainer {
2      constructor (texture: PIXI.Texture);
3      static fromFrame: (frameId: string | number) => PIXI.Sprite;
4      static fromImage: (imageId: string, crossorigin: any,
5                         scaleMode: any) => PIXI.Sprite;
6      _height: number;
7      _width: number;
8      anchor: PIXI.Point;
9      blendMode: number;
10     onTextureUpdate: () => void;
11     setTexture: (texture: PIXI.Texture) => void;
12     shader: any;
13     texture: PIXI.Texture;
14     tint: number;
15 }
```

Fig. 1. Example output from TSINFER, when run on PixiJS version 2.2.

the rapid evolution of the library. At the time of writing, the current version of PixiJS is 4.0, and the co-evolution of the declaration file continues to require substantial manual effort as testified by the numerous commits and issues in the repository. Hundreds of library developers face similar challenges with building TypeScript declaration files and updating them as the libraries evolve.

From Checking to Inferring Declaration Files. To our knowledge, only one tool exists that may alleviate the manual effort required: TSCHECK [8]. This tool detects mismatches between a JavaScript library and a TypeScript declaration file. It works in three phases: (1) it executes the library's initialization code and takes a snapshot of the resulting runtime state; (2) it then type checks the objects in the snapshot, which represent the structure of the library API, with respect to the TypeScript type declarations; (3) it finally performs a light-weight static analysis of each library function to type check the return value of each function signature. This works well for detecting errors, but not for inferring and evolving the declaration files. For example, running TSCHECK on PixiJS version 2.2 and a declaration file with an empty PIXI module (mimicking the situation where the module is known to exist but its API has not yet been declared) reports nothing but the missing properties of the PIXI module, which is practically useless. In comparison, our new tool TSINFER is able to infer a declaration file that is quite close to the manually written one. Figure 1 shows the automatically inferred declaration for one of the classes in PixiJS version 2.2. The declaration is not perfect (the types of frameId, crossorigin, scaleMode, and shader could be more precise), but evidently such output is a better starting point when creating the initial version of a declaration file than starting completely from scratch.

Evolving Declaration Files. The PixiJS library has recently been updated from version 3 to version 4. Using TSCHECK as a help to update the declaration file would not be particularly helpful. For example, running TSCHECK on version 4 of the JavaScript file and the existing version 3 of the declaration file reports that 38 properties are

```
Property PrimitiveShader removed from object on window.PIXI
Property FXAAFilter removed from object on window.PIXI
Property TransformManual added to object on window.PIXI
  Type: typeof PIXI.TransformBase
Property TransformBase added to object on window.PIXI
  Type:  class TransformBase { ... }
Property Transform added to object on window.PIXI
  Type: class Transform extends PIXI.TransformBase { ... }
```

(a) Some of the added or removed properties.

```
Type changed on
  window.PIXI.RenderTarget.[constructor].[return].stencilMaskStack
from StencilMaskStack to PIXI.Graphics[]
```

(b) A modified property.

Fig. 2. Example output from TSEVOLVE, when run on PixiJS versions 3 and 4.

missing on the PIXI object, without any information about their types. Moreover, 15 of these properties are also reported if running TSCHECK on version 3 of the JavaScript file, since they are due to the developers intentionally leaving some properties undocumented. Our experiments presented in Sect. 5 show that many libraries have such intentionally undocumented features, and some also have properties that intentionally exist in the declaration file but not in the library.[4] While TSINFER does suggest a type for each of the new properties, it does not have any way to handle the intentional discrepancies. Our other tool TSEVOLVE attempts to solve that problem by looking only at differences between two versions of the JavaScript implementation and is thereby better at only reporting actual changes. When running TSEVOLVE on PixiJS version 3 and 4, it reports (see Fig. 2(a)) that 8 properties have been removed and 24 properties have been added on the PIXI object. All of these correctly reflect an actual change in the library implementation, and the declaration file should therefore be updated accordingly. This update inevitably requires manual intervention, though; in this specific case, PrimitiveShader has been removed from the PIXI object but the developers want to keep it in the declarations as an internal class, and TransformManual, although it is new to version 4, is a deprecated alias for the also added TransformBase.

Changes in a library API from one version to the next often consist of extensions, but features are also sometimes removed, or types are changed. As an example of the latter, one of the changes from version 3 to 4 for PixiJS was changing the type of the field stencilMaskStack in the class RenderTarget from type PIXI.StencilMaskStack to type PIXI.Graphics[]. The developer updating the declaration file noticed that the field was now an array, but not that the elements were changed to type PIXI.Graphics, so the type was erroneously updated to PIXI.StencilMaskStack[]. In comparison, TSINFER reports the change correctly as shown in Fig. 2(b).

---

[4] This situation is rare, but can happen if, for example, documentation is needed for a class that is not exported, see e.g. https://github.com/pixijs/pixi.js/issues/2312/#issuecomment-174608951.

A Study of Evolution of Type Declarations. To further motivate the need for new tools to support the co-evolution of declaration files as the libraries evolve, we have measured to what extent existing declaration files lag behind the libraries.[5] We collected every JavaScript library that satisfies the following conditions: it is being actively developed and has a declaration file in the DefinitelyTyped repository, the declaration file contains a recognizable version number, and the library uses git tags for marking new versions, where we study the commits from January 2014 to August 2016. This resulted in 49 libraries. By then comparing the timestamps of the version changes for each library and its declaration file, respectively (where we ignore patch releases and only consider major.minor versioning), we find that for more than half of the libraries, the declaration file is lagging behind by at least a couple of months, and for some more than a year. This is notable, given that all the libraries are widely used according to the github ratings, and it seriously affects the usefulness of the declaration files in TypeScript application development.

Interestingly, we also find many cases where the version number found in the declaration file has not been updated correctly along with the contents of the file.[6] Not being able to trust version numbers of course also affects the usability of the declaration files. For some high-profile libraries, such as jQuery and AngularJS, the declaration files are kept up-to-date, which demonstrates that the developers find it necessary to invest the effort required, despite the lack of tool support. We hope our new tools can help not only those developers but also ones who do not have the same level of manual resources available.

Scalability. In addition to the limitations of TSCHECK described above, we find that its static analysis component, which we use as a foundation also for TSINFER and TSEVOLVE, is not sufficiently scalable to handle the sizes and complexity of contemporary JavaScript libraries. In Sect. 3.2 we explain how we replace the unification-based analysis technique used by TSCHECK with a more precise subset-based one, and in Sect. 5 we demonstrate that this modification, perhaps counterintuitively, leads to a significant improvement in scalability. As an example, the time required to analyze *Moment.js* is improved from 873 s to 12 s, while other libraries simply are not analyzable in reasonable time with the unification-based approach.

3   TSINFER: Inference of Initial Type Declarations

Our inference tool TSINFER works in three phases: (1) it concretely initializes the library in a browser and records a snapshot of the resulting runtime state, much like the first phase of TSCHECK (see Sect. 2); (2) it performs a static analysis of all the functions in that snapshot, similarly to the third phase of TSCHECK; (3) lastly it emits a TypeScript declaration file. As two of the phases are quite similar to the approach used by TSCHECK, we here focus on what TSINFER does differently.

3.1   The Snapshot Phase

In JavaScript, library code needs to actively put entry points into the heap in order for it to be callable by application code. This initialization, however, often involves complex

---

[5] Our data material from this study is available at http://www.brics.dk/tstools/.

[6] An example is Backbone.js, until our patch https://github.com/DefinitelyTyped/DefinitelyTyped/pull/10462.

metaprogramming, and statically analyzing the initialization of a library like jQuery can therefore be extremely complicated [2]. We sidestep this challenge by concretely initializing the library in a real browser and recording a snapshot of the heap after the top-level code has finished executing. This is done in the same way as described by TSCHECK, and we work under the same assumptions, notably, that the library API has been established after the top-level code has executed. We have, however, changed a few things.

For all functions in the returned snapshot, we record two extra pieces of information compared to TSCHECK: (1) the result of calling the function with the new operator (if the call returned normally), which helps us determine the structure of a class if the function is found to be a constructor; (2) all calls to the function that occur during the initialization, which we use to seed the static analysis phase.

The last step is to create a class hierarchy. JavaScript libraries use many different and complicated ways of creating their internal class structures, but after the initialization is done, the vast majority of libraries end up with constructor functions and prototype chains. The class hierarchy is therefore created by making a straightforward inspection of the prototype chains.

3.2   The Static Analysis Phase

The static analysis phase takes the produced snapshot as input and performs a static analysis of each of the functions. It produces types for the parameters and the return value of each function.

The analysis is an unsound, flow-insensitive, context-insensitive analysis that has all the features described in previous work [8], including the treatment of properties and native functions. There are, however, some important changes.

TSCHECK analyzes each function separately, meaning that if a function f calls a function g, this information is ignored when analyzing function g. This works well for creating an analysis such as TSCHECK that only infers the return type of functions. When creating an analysis that also infers function parameter types, the information gained by observing calls to a function is important. Our analysis therefore does not analyze each function separately, but instead performs a single analysis that covers all the functions.

While TSCHECK opts for a unification-based analysis, we find that switching to a subset-based analysis is necessary to gain the scalability needed to infer types for the bigger JavaScript libraries, as discussed in Sect. 2. The subset-based analysis is similar to the one described by Pottier [15], as it keeps separate constraint variables for upper-bounds and lower-bounds. After the analysis, the types for the upper-bound and lower-bound constraint variables are merged to form a single resulting type for each expression.

Compared to TSCHECK, some constraints have been added to improve precision for parameter types, for example, so that the arguments to operators such as - and * are treated as numbers. (Due to the page limit, we omit the actual analysis constraints used by TSINFER.)

A subset-based analysis gives more precise dataflow information compared to a unification-based analysis, however, more precise dataflow information does not necessarily result in more precise type inference. For example, consider the expression foo = bar || "", where bar is a parameter to a function that is never called within the library. A unification-based analysis, such as TSCHECK, will unify the types of foo, bar and "", and thereby conclude that the type of `bar` is possibly a string. A more precise subset-based analysis will only constrain the possible types of `foo` to be a superset of the types of `bar` and "", and thereby conclude that the type of `bar` is unconstrained. In a subset-based analysis with both upper-bound and lower-bound constraint variables, the example becomes more complicated, but the result remains the same. This shows that changing from unification-based to subset-based analysis does not necessarily improve the precision of the type inference. We investigate this experimentally in Sect. 5.

3.3   The Emitting Phase

The last phase of TSINFER uses the results of the preceding phases to emit a declaration for the library. A declaration can be seen as a tree structure that resembles the heap snapshot, so we create the declaration by traversing the heap snapshot and converting the JavaScript values to TypeScript types, using the results from the static analysis when a function is encountered.

Implementing this phase is conceptually straightforward, although it does involve some technical complications, for example, handling cycles in the heap snapshot and how to combine a set of recursive types into a single type.

4   TSEVOLVE: Evolution of Type Declarations

The goal of TSEVOLVE is to create a list of changes between an old and a new version of a JavaScript library. To do this it has access to three input files: the JavaScript files for the old version `old.js` and the new version `new.js` and an existing TypeScript declaration file for the old version `old.d.ts`.

To find the needed changes for the declaration file, a naive first approach would be to compare `old.d.ts` with the output of running TSINFER on `new.js`. However, this will result in a lot of spurious warnings, both due to imprecisions in the analysis of `new.js`, but also because of intentional discrepancies in `old.d.ts`, as discussed in Sect. 2.

Instead we choose a less obvious approach, where TSEVOLVE uses TSINFER to generate declarations for both `old.js` and `new.js`. These declarations are then traversed as trees, and any location where the two disagree is marked as a change. The output of this process will still contain spurious changes, but unchanged features in the implementation should rarely appear as changes, as imprecisions in unchanged features are likely the same in both versions. We then use `old.d.ts` to filter out the changes that concern features that are not declared in `old.d.ts`, which removes many of the remaining spurious changes. Relevant function sources code from `old.js` and `new.js` are also printed as part of the output, which allows for easy manual identification of many of the remaining spurious changes. As the analysis does not have perfect precision, it is necessary to manually inspect and potentially adjust the suggested changes before modifying the declaration file.

As an extra feature, in case a partially updated declaration file for the new version is available, TSEVOLVE can use that file to filter out some of the changes that have already been made.

5   Experimental Evaluation

Our implementations of TSINFER and TSEVOLVE, which together contain around 20000 lines of Java code and 1000 lines of JavaScript code, are available at http://www.brics.dk/tstools/.

We evaluate the tools using the following research questions.

– RQ1: Does the subset-based approach used by TSINFER improve analysis speed and precision compared to the unification-based alternative?
– RQ2: A tool such as TSCHECK that only aims to check existing declarations may blindly assume that some parts of the declarations are correct, whereas a tool such as TSINFER must aim to infer complete declarations. For this reason, it is relevant to ask: How much information in declarations is blindly ignored by TSCHECK but potentially inferred by TSINFER?
– RQ3: Can TSINFER infer useful declarations for libraries? That is, how accurate is the structure of the declarations and the quality of the types compared to handwritten declarations?
– RQ4: Is TSEVOLVE useful in the process of co-evolving declaration files as the underlying libraries evolve? In particular, does the tool make it possible to correctly update a declaration file in a short amount of time?

We answer these questions by running the tools on randomly selected JavaScript libraries, all of which have more than 5000 stars on GitHub and a TypeScript declaration file of at least 100 LOC. Our tools do not yet support the `require` function from Node.js,[7] so we exclude Node.js libraries from this evaluation. All experiments have been executed on a Windows 10 laptop with 16 GB of RAM and an Intel i7-4712MQ processor running at 1.5 GHz.

RQ1 (Subset-Based vs. Unification-Based Static Analysis)

To compare the subset-based and unification-based approaches, we ran TSINFER on 20 libraries. The results can be found in the left half of Table 1. The *Funcs* column shows the number of functions analyzed for each library. The *Unification* and *Subset* columns show the analysis time for the unification-based and subset-based analysis, respectively, using a timeout of 30 min.

The results show that our subset-based analysis is significantly faster than the unification-based approach. This is perhaps counterintuitive for readers familiar with Andersen-style [1] (subset-based) and Steengaard-style [20] (unification-based) pointer analysis for e.g. C or Java. However, it has been observed before for JavaScript, where the call graph is usually inferred as part of the analysis, that increased precision often boosts performance [2,19].

We compared the precision of the two approaches by their ability to infer function signatures on the libraries where the unification-based approach does not reach a timeout. Determining which of two machine generated function signatures is the most precise is difficult to do objectively, so we randomly sampled some of the function signatures and manually determined their precision. To minimize bias, each pair of generated function signatures was shown randomly.

---

[7] https://nodejs.org/

Table 1. Analysis speed and precision.

Library	Speed			Precision			
	Funcs	Unification	Subset	Unification	Subset	Equal	Unclear
Ace	1 249	timeout	13.8 s	-	-	-	-
AngularJS	609	193.3 s	7.8 s	1	14	17	0
async	169	28.2 s	4.9 s	2	22	20	6
Backbone.js	176	28.7 s	4.8 s	1	9	44	0
D3.js	1 030	181.7 s	15.8 s	4	19	44	2
Ember.js	2 902	timeout	319.7 s	-	-	-	-
Fabric.js	1 032	timeout	15.7 s	-	-	-	-
Hammer.js	122	32.5 s	3.2 s	0	2	61	3
Handlebars.js	280	9.2 s	6.9 s	0	3	12	1
Jasmine	51	135.4 s	4.6 s	2	4	71	0
jQuery	500	timeout	41.2 s	-	-	-	-
Knockout	325	168.8 s	14.4 s	2	7	41	8
Leaflet	758	timeout	11.6 s	-	-	-	-
Moment.js	446	872.6 s	12.4 s	1	27	21	2
PixiJS	1 527	timeout	308.0 s	-	-	-	-
Polymer.js	748	424.2 s	8.5 s	1	10	41	3
React	1 261	timeout	14.0 s	-	-	-	-
three.js	1 243	timeout	208.8 s	-	-	-	-
Underscore.js	298	81.2 s	4.2 s	0	4	47	0
vue.js	433	timeout	6.2 s	-	-	-	-
Total	15 159	-	1 026.5 s	14	121	419	25

The results from these tests are shown in the right half of Table 1 where the function signatures have been grouped into four categories: *Unification* (the unification-based analysis inferred the most precise signature), *Subset* (the subset-based analysis was the most precise), *Equal* (the two approaches were equally precise), and *Unclear* (no clear winner). The results show that the subset-based approach in general infers better types than the unification-based approach. The unification-based did in some cases infer the best type, which is due to the fact that a more precise analysis does not necessarily result in a more precise type inference, as explained in Sect. 3.2.

RQ2 (Information Ignored by TSCHECK but Considered by TSINFER)

TSCHECK only checks the return types of the functions where the corresponding signature in the declaration file do not have a void/any return type, which may detect many errors, but the rest of the declaration file is blindly assumed to be correct. In contrast, TSINFER infers types for all functions, including their parameters, and it also infers classes and fields.

Table 2. Features in handwritten declaration files ignored by TSCHECK but taken into account by TSINFER.

Library	void/any functions (all)	Parameters	Classes	Fields
Ace	301 (460)	370	2	4
AngularJS	8 (26)	39	0	0
async	64 (80)	222	0	0
Backbone.js	67 (149)	210	7	31
D3.js	7 (219)	271	5	12
Ember.js	270 (629)	991	58	103
Fabric.js	93 (330)	382	25	17
Hammer.js	33 (53)	53	16	24
Handlebars.js	20 (20)	19	1	0
Jasmine	1 (1)	1	1	0
jQuery	19 (53)	88	1	0
Knockout	68 (125)	226	6	0
Leaflet	48 (325)	435	26	17
Moment.js	0 (70)	71	0	0
PixiJS	338 (522)	639	86	584
Polymer.js	3 (4)	3	0	0
React	3 (21)	30	1	4
three.js	328 (993)	1 295	180	632
Underscore.js	36 (121)	241	0	0
vue.js	7 (23)	42	1	8
Total	1 714 (4 224)	5 628	416	1 436

Table 2 gives an indication of the amount of extra information that TSINFER can reason about compared to TSCHECK. For each library, we show the number of functions that have return type void or any (and in parentheses the total number of functions), and the number of parameters, classes, and fields, respectively. The numbers are based on the existing handwritten declaration files.

We see that on the 20 benchmarks, TSCHECK ignores 1714 of the 4224 functions, silently assumes 5628 parameter types to be correct, and ignores 1436 instance fields spread over 416 classes. In contrast TSINFER, and thereby also TSEVOLVE, does consider all these kinds of information.

RQ3 (Usefulness of TSINFER)

As mentioned in Sect. 2, TSCHECK is effective for checking declarations, but not for inferring them. We are not aware of any other existing tool that could be considered as an alternative to TSINFER. To evaluate the usefulness of TSINFER, we therefore evaluate against existing handwritten declaration files, knowing that these contain imprecise information.

We first investigate the ability of TSINFER to identify classes, modules, instance fields, methods, and module functions (but without considering inheritance relationships between the classes and types of the fields, methods, and functions). These features form a hierarchy in a declaration file. For example, `PIXI.Matrix.invert` identifies the `invert` method in the `Matrix` class in the `PIXI` module of *PixiJS*. When comparing the inferred features with the ones in the handwritten declaration files, a true positive (*TP*) is one that appears in both, a false positive (*FP*) exists only in the inferred declaration, and a false negative (*FN*) exists only in the handwritten declaration. In case of *FP* or *FN* we exclude the sub-features from the counts. The quality of the types of the fields and methods is investigated later in this section; for now we only consider their existence.

The counts are shown in Table 3, together with the resulting precision (*Prec*) and recall (*Rec*). We see that TSINFER successfully infers most of the structure of the declaration files, although some manual post-processing is evidently necessary. For example, 80.9% of the classes and 95.7% of the fields are found by TSINFER. Having false positives in an inferred declaration (i.e., low precision) is less problematic than false negatives (i.e., low recall): it is usually easier to manually filter away extra unneeded information than adding information that is missing in the automatically generated declarations.

The identification of classes, modules, methods, and module functions in TSINFER is based entirely on the snapshots (Sect. 3.1), so one might expect 100% precision for those counts. (Identification of fields is partly also based on the static analysis.) The main reason for the non-optimal precision is that many features are undocumented in the

Table 3. Precision of inferring various features of a declaration file.

Library	Classes			Modules			Class fields			Class methods			Module functions		
	TP	FP	FN	TP	FP	FN	TP	FP	FN	TP	FP	FN	TP	FP	FN
Ace	0	2	0	1	0	1	0	0	0	0	0	0	3	2	0
AngularJS	0	0	0	2	1	0	0	0	0	0	0	0	22	2	4
async	0	0	0	1	1	0	0	0	0	0	0	0	88	6	0
Backbone.js	5	0	2	1	1	0	18	3	12	183	8	3	12	10	2
D3.js	5	13	0	1	9	9	12	4	0	15	4	2	56	247	12
Ember.js	62	64	54	16	32	7	8	187	35	40	54	74	333	678	112
Fabric.js	25	21	0	7	3	1	16	193	1	248	402	8	165	24	3
Hammer.js	8	8	7	2	0	1	7	64	0	39	6	0	16	9	9
Handlebars.js	2	4	0	4	3	2	0	3	0	20	4	0	28	8	3
Jasmine	2	22	0	1	4	0	0	0	0	0	8	0	28	33	3
jQuery	2	6	0	4	29	2	0	6	0	0	6	0	90	59	6
Knockout	5	3	1	14	11	1	0	4	0	14	3	0	91	63	2
Leaflet	33	10	0	22	21	1	5	75	12	241	248	2	137	135	1
Moment.js	0	2	0	1	0	0	0	0	0	0	0	0	89	25	6
PixiJS	70	2	16	31	8	2	812	46	52	450	37	7	128	14	16
Polymer.js	0	2	0	1	19	0	0	0	0	0	0	0	2	9	0
React	1	0	0	4	3	0	3	7	1	2	0	1	26	6	130
three.js	169	12	11	12	18	0	2 348	71	33	907	105	24	241	26	8
Underscore.js	0	1	0	1	0	0	0	0	0	0	0	0	117	1	3
vue.js	1	1	0	2	4	0	8	22	0	23	21	0	12	1	1
Total	390	173	91	128	167	27	3 237	685	146	2 182	906	121	1 684	1 358	321
Precision/Recall	Prec: 69.3%			Prec: 43.4%			Prec: 82.5%			Prec: 70.7%			Prec: 55.36%		
	Rec: 80.9%			Rec: 82.6%			Rec: 95.7%			Rec: 94.8%			Rec: 84.0%		

manually written declarations. By manually inspecting these cases, we find that most of these are likely intentional: although they are technically exposed to the applications, the features are meant for internal use in the libraries and not for use by applications. Non-optimal recall is often caused by intentional discrepancies as discussed in Sect. 2 or by libraries that violate our assumption explained in Sect. 3.1 about the API being fully established after the initialization code has finished. Other reasons for non-optimal precision or recall are simply that the handwritten declaration files contain errors or, in cases where the version number is not clearly stated in declaration file, we were unable to correctly determine which library version it is supposed to match.

To measure the quality of the inferred types of fields and methods, we again used the handwritten declaration files as gold standard and this time manually compared the types, in places where the inferred and handwritten declaration files agreed about the existence of a field or method. Such a comparison requires some manual work, so we settled for sampling: for each library, we compared 50 fields and 100 methods (thereof 50 that were classified as constructors), or fewer if not that many were found in the library.

The result of this comparison can be seen in Table 4 where *Perfect* means that the inferred and handwritten type are identical, *Good* means that the inferred type is better than having nothing, *Any* means that the main reason for the sample not being perfect is that either the inferred or the handwritten type is any, *Bad* means that the inferred type is far from correct, and *No params* means that the inferred type has no parameters while the handwritten does. Obviously, this categorization to some extent relies on human judgement, but we believe it nevertheless gives an indication of the quality of the inferred types. An example in the *Good* category is in *PixiJS* where TSINFER infers a perfect type for the `PIXI.Matrix().applyInverse` method, except for the first argument where it infers the type `{x: number, y: number}` instead of the correct `PIXI.Point`.

As can be seen in Table 4, the types inferred for fields are perfect in most cases, and none of them are categorized as *Bad*. The story is more mixed for method types. Here, there are relatively fewer perfect types, but function signatures are also much more complex, given that they often contain multiple parameters as well as a return type, and parameters can sometimes be extremely difficult to infer correctly. For many method types categorized as *Good*, the overall structure of the inferred type is correct but some spurious types appear in type unions for some of the parameters or the return type, or, as in the example with `applyInverse`, an object type is inferred whose properties is a subset of the properties in the handwritten type. The main reason that some method types are categorized as *No params* is that our analysis is unable to reason precisely about the built-in function `Function.prototype.apply` and the `arguments` object. We leave it as future work to explore more precise abstractions of these features.

RQ4 (Usefulness of TSEVOLVE)

To evaluate if TSEVOLVE can assist in evolving declaration files, we performed a case study where TSEVOLVE was used for updating declaration files in 7 different evolution scenarios. In each case, we used the output from TSEVOLVE to make a pull request to the relevant repository. All of these libraries have more than 10000 stars on GitHub and had a need for the declaration file to be updated, but were otherwise randomly selected. We had no prior experience in using any of the libraries.

Table 4. Measuring the quality of inferred types of fields and methods.

Library	Class fields				Class methods and module functions				
	Perfect	Good	Any	Bad	Perfect	Good	Any	Bad	No params
Ace	0	0	0	0	0	3	0	0	0
AngularJS	0	0	0	0	10	10	2	0	0
async	0	0	0	0	0	26	18	0	6
Backbone.js	14	2	2	0	12	6	30	0	7
D3.js	3	0	9	0	11	36	5	2	1
Ember.js	3	3	2	0	42	37	11	5	5
Fabric.js	13	0	3	0	22	18	10	3	22
Hammer.js	0	0	1	0	7	17	9	0	8
Handlebars.js	0	0	0	0	6	22	9	2	7
Jasmine	0	0	0	0	1	12	6	0	9
jQuery	0	0	0	0	5	21	20	1	0
Knockout	0	0	0	0	5	25	24	0	1
Leaflet	3	2	0	0	14	36	7	0	19
Moment.js	0	0	0	0	8	15	21	0	6
PixiJS	32	5	13	0	38	40	21	1	0
Polymer	0	0	0	0	1	1	2	0	0
React	2	0	1	0	0	32	5	0	0
three.js	37	3	10	0	44	46	10	0	0
Underscore.js	0	0	0	0	0	11	35	3	1
vue.js	2	0	6	0	6	15	2	1	0
Total	109	15	47	0	232	429	247	18	92

The output from TSEVOLVE is a list of changes for each declaration file. We took the output lists from each of the 7 updates and classified each entry in each list based upon how useful it was in the process of evolving the specific library.

The result of this can be seen in Table 5 where each change listed by TSEVOLVE is counted in one of the four columns. *TP* counts true positives, i.e. changes that reflect an actual change in the library that should be reflected in the declaration file. Both *FP* and *FP** count false positives, the difference being that changes counted in *FP** could easily be identified as spurious by looking at the output from TSEVOLVE, as explained in Sect. 4. *Unclear* counts the listed changes that could not be easily categorized.

In the update from *Ember.js* version 1.13 to version 2.0, all of the 24 in the *Bad* category are due to *Ember.js* breaking our assumption about the API being fully established after the top-level code has executed. None of the other libraries violate that assumption.

In the update of *Handlebars.js* from version 3 to 4, all the 59 in the *Unclear* category are due to the structures of the handwritten and the inferred declaration files being substantially different. TSEVOLVE is therefore not able to automatically filter out undocumented features, and all 59 entries are therefore filtered out manually.

Table 5. Classification of TSEVOLVE output.

Library	TP	FP	FP*	Unclear
async 1.4 → 2.0	38	0	52	2
Backbone.js 1.0 → 1.3	34	0	42	2
Ember.js 1.13 → 2.0	55	24	40	0
Ember.js 2.0 → 2.7	44	0	54	0
Handlebars.js 3 → 4	37	3	8	59
Moment.js 2.11 → 2.14	10	0	54	2
PixiJS 3 → 4	270	13	41	2
Total	488	40	291	67

From Table 5 we can see that the output from TSEVOLVE mostly points out changes that should be reflected in the corresponding declaration file. Among the spuriously reported changes, most of them can easily be identified as being spurious and are therefore not a big problem.

These outputs of TSEVOLVE were used to create pull requests, which are described in Table 6. For each pull request, we show how many lines the pull request added and removed in the declaration file,[8] along with a response from a library developer, if one was given. For *Handlebars.js*, the pull request additionally contains a few corrections of errors in the declaration file that were spotted while reviewing the report from

Table 6. Pull requests sent based in TSEVOLVE output (The pull requests: https://gist.github.com/webbiesdk/f82c135fc5f67b0c7f175e985dd0c889).

Library	Lines added	Lines removed	Library author response
async 1.4 → 2.0	46	13	"pretty thorough and seems to follow the 2.x API much better than what we currently have"
Backbone.js 1.0 → 1.3	27	3	
Ember.js 1.13 → 2.0	8	508	"LGTM[a] 👍"
Ember.js 2.0 → 2.7	96	92	"👍"
Handlebars.js 3 → 4	49	2	
Moment.js 2.11 → 2.14	4	0	"thank you, looks good"
PixiJS 3 → 4 (pre-release)	158	261	"Awesome PR"
PixiJS 3 → 4	19	4	"I went through all of your changes and can confirm everything is perfect"

[a] An acronym for "Looks Good To Me".

---

[8] The complete pull requests in some cases contain more lines changed, due to minor refactorings or copying and renaming of files to match the version numbers.

TSINFER. All 7 pull requests were accepted without any modifications to the changes derived from the TSEVOLVE output.

The total working time spent going from TSEVOLVE output to finished pull requests was approximately one day, despite having no prior experience using any of the libraries. Without tool support, creating such pull requests, involving a total of 407 lines added and 883 lines removed, for libraries that contain a total of 129365 lines of JavaScript code across versions and declaration files containing 3938 lines (after the updates), clearly could not have been done in the same amount of time.

6 Related Work

The new tools TSINFER and TSEVOLVE build on the previous work on TSCHECK [8], as explained in detail in the preceding sections. Other research on TypeScript includes formalization and variations of its type system [4,17,18,22], and several alternative techniques for JavaScript type inference exist [6,11,16], however, none of that work addresses the challenges that arise when integrating JavaScript libraries into typed application code.

The need for co-evolving declaration files as the underlying libraries evolve can be viewed as a variant of collateral evolution [14]. By using our tools to increase confidence that the declaration files are consistent with the libraries, the TypeScript type checker becomes more helpful when developers upgrade applications to use new versions of libraries.

Our approach to analyze the JavaScript libraries differs from most existing dataflow and type analysis tools for JavaScript, such as, TAJS [2,9] and SAFE [3], which are whole-program analyzers and not sufficiently scalable and precise for typical JavaScript library code. We circumvent those limitations by concretely executing the library initialization code and using a subset-based analysis that is inspired by Pottier [15], Rastogi et al. [17], and Chandra et al. [6].

Other languages, such as typed dialects of Python [10,23], Scheme [21], Clojure [5], Ruby [12], and Flow for JavaScript [7], have similar challenges with types and cross-language library interoperability, though not (yet) at the same scale as TypeScript. Although TSINFER and TSEVOLVE are designed specifically for TypeScript, we believe our solutions may be more broadly applicable.

7 Conclusion

We have presented the tools TSINFER and TSEVOLVE and demonstrated how they can help programmers create and maintain TypeScript declaration files. By making the tools publicly available, we hope that the general quality of declaration files will improve, and that further use of the tools will provide opportunities for fine-tuning the analyses towards the intentional discrepancies found in real-world declarations.

Acknowledgments. This work was supported by the European Research Council (ERC) under the European Union's Horizon 2020 research and innovation program (grant agreement No 647544).

References

1. Andersen, L.O.: Program analysis and specialization for the C programming language. PhD thesis, University of Copenhagen (1994)
2. Andreasen, E., Møller, A.: Determinacy in static analysis for jQuery. In: Proceeding ACM International Conference on Object Oriented Programming Systems Languages & Applications (2014)
3. Bae, S., Cho, H., Lim, I., Ryu, S.: SAFE$_{WAPI}$: web API misuse detector for web applications. In: Proceeding 22nd ACM SIGSOFT International Symposium on Foundations of Software Engineering (2014)
4. Bierman, G.M., Abadi, M., Torgersen, M.: Understanding typescript. In: Proceeding 28th European Conference on Object-Oriented Programming (2014)
5. Bonnaire-Sergeant, A., Davies, R., Tobin-Hochstadt, S.: Practical optional types for clojure. In: Thiemann, P. (ed.) ESOP 2016. LNCS, vol. 9632, pp. 68–94. Springer, Heidelberg (2016). doi:10.1007/978-3-662-49498-1_4
6. Chandra, S., Gordon, C.S., Jeannin, J.-B., Schlesinger, C., Sridharan, M., Tip, F., Choi, Y.-I.: Type inference for static compilation of JavaScript. In: Proceeding ACM SIGPLAN Conference on Object-Oriented Programming, Systems, Languages, and Applications (2016)
7. Facebook. Flow (2016). http://flowtype.org/
8. Feldthaus, A., Møller, A.: Checking correctness of TypeScript interfaces for JavaScript libraries. In: Proceeding ACM SIGPLAN Conference on Object-Oriented Programming, Systems, Languages, and Applications (2014)
9. Jensen, S.H., Møller, A., Thiemann, P.: Type analysis for JavaScript. In: Proceeding 16th International Static Analysis Symposium (2009)
10. Lehtosalo, J., et al.: Mypy (2016). http://www.mypy-lang.org/
11. Lerner, B.S., Politz, J.G., Guha, A., Krishnamurthi, S.: TeJaS: retrofitting type systems for JavaScript. In: Proceeding 9th Symposium on Dynamic Languages (2013)
12. 'Matz' Matsumoto, Y.: RubyConf 2014 – opening keynote (2014). http://confreaks.tv/videos/rubyconf2014-opening-keynote
13. Microsoft. TypeScript language specification, February 2015. https://github.com/Microsoft/TypeScript/blob/master/doc/spec.md
14. Padioleau, Y., Lawall, J.L., Hansen, R.R., Muller, G.: Documenting and automating collateral evolutions in Linux device drivers. In: Proceeding EuroSys Conference. ACM (2008)
15. Pottier, F.: A framework for type inference with subtyping. In: Proceeding 3rd ACM SIGPLAN International Conference on Functional Programming (1998)
16. Rastogi, A., Chaudhuri, A., Hosmer, B.: The ins and outs of gradual type inference. In: Proceeding 39th ACM SIGPLAN-SIGACT Symposium on Principles of Programming Languages (2012)
17. Rastogi, A., Swamy, N., Fournet, C., Bierman, G.M., Vekris, P.: Safe & efficient gradual typing for TypeScript. In: Proceeding 42nd ACM SIGPLAN-SIGACT Symposium on Principles of Programming Languages (2015)
18. Richards, G., Zappa Nardelli, F., Vitek, J.: In: Proceeding 29th European Conference on Object-Oriented Programming (2015)
19. Sridharan, M., Dolby, J., Chandra, S., Schäfer, M., Tip, F.: Correlation tracking for points-to analysis of JavaScript. In: Noble, J. (ed.) ECOOP 2012. LNCS, vol. 7313, pp. 435–458. Springer, Heidelberg (2012). doi:10.1007/978-3-642-31057-7_20

20. Steensgaard, B.: Points-to analysis in almost linear time. In: Proceeding 23rd ACM SIGPLAN-SIGACT Symposium on Principles of Programming Languages (1996)
21. Tobin-Hochstadt, S., Felleisen, M.: The design and implementation of typed Scheme (2008)
22. Vekris, P., Cosman, B., Jhala, R.: Refinement types for TypeScript. In: Proceeding 37th ACM SIGPLAN Conference on Programming Language Design and Implementation (2016)
23. Vitousek, M.M., Kent, A.M., Siek, J.G., Baker, J.: Design and evaluation of gradual typing for Python. In: Proceeding 10th ACM Symposium on Dynamic Languages (2014)

Explicit Connection Actions in Multiparty Session Types

Raymond Hu$^{(\boxtimes)}$ and Nobuko Yoshida

Imperial College London, London, UK
rhu@doc.ic.ac.uk

Abstract. This work extends asynchronous multiparty session types
(MPST) with *explicit connection actions* to support protocols with
optional and dynamic participants. The actions by which endpoints
are connected and disconnected are a key element of real-world protocols that is not treated in existing MPST works. In addition, the use
cases motivating explicit connections often require a more relaxed form
of multiparty choice: these extensions do not satisfy the conservative
restrictions used to ensure safety in standard syntactic MPST. Instead,
we develop a modelling-based approach to validate MPST safety and
progress for these enriched protocols. We present a toolchain implementation, for distributed programming based on our extended MPST in
Java, and a core formalism, demonstrating the soundness of our approach. We discuss key implementation issues related to the proposed
extensions: a practical treatment of choice subtyping for MPST progress,
and multiparty correlation of dynamic binary connections.

1 Introduction

Multiparty session types (MPST) is a type systems theory for verifying message
passing concurrent processes, originally developed in the π-calculus [21]. A standard top-down presentation of syntactic MPST systems consists of three layers:
(1) a global specification of an asynchronous message passing protocol as a *global
type*, with the participants abstracted as *roles*; (2) a syntactic *projection* to a
localised view of the protocol for each role as a *local type*; which are in turn used
to (3) type check the endpoint *processes* implementing the roles. A well-typed
system of session endpoint implementations is guaranteed free from communication safety errors, such as unexpected message receptions and deadlocks.

In our view, the central design point of practical languages and tools based
on session types is: (a) to identify a class of protocols, through the constraints
of the type syntax and accompanying well-formedness conditions; such that
MPST safety is indeed guaranteed by (b) (independent) verification of endpoint programs against their local projections. Much research, both multiparty
and the special case of *binary* sessions, has focused on addressing (b) in various ways: extending existing languages to support static session typing (e.g.,
Links [32]) via pre-processing tools (Java [25,45]), embedding into existing languages via encodings (Haskell [26,40], Rust [27]), dynamic session typing by runtime monitoring (Python [15], Erlang [19]), hybrid (part static, part dynamic)
approaches (Java [24], Scala [42], ML [36]), and code generation (MPI/C [35]).

© Springer-Verlag GmbH Germany 2017
M. Huisman and J. Rubin (Eds.): FASE 2017, LNCS 10202, pp. 116–133, 2017.
DOI: 10.1007/978-3-662-54494-5_7

Regarding (a), the multiparty works of the above mostly follow the core theoretical systems [12,22], where protocol well-formedness is directly derived from syntactic restrictions in conjunction with various simplifying assumptions. Unfortunately, these restrictions are too conservative for many useful patterns found in practice. For example, consider a basic, generic pattern starting with interactions between two session participants that, in *some* cases, leads to the later involvement of a third party. By contrast, the standard MPST notion of session initiation is assumed to be a single, atomic synchronisation between *all* parties (as in all of the above works), which inherently rules out any instance of this pattern. Standard MPST basically do not support protocols with *dynamic joining/leaving* of participants during a session, nor *optional* participation.

This paper. We develop an MPST toolchain to address limitations w.r.t. to (a) as discussed above, that can be readily integrated with some of the existing approaches for (b). There are two main contributions.

One is to extend MPST to support *explicit connection actions* in protocol specifications, in a manner that is closely guided by the practical motivations. Rather than a globally interconnected structure between a fixed number of participants, we consider a multiparty session as a dynamically evolving configuration of *binary* bidirectional connections that are established and closed (and possibly re-established) as the session progresses. Concretely, we extend an existing MPST-based protocol description language, Scribble [44,47]. The following is an instance of the pattern from above in our extended Scribble:

```
explicit global protocol OptionalDynamicThirdParty(role A, role B, role C) {
    hello() connect A to B;    // A connects to B; sends a message labelled hello
    goodday() from B to A;     // B replies to A on the established connection
    choice at A { opt1() from A to B; // A has two choices: send opt1 or opt2 to B
                  greetings() connect B to C; }  // B connects to C; sends greetings
            or { opt2() from A to B; } }          // Session ends without involving C
```

(The syntax is explained more in Sect. 2.) Explicit connection actions allow MPST to better fit real-world use cases from domains such as Internet applications and Web services, where multiparty systems are often implemented over binary transports like TCP and HTTP. As we shall see in examples, many patterns involving explicit connections also require a more relaxed form of choice than in standard MPST, with mixed action kinds and destination roles.

The second aspect relates to global type *validation* in our extended MPST. The proposed extensions do not satisfy the conservative restrictions used to ensure safety in standard syntactic MPST: they allow writing additional use cases, but also introduce the potential for errors that were previously precluded.

```
/* Standard MPST: all roles interconnected      // Explicit connection actions
 * on session init. (Scribble default) */       explicit global protocol
global protocol                                         P2(role A, role B, role C) {
        P1(role A, role B, role C) {            choice at A { 1() connect A to B;
    choice at A { 1() from A to B; }                          disconnect A and B; }
            or { 2() from A to C; }                     or { 2() connect A to C;
    do P1(A, B, C);                                          disconnect A and C; }
}                                               do P2(A, B, C); }
```

The minimal examples above illustrate some of the issues at hand. P1 features a choice involving only A and B in one case, and A and C in the other (which is not permitted in [12,17,18,22]), that is repeated continuously by the recursion (not permitted in [18]). However, P1 *does* satisfy the intuitive notion of MPST *safety* (e.g., no reception errors or deadlocks); and under an assumption of *output choice fairness*, i.e., provided A does not starve B or C of messages, P1 also satisfies MPST *progress* (otherwise, if, e.g., A talks only to B, then C remains in the session but never progresses). Using explicit connection actions, this pattern can be rewritten in P2 to satisfy both safety and progress *without* such an assumption.

Our approach is to develop a modelling-based validation for MPST protocols. Specifically, we derive a model of a global type from the *1-bounded* execution of the induced multiparty session, i.e., where the capacity of each dynamically established, asynchronous channel is limited to one message; and explicitly check the model is free of the traditional MPST safety and progress errors, as well as the additional kinds of errors introduced by our extensions, such as unexpected or duplicate (dis)connections. The key to this approach is that the characteristics of syntactic MPST can be leveraged to serve the soundness of the bounded validation; as opposed to solely relying on syntactic restrictions for outright safety. We treat output choice fairness by a structural transformation in the model construction, that reflects the underlying issue of session subtyping [37]; e.g., our validation accepts P1 (above) only if fairness is assumed.

Techniques based on "minimal asynchrony" have been employed for various purposes in related theoretical works (Sect. 5); e.g., to show the decidability of choreography realisability [4], classifying session types in the context of communicating FSMs [18], and the study of properties of half-duplex binary systems [11]. The advance of this work is to formulate the 1-bounded validation for our extended MPST; and its application in a practical toolchain, from the validation of our extended Scribble specifications to safe implementations of distributed Java endpoints. We believe that such an approach may offer a practical, uniform validation methodology for MPST-based protocols, towards incorporating further MPST extensions (e.g., [5,6,15,29,46]) together in an integrated toolchain.

2   Use Case and Overview

2.1   Use Case: Travel Agency Web Service (Revisited)

Travel Agency is one of the widely-used examples in session types literature, based on a W3C Web services choreography use case;[1] we follow the version in [1]. The basic scenario starts by a *Client* (C) initiating a session with the *Travel Agent* (A) to negotiate a product quote. The client may eventually choose to reject all quotes, ending the session; or to accept one, leading to a payment transaction between the client and a third-party *Service* (S). Although this is a natural multiparty use case, it is not actually fully supported by standard MPST. To see the potential problems, consider the following fragment from the latter part of the protocol:

---

[1] https://www.w3.org/TR/2004/WD-ws-chor-reqs-20040311/ Sect. 3.1.1.

```
1   explicit global protocol TravelAgency      17   // So far, only C and A are connected
2       (role C, role A, role S) {              18   aux global protocol Pay
3       connect C to A;                         19       (role C, role A, role S) {
4       do Nego(C, A, S);                       20       choice at C {
5   }                                           21         // C connects to S, sends pay info
6   // aux subprotocols                         22         pay(Str) connect C to S;
7   aux global protocol Nego                    23         // S returns a payment reference
8       (role C, role A, role S) {              24         confirm(Int) from S to C;
9       choice at C {                           25         // C forwards the payref to A
10        query(Str) from C to A;               26         accpt(Int) from C to A;
11        quote(Int) from A to C;               27       } or {
12        do Nego(C, A, S);                      28         reject() from C to A;
13      } or {                                   29       }
14        do Pay(C, A, S);                       30   } // End of protocol
15    } }                                        31
```

Fig. 1. The Travel Agency choreography use case[1] using explicit connection actions.

choice at C { pay(Str) from C to S; confirm(Int) S to C; accpt(Int) from C to A;}
   or { reject () from C to A; } // S not involved   [i]

In standard MPST, the execution model is that all three roles are synchronised on session initiation, and there are no further implicit messages (e.g., no session termination handshake). Under these assumptions, the above fragment is unsafe because, in the second case, there is no way for an implementation of S to *locally* determine that the session is finished. Consequently, specifications in existing MPST use workarounds that are less rigorous (e.g., decomposing the protocol into separate global types, losing some of the message causalities) or less realistic/efficient (e.g., by introducing extra messages, or *delegation* [12]).

The above fragment is also not permitted as a standard MPST choice due to the *directed choice* restriction: the messages from a branch point must be sent to the *same* role in all cases (e.g., r' in the type grammar $r \rightarrow r' : \{l_i.G_i\}_{i \in I}$ [12,22]; similarly in automata-based works [17,18]) as a conservative element towards ensuring safety. The superficial quick fix by simply moving the accpt message to the start of the first case is not possible in this example, because the Int payload of this message is intended to be the value (the payment reference Int) received by C in the preceding confirm message.

Explicit connection actions allow this use case to be safely captured as a single global type, as given by TravelAgency and its two subprotocols (aux) in our extended Scribble in Fig. 1. Line 1 declares the root protocol with the three roles C, A and S. The new explicit modifier means that every inter-role connection used for message passing must first be established by explicitly specified connection actions. A session starts by C connect to A (line 3), creating a bidirectional channel (e.g., TCP) between client C and server A.

We then enter the Nego subprotocol by the do-statement, with the do argument roles playing the target parameter roles (given the same names in this example). The choice at C on line 9 means C makes an *internal* choice between the two cases (the or-separated blocks), to be explicitly communicated as an *external* choice to other roles as appropriate. In the first case, a message of *signature* `query(Str)` (a message with header/label `query`, and one payload value of type `Str`) is sent `from C to A`. `A` replies with a `quote(Int)`, and the choice is repeated by the recursive `do` on line 12. `A` and `C` thus perform the `query`/`quote` exchange some number of times (possibly zero, in this simplified version). Finally, in `Pay`, `C` has two further options. `C` may `connect` to `S`, thereby *dynamically* bringing `S` into the session: `C` exchanges payment details `pay(Str)` for a payment reference `confirm(Int)` with `S`, and forwards the reference to `A`. Otherwise, `C` sends a `reject` to `A`, and the session ends without involving `S`. Note that these syntactically nested choices actually amount to a single choice at `C`, between *mixed* kinds of actions to *different* roles: the connect to `S`, and the sends to `A`.

Extending MPST with explicit connection actions allows such protocols because, e.g., the `connect from C to S`, serves to delimit the scope of `S`'s involvement to the relevant choice case only. From `S`'s view, the *whole* session starts and ends, by interactions with `C`, in this one case, if the session indeed proceeds this way at run-time: while `S` remains unconnected, we can consider it as "inactive" with regards to session safety and progress. At the same time, this solution reduces the gap between MPST-based descriptions and real protocols, like Internet application RFCs, by recognising that the client/server connection actions are as important to a rigorous specification as the message passing (e.g., the `STARTTLS` "re-connection" in SMTP [28], and FTP's active/passive modes [39]).

The communication model promoted by our extended MPST is *at most* one (as opposed to *exactly* one) connection between any pair of roles. Consider the following `explicit` protocol with roles `A`, `B` and `C`:

connect A to B; rec X {   [ii]
choice at A { 1() from A to B; 2() connect B to C; disconnect B and C;continue X;
    } or { 3() from A to B; } }

The `disconnect` is necessary, inside the *recursion* rec X { ...`continue X`; }, to ensure there is never more than one connection between `B` and `C` (similarly in `P2` in Sect. 1). We can assume implicit `disconnect` actions at the end of a protocol.

2.2   Overview of 1-Bounded Global Type Validation and Examples

The restrictions employed in standard MPST are convenient for reasoning about the MPST safety properties. Aside from surface syntax details, systems like [12] ensure safety by essentially requiring pairwise *syntactic* duality of per-role views at all points in a protocol (called *consistency* [12] or *coherence* [22]). By contrast, our proposed extensions allow additional safe protocols, but also (syntactically) allow protocols with errors that were previously precluded. E.g., consider the choice from `P1` in Sect. 1, where it is safe, but now without the recursion: either `B` or `C` is unsafely left hanging at the end of a session.

choice at A { 1() from A to B; } or { 2() from A to C; }   [iii]

To deal with such additional errors, and those related to explicit connection actions, we validate global types by (1) a lighter set of syntactic conditions, in comparison to standard MPST; complemented by (2) explicit error checking on a *1-bounded model* of the protocol. The key conditions of (1) are:

Role Enabling. For any given choice, we consider the subject (the at role) to be *enabled* by default; other roles become enabled after receiving a message. Only enabled roles may connect or send messages to other roles. Role enabling checks that this transitive propagation of the enabled status is respected.

Consistent External Choice Subjects. Every potentially incoming message in an *input* choice (i.e., accepts or receives) must be directed *from* the *same* role.

These basic conditions, in conjunction with the inherent pairing of role-to-role actions in global types, serve the soundness of (2) in the presence of asynchrony and recursion (in general, the state space of an MPST protocol may be unbounded; e.g., P1 in Sect. 1). We note that the latter condition is implicitly imposed by the standard projection in existing MPST [12,22] (and by projections extended with *merging* [18,46]), with the additional restriction of directed choice to *send* every *output* choice message to the same role.

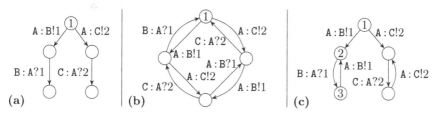

(a)   (b)   (c)

We first demonstrate the validation by illustrating some models used by our tool for some previous examples; the details will be covered in Sects. 3 and 4. Initial states are labelled 1; the notation, e.g., A:B!1 means A performs the local send B!1. **(a)** is for Ex. [iii]: the two terminals are *unfinished role* errors (Sect. 3.2), where the system is terminated but either B or C is not locally terminated. **(b)** is for P1 from Sect. 1 assuming output choice fairness, i.e., that both the B!1 and C!2 options are always viable; this model passes the validation. **(c)** is the contrary view for P1, where A commits exclusively to a single choice case after the first selection. Our tool additionally constructs this variant to expose such *role progress* violations (Sect. 3.2), where an unfinished role never progresses along some infinite execution, e.g., C does not progress in the cycle between 2 and 3. **(a)** is not affected by the fairness assumption, as there is no recursion.

The "unfair" model for P2 (not shown) has the same structure as **(c)**, but with connects/disconnects in place of the sends/receives. It would *not* violate progress because either B or C remains in a local connection-accept "guard" state, which is not considered unfinished (rather, "inactive"). TravelAgency satisfies progress (i.e., wrt. S) regardless of output choice fairness for the same reason.

3 MPST with Explicit Connection Actions

3.1 Global Types, Local Types and Sessions

Syntax. A core syntax of *global types* G and *local types* L is defined in Fig. 2. Global types have *guarded choices* $\Sigma_{i \in I} \pi_i.G_i$, with *connection* $r \twoheadrightarrow r' : l$, *messaging* $r \rightarrow r' : l$ and *disconnection* $r \# r'$ actions; *recursion* $\mu X.G$ and X; and *termination* end. As an example, TravelAgency from Fig. 1 may be written (assuming

Roles	$A, B, \ldots \in \mathbb{R}$	ranged over by	$r, r', \ldots$
Message labels	$1, 2, 3, \ldots \in \mathbb{L}$		$l, l', \ldots$
Recursion variables	$X, Y, \ldots \in \mathbb{X}$		$X, Y, \ldots$
Paired interactions	$(\mathbb{R} \times \{\rightarrow, \twoheadrightarrow\} \times \mathbb{R} \times \mathbb{L}) \cup (\mathbb{R} \times \{\#\} \times \mathbb{R})$		$\pi, \pi', \ldots$
Localised actions	$\mathbb{A} \subseteq (\mathbb{R} \times \{!, ?, !!, ??\} \times \mathbb{L}) \cup (\mathbb{R} \times \{\#\})$		$\alpha, \alpha', \ldots$

$$G ::= \Sigma_{i \in I} \pi_i.G_i \mid \mu X.G \mid X \mid \mathsf{end} \qquad L ::= \Sigma_{i \in I} \alpha_i.L_i \mid \mu X.L \mid X \mid \mathsf{end} \qquad |I| \geq 1$$

$$r_1 \dagger r_2 : l.G \restriction_\Delta r = \begin{cases} r_2[\dagger]_\bullet l.(G \restriction_\emptyset r) & r = r_1 \\ r_1[\dagger]_\circ l.(G \restriction_\emptyset r) & r = r_2 \\ G \restriction_\Delta r & r \notin \{r_1, r_2\} \end{cases} \qquad r_1 \# r_2.G \restriction_\Delta r = \begin{cases} r'\#.(G \restriction_\emptyset r) & r, r' \in \{r_1, r_2\}, r \neq r' \\ G \restriction_\Delta r & \text{otherwise} \end{cases}$$

$$[\rightarrow]_\bullet = ! \qquad [\rightarrow]_\circ = ? \qquad [\twoheadrightarrow]_\bullet = !! \qquad [\twoheadrightarrow]_\circ = ??$$

$$\Sigma_{i \in I} G_i \restriction_\Delta r \underset{(|I| > 1)}{=} \begin{cases} X \ (\text{resp. } \mathsf{end}) & \forall i \in I.G_i \restriction_\Delta r = X \ (\text{resp. } \forall i \in I.G_i \restriction_\Delta r = \mathsf{end}) \\ \Sigma_{j \in J \subseteq I}(L_j = G_j \restriction_\Delta r) & |J| > 0, \forall k \in I \setminus J(G_k \restriction_\Delta r = \mathsf{end} \text{ or } X \in \Delta), \text{ and} \\ & \text{either} \begin{cases} \forall j \in J.L_j = \alpha_j^\bullet.L_j' \\ \exists r' \forall j \in J.L_j = \alpha_j^\circ.L_j' \wedge \mathsf{subj}(\alpha_j^\circ) = r' \end{cases} \end{cases}$$

$$\mu X.G \restriction_\Delta r = \begin{cases} \mathsf{end} & G \restriction_{\Delta \cup \{X\}} r = X' \text{ or } \mathsf{end} \\ \mu X.(G \restriction_{\Delta \cup \{X\}} r) & \text{otherwise} \end{cases} \qquad X \restriction_\Delta r = X \qquad \mathsf{end} \restriction_\Delta r = \mathsf{end}$$

Fig. 2. Core syntax and global-to-local type projection.

an empty label `nil` for the initial connect, and "flattening" the nested `choices`):

$\mathtt{C} \twoheadrightarrow \mathtt{A} : \mathtt{nil}.\mu\mathtt{TravelAgency}. \, (\mathtt{C} \rightarrow \mathtt{A} : \mathtt{query}.\mathtt{A} \rightarrow \mathtt{C} : \mathtt{quote}.\mathtt{TravelAgency}$

$\qquad + \mathtt{C} \rightarrow \mathtt{S} : \mathtt{pay}.\mathtt{S} \rightarrow \mathtt{C} : \mathtt{confirm}.\mathtt{C} \rightarrow \mathtt{A} : \mathtt{accpt}.\mathsf{end} + \mathtt{C} \rightarrow \mathtt{A} : \mathtt{reject}.\mathsf{end})$

Local types are the same except for localised actions: *connect* $r!!l$, *accept* $r??l$, *send* $r!l$, *receive* $r?l$, and *disconnect* $r\#$. For a local action $\alpha = r \dagger l$, the annotation α° means $\dagger \in \{?, ??\}$; and $\alpha^\bullet$ means either α with $\dagger \in \{!, !!\}$ or an action $r\#$. We sometimes omit end.

The *projection of* G *onto* r, written $G \restriction r$, is the L given by $G \restriction_\emptyset r$ in Fig. 2, where the Δ is a set $\{X_i\}_{i \in I}$. Our projection is more "relaxed" than in standard MPST, in that we seek only to regulate some basic conditions to support the later validation (see below). Δ is simply used to prune X that become unguarded in choices during projection onto r, when the recursive path does not involve r; e.g., projecting `TravelAgency` onto S: `C??pay.C!confirm.end`). Note: we make certain simplifications for this core formulation, e.g., we omit payload types and flattening of nested choice projections [23].

We assume some basic constraints (typical to MPST) on any given G. **(1)** For all $\pi_\dagger = r \dagger r' : l$, $\dagger \in \{\rightarrow, \twoheadrightarrow\}$, and all $\pi_\# = r\#r'$, we require $r \neq r'$. We then define: $\mathsf{subj}(\pi_\dagger) = \{r\}, \mathsf{obj}(\pi_\dagger) = \{r'\}, \mathsf{lab}(\pi_\dagger) = l$; and $\mathsf{subj}(\pi_\#) = \{r, r'\}, \mathsf{obj}(\pi_\#) = \emptyset$. **(2)** G is closed, i.e., has no free recursion variables. **(3)** G features only deterministic choices in its projections. We write: $r \in G$ to mean r occurs in G; and $\alpha \in L$ to mean $L' = \Sigma_{i \in I} \alpha_i.L_i$, where L' is obtained from L by some number (possibly zero) of recursion unfoldings, with $\alpha = \alpha_i$ for some i.

(Sessions) $S ::= (P, Q)$ $P ::= \{L_r\}_{r \in \mathbb{R}}$ $Q : (\mathbb{R} \times \mathbb{R}) \mapsto \{\bot\} \cup \vec{l}$

[CONN] $\dfrac{\exists i' \in I, j' \in J \quad \alpha_{i'} = r'!!l \quad \alpha'_{j'} = r??l \quad Q(r, r') = Q(r', r) = \bot}{(\{(\Sigma_{i \in I} \alpha_i.L_i)_r, (\Sigma_{j \in J} \alpha'_j.L'_j)_{r'}\} \cup P, Q) \to_k (\{(L_{i'})_r, (L'_{j'})_{r'}\} \cup P, Q[r, r' \mapsto \epsilon][r', r \mapsto \epsilon])}$

[SEND] $\dfrac{\exists j \in I \quad \alpha_j = r'!l \quad Q(r, r') \neq \bot \quad Q(r', r) = \vec{l} \quad |\vec{l}| < k}{(\{\Sigma_{i \in I} \alpha_i.L_i\}_r \cup P, Q) \to_k (\{L_j\}_r \cup P, Q[r', r \mapsto \vec{l} \cdot l])}$

[RECV] $\dfrac{\exists j \in I \quad \alpha_j = r'?l \quad Q(r, r') = l \cdot \vec{l}}{(\{\Sigma_{i \in I} \alpha_i.L_i\}_r \cup P, Q) \to_k (\{L_j\}_r \cup P, Q[r, r' \mapsto \vec{l}])}$

[DIS] $\dfrac{Q(r, r') = \epsilon}{(\{r'\#.L\}_r \cup P, Q) \to_k (\{L\}_r \cup P, Q[r, r' \mapsto \bot])}$ [REC] $\dfrac{(\{L[\mu X.L/X]\}_r \cup P, Q) \to_k (P', Q')}{(\{\mu X.L\}_r \cup P, Q) \to_k (P', Q')}$

Fig. 3. Sessions (pairs of participants and message queues), and session reduction.

(Unfolding is the substitution on recursions $\mathsf{unf}(\mu X.G) = G[\mu X.G/X]$; $\mathsf{unf}(G) = G$ otherwise.) We use $\mathbb{R}_G$ to denote $\{r \mid r \in G\}$, omitting the subscript G where clear from context.

Well-formed global type. For a given G, let $\varphi(G)$ be the global type resulting from the *once-unfolding* of every recursion $\mu X.G'$ occurring within G (defined by $\varphi(\mu X.G) = \varphi(G[\mathsf{end}/X])$, and homomorphic for the other constructors). *Role enabling* (outlined in Sect. 2) on global types $R \vdash G$, $R \subseteq \mathbb{R}$, is defined by $R \vdash \mathsf{end}$ for any R, and:

$$\dfrac{\mathsf{subj}(\pi) \subseteq R \quad R \cup \mathsf{obj}(\pi) \vdash G}{R \vdash \pi.G} \qquad \dfrac{|I| > 1 \quad \exists r \in R \, \forall i \in I.\mathsf{subj}(\pi_i) = \{r\} \wedge \{r\} \cup \mathsf{obj}(\pi_i) \vdash G_i}{R \vdash \Sigma_{i \in I} \pi_i.G_i}$$

A global type G is *well-formed*, $\mathsf{wf}(G)$, if $\mathbb{R}_G \vdash \varphi(G)$, and for all $r \in \mathbb{R}_G$, $G \upharpoonright r$ *is defined*. A consequence is that disconnects are not prefixes in non-unary choices. Also, every local choice in a projection of a $\mathsf{wf}(G)$ comprises only $\alpha^\bullet$ or α° actions, with a consistent subject r in all cases of the latter.

Sessions (Fig. 3) are pairs of a set of *participant* local types P and inter-role *message queues* Q. $\bot$ designates a *disconnected* queue. We use the notation $Q[K \mapsto V]$ to mean Q' where $Q'(K) = V$, and $Q'(K') = Q(K')$ for $K \neq K'$. *Session reduction* (Fig. 3), $S \to_k S'$, is parameterised on a maximum queue size $k \in \mathbb{N}_1 \cup \{\omega\}$. If two roles are mutually disconnected, [CONN] establishes a connection, synchronising on a common label l. If both sides are connected, [SEND] asynchronously appends a message to destination queue if there is space. If the local queue is still connected: [RECV] consumes the first message, if any; and [DIS] disconnects the queue if it is empty.

For a $\mathsf{wf}(G)$ with roles $\mathbb{R}$, we define: **(1)** $\to_k^*$ is the reflexive and transitive closure of $\to_k$; **(2)** the *k-reachable set* of a session S for some k is $RS_k(S) = \{S' \mid S \to_k^* S'\}$; we say $S' \in RS_k(S)$ *is k-reachable from* S; **(3)** the *initial session* is the session $S_0 = (\{G \upharpoonright r\}_{r \in \mathbb{R}}, Q_{\mathbb{R}_0})$, where $Q_{\mathbb{R}_0} = \{r, r' \mapsto \bot \mid r, r' \in \mathbb{R}\}$; and **(4)** a *k-final session* S is such that $\nexists S'(S \to_k S')$. We may annotate a reduction step $S \xrightarrow{r}_k S'$ by a *subject role* r of the step: in Fig. 3, in [SEND], [RECV] and [DIS] the subject is r; in [CONN], both r and r' are subjects. Given S, r and k, $S \xrightarrow{r}_k$ stands for $\exists S'(S \xrightarrow{r}_k S')$. For $k = \omega$, we often omit ω.

3.2 MPST Safety and Progress

The following defines MPST safety errors and progress for this formulation. Assume a $\mathsf{wf}(G)$ with initial session S_0 and $S \in RS_k(S_0)$ for some k. For $r \in G$, we say: r *is inactive in* S, with $S = (P, Q)$ and $L_r \in P$, if **(1)** $L_r = \mathsf{end}$; or **(2)** $L_r = G \upharpoonright r$ and $\forall \alpha \in L_r \exists l(\alpha = r'??l)$. Otherwise, r *is active in* S.

Then, session $S = (P, Q)$ is a *safety error*, Err, if:

(i) $L_r \in P$ and one of the following holds:
  (*Connection error*) $\alpha \in L_r$, $\alpha = r'!!l$ or $r'??l$, and $Q(r, r') \neq \bot$;
  (*Disconnect error*) $r' \# \in L_r$ and $Q(r, r') \neq \epsilon$;
  (*Unconnected error*) $\alpha \in L_r$, $\alpha = r'!l$ or $r'?l$, and $Q(r, r') = \bot$;
  (*Synchronisation error*) $r'!!l \in L_r$, $(\Sigma_{i \in I} r'??l_i . L_i)_{r'} \in P$, and $l \notin \{l_i\}_{i \in I}$;
  (*Reception error*) $L_r = \Sigma_{i \in I} r'?l_i . L_i$, $Q(r, r') = l \cdot \vec{l}$ and $l \notin \{l_i\}_{i \in I}$;
or *(ii)* S is either:
  (*Unfinished role*) S is k-final and $r \in G$ is active in S;
  (*Orphan message*) $r \in G$ is inactive in S and $\exists r'(Q(r, r') \notin \{\bot, \epsilon\})$.

Session S *satisfies* k-progress if, for all $S' = (P, Q) \in RS_k(S)$, we have both: (*Role progress*) for all $r \in \mathbb{R}$, if r is active in S', then $S' \xrightarrow{*}_k \xrightarrow{r}_k$; and (*Eventual reception*) if $Q(r, r') = l \cdot \boldsymbol{l}$, then $S' \rightarrow^*_k (P', Q')$ where $L_r \in P'$ and $r'?l \in L_r$.

A session S *is* k-*safe* if $\nexists \mathsf{Err} \in RS_k(S)$. We simply say session *S is safe* if it is ω-safe; and *S satisfies progress* if it satisfies ω-progress.

The following establishes the soundness of our framework. Our approach is to adapt the CFSM-based methodology of [6,18], by reworking the notion of *multiparty compatibility* developed there, in terms of the syntactic conditions and explicitly checked 1-bounded properties of our extended setting. The omitted/expanded definitions and proofs can be found at [23].

Theorem 1 (*Soundness of 1-bounded validation*). *Let* S_0 *be the initial session of a* $\mathsf{wf}(G)$ *that is 1-safe and satisfies 1-progress. Then* S_0 *is safe and satisfies progress.*

4 Implementation

4.1 Modelling MPSTs by CFSMs with Dynamic Connections

We present a prototype implementation [43] that adapts the preceding formulation by constructing and checking explicit state models of our extended global types, based on a correspondence between MPST and communicating FSMs

(CFSMs) [15,18,30]. In this setting, our extensions correspond to CFSMs with *dynamic connection actions*. An *Endpoint FSM* (EFSM) for a role is:

(EFSM) $M = (\mathbb{S}, \mathbb{R}, s_0, \mathbb{L}, \delta)$ (States) $s, s', \ldots \in \mathbb{S}$ (Transitions) $\delta \subseteq \mathbb{S} \times \mathbb{A} \times \mathbb{S}$

where s_0 is the *initial state*; $\mathbb{R}$, $\mathbb{L}$ and $\mathbb{A}$ are as defined in Fig. 2. We write $\delta(s)$ to denote $\{\alpha \mid \exists s'.\delta(s, \alpha) = s'\}$. EFSMs are given by a (straightforward) translation from local types, for which we omit the full details [23]: an EFSM essentially captures the structure of the syntactic local type with recursions reflected as cycles. E.g., for C in TravelAgency (Fig. 1), omitting payload types:

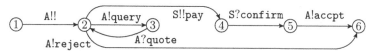

The execution of EFSM systems is adapted from basic CFSMs [9] following Fig. 3 in the expected way [23]. Then, assuming an *initial configuration* c_0 (the system with all endpoints in their initial EFSM states and unconnected) for a wf(G), the (base) *model of* G is the set of configurations that can be reached by *1-bounded* execution from c_0. We remark that the model of a wf(G) is finite.

Based on Sect. 3.2, G can be validated by its model as follows. The MPST safety errors pertain to individual configurations: this allows to simply check each configuration by adapting the Err-cases to this setting. E.g., an *unfinished role* error is a terminal configuration where role r is in a non-terminal state s_r, and s_r is not an accept-guarded initial state. MPST progress for potentially non-terminating sessions can be characterised on the finite model in terms of closed subsets of mutually reachable configurations (sometimes called *terminal sets*). E.g., a *role progress* violation manifests as such a closure in which an active role is not involved in any transition (e.g., configs. 2 and 3, wrt. C, in (c) on p. 6).

Choice subtyping vs. progress. A projected local choice is either an output choice (connects, sends) or an input choice (accepts, receives). While input choices are driven by the received message, output choices are driven by *process*-level procedures that global and local types abstract from. The notion of *session subtyping* [13,20] was developed to allow more flexible implementations against a local type. E.g., the projection of P1 from Sect. 1 for A is $\mu X.(\mathtt{B}!1.X + \mathtt{C}!2.X)$ which says A repeatedly has the choice of sending 1 to B or 2 to C: intuitively, it is *safe* here to implement an A that always opts to send 1 (e.g., a process $P(x) = x \oplus \langle \mathtt{B}, 1 \rangle.P\langle x \rangle$, where x is A's session channel, $\oplus$ is the select primitive [12]). For our relaxed form of multiparty choice, however, such an (naive) interpretation of subtyping raises the possibility of *progress* errors (in this case, for C).

To allow our validation approach to be integrated with the various methods of verifying local types in real-world languages, we consider this issue from the perspective of two basic assumptions on implementations of output choices. One is to simply assume *output choice fairness* (the basic interpretation that an infinite execution of an output choice selects each recursive case infinitely many times), which corresponds to the model construction defined so far.

The other interpretation is developed as a "worst case" view, where we do not assume any direct support for session typing or subtyping (fair or otherwise) in the target language (e.g., native Java), and allow the implementation of every recursive output choice to be reduced to only ever following one particular case. Our tool implements this notion as a transformation on each EFSM, by refining the continuations of output choices such that the *same* case is always selected if that choice is repeated in the future. We outline the transformation below (see [23] for the definition):

- For each non-unary output choice $s^\bullet$, we clone the subgraph reachable via an action $\alpha \in \delta(s^\bullet)$ in each case that $s^\bullet$ is reachable via α, i.e., if $s^\bullet \in RS(\delta(s^\bullet, \alpha))$.
- In each subgraph cloned via α, all $\alpha' \in \delta(s^\bullet)$ edges, s.t. $\alpha' \neq \alpha$, are pruned from the clone of $s^\bullet$. We redirect the α-edge from $s^\bullet$ to the clone of its successor $\delta(s^\bullet, \alpha)$ in the cloned subgraph. (States no longer connected are discarded.)
- This transformation is applied recursively on the cloned subgraphs, until every recursive output choice is reduced to a single action.

This transformation reflects endpoint implementations that push output choice subtyping to exercise a *minimum* number of different recursive cases along a path. To expose progress violations under subtyping when fairness is not assumed, our tool uses the transformed EFSMs to additionally construct and check the "unfair" 1-bounded global model in the same manner as above.

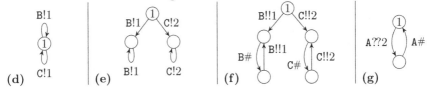

We illustrate some examples. **(d)** is the base EFSM, i.e., assuming output choice fairness, for A in P1 from Sect. 1. **(e)** is the transformed EFSM: if A starts by selecting the 1 case it will continue to select this case only; similarly for 2. (The transformation does not change B or C.) Using **(e)** gives the global model for P1 in **(c)** on p. 6, raising the role progress violations for B and C. By contrast, **(f)** is the transformed EFSM for A in P2 from Sect. 1: as in **(e)**, A commits exclusively to whichever case is selected first. However, P2 does not violate progress, despite the transformation of A in **(f)**, because the involvement of C is guarded by the initial connection-accept actions in **(g)**; similarly for B.

4.2   Type-Checking Endpoint Programs by Local Type Projections

Java endpoint implementation via API generation. We demonstrate an integration of the above developments with an existing approach for using local types to verify endpoint programs. Concretely, we extend the approach of [24], to *generate* Java APIs for implementing each role of a global type, including explicit connection actions, via the translation of projections to EFSMs. The idea is to reify each EFSM state as a Java class for a *state-specific* channel, offering methods for exactly the permitted I/O actions. These channel classes are linked by

```
1   TravelAgency sess = new TravelAgency();              // Generated session class
2   try (ExplicitEndpoint<TravelAgency, C> ep = new ExplicitEndpoint<>(sess, C) {
3     Buf<Integer> b = new Buf<>();
4     TravelAgency_C_2 C2 = new TravelAgency_C_1(ep)     // Generated channel classes
5         .connect(A, SocketChannelEndpoint::new, host_A, port_A);    // TCP client
6     for (int i = 0; i < queries.length; i++)           // Assume queries: String[]
7       C2 = C2.send(A, query, queries[i]).receive(A, quote, b);
8     C2.connect(S, SocketChannelEndpoint::new, host_S, port_S,       // TCP client
9         pay, "..paymentInfo..").receive(S, confirm, b)
10       .send(A, accpt, b.val);           // C simplified to always accept the quote
11  }                                                    // (reject option unused)
```

Fig. 4. Safe Java implementation of C in TravelAgency (Fig. 1) using generated APIs.

setting the return type of each method to its successor state. Session safety is assured by static (Java) typing of the I/O method calls, combined with run-time checks (built into the API) that each instance of a channel class is used *exactly once*, for the linear aspect of session typing. An endpoint implementation thus proceeds, from a channel instance of the initial state, by calling one I/O method on the current channel to obtain the next, up to the end of the session (if any).

Figure 4 illustrates the incorporation of explicit connect, accept and disconnect actions from local types into the API generated for C in TravelAgency; this code can be compared against the EFSM on p. 10. TravelAgency_C_1 is the initial state channel (cf. EFSM state 1), for which the *only* permitted I/O method is the connect to A; attempting any other session operation is simply a Java type error. (The various constants, such as A and query, are *singleton type values* in the API.) The connect returns a new instance of TravelAgency_C_2, offering exactly the mixed choice between the non-blocking query (line 7) or reject (*unused*, cf. Sect. 4.1, output choice subtyping) to A, or the blocking connect to S (line 8).

If the programmer respects the linear channel usage condition of the generated API, as in Fig. 4, then Java typing statically ensures the session code (I/O actions and message types) follows its local type. The only way to violate the protocol is to violate linearity, in which case the API will raise an exception without actually performing the offending I/O action. Our toolchain, from validated global types to generated APIs, thus assures safe executions of endpoint implementations up to premature termination.

Correlating dynamic binary connections in multiparty sessions. Even aside from explicit connections, session initiation is one aspect in which applications of session type theory, binary and multiparty, to real distributed systems raises some implementation issues. The standard π-calculus theory assumes a so-called *shared channel* used by all the participants for the initiation synchronisation.[2] The formal typing checks, on a "centralised" view of the entire process system, that each and every role is played by a compliant process, initiated via the shared channel. These assumptions transfer to our distributed, binary-connection programs as relying on correct host and port argument values in, e.g., the

---

[2] E.g., a in $a[1](y).P_1 \mid ... \mid a[n-1](y).P_{n-1} \mid \bar{a}[n](y).P_n$, initiating a session between n processes [12].

connect calls in C in Fig. 4 (lines 5 and 8); similarly for the arguments to the SocketChannelServer constructor and accept call in the A and S programs [23].

Existing π-calculus systems could be naively adapted to explicit connection actions by assigning a (binary) shared channel to each accept-point in the session, since the type for any given point in a protocol is fixed. Unfortunately, reusing a shared channel for dynamic accepts across *concurrent* sessions may lead to incorrect *correlation* of the underlying binary connections. E.g., consider $A \twoheadrightarrow B..A \twoheadrightarrow C..B \twoheadrightarrow C..$, where the C process uses multithreading to concurrently serve multiple sessions: if the *same* shared channel is used to accept *all* connections from the A's, and likewise for B's, there is no inherent guarantee that the connection accepted from a B by a given server thread will belong to the same *session* as the earlier connection from A, despite being of the expected type.

In practice, the correlation of connections to sessions may be handled by various mechanisms, such as passing session identifiers or port values. Consider the version of the Pay subprotocol (from Fig. 1), modified to use port passing (cf. FTP [39]), on the left:

choice at C { accpt() from C to A;
        connect A to S;
        port(Int) from S to A;
        port(Int) from A to C;
        pay(Str) connect C to S;
        confirm(Int) from S to C;
    } or { reject() from C to A; }
	// *Extended Scribble annotations:* [iv]
	// *S opens a (fresh) Int port for C*
	port(p:Int) from S to A; @open=p:C
	port(p) from A to C; // *A forwards p*
	pay(Str) connect C to S; @port=p
	    // *C connects using p as the port*

C sends accpt to A, and then A connects to S; S sends A an Int port value, which A forwards to C; C then connects to S at that port. To capture this intent explicitly, we adapt an extension of Scribble with assertions [34] to support the specification on the right. In general, *value*-based constraints, like forwarding and connecting to p, can be generated into the API as implicit run-time Java assertions. However, we take advantage of the API generation approach to directly generate *statically* safe operations for these actions. *N.B., in the following, port is simply the message label API constant*; assigning, sending and using the actual port *value* is safely handled *internally* by the generated operations.

In S: S.send(A, port).accept(C, pay, b).. // 'port' *is the msg label (API const.)*
        // *API internally opens fresh port p, and sends value; accepts conn. on p*
In A: A.receive(S, port).send(C, port)...
        // *API internally caches the received value of p; and forwards that value*
In C: C.receive(A, port).connect(S, SocketChanEndpoint::new, host_S, pay, "..")..
        // *API internaly caches the value of p; and connects using p as the port*

This combination of explicit connection actions, assertions, and typed API generation is essentially a practical realisation of (private) *shared channel passing* from session π-calculi for our binary connection setting in Java.

To facilitate integration with some existing implementations of session typed languages, our toolchain also supports an optional syntactic restriction on types where: each projection of a Scribble protocol may contain at most one *accept*-choice constructor, and only as the top-most choice constructor (cf. the commonly used replicated-server process primitives in process calculus works).

This constraint allows many useful explicit connection action patterns, including nested connects and recursive accepts, while ruling out correlation errors; apart from Ex. [iv], all of the examples in this paper satisfy this constraint.

5 Related Work and Concluding Remarks

Dynamic participants in typed process calculi and message sequence charts. To our knowledge, this paper is the first session types work that allows a single session to have optional roles, and dynamic joining and leaving of roles.

[16] presents a version of session types where a role designates a dynamic *set* of one or more participant processes. Their system does not support optional nor dynamic roles (every role is played by at least one process; the number of processes varies, but the set of *active roles* is fixed). It relies on a special-purpose run-time locking mechanism to block dynamically joining participants until some safe entry point, hindering its use in existing applications. Implementations of sessions in Python [15] and Erlang [19] have used a notion of *subsession* [14] as a coarse-grained mechanism for dynamically introducing participants. The idea is to launch a *separate* child session, by the heavyweight atomic multiparty initiation, involving a subset of the current participants along with other new participants; unlike this paper, where additional roles enter the same, running session by the connect and accept actions between the two relevant participants.

The *conversation calculus* [10] models conversations between dynamic *contexts*. A behavioural typing ensures error-freedom by characterising processes more directly; types do not relate to roles, as in MPST. Their notion of dynamic joining is more abstract (akin to standard MPST initiation), allowing a context n to interact with all other conversation members after a single atomic join action by n; whereas our explicit communication actions are designed to map more closely to concrete operations in standard network APIs.

Dynamic message sequence charts (DMSCs) in [31] support fork-join patterns with potentially unbounded processes. Model checking against a monadic second order logic is decidable, but temporal properties are not studied. [7] studies the implementability of *dynamic communication automata* (DCA) [8] against MSCs as specifications. The focus of study of DCA and DMSCs is more about dynamic *process spawning*; whereas we target dynamic *connections* (and disconnects) between a set of roles with specific concern for MPST safety and progress. Our implementation goes another "level" down from the automata model, applying the validated session types to Java programs with consideration of issues such as choice subtyping and connection correlation.

Well-formedness of session types and choreographies. Various techniques involving bounded executions have been used for multiparty protocols and choreographies. [3,4,41] positions choreography realisability in terms of *synchronisability*, an equivalence between a synchronous global model and the 1-bounded execution of local FSMs; this reflects a stricter perspective of protocol compliance, demanding stronger causality between global steps than session type safety. Their communication model has a single input queue per endpoint, while asynchronous session types has a separate input queue per peer: certain patterns are not synchronisable in the former while valid in the latter. [2] develops more general realisability conditions (in the single-queue model) than the above by determining an upper-bound on queue sizes wrt. equivalent behaviours. Our validation of MPST with explicit connection actions remains within a 1-bounded model.

[18] characterises standard MPST wrt. CFSMs by *multiparty compatibility*, a well-formedness condition expressed in terms of 1-reachability; it corresponds to the syntactic restrictions of standard MPST in ensuring safety. This paper relaxes some of these restrictions with other extensions, by our 1-bounded validation, to support our use cases. [30] develops a bottom-up synthesis of graphical choreographies from CFSMs via a correspondence between synchronous global models and local CFSMs. These works and the above works on choreographies: (1) do not support patterns with optional or dynamic participants; and (2) study single, pre-connected sessions in isolation without consideration of certain issues of implementing endpoint programs in practice (type checking, subtyping, concurrent connection correlation).

Advanced subtyping of local types with respect to liveness is studied theoretically in [37]. Our present work is based on a coarser-grained treatment of fairness in the global model, to cater for applications to existing (mainstream) languages where it may be difficult to precisely enforce a particular subtyping for sessions via the native type system. We plan to investigate the potential for incorporating their techniques into our approach in future work.

Implementations of session types. The existing version of Scribble [24,47] follows the established theory through syntactic restrictions to ensure safety (e.g., the same set of roles must be involved in every choice case, precluding optional participation). [24] concerns only the use of local types for API generation; it has no formalism, and does not discuss global type validation or projection. This paper is motivated by use cases to relax existing restrictions and add explicit connection actions to types. [38] develops a tool for checking or testing compatibility, adapted from [18], in a local system of abstract concurrent objects. It does not consider global types nor endpoint programs.

Recent implementation works [24–27,32,35,36,40,42,45], as discussed in Sect. 1, have focused more on applying standard session types, rather than developing session types to better support real use cases. This is in contrast to the range of primarily theoretical extensions (e.g., time [6,33], asynchronous interrupts [15], nested subsessions [14], assertions [5], role parameterisation [46], event handling [29], multi-process roles [16], etc.), which complicates tool implementation because each has its own specific restrictions to treat the subtleties of its setting. The approach of this paper, shifting the emphasis from outright syntactic well-formedness to a more uniform validation of the types, may be one way to help bring some of these scattered features (and those in this paper) together in practical MPST implementations. We plan to investigate such directions in future work, in addition to closer integrations of MPST tools, that treat concepts like role projections, endpoint program typing, subtyping and channel passing, with established model checking tools and optimisations.

Acknowledgements. We thank Gary Brown and Steve Ross-Talbot for collaborations, and Rumyana Neykova for comments. This work is partially supported by EPSRC projects EP/K034413/1, EP/K011715/1, EP/L00058X/1, EP/N027833/1, and EP/N028201/1; and by EU FP7 612985 (UPSCALE).

References

1. Ancona, D., et al.: Behavioral types in programming languages. Found. Trends Program. Lang. **3**(2–3), 95–230 (2016)
2. Basu, S., Bultan, T.: Automatic verification of interactions in asynchronous systems with unbounded buffers. In: ASE 2014, pp. 743–754. ACM (2014)
3. Basu, S., Bultan, T.: Automated choreography repair. In: Stevens, P., Wąsowski, A. (eds.) FASE 2016. LNCS, vol. 9633, pp. 13–30. Springer, Heidelberg (2016). doi:10.1007/978-3-662-49665-7_2
4. Basu, S., Bultan, T., Ouederni, M.: Deciding choreography realizability. In: POPL 2012, pp. 191–202. ACM (2012)
5. Bocchi, L., Honda, K., Tuosto, E., Yoshida, N.: A theory of design-by-contract for distributed multiparty interactions. In: Gastin, P., Laroussinie, F. (eds.) CONCUR 2010. LNCS, vol. 6269, pp. 162–176. Springer, Heidelberg (2010). doi:10.1007/978-3-642-15375-4_12
6. Bocchi, L., Lange, J., Yoshida, N.: Meeting deadlines together. In: CONCUR 2015. LIPIcs, vol. 42, pp. 283–296. Schloss Dagstuhl (2015)
7. Bollig, B., Cyriac, A., Hélouët, L., Kara, A., Schwentick, T.: Dynamic communicating automata and branching high-level MSCs. In: Dediu, A.-H., Martín-Vide, C., Truthe, B. (eds.) LATA 2013. LNCS, vol. 7810, pp. 177–189. Springer, Heidelberg (2013). doi:10.1007/978-3-642-37064-9_17
8. Bollig, B., Hélouët, L.: Realizability of dynamic MSC languages. In: Ablayev, F., Mayr, E.W. (eds.) CSR 2010. LNCS, vol. 6072, pp. 48–59. Springer, Heidelberg (2010). doi:10.1007/978-3-642-13182-0_5
9. Brand, D., Zafiropulo, P.: On communicating finite-state machines. J. ACM **30**, 323–342 (1983)
10. Caires, L., Vieira, H.T.: Conversation types. Theor. Comput. Sci. **411**(51–52), 4399–4440 (2010)
11. Cécé, G., Finkel, A.: Verification of programs with half-duplex communication. Inf. Comput. **202**(2), 166–190 (2005)
12. Coppo, M., Dezani-Ciancaglini, M., Yoshida, N., Padovani, L.: Global progress for dynamically interleaved multiparty sessions. Math. Struct. Comput. Sci. **760**, 1–65 (2015)
13. Demangeon, R., Honda, K.: Full abstraction in a subtyped pi-calculus with linear types. In: Katoen, J.-P., König, B. (eds.) CONCUR 2011. LNCS, vol. 6901, pp. 280–296. Springer, Heidelberg (2011). doi:10.1007/978-3-642-23217-6_19
14. Demangeon, R., Honda, K.: Nested protocols in session types. In: Koutny, M., Ulidowski, I. (eds.) CONCUR 2012. LNCS, vol. 7454, pp. 272–286. Springer, Heidelberg (2012). doi:10.1007/978-3-642-32940-1_20
15. Demangeon, R., Honda, K., Hu, R., Neykova, R., Yoshida, N.: Practical interruptible conversations: distributed dynamic verification with multiparty session types and python. In: Formal Methods in System Design, pp. 1–29 (2015)
16. Deniélou, P.-M., Yoshida, N.: Dynamic multirole session types. In: POPL 2011, pp. 435–446. ACM (2011)

17. Deniélou, P.-M., Yoshida, N.: Multiparty session types meet communicating automata. In: Seidl, H. (ed.) ESOP 2012. LNCS, vol. 7211, pp. 194–213. Springer, Heidelberg (2012). doi:10.1007/978-3-642-28869-2_10

18. Deniélou, P.-M., Yoshida, N.: Multiparty compatibility in communicating automata: characterisation and synthesis of global session types. In: Fomin, F.V., Freivalds, R., Kwiatkowska, M., Peleg, D. (eds.) ICALP 2013. LNCS, vol. 7966, pp. 174–186. Springer, Heidelberg (2013). doi:10.1007/978-3-642-39212-2_18

19. Fowler, S.: An erlang implementation of multiparty session actors. In: ICE 2016. EPTCS, vol. 223, pp. 36–50 (2016)

20. Gay, S., Hole, M.: Subtyping for session types in the pi-calculus. Acta Informatica 42(2/3), 191–225 (2005)

21. Honda, K., Yoshida, N., Carbone, M.: Multiparty asynchronous session types. In: POPL 2008, pp. 273–284. ACM (2008)

22. Honda, K., Yoshida, N., Carbone, M.: Multiparty asynchronous session types. J. ACM 63(1), 9 (2016)

23. Hu, R., Yoshida, N.: Explicit Connection Actions in Multiparty Session Types (Long Version). https://www.doc.ic.ac.uk/rhu/~scribble/explicit.html

24. Hu, R., Yoshida, N.: Hybrid session verification through endpoint API generation. In: Stevens, P., Wąsowski, A. (eds.) FASE 2016. LNCS, vol. 9633, pp. 401–418. Springer, Heidelberg (2016). doi:10.1007/978-3-662-49665-7_24

25. Hu, R., Yoshida, N., Honda, K.: Session-based distributed programming in java. In: Vitek, J. (ed.) ECOOP 2008. LNCS, vol. 5142, pp. 516–541. Springer, Heidelberg (2008). doi:10.1007/978-3-540-70592-5_22

26. Imai, K., Yuen, S., Agusa, K.: Session type inference in haskell. In: PLACES. EPTCS, vol. 69, pp. 74–91 (2010)

27. Jespersen, T.B.L., Munksgaard, P., Larsen, K.F.: Session types for rust. In: WGP 2015, pp. 13–22. ACM (2015)

28. Klensin, J.: IETF RFC 5321 Simple Mail Transfer Protocol. https://tools.ietf.org/html/rfc5321

29. Kouzapas, D., Yoshida, N., Hu, R., Honda, K.: On asynchronous eventful session semantics. Math. Struct. Comput. Sci. 26(2), 303–364 (2016)

30. Lange, J., Tuosto, E., Yoshida, N.: From communicating machines to graphical choreographies. In: POPL 2015, pp. 221–232. ACM (2015)

31. Leucker, M., Madhusudan, P., Mukhopadhyay, S.: Dynamic message sequence charts. In: Agrawal, M., Seth, A. (eds.) FSTTCS 2002. LNCS, vol. 2556, pp. 253–264. Springer, Heidelberg (2002). doi:10.1007/3-540-36206-1_23

32. Lindley, S., Morris, J.G.: Lightweight Functional Session Types. http://homepages.inf.ed.ac.uk/slindley/papers/fst-draft-february2015.pdf

33. Neykova, R., Bocchi, L., Yoshida, N.: Timed runtime monitoring for multiparty conversations. In: BEAT 2014. EPTCS, vol. 162, pp. 19–26 (2014)

34. Neykova, R., Yoshida, N., Hu, R.: SPY: local verification of global protocols. In: Legay, A., Bensalem, S. (eds.) RV 2013. LNCS, vol. 8174, pp. 358–363. Springer, Heidelberg (2013). doi:10.1007/978-3-642-40787-1_25

35. Ng, N., Figueiredo Coutinho, J.G., Yoshida, N.: Protocols by default. In: Franke, B. (ed.) CC 2015. LNCS, vol. 9031, pp. 212–232. Springer, Heidelberg (2015). doi:10.1007/978-3-662-46663-6_11

36. Padovani, L.: FuSe homepage. http://www.di.unito.it/padovani/Software/FuSe/FuSe.html

37. Padovani, L.: Fair subtyping for multi-party session types. Math. Struct. Comput. Sci. 26(3), 424–464 (2016)

38. Perera, R., Lange, J., Gay, S.J.: Multiparty compatibility for concurrent objects. In: PLACES 2016. EPTCS, vol. 211, pp. 73–82 (2016)
39. Postel, J., Reynolds, J.: IETF RFC 959 File Transfer Protocol. https://tools.ietf.org/html/rfc959
40. Pucella, R., Tov, J.A.: Haskell session types with (almost) no class. In: Haskell 2008, pp. 25–36. ACM (2008)
41. Salaün, G., Bultan, T., Roohi, N.: Realizability of choreographies using process algebra encodings. IEEE Trans. Serv. Comput. 5(3), 290–304 (2012)
42. Scalas, A., Yoshida, N.: Lightweight session programming in scala. In: ECOOP 2016. LIPIcs, vol. 56, pp. 21:1–21:28. Schloss Dagstuhl (2016)
43. Scribble.: GitHub repository. https://github.com/scribble/scribble-java
44. Scribble homepage. http://www.scribble.org
45. Sivaramakrishnan, K.C., Qudeisat, M., Ziarek, L., Nagaraj, K., Eugster, P.: Efficient sessions. Sci. Comput. Program. 78(2), 147–167 (2013)
46. Yoshida, N., Deniélou, P.-M., Bejleri, A., Hu, R.: Parameterised multiparty session types. In: Ong, L. (ed.) FoSSaCS 2010. LNCS, vol. 6014, pp. 128–145. Springer, Heidelberg (2010). doi:10.1007/978-3-642-12032-9_10
47. Yoshida, N., Hu, R., Neykova, R., Ng, N.: The scribble protocol language. In: Abadi, M., Lluch Lafuente, A. (eds.) TGC 2013. LNCS, vol. 8358, pp. 22–41. Springer, Cham (2014). doi:10.1007/978-3-319-05119-2_3

Change and Delay Contracts for Hybrid System Component Verification

Andreas Müller[1]([✉]), Stefan Mitsch[2], Werner Retschitzegger[1],
Wieland Schwinger[1], and André Platzer[2]

[1] Department of Cooperative Information Systems, Johannes Kepler University,
Altenbergerstr. 69, 4040 Linz, Austria
{andreas.mueller,wieland.schwinger,werner.retschitzegger}@jku.at
[2] Computer Science Department, Carnegie Mellon University,
Pittsburgh, PA 15213, USA
{smitsch,aplatzer}@cs.cmu.edu

Abstract. In this paper, we present reasoning techniques for a component-based modeling and verification approach for hybrid systems comprising discrete dynamics as well as continuous dynamics, in which the components have local responsibilities. Our approach supports component contracts (i.e., input assumptions and output guarantees of interfaces) that are more general than previous component-based hybrid systems verification techniques in the following ways: We introduce *change contracts*, which characterize how current values exchanged between components along ports relate to previous values. We also introduce *delay contracts*, which describe the change relative to the time that has passed since the last value was exchanged. Together, these contracts can take into account what has changed between two components in a given amount of time since the last exchange of information. Most crucially, we prove that the safety of compatible components implies safety of the composite. The proof steps of the theorem are also implemented as a tactic in KeYmaera X, allowing automatic generation of a KeYmaera X proof for the composite system from proofs of the concrete components.

Keywords: Component-based development · Hybrid systems · Formal verification

1 Introduction

Cyber-physical systems (CPS) feature discrete dynamics (e.g., autopilots in airplanes, controllers in self-driving cars) as well as continuous dynamics (e.g., motion of airplanes or cars) and are increasingly used in safety-critical areas. Models of such CPS (i.e., hybrid system models, e.g., hybrid automata [8], hybrid programs [23]) are used to capture properties of these CPS as a basis to analyze their behavior and ensure safe operation with formal verification methods.

This material is based on research sponsored by DARPA under agreement DARPA FA8750-12-2-0291, and by the Austrian Science Fund (FWF) P28187-N31.

© Springer-Verlag GmbH Germany 2017
M. Huisman and J. Rubin (Eds.): FASE 2017, LNCS 10202, pp. 134–151, 2017.
DOI: 10.1007/978-3-662-54494-5_8

However, as the complexity of these systems increases, monolithic models and analysis techniques become unnecessarily challenging.

Since complex systems are typically composed of multiple subsystems and interact with other systems in their environment, it stands to reason to apply *component-based modeling* and split the analysis into isolated questions about subsystems and their interaction. However, approaches supporting component-based *verification* of hybrid system models are rare and differ strongly in the supported class of problems (cf. Sect. 5). Component-based techniques for hybrid (I/O) automata are based on *assume-guarantee reasoning* (AGR) [3,6,9] and focus on reachability analysis. Complementarily, hybrid systems theorem proving provides proofs, which are naturally compositional [22] (improves modularity) and support nonlinear dynamics, but so far limit components [15,16] to contracts over constant ranges (e.g., speed of a robot is non-negative and at most 10). Such contracts require substantial static independence of components, which does not fit to dynamic interactions frequently found in CPS. For example, one might show that a robot in the kitchen will not collide with obstacles in the physically separated back yard, but nothing can be said about what happens when both occupy the same parts of the space at different times to be safe. We, thus, extend CPS contracts [15,16] to consider change of values and timing.

In this paper, we introduce a component-based modeling and verification approach, which improves over previous approaches in the following critical ways. We introduce *change contracts* to specify the *change* of a variable between two states (e.g., current speed is at most twice the previous speed). We further add *delay contracts* to capture the *time delay* between the states (e.g., current speed is at most previous speed increased by accelerating for some time ε). Together, change and delay contracts make the hybrid (continuous-time) behavior of a component available as a discrete-time measurement abstraction in other components. That way, the joint hybrid behavior of a system of components simplifies to analyzing each component separately for safety and for satisfying its contracts (together with checks of compatibility and local side conditions). The isolated hybrid behavior of a component in question is, thus, analyzed with respect to simpler discrete-time abstractions of all other components in the system. We prove that this makes safety proofs about components transfer to the joint hybrid behavior of the composed system built from these compatible components. Moreover, we automate constructing the safety proof of the joint hybrid behavior from component proofs with a proof tactic in KeYmaera X [7]. This enables a small-core implementation [4] of the theory we develop here.

2   Preliminaries: Differential Dynamic Logic

For specifying and verifying correctness statements about hybrid systems, we use *differential dynamic logic* (dL) [19,21], which supports *hybrid programs* as a program notation for hybrid systems, according to the following EBNF grammar:

$$\alpha ::= \alpha; \beta \mid \alpha \cup \beta \mid \alpha^* \mid x := \theta \mid x := * \mid (x_1' = \theta_1, \ldots, x_n' = \theta_n \ \& \ H) \mid ?H$$

For details on the formal semantics of hybrid programs see [19, 21]. The sequential composition $\alpha; \beta$ expresses that β starts after α finishes. The non-deterministic choice $\alpha \cup \beta$ follows either α or β. The non-deterministic repetition operator α^* repeats α zero or more times. Discrete assignment $x := \theta$ instantaneously assigns the value of the term θ to the variable x, while $x := *$ assigns an arbitrary value to x. The ODE $(x' = \theta \ \& \ H)$ describes a continuous evolution of x (x' denotes derivation with respect to time) within the evolution domain H. The test $?H$ checks that a condition expressed by property H holds, and aborts if it does not. A typical pattern $x := *; ?a \leq x \leq b$, which involves assignment and tests, is to limit the assignment of arbitrary values to known bounds. Other control flow statements can be expressed with these primitives [19].

To specify safety properties about hybrid programs, d$\mathcal{L}$ provides modal operator $[\alpha]$. When ϕ is a d$\mathcal{L}$ formula describing a state and α is a hybrid program, then the d$\mathcal{L}$ formula $[\alpha]\phi$ expresses that all states reachable by α satisfy ϕ. The set of d$\mathcal{L}$ formulas relevant in this paper is generated by the following EBNF grammar (where $\sim \ \in \{<, \leq, =, \geq, >\}$ and θ_1, θ_2 are arithmetic expressions in $+, -, \cdot, /$ over the reals):

$$\phi ::= \theta_1 \sim \theta_2 \mid \neg\phi \mid \phi \wedge \psi \mid \phi \vee \psi \mid \phi \rightarrow \psi \mid \phi \leftrightarrow \psi \mid \forall x\phi \mid \exists x\phi \mid [\alpha]\phi$$

Proof for properties containing non-deterministic repetitions often use *invariants*, representing a property that holds before and after each repetition. Even though there is no unified approach for invariant generation, if a safety property including a non-deterministic repetition is valid, an invariant exists.

We use V to denote a set of variables. $FV(.)$ is used as an operator on terms, formulas and hybrid programs returning the free variables, whereas $BV(.)$ is an operator returning the bound variables.[1] Similarly, $V(.) = FV(.) \cup BV(.)$ returns all variables occurring in terms, formulas and hybrid programs. We use d$\mathcal{L}$ in definitions and formulas to denote the set of all d$\mathcal{L}$ formulas. We use "$\mapsto$" to define functions. $f = (a \mapsto b)$ means that the (partial) function f maps argument a to result b and is solely defined for a.

3   Hybrid Components with Change and Delay Contracts

In this section, we extend *components* (defined as hybrid programs) and their *interfaces* [16] with time and delay concepts. Interfaces identify assumptions about component inputs and guarantees about component outputs. We define what it means for a component to *comply with its contract* by a d$\mathcal{L}$ formula expressing safe behavior and compliance with its interface. And we define the *compatibility of component connections* rigorously as d$\mathcal{L}$ formulas as well. The main result of this paper is a proof showing that the safety properties of components transfer to a composed system, given proofs of contract compliance, compatibility and satisfaction of local side conditions. Users only provide a *specification* of components, interfaces, and how the components are connected, and

---

[1] *Bound variables* of a hybrid program are all those that may potentially be written to, while *free variables* are all those that may potentially be read [25].

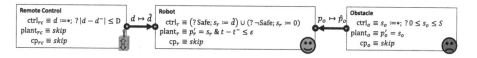

Fig. 1. Components for a collision avoidance system with remote control

show *proof obligations* about component contract compliance, compatibility and local side conditions; system safety follows automatically.

To illustrate the concepts, we use a running example of a tele-operated robot with collision avoidance inspired by [10,13], see Fig. 1: a *robot* reads speed advice d at least every ε time units from a *remote control* (RC), but automatically overrides the advice to avoid collisions with an *obstacle* that moves with an arbitrary but bounded speed $0 \leq s_o \leq S$ (e.g., a moving person). Two consecutive speed advisories from the RC should be at most D apart ($|d - d^-| \leq D$). The RC issues speed advice to the robot, but has no physical part. The obstacle chooses a new non-negative speed but at most S and moves according to the ODE $p'_o = s_o$. The robot measures the obstacle's position. If the distance is safe, the robot chooses the speed suggested by the RC; otherwise, the robot stops.

The RC satisfies a change contract (two consecutive speed advisories are not too far apart), while the obstacle and the robot satisfy delay contracts (their positions change according to speed and how much time passed). Formal definitions of these three components, their interfaces, and the respective contracts, will be introduced step-by-step along the definitions in subsequent sections. A comprehensive explanation of the running example can be found in [17].

3.1   Specification: Components and Interfaces

Change components and interfaces specify what a component assumes about the change of each of its inputs, and what it guarantees about the change on its outputs. To make such conditions expressible, every component will use additional variables to store both the current and the previous value communicated along a port. These so-called Δ-ports can be used to model jumps in discrete control, and for measurement of physical behavior if the rate of change is irrelevant.

Components may consist of a discrete control part and a continuous plant, cf. Definition 1. Definition 1 does not prescribe how control and plant are composed; the composition to a hybrid program is specified later in Definition 5. We allow components to be hierarchically composed from sub-components, so components list the internally connected ports of sub-components.

Definition 1 (Component). *A component* $C = (\text{ctrl}, \text{plant}, \text{cp})$ *is defined as*

- ctrl *is the discrete part without differential equations,*
- plant *is a differential equation* $(x'_1 = \theta_1, \ldots, x'_n = \theta_n \& H)$ *for* $n \in \mathbb{N}$,
- cp *are deterministic assignments connecting ports of sub-components, and*
- $V(C_i) \overset{def}{=} V(\text{ctrl}) \cup V(\text{plant}) \cup V(\text{cp})$, *correspondingly for* $BV(C_i)$.

If a component is atomic, i.e., not composed from sub-components, the port connections cp are empty (skip statement of no effect). The variables of a component are the sum of all used variables. We aim at components that can be analyzed in isolation and that communicate solely through ports. Global shared constants (read-only and thus not used for communication purposes) are included for convenience to share common knowledge for all components in a single place.

Definition 2 (Variable Restrictions). *A system of components $C_1, ..., C_n$ is well-defined if*

- *global variables V^{global} are read-only and shared by all components:*
  $V^{\text{global}} \cap BV(C_i) = \emptyset$,
- *$\forall i \neq j \,.\, V(C_i) \cap V(C_j) \subseteq V^{\text{global}}$ such that no variable of other components can be read or written.*

Consider the robot collision avoidance system. Its global variables are the maximum obstacle speed S and the maximum difference D between two speed advisories, i.e., $V^{global} = \{S, D\}$. They can neither be bound in control nor plant, cf. Definition 2. The RC component's controller picks a new demanded speed d that is not too far from the previous demanded speed d^-. Since it is not composed from sub-components the cp_{rc} part is skip in Fig. 1. The obstacle's controller chooses any speed s_o that does not exceed the maximum speed S. The plant ODE $p'_o = s_o$ describes how the position of the obstacle changes according to its speed. Since the obstacle is an atomic component, cp_o is skip, cf. Fig. 1.

An interface defines how a component may interact with other components through its ports, what assumptions the component makes about its inputs, and what guarantees it provides for its outputs, see Definition 3.

Definition 3 (Admissible Interface). *An admissible interface I^Δ for a component C is a tuple $I^\Delta = \left(V^{\text{in}}, \pi^{\text{in}}, V^{\text{out}}, \pi^{\text{out}}, V^\Delta, V^-, pre\right)$ with*

- *$V^{\text{in}} \subseteq V(C)$ and $V^{\text{out}} \subseteq V(C)$ are disjoint sets of input- and output variables,*
- *$V^{\text{in}} \cap BV(C) = \emptyset$, i.e., input variables may not be bound in the component,*
- *$\pi^{\text{in}} : V^{\text{in}} \to d\mathcal{L}$ is a function specifying exactly one formula per input variable (i.e., input port), representing input requirements and assumptions,*
- *$\pi^{\text{out}} : V^{\text{out}} \to d\mathcal{L}$ specifies output guarantees for output ports,*
- *$\forall v \in V^{\text{in}} \;:\; V(\pi^{\text{in}}(v)) \subseteq \left(V(C) \setminus \left(V^{\text{in}} \cup V^{\text{out}}\right)\right) \cup \{v\}$ such that input formulas are local to their port,*
- *$V^\Delta = V^{\Delta+} \cup V^{\Delta i} \subseteq V(C)$ is a set of Δ-port variables of unconnected public $V^{\Delta+} \subseteq V^{\text{in}} \cup V^{\text{out}}$, and connected private $V^{\Delta i}$, with $V^{\Delta i} \cap \left(V^{\text{in}} \cup V^{\text{out}}\right) = \emptyset$, so $V^{\Delta+} \cap V^{\Delta i} = \emptyset$,*
- *$V^- \subseteq V(C)$ with $V^- \cap BV(C) = \emptyset$ is a read-only set of variables storing the previous values of Δ-ports, disjoint from other interface variables $V^- \cap (V^{\text{in}} \cup V^{\text{out}} \cup V^\Delta) = \emptyset$,*
- *$pre : V^\Delta \to V^-$ is a bijective function, assigning one variable to each Δ-port to store its previous value.*

The definition is accordingly for vector-valued ports that share multiple variables along a single port, provided that each variable is part of exactly one vectorial port. This leads to *multi-ports*, which transfer the values of multiple variables, but have a single joint output guarantee/input assumption over the variables in the multi-port vector. Input assumptions are local to their port, i.e., no input formula can mention other input variables (which lets us reshuffle port ordering) nor any output variables (which prevents cyclic port definitions). Not all ports of a component need to be connected to other components; unconnected ports simply remain input/output ports of the resulting composite system.

Considering our example, the RC interface I_{rc}^{Δ} from (1) contains one output port d in V^{out}, where the robot can retrieve the demanded speed. The RC guarantees that the new demanded speed d will not deviate too far from the previous speed d^-, so $|d - d^-| \leq D$. Since the current and the previous demanded speed are related, d is a Δ-port in V^{Δ} with its previous value d^- in V^- per pre.

$$I_{rc}^{\Delta} = \big(\underbrace{\{\}}_{V^{in}}, \underbrace{()}_{\pi^{in}}, \underbrace{\{d\}}_{V^{out}}, \underbrace{\big(d \mapsto |d - d^-| \leq D\big)}_{\pi^{out}}, \underbrace{\{d\}}_{V^{\Delta}}, \underbrace{\{d^-\}}_{V^-}, \underbrace{\big(d \mapsto d^-\big)}_{pre} \big) \qquad (1)$$

3.2   Specification: Time and Delay

In a monolithic hybrid program with a combined plant for all components, time passes synchronously for all components and their ODEs evolve for the same amount of time. When split into separate components, the ODEs are split into separate plants too, thereby losing the connection of evolving for identical amounts of time. From the viewpoint of a single component, other plants reduce to discrete abstractions through input assumptions on Δ-ports. These input assumptions are phrased in terms of worst-case behavior (e.g., from the viewpoint of the robot, the obstacle may jump at most distance $S \cdot \varepsilon$ between measurements because it lost a precise model). The robot's ODE, however, still runs for some arbitrary time, which makes the measurements and the continuous behavior of the robot drift (i.e., robot and obstacle appear to move for different durations). To address this issue, we introduce *delay* as a way of ensuring that the changes are consistent with the time that passes in a component.

To unify the timing for all components of a system, we introduce a globally synchronized time t and a global variable t^- to store the time before each run of plant. Both are special global variables, which cannot be bound by the user, but only on designated locations specified through the contract, cf. Definition 4.

Definition 4 (Time). *Let C_i, $i \in \mathbb{N}$ be any number of components with variables according to Definition 2. When working with* delay *contracts, we assume*

– *the global system time t changes with constant rate $t' = 1$,*
– *t^- is the initial plant time at the start of the current plant run,*
– *$\{t, t^-\} \cap BV(C_i) = \emptyset$, thus clocks t, t^- are not written by a component.*

Let us continue our running example with the obstacle's interface, which has one output port (providing the current obstacle position) that uses the introduced global time in its output property to restrict the obstacle's position relative to its previous position and maximum speed, i.e.,

$$I_o^\Delta = \Big(\underbrace{\{\}}_{V^{in}}, \underbrace{()}_{\pi^{in}}, \underbrace{\{p_o\}}_{V^{out}}, \underbrace{(p_o \mapsto |p_o - p_o^-| \le S \cdot (t - t^-))}_{\pi^{out}}, \underbrace{\{p_o\}}_{V^\Delta}, \underbrace{\{p_o^-\}}_{V^-}, \underbrace{(p_o \mapsto p_o^-)}_{pre} \Big).$$

3.3   Proof Obligations: Change and Delay Contract

Contract compliance ties together components and interfaces by showing that a component guarantees the output changes that its interface specifies under the input assumptions made in the interface. Contract compliance further shows a local safety property, which describes the component's desired safe states. For example, a safety property of a robot might require that the robot will not drive too close to the last measured position of the obstacle. Together with the obstacle's output guarantee of not moving too far from its previous position, the local safety property implies a system-wide safety property (e.g., robot and obstacle will not collide), since we know that a measurement previously reflected the real position. Contract compliance can be verified using KeYmaera X [7].

In order to make guarantees about the behavior of a composed system we use the synchronized system time t to measure the delay $(t - t^-)$ between controller runs in delay contract compliance proof obligations, cf. Definition 5.

Definition 5 (Contract Compliance). *Let C be a component with its admissible interface I^Δ (cf. Definition 3). Let formula ϕ describe initial states of C and formula ψ^{safe} the safe states, both over the component variables $V(C)$. The output guarantees $\Pi^{\text{out}} \equiv \bigwedge_{v \in V^{\text{out}}} \pi^{\text{out}}(v)$ extend safety to $\psi^{\text{safe}} \wedge \Pi^{\text{out}}$. Change contract compliance $\text{CC}(C, I^\Delta)$ of C with I^Δ is defined as the $d\mathcal{L}$ formula:*

$$\text{CC}(C, I^\Delta) \stackrel{def}{\equiv} \phi \rightarrow [(\Delta; \text{ctrl}; \text{plant}; \text{in}; \text{cp})^*](\psi^{\text{safe}} \wedge \Pi^{\text{out}})$$

and delay contract compliance $\text{DC}(C, I^\Delta)$ *is defined as the $d\mathcal{L}$ formula:*

$$\text{DC}(C, I^\Delta) \stackrel{def}{\equiv} t = t^- \wedge \phi \rightarrow [(\Delta; \text{ctrl}; t^- := t; (t' = 1, \text{plant}); \text{in}; \text{cp})^*](\psi^{\text{safe}} \wedge \Pi^{\text{out}})$$

where
$$\text{in} \stackrel{def}{\equiv} (v := *; ?\pi^{\text{in}}(v)) \text{ for all } v \in V^{\text{in}},$$

are (vectorial) assignments to input ports satisfying input assumptions $\pi^{\text{in}}(v)$ and Δ are (vectorial) assignments storing previous values of Δ-port variables:

$$\Delta \stackrel{def}{\equiv} \text{pre}(v) := v \text{ for all } v \in V^\Delta.$$

The order of the assignments in both *in* and Δ is irrelevant because the assignments are over disjoint variables and $\pi^{in}(v)$ are local to their port, cf. Definition 3. The function pre can be used throughout the component to read the initial value of a Δ-port. Since $\text{pre}(v) \in V^-$ for all $v \in V^\Delta$, Definitions 3 and 5 require that the resulting initial variable is not bound anywhere outside Δ.

This notion of contracts crucially changes compared to [16] with respect to where ports are read and how change is modeled: reading from input ports at the beginning of a component's loop body (i.e., before the controller runs) as in [16] may seem intuitive, but it would require severe restrictions to a component's plant in order to make inputs and plant agree on duration. Instead, we prepare the next loop iteration at the end of the loop body (i.e., after *plant*), so that actual plant duration can be considered for computing the next input values.

Example: Change Contract. We continue the collision avoidance system with a change contract (2) according to Definition 5 for the RC from Fig. 1. The difference between speed advisories should be non-negative, whereas the output port's previous value d^- is bootstrapped from the current demanded speed d to guarantee contract compliance even without component execution, since non-deterministic repetitions can execute 0 times, so $\phi_{rc} \equiv D \geq 0 \wedge d = d^-$. The RC guarantees that consecutive speed advisories are at most D apart, see Π_{rc}^{out} ($\psi_{rc}^{safe} \equiv \top$).

$$\phi_{rc} \rightarrow [(\underbrace{d^- := d; d := *; ? |d - d^-| \leq D}_{\Delta_{rc}}; \underbrace{skip}_{ctrl_{rc}}; \underbrace{skip}_{plant_{rc}}; \underbrace{skip}_{in_{rc}}; \underbrace{skip}_{cp_{rc}})^*] \underbrace{(|d - d^-| \leq D)}_{\Pi_{rc}^{out}}$$

(2)

We verified the RC contract using KeYmaera X and thus know that the component is safe and complies with its interface. Compared to contracts with fixed ranges as in approaches [3,16], we do not have to assume a global limit for demanded speeds d, but consider the previous advice d^- as a reference value when calculating the next speed advice.

Example: Delay Contract. Change in obstacle position depends on speed and on how much time passed. Hence, we follow Definition 5 to specify the obstacle delay contract (3). For simplicity, assume that maximum speed S is non-negative and the obstacle stopped initially. As before, the previous position p_o^- is bootstrapped from the current position p_o, so $\phi_o \equiv S \geq 0 \wedge p_o = p_o^- \wedge s_o = 0$. We model an adversarial obstacle, which does not care about safety. Thus, the output property only guarantees that positions change at most by $S \cdot (t - t^-)$, which is a discrete abstraction of the obstacle's physical movement. Such an abstraction can be found by solving the plant ODE or from differential invariants [24]. Again, we verified the obstacle's contract compliance using KeYmaera X.

$$t = t^- \wedge \phi_o \rightarrow [(\overbrace{p_o^- := p_o}^{\Delta_o}; \overbrace{s_o := *; ?(0 \leq s_o \leq S)}^{ctrl_o}; t^- := t; \overbrace{\{t' = 1, p_o' = s_o\}}^{plant_o};$$
$$\underbrace{skip}_{in_o}; \underbrace{skip}_{cp_o})^*] \underbrace{(|p_o - p_o^-| \leq S \cdot (t - t^-))}_{\Pi_o^{out}}$$

(3)

3.4   Proof Obligations: Compatible Parallel Composition

From components with verified contract compliance, we now compose systems and provide safety guarantees about them, without redoing system proofs. For this, Definition 6 introduces a quasi-parallel composition, where the discrete *ctrl* parts of the components are executed sequentially in any order, while the continuous *plant* parts run in parallel. The connected ports *cp* of all components are composed sequentially in any order, since the order of independent deterministic assignments (i.e., assignments having disjoint free and bound variables) is irrelevant. Such a definition is natural in d$\mathcal{L}$, since time only passes during continuous evolution in hybrid programs, while the discrete actions of a program do not consume time and thus happen instantaneously at a single real point in time, but in a specific order. The actual execution order of independent components in a real system is unknown, which we model with a non-deterministic choice between all possible controller execution orders. Values can be exchanged between components using Δ-ports; all other variables are internal to a single component, except global variables, which can be read everywhere, but never bound, and system time t, t^-, which can be read everywhere, but only bound at specific locations fixed by the delay contract, cf. Definition 5. Δ-ports store their previous values in the composite component, regardless if connected or not. For all connected ports, Definition 6 replaces the non-deterministic assignments to open inputs (cf. *in*) with a deterministic assignment from the connected port (cf. *cp*). This represents an instantaneous and lossless interaction between components.

Definition 6 (Parallel Composition). *Let* $C_i = (\text{ctrl}_i, \text{plant}_i, \text{cp}_i)$ *denote components with their corresponding admissible interfaces*

$$I_i^\Delta = \left(V_i^{\text{in}}, \pi_i^{\text{in}}, V_i^{\text{out}}, \pi_i^{\text{out}}, V_i^\Delta, V_i^-, \text{pre}_i \right) \text{ for } i \in \{1, \ldots, n\},$$

sharing only V^{global} *and global times such that* $V(C_i) \cap V(C_j) \subseteq V^{\text{global}} \cup \{t, t^-\}$ *for* $i \neq j$. *Let further*

$$\mathcal{X} : \left(\bigcup_{1 \leq j \leq n} V_j^{\text{in}} \right) \rightharpoonup \left(\bigcup_{1 \leq i \leq n} V_i^{\text{out}} \right), \text{ provided } \mathcal{X}(v) \notin V_j^{\text{out}}, \text{ for all } v \in V_j^{\text{in}}$$

be a partial (i.e., not every input must be mapped), injective (i.e., every output is only mapped to at most one input) function, connecting some inputs to some outputs, with domain $\mathcal{I}^{\mathcal{X}} = \{x \in V^{\text{in}} \mid \mathcal{X}(x) \text{ is defined}\}$ *and image* $\mathcal{O}^{\mathcal{X}} = \{y \in V^{\text{out}} \mid y = \mathcal{X}(x) \text{ for some } x \in V^{\text{in}}\}$. *The composition of n components and their interfaces* $(C, I^\Delta) \overset{\text{def}}{\equiv} ((C_1, I_1^\Delta) \| \ldots \| (C_n, I_n^\Delta))_{\mathcal{X}}$ *according to* $\mathcal{X}$ *is defined as:*

- *controllers are executed in non-deterministic order of all the n! possible permutations of* $\{1, \ldots, n\}$,

$$\text{ctrl} \equiv (\text{ctrl}_1; \text{ctrl}_2; \ldots; \text{ctrl}_n) \cup (\text{ctrl}_2; \text{ctrl}_1; \ldots; \text{ctrl}_n)$$
$$\cup \ldots \cup (\text{ctrl}_n; \ldots; \text{ctrl}_2; \text{ctrl}_1)$$

- *plants are executed in parallel, with evolution domain* $H \equiv \bigwedge_{i \in \{1, \ldots, n\}} H_i$

$$\text{plant} \equiv \underbrace{x_1^{(1)\prime} = \theta_1^{(1)}, \ldots, x_1^{(k)\prime} = \theta_1^{(k)}}_{\text{component } C_1}, \ldots, \underbrace{x_n^{(1)\prime} = \theta_n^{(1)}, \ldots, x_n^{(m)\prime} = \theta_n^{(m)}}_{\text{component } C_n} \& H,$$

– *port assignments are extended with connections for some* $\{v_j, \ldots, v_r\} = \mathcal{I}^{\mathcal{X}}$

$$\mathrm{cp} \stackrel{def}{\equiv} \underbrace{\mathrm{cp}_1; \mathrm{cp}_2; \ldots; \mathrm{cp}_n}_{components'\ \mathrm{cp}}; \underbrace{v_j := \mathcal{X}(v_j); \ldots; v_r := \mathcal{X}(v_r)}_{connected\ inputs},$$

– *previous values* $V^- \stackrel{def}{\equiv} \bigcup_{1 \leq i \leq n} V_i^-$ *are merged; connected ports become private* $V^{\Delta i} \stackrel{def}{\equiv} \left(\bigcup_{1 \leq i \leq n} V_i^{\Delta i} \right) \cup \mathcal{I}^{\mathcal{X}} \cup \mathcal{O}^{\mathcal{X}}$; *unconnected ports remain public* $V^{\Delta +} \stackrel{def}{\equiv}$
$\left(\bigcup_{1 \leq i \leq n} V_i^{\Delta +} \right) \setminus (\mathcal{I}^{\mathcal{X}} \cup \mathcal{O}^{\mathcal{X}})$,

– pre_i *are combined such that* $pre(v) \equiv pre_i(v)$ *if* $v \in V_i^{\Delta}$ *for all* $i \in \{1, \ldots, n\}$,

– *unconnected inputs* $V^{\mathrm{in}} = \left(\bigcup_{1 \leq i \leq n} V_i^{\mathrm{in}} \right) \setminus \mathcal{I}^{\mathcal{X}}$ *and unconnected outputs* $V^{\mathrm{out}} =$
$\left(\bigcup_{1 \leq i \leq n} V_i^{\mathrm{out}} \right) \setminus \mathcal{O}^{\mathcal{X}}$ *are merged and their requirements preserved*

$$\pi^{\mathrm{in}}(v) \equiv \pi_i^{\mathrm{in}}(v) \text{ if } v \in V_i^{\mathrm{in}} \setminus \mathcal{I}^{\mathcal{X}} \text{ for all } i \in \{1, \ldots, n\}$$
$$\pi^{\mathrm{out}}(v) \equiv \pi_i^{\mathrm{out}}(v) \text{ if } v \in V_i^{\mathrm{out}} \setminus \mathcal{O}^{\mathcal{X}} \text{ for all } i \in \{1, \ldots, n\}.$$

The order of port assignments is irrelevant because all sets of variables are disjoint and a port can only be either an input port or output port, cf. Definitions 1 and 3, and thus the assignments share no variables. This also entails that the merged pre, π^{in} and π^{out} are well-defined since V_i^{Δ}, V_i^{in}, respectively V_i^{out}, are disjoint between components by Definition 2.

The user provides component specifications (C_i, I_i^{Δ}) and a mapping function $\mathcal{X}$, defining which output is connected to which input. The composed system of parallel components can be derived automatically from Definition 6. It follows that the set of variables of the composite component $V(C)$ is the union of all involved components' variable sets $V(C_i)$, i.e., $V(C) = \bigcup_{1 \leq i \leq n} V(C_i)$. The set of global variables V^{global} contains all global variables in the system (i.e., in all components) and thus, its contents do not change. Since $V^{\Delta} = \bigcup_{1 \leq i \leq n} V_i^{\Delta}$, this definition implies that internally connected Δ-ports $V^{\Delta i}$ of sub-components, as well as the previous values $V^{\Delta +}$ for all open Δ-ports are still stored. As a result, the current and previous values of Δ-ports can still be used internally in the composite, even when the ports are no longer exposed through the external interface of the composed system.

Returning to our running example of Fig. 1 the component C_{sys} in (4) and interface I_{sys}^{Δ} in (5) result from parallel composition of the RC, the robot, and the obstacle. The robot controller follows the speed advice received on input port $\hat{d}$ if the robot is at a safe distance from the obstacle position measured with input port $\hat{p}_o$; otherwise it stops. The robot plant changes the robot's position according to its speed, where the controller executes at least every ε time-units. The robot's input ports are connected to the RC's and obstacle's output ports.[2]

$$C_{sys} = ((\underbrace{ctrl_{rc}; ctrl_r; ctrl_o \cup ctrl_o; \ldots}_{ctrl_{sys}}), (\underbrace{plant_r, plant_o}_{plant_{sys}}), \underbrace{\hat{p}_o := p_o; \hat{d} := d}_{cp_{sys}}) \quad (4)$$

---

[2] For the detailed robot component C_r and interface I_r^{Δ}, see [17].

$$\mathrm{I}_{sys}^{\Delta} = \Big(\underbrace{\{\}}_{V^{in}}, \underbrace{()}_{\pi^{in}}, \underbrace{\{\}}_{V^{out}}, \underbrace{()}_{\pi^{out}}, \underbrace{\{p_o, d, \hat{p}_o, \hat{d}\}}_{V^{\Delta}}, \underbrace{\{p_o^-, d^-, \hat{p}_o^-, \hat{d}^-\}}_{V^-}, \underbrace{(p_o \mapsto p_o^-, ...)}_{pre} \Big) \quad (5)$$

During composition, the tests guarding the input ports of an interface are replaced with a deterministic assignment modeling the port connection of the components, which is only safe if the respective output guarantees and input assumptions match. Hence, in addition to contract compliance, users have to show compatibility of components as defined in Definition 7.

Definition 7 (Compatible Composite). *A composite of n components with interfaces* $\big((C_1, I_1^{\Delta}) \| ... \| (C_n, I_n^{\Delta})\big)_{\mathcal{X}}$ *is a compatible composite iff* d$\mathcal{L}$ *formula*

$$\mathrm{CPO}(I_i^{\Delta}) \stackrel{def}{\equiv} \big(pre(\mathcal{X}(v)) = pre(v)\big) \to [v := \mathcal{X}(v)](\pi_j^{out}(\mathcal{X}(v)) \to \pi_i^{in}(v))$$

is valid over (vectorial) equalities and assignments for input ports $v \in \mathcal{I}^{\mathcal{X}} \cap V_i^{in}$ *from* I_i^{Δ} *connected to* $\mathcal{X}(v) \in \mathcal{O}^{\mathcal{X}} \cap V_j^{out}$ *from* I_j^{Δ}. *We call* $\mathrm{CPO}(I_i^{\Delta})$ *the compatibility proof obligation for the interfaces* I_i^{Δ} *and say the interfaces* I_i^{Δ} *are compatible (with respect to* $\mathcal{X}$) *if* $\mathrm{CPO}(I_i^{\Delta})$ *is valid for all i.*

Components are compatible if the output properties imply the input properties of connected ports. Compatibility guarantees that handing an output port's value over to the connected input port ensures that the input port's input assumption π^{in} holds, which is no longer checked explicitly by a test, so $\pi_j^{out}(\mathcal{X}(v)) \to \pi_i^{in}(v)$. To achieve local compatibility checks for pairs of connected ports, instead of global checks over entire component models, we restrict output guarantees, respectively input assumptions to the associated output ports, respectively input ports (cf. Definition 3). In our example, the robot and the obstacle, respectively the RC are compatible, as witnessed by proofs of $CPO(\mathrm{I}_{rc}^{\Delta})$ and $CPO(\mathrm{I}_o^{\Delta})$, cf. [17].

3.5   Transferring Local Component Safety to System Safety

After verifying contract compliance and compatibility proof obligations, Theorem 1 below ensures that the safety properties in component contracts imply safety of the composed system. Thus, to ensure a safety property of the monolithic system, we no longer need a (probably huge) monolithic proof, but can apply Theorem 1 (proof available in [17]).

Theorem 1 (Composition Retains Contracts). *Let* C_1 *and* C_2 *be components with admissible interfaces* I_1^{Δ} *and* I_2^{Δ} *that are delay contract compliant (cf. Definition 5) and compatible with respect to* $\mathcal{X}$ *(cf. Definition 7). Initially, assume* $\phi^p \stackrel{def}{\equiv} \bigwedge_{v \in \mathcal{I}^{\mathcal{X}}} \mathcal{X}(v) = v$ *to bootstrap connected ports. Then, if the side condition (6) holds (*φ_i *is the loop invariant used to prove the component's contract)*

$$\models \varphi_i \to [\Delta_i][\mathrm{ctrl}_i][t^- := t][(t' = 1, \mathrm{plant}_i)]\Pi_i^{out} \quad (6)$$

for all components C_i, the parallel composition $(C, I^\Delta) = ((C_1, I_1^\Delta) \| (C_2, I_2^\Delta))_\chi$ then satisfies the contract (7) with in, cp, ctrl, *and* plant *according to Definition 6:*

$$\models (t = t^- \wedge \phi_1 \wedge \phi_2 \wedge \phi^p) \rightarrow [(\Delta; \mathrm{ctrl}; t^- := t; (t' = 1, \mathrm{plant});$$
$$\mathrm{in}; \mathrm{cp})^*] \left(\psi_1^{\mathrm{safe}} \wedge \Pi_1^{\mathrm{out}} \wedge \psi_2^{\mathrm{safe}} \wedge \Pi_2^{\mathrm{out}}\right). \tag{7}$$

The composite contract's precondition ϕ^p ensures that the values of connected ports are consistent initially. Side condition (6) shows that a component already produces the correct output from just its *ctrl* and *plant*; preparing the port inputs for the next loop iteration does not change the current output.

The side condition (6) is trivially true for components without output ports, since $\Pi_i^{out} \equiv true$. For atomic components without input ports, the proof of (6) automatically follows from the contract proof, since *in; cp* is empty. Because of the precondition ϕ^p and because *cp* is executed after every execution of the main loop (cf. Definition 5), we know that the values of connected input and output ports coincide in the safety property, as one would expect. Thus, for instance, if the local safety property of a single component mentions an input port (e.g., $\psi_1^{safe} \equiv |p_r - \hat{p}_o| > 0$, we can replace the input port with the original value as provided by the output port for the composite safety property (e.g., $\psi^{safe} \equiv |p_r - \hat{p}_o| > 0 \equiv |p_r - p_o| > 0$). Theorem 1 easily extends to n components (cf. proof sketch in [17]) and also holds for change contracts. A change port cannot be attached to a delay port and vice versa.

Going back to our example, the overall system property of our collision avoidance system follows from Theorem 1, given the local safety property of the robot, the change contract compliance of the RC, the delay contract compliance of the obstacle, and the compatibility of the connections. Since we verified all component contracts as well as the compatibility proof obligations and since the components with output ports are atomic and have no input ports (i.e., the side condition holds), safety of the collision avoidance system follows.

Automation. We implemented the proof steps of Theorem 1 as a KeYmaera X tactic, which automatically reduces a system safety proof to separate proofs about components[3]. This gave us the best of the two worlds: the flexibility of reasoning with components that our Theorem 1 provides, together with the soundness guarantees we inherit from KeYmaera X, which derives proofs by uniform substitution from axioms [25]. This is to be contrasted with the significant soundness-critical changes we would have to do if we were to add Theorem 1 as a built-in rule into the KeYmaera X prover core. Uniform substitution guarantees, e.g., that the subtle conditions on how and where input and output variables can be read or written in components are checked correctly.

---

[3] Implementation and full models available online at http://www.cs.cmu.edu/~smitsch/resource/fase17.

4 Case Studies

To evaluate our approach (See footnote 3), we use the running example of a remote-controlled robot (RC robot) and revisit prior case studies on the European Train Control System (i.e., ETCS) [26], two-component robot collision avoidance (i.e., Robix) [13], and adaptive cruise control (i.e., LLC) [10]. In *ETCS*, a radio-block controller (RBC) communicates speed limits to a train, i.e., it requires the train to have at most speed d after some point m. The RBC multi-port change contract relates distances m, m^- and demanded speeds d, d^- in input assumptions/output guarantees of the form $d \geq 0 \wedge (d^-)^2 - d^2 \leq 2b(m - m^-) \wedge state = drive$, thus avoiding physically impossible maneuvers.

In *Robix*, a robot measures the position of a moving obstacle with a maximum speed S. The obstacle guarantees to not move further than $S \cdot (t - t^-)$ in either axis between measurements, using a delay contract.

In *LLC*, a follower car measures both speed v_l and position x_l of a leader car, with maximum acceleration A and braking capabilities B. Hence, we use a multi-port delay contract with properties of the form $2 \cdot (x_l - x_l^-) \geq v_l + v_l^- \cdot t \wedge 0 \leq v_l \wedge -B \cdot t \leq v_l - v_l^- \leq A \cdot t$ tying together speed change and position progress.

Table 1 summarizes the experimental results of the component-based approach in comparison to monolithic models in terms of duration and degree of proof automation. The column *Contract* describes the kind of contract used in the case study (i.e., multiport, delay contract or change contract), as well as whether or not the models use non-linear differential equations. The column *Automation* indicates fully automated proofs with checkmarks; it indicates the number of built-in tactics composed to form a proof script when user input is required. The column *Duration* compares the proof duration, using Z3 [14] as a back-end decision procedure to discharge arithmetic. The column *Sum* sums up the proof durations for the components (columns C_1 and C_2) and Theorem 1 (column *Th. 1*, i.e., checking compatibility, condition (6) and the execution of our composition proof). Checking the composition proof is fully automated, following the proof steps of Theorem 1.

All measurements were conducted on an Intel i7-6700HQ CPU@2.6 GHz with 16 GB memory. In summary, the results indicate that our approach verification leads to performance improvements and smaller user-provided proof scripts.

Table 1. Experimental results for case studies

	Contract				Automation				Duration [s]				
	Multi	Change	Delay	Non-linear	C_1	C_2	Th. 1	Monolithic	C_1	C_2	Th. 1	Sum	Monolithic
RC robot			✓		✓	✓	✓	✓	32	101	56	**189**	1934
ETCS [26]	✓	✓			✓	✓	✓	✓	127	608	179	**873**	15306
Robix [13]			✓	✓	(31)	✓	✓	(96)	469	117	132	**718**	902
LLC [10]	✓		✓		✓	(50)	✓	(131)	135	351	267	**753**	568

5 Related Work

We group related work into hybrid automata, hybrid process algebras, and hybrid programs.

Hybrid Automata and Assume-Guarantee Reasoning. Hybrid automata [1] can be composed in parallel. However, the associated verification procedure (i.e., verify that a formula holds throughout all runs of the automaton) is not compositional, but requires verification of the exponential product automaton [1]. Thus, for a hybrid automaton it is not sufficient to establish a property about its parts in order to establish a property about the automaton. We, instead, decompose *verification* into local proofs and get system safety automatically. Hybrid I/O automata [11] extend hybrid automata with a notion of external behavior. The associated implementation relation (i.e., if automaton A implements automaton B, properties verified for B also hold for A) is respected by their composition operation in the sense that if A_1 implements A_2, then the composition of A_1 and B implements the composition of A_2 and B. Hybrid (I/O) automata are mainly verified using reachability analysis. Therefore, techniques to prevent state-space explosion are needed, like assume-guarantee reasoning (AGR, e.g., [3,6,9]), which was developed to decompose a verification task into subtasks. In [6], timed transition systems are used to approximate a component's behavior by discretization. These abstractions are then used in place of the more complicated automata to verify refinement properties. The implementation of their approach is limited to linear hybrid automata. In analogy, we discretize plants to delay contracts; however, in our approach, contracts completely replace components and do not need to retain simplified transition systems. A similar AGR rule is presented in [9], where the approximation drops continuous behaviors of single components entirely. As a result, the approach only works when the continuous behavior is irrelevant to the verified property, which rarely happens in CPS. Our change and delay contracts still preserve knowledge about continuous behavior. The AGR approach of [3] uses contracts consisting of input assumptions and output guarantees to verify properties about single components: a component is an abstraction of another component if it has a stricter contract. The approach is restricted to constant intervals, i.e., static global contracts as in [16].

In [5], a component-based design framework for controllers of hybrid systems with linear dynamics based on hybrid automata is presented. It focuses on checking interconnections of components: alarms propagated by an out-port must be handled by the connected in-ports. We, too, check component compatibility, but for contracts, and focus on transferring proofs from components to the system level. We provide parallel composition, while [5] uses sequential composition. The compositional verification approach in [2] bases on linear hybrid automata using invariants to over-approximate component behavior and interactions. However, interactions between components are restricted to synchronization. (i.e., no variable state can be transferred between components).

In summary, aforementioned approaches are limited to linear dynamics [5] or even linear hybrid automata [2], use global contracts [3], focus on sequential composition [5] or rely on reachability analysis, over-approximation and model checking [3,6,9]. We, in contrast, focus on *theorem proving* in d$\mathcal{L}$, using change and delay contracts and handle *non-linear dynamics* and parallel composition. Most crucially, we focus on transfer of safety properties from components to composites, while related approaches are focused on property transfer between different levels of abstraction [3,6,9].

Hybrid process algebras are compositional modeling formalisms for the description of behavior and interaction of processes, based on algebraic equations. Examples are Hybrid χ [27], HyPA [18] or the Φ-Calculus [28]. Although the modeling is compositional, for verification purposes the models are again analyzed using simulation or reachability analysis in a non-compositional fashion (e.g., Hybrid χ using PHAVer [30], HyPA using HyTech [12], Φ-Calculus using SPHIN [29]), while we focus on exploiting compositionality in the proof.

Hybrid Programs. Quantified hybrid programs enable a compositional verification of hybrid systems with an arbitrary number of components [20], if they all have the same structure (e.g., many cars, or many robots). They were used to split monolithic hybrid program models into smaller parts to show that adaptive cruise control prevents collisions for an arbitrary number of cars on a highway [10]. We focus on different components. Similarly, the approach in [15] presents a component-based approach limited to traffic flow and global contracts.

Our approach extends [16], which was restricted to contracts over constant ranges. Such global contracts are well-suited for certain use cases, where the change of a port's value does not matter for safety, such as the traffic flow models of [15]. However, for systems such as the remote-controlled robot obstacle avoidance from our running example (cf. Sect. 3.1), which require knowledge about the change of certain values, global contracts only work for considerably more conservative models (e.g., robot and obstacle must stay in fixed globally known regions, since the obstacle's last position is unknown). Contracts with change and delay allow more liberal component interaction.

6   Conclusion and Future Work

Component-based modeling and verification for hybrid systems splits monolithic system verification into proofs about components with local responsibilities. It reduces verification effort compared to proving monolithic models, while change and delay contracts preserve crucial properties about component behavior to allow liberal component interaction.

Change contracts relate a port's previous value to its current value (i.e., the change since the last port transmission), while delay contracts additionally relate to the delay between measurements. Properties of components, described by component contracts and verified using KeYmaera X, transfer to composed systems of multiple compatible components without re-verification of the entire system. We have shown the applicability of our approach on a running example and three existing case studies, which furthermore demonstrated the potential reduction of verification effort. We implemented our approach as a KeYmaera X tactic, which automatically verifies composite systems based on components with verified contracts without increasing the trusted prover core.

For future work, we plan to (i) introduce further composition operations (e.g., error-prone transmission), and (ii) provide support for system decomposition by discovery of output properties (i.e., find abstraction for port behavior).

References

1. Alur, R., Courcoubetis, C., Henzinger, T.A., Ho, P.-H.: Hybrid automata: an algorithmic approach to the specification and verification of hybrid systems. In: Grossman, R.L., Nerode, A., Ravn, A.P., Rischel, H. (eds.) HS 1991-1992. LNCS, vol. 736, pp. 209–229. Springer, Heidelberg (1993). doi:10.1007/3-540-57318-6_30
2. Aştefănoaei, L., Bensalem, S., Bozga, M.: A compositional approach to the verification of hybrid systems. In: Ábrahám, E., Bonsangue, M., Johnsen, E.B. (eds.) Theory and Practice of Formal Methods. LNCS, vol. 9660, pp. 88–103. Springer, Cham (2016). doi:10.1007/978-3-319-30734-3_8
3. Benvenuti, L., Bresolin, D., Collins, P., Ferrari, A., Geretti, L., Villa, T.: Assume-guarantee verification of nonlinear hybrid systems with Ariadne. Int. J. Robust Nonlinear Control 24(4), 699–724 (2014)
4. Bohrer, B., Rahli, V., Vukotic, I., Völp, M., Platzer, A.: Formally verified differential dynamic logic. In: Bertot, Y., Vafeiadis, V. (eds.) Proceedings of the 6th ACM SIGPLAN Conference on Certified Programs and Proofs, pp. 208–221. ACM (2017)
5. Damm, W., Dierks, H., Oehlerking, J., Pnueli, A.: Towards component based design of hybrid systems: safety and stability. In: Manna, Z., Peled, D.A. (eds.) Time for Verification. LNCS, vol. 6200, pp. 96–143. Springer, Heidelberg (2010). doi:10.1007/978-3-642-13754-9_6
6. Frehse, G., Han, Z., Krogh, B.: Assume-guarantee reasoning for hybrid I/O-automata by over-approximation of continuous interaction. In: 43rd IEEE Conference on Decision and Control, CDC, vol. 1, pp. 479–484 (2004)
7. Fulton, N., Mitsch, S., Quesel, J.-D., Völp, M., Platzer, A.: KeYmaera X: an axiomatic tactical theorem prover for hybrid systems. In: Felty, A.P., Middeldorp, A. (eds.) CADE 2015. LNCS (LNAI), vol. 9195, pp. 527–538. Springer, Cham (2015). doi:10.1007/978-3-319-21401-6_36
8. Henzinger, T.A.: The theory of hybrid automata. In: Proceedings, 11th Annual IEEE Symposium on Logic in Computer Science, pp. 278–292. IEEE Computer Society (1996)
9. Henzinger, T.A., Minea, M., Prabhu, V.: Assume-guarantee reasoning for hierarchical hybrid systems. In: Di Benedetto, M.D., Sangiovanni-Vincentelli, A. (eds.) HSCC 2001. LNCS, vol. 2034, pp. 275–290. Springer, Heidelberg (2001). doi:10.1007/3-540-45351-2_24
10. Loos, S.M., Platzer, A., Nistor, L.: Adaptive cruise control: hybrid, distributed, and now formally verified. In: Butler, M., Schulte, W. (eds.) FM 2011. LNCS, vol. 6664, pp. 42–56. Springer, Heidelberg (2011). doi:10.1007/978-3-642-21437-0_6

11. Lynch, N.A., Segala, R., Vaandrager, F.W.: Hybrid I/O automata. Inf. Comput. **185**(1), 105–157 (2003)

12. Man, K.L., Reniers, M.A., Cuijpers, P.J.L.: Case studies in the hybrid process algebra Hypa. Int. J. Softw. Eng. Knowl. Eng. **15**(2), 299–306 (2005)

13. Mitsch, S., Ghorbal, K., Platzer, A.: On provably safe obstacle avoidance for autonomous robotic ground vehicles. In: Newman, P., Fox, D., Hsu, D. (eds.) Robotics: Science and Systems IX (2013)

14. de Moura, L., Bjørner, N.: Z3: an efficient SMT solver. In: Ramakrishnan, C.R., Rehof, J. (eds.) TACAS 2008. LNCS, vol. 4963, pp. 337–340. Springer, Heidelberg (2008). doi:10.1007/978-3-540-78800-3_24

15. Müller, A., Mitsch, S., Platzer, A.: Verified traffic networks: component-based verification of cyber-physical flow systems. In: 18th International Conference on Intelligent Transportation Systems, pp. 757–764 (2015)

16. Müller, A., Mitsch, S., Retschitzegger, W., Schwinger, W., Platzer, A.: A component-based approach to hybrid systems safety verification. In: Ábrahám, E., Huisman, M. (eds.) IFM 2016. LNCS, vol. 9681, pp. 441–456. Springer, Cham (2016). doi:10.1007/978-3-319-33693-0_28

17. Müller, A., Mitsch, S., Retschitzegger, W., Schwinger, W., Platzer, A.: Change and delay contracts for hybrid system component verification. Technical report CMU-CS-17-100, Carnegie Mellon (2017)

18. Cuijpers, P.J.L., Reniers, M.A.: Hybrid process algebra. J. Log. Algebr. Program. **62**(2), 191–245 (2005)

19. Platzer, A.: Differential-algebraic dynamic logic for differential-algebraic programs. J. Log. Comput. **20**(1), 309–352 (2010)

20. Platzer, A.: Quantified differential dynamic logic for distributed hybrid systems. In: Dawar, A., Veith, H. (eds.) CSL 2010. LNCS, vol. 6247, pp. 469–483. Springer, Heidelberg (2010). doi:10.1007/978-3-642-15205-4_36

21. Platzer, A.: A complete axiomatization of quantified differential dynamic logic for distributed hybrid systems. Logical Methods Comput. Sci. **8**(4), 1–44 (2012)

22. Platzer, A.: The complete proof theory of hybrid systems. In: Proceedings of the 27th Annual IEEE Symposium on Logic in Computer Science, pp. 541–550. IEEE Computer Society (2012)

23. Platzer, A.: Logics of dynamical systems science. In: Proceedings of the 27th Annual IEEE Symposium on Logic in Computer Science, pp. 13–24. IEEE Computer Society (2012)

24. Platzer, A.: The structure of differential invariants and differential cut elimination. Logical Methods Comput. Sci. **8**(4), 1–38 (2012)

25. Platzer, A.: A complete uniform substitution calculus for differential dynamic logic. J. Autom. Reas. 1–47 (2016). doi:10.1007/s10817-016-9385-1

26. Platzer, A., Quesel, J.-D.: European train control system: a case study in formal verification. In: Breitman, K., Cavalcanti, A. (eds.) ICFEM 2009. LNCS, vol. 5885, pp. 246–265. Springer, Heidelberg (2009). doi:10.1007/978-3-642-10373-5_13

27. Schiffelers, R.R.H., van Beek, D.A., Man, K.L., Reniers, M.A., Rooda, J.E.: Formal semantics of hybrid Chi. In: Larsen, K.G., Niebert, P. (eds.) FORMATS 2003. LNCS, vol. 2791, pp. 151–165. Springer, Heidelberg (2004). doi:10.1007/978-3-540-40903-8_12

28. Rounds, W.C., Song, H.: The Ö-calculus: a language for distributed control of reconfigurable embedded systems. In: Maler, O., Pnueli, A. (eds.) HSCC 2003. LNCS, vol. 2623, pp. 435–449. Springer, Heidelberg (2003). doi:10.1007/3-540-36580-X_32

29. Song, H., Compton, K.J., Rounds, W.C.: SPHIN: a model checker for reconfigurable hybrid systems based on SPIN. Electr. Notes Theor. Comput. Sci. **145**, 167–183 (2006)

30. Xinyu, C., Huiqun, Y., Xin, X.: Verification of hybrid Chi model for cyber-physical systems using PHAVer. In: Barolli, L., You, I., Xhafa, F., Leu, F.Y., Chen, H.C. (eds.) 7th International Conference on Innovative Mobile and Internet Services in Ubiquitous Computing, pp. 122–128. IEEE Computer Society (2013)

Precise Version Control of Trees
with Line-Based Version Control Systems

Dimitar Asenov[1], Balz Guenat[1], Peter Müller[1(✉)], and Martin Otth[2]

[1] Department of Computer Science, ETH Zurich, Zurich, Switzerland
{dimitar.asenov,peter.mueller}@inf.ethz.ch, guenatb@student.ethz.ch
[2] Ergon Informatik AG, Zurich, Switzerland
martin.otth@ergon.ch

Abstract. Version control of tree structures, ubiquitous in software engineering, is typically performed on a textual encoding of the trees, rather than the trees directly. Applying standard line-based diff and merge algorithms to such encodings leads to inaccurate diffs, unnecessary conflicts, and incorrect merges. To address these problems, we propose novel algorithms for computing precise diffs between two versions of a tree and for three-way merging of trees. Unlike most other approaches for version control of structured data, our approach integrates with mainstream version control systems. Our merge algorithm can be customized for specific application domains to further improve merge results. An evaluation of our approach on abstract syntax trees from popular Java projects shows substantially improved merge results compared to Git.

Keywords: Version control · Trees · Structured editor · Software evolution

1 Introduction

Tree structures such as XML, JSON, and source code are ubiquitous in software engineering, but support for precise version control of trees is lacking. Mainstream version control systems (VCSs) such as Git, Mercurial, and SVN treat all data as sequences of lines of text. Standard diff and merge algorithms disregard the structure of the data they manipulate, which has three major drawbacks for versioning trees. First, standard line-based diff algorithms may lead to *inaccurate and confusing diffs*, for instance when differences in formatting (e.g., added indentation) blend with real changes or when lines are incorrectly matched across different sub-trees (e.g., across method boundaries in a program). Inaccurate diffs do not only waste developers' time, but may also corrupt the result of subsequent merge operations. Second, standard merge algorithms may lead to *unnecessary conflicts*, which occur for incompatible changes to the formatting (e.g., breaking a line at different places), but also for more substantial changes such as merging two revisions that each add an element to an un-ordered list (for instance, a method at the end of the same class). Unnecessary conflicts

M. Huisman and J. Rubin (Eds.): FASE 2017, LNCS 10202, pp. 152–169, 2017.
DOI: 10.1007/978-3-662-54494-5_9

could be merged automatically, but instead require manual intervention from the developer. Third, standard merge algorithms may lead to *incorrect merges*; for instance, if two developers move the same tree node to two different places, a line-based merge might incorrectly duplicate the node. Incorrect merges lead to errors that developers need to detect and fix manually.

To solve these problems, we propose a novel approach to versioning trees. Our approach builds on a standard line-based VCS (in our case, Git), but provides diff and merge algorithms that utilize the tree structure to provide accurate diffs, conflict detection, and merging. In contrast to VCSs that require a dedicated backend for trees [14,15,21,24,25], employing a standard VCS allows developers to use established infrastructures and workflows (such as GitHub or BitBucket) and to version trees and text files such as documentation in the same VCS. Our diff algorithm relies on the optimized line-based diff of the underlying VCS, but utilizes the tree structure to accurately report changes. Building on the diff algorithm, we designed a three-way merge algorithm that reduces unnecessary conflicts and incorrect merges by using the tree structure and, optionally, domain knowledge such as whether the order of elements in a list is relevant.

Diff and merge algorithms rely on matching different revisions of a tree to recognize commonalities and changes. One option to obtain such a matching is to associate each tree node with a unique ID that remains unchanged across revisions. This approach yields precise matchings and makes it easy to recognize changed and moved nodes, but requires a custom storage format and support from an editor such as MPS [30] or Envision [5]. Alternatively, one can use traditional textual encodings of trees without IDs (e.g., source code to represent an AST) and compute matchings using an algorithm such as ChangeDistiller [10] or GumTree [9]. However, such algorithms require significant time and produce results that are approximate and, thus, lead to less precise diffs and merges. Our approach supports both options; it benefits from the precise matchings provided by node IDs when available, but can also utilize the results of matching algorithms and, thus, be used with standard editors. We will present the approach for a storage format that includes node IDs, but our evaluation shows that even with approximate matchings computed on standard Java code, our approach achieves substantially better results than a standard line-based merge.

The contributions of this paper are:

- A textual encoding of generic trees that enables their precise version control within standard line-based VCSs such as Git.
- A novel algorithm for computing the difference between two versions of a tree based on the diff reported by a line-based VCS.
- A novel algorithm for a three-way merge of trees, which allows the customization of conflict detection and resolution.
- An implementation of the algorithms in the Envision IDE and an evaluation on several popular open-source Java code bases.

The rest of this paper is structured as follows. In Sect. 2, we present a textual encoding of trees and a corresponding diff algorithm, which builds on a line-based diff. We describe a generic algorithm for merging trees and two customizations that improve the merge result in Sect. 3. In Sect. 4, we discuss the results of our evaluation. We discuss related work in Sect. 5 and conclude in Sect. 6. More details of the algorithms can be found in the PhD thesis of the first author [6].

2   Tree Versioning with a Line-Based VCS

The algorithms we designed work on a general tree structure. In order to enable precise version control of trees, we assume, without loss of generality, that each tree *node* is a tuple with the following elements:

- *id*: a globally unique ID. This ID is used to match and compare nodes from different versions and track node movement. IDs can be randomly generated, as long as matching nodes from different versions have the same ID, which can be achieved by using a tree-matching algorithm such as GumTree [9]. We use a standard 128-bit universally unique identifier (UUID).
- *parentId*: the ID of the parent node. The parent ID of the root node is a null UUID. All other nodes must have a parentId that matches the ID of an existing node.
- *label*: a name that is unique among sibling nodes. The label is essentially the name of the edge from parent to child node. This could be any string or number, e.g., 1, 2, 3, ... for the children of nodes representing lists.
- *type*: an arbitrary type name from the target domain. For example, types of AST nodes could be `Method` or `IntegerLiteral`. Types enable additional customization of the version control algorithms, used to improve conflict detection and resolution. In domains without different node types, one type can be used for all nodes.
- *value*: an optional value.

A *valid tree* is a set of nodes which form a tree and meet the requirements above.

2.1   Textual Encoding of Valid Trees

In order to efficiently perform version control of trees within a line-based VCS, we encode trees in a specific text format, which enables using the existing line-based diff in the first of two stages for computing the changes between two tree versions. A valid tree is encoded into text files as illustrated in Fig. 1. The key property of the encoding is that a single line contains the encoding of exactly one tree node with all its elements. In Fig. 1, each line encodes a node's label, type, UUID, the UUID of the parent node, and the optional value in that order. A reserved node type *External* indicates that a subtree is stored in a different file (Fig. 1b).

This encoding allows two versions of a set of files to be efficiently compared using a standard line-based diff. The different lines reported by such a diff correspond directly to a set of nodes that is guaranteed to be an overapproximation of the nodes that have changed between the two versions of the encoded tree.

```
 2 Method {9c2c..} {e0b6..}
   modifiers Modifier {8842..} {9c2c..} 1          12 Class {5414..} {425d..}
   name Name {3269..} {9c2c..} foo                    methods List {e0b6..} {5414..}
   body StatementList {1023..} {9c2c..}               0 External {e239..} {e0b6..}
     0 If {f3c2..} {1023..}                           1 External {5db1..} {e0b6..}
       condition BinOp {b0a0..} {f3c2..}              2 External {9c2c..} {e0b6..}
         left Text {f7c3..} {b0a0..} two\nlines
                                                                   (b)
                  (a)
```

Fig. 1. (a) An example encoding of an AST fragment. For brevity, only the first 2 bytes of UUIDs are shown here. (b) A file that references external files, which contain the subtrees of a class's methods. The last line refers to the file from (a). At most two lines in different files may have the same ID, and one of them must be of type *External*.

For efficient parsing, we indent each child node and insert children after their parents (Fig. 1), enabling simple stack-based parsing. The names of the files that comprise a single tree is irrelevant, but for quickly finding subtrees, it is advisable to include the UUID of the root of each file's subtree in the file name.

2.2 Diff Algorithm

The diff algorithm computes the delta between two versions of a tree (T_{old} and T_{new}). The delta is a set of changes, where each change represents the evolution of one node and is a tuple consisting of:

- *oldNode*: the node tuple from T_{old}, if it exists (node was not inserted).
- *newNode*: the node tuple from T_{new}, if it exists (node was not deleted).
- *kind*: the kind of the change – one of *Insertion*, *Deletion*, *Move* (change of parent and possibly label, type, or value), *Stationary* (no change of parent, but change in at least one of label, type, or value).

These elements provide the full information necessary to report precisely how a node has changed. The encoding from Sect. 2.1 enables an efficient two-stage algorithm for computing the delta between two versions of a tree. The operation of the algorithm is illustrated in Fig. 2.

The **first stage** computes two sets of nodes *oldNodes* $\subseteq T_{old}$ and *newNodes* $\subseteq T_{new}$, which overapproximate the nodes that have changed between T_{old} and T_{new}. The sets are computed by comparing the encodings of T_{old} and T_{new} using a standard line-based diff [20, 22, 29]. Given two text files, a line-based diff computes a longest common subsequence (LCS), where each line is treated as an atomic element. The LCS is a subset of all identical lines between T_{old} and T_{new}. The diff outputs the lines that are not in the LCS, thus overapproximating changes: lines from the "old" file are marked as deleted and lines from the "new" file are marked as inserted. In the middle of Fig. 2, lines B, E, G, H, and D on the left are marked as removed and lines B', E', G, H, and X on the right are marked as inserted. The combined diff output for all files is two sets of removed and inserted lines. The nodes corresponding to these two sets, ignoring nodes of type External, are the inputs to the second stage of the diff algorithm.

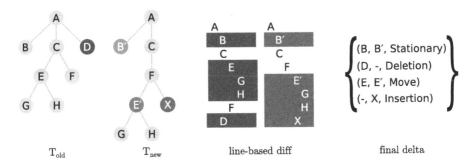

Fig. 2. A tree modification and the outputs of the two stages of the diff algorithm.

The **second stage** (Algorithm 2.1) filters the overapproximated nodes and computes the final, precise delta between T_{old} and T_{new}. The algorithm essentially compares nodes with the same id from *oldNodes* and *newNodes* and if they are different, adds a corresponding change to the delta. A node from oldNodes might be identical to a node from newNodes, for example, if its corresponding line has moved, but is otherwise unchanged. This is the case for nodes G and H in Fig. 2, where the final delta consist only of real changes to the nodes B, D, E, and X. This is in contrast to a line-based diff, which will also report G and H as changed, even though they have not.

In the absence of unique IDs stored with the tree, it is possible to compute matching nodes using a tree match algorithm, enabling our diff and merge algorithms to be used for traditional encodings of trees, such as Java files. To achieve this, the first stage needs to be replaced so that it parses the input files, computes a tree matching, and assigns new IDs according to the matching.

```
1: function TREEDIFFSTAGETWO(oldNodes, newNodes)
2:     changes ← ∅
3:     for all {(old, new) ∈ (oldNodes × newNodes) | old.id=new.id ∧ old≠new} do
4:         if old.parentId = new.parentId then
5:             changes ← changes ∪ {(old, new, Stationary)}
6:         else
7:             changes ← changes ∪ {(old, new, Move)}
8:         end
9:     end
10:    for all {old ∈ oldNodes | old.id ∉ IDs(newNodes)} do
11:        changes ← changes ∪ {(old, NIL, Deletion)}
12:    end
13:    for all {new ∈ newNodes | new.id ∉ IDs(oldNodes)} do
14:        changes ← changes ∪ {(NIL, new, Insertion)}
15:    end
16:    return changes
17: end
```

Algorithm 2.1. The second stage of the *TreeDiff* algorithm. IDs is the set of all identifiers of nodes from the input set. A more detailed version of this algorithm and a proof of correctness can be found in [12].

The described diff algorithm eliminates (with unique IDs), or greatly reduces (using a tree matching algorithm) inaccurate diffs. This is because the formatting of the encoding is irrelevant, changes are expressed in term of tree nodes, and moved nodes are tracked, even across files. The diff provides a basis for improved merges, discussed next.

3 Merging Trees and Domain-Specific Customizations

Building on the diff algorithm from Sect. 2.2, we designed an algorithm for merging two tree revisions T_A and T_B given their common ancestor T_{base}. At the core of the merge is the change graph – a graph of changes performed by the two revisions, which includes conflicts and dependencies. In this section, we will first describe the change graph and how it is used to merge files, and then we will outline additional merge customizations, which use knowledge about the domain of the tree to improve conflict detection and resolution. Unlike the diff algorithm, the merge does not build on its line-based analog, which is unaware of the tree structure and may produce invalid results. For example, if two revisions move the same node (line) to two different parents, which are located in different parts of a file or in different files, a line-based algorithm would simply keep both lines, incorrectly duplicating the subtree, whereas our algorithm will report a conflict.

3.1 Change Graph and Merge Algorithm

The purpose of the *change graph* (CG) is to bring together changes from two diverging revisions and facilitate the creation of a merged tree. The nodes of the CG are changes, similar to the ones reported by the diff. The changes are connected with two types of edges, which constrain when changes may be applied. A change may require another change to be applied first, expressed as a directed *dependency edge*. For example, a change inserting a node might depend on the change inserting the parent node. Two changes may be in conflict with each other, expressed as an undirected *conflict edge*. For example, if both revisions change the same node differently, these changes will be in conflict. An example change graph is illustrated in Fig. 3.

To merge T_A and T_B into a tree T_{merged}, first an inverse topological ordering of the CG is computed using the dependency edges. Changes are applied according to this ordering, if possible. A change is applicable if it does not depend on any other change and has no conflict edges. Changes that form cycles in the CG may be applied together, in one atomic step, provided that all changes (i) have no conflict edges; (ii) are made by the same revision or by both revisions simultaneously; and (iii) do not depend on any change outside the cycle. Essentially, changes in such cycles are independent of other changes and are compatible with both revisions, making them safe to apply. These restrictions ensure that applying changes preserves the validity of the tree (see Sect. 7.3.1 in [6] for details).

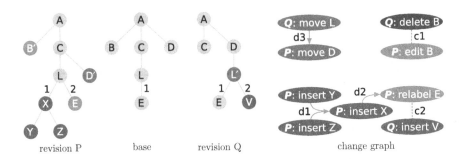

Fig. 3. A base tree with two modifying revisions and the corresponding CG. Each edge in the CG is labeled with the dependency or conflict type that the edge represents.

Applied changes are removed from the CG along with any incoming dependency edges. Once all applicable changes have been applied, any remaining changes represent conflicts and will be reported to the user. Next, we explain how the CG is constructed.

Merge Changes. A *merge change* is a tuple that extends the change tuple from the diff algorithm with one new element, *revisions*, which indicates which revisions make this change: *RevA*, *RevB*, or *Both*. The nodes of the CG are the merge changes obtained by running the diff algorithm twice to compute the delta between T_{base} and T_A and between T_{base} and T_B, respectively. First, each change from the two deltas is associated with either *RevA* or *RevB* to create a corresponding merge change. Then, we organize the elements of a tree node into two *element groups*: (i) parent and label; and (ii) type and value. Each group contains tuple elements whose modification by different revisions is a conflict. Any merge changes that modify both element groups are split into two merge changes: one for each element group. For example, if a node is moved to a new parent and its value is modified, this will appear as two separate and independent merge changes within the CG. This separation reduces conflicts and dependencies in the CG, since the two groups are independent. Finally, any identical changes made by different revisions are combined into a single merge change with *revisions=Both*, which ensures that identical changes are applied only once.

Dependencies Between Merge Changes. A dependency $X \rightarrow Y$ means that change X cannot be applied before Y, and is the first of two means that restrict applicable changes. Dependencies prevent three cases of tree structure violations.

(d1) orphan nodes: (a) Before a change *IM* inserts or moves a node N, N's parent destination node P must exist. If P does not already exist in T_{base}, then there must be an insertion change I, which inserts it. An edge $IM \rightarrow I$ is added to indicate that I must be applied before *IM* can be applied. In Fig. 3, nodes

Y and Z depend on the insertion of X. (b) Before a change D deletes a node N, all of N's children must be deleted or moved. An edge $D \rightarrow DM$ is added between D and each change DM that moves or deletes a child of N. In both (a) and (b), the changes I and DM are guaranteed to exist if they are necessary, because the merge changes were computed from the deltas of valid trees. Note that dependencies that prevent orphan nodes cannot form cycles on their own.

(d2) clashing labels: Before a change IMR inserts, moves, or relabels (modifies the label of) a node N, there must be no sibling at the destination of N with the same label. If a node with the same label as N's final label exists in T_{base} at the destination parent of N then there must be a change DMR that deletes, moves, or relabels that sibling. An edge $IMR \rightarrow DMR$ is added to the CG. In Fig. 3, node X depends on the relabeling of E. Such dependencies may form cycles. For example, swapping two elements in a list yields two relabel changes, where each change depends on the other.

(d3) cycles: If a change M_N moves a node N, N must not become its own ancestor. Such a situation occurs, for example, if a revision A moves an if-statement IF_1 into an if-statement IF_2, and revision B moves IF_2 into IF_1. To prevent such issues, move changes are applied only if the destination subtree does not need to be moved. This is enforced using dependencies. If M_N moves N to a subtree that needs to be moved, let M_P be the change that moves the subtree. An edge $M_N \rightarrow M_P$ is added to the CG. Move changes from different revisions may create dependency chains that form a cycle in the CG. For example, the move of IF_1 will depend on the move of IF_2, which will itself depend on the move of IF_1. Such a cycle means that the two revisions perform incompatible moves and the changes from the cycle cannot be applied. Move changes from different revisions do not always result in a cycle. For example, in Fig. 3, the move of L depends on the move of D, which is independent.

Conflicting Merge Changes. Conflicts that would result in a node becoming its own ancestor are indirectly represented in the CG in the form of dependency cycles described above. Other conflicts cannot be expressed with dependencies and appear directly as conflict edges, which are the second means for restricting change application. There are three cases of direct conflicts.

(c1) same node: If two revisions make non-identical changes X and Y to the same node, these changes may be conflicting. Deletions conflict with all other changes. Other changes conflict only with changes of the same element group. Conflicting changes are connected with an undirected edge $X \sim Y$ in the CG. An example of such a conflict is the modification and deletion of B in Fig. 3.

(c2) label clash: If a change IMR_N inserts, moves, or relabels a node N, and another change IMR_Q inserts, moves, or relabels a node Q such that N and Q have identical final labels and parent nodes, the two changes are in conflict. An edge $IMR_N \sim IMR_Q$ is added to the CG. In Fig. 3, such a conflict is the relabeling of E and the insertion of V.

(c3) deletion clash: If a change D_N deletes a node N, and another change IM_Q inserts or moves a node Q as a child of N, the two are in conflict. An edge $D_N \sim IM_Q$ is added to the CG.

In contrast to line-based merges, applying changes using the CG prevents incorrect merges by considering the tree structure. The algorithm, as described so far, has no knowledge about the domain of the tree, and misses opportunities for improved merges and better error reporting. Next, we explain customizations, that improve the merge results and report potential semantic issues.

3.2   Domain-Specific Customizations

Merging two tree revisions without any domain knowledge, as described so far, can lead to suboptimal merges. Figures 3 and 4 illustrate one such example, where revision P inserts a node X in the beginning of list L and revision Q inserts a node V at the end. These two changes conflict, because the label of E in P is identical to the label of V in Q. Despite this conflict, intuitively these changes can be merged by relabeling V. To achieve better merge results, we allow the merge process to be customized by taking domain knowledge into account. Customizations use domain knowledge, such as the semantics of specific node types or values, to tweak the CG, eliminating conflicts and dependencies, and thus, enabling additional changes to be applied. Customizations may also produce *review items*, which are messages that inform the user of a potential semantic issue with the final merge. Review items have two advantages over conflicts. First, unlike changes in a conflict or their depending changes (even if not in a conflict), which are not applicable, review items are not part of the CG and do not prevent the application of changes. Applying more changes is desirable because the final merge more closely represents both revisions and the user has to review issues with only a selected group of nodes, instead of manually exploring many unapplied changes. Second, review items provide semantic information to the user, making it easier to take corrective action, unlike conflicts, which represent generic constraints on the tree structure. Similarly, review

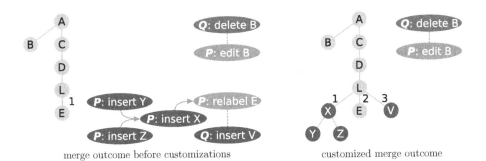

merge outcome before customizations   customized merge outcome

Fig. 4. The resulting T_{merged} and CG after applying all possible changes from Fig. 3 (left) and after additional customizations (right).

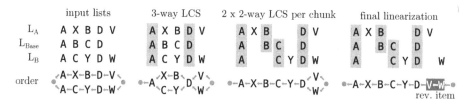

Fig. 5. Computing a total order for the elements of a merged list. Stable chunks have a light-gray background. At the end, V and W are linearized and added to a review item. In the merged list, B and C will be removed to reflect changes from revisions.

items are preferable to conflicts in line-based merges, because review items are more focused and provide semantic information. Next, we present two examples of customizations, which we have found useful for achieving high-quality merges.

List-Merge Customization. Data from many domains (e.g., ASTs, UML models) has list entities. Merging lists is challenging [13,28], as it is not trivial to determine the order of the merged elements and to detect and resolve conflicts. In addition, the CG often contains label clash conflicts in lists (e.g., for nodes E and V in Fig. 4), which are usually easy to resolve automatically. We developed the List-Merge customization, which is crucial for merging list nodes well. Essentially, the customization computes a total order of all list elements from both revisions. This total order is used to relabel all elements, giving each element a unique label. Thus, all conflicts or dependencies due to previously clashing labels are removed from the CG, allowing many more changes to be merged. Next, we describe the computation of the total order and how ambiguities are handled.

The total order is computed in three steps as illustrated in Fig. 5. In the **first step**, a three-way longest common subsequence (LCS) between L_{Base}, L_A, and L_B is computed and used to create an alternating sequence of stable and unstable chunks. The *stable chunks* are a partition of the LCS – elements in a single chunk are adjacent in all lists. There are two stable chunks in Fig. 5: $[A]$ and $[D]$. An *unstable chunk* consists of one element span per list, each span containing elements that are not in the LCS. There are two unstable chunks in Fig. 5: $[XB, BC, CY]$ and $[V, \epsilon, W]$. Elements from different chunks are totally ordered using the order of the chunks, e.g., A before X and D. Elements from the same stable chunk are totally ordered using their order within the chunk. In the **second step**, for each unstable chunk C, two two-way LCSs $lcs_a = LCS(C_{base}, C_a)$ and $lcs_b = LCS(C_{base}, C_b)$ are computed. Elements from lcs_a are totally ordered with respect to elements from lcs_b using the order in C_{base}. In Fig. 5 these are B and C. The remaining elements from C_a and C_b are ordered with respect to elements from lcs_a and lcs_b, respectively. Such elements are totally ordered using the order from one revision, if there are no elements from the other revision in the corresponding chunk (X and Y in Fig. 5). Otherwise, the elements are not totally ordered (V and W in Fig. 5). In the **third step**, unordered elements are linearized in an arbitrary order. If the list represents an ordered collection within the domain, a review item is created to inform the user of the ambiguity.

The List-Merge customization brings essential domain knowledge about lists to the merge algorithm. The customization not only resolves many conflicts automatically, but also reports merge ambiguities on a semantic level. Thus, it lets developers deal with less conflicts and do so more easily, saving time.

Conflict Unit Customization. Our merge algorithm is able to merge changes at the very fine-grained level of tree nodes, which is not desirable in some domains. For example, if $x < y$ in an AST is changed to $x \leq y$ in one revision, and to $x < y + 1$ in another, these two changes can be merged as $x \leq y + 1$, which is not intended. A common case where fine-grained merges might result in semantic issues is when changes affect nodes that are "very close" according to the semantics of the tree domain. We designed the Conflict Unit (CU) customization to detect such situations. In essence, the customization partitions the tree into small regions called CUs and creates review items for each CU that is changed by both revisions. The customization does not alter the change graph.

The CU customization is parametrized by a set of node types – the *CU types*. The *conflict root* of a node is its closest reflexive ancestor of a CU type. The tree root is always a conflict root. The set of nodes that have the same conflict root constitute a CU (see Fig. 6). If two revisions change nodes from the same CU, there is a potential for a semantic issue and this is reported with a review item.

With an appropriate choice of CU types, the CU customization can be useful in identifying potential semantic issues. For example, in ASTs, if statements are CU types, like in Fig. 6, a change in one statement is semantically independent from a change in another statement, but two changes in the subtree of the same statement will result in a review item. In this setting, if a developer changes one part of the $i \geq 0$ expression, while another developer changes another part, these changes will no longer be silently merged, but a semantic issue will be reported.

Structure- and semantics-based review items are more precise and meaningful than the line-based conflicts produced by standard algorithms. A line-based

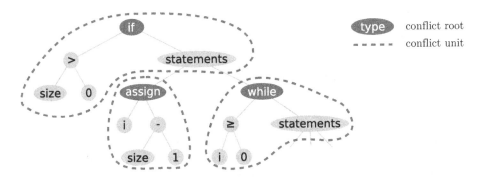

Fig. 6. A tree with three conflict units.

conflict might incorrectly arise due to compatible changes (e.g., moving a declaration in one revision and adding a comment in another revision) or it might be due to formatting (e.g., renaming a method in one revision and moving the opening brace to a new line in another revision). In contrast, our CU approach is precise, predictable, and uses domain knowledge to report issues on a semantic level.

4   Evaluation and Discussion

To evaluate our approach, we implemented our version control algorithms in the Envision IDE [5]. Even though Envision supports unique node IDs, we use Gumtree [9] to evaluate our approach on large existing Java projects to show its applicability on large trees with a long history. We inspected the default branch of the most popular (having more than 10000 stars) Java projects on GitHub, 19 in total. Six of the projects did not contain any merges of Java files. In the remaining 13 projects, we evaluate each merge of a Java file by comparing the merge results of Git and our implementation. We focus on the merge here since the merge operation depends on the diff and thus, reflects its quality. The results are presented in Table 1. All tests were run on an Intel i7-2600K CPU running at 3.4 GHz, 32 GB RAM, and an SSD.

A *divergent merge* (DM) is one that results in conflicts (C) or one where the automatically merged file is different from the file committed by the developer. One exception are successful automatic merges in Envision that only differ from the developer committed version by the order of methods or import declarations. Since this order is semantically irrelevant, we do not consider such merges divergent – they are counted as *order difference* (OD). For Envision, we also list the number of files whose merge produced review items due to linearized list elements (RI_l) or changes to the same conflict unit by two revisions (RI_{cu}). For conflict unit types we use all statement and declaration node types. The total and average merge times are reported for both tools (merge and avg. merge). Merging Java sources with Envision incurs a significant overhead (ovrhd.) in addition to the merge time, because (i) the sources have to be parsed, (ii) the different revisions have to be matched to the base using Gumtree, and (iii) these two-way matchings are tweaked to enable a three-way merge. Almost all of this overhead can be avoided by using IDs directly stored on disk.

Tree-based merging results in significantly fewer divergent merges, 717, compared to the standard line-based approach, 1100. The difference in conflicts is even more substantial, with 362 for the tree-based approach, and 1039 for Git. Our approach also reports a significant number of files with review items for lists, 222, and conflict units, 662. Unlike textual conflicts, review items describe the semantic issue they reflect and report the minimal set of nodes that are affected, which makes it easier for developers to understand and act on review items.

To get more insight, we manually investigated all 46 cases of Envision's diverging merges in the RxJava project. All of these merges also diverge when using Git. There are 34 merges with real conflicts or merges where the developer

Table 1. Comparison between merges by Git (G) and Envision (E). DM – divergent merge; C – merge with conflicts; OD – merge where only order differs; RI – review item (l – due to linearized list elements, cu – due to multiple changes in a CU).

project	all merges	number of files							merge [s]		ovrhd. [min]	avg.merge [ms]	
		DM		C		OD	RI_l	RI_{cu}					
		G	E	G	E	E	E	E	G	E	E	G	E
ReactiveX/RxJava	354	82	46	74	12	19	22	38	3	125	122	9	353
elastic/ elasticsearch	2677	863	547	821	281	29	157	525	10	276	266	4	103
square/retrofit	49	14	13	12	10	0	3	12	0	3	4	3	53
square/okhttp	163	4	4	4	1	0	1	11	1	23	22	4	138
nostra13/Android-Universal-Image-Loader	56	15	10	14	6	0	4	8	0	2	4	5	36
iluwatar/java-design-patterns	59	2	1	2	0	0	1	1	0	0	3	5	3
JakeWharton/butterknife	18	0	0	0	0	0	0	0	0	1	2	6	73
greenrobot/EventBus	10	4	3	4	2	0	0	4	0	1	1	7	54
square/picasso	40	0	0	0	0	0	0	3	0	3	4	5	75
PhilJay/MPAndroidChart	169	32	35	24	20	0	9	21	1	13	15	4	76
square/leakcanary	13	1	0	1	0	0	0	2	0	0	1	7	31
bumptech/glide	76	69	54	69	29	2	22	32	0	3	6	3	39
spring-projects/spring-framework	339	14	4	14	1	0	3	5	1	2	19	3	5
total	4023	1100	717	1039	362	50	222	662	16	452	469	5	80

made a semantic change, neither of which can be automatically handled. In the remaining 12 cases, we observed two reasons for divergence in Envision.

First, in six cases the result of a tree merge was, in fact, correct, but the version committed by the developer was incorrect. This occurred when a Git merge results in a conflict which the developer resolves incorrectly, even though the resulting code compiles. For example, a conflict marker (<<<<<<< HEAD) inserted by Git was forgotten inside a block comment. Another example is the accidental omission of an @Test annotation which appeared just before a conflict marker. This omission potentially disabled one of the test cases in the code and went unnoticed for nearly three years until the RxJava developers accepted our patch for fixing it. Our approach automatically merges all of these cases correctly.

Second, six merges diverge due to the suboptimal matchings produced by GumTree. For example, if a particular Java import declaration is present in the base version, but is deleted in both revisions, GumTree may match the deleted import to two different newly inserted imports from the different revisions. Our merge algorithm detects this as a conflict and fails to merge the file.

In terms of run-time, merging files with Envision is, on average, 16 times slower compared to Git. Nevertheless, Envision still allows merging at a rate of 12.5 files a second, which is significantly faster than manually resolving conflicts.

However, if the files are not stored using the format we described in Sect. 2.1, and require parsing and tree-matching, there is significant overhead, which further slows down Envision by a factor of 60. In this case merging a single file could take about one minute. To further investigate the effect of the matching on the merge result, we implemented a simple tree-matching algorithm and used it instead of Gumtree on the RxJava project. Our tree-matching produces worse matchings compared to GumTree, but incurs less overhead (81 minutes instead of 122). The simpler matcher resulted in more divergent merges (70) and more conflicts (40), compared to using GumTree, but the results are still better than using Git. These results suggest that our approach is most useful for storage formats that include unique node IDs such that matching algorithms are avoided altogether.

Threats to Validity. We evaluated our implementation on 13 Java repositories. Our results might not apply to other projects, other languages, or trees that are not ASTs. Nevertheless, the code bases we used provide a wide variety of tree-merge situations, and we used popular projects in order to increase the ecological validity of the results.

The tool we used to convert Java files into files encoded as we described in Sect. 2.1 omits some rarely-used Java constructs such as multiple type bounds for generic types. It is possible that a conflict in Git is due to a part of the code, which is missing in the new encoding. We are not aware of such cases.

We discard the text formatting and some comments. To handle such unstructured data with our approach the data would have to be encoded as part of the AST, e.g., by attaching a textual prefix node to each AST node.

5   Related Work

Researches have proposed a number of systems for version control of structured data. Molhado [24] is a powerful stand-alone framework for versioning object-oriented data. It is based on an extensible model that could be used to version arbitrary types of objects. Molhado requires deep integration with the development environment, making Molhado the "heart of the environment", in contrast to our more lightweight approach. OperV [25] is another approach for versioning of structured tree data with fine granularity, which, unlike our system, is operation-based, thereby requiring additional data and more complex tool support. Unlike our approach, both Molhado and OperV introduce a custom storage backend and do not integrate with an existing VCS.

Altmanninger has surveyed various systems for versioning models [2]. One of the most popular model repositories is EMFStore [14], part of the Eclipse Modeling Framework. There is continued interest in the research community in improving EMFStore, e.g., by formalizing merging for models [31] or performing semantics-based mering [1]. Odyssey [21,26] is another model VCS, which targets UML models and features advanced merge capabilities. EMFStore, Odyssey, and most systems for versioning models are not often used to version trees, and unlike our approach, they use a custom backend and do not integrate with standard line-based VCSs. Our approach may be applied to graph models, e.g., by expressing them as containment trees, similar to Mikhaiel et al. [19].

Mens [18] provides an overview of different approaches for merging program sources. Newer approaches based on the full [3] or partial structure [4] of source files have been proposed by Apel et al. These approaches improve on the merge results of Git, and can be fast and practical, but unlike our approach they do not work with unique IDs stored as part of the files, and thus may be inaccurate. Other approaches, rely on storing unique IDs, for example, the version control system of TouchDevelop [27] or MolhadoRef [7]. However, TouchDevelop is designed for a specific language and automatically resolves conflicts by ignoring one of the revisions, and MolhadoRef is an operation-based system, in contrast to our approach. Neither of the two integrate with a standard VCS like our approach.

There are also approaches to enhance VCSs for software with additional knowledge about the semantics of code and refactoring in order to improve merging [7,8,23]. Our customization mechanism can also be used to provide similar semantics-based improvements to the merge.

Ghezzi et al. [11] propose that a pluggable framework be built on top of traditional VCSs in order to provide additional services and analysis capabilities. Our algorithms can be seen as an instance of their suggestion.

Lorenz and Rosenan [17] propose a JSON format for storing structured data and integrating it with a traditional VCS. Their proposal however uses the VCS only for storage and performs versioning on its own – one version of the JSON file in the VCS stores itself all previous versions of the objects that comprise it. In contrast, our approach uses the underlying VCS for both storage and versioning.

Lindholm [16] proposes a way to merge XML documents using the XML tree structure. Their approach focuses on the particular class of document-oriented XML files, whereas our approach is designed for arbitrary trees.

MPS [30] is a commercial system which stores programs as XML files and implements custom merge hooks to integrate with traditional VCSs. It relies on IDs for precise merging, but the system does not seem to be customizable or easily usable for other data.

Schwägerl et al. have designed a graph-based algorithm [28] for merging ordered collections. Unlike our List-Merge customization, their algorithm only works with inserted, deleted, and relabeled elements, and there is no treatment for elements which are moved in or out of the list to another subtree and possible conflicts with these operations.

6   Conclusion

We described an approach for accurate version control of tree structures using a mainstream line-based VCS. Our diff algorithm can work with either stored node identifiers or tree matching algorithms. It provides accurate deltas with respect to the input matching, which prevents inaccurate or confusing diffs. Our merge algorithm and domain-specific customizations eliminate incorrect merges, reduce unnecessary conflicts, and report semantic issues, improving the merge result.

We evaluated our approach on traditional Java ASTs with the help of the Gumtree tree-matching algorithm. We observed a substantial reduction in merge conflicts compared to a line-based approach. It will be worth to experiment with trees with stored IDs instead of computing node matchings, which would allow us to further quantify the performance of our approach.

Another promising research direction is the design of additional merge customizations that understand trees at a more semantic level. For example, we have started exploring a customization that can detect renamings of declarations in an AST in one revision and apply them automatically to another on merge. Such high-level customizations might help to further reduce conflicts in particular domains and detect additional semantic incompatibilities between revisions.

References

1. Altmanninger, K., Schwinger, W., Kotsis, G.: Semantics for accurate conflict detection in SMoVer: specification, detection and presentation by example. IJEIS **6**(1) (2010)
2. Altmanninger, K., Seidl, M., Wimmer, M.: A survey on model versioning approaches. Int. J. Web Inf. Syst. **5**(3), 271–304 (2009)
3. Apel, S., Leßenich, O., Lengauer, C.: Structured merge with auto-tuning: balancing precision and performance. In: Proceedings of the 27th IEEE/ACM International Conference on Automated Software Engineering, ASE 2012. ACM (2012)
4. Apel, S., Liebig, J., Brandl, B., Lengauer, C., Kästner, C.: Semistructured merge: rethinking merge in revision control systems. In: Proceedings of the 19th ACM SIGSOFT Symposium and the 13th European Conference on Foundations of Software Engineering, ESEC/FSE 2011. ACM (2011)
5. Asenov, D., Müller, P.: Envision: A fast and flexible visual code editor with fluid interactions (overview). In: 2014 IEEE Symposium on Visual Languages and Human-Centric Computing (VL/HCC), July 2014
6. Asenov, D.: Envision: Reinventing the Integrated Development Environment. Ph.D. thesis, ETH Zurich (to appear, 2017)
7. Dig, D., Manzoor, K., Johnson, R., Nguyen, T.N.: Refactoring-aware configuration management for object-oriented programs. In: 29th International Conference on Software Engineering (ICSE 2007), May 2007
8. Ekman, T., Asklund, U.: Refactoring-aware versioning in Eclipse. Electron. Not. Theor. Comput. Sci. **107**, 57–69 (2004)
9. Falleri, J.R., Morandat, F., Blanc, X., Martinez, M., Montperrus, M.: Fine-grained and accurate source code differencing. In: Proceedings of the 29th ACM/IEEE International Conference on Automated Software Engineering, ASE 2014. ACM (2014)
10. Fluri, B., Wuersch, M., Pinzger, M., Gall, H.: Change distilling: tree differencing for fine-grained source code change extraction. IEEE Trans. Softw. Eng. **33**(11), 725–743 (2007)

11. Ghezzi, G., Würsch, M., Giger, E., Gall, H.C.: An architectural blueprint for a pluggable version control system for software (evolution) analysis. In: Proceedings of the Second International Workshop on Developing Tools As Plug-Ins, TOPI 2012. IEEE Press (2012)

12. Guenat, B.: Tree-based Version Control in Envision. BSc. Thesis, ETH Zurich (2015)

13. Kehrer, T., Kelter, U.: Versioning of ordered model element sets. Technical report 2, University of Siegen (2014)

14. Koegel, M., Helming, J.: EMFstore: a model repository for EMF models. In: Proceedings of the 32nd ACM/IEEE International Conference on Software Engineering, ICSE 2010, vol. 2. ACM (2010)

15. Koegel, M., Herrmannsdoerfer, M., von Wesendonk, O., Helming, J.: Operation-based conflict detection. In: Proceedings of the 1st International Workshop on Model Comparison in Practice, IWMCP 2010 (2010)

16. Lindholm, T.: A three-way merge for XML documents. In: Proceedings of the 2004 ACM Symposium on Document Engineering, DocEng 2004. ACM (2004)

17. Lorenz, D.H., Rosenan, B.: Source code management for projectional editing. In: Proceedings of the 2013 Companion Publication for Conference on Systems, Programming, Languages & Applications: Software for Humanity, SPLASH 2013. ACM (2013)

18. Mens, T.: A state-of-the-art survey on software merging. IEEE Trans. Softw. Eng. **28**(5), 449–462 (2002)

19. Mikhaiel, R., Tsantalis, N., Negara, N., Stroulia, E., Xing, Z.: Differencing UML models: a domain-specific vs. a domain-agnostic method. In: International Summer School on Generative and Transformational Techniques in Software Engineering IV, GTTSE 2011 (2013)

20. Miller, W., Myers, E.W.: A file comparison program. Softw. Pract. Exp. **15**(11), 1025–1040 (1985)

21. Murta, L., Corrêa, C., Prudêncio, J.G., Werner, C.: Towards Odyssey-VCS 2: improvements over a UML-based version control system. In: Proceedings of the 2008 International Workshop on Comparison and Versioning of Software Models, CVSM 2008. ACM (2008)

22. Myers, E.W.: An O(ND) difference algorithm and its variations. Algorithmica **1**(1) (1986)

23. Nguyen, H.V., Nguyen, M.H., Dang, S.C., Kästner, C., Nguyen, T.N.: Detecting semantic merge conflicts with variability-aware execution. In: Proceedings of the 2015 10th Joint Meeting on Foundations of Software Engineering, ESEC/FSE 2015. ACM (2015)

24. Nguyen, T., Munson, E., Boyland, J.: An infrastructure for development of object-oriented, multi-level configuration management services. In: Proceedings of the 27th International Conference on Software Engineering, (ICSE 2005), May 2005

25. Nguyen, T.T., Nguyen, H.A., Pham, N.H., Nguyen, T.N.: Operation-based, fine-grained version control model for tree-based representation. In: Rosenblum, D.S., Taentzer, G. (eds.) FASE 2010. LNCS, vol. 6013, pp. 74–90. Springer, Heidelberg (2010). doi:10.1007/978-3-642-12029-9_6

26. Oliveira, H., Murta, L., Werner, C.: Odyssey-VCS: a flexible version control system for UML model elements. In: Proceedings of the 12th International Workshop on Software Configuration Management, SCM 2005. ACM (2005)

27. Protzenko, J., Burckhardt, S., Moskal, M., McClurg, J.: Implementing real-time collaboration in TouchDevelop using AST merges. In: Proceedings of the 3rd International Workshop on Mobile Development Lifecycle, MobileDeLi 2015. ACM (2015)

28. Schwägerl, F., Uhrig, S., Westfechtel, B.: A graph-based algorithm for three-way merging of ordered collections in EMF models. Sci. Comput. Program. **113**(Pt. 1), 51–81 (2015). Model Driven Development (Selected & extended papers from MODELSWARD 2014)

29. Ukkonen, E.: International conference on foundations of computation theory algorithms for approximate string matching. Inf. Control **64**(1), 100–118 (1985)

30. Voelter, M., Siegmund, J., Berger, T., Kolb, B.: Towards user-friendly projectional editors. In: Combemale, B., Pearce, D.J., Barais, O., Vinju, J.J. (eds.) SLE 2014. LNCS, vol. 8706, pp. 41–61. Springer, Cham (2014). doi:10.1007/978-3-319-11245-9_3

31. Westfechtel, B.: A formal approach to three-way merging of EMF models. In: Proceedings of the 1st International Workshop on Model Comparison in Practice, IWMCP 2010. ACM (2010)

Graph Modelling and Transformation

Static Gen: Static Generation of UML Sequence Diagrams

Chris Alvin[1]([✉]), Brian Peterson[2], and Supratik Mukhopadhyay[2]

[1] Bradley University, Peoria, IL 61625, USA
calvin@bradley.edu
[2] Louisiana State University Baton Rouge, Baton Rouge, LA 70803, USA
{brian,supratik}@csc.lsu.edu

Abstract. UML sequence diagrams are visual representations of object interactions in a system and can provide valuable information for program comprehension, debugging, maintenance, and software archeology. Sequence diagrams generated from legacy code are independent of existing documentation that may have eroded. We present a framework for static generation of UML sequence diagrams from object-oriented source code. The framework provides a query refinement system to guide the user to interesting interactions in the source code. Our technique involves constructing a hypergraph representation of the source code, traversing the hypergraph with respect to a user-defined query, and generating the corresponding set of sequence diagrams. We implemented our framework as a tool, *StaticGen*, analyzing a corpus of 30 Android applications. We provide experimental results demonstrating the efficacy of our technique.

1 Introduction

Legacy object-oriented code may be accompanied by high-level documentation and/or descriptive source code comments, each of which may contain omissions or erroneous information. As documentation erodes, an engineer can trust only the source code. A necessary component of software archeology in object-oriented systems is the interactions among objects. A sequence diagram is a visual representation of those object interactions as well as their lifelines.

Sequence diagrams generated from legacy code are independent of existing documentation. Dynamic techniques for generation of sequence diagrams from legacy code [5,16,17,22,25] can synthesize a subset of all possible sequence diagrams based on runtime traces. Existing static techniques [34] result in sequence diagrams that replicate the original legacy source code, including conditionals and loops, without providing further intuitive notions beyond the code itself.

We present a technique, depicted in Fig. 1, for static generation of UML sequence diagrams together with a query system to guide the user to the most interesting interactions in the (unobfuscated) source code. Given an existing object-oriented code base as input, our technique involves three distinct steps as shown in Fig. 1. The first step in our technique (Fig. 1) takes the input code base and transforms it into a *typed control flow graph* (TCFG): a control flow

© Springer-Verlag GmbH Germany 2017
M. Huisman and J. Rubin (Eds.): FASE 2017, LNCS 10202, pp. 173–190, 2017.
DOI: 10.1007/978-3-662-54494-5_10

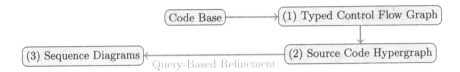

Fig. 1. The *StaticGen* system flowchart

```
public class Main extends ActionBarActivity {
    private int goodId, btnID = 2131296336; private Button b;
    private Random r = new Random();

    public boolean onOptionsItemSelected(MenuItem item) {
        int id = item.getItemId();
        return super.onOptionsItemSelected(item);
    }
    public void middleButtonOnClick(View v) {
        ((Button)v).setText("Clicked");

        int c = 0;
        if (r.nextBoolean()) c = getRed();
        else c = getBlue();

        int opt = r.nextInt(4);
        if (opt == 0) SetUpperLeftButton(c);
        else if (opt == 1) SetUpperRightButton(c);
        else if (opt == 2) SetLowerLeftButton(c);
        else SetLowerRightButton(c);
    }
    // Other Set methods omitted for redundancy
    private void SetUpperRightButton(int c) {
        b = (Button)findViewById(btnID);
        SetBtnColor(b, c);
    }
    private void SetBtnColor(Button b, int c) {
        b.setBackgroundColor(c);
        goodId = b.getId();
    }
    private int getRed() { return Color.RED; }
    private int getBlue() { return Color.BLUE; }
}
```

Fig. 2. Example android source code

graph annotated with type information—a familiar structure in static analysis acquired from an existing front-end tool such as Soot [29] or goto-cc [15].

The TCFG for a program P captures the execution of P, but does not capture (a) the interactions among the objects constituting P, (b) their context, and (c) the *causal ordering* of their interactions. Hence, the second step of our methodology involves constructing a directed *code hypergraph* [6, Ch. 1] (Sect. 3) that captures (1) intra- and inter-procedural control flow, (2) message *interactions* among objects, (3) message *context*, and (4) *causal ordering* of messages. From the source code in Fig. 2, we consider a portion of the generated *code hypergraph* (corresponding to a hyperpath [6, Ch. 1]) in Fig. 3. A code hypergraph corresponding to the input source code contains two categories of nodes. The first category refers to *code objects*: objects and their datatypes (rounded corners in Fig. 3). The second category of nodes, called *trace* nodes, capture a trace of a

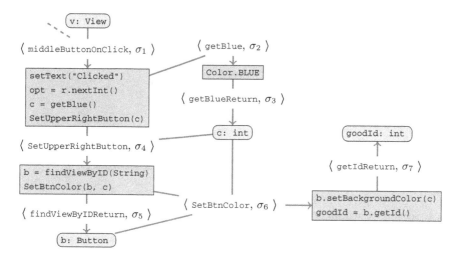

Fig. 3. A portion of the code hypergraph corresponding to the code in Fig. 2

method (rectangles in Fig. 3). For example, it is clear that `middleButtonOnClick` in Fig. 2 has $2 * 4 = 8$ possible traces due to the permutation of respective branches; Fig. 3 depicts one of those 8 trace nodes.

A directed hyperedge captures a message context in the form of an origin hypernode (a set of nodes) and causal ordering by virtue of directedness of hyperedges. The annotation of each hyperedge defines corresponding messages. For example, a call to `middleButtonOnClick` in Fig. 2 requires the context of an object of type `View` and a callee; the corresponding hyperedge in Fig. 3 is labeled accordingly with the destination method and program state information for context.

The third step in our technique (Fig. 1) constructs sequence diagrams (Sect. 4) given a *code hypergraph* corresponding to an input code base. Each hyperpath [6, Ch. 1] in that hypergraph encodes all object interactions in an execution of the code base and therefore a corresponding sequence diagram can be generated. The hyperpath in Fig. 3 corresponds to the sequence diagram shown in Fig. 4. To empower the user to identify 'interesting' interactions, we provide a *query-based refinement* interface that allows the user to narrow the resultant set of generated sequence diagrams based on their criteria and guides the user to the most interesting interactions in the source code.

We evaluated the effectiveness of our tool, *StaticGen*, on 30 open source Android applications [1,35]. *StaticGen* generated 647.1 sequence diagrams on average per package taking a mean of 96.78 s for each package. In addition to helping developers comprehend legacy code, *StaticGen* could fill an important security role for normal users as well. In a second experiment, we conducted a case study of using *StaticGen* to uncover *security vulnerabilities*. The query refinement system of *StaticGen* using the notions of 'interesting' and 'refinement', allowed us to narrow down the set of all sequence diagrams of a program to a subset that exposed a vulnerability.

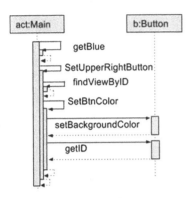

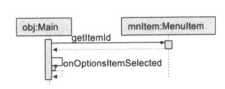

Fig. 4. Sequence diagram for an execution path in Fig. 2

Fig. 5. Uninteresting sequence diagram for Fig. 2

This paper makes the following contributions:

- Section 2 formalizes a sequence diagram with respect to a hyperpath in a hypergraph.
- We describe a tool, *StaticGen*, for statically generating sequence diagrams by constructing (Sect. 3) and exploring (Sect. 4) a *code hypergraph* for an input code base.
- *StaticGen* provides a query system to refine the set of generated diagrams and guide the user to the most interesting interactions in the source code. (Sect. 5).
- We illustrate the efficacy of our technique (Sect. 6) with quantitative analyses and a case study to identify a security vulnerability.

2   Program Abstraction and Code Hypergraphs

In this section, we describe an abstract model for programs, formalize the notion of a *code hypergraph*, define a sequence diagram in that context, and define terms related to the features and quality of a given sequence diagram.

2.1   Program Abstraction Model

To define a framework for static generation of sequence diagrams not tied to a particular object-oriented language, we introduce a *typed control flow graph* (TCFG), an abstract model that will serve as the basis for our analysis. The model maintains both data flow (i.e. program points with state information attributed to collecting semantics, alias analysis, etc.) and control flow information (i.e. intra-procedural instructions and inter-procedural method calls). A program is abstracted by a typed control flow graph (Definition 1) containing two types of edges: intra-procedural transfer edges and inter-procedural call edges.

Definition 1 (Typed Control-Flow Graph). A typed control-flow graph for a program P is a control flow graph $G_{N_T} = (N_T, X, C, n_0)$ where N_T is the set of program points including *type* information for all variables, X is the set of intra-procedural transfer edges, C is the set of inter-procedural call edges, and n_0 is the entry point of the program.

For acyclic TCFGs, we assume the standard notion of *sequential ordering of instructions* as induced by the directed nature of the representative graph. We describe our approach in the context of a simple object-oriented programming language with conditionals, assignments, loops, references, and methods with call-by-value. We omit the details of the language as the operational and denotational semantics are defined in the usual way.

2.2   The Code Hypergraph

For a program P, we use a *directed hypergraph* [6, Ch. 1] data structure where *hypernodes* (sets of nodes) capture the context of interactions and *directed hyperedges* capture the interactions of objects constituting P. The order of hyperedges in a hypergraph captures the notion of *causal ordering* [2]; for events (invocations or returns of methods) U and V, we write $U \to V$ if event U is causally ordered before event V. In our model, hyperedges consist of a set of origin nodes and a single target node; a many-to-one relationship.

We formally introduce an abstract, many-to-one directed hypergraph called an *annotated hypergraph* where all hyperedges are annotated according to the problem space. A simple annotation may consist of a boolean expression indicating if a hyperedge is to be considered (in)active; that is, all the context information corresponding to the hyperedge is available or not.

Definition 2 (Annotated Hypergraph). An annotated hypergraph is a directed hypergraph $H(N, E_\mathcal{A})$ where N is a set of nodes and $E_\mathcal{A} \subseteq 2^N \times N \times \mathcal{A}$ a set of directed annotated hyperedges over a set of annotations $\mathcal{A}$. Each directed hyperedge $e \in E_\mathcal{A}$ is defined as an ordered pair $e = (S, t, A)$ where $S \subseteq N$, $t \in N$, and $A \in \mathcal{A}$.

Hyperedge annotations correspond to events in the program. Given two hyperedges, $E_A = (S_1, t_1, A)$ and $E_B = (S_2, t_2, B)$ with origin hypernodes S_1 and S_2, respectively, t_1 and t_2 target nodes, respectively, and annotations A and B respectively, we say $A \twoheadrightarrow B$ if $t_1 \in S_2$. We define $\to$ to be the transitive closure of $\twoheadrightarrow$. An important component of our technique is the hyperpath construction; we define hyperpath in the context of an annotated hypergraph.

Definition 3 (Hyperpath). Let $H(N, E_\mathcal{A})$ be an annotated hypergraph, $G \subset N$, and $g \in N$. A *hyperpath* Y (of length n) from G to g is a sequence of hypernodes $G_0, G_1, G_2, \ldots, G_{n-1}$ where $G_0 = G$ and $G_{n-1} = \{g\}$ such that for each $1 \leq i \leq n-1$ there exists a hyperedge $(G_{i-1}, g_i, A_i) \in E$ where $g_i \in G_i$ and $A_i \in \mathcal{A}$.

The annotated hypergraph in Definition 2 is an abstract structure that we instantiate to encode interactions, context, and causal ordering through nodes and hyperedges. We call the resulting hypergraph a *code hypergraph*. Before we formally define a *code hypergraph*, we define the set of nodes and hyperedges that will constitute it.

Nodes. The nodes of a code hypergraph are of two types: *code object* and (method) *trace*. A code object captures the notion of an object in an object-oriented program. A trace is more than just a basic block in a TCFG, it is a sequential set of instructions corresponding to an execution path for an entire method. For example, in Fig. 3, the trace node corresponding to the `middleButtonOnClick` method is composed of instructions that would span many basic blocks in a TCFG.

Definition 4 (Code Object). A code object v of type T in an object-oriented program P is an instantiated object variable of type T. For code object v of type T, we say $\mathsf{Datatype}\,(v) = T$.

Definition 5 (Trace). For a method M with entry instruction m_0 and set of exit instructions M_{exit}, a *method trace* is a path in a TCFG consisting of intra-procedural instructions from m_0 to m_{exit} for $m_{exit} \in M_{exit}$.

Hyperedges. There are two varieties of hyperedges we consider: one based on method invocations and the other based on objects being returned from non-void methods. Each *call hyperedge* is a many-to-one, annotated relationship among nodes in the hypergraph and is constructed for each method invocation. For a method invocation m in a method trace t, a hyperedge is constructed with the set of source nodes consisting of the node corresponding to t and the set of nodes corresponding to the formal parameter types of method m. The target of the hyperedge is a node corresponding to a method trace for method m. We annotate this node with the program state information for context as well as the method name. For a set of annotated hyperedges $E_{\mathcal{A}}$, $\mathsf{CallEdges}\,(E_{\mathcal{A}})$ defines the set of call hyperedges. Each *return hyperedge* is a one-to-one relationship between an origin trace node and a target code object with an annotation comprising of the method name for the origin node and program state information for context. For a program P, we say a *program state* σ of a program P is data store for all variables at a given execution point in P.

Definition 6 (Code Hypergraph). Let Π be the set of all program states for a program P with TCFG $\mathcal{T}$. A *code hypergraph* corresponding to a TCFG $\mathcal{T}$ is an annotated hypergraph $H\,(N, E_{\mathcal{A}})$ where, for each $n \in N$, n corresponds to either a (1) code object or (2) a method trace (acquired from an analysis of $\mathcal{T}$). Each directed hyperedge $e \in E_{\mathcal{A}}$ is defined by the ordered pair $e = (S, t, A)$ where $S \subseteq N$ and $t \in N$ is a target set of instructions corresponding to some method call. Each hyperedge annotation, $A \in \mathcal{A}$, is defined as a pair $A = (m, \sigma)$ where m is a method in the source code and $\sigma \in \Pi$. We say that a hyperedge (S, t, A) is labeled by m if $A = (m, \sigma)$ for some $\sigma \in \Pi$.

It is clear from Definition 6 that we can encode method invocations and returns as events and thus as annotations of hyperedges in a *code hypergraph*.

2.3 Sequence Diagrams

A sequence diagram is an instance of the more general *message sequence chart*. Succinctly, a message sequence chart [11, Ch. 4] [2,18] can be described as a set of partially-ordered, labeled events over a set of "processes". We will define a sequence diagram as a *code hyperpath* in a *code hypergraph*. A *code hyperpath* in a code hypergraph $H(N, E_A)$, constructed from a TCFG $\mathcal{T}$, is a hyperpath in H.

We now define a sequence diagram in terms of a (code) hyperpath in a *code hypergraph*.

Definition 7 (Hypergraph Sequence Diagram). Let $H(N, E_A)$ be a *code hypergraph*. Also let m be a method with entry point m_0 and let m_{exit} be an exit point of m. A *hypergraph sequence diagram* for method m corresponds to a hyperpath in H from the source hypernode of a hyperedge labeled m_0 to the target node of a hyperedge labeled m_{exit} and is denoted by $Y(H, m_0, m_{exit})$. The set of sequence diagrams $\mathcal{Y}(H, m_0, m_{exit})$ for a fixed pair of entry and exit points, m_0 and m_{exit} respectively, is the set of all $Y(H, m_0, m_{exit})$. Since a method has one fixed entry point and many possible exit points (given by M_{exit}), the collection of all such sequence diagrams (code hyperpaths) is given by $\mathcal{Y} = \bigcup_{m_{exit} \in M_{exit}} \mathcal{Y}(H, m_0, m_{exit})$.

We prove the equivalence of a message sequence chart with our notion of a sequence diagram as a hyperpath in [3].

To generate sequence diagrams, the *code hypergraph* is extracted according to the discussion in Sect. 3 where method m is a parameter specified by the user.

2.4 Characteristics of Sequence Diagrams

In this subsection, we formalize some properties of sequence diagrams that will be used by the query-based refinement interface for narrowing down the set of sequence diagrams generated to those that would be most "informative" to the user.

Depth of a Sequence Diagram. As a metric for code complexity, we define *depth* which relates the longest sequence of causally ordered messages without returning. We call $\mathcal{O}_1, \ldots, \mathcal{O}_n = \{\mathcal{O}\}_i$ an *object sequence* where for all $1 \leq i \leq n$, $\mathcal{O}_i$ are code objects. The *length* of the object sequence $\mathcal{O}_1, \ldots, \mathcal{O}_n$ is n. We define depth for a sequence diagram independent of the hypergraph definitions.

Definition 8 (Depth of a Sequence Diagram). The depth of a sequence diagram D is the greatest length d of the object sequence $\mathcal{O}_1, \ldots, \mathcal{O}_d$ in the diagram such that for each $1 \leq i \leq d - 1$, there exists a message m_i from $\mathcal{O}_i$ to $\mathcal{O}_{i+1}$ and for each $1 \leq j \leq d - 2$, $m_j \to m_{j+1}$ (m_j causally precedes m_{j+1}) and there does not exist any message m either from $\mathcal{O}_j$ to $\mathcal{O}_{j+1}$ or vice versa such that $m_j \to m$ and $m \to m_{j+1}$.

Interesting Sequence Diagrams. Not all sequence diagrams are of particular interest to a user. Requiring user interaction for refinement from the set of all sequence diagrams corresponding to a program is not ideal in terms of time and effort; therefore, we suggest a first step in formalizing the notion of an interesting sequence diagram to make interactions with *StaticGen* more efficient.

Formally defining an interesting sequence diagram requires quantification of some characteristic(s) of a sequence diagram. For a code hypergraph $H(N, E_A)$, we define function $\mathsf{Msg} : H \rightarrow \mathbb{N}$, as $\mathsf{Msg}(H) = |\mathsf{CallEdges}(E_A)|$. For a hypergraph sequence diagram D in $H(N, E_A)$, we define $\mathsf{Msg}(D) = \mathsf{Msg}(H)_D$ where the subscript denotes restriction to D and note that Msg is a measure that specifies the number of messages (method invocations) in the sequence diagram.

Let $\mathcal{D}_P$ be the set of all sequence diagrams for a program P. For $D \subseteq \mathcal{D}_P$, let $Msgs(D) = \{u \mid \exists D \in D \text{ s.t. } \mathsf{Msg}(D) = u \in \mathbb{N}\}$ and let $Msgs(D)_k$ denote the set of the k greatest elements of $Msgs(D)$ where $1 \leq k \leq |D|$. We define a function $\mathsf{select} : \mathbb{N} \rightarrow \mathcal{D}_P$ that, for a $u \in \mathbb{N}$, returns a sequence diagram $D \in \mathcal{D}_P$ such that $\mathsf{Msg}(D) = u$. If there exists multiple $D \in \mathcal{D}_P$ with $\mathsf{Msg}(D) = u$, ties are broken arbitrarily; $\mathsf{select}(u)$ is undefined if there does not exist any sequence diagram $D \in \mathcal{D}_P$ such that $\mathsf{Msg}(D) = u$. We define a function top that, for a set of sequence diagrams $\mathcal{D} \subseteq \mathcal{D}_P$ and a fixed number $0 \leq k \leq |\mathcal{D}|$, returns k sequence diagrams in $\mathcal{D}$ having the greatest number of messages. Formally, $\mathsf{top}(\mathcal{D}, k) = \{\mathsf{select}(u) \mid u \in Msgs(\mathcal{D})_k\}$ where $\mathcal{D} \subseteq \mathcal{D}_P$ and $1 \leq k \leq |\mathcal{D}|$.

Definition 9 (Interesting Sequence Diagram). For a program P with the set of sequence diagrams $\mathcal{D}_P$ with $|\mathcal{D}_P| = n$ and a fixed $0 < k \leq n$, D_P is an *interesting sequence diagram* if $D_P \in \mathsf{top}(\mathcal{D}_P, k)$.

For example, consider method `middleButtonOnClick` in Fig. 2 with generated set of sequence diagrams $\mathcal{D}$. The sequence diagram in Fig. 4 is interesting for $0 < k \leq 8$, since $\mathsf{Msg}(D) = 6$ for each $D \in \mathcal{D}$ describing a trace of `middleButtonOnClick`. The sequence diagram in Fig. 5 contains two messages and is therefore uninteresting for $0 < k \leq 8$.

While it is arguable that Definition 9 may not be ideal for every user, we believe that code complexity is often rooted in the number of method invocations and thus the probability is greater that a single trace can provide more information and thus is more likely to expose bugs and vulnerabilities.

3   Constructing the Hypergraph

In this section, we describe how *StaticGen* constructs a *code hypergraph* from an input set of code files; see [3] for pseudocode of the algorithms described here. The input to *StaticGen* is a set of (unobfuscated) code files in an object-oriented language. We assume that the code is processed by an intermediate system [15,29] into a TCFG. We construct a corresponding H and populate the nodes and hyperedges.

Nodes. As in Definition 6, there are two types of nodes in a *code hypergraph*. To construct both types of nodes, we parse the TCFG. For code objects, if a particular instruction is a declaration or a formal parameter, we add a corresponding node to H. If a node m defines a method prototype, we construct all possible traces for m using a process that identifies all possible naive execution paths for a method m over a control-flow graph; we then add each trace to the *code hypergraph*.

Hyperedges. We consider the two varieties of hyperedges in turn: *call hyperedge* and *return hyperedge*. A *call hyperedge* captures the callee trace, context of a caller through the set of input objects, and annotation of the method. For method calls, the hyperedge origin nodes consist of the callee trace nodes and the set of nodes corresponding to the actual parameters in the method call. The target node is then a node corresponding to a trace of the called method. The result is a call hyperedge for the *code hypergraph* with an annotation consisting of the name of the called method and an empty program state. For non-void methods, we construct a *return hyperedge* relating the current trace node as source and the object being returned as target annotated with the called method name and empty program state and an indicator that it is a return hyperedge.

4   Static Sequence Diagram Construction

Sequence diagram generation consists of three phases: (1) sub-hypergraph identification through pebbling [8], (2) hyperpath identification, and (3) converting from a hyperpath to a sequence diagram. For a more detailed description and pseudocode of each phase, see the extended paper [3].

Pebbling. Pebbling is a linear-time traversal over an annotated hypergraph that identifies a sub-hypergraph [6, Ch. 1] satisfying constraints placed on code objects and methods by the user. Pebbling is a breadth-first traversal over an annotated hypergraph where we mark each node with a pebble once it is visited using the rule "once all source nodes in a hyperedge have been pebbled, the target node is pebbled" (similar to the Dowling and Gallier [8] marking algorithm for satisfiability of propositional horn clauses). For example, in Fig. 3, if we pebble the trace node for `middleButtonOnClick`, we immediately pebble the trace node for `getBlue`. In turn, we pebble the code object node for c. Then, since both source nodes are pebbled, we pebble the target trace node for `SetUpperRightButton`. We assume that a *code hypergraph* has been pebbled resulting in a *pebbled code hypergraph*.

Hyperpath Identification. For a given method m, we construct the corresponding set of all hyperpaths in a *code hypergraph* H. Our algorithm maintains the same information for a sequence diagram as stated in Definition 7, but instead of maintaining a code hyperpath the result is an equivalent *path* consisting of one-to-one edges and an associated set of objects. For simplicity, we consider constructing a single path $\mathcal{P}$ by considering a single trace T of m. Recall that a trace T is a sequential set of instructions. For each instruction $i \in T$, we consider if i is a method invocation. If i is not a method invocation, we add i to $\mathcal{P}$ maintaining sequential order of instructions. If i is a method invocation, we recur with a trace of the method called in i. $\mathcal{P}$ is then a valid, sequential ordering of instructions for method m.

Hyperpath to Sequence Diagram Conversion. Given a path $\mathcal{P}$ corresponding to a hyperpath in a *code hypergraph*, we construct the corresponding sequence diagram D. For each method invocation instruction i in $\mathcal{P}$, we add to D each of the following: (a) the invocation of method m in i as a message, (b) a recursively constructed sub-sequence diagram of m, and (c) a message indicating a return from m.

5   Interface for Diagram Generation

A sequence diagram D has features such as: depth as defined in Definition 8, number of messages (number of call hyperedges), types of all code objects, method coverage, and branch coverage. In this section, we describe the query language, the interface for query-based refinement, and provide some examples.

5.1   Query over the Language of Sequence Diagrams

We define a query over the language of sequence diagrams. The language of sequence diagrams $\mathcal{L}$ is defined over the alphabet Σ consisting of code objects and method traces. For simplicity, we will refer to code objects as c_i with $i \in \mathbb{Z}^+$, method traces as m_j with $j \in \mathbb{Z}^+$ with corresponding method returns m'_j. Hence, $\Sigma = \{c\}_i \cup \{m\}_j \cup \{m\}'_j$ for i and j finite in $\mathbb{Z}^+$ and $i \geq 1$ and $j \geq 1$.

We note that a hyperpath Y in a *code hypergraph* H is a string in $\mathcal{L}$ [3] since a topological sort of the DAG corresponding to Y results in a string $s \in \mathcal{L}$. We note that distinct orders of topological sorts on a DAG corresponding to a hyperpath will result in distinct strings; however, each such string is unique in $\mathcal{L}$ over the original program. A query is defined over a set of sequence diagrams $\mathcal{D} \subseteq \mathcal{L}$ generated using the techniques described in Sect. 4; however, generation can be more targeted. It is often cumbersome and unnecessary to generate all sequence diagrams beginning at a `main` method in a program. Generation can be performed on-demand beginning at any method reducing the size of the corresponding hypergraph. In order to acquire the initial set of sequence diagrams D_S, we may use the predicate "`start M`," where M is a method dictating where the resultant sequence diagram(s) will begin.

Query Operations. A query $Q = \{q\}_i$ over $\mathcal{L}$ consists of a finite sequence of operations $\{q\}_i$ that *refine* the given set of sequence diagrams $\mathcal{D} \subseteq \mathcal{L}$ into the resulting set $Q(\mathcal{D}) = F \subseteq \mathcal{D}$.

- For a method trace $\ell \in \Sigma$, "`filter ℓ D`" prunes the substring from ℓ to ℓ' in each sequence diagram in $\mathcal{D}$. This removal process efficiently eliminates calls to library-based functionality or method definitions that are not of interest.

For a set of code objects $\ell \subseteq \Sigma$, "`filter` ℓ $\mathcal{D}$" prunes all characters $c \in \ell$ from each string in $\mathcal{D}$. Removal of a code object allows the user to refine the set of sequence diagrams by omitting specific variables.

- For a set of predicates R describing strings in $\mathcal{L}$, "`remove` R $\mathcal{D}$" will remove all resulting sequence diagrams for which all $r \in R$ evaluate to `true`. The complementary operation "`accept` R $\mathcal{D}$" will collect all sequence diagrams for which all $r \in R$ evaluate to `true`.
- For an integer k, "`top-interesting` k $\mathcal{D}$" returns $\text{top}\,(\mathcal{D}, k)$.
- "`meth-cover` p $\mathcal{D}$" and "`br-cover` p $\mathcal{D}$" each return sequence diagrams ensuring minimal method and branch coverage respectively for a lower bound percentage p ([3] formally defines method and branch coverage).

We define a simple grammar for a query Q over $\mathcal{L}$; the terminal symbols include ℓ, R, $0 \le p \le 1$, and $k \in \mathbb{Z}^+$ as defined above.

$$Q(\mathcal{D}) \rightarrow \mathcal{D} \mid \texttt{filter } \ell \ Q(\mathcal{D}) \mid \texttt{remove } R \ Q(\mathcal{D}) \mid \texttt{accept } R \ Q(\mathcal{D})$$
$$\mid \texttt{top-interesting } k \ Q(\mathcal{D}) \mid \texttt{meth-cover } p \ Q(\mathcal{D})$$
$$\mid \texttt{br-cover } p \ Q(\mathcal{D})$$

5.2 Query Interface to Diagram Generation

We present an interface where a user of *StaticGen* can query over the set of sequence diagram features to obtain a subset of sequence diagrams. Our methodology requires manual input of the code as well as a query Q as previously described. Depending on the specification of Q, we may omit, through the pebbling process, call hyperedges corresponding to method calls that may be removed. Given a pebbled code hypergraph, we construct the corresponding set of all sequence diagrams. We then `filter` the resulting set of sequence diagrams related to method removal, coverage, or `top` into the desired set of sequence diagrams.

If the user wishes to refine Q into Q' we may re-pebble the code hypergraph and generate according to Q'. Our query system provides continual refinement until the appropriate set of sequence diagrams is acquired. That is, initially, a user might simply request a set of interesting sequence diagrams. Then, as the user becomes more familiar with the code base, they may define a more restricted query. This process of query refinement can continue ad nauseum.

Within the bounds of the user selected query, we prioritize what the user sees by first eliminating strictly isomorphic diagrams [3] and diagrams which are "subsets" of other diagrams. We then determine the set of sequence diagrams S that match the user's query. Using a method coverage metric for the code, we prioritize the diagrams into a list I.

5.3 Sample Queries

Assume the user specifies as input the code base containing the source code in Fig. 2. To filter elements from the set of resulting sequence diagrams, the user defines a query Q with `start` being `middleButtonOnClick` and filters object r and its corresponding methods as well as the `setText` method. The result is eight diagrams, seven of which are strictly isomorphically unique [3], and one of which is shown in Fig. 4. If we append to Q an `accept` predicate with method `SetUpperRightButton(int)`, the only diagram returned is shown in Fig. 4.

As another example, Fig. 5 arises from a query requesting the least interesting diagram from analyzing all methods.

6   Experimental Results

Timely generation of sequence diagrams depends on two factors: (1) complexity of branching in the given code and (2) user-defined queries to pebble the hypergraph and prune the resultant set sequence diagrams. For our experiments, we limit diagram generation to package prefixes. This limitation allows the user to visualize internal package interactions without dealing with bloat from exterior execution paths to that package. We ran our generation algorithm on a desktop with Intel Core i5-4460 at 3.2 GHz with 8 GB RAM on 64-bit Linux Mint operating system.

Benchmark Code. Our initial tests have focused on open-source Android bytecode applications taken from [1,35] with wide-ranging focus, including: ad blocking, email, and web browsing. The bytecode was input into the Soot framework [29] which can process bytecode or source code thus bringing the same capabilities to bear, independent of input format. [3] lists the projects and corresponding facts about each code base in the chosen corpus, including the package we analyzed, the number of constituent classes, processing time, and the operation count.

Soot analyzes bytecode by breaking down classes into groups of methods, and methods into groups of abstract statements; the number of abstract statements is referred to as the operation count. While operation count may not correspond one to one with source lines of code, it does correspond to essential logical statements executed by the processor, and is a useful measurement of the complexity of the program analyzed. The operation count for our corpus is shown in [3].

As another measure of complexity of the target Android code, we consider the histogram in Fig. 6 depicting the mean depth of diagrams for non-library functionality for each benchmark Android package. Our event-driven benchmarks are generally shallow as is evident in Fig. 6; the mean depth among all packages is 1.29 with standard deviation 0.92. We view the depth metric as a guide to the number of corresponding sequence diagrams; the greater the depth, the more diagrams should result. Figure 7 is a scatterplot of the relationship between mean depth and number of diagrams generated. We see a linear model given by $y = 887.58x - 496.56$, where y is the number of diagrams generated, and x is the mean depth of the set of diagrams for an Android package. The correlation is moderate with correlation coefficient $r^2 = 0.5643$.

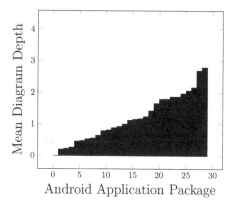

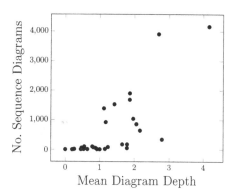

Fig. 6. Mean sequence diagram depth per android application package

Fig. 7. No. generated sequence diagrams vs. mean diagram depth for the entire corpus

Time and Scope of Synthesis. We measure tool efficiency by considering generation time. Our reported execution times include Soot's Simplification [29] procedure, hypergraph construction, diagram generation, and refinement. In Fig. 8, several Android packages are processed quickly. However, the mean of 96.78s and the standard deviation of 174.58s indicates more complex packages result in greater time dispersion. For each Android package, Fig. 9 describes the number of diagrams that give complete method coverage. Some of the more complex packages skew the distribution (std. dev. 1085.23 and mean 647.1) with a strongly correlated linear model ($r^2 = 0.9082$) comparing the number of diagrams with respect to generation time. This is strong evidence indicating our technique does not require a significant amount of processing time for code bases with large sets of sequence diagrams.

Comparison with Dynamic Synthesis Tools. Several existing tools for sequence diagram generation are based on traces saved from debug runs of a program [10,24]. While our approach differs significantly in that we utilize static analysis to generate diagrams from a large number of potential execution paths, we did compare our approach against Diver [24]. We found that *StaticGen* was able to construct similar sequence diagrams compared to Diver which uses a dynamic approach. The full text of this comparison is available at [3].

Evaluation of Interestingness. We test the usefulness of our interestingness metric by examining the possibility of using it in uncovering *security vulnerabilities in code*. We selected an independently studied example for assessing our definition of interestingness. Both Livshits [19] and Sampaio [31] used a web application named BlueBlog [7] in their corpora of applications with security vulnerabilities. In addition, [31] provided a software tool, ESVD [30], to analyze code for vulnerabilities.

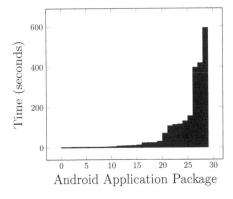

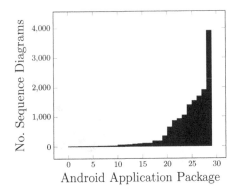

Fig. 8. Time per android application package

Fig. 9. Number of sequence diagrams per android application package

We focus on a vulnerability evident in the unsafe http request in the code in Fig. 10 that was originally detected by ESVD [30]. The value returned by the getServletPath function is stored in the variable url and is not sanitized by both branches. Without any filtering, *StaticGen* generated 2800 diagrams from BlueBlog, while the interestingness criterion narrowed it down to 45 diagrams ranked according to top defined in Sect. 5. The doGet method was the subject of the diagrams ranked 22 and 32 of the 45 interesting diagrams; a fragment of the rank-22 diagram is shown in Fig. 11. This example shows that prioritizing novel information allows us to reduce a set of diagrams to a useful fraction, while retaining information about crucial code paths, that can then be delegated to a human expert or a vulnerability analysis tool for further analysis for security vulnerabilities. It is possible that an excluded diagram may contain the vulnerability; however, our query focusing on interestingness, by definition, includes diagrams that provide novel information. Hence, a vulnerability as we have described cannot hide only in the discarded diagrams.

```
protected void doGet(HttpServletRequest request, HttpServletResponse response)
  throws ServletException, IOException
{
  String url = request.getServletPath() + toPath;
  if( forward ) {
    RequestDispatcher disp = getServletContext().getRequestDispatcher(url);
    disp.forward(request, response);
  } else {
    response.sendRedirect(url);
  }
}
```

Fig. 10. BlueBlog [7] doGet function

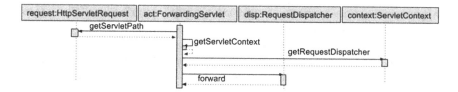

Fig. 11. BlueBlog [7] doGet sequence diagram fragment

7 Related Work

In [16,17,22], Lo, et al., propose techniques for dynamic specification mining by inferring sequence diagrams over execution traces that include inter-object behavior and causal ordering. Lo, et al. use a graph of symbolic message sequence charts as an intermediate representation while we invoke a hypergraph representation. Tools such as jTracert [5] and Object-Aid [25] generate sequence diagrams directly from application runtime while [25] uses the Eclipse IDE [9] to reverse engineer all or part of a stack trace. Similarly, [12] divides a long dynamic trace of a Java program into a series of smaller diagrams culminating in a sequence diagram. Finally, [36] describes an approach for generating sequence diagrams dynamically using a k-tail merging algorithm that merges the collected traces. The goal of merging by [36] is to construct a single sequence diagram. Our technique does not limit generation to a single diagram, but generates a complete space of sequence diagrams that is refined by query.

There are several tools that statically generate sequence diagrams. Visual paradigm [34] is a simple tool for sequence diagram generation that is in one-to-one correspondence with the source code without refinement. Other tools such as eUML2 Modeler [32] and Visual Studio [23] generate diagrams statically, but also offer the ability for the user to refine the diagram by selection or omission of methods. Similarly, Architexa [4] generates sequence diagrams, but is completely interactive with the user during construction. While all of these tools are based on a static analysis of the target code, none of these tools automate the refinement process based on a query scheme over the set of all possible diagrams.

The Interaction Scenario Visualizer (ISVis) [13], employs a combination of static and trace-based information and communicates the overall importance of visualizing source code. Tonella and Potrich [33] describe static extraction of UML sequence diagrams from C++ code using partial analysis and focusing, but do not perform analysis of intraprocedural flow of control. The CPP2XMI tool [14] processes XMI into sequence diagrams with no means of user-based refinement as with *StaticGen*. I2SD [26] is a static generation tool that leverages metadata through interceptors whereas our technique does not rely on such information. The RED tool [27,28] was a significant step forward in reverse-engineering diagrams by mapping reducible CFGs to interactions. In contrast, our use of an annotated hypergraph provides the means to refine the object interactions, context, and causal ordering based on user query; in some respects, our approach attempts to fill the "exploration mode" described in [27]. In total, our approach seeks to empower the user by supporting query-based refinement over the set of all sequence diagrams.

In [20,21] authors present techniques for *user-guided specification mining* over executions traces by proposing approaches to filter mined sequence diagrams. We similarly aim to support property discovery through an iterative and interactive approach by incorporating a notion of interestingness.

8   Conclusions

This paper describes a framework for static generation of sequence diagrams using a directed hypergraph to encode message context, interactions, and causality. Based on a user-query, we prune the sequence diagram space through a pebbling procedure to generate the desired set of sequence diagrams. We showed that, in practice, our framework provides the basis for interactive software archeology as well as an important tool for debugging legacy code.

References

1. List of Open-Source Android Apps (2013). http://forum.xda-developers.com/showthread.php?t=2124002
2. Alur, R., Etessami, K., Yannakakis, M.: Inference of message sequence charts. In: ICSE 2000, pp. 304–313 (2000). http://doi.acm.org/10.1145/337180.337215
3. Alvin, C., Peterson, B., Mukhopadhyay, S.: StaticGen: Static Generation of UML Sequence Diagrams - Technical Report (2017). http://hilltop.bradley.edu/~calvin/papers/fase17-technical.pdf
4. Architexa.com: Introduction to Architexa—Sequence Diagram Generation (2015). http://www.architexa.com/support/videos/sequence-diagrams
5. Bedrin, D.: jtracert (2015). https://code.google.com/p/jtracert/
6. Berge, C.: Graphs and Hypergraphs, vol. 45. North-Holland Mathematical Library, Elsevier Science Publishers B.V. (1989)
7. Burén, R.: BlueBlog. https://sourceforge.net/projects/blueblog/. Accessed 16 Oct 2016
8. Dowling, W.F., Gallier, J.H.: Linear-time algorithms for testing the satisfiability of propositional horn formulae. J. Log. Program. **1**(3), 267–284 (1984). dx.doi.org/10.1016/0743-1066(84)90014-1
9. Eclipse Foundation Inc: Eclipse (2015). https://eclipse.org/
10. Gestwicki, P.V., Jayaraman, B.: JIVE: Java interactive visualization environment. In: OOPSLA 2004, pp. 226–228. ACM, New York (2004). http://doi.acm.org/10.1145/1028664.1028762
11. Harel, D., Thiagarajan, P.: Message sequence charts. In: Lavagno, L., Martin, G., Selic, B. (eds.) UML for Real: Design of Embedded Real-time Systems, 1st edn. Kluwer Academic Publishers (2003)
12. Ishio, T., Watanabe, Y., Inoue, K.: AMIDA: A sequence diagram extraction toolkit supporting automatic phase detection. In: ICSE 2008, pp. 969–970 (2008). http://doi.acm.org/10.1145/1370175.1370212

13. Jerding, D.F., Stasko, J.T., Ball, T.: Visualizing interactions in program executions. In: ICSE 1997, pp. 360–370 (1997). http://doi.acm.org/10.1145/253228. 253356
14. Korshunova, E., Petkovic, M., van den Brand, M.G.J., Mousavi, M.R.: CPP2XMI: Reverse engineering of UML class, sequence, and activity diagrams from C++ source code. In: WCRE 2006, pp. 297–298 (2006). http://dx.doi.org/10.1109/WCRE.2006.21
15. Kroening, D.: goto-cc–A C/C++ Front-End for Verification (2015). http://www.cprover.org/goto-cc/
16. Kumar, S., Khoo, S., Roychoudhury, A., Lo, D.: Mining message sequence graphs. In: ICSE 2011, pp. 91–100 (2011). http://doi.acm.org/10.1145/1985793.1985807
17. Kumar, S., Khoo, S., Roychoudhury, A., Lo, D.: Inferring class level specifications for distributed systems. In: ICSE 2012, pp. 914–924 (2012). http://dx.doi.org/10.1109/ICSE.2012.6227128
18. Leucker, M., Madhusudan, P., Mukhopadhyay, S.: Dynamic message sequence charts. In: Agrawal, M., Seth, A. (eds.) FSTTCS 2002. LNCS, vol. 2556, pp. 253–264. Springer, Heidelberg (2002). doi:10.1007/3-540-36206-1_23
19. Livshits, V.B., Lam, M.S.: Finding security vulnerabilities in java applications with static analysis. In: SSYM 2005, pp. 18–18. USENIX Association, Berkeley (2005). http://dl.acm.org/citation.cfm?id=1251398.1251416
20. Lo, D., Maoz, S.: Mining scenario-based triggers and effects. In: ASE 2008, pp. 109–118 (2008). http://dx.doi.org/10.1109/ASE.2008.21
21. Lo, D., Maoz, S.: Mining hierarchical scenario-based specifications. In: ASE 2009, pp. 359–370 (2009). http://dx.doi.org/10.1109/ASE.2009.19
22. Lo, D., Maoz, S., Khoo, S.: Mining modal scenario-based specifications from execution traces of reactive systems. In: ASE 2007, pp. 465–468 (2007). http://doi.acm.org/10.1145/1321631.1321710
23. Msdn.microsoft.com: Visualize Code on Sequence Diagrams (2015). https://msdn.microsoft.com/en-us/library/ee317485.aspx
24. Myers, D., Storey, M.A.: Using dynamic analysis to create trace-focused user interfaces for IDEs. In: FSE 2010, pp. 367–368. ACM, New York (2010). http://doi.acm.org/10.1145/1882291.1882351
25. Objectaid.com: UML Explorer (2015). http://www.objectaid.com/sequence-diagram
26. Roubtsov, S.A., Serebrenik, A., Mazoyer, A., van den Brand, M.G.J., Roubtsova, E.E.: I2SD: Reverse engineering sequence diagrams from enterprise java beans with interceptors. IET Softw. 7(3) (2013). http://dx.doi.org/10.1049/iet-sen.2012.0056
27. Rountev, A., Connell, B.H.: Object naming analysis for reverse-engineered sequence diagrams. In: ICSE 2005, pp. 254–263 (2005). http://doi.acm.org/10.1145/1062455.1062510
28. Rountev, A., Volgin, O., Reddoch, M.: Static control-flow analysis for reverse engineering of UML sequence diagrams. In: PASTE 2005, pp. 96–102 (2005). http://doi.acm.org/10.1145/1108792.1108816
29. Sable Research Group: Soot: A framework for Analyzing and Transforming Java and Android Applications (2015). http://sable.github.io/soot/
30. Sampaio, L.: Early Security Vulnerability Detector. https://marketplace.eclipse.org/content/early-security-vulnerability-detector-esvd. Accessed 16 Oct 2016
31. Sampaio, L., Garcia, A.: Exploring context-sensitive data flow analysis for early vulnerability detection. J. Syst. Softw. **113**, 337–361 (2016). http://www.sciencedirect.com/science/article/pii/S0164121215002873

32. Soyatec.com: Soyatec - Sequence diagram generation (2015). http://www.soyatec.com/euml2/features/eUML2%20Modeler/
33. Tonella, P., Potrich, A.: Reverse engineering of the interaction diagrams from C++ code. In: ICSM 2003, pp. 159–168 (2003). http://dx.doi.org/10.1109/ICSM.2003.1235418
34. Visual-paradigm.com: Reverse Engineering Sequence Diagram from Java Source Code (2015). https://www.visual-paradigm.com/tutorials/seqrev.jsp
35. Wikipedia: List of Free and Open-Source Android Applications (2015). http://en.wikipedia.org/wiki/List_of_free_and_open-source_Android_applications
36. Ziadi, T., da Silva, M.A.A., Hillah, L., Ziane, M.: A fully dynamic approach to the reverse engineering of UML sequence diagrams. In: ICECCS 2011, pp. 107–116 (2011). http://dx.doi.org/10.1109/ICECCS.2011.18

Inter-model Consistency Checking Using Triple Graph Grammars and Linear Optimization Techniques

Erhan Leblebici[1]([⊠]), Anthony Anjorin[2], and Andy Schürr[1]

[1] Technische Universität Darmstadt, Darmstadt, Germany
{erhan.leblebici,andy.schuerr}@es.tu-darmstadt.de
[2] Universität Paderborn, Paderborn, Germany
anthony.anjorin@uni-paderborn.de

Abstract. An important task in *Model-Driven Engineering* (MDE) is to *check consistency* between two *concurrently developed yet related* models. Practical approaches to consistency checking, however, are scarce in MDE. *Triple Graph Grammars* (TGGs) are a rule-based technique to describe the consistency of two models together with correspondences. While TGGs seem promising for consistency checking with their precise consistency notion and explicit traceability information, the substantial search space involved in determining the "optimal" set of rule applications in a consistency check has arguably prevented mature tool support so far. In this paper, we close this gap by combining TGGs with *linear optimization* techniques. We formulate decisions between single rule applications of a consistency check as integer inequalities, which serve as input for an optimization problem used to detect maximum consistent portions of two models. To demonstrate our approach, we provide an experimental evaluation of the tool support made feasible by this formalization.

Keywords: Consistency check · Traceability · Linear optimization

1 Introduction and Motivation

Models are used in Model-Driven Engineering (MDE) to represent abstractions of a system with respect to a certain perspective. In a typical MDE process, especially when different disciplines are involved, there are often models containing related information but maintained by different engineers concurrently giving rise to *consistency* challenges. A crucial task in MDE is thus to perform a *consistency check*, i.e., to determine if, or to what extent, two models are consistent, before applying any consistency restoration. We discuss in this paper consistency checking with *Triple Graph Grammars* (TGGs) [25], a rule-based language for specifying a consistency relation between two modeling languages.

The basic idea of TGGs is to specify a set of rules (a grammar) describing how consistent model pairs are constructed together with a *correspondence* model

© Springer-Verlag GmbH Germany 2017
M. Huisman and J. Rubin (Eds.): FASE 2017, LNCS 10202, pp. 191–207, 2017.
DOI: 10.1007/978-3-662-54494-5_11

representing explicit traceability information. Given such a specification and two models, the goal of a consistency check is to determine whether the models can be constructed by the grammar and, if so, to create a respective correspondence model. If the model pair is not completely consistent, we propose to determine a partial correspondence model referencing consistent subparts of the models.

Establishing consistency checking with TGGs is crucial as practical solutions to consistency checking are currently scarce in MDE. QVT-R [22] (in particular its *checkonly mode*) is the only available standard for consistency checking in MDE. The QVT-R implementation candidate Medini QVT [20], however, is able to check consistency only if one of the models is generated by the tool itself via model transformation and auxiliary traces are already available. Consistency checking for models developed *concurrently* (in independent environments by different developers) where traces are not available beforehand is not addressed so far. Our goal is to tackle this general consistency challenge in concurrent MDE activities by clearing the last obstacles for the applicability of TGGs.

The pioneer work for consistency checking with TGGs is [4] which derives consistency checking rules from a TGG. How to conclude consistency (or inconsistency) of two models with these rules, however, remains open due to the substantial state space regarding decisions among possible rule applications. Finding the *best* partial correspondence model between two inconsistent models (e.g., relating as many elements as possible) is consequently also an open issue. We close this gap by formulating a *linear optimization problem* for choices among rules, and discuss the respective tool support made feasible by this novel formalization. While we discuss relating a maximum number of model elements as a general objective fort the optimization problem, our approach can be extended with custom objectives reflecting case-specific policies for handling inconsistency (e.g., covering as many elements as possible of a certain type, model, or property).

As a running example, we consider consistency between Java code and UML class diagrams throughout the paper. Note that many UML tools generate Java code from UML class diagrams (or vice versa) in a consistent way but no practical solution exists to check consistency between these artifacts if they are developed concurrently (similar to the shortcomings of QVT-R implementations as discussed above). The excerpt we focus on in our running example is a one-to-one mapping between Java and UML classes, methods, and parameters but already reveals the complexity of consistency checking. The challenging part of our case study arises from *overloaded methods*: Determining the corresponding pairs of methods belonging to the same class and sharing the same name can require a careful decision making. Consider, for example, the consistent Java and UML class pair in Fig. 1. The dashed lines represent correct decisions of corresponding remove methods (and consequently corresponding parameters), while the dotted lines represent wrong decisions. In fact, such local decisions while relating two models are not specific to this example and wrong decisions can be chosen by a

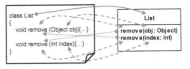

Fig. 1. A consistent model pair

TGG-based consistency check. In this case, our consistent model pair would be identified erroneously as inconsistent (due to incompatible parameters of mistakenly corresponding methods). Our experiments with HenshinTGG [8], the only TGG tool we are aware of with consistency checking support, showed that consistency checking indeed fails in cases where such decisions are necessary.

Our approach considers alternative steps of a consistency check and uses logical dependencies between single steps to calculate a correct subset. This corresponds to creating all lines together in Fig. 1, solving a suitable optimization problem to maximize the number of related elements, and eliminating the dotted lines in retrospect. Intuitively, the dashed and dotted lines in Fig. 1 are alternatives where the dashed ones relate a larger number of elements.

After reviewing basic TGG theory in Sect. 2, we formalize in Sect. 3 choices between alternative decisions in a consistency check as integer inequalities. Our basic formal result in Theorem 1 states that any choice satisfying these inequalities leads to some consistent portions of models. Subsequently, we state a sufficient (Corollary 1) as well as a sufficient and necessary (Corollary 2) condition for consistency by maximizing these portions. Section 4 evaluates our tool support. Section 5 discusses related work, and Sect. 6 concludes the paper.

2   Preliminaries

In line with the algebraic formalization of graph grammars [6], we represent *models* as *graphs*. We then introduce *triples* of graphs (Fig. 2) as we shall be dealing with *source*, *target*, and *correspondence* models (denoted with S, T, or C prefix, respectively). The notion of triple graphs provides a precise means for describing correspondences as graph patterns that are amenable to mature graph transformation tools. We provide our formalization without type and attribute information in graphs for brevity. The formalization can be extended compatibly to attributed typed graphs with inheritance according to [6].

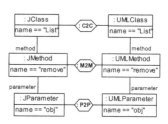

Fig. 2. A triple graph

Definition 1 (Graph, Triple Graph). *A graph $G = (V, E, s, t)$ consists of a set V of vertices, a set E of edges, and two functions $s, t : E \to V$ assigning to each edge a source and target vertex, respectively. elements(G) denotes the union $V \cup E$ where each $e \in$ elements(G) is an element of G. A graph morphism $f : G \to G'$, with $G' = (V', E', s', t')$, is a pair of functions $f_V : V \to V'$, $f_E : E \to E'$ such that $f_V \circ s = s' \circ f_E \wedge f_V \circ t = t' \circ f_E$. f is a monomorphism iff f_V and f_E are injective.*

A triple graph $G = G_S \xleftarrow{\gamma_S} G_C \xrightarrow{\gamma_T} G_T$ consists of graphs G_S, G_C, G_T, and graph morphisms $\gamma_S : G_C \to G_S$ and $\gamma_T : G_C \to G_T$. elements(G) denotes the union elements$(G_S) \cup$ elements$(G_C) \cup$ elements(G_T). A triple morphism $f : G \to G'$ with $G' = G'_S \xleftarrow{\gamma'_S} G'_C \xrightarrow{\gamma'_T} G'_T$, is a triple $f = (f_S, f_C, f_T)$ of graph morphisms *where $f_X : G_X \to G'_X$ and $X \in \{S, C, T\}$, $f_S \circ \gamma_S = \gamma'_S \circ f_C$ and $f_T \circ \gamma_T = \gamma'_T \circ f_C$. f is a triple monomorphism iff f_S, f_C, and f_T are monomorphisms.*

A TGG comprises monotonic (i.e., non-deleting) *triple rules* that generate and thus define the language of consistent source and target graphs.

Definition 2 (Triple Rule and Derivation). *A triple rule r : $L \to R$ is a triple monomorphism. A direct derivation via a triple rule r, denoted as $G \xRightarrow{r@m} G'$, is constructed, as depicted to the right, by a pushout over r and a triple monomorphism $m : L \to G$ where m is called* match. *A derivation $D : G \xRightarrow{r_1@m_1} G_1 \xRightarrow{r_2@m_2} \ldots \xRightarrow{r_n@m_n} G_n$ (short $D : G \xRightarrow{*} G_n$) is a sequence of direct derivations. We refer to the set $\mathcal{D} = \{d_1, \ldots, d_n\}$ of direct derivations included in D as the underlying set of D.*

$$
\begin{array}{ccc}
L & \xrightarrow{r} & R \\
\downarrow{m} & PO & \downarrow{m'} \\
G & \xrightarrow{g} & G'
\end{array}
$$

Example 1. Figure 3 depicts four TGG rules for our running example where created elements of a rule (i.e., elements in R but not in L) are depicted green with a ++-markup. Context elements (L) are depicted black. Triple rule r_1 creates a Java class and a UML class together with a correspondence. Triple rule r_2 does the same with additional inheritance links on both sides. Triple rule r_3 creates a corresponding pair of Java and UML methods, while triple rule r_4 creates parameters. The attribute constraints (e.g., *jc.name == uc.name* in r_1) enforce name equality of corresponding classes, methods, and parameters.

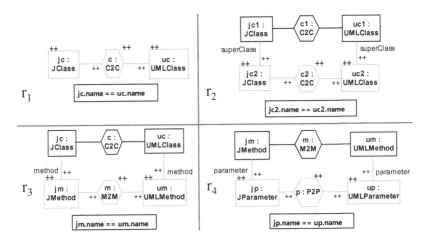

Fig. 3. TGG rules describing how consistent models are constructed

Definition 3 (Triple Graph Grammar and Consistency). *A triple graph grammar $TGG : \mathcal{R}$ consists of a set $\mathcal{R}$ of triple rules. The generated language*

$\mathcal{L}(TGG)$ is defined as follows: $\mathcal{L}(TGG) = \{G_\emptyset\} \cup \{G \mid \exists D : G_\emptyset \xrightarrow{r_1@m_1} G_1 \xrightarrow{r_2@m_2}$
$\cdots \xrightarrow{r_n@m_n} G_n = G\}$, where $G_\emptyset$ is the empty triple graph and, $\forall i \in \{1, \ldots, n\}$,
$r_i \in \mathcal{R}$. A source graph G_S and a target graph G_T are consistent with respect to
TGG iff $\exists G \in \mathcal{L}(TGG)$ with $G = G_S \leftarrow G_C \rightarrow G_T$.

Finally, we define *consistency rules* derived from the original triple rules.
They *mark* source and target elements that would be created by the original
TGG rules. This way, it can be determined whether a given pair of source and
target graphs can be constructed by applying the original triple rules of a TGG.

Definition 4 (Consistency Rule and Marking Elements).

Given a triple rule $r : L \rightarrow R$
with $L = L_S \leftarrow L_C \rightarrow L_T$
and $R = R_S \leftarrow R_C \rightarrow$
R_T, *the respective consis-*
tency rule $cr : CL \rightarrow CR$
is constructed, as depicted to

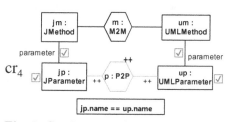

the right, such that CL is a pushout of L and $R_S \leftarrow \emptyset \rightarrow R_T$ *over* $L_S \leftarrow \emptyset \rightarrow L_T$,
and $CR = R$ *($cr : CL \rightarrow CR$ is induced as the universal property of the pushout).*
An element $e \in$ elements$(R_S) \cup$ elements(R_T) *is referred to as a* marking element
of cr iff $\nexists e' \in$ elements$(L_S) \cup$ elements(L_T) *with* $r_S(e') = e$ *or* $r_T(e') = e$.

Example 2. The consistency rule cr_4
derived from the original triple rule
r_4 is depicted to the right together
with its marking elements. Intuitively,
a consistency rule *marks* exactly those
source and target elements that are
created by the original triple rule (++-
markup is replaced by a gray checked
box on the source and target side),
and creates the same correspondences.
Consistency rules cr_1, cr_2, and cr_3 for

Fig. 4. Consistency rule cr_4 derived from
r_4 in Fig. 3

the respective triple rules r_1, r_2, and r_3 are derived analogously.

3   Choices Between Markings as an Optimization Problem

Our goal in this section is to check consistency for a given model pair G_S and G_T
with respect to a TGG, i.e., to find a triple graph $G'_S \leftarrow G_C \rightarrow G'_T \in \mathcal{L}(TGG)$
where G'_S and G'_T refer to the consistent portions of G_S and G_T, respectively
($G'_S = G_S$ and $G'_T = G_T$ if G_S and G_T are consistent). Direct derivations via
consistency rules represent the single steps of such a consistency check. Markings
simulate the creation of G_S and G_T by the original triple rules and correspondences (G_C) are created in the process serving as traceability information. As
we have discussed in Sect. 1, however, this process can result in wrong markings
and correspondence creations if it is not suitably controlled.

In the following, we consider derivations with consistency rules that possibly mark model elements multiple times and thus represent a superset of correct markings. We consider each direct derivation of such a derivation as an integer between 0-1 and formulate integer inequalities for exclusion and implication dependencies between direct derivations which were discussed in previous work [17]. In sum, we combine two techniques: Graph pattern matching (via consistency rules) is performed on triple graphs and logical constraints over matched patterns are solved. While the first reduces the search space via structural patterns (as compared to purely constraint-based solutions such as [18,19]), the latter leads to a final choice between matchings.

Moreover, we handle the logical constraints as an *optimization problem* to address consistency and inconsistency in a unified manner. This allows us to use an *objective function* that governs the process to find a best choice among collected direct derivations, which is especially crucial in case of inconsistency. In this paper, we only focus on maximizing the number of related elements as the objective while our approach can be extended by further custom objectives reflecting case-specific consistency policies (e.g., marking as many UML elements as possible while marking Java elements is not of uppermost priority). The main idea is depicted schematically in Fig. 5 based on our exemplary model pair.

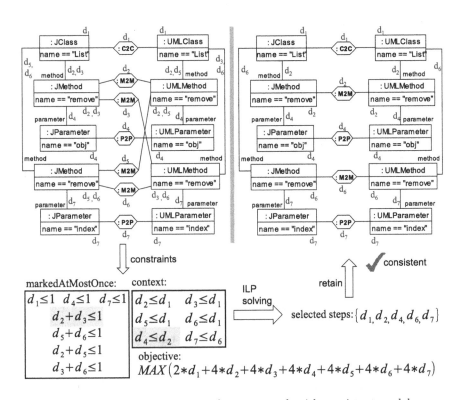

Fig. 5. A schematic overview of our approach with consistent models

In the upper left part of Fig. 5, a derivation of seven direct derivations $\{d_1, \ldots, d_7\}$ with consistency rules marks the source and target model elements. Every source and target model element is annotated with its marking direct derivations. Similarly, each correspondence is annotated with its creating direct derivation. Without taking a decision, for instance, all overloaded remove methods are marked twice due to multiple options. Sets of *constraints* then state logical dependencies between direct derivations. For example, both d_2 and d_3 mark the same remove method on the Java side as alternatives and thus cannot be chosen together, leading to $d_2 + d_3 \leq 1$ (highlighted with a gray shading in Fig. 5). Furthermore, d_2 creates a correspondence and marks source and target elements used by d_4 as context to mark obj parameters. Hence, d_4 can only be chosen if d_2 is chosen (leading to $d_4 \leq d_2$). Finally, an *objective function* maximizes the number of marked elements while satisfying the inequalities (each direct derivation is weighted with the number of its marked elements). This forms a linear optimization problem and can be appropriately handled with *Integer Linear Programming* (ILP) techniques in practice (in fact, a special case of ILP with 0-1 integers). The model pair in Fig. 5 is identified to be consistent as the outcome of the optimization problem marks each model element exactly once (as they would be if created by the original TGG rules).

To formalize this idea, we first define sets of *marked, required,* and *created* elements of a direct derivation, which are decisive for formulating constraints.

Definition 5 (Marked, Required, and Created Elements). *For a direct derivation* $d : G \xLongrightarrow{cr@cm} G'$ *via a consistency rule* $cr : CL \to CR$ *with* $G = G_S \leftarrow G_C \to G_T$ *and* $G' = G_S \leftarrow G'_C \to G_T$, *we define the following sets:*

- *marks*$(d) = \{e \in elements(G_S) \cup elements(G_T) \mid \exists e' \in elements(CL)$ *with* $cm(e') = e$ *where* e' *is a marking element of* $cr\}$
- *requiresSrcTrg*$(d) = \{e \in elements(G_S) \cup elements(G_T) \mid \exists e' \in elements(CL)$ *with* $cm(e') = e$ *where* e' *is not a marking element of* $cr\}$
- *requiresCorr*$(d) = \{e \in elements(G_C) \mid \exists e' \in elements(CL)$ *with* $cm(e') = e\}$
- *creates*$(d) = elements(G'_C) \setminus elements(G_C)$.

Given a model pair $G_0 = G_S \leftarrow \emptyset \to G_T$, a derivation constraint is a set of integer inequalities representing exclusions and implications between direct derivations collected in a consistency check process starting from G_0.

Definition 6 (Constraints for Consistency Check Derivations). *Given a triple graph* $G_0 : G_S \leftarrow \emptyset \to G_T$, *let* $D : G_0 \overset{*}{\Rightarrow} G_n$ *be a derivation via consistency rules with the underlying set* $\mathcal{D}$ *of direct derivations. For each direct derivation* $d_1, \ldots, d_n \in \mathcal{D}$, *we define respective integer variables* $\delta_1, \ldots, \delta_n$ *with* $0 \leq \delta_1, \ldots, \delta_n \leq 1$. *A constraint* $\mathcal{C}$ *for* D *is a conjunction of linear inequalities which involve* $\delta_1, \ldots, \delta_n$. *A set* $\mathcal{D}' \subseteq \mathcal{D}$ *fulfills* $\mathcal{C}$, *denoted as* $\mathcal{D}' \vdash \mathcal{C}$, *iff* $\mathcal{C}$ *is satisfied for variable assignments* $\delta_i = 1$ *if* $d_i \in \mathcal{D}'$ *and* $\delta_i = 0$ *if* $d_i \notin \mathcal{D}'$.

Our first constraint markedAtMostOnce(G_0) requires that each source and target element of a model pair G_0 be marked at most once, i.e., a choice between alternative markings of the same element(s) is enforced. As a result of a consistency check, an element can either remain unmarked (due to inconsistency) or it can be marked once. Definition 7 introduces the sum of alternative markings of the same element and Definition 8 restricts it to 0–1 as a constraint.

Definition 7 (Sum of Alternative Markings for an Element). *Given a triple graph* $G_0 = G_S \leftarrow \emptyset \rightarrow G_T$, *let* $D : G_0 \overset{*}{\Rightarrow} G_n$ *be a derivation via consistency rules with the underlying set* $\mathcal{D}$ *of direct derivations. For each element* $e \in elements(G_0)$, *let* $\mathcal{E} = \{d \in \mathcal{D} \mid e \in marks(d)\}$. *The integer* $markersSum(e)$ *denotes the sum of variables for each* $d \in \mathcal{E}$ *as follows:* *If* $\mathcal{E} = \emptyset$, $markersSum(e) = 0$. *If* $\mathcal{E} = \{d_1\}$, $markersSum(e) = \delta_1$. *If* $\mathcal{E} = \{d_1, \dots, d_n\}$, $markersSum(e) = \delta_1 + \dots + \delta_n$.

Definition 8 (Constraint 1: Marking Each Element at Most Once). *Given a triple graph* $G_0 = G_S \leftarrow \emptyset \rightarrow G_T$, *let* $D : G_0 \overset{*}{\Rightarrow} G_n$ *be a derivation via consistency rules with the underlying set* $\mathcal{D}$ *of direct derivations. The constraint* $markedAtMostOnce(G_0)$ *denotes* $\bigwedge\limits_{e \in elements(G_0)} markersSum(e) \leq 1$.

The next constraint context(D) defines dependencies as implications between direct derivations due to their required context: A direct derivation is either not chosen, or its required source and target elements must be marked and its required correspondences must be created by some other chosen direct derivations. This is necessary as each chosen marking should be traced back to a derivation by the original TGG rules, where the context must always be provided.

Definition 9 (Constraint 2: Providing Context for Markings). *Given a triple graph* $G_0 = G_S \leftarrow \emptyset \rightarrow G_T$, *let* $D : G_0 \overset{*}{\Rightarrow} G_n$ *be a derivation via consistency rules with the underlying set* $\mathcal{D}$ *of direct derivations. For each direct derivation* $d_i \in D$, *we define the following constraints:* $contextSrcTrg(d_i) = \bigwedge\limits_{e \in requiresSrcTrg(d_i)} \delta_i \leq markersSum(e), contextCorr(d_i) = \bigwedge\limits_{d_j \in \mathcal{D}, requiresCorr(d_i) \cap creates(d_j) \neq \emptyset} \delta_i \leq \delta_j,$ *The constraint* $context(D)$ *denotes* $\bigwedge\limits_{d_i \in \mathcal{D}} contextSrcTrg(d_i) \wedge contextCorr(d_i)$.

Example 3. In Fig. 5, the constraints $markedAtMostOnce(G_0)$ and $context(D)$ are depicted (after some logical simplifications) for our example.

The constraint context(D) ensures that the context for each chosen direct derivation is supplied but *cycles* must still be avoided. Intuitively, two chosen direct derivations may not provide context for each other (also not transitively) as such derivations cannot be sequenced in terms of the underlying TGG.

Definition 10 (Cyclic Markings). *Let* $D : G_0 \overset{*}{\Rightarrow} G_n$ *be a derivation via consistency rules with the underlying set* $\mathcal{D}$ *of direct derivations. We define a relation* $\rhd \subseteq \mathcal{D} \times \mathcal{D}$ *between two direct derivations* $d_i, d_j \in \mathcal{D}$ *as follows:* $d_i \rhd d_j$ *iff* $requiresSrcTrg(d_i) \cap marks(d_j) \neq \emptyset$ *or* $requiresCorr(d_i) \cap creates(d_j) \neq \emptyset$. *A sequence* $cy \subseteq \mathcal{D}$ *with* $cy = \{d_1, \dots, d_n\}$ *of direct derivations is a* cycle *iff* $d_1 \rhd \dots \rhd d_n \rhd d_1$.

Definition 11 (Constraint 3: Eliminating Cycles). *Given a triple graph* $G_0 = G_S \leftarrow \emptyset \rightarrow G_T$, *let* $D : G_0 \stackrel{*}{\Rightarrow} G_n$ *be a derivation via consistency rules with the underlying set $\mathcal{D}$ of direct derivations and let $\mathcal{CY}$ be the set of all cycles* $cy \subseteq \mathcal{D}$. *We define a constraint acyclic(D) as follows:*

$$acyclic(D) = \bigwedge_{\substack{cy \in \mathcal{CY}, \\ cy = \{d_1, \ldots, d_n\}}} \delta_1 + \ldots + \delta_n < |cy| \text{ where } |cy| \text{ is the cardinality of } cy.$$

Example 4. The derivation depicted in Fig. 5 exhibits no cycles. In Fig. 6, however, two direct derivations (d_2 and d_3, both via the consistency rule cr_2 derived from r_2) mark each others required elements ($d_2 \rhd d_3$ and $d_3 \rhd d_2$).

Given two classes List and Queue with cyclic inheritance relation on both sides, d_2 marks the Queue classes and requires List classes, and conversely for d_3. Although d_2 and d_3 mark the model pair entirely (without being alternatives to each other for any element), they cannot be chosen together as they cannot be sequenced in terms of the original grammar. In fact, these models are inconsistent (they just exhibit the same type of inconsistency on both sides) as our TGG (in particular the triple rule r_2) cannot create cyclic inheritance relations.

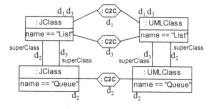

Fig. 6. Cyclic markings of d_2 and d_3

Our constraints so far enforce that (i) each element is marked at most once, (ii) chosen direct derivations completely satisfy their context with other direct derivations, and (iii) direct derivations do not provide context in a cyclic manner to each other. Theorem 1 in the following states that, given a model pair $G_0 = G_S \leftarrow \emptyset \rightarrow G_T$ and a derivation D via consistency rules, each subset of direct derivations in D satisfying these constraints leads to a triple graph representing a consistent portion of G_S and G_T. The consistent triple graph consists of elements marked and created by the chosen subset of direct derivations.

Theorem 1 (Consistent Portions of Source and Target Graphs). *Given a TGG : (TG, R) with the set $\mathcal{CR}$ of respective consistency rules and a triple graph $G_0 = G_S \leftarrow \emptyset \rightarrow G_T$, let $D : G_0 \stackrel{*}{\Rightarrow} G_n$ be a derivation via rules in $\mathcal{CR}$ with the underlying set $\mathcal{D}$ of direct derivations. For any set $\mathcal{D}' \subseteq \mathcal{D}$ with $\mathcal{D}' \vdash markedAtMostOnce(G_0) \land context(D) \land acyclic(D)$, we get a triple graph $G' = G'_S \leftarrow G'_C \rightarrow G'_T$ such that $G' \in \mathcal{L}(TGG)$, elements$(G'_S) \subseteq$ elements(G_S), elements$(G'_T) \subseteq$ elements(G_T), and elements$(G') = \bigcup_{d \in \mathcal{D}'} (marks(d) \cup creates(d))$.*

Proof. For each direct derivation d in $\mathcal{D}'$, the required source and target elements are marked and the required correspondences are created by some other direct derivations in $\mathcal{D}'$ (context(D)). Furthermore, direct derivations in $\mathcal{D}'$ provide context for each other in an acyclic manner (acyclic(D)). Hence, all direct derivations in $\mathcal{D}'$ can be sequenced to a derivation D' via rules in $\mathcal{CR}$. Marked and created elements of each direct derivation in D' are equal to created elements by the respective original triple rule (cf. consistency rule construction in Definition 4). Consequently, the union of marked and created elements of D' leads to a triple graph $G' = G'_S \leftarrow G'_C \rightarrow G'_T \in \mathcal{L}(TGG)$. Moreover, G'_S and G'_T are composed by picking each element of G_S and G_T at most once as markedAtMostOnce(G_0) holds, i.e., we get elements(G'_S) $\subseteq$ elements(G_S) and elements(G'_T) $\subseteq$ elements(G_T). $\qquad\square$

In practice, when applying Theorem 1, we employ an ILP solver together with an objective maximizing the number of marked elements as depicted in Fig. 5. Consistency of two models can be concluded if the maximally marked portions in Theorem 1 are equal to the entire models.

Corollary 1 (A Sufficient Condition for Consistency). *Given a TGG : $(TG, \mathcal{R})$ with the set $\mathcal{CR}$ of respective consistency rules and a triple graph $G_0 : G_S \leftarrow \emptyset \rightarrow G_T$, let $D : G_0 \overset{*}{\Rightarrow} G_n$ be a derivation via rules in $\mathcal{CR}$ with the underlying set $\mathcal{D}$ of direct derivations. G_S and G_T are consistent if a set $\mathcal{D}' \subseteq \mathcal{D}$ exists with $\mathcal{D}' \vdash$ markedAtMostOnce(G_0) $\wedge$ context(D) $\wedge$ acyclic(D) and $\bigcup_{d \in \mathcal{D}'}$ marks(d) = elements(G_0).*

Proof. This is a special case of Theorem 1 where elements marked and created by direct derivations in $\mathcal{D}'$ result in $G_S \leftarrow G_C \rightarrow G_T \in \mathcal{L}(TGG)$. $\qquad\square$

Example 5. In Fig. 5, two models G_S and G_T are given together with a derivation that marks some model elements multiple times. A subset of direct derivations satisfying the constraints is then determined leading to a triple graph $G_S \leftarrow G_C \rightarrow G_T$, i.e., G_S and G_T are marked entirely.

Corollary 1 is a sufficient condition for consistency and already useful to conclude consistency from arbitrarily collected markings. If no subset of markings in a derivation D is found that satisfies constraints and marks all elements, however, it is unclear if the models are really inconsistent or if there are some further markings that were not collected in D. We thus characterize *final* derivations with consistency rules providing *all possible markings*, and lift our result to a sufficient and necessary condition for consistency. We restrict ourselves in the following to TGGs whose consistency rules mark at least one element (called *progressive* TGGs). Consistency rules that only create correspondences but do not contribute any markings are excluded as it is unclear how often to apply such rules for collecting a complete set of markings. This restriction does not have any significant consequence in practice according to our experience, and is fulfilled by all industrial and academic case studies we have worked on so far.

Definition 12 (Progressive TGG). *A TGG : $(TG, \mathcal{R})$ with the set $\mathcal{CR}$ of respective consistency rules is progressive iff each $cr \in \mathcal{CR}$ has at least one marking element.*

Definition 13 (Final Derivations with Consistency Rules). *Given a progressive TGG* : $(TG, \mathcal{R})$ *with the set* $\mathcal{CR}$ *of respective consistency rules and a triple graph* G_0 : $G_S \leftarrow \emptyset \rightarrow G_T$, *let* $D : G_0 \overset{*}{\Rightarrow} G_n$ *be a derivation via rules in* $\mathcal{CR}$ *with the underlying set* $\mathcal{D}$ *of direct derivations.* D *is final iff* $\forall d_{n+1} : G_n \xrightarrow{cr_{n+1}@cm_{n+1}} G_{n+1}$ *with* $cr_{n+1} \in \mathcal{CR}$, $\exists d_i : G_{i-1} \xrightarrow{cr_i@cm_i} G_i$ *where* $d_i \in \mathcal{D}$, $cr_i = cr_{n+1}$, *and* $cm_i = cm_{n+1}$.

Remark 1. An interesting issue is the existence of a final derivation for a given *TGG* and a model pair. In some cases, the search for a final derivation does not terminate when consistency rules create new matches for each other in a cyclic manner (e.g., in case of a cyclic inheritance in our example as depicted in Fig. 6, direct derivations via cr_2 continuously create new correspondences and thus new matches for each other). The problem is similar to the termination problem of graph grammars which is in general undecidable [23]. In practice, such cycles can either be detected and aborted at runtime, or additional restrictions for the model pair or for the TGG can be imposed. For example, a TGG can be specified in the style of a Layered Graph Grammar [5, 24] whose termination with distinct matches is shown in [5], or models can be constrained to avoid cyclic matches (cyclic inheritance must be prohibited in our concrete case). We leave it to future work to explore a restricted yet sufficiently expressive class of TGGs (statically) guaranteeing the existence of a final derivation.

A final derivation provides all possible markings. In this case, inconsistency can be concluded if a subset of direct derivations satisfying our constraints and marking all elements does not exist. Corollary 2 in the following thus extends our result from Corollary 1 to a sufficient and necessary condition for final derivations via consistency rules of progressive TGGs.

Corollary 2 (A Sufficient and Necessary Condition for Consistency). *Given a progressive TGG* : $(TG, \mathcal{R})$ *with the set* $\mathcal{CR}$ *of respective consistency rules, and a triple graph* G_0 : $G_S \leftarrow \emptyset \rightarrow G_T$, *let* $D : G_0 \overset{*}{\Rightarrow} G_n$ *be a final derivation via rules in* $\mathcal{CR}$ *with the underlying set* $\mathcal{D}$ *of direct derivations.* G_S *and* G_T *are consistent iff a set* $\mathcal{D}' \subseteq \mathcal{D}$ *exists with* $\mathcal{D}' \vdash$ markedAtMostOnce$(G_0) \wedge$ context$(D) \wedge$ acyclic(D) *and* $\bigcup_{d \in \mathcal{D}'}$ marks(d) = elements(G_0).

Proof. If $\mathcal{D}'$ exists, the same arguments as in Corollary 1 apply to conclude consistency of G_S and G_T. We show in the following that inconsistency can be concluded if $\mathcal{D}'$ does not exist: TGG is progressive and D is final. Hence, there does not exist any further direct derivation via consistency rules that contribute new markings with a different match to D. If $\mathcal{D}'$ does not exist, there does not exist any derivation D' via consistency rules whose marked and created elements compose a triple graph $G_S \leftarrow G_C \rightarrow G_T \in \mathcal{L}(TGG)$. As a result of the consistency rule construction (Definition 4), furthermore, for each derivation via original triple rules in $\mathcal{R}$ there exists a unique derivation via consistency rules in $\mathcal{CR}$. Thus, the absence of D' leads to the absence of a derivation via triple rules in $\mathcal{R}$, i.e., G_S and G_T cannot be constructed together by the grammar. $\square$

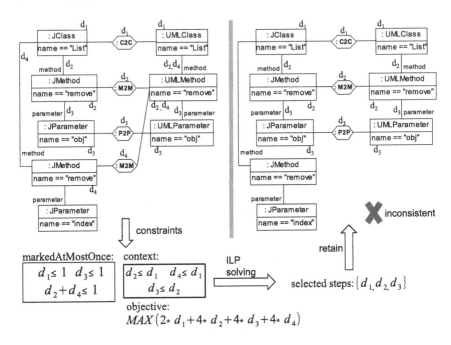

Fig. 7. A further example with inconsistent models

Example 6. Figure 7 shows an example where inconsistency of two models is concluded (we have less methods on the UML side). In the upper left part, we have a final derivation consisting of four direct derivations where d_2 and d_4 mark the same remove method on the UML side. The upper right part depicts a subset of direct derivations satisfying our constraints with the maximum number of marked elements (d_2 is preferred over d_4 in order to mark obj parameters with d_3). Having still unmarked elements on the Java side, however, the models are identified to be inconsistent. Nevertheless, the retained markings and correspondences refer to the maximum consistent portions of these models.

4   Experimental Evaluation

Our goal in this section is to evaluate the applicability of our tool support for consistency checking with regard to performance. To this end, we state the following two research questions to be investigated with our experiments:

RQ1: Are consistency checks by combining TGGs and linear optimization applicable to real-world model pairs?

RQ2: How is the scalability of our implementation affected by different factors including model size and numbers of collected/chosen marking steps?

Evaluation set-up. We approach both research questions with an extended version of our running example. We extracted Java and UML model pairs from real and synthetically generated software projects using the MoDisco tool [21] and performed consistency checks using our TGG tool. Our TGG tool collects alternative markings between two models and utilizes an ILP solver, namely Gurobi [13], for a decision in retrospect (we chose Gurobi due to its performance, available academic licence, and Java API). The TGG in our experiments has 17 rules and relates packages, types, attributes, methods, and parameters on both sides. Method bodies in Java models are ignored as they do not have any counterpart in UML models. In all cases, the only inconsistency detected with our TGG was the primitive type **string** in UML models (which is not primitive in Java). We repeated our measurements 15 times with Intel i5@3.30 GHz, Windows 7 (64 bit), Java 8, Eclipse Neon, and 15 GB memory, and show the median.

Evaluation results and discussion. The upper part of Table 1 shows measurement results with four real software projects with diverse sizes. The number of marked source elements is generally larger than the number of marked target elements as Java models represent the same information with more vertices and edges as compared to UML models. Moreover, there is always a difference between the number of all marking steps and the number of chosen marking steps (as a result of the optimization problem) due to alternative markings of overloaded methods as we have exemplified throughout the paper. Especially the project modisco.java makes intensive usage of method overloading and is thus the most noticeable one among our real software projects with respect to this difference (ca. 3.8 K of 30 K marking steps are chosen). In all experiments with real software projects, ILP solving requires under 1 s while collecting all markings requires between 5 s and 2.5 min depending on the model size. Removing eliminated markings and correspondences has negligible runtime.

Table 1. Measurement results with real and synthetically generated software projects

	Model size		ILP problem size		Runtime			
	# src. elts.	# trg. elts.	# all marking steps	# chosen steps	Collect markings (sec)	ILP solving (sec)	Retain chosen (sec)	Total (sec)
tgg.core	8,484	5,594	2,007	1,919	**5.29**	0.11	0.01	**5.39**
modisco.java	16,705	11,279	29,977	3,791	**15.28**	0.94	0.12	**16.34**
eclipse.graphiti	33,778	21,778	8,819	7,271	**63.20**	0.36	0.03	**63.60**
eclipse.compare	53,391	31,912	11,670	10,700	**143.63**	0.42	0.03	**144.09**
Synthetic ($n = 25$)	2,300	1,081	6,162	362	**1.70**	0.51	0.05	**2.26**
Synthetic ($n = 50$)	8,950	4,006	45,437	1,337	**6.18**	7.64	0.31	**14.13**
Synthetic ($n = 75$)	19,975	8,806	149,087	2,937	**23.53**	53.50	2.64	**79.665**
Synthetic ($n = 100$)	35,375	15,481	348,362	5,162	**67.51**	201.33	13.89	**282.73**
Synthetic ($n = 125$)	55,150	24,031	674,512	8,012	**164.70**	674.08	51.91	**890.69**

In order to explore the limits of the ILP solver (which is not challenged by real models), we furthermore generated synthetic projects consisting of a class with n overloaded methods including 1 to n parameters. We used the same naming convention for all parameters as depicted to the right. With this strategy, we get n^2 possible markings for methods where n of them must be chosen. For parameters, the number of all markings is given by $\sum_{i=1}^{n} i^2$ and the number of chosen ones by $\sum_{i=1}^{n} i$. In all cases, there are 12 further alternativeless markings for (primitive) types and packages. Measurement results in the lower part of Table 1 show that collecting markings requires similar runtime as in real models of similar size, while ILP solving requires more than 3 min for $n = 100$ (ca. 5 K of 348 K markings are chosen) and more than 11 min for $n = 125$ (ca. 8 K of 674 K markings are chosen). This time, removing eliminated markings has also observable runtime (52 s) in the largest case.

In line with our results, we conclude the following for **RQ1** and **RQ2**:

RQ1: Our approach is applicable to realistic models, terminating in the order of only a few minutes for large models with up to 50 K elements. ILP solving can easily cope with our specific type of constraints and objectives if the number of alternative markings is not exceptionally large. Collecting all markings, however, is currently the limiting factor for applicability to larger models.

RQ2: Scalability of collecting all markings strictly depends on the model size but not necessarily on the number of collected markings. This step shows similar runtime behaviour for real and synthetic projects although much more markings are collected in the latter. Apparently, searching for markings between large models (*pattern matching*) is the most costly operation which we also confirmed by profiling. Conversely, scalability of ILP solving has a strict dependency on the number of collected markings (as they form together the optimization problem).

Finally, we believe to have come up with a consistency checking approach which (i) is already applicable to realistic models in its current form, (ii) has reasonable runtime even for corner cases with lots of alternative markings, and (iii) has potential for improvements, especially with respect to pattern matching.

Threats to validity. *External validity* is our primary concern as generalizability of our results requires further non-trivial case studies. We argue, nevertheless, that our synthetically generated models address ultimately challenging cases for their sizes. Furthermore, expectations and research interests of the authors may be a threat to *conclusion validity*. We thus used real-world and randomly chosen models to make experiments unpredictable and carefully utilized profiling tools to draw conclusions on the scalability of individual components.

5   Related Work

We consider two groups of related work: (i) consistency checking approaches in MDE and (ii) MDE-related applications of *optimization techniques*.

Consistency checking approaches. QVT-R [22] proposed by OMG is the only current standard for consistency checking and describes consistency as a set of relations between two models. Seminal contributions to QVT-R, however, primarily address its ambiguous semantics due to a missing formalization in the standard. In [26], a game-theoretic approach is proposed to define semantics of consistency checking with QVT-R, later extended by recursive relations in [1]. In this setting, consistency checking is a game between a verifier and a refuter whose interest is to satisfy or to contradict relations, respectively. In [12], QVT-R is translated to graph constraints using similar formal foundations as for TGGs. Due to the nature of QVT-R, however, consistency must be designed in two directions in these formalisms (there is a forward and backward consistency check) and direction-agnostic traceability information is not provided [26]. An interesting approach is proposed in [18,19] defining QVT-R semantics as a constraint solving problem. While constraint solving is employed for entire models in this case, our approach is in contrast rule-based and formulates only decisions between rule applications as constraints. Our constraints are thus more compact and manageable for state-of-the-art solvers. This claim is supported by the order of processable model sizes of our approach (currently up to 50 K elements) as compared to experimental results in [19] (hundreds of elements). It is, nonetheless, crucial to establish benchmarks for a direct comparison of different approaches. Considering recent work on TGGs, reusing existing markings and correspondences from former runs is proposed in [7,14] when relating two models. Decision making for remaining parts, however, is still open and can be tackled with our approach. Combining our approach with [7,14] could yield performance gains via incrementality and is thus important future work.

Optimization techniques in MDE. We observe a close relation between our work and [10] which combines search-based optimization techniques with model transformation. Given a set of rules, input model(s), and an objective, the idea is to calculate an "optimal" sequence of rule applications via search-based algorithms. Interestingly, this can reverse the complexity distribution of our approach: While we invest substantial effort in rule applications (collecting all markings) and solve a rather simple optimization problem (at least in case of realistic models) in retrospect, more effort is put into optimization in [10] and necessary rule applications are determined in advance. Different MDE tasks are addressed with search-based optimization including change detection [9] and refactoring [11]. Further investigation is needed to understand to what extent the same methodologies are applicable to our goals. Other applications of optimization techniques in MDE include bidirectional model transformation [2] and learning model transformation by examples [15]. Applicability to large models, however, is again a critical limitation in these cases as the papers openly discuss.

6   Conclusion and Future Work

We presented an approach to inter-model consistency checking by combining TGGs with linear optimization techniques. We evaluated our respective tool support and explored its scalability with realistic and synthetically generated models. Our results show that the idea of combining a model transformation engine with optimization techniques is promising and we believe that it can be transferred to other approaches (e.g., QVT-R) to facilitate decision making. Tasks for future work include (i) experimenting with further industrial case studies as well as with academic non-trivial examples as collected in the *bx* example repository [3], (ii) comparing our approach to hand-written solutions of the same problem (developed with general purpose or bidirectional programming languages such as [16]), (iii) utilizing novel pattern matching techniques (e.g., [27,28]) to attain applicability to larger models, (iv) incremental consistency checking by reusing results from former runs, and (v) exploring new types of optimization problems beyond identifying maximal consistent portions and represent case-specific policies. Finally, our contribution paves the way to *bidirectional model integration*. Starting with two inconsistent models, consistent parts can be detected with the current contribution. Remaining parts can be synchronized again by TGGs (possibly after a conflict resolution).

Acknowledgement. This work has been funded by the German Federal Ministry of Education and Research within the Software Campus project GraTraM at TU Darmstadt, funding code 01IS12054.

References

1. Bradfield, J., Stevens, P.: Recursive checkonly QVT-R transformations with general *when* and *where* clauses via the modal Mu calculus. In: Lara, J., Zisman, A. (eds.) FASE 2012. LNCS, vol. 7212, pp. 194–208. Springer, Heidelberg (2012). doi:10.1007/978-3-642-28872-2_14
2. Callow, G., Kalawsky, R.: A satisficing bi-directional model transformation engine using mixed integer linear programming. J. Object Technol. **12**(1), 1–43 (2013)
3. Cheney, J., McKinna, J., Stevens, P., Gibbons, J.: Towards a repository of BX examples. In: Candan, K.S., Amer-Yahia, S., Schweikardt, N., Christophides, V., Leroy, V. (eds.) BX 2014. CEUR Workshop Proceedings, vol. 1133, pp. 87–91 (2014). CEUR-WS.org
4. Ehrig, H., Ehrig, K., Hermann, F.: From model transformation to model integration based on the algebraic approach to triple graph grammars. ECEASST **10**, 1–15 (2008)
5. Ehrig, H., Ehrig, K., Lara, J., Taentzer, G., Varró, D., Varró-Gyapay, S.: Termination criteria for model transformation. In: Cerioli, M. (ed.) FASE 2005. LNCS, vol. 3442, pp. 49–63. Springer, Heidelberg (2005). doi:10.1007/978-3-540-31984-9_5
6. Ehrig, H., Ehrig, K., Prange, U., Taentzer, G.: Fundamentals of Algebraic Graph Transformation. Monographs in Theoretical Computer Science. An EATCS Series. Springer, Heidelberg (2006)
7. Ehrig, H., Ermel, C., Golas, U., Hermann, F.: Graph and Model Transformation - General Framework and Applications. Monographs in Theoretical Computer Science. An EATCS Series. Springer, Heidelberg (2015)
8. Ermel, C., Hermann, F., Gall, J., Binanzer, D.: Visual modeling and analysis of EMF model transformations based on triple graph grammars. ECEASST **54**, 1–12 (2012)

9. Fadhel, A.B., Kessentini, M., Langer, P., Wimmer, M.: Search-based detection of high-level model changes. ICSM **2012**, 212–221 (2012)
10. Fleck, M., Troya, J., Wimmer, M.: Marrying search-based optimization and model transformation technology. In: Proceedings of NasBASE (2015)
11. Fleck, M., Troya, J., Wimmer, M.: Search-based model transformations with MOMoT. In: Van Gorp, P., Engels, G. (eds.) ICMT 2016. LNCS, vol. 9765, pp. 79–87. Springer, Cham (2016). doi:10.1007/978-3-319-42064-6_6
12. Guerra, E., de Lara, J.: An algebraic semantics for QVT-relations check-only transformations. Fundam. Inform. **114**(1), 73–101 (2012)
13. Gurobi: (2016). http://www.gurobi.com/
14. Hermann, F., Ehrig, H., Orejas, F., Czarnecki, K., Diskin, Z., Xiong, Y., Gottmann, S., Engel, T.: Model synchronization based on triple graph grammars: correctness, completeness and invertibility. Softw. Syst. Model. **14**(1), 241–269 (2015)
15. Kessentini, M., Sahraoui, H., Boukadoum, M.: Model transformation as an optimization problem. In: Czarnecki, K., Ober, I., Bruel, J.-M., Uhl, A., Völter, M. (eds.) MODELS 2008. LNCS, vol. 5301, pp. 159–173. Springer, Heidelberg (2008). doi:10.1007/978-3-540-87875-9_12
16. Ko, H., Zan, T., Hu, Z.: BiGUL: a formally verified core language for putback-based bidirectional programming. In: Erwig, M., Rompf, T. (eds.) PEPM 2016, pp. 61–72 (2016)
17. Leblebici, E.: Towards a graph grammar-based approach to inter-model consistency checks with traceability support. In: Anjorin, A., Gibbons, J. (eds.) BX 2016. CEUR Workshop Proceedings, vol. 1571, pp. 35–39 (2016). CEUR-WS.org
18. Macedo, N., Cunha, A.: Implementing QVT-R bidirectional model transformations using alloy. In: Cortellessa, V., Varró, D. (eds.) FASE 2013. LNCS, vol. 7793, pp. 297–311. Springer, Heidelberg (2013). doi:10.1007/978-3-642-37057-1_22
19. Macedo, N., Cunha, A.: Least-change bidirectional model transformation with QVT-R and ATL. Softw. Syst. Model. **15**(3), 783–810 (2016)
20. Medini-QVT: (2016). http://projects.ikv.de/qvt
21. MoDisco: (2016). http://www.eclipse.org/MoDisco/
22. OMG: QVT Specification, V1.2 (2015). http://www.omg.org/spec/QVT/
23. Plump, D.: Termination of graph rewriting is undecidable. Fundam. Inform. **33**(2), 201–209 (1998)
24. Rekers, J., Schürr, A.: Defining and parsing visual languages with layered graph grammars. J. Vis. Lang. Comput. **8**(1), 27–55 (1997)
25. Schürr, A.: Specification of graph translators with triple graph grammars. In: Mayr, E.W., Schmidt, G., Tinhofer, G. (eds.) WG 1994. LNCS, vol. 903, pp. 151–163. Springer, Heidelberg (1995). doi:10.1007/3-540-59071-4_45
26. Stevens, P.: A simple game-theoretic approach to checkonly QVT relations. In: Paige, R.F. (ed.) ICMT 2009. LNCS, vol. 5563, pp. 165–180. Springer, Heidelberg (2009). doi:10.1007/978-3-642-02408-5_12
27. Ujhelyi, Z., Bergmann, G., Hegedüs, Á., Horváth, Á., Izsó, B., Ráth, I., Szatmári, Z., Varró, D.: EMF-IncQuery: an integrated development environment for live model queries. Sci. Comput. Program. **98**, 80–99 (2015)
28. Varró, G., Deckwerth, F.: A Rete network construction algorithm for incremental pattern matching. In: Duddy, K., Kappel, G. (eds.) ICMT 2013. LNCS, vol. 7909, pp. 125–140. Springer, Heidelberg (2013). doi:10.1007/978-3-642-38883-5_13

GTS Families for the Flexible Composition of Graph Transformation Systems

Steffen Zschaler[1(✉)] and Francisco Durán[2]

[1] Department of Informatics, King's College London, London WC2R 2LS, UK
szschaler@acm.org
[2] Dpto. de Lenguajes y Ciencias de la Computación,
University of Málaga, Málaga, Spain
duran@lcc.uma.es

Abstract. Morphisms between graph-transformation systems (GTSs) have been successfully used for the refinement, reuse, and composition of GTSs. All these uses share a fundamental problem: to be able to define a morphism, source and target GTSs need to be quite similar in their structure (in terms of both the type graphs and the set of rules and their respective structures). This limits the applicability of these approaches by excluding a wide range of mappings that would intuitively be accepted as meaningful, but that cannot be captured formally as a morphism. Some researchers have attempted to introduce some flexibility, but these attempts either focus only on the type graphs (e.g., Kleisli morphisms between type graphs) or only support specific forms of deviation (e.g., supporting sub-typing in type graphs through clan morphisms). In this work, we introduce the notion of GTS families, which provide a general mechanism for explicitly expressing the amount of acceptable adaptability of the involved GTSs so that the intended morphisms can be defined. On this basis, we demonstrate how GTS families that are extension preserving can be used to enable flexible GTS amalgamation.

1 Introduction

Graph transformation systems (GTSs) were proposed in the late seventies as a formal technique for the rule-based specification of the dynamic behaviour of systems [1]. Since then, GTSs have been used in different contexts in computer science, including the formalisation of systems, programming languages and model-driven engineering.

In the many contexts in which GTSs have been used, a key ingredient for exploiting their power is that of GTS morphisms. GTS morphisms have been used for different purposes in system specification, for instance, to characterise the relationship between a system and views of it [2], for expressing refinements [3,4], or for modelling import and export interfaces of modules [5]. Recent uses of GTSs in the context of Model-Driven Engineering (MDE) have gone one step further, proposing practical uses of different forms of parametric GTSs for reusing model transformations, and reusing and composing domain specific language

M. Huisman and J. Rubin (Eds.): FASE 2017, LNCS 10202, pp. 208–225, 2017.
DOI: 10.1007/978-3-662-54494-5_12

(DSL) definitions. In [6], de Lara and Guerra proposed the use of transformation templates, typed by a graph, that they call *concept*, which can then be instantiated by binding the concept to a concrete graph. Durán et al. proposed in [7,8] what they call *parameterised GTSs*, where the parameter is not just a type graph, but a complete GTS, and where composition of GTSs is based on a GTS amalgamation construction. In the same way concepts gather the structural requirements, the set of rules of parameter GTSs are behavioural requirements over the concrete GTSs used in the instantiation. In each of these cases, using GTS morphisms enables useful syntactic or semantic guarantees to be given. For example, in [6] the use of morphisms means that transformations can be guaranteed to be syntactically reusable. In the case of [8], the use of suitable morphisms enables guarantees on behaviour protection of amalgamated GTSs.

For reuse and composition, the main difficulty is the flexibility of the mechanisms available. In specific domains, *ad hoc* definitions of GTS morphisms have been proposed. For example, an alternative notion of refinement relation is given for transactional graph transformation systems in [9], where a graph typing mechanism induces a distinction between stable and unstable graph items and where implementation morphisms map single productions to whole transactions so that morphisms define simulations. Taentzer [10] uses a subset of UML extended by reconfiguration and import/export view facilities, represented as embedding morphisms, to propose a formal framework for visual modeling of distributed object systems. Component composition is defined by only allowing embedding morphisms between import and export rules where each two rules connected by an embedding morphism are named equally. These specialised solutions do not easily extend to the general setting. The use of GTSs in MDE introduces even more challenges, as we need to consider more complex graphs including attributes and node-type inheritance [11].

The need for a mechanism for relating different GTSs, or their type graphs, that is more flexible than direct morphisms—to broaden opportunities for GTS reuse—has been recognised before: In the case of models, represented as graphs, this has been resolved more or less pragmatically by supporting a specific, fixed set of adaptations to be applied prior to applying the morphism (see, *e.g.*, [6,11–13]). For example, Diskin *et al.* [12] propose using Kleisli categories for relating models. De Lara and Guerra extended their work on concepts in [13] by using adapters to allow heterogeneities between the concept and the concrete graph. Each of these works "hard wires" a specific set of flexibilities.

To support complete GTSs, rules must also be related in a flexible manner. In [4,14], Große-Rhode *et al.* introduce temporal and spatial refinement relations. In a spatial refinement, each rule is refined by an amalgamation (*i.e.*, a parallel composition with sharing) of rules, while in a temporal refinement it is refined by a sequential composition. Engels *et al.* [5] present a framework for classifying and systematically defining GTS morphisms. Different types of morphisms are characterised by their relationship between the behaviours of source and target GTSs. For instance, refinements are a case of behaviour-preserving morphisms, while views are a case of behaviour-reflecting morphisms. Durán *et al.* [8] similarly introduce different behaviour-aware GTS morphisms.

These solutions are, however, far from satisfactory. Even though the intro-duction of derived attributes and links as in [12] or [13], and the behavioural relations provided for GTS morphisms as in [8] improve the chances of defining the required morphisms, structural mismatch remains a problem. Often even where there is an intuitive match, no morphism can be established. This sub-stantially limits the reuse potential of these approaches. In many cases, a simple restructuring of the GTSs involved could easily allow a valid mapping to be established. However, there is currently no support for capturing such restruc-turings, and in particular for capturing exactly the set of restructurings the designer of a GTS would consider valid and meaningful.

In this work, we propose the use of GTS transformers to refactor GTSs with the goal of resolving the structural mismatches between source and target GTSs so that GTS morphisms can be defined. In fact, GTS transformers may be seen as re-factoring mechanisms, which provide a general setting for defining adaptations. GTS transformers are functions, and can successively be applied to our source GTS to find the one on which the morphism can be defined. To systematise this, we introduce the notion of *GTS families*. Given a set of transformers T, the T-family of a GTS GTS_0 is the set of GTSs reachable from GTS_0 using the transformers in T. The problem of defining a mapping morphism between a GTS GTS_0 and a target GTS GTS_1 then amounts to finding a GTS in the family of GTS_0 from which the morphism can be defined. This way, the problem becomes a *model-based search problem* [15].

Of course, any mechanisms enabling more flexibility must balance this against the required level of control so that suitable semantic properties can be guaranteed. We provide different transformers and prove that they preserve *extensions* [16] between GTSs. As a result, we show how these transformers can be used to enable flexible composition of GTSs.

The remainder of this paper is structured as follows. In Sect. 2, we introduce a running example and motivate the limitations of GTS morphisms and the need for more flexibility. After providing some formal background on typed attributed graphs, GTSs, and their morphisms in Sect. 3, Sect. 4 introduces the notions of GTS transformers and GTS families as well as three example GTS transformers. In Sect. 4.3, we show that these transformers are *extension preserving* and can, thus, be used to compose GTSs using the mechanism from [16]. We wrap up in Sect. 5 with some conclusions and lines of future research.

2   Running Example

Let us consider a simple production-line system (PLS) GTS, part of which is depicted in Fig. 1. This GTS models a PLS for making hammers out of hammer heads and handles. In the type graph TG_{PLS} in Fig. 1a we find different types of machines, different types of parts, and different containers of parts.[1] The behaviour of such systems is defined through a number of graph-transformation rules, like the one in Fig. 1b, which models the polishing of a part by a polishing

---

[1] We use the hollow-arrow notation from UML to denote inheritance relationships.

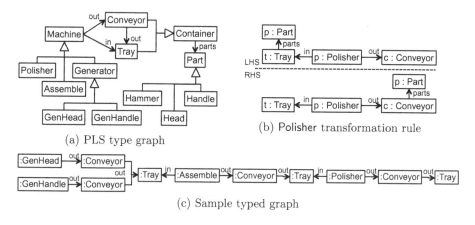

(a) PLS type graph

(b) Polisher transformation rule

(c) Sample typed graph

Fig. 1. Production line system

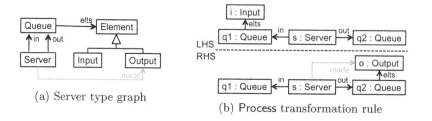

(a) Server type graph

(b) Process transformation rule

Fig. 2. Server tracking system

machine. Other actions, like the generation of head and handle parts in generator machines, the assembling of hammers out of hammer heads and handles, the moving of parts along conveyors, or the collection of parts from final trays is modelled by corresponding rules. A sample graph conforming to such type graph, providing an instance of the system, is shown in Fig. 1c. In it, we can see how machines take parts from input trays and put their outputs in corresponding conveyors, which move parts towards trays.

Let us suppose now that we wanted to keep track of the elements polished in our production line system. Instead of modifying our PLS GTS, we may use the mechanism in [16] to compose it with a generic tracker system, the Tracker GTS defined in Fig. 2. Its type graph $TG_{Tracker}$ is depicted in Fig. 2a. It describes the concepts related to servers that process elements taken from input queues into resulting elements that are placed in output queues. The action of processing an input element is then modelled by the transformation rule in Fig. 2b. The made association allows servers to keep track of all processed instances.

To compose the Tracker and the PLS GTSs following the construction in [16], we take the Tracker GTS as a parameterized GTS. The Server GTS, shown in Fig. 3, defines a generic behaviour, the structural and behavioural requirements the Tracker GTS builds on. Note that we can easily establish an inclusion g to

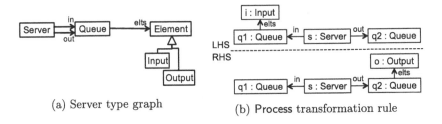

(a) Server type graph   (b) Process transformation rule

Fig. 3. Server system parameter GTS

the Tracker GTS. Then, we can compose the Tracker GTS with the PLS GTS so that polisher machines would keep track of the parts it processes:

$$
\begin{array}{ccc}
GTS_0 & \xrightarrow{\;f\;} & GTS_2 \\
\Big\downarrow{\scriptstyle g} & & \Big\downarrow{\scriptstyle \widehat{g}} \\
GTS_1 & \dashrightarrow & \widehat{GTS}
\end{array}
$$

where GTS_0 is the parameter GTS Server, GTS_1 is the parameterized GTS Tracker, and GTS_2 is the PLS GTS used in the instantiation.

For this to work, we need to establish a GTS morphism between the Server GTS (the parameter) and the PLS GTS. Intuitively, the PLS GTS might be seen as a concrete interpretation of the Server GTS—e.g., polishing of parts can be seen as particular case of the server processing. A morphism between the two GTSs would be the formal expression of this. Let us first focus on the type graphs. At first sight, it may seem quite reasonable to define a binding between TG_{Server} and TG_{PLS} by mapping *Server* into Polisher, and Queue into Container,[2] with the in and out associations going to the corresponding ones in the PLS system type graph. However, in TG_{PLS} input and output "queues" are represented by two different types: Tray and Conveyor, respectively. As a result, we cannot establish a valid morphism. Whether source and target queues are of the same type is not actually relevant to our specification of *Server* nor to the definition of tracking. We would like to be able to express the intuition that this particular mapping should be considered valid. Even where we can establish a morphism between the type graphs, there may still be problems establishing morphisms between the rule sets.

In this paper, we introduce the notions of GTS transformers and GTS families and show how they can be used to automatically rewrite the Server and Tracker GTSs in sync to find the GTS depicted in Fig. 4, for which a morphism to the PLS GTS can straightforwardly be defined. Thus, GTS families enable expressing the above intuition about what GTS mappings we would like to allow.

---

[2] Notice that although we use Queue to name the device in which input and output elements are placed, no specific order is assumed on its elements in the server GTS.

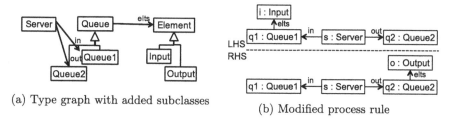

(a) Type graph with added subclasses

(b) Modified process rule

Fig. 4. Modified GTS

3   Preliminaries on GTSs, Clans, and Clan Morphisms

We focus on the double pushout (DPO) approach to graph transformation [3]. In this section, we introduce some of the basic definitions concerning typed graphs and the algebraic approaches to the rewriting of typed graphs, and provide background definitions underpinning our discussion throughout this paper. The notation and most of the definitions in this section follow very closely those in, e.g., [3,8,13,17].

3.1   Graph Transformation Systems

Given some category of graphs and graph morphisms **Graph**, and given a distinguished graph TG, called *type graph*, a TG-*typed graph* (G, g_G), or simply *typed graph* if TG is known, consists of a graph G and a typing homomorphism $g_G : G \rightarrow TG$ associating with each vertex and edge of G its type in TG. To enhance readability, we will use simply g_G to denote a typed graph (G, g_G), and when the typing morphism g_G can be considered implicit, we will often refer to a typed graph (G, g_G) just as G. A TG-typed graph morphism between TG-typed graphs $(G_i, g_i : G_i \rightarrow TG)$, with $i = 1, 2$, denoted $f : (G_1, g_1) \rightarrow (G_2, g_2)$, is a graph morphism $f : G_1 \rightarrow G_2$ which preserves types; that is, $g_2 \circ f = g_1$.

A graph transformation rule[3] p is of the form $L \xleftarrow{l} K \xrightarrow{r} R$ with graphs L, K, and R, called, resp., left-hand side, interface, and right-hand side, and some kind of monomorphisms (typically inclusions) l and r.

In the DPO approach to graph transformation, the application of a transformation rule $p = L \xleftarrow{l} K \xrightarrow{r} R$ to a graph G via a match $m : L \rightarrow G$ is constructed as two gluings (1) and (2), which are pushouts in the corresponding graph category, leading to a direct transformation $G \xLongrightarrow{p,m} H$.

$$
\begin{array}{ccccc}
L & \xleftarrow{\ l\ } & K & \xrightarrow{\ r\ } & R \\
{\scriptstyle m}\downarrow & (1) & \downarrow & (2) & \downarrow \\
G & \longleftarrow & D & \longrightarrow & H
\end{array}
$$

---

[3] As a simplification, we do not consider application conditions (*cf.*, *e.g.*, [8]).

A graph transformation system (GTS) over a type graph TG is a triple (TG, P, π) where P is a set of rule names and π is a function mapping each rule name p into a rule $L \xleftarrow{l} K \xrightarrow{r} R$ typed over TG.

Since we are interested in relating GTSs over different type graphs, we need to move graphs and graph morphisms along morphisms. Assuming $\mathbf{Graph}_{TG}$ the category of TG-typed graphs and TG-typed graph morphisms, a graph morphism $f\colon TG \to TG'$ induces *forward and backward retyping* functors $f^>\colon \mathbf{Graph}_{TG} \to \mathbf{Graph}_{TG'}$ and $f^<\colon \mathbf{Graph}_{TG'} \to \mathbf{Graph}_{TG}$. Since, as said above, we refer to a TG-typed graph $G \to TG$ just by its typed graph G, leaving TG implicit, given a morphism $f\colon TG \to TG'$, we may refer to the corresponding TG'-typed graph by $f^>(G)$. Since we can retype graphs and graph morphisms, we can retype rules. Given a rule p over a type graph TG and a graph morphism $f\colon TG \to TG'$, we will write things like $f^<(p)$ and $f^>(p)$ denoting, respectively, the backward and forward retyping of rule p.

3.2 Morphisms Between Graph Transformation Systems

Although the mechanisms presented in the following sections may be applicable to most notions of GTS morphisms defined in the literature, to simplify the presentation we will focus on a specific type of rule morphism and GTS morphism. We begin with rule morphisms, relating two graph-transformation rules.[4]

Definition 1. *Given rules* $p_i = L_i \xleftarrow{l_i} K_i \xrightarrow{r_i} R_i$, *for* $i = 0, 1$, *a rule morphism* $f\colon p_0 \to p_1$ *is a tuple* $f = (f_L, f_K, f_R)$ *of graph monomorphisms* $f_L\colon L_0 \to L_1$, $f_K\colon K_0 \to K_1$, *and* $f_R\colon R_0 \to R_1$ *such that the squares with the span morphisms* l_0, l_1, r_0, *and* r_1 *are pullbacks, as in the diagram below.*

$$
\begin{array}{ccccccc}
p_0 & : & L_0 & \xleftarrow{l_0} & K_0 & \xrightarrow{r_0} & R_0 \\
f\downarrow & & f_L\downarrow & pb & f_K\downarrow & pb & \downarrow f_R \\
p_1 & : & L_1 & \xleftarrow[l_1]{} & K_1 & \xrightarrow[r_1]{} & R_1
\end{array}
$$

We are now ready to introduce GTS morphisms.[5]

Definition 2. *Given GTSs* $GTS_i = (TG_i, P_i, \pi_i)$, *for* $i = 0, 1$, *a GTS morphism* $f\colon GTS_0 \to GTS_1$, *with* $f = (f_{TG}, f_P, f_r)$, *is given by a morphism* $f_{TG}\colon TG_0 \to TG_1$, *a surjective mapping* $f_P\colon P_1 \to P_0$ *between the sets of rule names, and a family of rule morphisms* $f_r = \{f^p\colon f_{TG}^>(\pi_0(f_P(p))) \to \pi_1(p)\}_{p \in P_1}$.

A special kind of GTS morphism is a GTS extension, which is essentially an inclusion such that everything being added to the rules of the extended GTS is typed by elements also added to the type graph.

---

[4] Similar definitions of rule morphisms can be found in the literature where the squares are pushouts instead of pullbacks, or simply commuting squares (*e.g.*, [18]), or where the relations are between a single rule and a collection of rules (*e.g.*, spatial and temporal refinements [4]). Requiring pullbacks is quite natural though: the intuition of morphisms is that they should preserve the "structure" of objects.

[5] See [5] for a systematic classification of other definitions of GTS morphisms.

Definition 3 *(GTS Extension* [16]*). Given GTSs* $GTS_i = (TG_i, P_i, \pi_i)$*, for* $i = 0, 1$*, a GTS morphism* $f: GTS_0 \to GTS_1$*, with* $f = (f_{TG}, f_P, f_r)$*, is an extension morphism if* f_{TG} *is a monomorphism and for each* $p \in P_1$*,* $\pi_0(f_P(p)) = f_{TG}^<(\pi_1(p))$*.*

3.3   Typed Attributed Graphs and Clan Morphisms

Our underlying graphs are attributed graphs typed over attributed type graphs with inheritance [3,11]. In these graphs, attributes are represented as edges between graph nodes and data nodes (captured by the notion of *E-graphs* in [3]). We use symbolic graphs [19,20] to enrich graphs with a set Φ of formulas over a signature $\Sigma = (S, \Omega)$, with S a set of sorts and Ω a set of operations. We assume that each formula is an equality between a variable and its value (grounded symbolic graphs in [19]). For simplicity, we assume attributed graphs on the same signature and omit a treatment of cardinalities and composition relations, which could be given as constraints as discussed in [21]. We refer the interested reader to [19,20] for a more general presentation of symbolic attributed graphs.

An attributed graph $ATG = (TG, \Phi)$ may be used as a type graph. As for any type of graph, a *typed attributed graph* (AG, t) over an attributed type graph ATG consists of an attributed graph AG together with an attributed morphism $t : AG \to ATG$. A typed attributed graph morphism $f : (AG_1, t_1) \to (AG_2, t_2)$ is an attributed graph morphism $f : AG_1 \to AG_2$ such that $t_2 \circ f = t_1$.

To deal with object-oriented systems we need some additional machinery. We follow [11] in defining attributed type graphs with inheritance.

Definition 4. *An attributed type graph with inheritance* $ATGI = (ATG, I, Ab)$ *consists of an attributed type graph* $ATG = (TG, \Phi)$*, with an E-graph* $TG = (V, E, A, D, s^E, t^E, s^A, t^A)$*, a set* $I \subseteq V \times V$ *of inheritance relations, and a set* $Ab \subseteq V$ *of abstract nodes.*

The typing of an object diagram with respect to a class diagram is typically represented as a clan morphism [11]. Intuitively, a clan morphism $f : AG \to ATGI$ from an attributed graph AG to an attributed type graph with inheritance $ATGI$ is an attributed graph morphism that takes into account the inheritance relation and abstraction definitions of the target $ATGI$.

Definition 5. *Let* $ATG_i = (TG_i, \Phi_{ATG_i})$*, with* $i = 1, 2$*, be attributed type graphs, with* $TG_i = (V_{TG_i}, E_{TG_i}, A_{TG_i}, D_{TG_i}, s^E_{TG_i}, t^E_{TG_i}, s^A_{TG_i}, t^A_{TG_i})$*, and let* $ATGI_2 = (ATG_2, I, Ab)$ *be an attributed type graph with inheritance. For each node* v *in* V_{TG_2}*,* $clan(v) = \{v' \in V_{TG_2} \mid (v', v) \in I^*\}$*, with* I^* *the reflexive and transitive closure of* I*. Then, given an algebra* $\mathcal{A}$*, a clan morphism* $f: ATG_1 \to ATGI_2$ *is an attributed graph morphism* $(f_V, f_E, f_A, f_D): ATG_1 \to ATG_2$ *such that*

1. $\forall e \in E_{TG_1}, f_V(s^E_{TG_1}(e)) \in clan(s^E_{TG_2}(f_E(e)))$ *and* $f_V(t^E_{TG_1}(e)) \in clan(t^E_{TG_2}(f_E(e)))$*, and*

2. $\forall a \in A_{TG_1}, f_A(s^A_{TG_1}(a)) \in clan(s^A_{TG_2}(f_A(a)))$ and $f_A(t^A_{TG_1}(a)) = t^A_{TG_2}(f_A(a))$.

Definition 6. *Given $ATGI_i = (ATG_i, I_i, Ab_i)$, for $i = 1, 2$, attributed type graphs with inheritance, and an algebra $\mathcal{A}$, a morphism $f : ATGI_1 \to ATGI_2$ is a clan morphism $f = (f_V, f_E, f_A, f_D) : ATG_1 \to ATGI_2$ that*

1. *preserves the inheritance relation, i.e., if $(a, b) \in I_1$ then $(f_V(a), f_V(b)) \in I_2^*$,*
2. *reflects subtyping, that is, for each $(a, b) \in I_2^*$ with some $a' \in V_1$ such that $f_V(a') = a$, there must be a $b' \in V_1$ such that $f_V(b') = b$ and $(a', b') \in I_1^*$, where V_1 is the node set of ATG_1, and*
3. *preserves the abstraction definitions, that is, $u \in Ab_1 \Leftrightarrow f_D(u) \in Ab_2$.*

Example 1. The mapping in Sect. 2 between TG_{Server} and TG_{PLS} does not satisfy the conditions to be part of a clan morphism. Specifically, the mapping for the in association fails condition 1 in Definition 5: $f_V(t^E_{Server}(\mathsf{in})) = \mathsf{Container} \notin clan(t^E_{PLS}(f_E(\mathsf{in}))) = \{\mathsf{Tray}\}$.

4   GTS Transformers and Families

Intuitively, a GTS family is a set of GTSs inductively defined from a source GTS GTS_0, capturing exactly the kind of flexibility we would like to permit when mapping GTS_0 to another GTS GTS_1. Given a set of transformers T, that model the different alterations that may be applied on GTSs, we denote by $[GTS_0]_T$ the family of GTS_0 using T. Mappings are then formally defined by selecting one GTS from the GTS family of GTS_0, written $[GTS_0]_T \rightsquigarrow GTS'_0$, and establishing a morphism between GTS'_0 and GTS_1. We first introduce the notion of GTS transformers, before using them to formally define GTS families. We then show how extension preserving transformers can be used to enable the flexible composition of GTSs and how individual members of a GTS family can be identified based on a given target GTS for a mapping.

4.1   GTS Transformers

GTS transformers, and the GTS families we generate with them, generalise the idea of adapters over transformations (also called adaptations in [13, 22, 23]). We start by defining GTS transformers as transformations between GTSs.[6]

Definition 7 (GTS transformer). *A GTS transformer t is a triple of three inter-related transformations $t = (t_{TG}, t_P, t_\pi)$:*

t_{TG} *takes GTSs to type graphs;*
t_P *takes GTSs to sets of rule names;*
t_π *takes GTSs to functions mapping rule names to rules.*

---

[6] In effect, GTS transformers are a form of higher-order transformation [24].

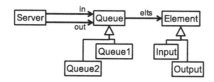

Fig. 5. *IntroSC*-modified type graph

GTS transformers define functions over the set of all ATGI-typed GTSs. Given a GTS $GTS_0 = (TG_0, P_0, \pi_0)$, $t(GTS_0) = (TG_1, P_1, \pi_1)$ such that: $TG_1 = t_{TG}(GTS_0)$, $P_1 = t_P(GTS_0)$, $\pi_1 = t_\pi(GTS_0)$, and for all $p \in P_1$, $\pi_1(p)$ is a rule typed over TG_1.

Note that while the three component functions are defined to range over the entire GTS, they each only transform one aspect of the GTS. For example, t_{TG} will only transform the type graph of the given GTS. However, we define them to range over the entire GTS so that they can ensure consistency of the result.

Remark 1. By definition, given a valid GTS as input, a well-defined GTS transformer will always produce a valid GTS as output.

To make this definition more concrete, we now introduce three examples of transformers, namely $t_{IntroSC}$, $t_{MvAssoc}$ and $t_{InhUnfld}$, which, respectively, add subclasses in the inheritance hierarchy, move associations in its type graph down in the inheritance hierarchy, and specialise rules to particular subclasses.

Definition 8. *The $t_{IntroSC}$ transformer modifies the type graph of a GTS by introducing a subclass to a class. It non-deterministically chooses a class from the type graph of the original GTS and adds a subclass with no attributes nor associations. All other classes, attributes, and associations are maintained. The set of rules is not changed.*

Example 2. By repeatedly applying $t_{IntroSC}$ to the Server GTS in Fig. 3 we could obtain, *e.g.*, a GTS Server v1 with the type graph shown in Fig. 5. The set of rules in the new GTS are identical to the rules in the original GTS.

Definition 9. *Given a GTS $GTS_0 = (TG_0, P_0, \pi_0)$, the $t_{InhUnfld}$ transformer produces a new GTS GTS_1 with the same type graph and a rule set resulting of modifying its rules as follows:*

1. *Non-deterministically picks a class $C \in TG_0$ that has a number of subclasses $SC_i \in TG_0$, $i = 1, \ldots, n$;*
2. *Non-deterministically picks a rule name $p \in P_0$ s.t. $\pi_0(p)$ contains objects that are typed by C;*
3. *Non-deterministically picks one subclass of C for every free object in $\pi_0(p)$ typed by C (different subclasses may be picked for different objects);*

4. *Generates a new rule $\pi_1(p)$ using the chosen subclasses to type the corresponding objects;*
5. *Copies all other rules as they are.*

Example 3. Given the Server v1 GTS resulting from the application of the $t_{IntroSC}$ transformer as in Example 2, the application of the $t_{InhUnfld}$ transformer on it may result in the GTS Server v2 with the same type graph and a rule as in Fig. 4b. All other rules remain as in the original GTS.

Definition 10. *Given a GTS, the $t_{MvAssoc}$ transformer produces a GTS with all rules as in the original GTS and where the type graph is modified as follows:*

1. *Non-deterministically picks a class C.*
2. *Non-deterministically picks an association $assoc$ that ends in C.*
3. *Non-deterministically picks a set SC of subclasses of C. At least every subclass S of C for which there is a rule in π_0 where $assoc$ refers to an object typed as S will be included in SC.*
4. *If C and $assoc$ are such that there are no rules that use $assoc$ to refer to an object typed as C, then $assoc$ is removed from the type graph, and a new replica of $assoc$ with the same source as the original is created and defined to point to each $S \in SC$.*

If the type graph modification is not possible, because the condition in Step 4 fails, $t_{MvAssoc}$ returns the original GTS.

The condition in Step 4 as well as the specific construction of the set SC are required to ensure that $t_{MvAssoc}$ produces a valid and well-typed GTS.

Example 4. Repeatedly applying $t_{MvAssoc}$ to the Server v2 GTS produced in Example 3, may result in a GTS Server v3 with the type graph in Fig. 4a and the rules as those of Server v2 GTS.

The three introduced transformers are just a sample of the kind of transformations we can define on GTSs. For our running example, we have used these transformers to reflect our intuition that the specific types of input and output queues are not important for the behaviour we want to abstract in the Server GTS. As we have mentioned at the beginning of this section, the mismatches may be both in the structure or in the transformation rules, and therefore more sophisticated transformers operating on the type graph and on the rules may be necessary in other cases. In the next subsection we introduce GTS families as a way of packaging the transformers representing our intuition about the behaviour we want to capture.

4.2   GTS Families

Given a set of GTS transformers, new GTSs can be derived from a GTS.

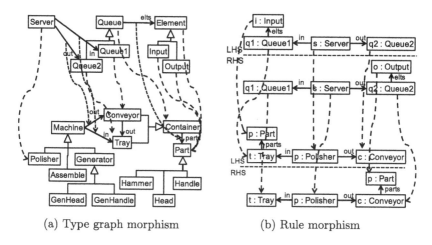

(a) Type graph morphism   (b) Rule morphism

Fig. 6. Sketch of the morphism between GTSs Server v3 and PLS

Definition 11. *Given a GTS GTS_0 and a GTS transformer t, a single-step GTS derivation $GTS_0 \Rightarrow_t GTS_1$ is induced iff $GTS_1 = t(GTS_0)$. Given a set $T = \{t_i | i = 1, \dots, n\}$ of GTS transformers, a GTS derivation of GTS_0 over T ($GTS_0 \Rightarrow_T^* GTS_m$) is given by a, possibly empty, sequence of single-step derivations $GTS_j \Rightarrow_{t_j} GTS_{j+1}$, $j = 0, \dots, m-1$, $t_j \in T$.*

Example 5. After the application of transformers $t_{IntroSC}$, $t_{InhUnfld}$, and $t_{MvAssoc}$ as in Examples. 2–4, the morphism between GTSs Server v3 and PLS can now be defined, as sketched in Fig. 6.

We call the (possibly infinite) set of all GTSs derivable from GTS_0 over a set of transformers T the T-family of GTS_0.

Definition 12. *Given a set of GTS transformers $T = \{t_i | i = 1, \dots, n\}$, and a GTS GTS_0, the T-family of GTS_0, denoted by $[GTS_0]_T$, is the (possibly infinite) reflexive-transitive closure of GTS derivations of GTS_0 over T: $GTS_0' \in [GTS_0]_T \Leftrightarrow GTS_0 \Rightarrow_T^* GTS_0'$.*

We will write $[GTS_0]_T \rightsquigarrow GTS_0'$ to denote the *selection* of some GTS_0' from the GTSs in $[GTS_0]_T$. Note that $GTS_0 \in [GTS_0]_T$.

The GTS transformers defined above, non-deterministically select elements of the type graph or rules to be modified. In analogy to graph-transformation rules, we allow transformer applications to be guided by providing a (partial) match for these elements. We will refer to the combination of a transformer and a complete match for each of the elements it would otherwise select non-deterministically as a *specific application of a transformer*.

Example 6. Consider the GTS Server v1 in Example 2. It results from the repeated application of the $t_{IntroSC}$ transformer (Definition 9). Specifically, given the Server GTS we may invoke the application of $t_{IntroSC}$ on class Queue, introducing subclass Queue1, followed again by its application on class Queue to introduce the subclass Queue2.

4.3   Extension Preserving Transformers and GTS Amalgamation

An interesting case, with direct application to parameterized GTSs, is the case of *extensions* (see Definition 3). Parametrization of GTSs establishes an inclusion between the parameter GTS (GTS_0) and the full, parametrized GTS (GTS_1)—for example, see [8]. Typically, these inclusions are extensions.

To improve the possibilities of instantiating a parameterized GTS, we would like to be able to consider as parameter GTS any of the GTSs we can reach using a given set of transformers. In other words, we would like to be able to consider as parameter, not a single GTS, but its entire family. To make this safe, we need to ensure that for any path of transformers $GTS_0 \Rightarrow_T^* GTS_0'$ we can find a corresponding path $GTS_1 \Rightarrow_T^* GTS_1'$ such that the extension $GTS_0 \hookrightarrow GTS_1$ leads to the extension $GTS_0' \hookrightarrow GTS_1'$; that is, a new parametrized GTS preserving the extension. The easiest way of finding such a corresponding path is by constructing it from the same transformer applications in both cases. Transformers for which this can be done, we will call *extension-preserving transformers*.

Definition 13. *A transformer t preserves extensions if for any GTS extension $GTS_0 \hookrightarrow GTS_1$, the exact same specific application of t to GTS_0 and GTS_1 results in an extension as depicted in the following diagram, where the dotted arrow means that the application of the transformer on GTS_1 is exactly the same as the one on GTS_0.*

$$
\begin{array}{ccc}
GTS_0 & \xrightarrow{\ \ t\ \ } & GTS_0' \\
\rotatebox{90}{$\hookrightarrow$} & & \rotatebox{90}{$\hookrightarrow$} \\
GTS_1 & \xrightarrow[t]{\ \ \ \ } & GTS_1'
\end{array}
$$

Note that it is enough to prove that each individual transformer is extension preserving for any combination of these transformers to be extension preserving, too. In particular, to be extension preserving, a transformer needs to be applicable both on GTS_0 and on GTS_1 without changes.

Proposition 1. *The $t_{IntroSC}$ transformer preserves extensions.*

Proof. Given GTSs $GTS_i = (TG_i, P_i, \pi_i)$, with $i = 0, 1$, and $\iota = (\iota_{TG}, \iota_P, \iota_r)$: $GTS_0 \hookrightarrow GTS_1$ an inclusion morphism, the first observation is that if the $t_{IntroSC}$ transformer is applicable to GTS_0, then it can also be applied to GTS_1 in exactly the same way. All classes in TG_0 are in TG_1, and specifically the class C to which the new subclass is added. Assume that the application of $t_{IntroSC}$ on GTS_0 results in a new GTS $GTS_0' = (TG_0', P_0, \pi_0)$, with rules as in GTS_0 and a type graph TG_0' as TG_0 but with a new class C' added, and declared subclass of C. Applying $t_{IntroSC}$ to GTS_1 results in the introduction of the new class C'' as a subclass of $\iota_{TG}(C)$, with no attributes or links. This produces a new GTS $GTS_1' = (TG_1', P_1, \pi_1)$, with the same rules as in GTS_1. The inclusion morphism $\iota' = (\iota_{TG}', \iota_P', \iota_r') : GTS_0' \hookrightarrow GTS_1'$ can trivially be defined by defining ι_{TG}' by extending ι_{TG} for the new class and subclass relation, mapping C' to C'', with the same components for the rules. Notice that if ι_{TG} is an attribute type graph morphism, then ι_{TG}' is as well, since it preserves the inheritance relation, reflects subtyping, and preserves the abstraction definitions. Since rules are not changed, if ι is an extension, then ι' is also an extension.

Proposition 2. *The $t_{InhUnfld}$ transformer preserves extensions.*

Proof. Let GTSs GTS_0 and GTS_1 and inclusion GTS morphism $\iota : GTS_0 \hookrightarrow GTS_1$ as in Proposition 1, and let us assume it is an extension. Since the type graph is not changed, if the transformer is applicable on GTS_0, it is obviously applicable on GTS_1 for same class C, rule p and subclasses of C. We can define the inclusion morphism $\iota' = (\iota_{TG}', \iota_P', \iota_r') : GTS_0' \hookrightarrow GTS_1'$ by taking the same type graph morphism and morphisms for non-modified rules. Since the transformer replaces rules $\pi_0(p)$ and $\pi_1(p)$ with rules $\pi_0'(p)$ and $\pi_1'(p)$, respectively in GTS_0 and GTS_1, with these new rules generated in exactly the same way, given $\iota^p : \iota_{TG}^>(\pi_0(\iota_P(p))) \to \pi_1(p)$ we have $\iota'^p : \iota_{TG}^>(\pi_0'(\iota_P'(p))) \to \pi_1'(p)$. Since ι is an extension, to have that ι' is also an extension we just need to check that $\pi_0'(f_P'(p)) = f_{TG}^<(\pi_1'(p))$. But this is the case, since the transformer is exactly making the same changes.

Proposition 3. *The $t_{MvAssoc}$ transformer preserves extensions.*

Proof. Let GTSs GTS_0 and GTS_1 and inclusion GTS morphism $\iota : GTS_0 \hookrightarrow GTS_1$ as in Proposition 1. The transformer just moves an association $assoc$ from class C to one or more of its subclasses, requiring that there is no rule in the source GTS using $assoc$ on instances of C. Assuming ι is an extension, then, if $t_{MvAssoc}$ is applicable on GTS_0 for some C, some subclass(es) of C and rule p, there cannot be in GTS_1 a new rule, or an extension of a rule in GTS_0, with such a link (to C or any of its subclasses), and therefore the same application of the transformer is possible on GTS_1. Since the transformer is changing associations consistently in TG_0 and TG_1, the definition of ι_{TG}' follows quite closely that of ι_{TG}. Rules are left unchanged, so the definitions of ι_P' and ι_r' are as those in ι. Thus, we can conclude that ι' is also an extension.

Let us go back to our example in Sect. 2. First, notice that Tracker is an extension of the Server GTS. A new association is added to its type graph, and its rules are modified just by adding instances of the new elements. Then, to apply the composition scheme from [16], we need a morphism f from the parameter GTS Server to the PLS GTS. However, as we have seen in Sect. 2, the morphism f cannot be established. To support this composition scenario, we can express our server GTS as a GTS family and follow the scheme below:

$$[GTS_0]_T \rightsquigarrow_T GTS_0' \xrightarrow{f} GTS_2$$
$$\Big\downarrow g \qquad \Big\downarrow g' \qquad \Big\downarrow \widehat{g}$$
$$[GTS_1]_T \rightsquigarrow_T GTS_1' \dashrightarrow \widehat{GTS}$$

In other words, we explicitly encode the variability we find acceptable by extending the parameter GTS GTS_0 into a GTS family $[GTS_0]_T$, providing transformers $t_{IntroSC}, t_{InhUnfld}$, and $t_{MvAssoc}$ in T. By using these transformers, we can derive a GTS GTS_0' (see Fig. 4) for which a GTS morphism f can be established to the PLS described in GTS_2. Because all the transformers in T are extension-preserving, we can derive a corresponding GTS_1' and the extension $g' : GTS_0' \hookrightarrow GTS_1'$. With these, we can finally apply the amalgamation scheme from [16] to produce the composed GTS $\widehat{GTS}$.

4.4 Finding GTS-Family Members

Finding the appropriate representative of a GTS family for a given composition problem is not trivial. Essentially, this requires searching through the space of GTSs spanned by the GTS family, looking for a GTS with the right structure, if any exists. Search-based problems have long been the subject of intense research interest [15]. More recently, there have been proposals for tools solving search problems in an MDE context [25–27]. Of particular interest in the context of GTS families is the work on MoMoT by Fleck *et al.* [27]. Here, new candidate solutions are found by applying a sequence of transformations to an initial model (*e.g.*, a GTS). The search is guided by appropriate fitness criteria (*e.g.*, the number of matching elements that could be used to construct a suitable morphism). Their approach keeps track of the transformation sequence at all time and thus guarantees that it will only find solutions for which there is a transformation sequence—a key criteria in finding representatives of GTS families.

Based on similar ideas, we have developed a basic automated search algorithm in Maude [28]. This prototype demonstrates that automated search of suitable GTSs in a GTS family is possible, but the prototype still suffers from inefficiencies. As part of our future work, we are exploring improving the implementation based on MoMoT or similar tools.

5   Conclusions

In this paper, we have presented GTS families as a mechanism for encoding controlled flexibility for morphisms between GTSs. This is achieved by extending a GTS GTS_0 to a set of GTSs that can be derived from GTS_0 given a set of GTS transformers T. This set is called the GTS T-family of GTS_0 and is taken to encode the full intent of what is expected to be preserved by any morphism from GTS_0. Then a direct morphism between GTS_0 and GTS_1 is replaced by selecting a suitable representative from the GTS family and defining the morphism from that representative. Thus, instead of direct morphisms $GTS_0 \rightarrow GTS_1$ we will use the construction $[GTS_0]_T \rightsquigarrow GTS_0' \rightarrow GTS_1$.

In addition to providing an explicit design mechanism for transformation developers, GTS families as a formal concept also open up a new research agenda: rather than relying on the pragmatic approaches taken to the definition of valid adaptations so far, we can now begin to study the fundamental properties of different types of GTS transformers, identifying different classes of GTS families that can be most appropriately used in different scenarios (*e.g.*, are there easily checked conditions that will guarantee extension preservation?). In this paper, we have shown how extension-preserving transformers can be used to construct GTS families that enable flexible GTS amalgamation. As part of our future work, we plan to study the properties required of GTS transformers to allow flexible reuse of transformations, extending the work by de Lara *et al.* to semantic transformation reuse.

Acknowledgements. This work has been partially supported by Spanish MINECO/FEDER project TIN2014-52034-R and Univ. Málaga, Campus de Excelencia Internacional Andalucía Tech.

References

1. Ehrig, H.: Introduction to the algebraic theory of graph grammars. In: Claus, V., Ehrig, H., Rozenberg, G. (eds.) 1st Graph Grammar Workshop, vol. 73, LNCS, pp. 1–69. Springer, Heidelberg (1979)
2. Engels, G., Heckel, R., Taentzer, G., Ehrig, H.: A combined reference model- and view-based approach to system specification. Int. J. Software Eng. Knowl. Eng. **7**(4), 457–477 (1997)
3. Ehrig, H., Ehrig, K., Prange, U., Taentzer, G.: Fundamentals of Algebraic Graph Transformation. Monographs in Theoretical Computer Science. An EATCS Series. Springer, Heidelberg (2006)
4. Große-Rhode, M., Parisi-Presicce, F., Simeoni, M.: Spatial and temporal refinement of typed graph transformation systems. In: Brim, L., Gruska, J., Zlatuška, J. (eds.) MFCS 1998. LNCS, vol. 1450, pp. 553–561. Springer, Heidelberg (1998). doi:10.1007/BFb0055805
5. Engels, G., Heckel, R., Cherchago, A.: Flexible interconnection of graph transformation modules. In: Kreowski, H.-J., Montanari, U., Orejas, F., Rozenberg, G., Taentzer, G. (eds.) Formal Methods in Software and Systems Modeling. LNCS, vol. 3393, pp. 38–63. Springer, Heidelberg (2005). doi:10.1007/978-3-540-31847-7_3
6. de Lara, J., Guerra, E.: From types to type requirements: Genericity for model-driven engineering. SoSyM **12**(3), 453–474 (2013)
7. Durán, F., Zschaler, S., Troya, J.: On the reusable specification of non-functional properties in DSLs. In: Czarnecki, K., Hedin, G. (eds.) SLE 2012. LNCS, vol. 7745, pp. 332–351. Springer, Heidelberg (2013). doi:10.1007/978-3-642-36089-3_19
8. Durán, F., Moreno-Delgado, A., Orejas, F., Zschaler, S.: Amalgamation of domain specific languages with behaviour. J. Log. Algebraic Methods Program. (2015)
9. Baldan, P., Corradini, A., Dotti, F.L., Foss, L., Gadducci, F., Ribeiro, L.: Towards a notion of transaction in graph rewriting. Electr. Notes Theor. Comput. Sci. **211**, 39–50 (2008)

10. Taentzer, G.: A visual modeling framework for distributed object computing. In: Jacobs, B., Rensink, A. (eds.) FMOODS 2002. IFIP, vol. 81, pp. 263–278. Springer, Boston, MA (2002). doi:10.1007/978-0-387-35496-5_18

11. de Lara, J., Bardohl, R., Ehrig, H., Ehrig, K., Prange, U., Taentzer, G.: Attributed graph transformation with node type inheritance. Theoret. Comput. Sci. **376**, 139–163 (2007)

12. Diskin, Z., Maibaum, T., Czarnecki, K.: Intermodeling, queries, and kleisli categories. In: Lara, J., Zisman, A. (eds.) FASE 2012. LNCS, vol. 7212, pp. 163–177. Springer, Heidelberg (2012). doi:10.1007/978-3-642-28872-2_12

13. de Lara, J., Guerra, E.: Towards the flexible reuse of model transformations: A formal approach based on graph transformation. J. Log. Algebraic Methods Program. **83**(5–6), 427–458 (2014)

14. Große-Rhode, M., Parisi Presicce, F., Simeoni, M.: Refinements of graph transformation systems via rule expressions. In: Ehrig, H., Engels, G., Kreowski, H.-J., Rozenberg, G. (eds.) TAGT 1998. LNCS, vol. 1764, pp. 368–382. Springer, Heidelberg (2000). doi:10.1007/978-3-540-46464-8_26

15. Harman, M.: The current state and future of search based software engineering. In: Briand, L.C., Wolf, A.L. (eds.) International Conference on Software Engineering, ISCE 2007, Workshop on the Future of Software Engineering, FOSE 2007, 23–25 May, Minneapolis, MN, USA, 342–357. IEEE Computer Society (2007)

16. Durán, F., Orejas, F., Zschaler, S.: Behaviour protection in modular rule-based system specifications. In: Martí-Oliet, N., Palomino, M. (eds.) WADT 2012. LNCS, vol. 7841, pp. 24–49. Springer, Heidelberg (2013). doi:10.1007/978-3-642-37635-1_2

17. Rozenberg, G. (ed.): Handbook of Graph Grammars and Computing by Graph Transformations, vol. 1: Foundations, World Scientific (1997)

18. Parisi-Presicce, F.: Transformations of graph grammars. In: Cuny, J., Ehrig, H., Engels, G., Rozenberg, G. (eds.) Graph Grammars 1994. LNCS, vol. 1073, pp. 428–442. Springer, Heidelberg (1996). doi:10.1007/3-540-61228-9_103

19. Orejas, F., Lambers, L.: Symbolic attributed graphs for attributed graph transformation. ECEASST **30** (2010)

20. Orejas, F.: Symbolic graphs for attributed graph constraints. J. Symbolic Comput. **46**(3), 294–315 (2011)

21. Taentzer, G., Rensink, A.: Ensuring structural constraints in graph-based models with type inheritance. In: Cerioli, M. (ed.) FASE 2005. LNCS, vol. 3442, pp. 64–79. Springer, Heidelberg (2005). doi:10.1007/978-3-540-31984-9_6

22. Cuadrado, J.S., Guerra, E., de Lara, J.: Flexible model-to-model transformation templates: an application to ATL. J. Object Technol. **11**(2), 4:1–4:28 (2012)

23. Guy, C., Combemale, B., Derrien, S., Steel, J.R.H., Jézéquel, J.-M.: On model subtyping. In: Vallecillo, A., Tolvanen, J.-P., Kindler, E., Störrle, H., Kolovos, D. (eds.) ECMFA 2012. LNCS, vol. 7349, pp. 400–415. Springer, Heidelberg (2012). doi:10.1007/978-3-642-31491-9_30

24. Tisi, M., Jouault, F., Fraternali, P., Ceri, S., Bézivin, J.: On the use of higher-order model transformations. In: Paige, R.F., Hartman, A., Rensink, A. (eds.) ECMDA-FA 2009. LNCS, vol. 5562, pp. 18–33. Springer, Heidelberg (2009). doi:10.1007/978-3-642-02674-4_3

25. Hegedüs, Á., Horváth, Á., Ráth, I., Varró, D.: A model-driven framework for guided design space exploration. In: Proceedings of the 26th IEEE/ACM International Conference Automated Software Engineering (ASE 2011), pp. 173–182, November 2011

26. Zschaler, S., Mandow, L.: Towards model-based optimisation: Using domain knowledge explicitly. In: Proceedings of Workshop on Model-Driven Engineering, Logic and Optimization (MELO 2016) (2016)
27. Fleck, M., Troya, J., Wimmer, M.: Marrying search-based optimization and model transformation technology. In: Proceedings of the 1st North American Search Based Software Engineering Symposium (NasBASE 2015) (2015) (Preprint). http://martin-fleck.github.io/momot/downloads/NasBASE_MOMoT.pdf
28. Clavel, M., Durán, F., Eker, S., Lincoln, P., Martí-Oliet, N., Meseguer, J., Talcott, C.L.: All About Maude, vol. 4350. LNCS. Springer, Heidelberg (2007)
29. Brim, L., Gruska, J., Zlatuška, J. (eds.): MFCS 1998. LNCS, vol. 1450. Springer, Heidelberg (1998)

Symbolic Model Generation
for Graph Properties

Sven Schneider[1(✉)], Leen Lambers[1], and Fernando Orejas[2]

[1] Hasso Plattner Institut, University of Potsdam, Potsdam, Germany
{sven.schneider,leen.lambers}@hpi.de
[2] Dpto de L.S.I., Universitat Politècnica de Catalunya, Barcelona, Spain
orejas@cs.upc.edu

Abstract. Graphs are ubiquitous in Computer Science. For this reason, in many areas, it is very important to have the means to express and reason about graph properties. In particular, we want to be able to check automatically if a given graph property is satisfiable. Actually, in most application scenarios it is desirable to be able to explore graphs satisfying the graph property if they exist or even to get a complete and compact overview of the graphs satisfying the graph property.

We show that the tableau-based reasoning method for graph properties as introduced by Lambers and Orejas paves the way for a symbolic model generation algorithm for graph properties. Graph properties are formulated in a dedicated logic making use of graphs and graph morphisms, which is equivalent to first-order logic on graphs as introduced by Courcelle. Our parallelizable algorithm gradually generates a finite set of so-called symbolic models, where each symbolic model describes a set of finite graphs (i.e., finite models) satisfying the graph property. The set of symbolic models jointly describes all finite models for the graph property (complete) and does not describe any finite graph violating the graph property (sound). Moreover, no symbolic model is already covered by another one (compact). Finally, the algorithm is able to generate from each symbolic model a minimal finite model immediately and allows for an exploration of further finite models. The algorithm is implemented in the new tool AUTOGRAPH.

Keywords: Graph properties · Nested graph conditions · Model generation · Tableau method · Satisfiability solving · Graph transformation

1 Introduction

Graphs are ubiquitous in Computer Science. For this reason, in many areas, it is (or it may be) very important to have the means to express and reason about graph properties. Examples may be, (a) model-based engineering where we may need to express properties of graphical models; (b) the verification of systems whose states are modeled as graphs; (c) to express properties about sets of semi-structured documents, especially if they are related by links; (d) graph

© Springer-Verlag GmbH Germany 2017
M. Huisman and J. Rubin (Eds.): FASE 2017, LNCS 10202, pp. 226–243, 2017.
DOI: 10.1007/978-3-662-54494-5_13

databases, where we may want to state integrity constraints in the form of graph properties or where we may want to be able to reason about the validity of graph queries and, in particular, to understand why queries might be valid or not.

Let us take a closer look at the latter application field to understand how the symbolic model generation approach for graph properties, as presented in this paper, will support a *typical usage scenario*. In general, a graph query for a graph database G (as formalized in [3] and used in extended form in [18]) formulates the search for occurrences of graph patterns of a specific form L satisfying some additional property in G. Since such a query can become quite complex it is important to have an intuitive query language to formulate it and to have additional support allowing for reasoning about the query to enhance understandability and facilitate debugging. *Validity* of a graph query means that there should exist a graph database G in which we find an occurrence of the pattern L satisfying the additional property for L encoded in the query, see e.g. Fig. 1b depicting a graph property p_1 expressing validity for a query taken from [9,35] explained in detail in Sect. 3. First of all automatic support to answer this validity question for a query is thus desired. Moreover, if validity is the case, then one wants to be able to inspect a graph database G as a *concrete example*, but this example should be of a *manageable size*. Moreover, if there are considerably different types of graph databases being witnessed for the validity of a query then we would like to get a *finite, complete, and compact overview* S of all these graph databases. Also a *flexible exploration* starting from some minimal example graph database to a bigger one still being a witness for validity is desirable. Finally, of course one wants to see all these results within a *reasonable amount of time*.

For a given graph property p, formulating more generically all requirements occurring in this usage scenario means that we would like to have an algorithm $\mathcal{A}$ returning for p a *finite set of so-called symbolic models* S such that

- S jointly covers each finite graph G satisfying p (*complete*),
- S does not cover any finite graph G violating p (*sound*),
- S contains no superfluous symbolic model (*compact*),
- S allows for each of its symbolic models the immediate extraction of a minimal finite graph G covered (*minimally representable*), and
- S allows an enumeration of further finite graphs G satisfying p (*explorable*).

The contribution of this paper is the presentation and implementation of a *parallelizable* symbolic model generation algorithm delivering a complete (provided termination), sound, compact, minimally representable, and explorable set of symbolic models. We illustrate the algorithm w.r.t. checking validity of some complex graph queries from [9,35]. Our algorithm takes as input graph properties formulated in an intuitive, dedicated logic making use of graphs and graph morphisms as first-class citizens. This *logic of so-called nested graph conditions* was defined by Habel and Pennemann [13]. A similar approach was first introduced by Rensink [30]. The origins can be found in the notion of graph constraint [15], introduced in the area of graph transformation [31], in connection with the notion of (negative) application conditions [8,12], as a form to limit the applicability of transformation rules. These graph constraints originally had a very limited expressive power, while nested conditions have been shown [13,26] to have the *same expressive power as first-order logic (FOL) on graphs* as introduced by Courcelle [4]. Note that because we support FOL on graphs our algorithm might in general not terminate. It is designed however (also if non-terminating) to gradually deliver better underapproximations of the complete set of symbolic models.

This paper is structured as follows: In Sect. 2 we give an overview over related work. In Sect. 3 we introduce our running example and we reintroduce the key notions of the tableau-based reasoning method that our symbolic model generation algorithm is based on. In Sect. 4 we present our algorithm and its formalization and in particular show that it fulfills all requirements. In Sect. 5 we describe the algorithm implementation in the new tool AUTOGRAPH. We conclude the paper in Sect. 6 together with an overview of future work. A more elaborate presentation including further evaluation and proofs is given in the technical report [33].

2   Related Work

Instead of using a dedicated logic for graph properties, one can define and reason about graph properties in terms of some existing logic and reuse its associated reasoning methods. In particular, Courcelle [4] studied systematically a graph logic defined in terms of first-order (or monadic second-order) logic. In that approach, graphs are defined axiomatically using predicates $node(n)$, asserting that n is a node, and $edge(n_1, n_2)$ asserting that there is an edge from n_1 to n_2. Such a *translation-based approach* for finding models of graph-like properties is followed, e.g., in [10], where OCL properties are translated into relational logic, and reasoning is then performed by KODKOD, a SAT-based constraint solver for relational logic. In a similar vein, in [1] reasoning for feature models is being provided based on a translation into input for different general-purpose reasoners. Analogously, in [34] the ALLOY analyzer is used to synthesize in this case large, well-formed and realistic models for domain-specific languages. Reasoning for domain specific modeling is addressed also in [16,17] using the FORMULA approach taking care of dispatching the reasoning to the state-of-the-art SMT solver Z3. In [32] another translation-based approach is presented to reason with so-called partial models expressing uncertainty about the information in the model during model-based software development. In principle, all the previously exemplarily presented approaches from the model-based engineering domain represent potential use cases for our dedicated symbolic model generation approach for graph-like properties. Since we are able to generate *symbolic models* being complete (in case of termination), sound, compact, minimally representable, and explorable in combination, we believe that our approach has the potential to enhance considerably the type of analysis results, in comparison with the results obtained by using off-the-shelf SAT-solving technologies.

Following this idea, in contrast to the translation-based approach it is possible, e.g., to formalize a graph-like property language such as OCL [29] by a dedicated logic for graph properties [13] and apply corresponding *dedicated automated reasoning methods* as developed in [20, 23–25]. The advantage of such a graph-dedicated approach as followed in this paper is that graph axioms are natively encoded in the reasoning mechanisms of the underlying algorithms and tooling. Therefore, they can be built to be more efficient than generic-purpose methods as demonstrated e.g. in [24–26], where such an approach outperforms some standard provers working over encoded graph conditions. Moreover, the translation effort for each graph property language variant (such as e.g. OCL) into a formal logic already dedicated to the graph domain is much smaller than a translation into some more generic logic, which in particular makes translation errors less probable. As most directly related work [24, 26] presents a satisfiability solving algorithm for graph properties as employed in this paper [13]. This solver attempts to find one finite model (if possible), but does not generate a compact and gradually complete finite set of symbolic models allowing to inspect all possible finite models including a finite set of minimal ones. In contrast to [24, 26] our symbolic model generation algorithm is interleaved directly with a refutationally complete tableau-based reasoning method [20], inspired by rules of a proof system presented previously in [25], but in that work the proof rules were not shown to be refutationally complete.

3   Preliminaries

In this section we first introduce our running example and then recall definitions and results from [20] simplified for their application in subsequent sections.

We consider as an example two social network queries as described in the Social Network Benchmark developed by the Linked Data Benchmark Council [9, 35]. The form of social networks to be queried is given by the type graph in Fig. 1a. Moreover, we forbid parallel edges of the same type. The first considered graph query (a variant of query 8 from [3]) looks for pairs of *Person*s and *Tag*s such that in such a pair a *Tag* is new in some *Post* by a friend of this *Person*. To be a *Post* of a friend, the *Post* must be from a second *Person* the *Person knows*. In order to be new, the *Tag* must be linked in the latest *Post* of the second *Person* (and thus in a *Post* that has no *successor Post*) and there has to be no former *Post* by any other or the same friend that is not her last one and where the same *Tag* has been already used. In both cases only *Tag*s that are not simply inherited from a *linked Post* should be considered. This query is valid if there is a graph database G in which such a *Person* and *Tag* pair can be found at least once. The corresponding graph property p_1 is depicted in Fig. 1b. The graph property p_2 for a variant of query 10 [9, 35] is given in Fig. 1c.

Technically, we express graph properties as a special case of nested graph conditions that are formulated over a graph C and satisfied by monomorphisms (monos for short) [13]. In particular, a graph property satisfied by a graph G is a graph condition over the empty graph $\emptyset$ satisfied by the unique mono $\emptyset \hookrightarrow G$.

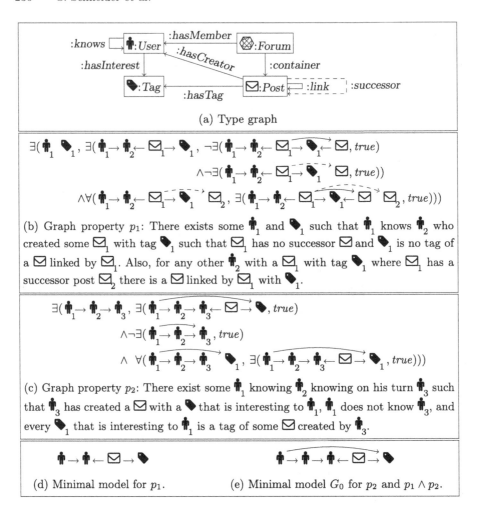

(a) Type graph

(b) Graph property p_1: There exists some 👤₁ and 🏷₁ such that 👤₁ knows 👤₂ who created some ✉₁ with tag 🏷₁ such that ✉₁ has no successor ✉ and 🏷₁ is no tag of a ✉ linked by ✉₁. Also, for any other 👤₂ with a ✉₁ with tag 🏷₁ where ✉₁ has a successor post ✉₂ there is a ✉ linked by ✉₁ with 🏷₁.

(c) Graph property p_2: There exist some 👤₁ knowing 👤₂ knowing on his turn 👤₃ such that 👤₃ has created a ✉ with a 🏷 that is interesting to 👤₁, 👤₁ does not know 👤₃, and every 🏷₁ that is interesting to 👤₁ is a tag of some ✉ created by 👤₃.

(d) Minimal model for p_1.   (e) Minimal model G_0 for p_2 and $p_1 \wedge p_2$.

Fig. 1. Graph properties for queries from the Social Network Benchmark [9,35].

Definition 1 (condition, property). *We define conditions inductively:*

- $\exists(m, c)$ *is a condition over a graph* C, *if* $m : C \hookrightarrow D$ *is a mono and* c *is a condition over* D,
- $\neg c$ *is a condition over* C, *if* c *is a condition over* C, *and*
- $\wedge(c_1, \ldots, c_k)$ *is a condition over* C, *if* $c_1, \ldots, c_k$ *are conditions over* C.

A graph property *is a condition over the empty graph* $\emptyset$.

Note, the empty conjunction $\wedge()$ serves as a base case for the inductive definition. Without extending expressiveness of the conditions, we define the following operators: $\vee(c_1, \ldots, c_k):=\neg \wedge (\neg c_1, \ldots, \neg c_k)$, $true:=\wedge()$, $false:=\vee()$, and $\forall(m, c):=\neg\exists(m, \neg c)$. Finally, we also use $\wedge(S)$ if S is a finite set instead of a list.

Definition 2 (satisfaction). *A graph mono* $q : C \hookrightarrow G$ *satisfies a condition* $\exists(m, c)$ *where* $m : C \hookrightarrow D$ *is a mono and where* c *is a condition over* D, *written* $q \models \exists(m, c)$, *if there is a mono* $q' : D \hookrightarrow G$ *such that* $q' \circ m = q$ *and* $q' \models c$. *The satisfaction relation* $\models$ *is defined on the other connectives as expected. Finally, if* G *is a graph,* p *is a graph property, and the unique mono* $i : \emptyset \hookrightarrow G$ *satisfies* p, *then* G *satisfies* p, *written* $G \models p$.

Note that we reintroduced these definitions for graphs, but our results can be generalized to variants of graphs such as, e.g., typed attributed graphs, Petri nets, or even algebraic specifications, since they belong to an $\mathcal{M}$-adhesive category [6,19] satisfying some additional categorical properties that the tableau-based reasoning method [20] requires. This is another advantage as opposed to using encodings as referred to in related work, since each kind of graph structure would otherwise need a different encoding.

Our symbolic model generation method will operate on the subset of conditions in conjunctive normal form (CNF), simplifying the corresponding reasoning. For example, $\wedge(\vee()) = \wedge(false)$ is a condition in CNF equivalent to *false*. We therefore assume an operation $[\cdot]$, similarly to operations in [20,25,26], translating conditions into equivalent conditions in CNF. This operation applies, besides the expected equivalences, like the equivalence for removal of universal quantification mentioned before Definition 2, an equivalence for the removal of literals with isomorphisms (e.g., $\exists(i : A \xrightarrow{\sim} B, \exists(m : B \hookrightarrow C, true))$ is replaced by $\exists((m \circ i) : A \hookrightarrow C, true)$ by moving the isomorphism i into the literals of the next nesting level). In particular, a negative literal in CNF is trivially satisfiable by the identity morphism, a property that will be exploited heavily in our symbolic model generation algorithm. Note, skolemization, which removes existential quantification in FOL SAT-reasoning, is not needed for graph conditions [26, p. 100]; we employ CNF-conversion on quantified subconditions separately.

Definition 3 (CNF). *A literal* ℓ *is either a positive literal* $\exists(m, c)$ *or a negative literal* $\neg\exists(m, c)$ *where* m *is no isomorphism and* c *is in CNF. A clause is a disjunction of literals. A conjunction of clauses is a condition in CNF.*

The tableau-based reasoning method as introduced in [20] is based on so-called nested tableaux. We start with reintroducing the notion of a regular tableau for a graph condition, which was directly inspired by the construction of tableaux for plain FOL reasoning [14]. Intuitively, provided a condition in CNF, such an iteratively constructed tableau represents all possible selections (computed using the extension rule in the following definition) of precisely one literal from each clause of the condition (note, a condition is unsatisfiable if it contains an empty clause). Such a selection is given by a maximal path in the tableau, which is called branch. In this sense, we are constructing a disjunctive normal form (DNF) where the set of nodes occurring in a branch of the resulting tableau corresponds to one clause of this DNF. Then, to discover contradictions in the literals of a branch and to prepare for the next step in the satisfiability analysis we merge (using the lift rule in the following definition) the selected literals into a single positive literal (note, if no positive literal is available the condition is always satisfiable), which is called opener. Note that the lift rule is based on a shifting translating a condition over a morphism into an equivalent condition [7,13].

Definition 4 (tableau, tableau rules, open/closed branches). *Given a condition c in CNF over C. A* tableau *T for c is a tree whose nodes are conditions constructed using the rules below. A* branch *in a tableau T for c is a maximal path in T. Moreover, a branch is* closed *if it contains false; otherwise, it is* open. *Finally, a tableau is* closed *if all of its branches are closed; otherwise, it is* open.

– initialization rule*: a tree with a single root node true is a tableau for c.*
– extension rule*: if T is a tableau for c, B is a branch of T, and $\vee(c_1, \ldots, c_n)$ is a clause in c, then if $n > 0$ and $c_1, \ldots, c_n$ are not in B, then extend B with n child nodes $c_1, \ldots, c_n$ or if $n = 0$ and false is not in B, then extend B with false.*
– lift rule*: if T is a tableau for c, B is a branch of T, $\exists(m, c')$ and ℓ are literals in B, $\ell' = \exists(m, [c' \wedge shift(m, \ell)])$ is not in B, then extend B with ℓ'.*

The operation $shift(\cdot, \cdot)$ allows to shift conditions over morphisms preserving satisfaction in the sense that $m_1 \circ m_2 \models c$ iff $m_1 \models shift(m_2, c)$ (see [20, Lemma 3]). Semi-saturated tableaux are the desired results of the iterative construction where no further rules need to be applied.

Definition 5 (semi-saturation, hook of a branch). *Let T be a tableau for condition c over C. A branch B of T is* semi-saturated *if it is either closed or*

– *B is not extendable with a new node using the extension rule and*
– *if $E = \{\ell_1, \ldots, \ell_n\}$ is nonempty and the set of literals added to B using the extension rule, then there is a positive literal $\ell = \exists(m, c')$ in E such that the literal in the leaf of B is equivalent to $\exists(m, c' \wedge_{\ell' \in (E - \{\ell\})} shift(m, \ell'))$. Also, we call ℓ the* hook *of B.*

Finally, T is semi-saturated *if all its branches are semi-saturated.*

In fact, a condition c is satisfiable if and only if the leaf condition of some open branch of a corresponding semi-saturated tableau is satisfiable. Hence, the next analysis step is required if there is a leaf $\exists(m : C \hookrightarrow C', c')$ of some open branch for which satisfiability has to be decided. That is, the next analysis step is to construct a tableau for condition c'. The iterative (possibly non-terminating) execution of this procedure results in (possibly infinitely many) tableaux where each tableau may result in the construction of a finite number of further tableaux. This relationship between a tableau and the tableaux derived from the leaf literals of open branches results in a so called nested tableau (see Fig. 2 for an example of a nested tableau).

Definition 6 (nested tableau, opener, context, nested branch, semi-saturation). *Given a condition c over C and a poset $(I, \leq, i_0)$ with minimal element i_0. A* nested tableau *NT for c is for some $I' \subseteq I$ a family of triples $\{\langle T_i, j, c_i \rangle\}_{i \in I'}$ constructed using the following rules.*

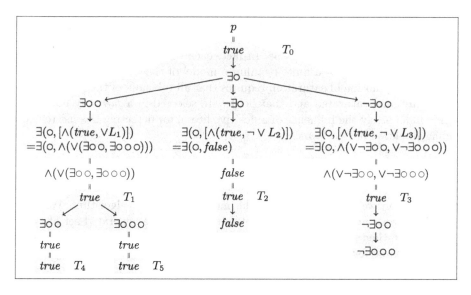

Fig. 2. Nested tableau (consisting of tableau T_0, ..., T_5) for graph property $p = \exists(\circ, \textit{true}) \land (\lor(\exists(\circ\circ, \textit{true}), \neg\exists(\circ, \textit{true}), \neg\exists(\circ\circ, \textit{true})))$. In• the middle branch *false* is obtained because $\neg \lor L_2$ is reduced to *false* because $\lor L_2$ is reduced to *true* because L_2 contains $\exists\circ$ due to shifting, which is reduced by $[\cdot]$ to *true* because of the used isomorphism. We extract from the nested branches ending in T_4, T_5, and T_3 the symbolic models $\langle \circ\circ, \textit{true}\rangle$, $\langle \circ\circ\circ, \textit{true}\rangle$, and $\langle \circ, \land(\neg\exists\circ\circ, \neg\exists\circ\circ\circ)\rangle$. Here $\langle \circ\circ\circ, \textit{true}\rangle$ is a refinement of $\langle \circ\circ, \textit{true}\rangle$ and, hence, would be removed by compaction as explained in Sect. 4.4.

- initialization rule: *If T_{i_1} is a tableau for c, then the family containing only $\langle T_{i_1}, i_0, \textit{true}\rangle$ for some index $i_1 > i_0$ is a nested tableau for c and C is called context of T_{i_1}.*
- nesting rule: *If NT is a nested tableau for c with index set I', $\langle T_n, k, c_k\rangle$ is in NT for index n, the literal $\ell = \exists(m_n : A_n \hookrightarrow A_j, c_n)$ is a leaf of T_n, ℓ is not the condition in any other triple of NT, T_j is a tableau for c_n, and $j > n$ is some index not in I', then add the triple $\langle T_j, n, \ell\rangle$ to NT using index j, ℓ is called* opener *of T_j, and A_j is called* context *of T_j.*

A nested branch NB of the nested tableau NT is a maximal sequence of branches $B_{i_1}, \ldots, B_{i_k}, B_{i_{k+1}}, \ldots$ of tableaux $T_{i_1}, \ldots, T_{i_k}, T_{i_{k+1}}, \ldots$ in NT starting with a branch B_{i_1} in the initial tableau T_{i_1} of NT, such that if B_{i_k} and $B_{i_{k+1}}$ are consecutive branches in the sequence then the leaf of B_{i_k} is the opener of $T_{i_{k+1}}$. NB is closed *if it contains a closed branch; otherwise, it is* open. *NT is* closed *if all its nested branches are closed. Finally, NT is* semi-saturated *if each tableau in NT is semi-saturated.*

It has been shown in [20] that the tableau based reasoning method using nested tableaux for conditions c is sound and refutationally complete. In particular, soundness means that if we are able to construct a nested tableau where all its branches are closed then the original condition c is unsatisfiable. Refutational completeness means that if a *saturated* tableau includes an open branch, then the original condition is satisfiable. In fact, each open finite or infinite branch in such a tableau defines a finite or infinite model of the property, respectively. Informally, the notion of saturation requires that all tableaux of the given nested tableau are semi-saturated and that hooks are selected in a *fair* way not postponing indefinitely the influence of a positive literal for detecting inconsistencies leading to closed nested branches.

4   Symbolic Model Generation

In this section we present our symbolic model generation algorithm. We first formalize the requirements from the introduction for the generated set of symbolic models, then present our algorithm, and subsequently verify that it indeed adheres to these formalized requirements. In particular, we want our algorithm to extract symbolic models from all open finite branches in a saturated nested tableau constructed for a graph property p. This would be relatively straightforward if each saturated nested tableau would be finite.

However, in general, as stated already at the end of the previous section this may not be the case. E.g., consider the conjunction $p_0 = \wedge(p_1, p_2, p_3)$ of the conditions $p_1 = \exists(①, \forall(\bigcirc\!\rightarrow\!①, \mathit{false}))$ (there is a node which has no predecessor), $p_2 = \forall(①, \exists(①\!\rightarrow\!\bigcirc, \mathit{true}))$ (every node has a successor), and $p_3 = \forall(\bigcirc\!\rightarrow\!\bigcirc\!\leftarrow\!\bigcirc, \mathit{false})$ (no node has two predecessors), which is only satisfied by the infinite graph $G_\infty = \bigcirc\!\rightarrow\!\bigcirc\!\rightarrow\!\bigcirc\!\rightarrow\!\bigcirc\!\rightarrow \cdots$.

Thus, in order to be able to find a complete set of symbolic models without knowing beforehand if the construction of a saturated nested tableau terminates, we introduce the key-notions of k-semi-saturation and k-termination to reason about nested tableaux up to depth k, which are in some sense a prefix of a saturated tableau. Note, the verification of our algorithm, in particular for completeness, is accordingly based on induction on k. Informally, this means that by enlarging the depth k during the construction of a saturated nested tableau, we eventually find all finite open branches and thus finite models. This procedure will at the same time guarantee that we will be able to extract symbolic models from finite open branches even for the case of an infinite saturated nested tableau. E.g., we will be able to extract $\emptyset$ from a finite open branch of the infinite saturated nested tableau for property $p_4 = \wedge(p_1 \vee \exists(①, \mathit{false}), p_2, p_3)$.

4.1   Sets of Symbolic Models

The symbolic model generation algorithm $\mathcal{A}$ should generate for each graph property p a set of symbolic models $\mathcal{S}$ satisfying all requirements described in the introduction. A symbolic model in its most general form is a graph condition over a graph C, where C is available as an explicit component. A symbolic model then represents a possibly empty set of graphs (as defined subsequently in Definition 10). A specific set of symbolic models $\mathcal{S}$ for a graph property p

satisfies the requirements soundness, completeness, minimal representability, and compactness if it adheres to the subsequent formalizations of these notions.

Definition 7 (symbolic model). *If c is a condition over C according to Definition 1, then $\langle C, c \rangle$ is a symbolic model.*

Based on the notion of m-consequence we relate symbolic models subsequently.

Definition 8 (m-consequence on conditions). *If c_1 and c_2 are conditions over C_1 and C_2, respectively, $m : C_1 \hookrightarrow C_2$ is a mono, and for all monos $m_1 : C_1 \hookrightarrow G$ and $m_2 : C_2 \hookrightarrow G$ such that $m_2 \circ m = m_1$ it holds that $m_2 \models c_2$ implies $m_1 \models c_1$, then c_1 is an m-consequence of c_2, written $c_2 \vdash_m c_1$. We can state the existence of such an m by writing $c_2 \vdash c_1$. We also omit m if it is the identity or clear from the context. Finally, conditions c_1 and c_2 over C are equivalent, written $c_1 \equiv c_2$, if $c_1 \vdash c_2$ and $c_2 \vdash c_1$.*

We define coverage of symbolic models based on the notion of m-refinement, which relies on an m-consequence between the contained conditions.

Definition 9 (m-refinement of symbolic model). *If $\langle C_1, c_1 \rangle$ and $\langle C_2, c_2 \rangle$ are symbolic models and $m : C_1 \hookrightarrow C_2$ is a mono, and $c_2 \vdash_m c_1$, then $\langle C_2, c_2 \rangle$ is an m-refinement of $\langle C_1, c_1 \rangle$, written $\langle C_2, c_2 \rangle \leq_m \langle C_1, c_1 \rangle$. The set of all such symbolic models $\langle C_2, c_2 \rangle$ is denoted by refined($\langle C_1, c_1 \rangle$).*

We define the graphs covered by a symbolic model as follows.

Definition 10 (m-covered by a symbolic model). *If $\langle C, c \rangle$ is a symbolic model, G is a finite graph, $m : C \hookrightarrow G$ is a mono, and $m \models c$ then G is an m-covered graph of $\langle C, c \rangle$. The set of all such graphs is denoted by covered($\langle C, c \rangle$). For a set S of symbolic models covered(S) $= \cup_{s \in S}$ covered(s).*

Based on these definitions, we formalize the first four requirements from Sect. 1 to be satisfied by the sets of symbolic models returned by algorithm $\mathcal{A}$.

Definition 11 (sound, complete, minimally representable, compact). *Let S be a set of symbolic models and let p be a graph property. S is sound w.r.t. p if covered(S) $\subseteq \{G \mid G \models p \wedge G$ is finite$\}$, S is complete w.r.t. p if covered(S) $\supseteq \{G \mid G \models p \wedge G$ is finite$\}$, S is minimally representable w.r.t. p if for each $\langle C, c \rangle \in S : C \models p$ and for each $G \in$ covered($\langle C, c \rangle$) there is a mono $m : C \hookrightarrow G$, and S is compact if all $(s_1 \neq s_2) \in S$ satisfy covered(s_1) $\not\subseteq$ covered(s_1).*

4.2 Symbolic Model Generation Algorithm $\mathcal{A}$

We briefly describe the two steps of the algorithm $\mathcal{A}$, which generates for a graph property p a set of symbolic models $\mathcal{A}(p) = S$. The algorithm consists of two steps: the generation of symbolic models and the compaction of symbolic models, which are discussed in detail in Sects. 4.3 and 4.4, respectively. Afterwards, in Sect. 4.5, we discuss the explorability of the obtained set of symbolic models S.

Step 1 (Generation of symbolic models in Sect. 4.3). We apply the tableau and nested tableau rules from Sect. 3 to iteratively construct a nested tableau. Then, we extract symbolic models from certain nested branches of this nested tableau that can not be extended. Since the construction of the nested tableau may not terminate due to infinite nested branches we construct the nested tableau in breadth-first manner and extract the symbolic models whenever possible. Moreover, we eliminate a source of nontermination by selecting the hook in each branch in a fair way not postponing the successors of a positive literal that was not chosen as a hook yet indefinitely [20, p. 29] ensuring at the same time refutational completeness of our algorithm. This step ensures that the resulting set of symbolic models is sound, complete (provided termination), and minimally representable. The symbolic models extracted from the intermediately constructed nested tableau NT for growing k is denoted $\mathcal{S}_{NT,k}$.

Step 2 (Compaction of symbolic models in Sect. 4.4). We obtain the final result $\mathcal{S}$ from $\mathcal{S}_{NT,k}$ by the removal of symbolic model that are a refinement of any other symbolic model. This step preserves soundness (as only symbolic models are removed), completeness (as only symbolic models are removed that are refinements, hence, the removal does not change the set of covered graphs), and minimal representability (as only symbolic models are removed), and additionally ensures compactness.

4.3   Generation of $\mathcal{S}_{NT,k}$

By applying a breadth-first construction we build nested tableaux that are for increasing k, both, k-semi-saturated, stating that all branches occurring up to index k in all nested branches are semi-saturated, and k-terminated, stating that no nested tableau rule can be applied to a leaf of a branch occurring up to index k in some nested branch.

Definition 12 (k-semi-saturation, k-terminated). *Given a nested tableau NT for condition c over C. If NB is a nested branch of length k of NT and each branch B contained at index $i \leq k$ in NB is semi-saturated, then NB is k-semi-saturated. If every nested branch of NT of length n is $min(n,k)$-semi-saturated, then NT is k-semi-saturated. If NB is a nested branch of NT of length n and the nesting rule can not be applied to the leaf of any branch B at index $i \leq min(n,k)$ in NB, then NB is k-terminated. If every nested branch of NT of length n is $min(n,k)$-terminated, then NT is k-terminated. If NB is a nested branch of NT that is k-terminated for each k, then NB is terminated. If NT is k-terminated for each k, then NT is terminated.*

We define the k'-remainder of a branch, which is a refinement of the condition of that tableau, that is used by the subsequent definition of the set of extracted symbolic models.

Definition 13 (k'-remainder of branch). *Given a tableau T for a condition c over C, a mono $q : C \hookrightarrow G$, a branch B of T, and a prefix P of B of length $k' > 0$. If R contains (a) each condition contained in P unless it has been used* *in P by the lift rule (being $\exists(m, c')$ or ℓ in the lift rule in Definition 4) and (b) the clauses of c not used by the extension rule in P (being $\vee(c_1, \ldots, c_n)$ in the extension rule in Definition 4), then $\langle C, \wedge R \rangle$ is the k'-remainder of B.*

The set of symbolic models extracted from a nested branch *NB* is a set of certain k'-remainders of branches of *NB*. In the example given in Fig. 2 we extracted three symbolic models from the four nested branches of the nested tableau.

Definition 14 (extracted symbolic model). *If NT is a nested tableau for a condition c over C, NB is a k-terminated and k-semi-saturated nested branch of NT of length $n \le k$, B is the branch at index n of length k' in NB, B is open, B contains no positive literals, then the k'-remainder of B is the symbolic model extracted from B. The set of all such extracted symbolic models from k-terminated and k-semi-saturated nested branches of NT is denoted $\mathcal{S}_{NT,k}$.*

Based on the previously introduced definitions of soundness, completeness, and minimal representability of sets of symbolic models w.r.t. graph properties we are now ready to verify the corresponding results on the algorithm $\mathcal{A}$.

Theorem 1 (soundness). *If NT is a nested tableau for a graph property p, then $\mathcal{S}_{NT,k}$ is sound w.r.t. p.*

Theorem 2 (completeness). *If NT is a terminated nested tableau for a graph property p, k is the maximal length of a nested branch in NT, then $\mathcal{S}_{NT,k}$ is complete w.r.t. p.*

As explained by the example at the beginning of Sect. 4 the algorithm may not terminate. However, the symbolic models extracted at any point during the construction of the nested tableau are a gradually extended underapproximation of the complete set of symbolic models. Moreover, the openers $\exists(m : G_1 \hookrightarrow G_2, c)$ of the branches that end nonterminated nested branches constitute an overapproximation by encoding a lower bound on missing symbolic models in the sense that each symbolic model that may be discovered by further tableau construction contains some G_2 as a subgraph.

Theorem 3 (minimal representability). *If NT is a nested tableau for a graph property p, then $\mathcal{S}_{NT,k}$ is minimally representable w.r.t p.*

For $p_1 \wedge p_2$ from Fig. 1 we obtain a terminated nested tableau (consisting of 114 tableaux with 25032 nodes) from which we generate 28 symbolic models (with a total number of 5433 negative literals in their negative remainders). For p from Fig. 2 we generate 3 symbolic models, which are given also in Fig. 2. In the next subsection we explain how to compact sets of symbolic models.

4.4   Compaction of $\mathcal{S}_{NT,k}$ into $\mathcal{S}$

The set of symbolic models $\mathcal{S}_{NT,k}$ as obtained in the previous section can be compacted by application of the following lemma. It states a sufficient condition for whether a symbolic model $\langle A_1, c_1 \rangle$ refines another symbolic model $\langle A_2, c_2 \rangle$, which is equivalent to $covered(\langle A_1, c_1 \rangle) \supseteq covered(\langle A_2, c_2 \rangle)$. In this case we can remove the covered symbolic model $\langle A_2, c_2 \rangle$ from $\mathcal{S}_{NT,k}$ without changing the graphs covered. Since the set of symbolic models $\mathcal{S}_{NT,k}$ is always finite we can apply the following lemma until no further coverages are determined.

Lemma 1 (compaction). *If $\langle A_1, c_1 \rangle$ and $\langle A_2, c_2 \rangle$ are two symbolic models, $m : A_1 \hookrightarrow A_2$ is a mono, and $\exists(i_2, c_2 \wedge \neg shift(i_2, \exists(i_1, c_1)))$ is not satisfiable by a finite graph, then $covered(\langle A_1, c_1 \rangle) \supseteq covered(\langle A_2, c_2 \rangle)$.*

This lemma can be applied when we determine a mono m such that $\exists(i_2, c_2 \wedge \neg shift(i_2, \exists(i_1, c_1)))$ is refutable. For this latter part we apply our tableau construction as well and terminate as soon as non-refutability is detected, that is, as soon as a symbolic model is obtained for the condition.

For the resulting set $\mathcal{S}$ of symbolic models obtained from iterated application of Lemma 1 we now state the compactness as defined before.

Theorem 4 (compactness). *If NT is a nested tableau for a graph property p, then $\mathcal{S} \subseteq \mathcal{S}_{NT,k}$ is compact.*

For $p_1 \wedge p_2$ from Fig. 1 we determined a single symbolic model with minimal model (given in Fig. 1e) that is contained by the minimal models of all 28 extracted symbolic models. However, this symbolic model covers only 2 of the other 27 symbolic models in the sense of Lemma 1. For p from Fig. 2 we removed one of the three symbolic models by compaction ending up with two symbolic models, which have incomparable sets of covered graphs as for the symbolic models remaining after compaction for $p_1 \wedge p_2$ from Fig. 1.

4.5 Explorability of $\mathcal{S}$

We believe that the exploration of further graphs satisfying a given property p based on the symbolic models is often desireable. In fact, $covered(\mathcal{S})$ can be explored according to Definition 10 by selecting $\langle C, c \rangle \in \mathcal{S}$, by generating a mono $m : C \hookrightarrow G$ to a new finite candidate graph G, and by deciding $m \models c$. Then, an entire automatic exploration can proceed by selecting the symbolic models $\langle C, c \rangle \in \mathcal{S}$ in a round-robin manner using an enumeration of the monos leaving C in each case. However, the exploration may also be guided interactively restricting the considered symbolic models and monos.

(a) Extension Candidate G_1 (b) Extension Candidate G_2

Fig. 3. Two extension candidates that include the graph G_0 from Fig. 1e with obvious monos $m_1 : G_0 \hookrightarrow G_1$ and $m_2 : G_0 \hookrightarrow G_2$.

For example, consider p_2 from Fig. 1c for which the algorithm $\mathcal{A}$ returns a single symbolic model $\langle G_0, c_0 \rangle$ of which the minimal model is given in Fig. 1c. In an interactive exploration we may want to decide whether the two graphs given in Fig. 3 also satisfy p_2. In fact, because $m_1 \models c_0$ and $m_2 \not\models c_0$ we derive $G_1 \models p_2$ and $G_2 \not\models p_2$ as expected.

5   Implementation

We implemented the algorithm $\mathcal{A}$ platform-independently using Java as our new tool AUTOGRAPH using xsd-based [36] input/output-format.

For $p_1 \wedge p_2$ from Fig. 1 we computed the symbolic models using AUTOGRAPH in 7.4 s, 4.6 s, 3.4 s, 2.7 s, and 2.1 s using 1, 2, 3, 4, and 13 threads (machine: 256 GB DDR4, 2 × E5-2643 Xeon @ 3.4 GHz × 6 cores × 2 threads). The minimal models derived using AUTOGRAPH for p_1, p_2, and $p_1 \wedge p_2$ from Fig. 1 are given in Fig. 1d and e. For p from Fig. 2 AUTOGRAPH terminates in negligible time.

While some elementary constructions used (such as computing CNF, existence of monos, and pair factorization) have exponential worst case executing time, we believe, based on our tool-based evaluation, that in many practical applications the runtime will be acceptable. Furthermore, we optimized performance by exploiting parallelizability of the tableaux construction (by considering each nested branch in parallel) and of the compaction of the sets of symbolic models (by considering each pair of symbolic models in parallel).

To limit memory consumption we discard parts of the nested tableau not required for the subsequent computation, which generates the symbolic models,

$$
\frac{1 : \text{REFUTE-FALSE}}{\dfrac{res = \exists(m, \wedge(\vee(\emptyset)))}{\emptyset}}
\qquad
\frac{2 : \text{SELECT-HOOK-FROM-PRE-QUEUE}}{\dfrac{res = \bot \quad q\text{-}pre = \ell \cdot \ell_s}{\{(\diamond, \ell, \diamond, \ell_s, \diamond, \diamond, \diamond)\}}}
\qquad
\frac{3 : \text{NO-HOOK}}{\dfrac{res = \bot \quad inp = \wedge()}{\emptyset}}
$$

$$
\frac{4 : \text{LIFT-NEGATIVE-LITERAL-INTO-BRANCHING-RESULT}}{\dfrac{res = \exists(m, c) \quad neg = \ell \cdot \ell_s \quad shift(m, \ell) = c'}{\{(\diamond, \exists(m, [c \wedge c']), \ell_s, \diamond, \diamond, \diamond)\}}}
$$

$$
\frac{5 : \text{LIFT-POSITIVE-LITERALS-FROM-PRE-QUEUE}}{\dfrac{res = \exists(m, c) \quad q\text{-}pre = \ell \cdot \ell_s \quad shift(m, \ell) = \vee L}{\begin{array}{c}\{(\diamond, \diamond, \diamond, \ell_s, q\text{-}post \cdot \exists(m', [c']), \diamond) \mid \exists(m', c') \in L \wedge \neg iso(m')\} \\ \cup \{(\diamond, \exists(m, [c \wedge \exists(m', c')]), \diamond, \ell_s, \diamond, \diamond) \mid \exists(m', c') \in L \wedge iso(m')\}\end{array}}}
$$

$$
\frac{6 : \text{CREATE-NESTED-TABLEAU}}{\dfrac{res = \exists(m, c) \quad inp = \wedge()}{\{(c, \bot, \diamond, q\text{-}post, \lambda, m \circ cm)\}}}
$$

$$
\frac{7 : \text{EXTEND-USING-FIRST-CLAUSE}}{\dfrac{inp = \wedge(cl_1, cl_2, \ldots, cl_n) \quad cl_1 = \vee L}{\begin{array}{c}\{(\wedge(cl_2, \ldots, cl_n), \diamond, \diamond, q\text{-}pre \cdot \exists(m, c), \diamond, \diamond) \mid \exists(m, c) \in L\} \\ \cup \{(\wedge(cl_2, \ldots, cl_n), \diamond, neg \cdot \neg\exists(m, c), \diamond, \diamond, \diamond) \mid \neg\exists(m, c) \in L\}\end{array}}}
$$

Fig. 4. Implemented construction rules: ℓ is a literal, ℓ_s is a sequence of literals, L is a set of literals, cl_i is a clause, and $\diamond$ is the unchanged value from the input.

as follows. The implemented algorithm operates on a queue (used to enforce the breadth-first construction) of configurations where each configuration represents the last branch of a nested branch of the nested tableau currently constructed (the parts of the nested tableau not given by theses branches are thereby not represented in memory). The algorithm starts with a single initial configuration and terminates if the queue of configurations is empty.

A configuration contains the information necessary to continue the further construction of the nested tableau (also ensuring fair selection of hooks) and to extract the symbolic models whenever one is obtained.

A configuration of the implementation is a tuple containing six elements $(inp, res, neg, q\text{-}pre, q\text{-}post, cm)$ where inp is a condition c over C in CNF and is the remainder of the condition currently constructed (where clauses used already are removed), res is $\bot$ or a positive literal $\exists(m : C \hookrightarrow D, c')$ into which the other literals from the branch are lifted, neg is a list of negative literals over C from clauses already handled (this list is emptied as soon as a positive literal has been chosen for res), $q\text{-}pre$ is a queue of positive literals over C from which the first element is chosen for the res component, $q\text{-}post$ is a queue of positive literals: once res is a chosen positive literal $\exists(m : C \hookrightarrow D, c')$ we shift the elements from $q\text{-}pre$ over m to obtain elements of $q\text{-}post$, and cm is the composition of the morphisms from the openers of the nested branch constructed so far and is used to obtain eventually symbolic models (if they exist).

Given a condition c over C the single initial configuration is $(c, \bot, \lambda, \lambda, \lambda, id_C)$. The implemented construction rules operating on these configurations are given in Fig. 4. Given a configuration c we check the rules in the order given for applicability and apply only the first rule found. For each rule, applicability is determined by the conditions above the line and each rule results in a set of configurations given below the rule.

Rule 1 stops further generation if the current result is unsatisfiable. Rule 2 ensures that hooks are selected from the queue (if the queue is not empty) to ensure fairness of hook selection. Rule 3 if the queue can not be used to select a hook and no clause remains, the nested branch is terminated and a symbolic model can be extracted by taking $\langle codomain(cm), \wedge neg \rangle$. Rule 4 implements the lifting rule (see Definition 4) for negative literals taken from neg. Rule 5 implements the lifting rule (see Definition 4) for positive literals taken from $q\text{-}pre$; if the morphism of the resulting positive literal is an isomorphism, as forbidden for literals in CNF, we move an equivalent condition in CNF into the current hook (also implementing the lift rule) instead of moving the literal to the queue $q\text{-}post$. Rule 6 implements the nesting rule (see Definition 6). Rule 7 deterministically implements the extension rule (see Definition 4) constructing for each literal of the first clause a new configuration to represent the different nested branches.

For soundness reconsider Definition 13 where the set R used in the condition $\wedge R$ recovers the desired information similarly to how it is captured in the configurations. The separation into different elements in the configurations then allows for queue handling and determinization.

6   Conclusion and Outlook

We presented a symbolic model generation procedure for graph properties being equivalent to FOL on graphs. Our algorithm is innovative in the sense that it is designed to generate a finite set of symbolic models that is sound, complete (upon termination), compact, minimally representable, and flexibly explorable. Moreover, the algorithm is highly parallelizable. The approach is implemented in a new tool, called AUTOGRAPH.

As future work we aim at applying, evaluating, and optimizing our approach further w.r.t. different application scenarios from the graph database domain [37] as presented in this paper, but also to other domains such as model-driven engineering, where our approach can be used, e.g., to generate test models for model transformations [2,11,22]. We also aim at generalizing our approach to more expressive graph properties able to encode, e.g., path-related properties [21,27,28]. Finally, the work on exploration and compaction of extracted symbolic models as well as reducing their number during tableau construction is an ongoing task.

References

1. Bak, K., Diskin, Z., Antkiewicz, M., Czarnecki, K., Wasowski, A.: Clafer: unifying class and feature modeling. SoSyM **15**(3), 811–845 (2016)
2. Baudry, B.: Testing model transformations: a case for test generation from input domain models. In: MDE4DRE (2009)
3. Beyhl, T., Blouin, D., Giese, H., Lambers, L.: On the operationalization of graph queries with generalized discrimination networks. In: [5], 170–186
4. Courcelle, B.: The expression of graph properties and graph transformations in monadic second-order logic. In: [31], 313–400
5. Echahed, R., Minas, M. (eds.): ICGT 2016. LNCS, vol. 9761. Springer, Cham (2016)
6. Ehrig, H., Ehrig, K., Prange, U., Taentzer, G.: Fundamentals of Algebraic Graph Transformation. Springer, Heidelberg (2006)
7. Ehrig, H., Golas, U., Habel, A., Lambers, L., Orejas, F.: $\mathcal{M}$-adhesive transformation systems with nested application conditions. part 2: embedding, critical pairs and local confluence. Fundam. Inform. **118**(1–2), 35–63 (2012)
8. Ehrig, H., Golas, U., Habel, A., Lambers, L., Orejas, F.: $\mathcal{M}$-adhesive transformation systems with nested application conditions. part 1: parallelism, concurrency and amalgamation. Math. Struct. Comput. Sci. **24**(4) (2014)
9. Erling, O., Averbuch, A., Larriba-Pey, J., Chafi, H., Gubichev, A., Prat-Pérez, A., Pham, M., Boncz, P.A.: The LDBC social network benchmark: interactive workload. In: Proceedings of the 2015 ACM SIGMOD International Conference on Management of Data, pp. 619–630. ACM (2015)
10. Gogolla, M., Hilken, F.: Model validation and verification options in a contemporary UML and OCL analysis tool. In: Modellierung 2016. LNI, vol. 254, pp. 205–220. GI (2016)
11. González, C.A., Cabot, J.: Test data generation for model transformations combining partition and constraint analysis. In: Ruscio, D., Varró, D. (eds.) ICMT 2014. LNCS, vol. 8568, pp. 25–41. Springer, Cham (2014). doi:10.1007/978-3-319-08789-4_3

12. Habel, A., Heckel, R., Taentzer, G.: Graph grammars with negative application conditions. Fundam. Inform. **26**(3/4), 287–313 (1996)
13. Habel, A., Pennemann, K.: Correctness of high-level transformation systems relative to nested conditions. MSCS **19**(2), 245–296 (2009)
14. Hähnle, R.: Tableaux and related methods. In: Handbook of Automated Reasoning (in 2 vols.), pp. 100–178 (2001)
15. Heckel, R., Wagner, A.: Ensuring consistency of conditional graph rewriting - a constructive approach. ENTCS **2**, 118–126 (1995)
16. Jackson, E.K., Levendovszky, T., Balasubramanian, D.: Reasoning about meta-modeling with formal specifications and automatic proofs. In: Whittle, J., Clark, T., Kühne, T. (eds.) MODELS 2011. LNCS, vol. 6981, pp. 653–667. Springer, Heidelberg (2011). doi:10.1007/978-3-642-24485-8_48
17. Jackson, E.K., Sztipanovits, J.: Constructive techniques for meta- and model-level reasoning. In: Engels, G., Opdyke, B., Schmidt, D.C., Weil, F. (eds.) MODELS 2007. LNCS, vol. 4735, pp. 405–419. Springer, Heidelberg (2007). doi:10.1007/978-3-540-75209-7_28
18. Krause, C., Johannsen, D., Deeb, R., Sattler, K., Knacker, D., Niadzelka, A.: An SQL-based query language and engine for graph pattern matching. In: Echahed and Minas [5], 153–169
19. Lack, S., Sobocinski, P.: Adhesive and quasiadhesive categories. ITA **39**(3), 511–545 (2005)
20. Lambers, L., Orejas, F.: Tableau-based reasoning for graph properties. In: Giese, H., König, B. (eds.) ICGT 2014. LNCS, vol. 8571, pp. 17–32. Springer, Cham (2014). doi:10.1007/978-3-319-09108-2_2
21. Milicevic, A., Near, J.P., Kang, E., Jackson, D.: Alloy*: a general-purpose higher-order relational constraint solver. In: 37th IEEE/ACM International Conference on Software Engineering, ICSE 2015, vol. 1, pp. 609–619 (2015)
22. Mougenot, A., Darrasse, A., Blanc, X., Soria, M.: Uniform random generation of huge metamodel instances. In: Paige, R.F., Hartman, A., Rensink, A. (eds.) ECMDA-FA 2009. LNCS, vol. 5562, pp. 130–145. Springer, Heidelberg (2009). doi:10.1007/978-3-642-02674-4_10
23. Orejas, F., Ehrig, H., Prange, U.: Reasoning with graph constraints. Formal Asp. Comput. **22**(3–4), 385–422 (2010)
24. Pennemann, K.: An algorithm for approximating the satisfiability problem of high-level conditions. ENTCS **213**, 75–94 (2008)
25. Pennemann, K.-H.: Resolution-like theorem proving for high-level conditions. In: Ehrig, H., Heckel, R., Rozenberg, G., Taentzer, G. (eds.) ICGT 2008. LNCS, vol. 5214, pp. 289–304. Springer, Heidelberg (2008). doi:10.1007/978-3-540-87405-8_20
26. Pennemann, K.H.: Development of Correct Graph Transformation Systems, PhD Thesis. Dept. Informatik, Univ. Oldenburg (2009)
27. Poskitt, C.M., Plump, D.: Verifying monadic second-order properties of graph programs. In: Giese, H., König, B. (eds.) ICGT 2014. LNCS, vol. 8571, pp. 33–48. Springer, Cham (2014). doi:10.1007/978-3-319-09108-2_3
28. Radke, H.: Hr* graph conditions between counting monadic second-order and second-order graph formulas. ECEASST **61** (2013)
29. Radke, H., Arendt, T., Becker, J.S., Habel, A., Taentzer, G.: Translating essential OCL invariants to nested graph constraints focusing on set operations. In: Parisi-Presicce, F., Westfechtel, B. (eds.) ICGT 2015. LNCS, vol. 9151, pp. 155–170. Springer, Cham (2015). doi:10.1007/978-3-319-21145-9_10

30. Rensink, A.: Representing first-order logic using graphs. In: Ehrig, H., Engels, G., Parisi-Presicce, F., Rozenberg, G. (eds.) ICGT 2004. LNCS, vol. 3256, pp. 319–335. Springer, Heidelberg (2004). doi:10.1007/978-3-540-30203-2_23
31. Rozenberg, G. (ed.): Handbook of Graph Grammars and Computing by Graph Transformations. Foundations, vol. 1. World Scientific, Singapore (1997)
32. Salay, R., Chechik, M.: A generalized formal framework for partial modeling. In: Egyed, A., Schaefer, I. (eds.) FASE 2015. LNCS, vol. 9033, pp. 133–148. Springer, Heidelberg (2015). doi:10.1007/978-3-662-46675-9_9
33. Schneider, S., Lambers, L., Orejas, F.: Symbolic Model Generation for Graph Properties (Extended Version). No. 115 in Technische Berichte des Hasso-Plattner-Instituts für Softwaresystemtechnik an der Universität Potsdam, Universitätsverlag Potsdam, Hasso Plattner Institute (Germany, Potsdam), 1 edn. (2017)
34. Semeráth, O., Vörös, A., Varró, D.: Iterative and incremental model generation by logic solvers. In: Stevens, P., Wąsowski, A. (eds.) FASE 2016. LNCS, vol. 9633, pp. 87–103. Springer, Heidelberg (2016). doi:10.1007/978-3-662-49665-7_6
35. The Linked Data Benchmark Council (LDBC): Social network benchmark (2016). http://ldbcouncil.org/benchmarks/snb
36. T.W.W.W.C. (W3C): W3C xml schema definition language (xsd) 1.1 part 1: structures (2012)
37. Wood, P.T.: Query languages for graph databases. SIGMOD Rec. 41(1), 50–60 (2012)

Model Transformations

Traceability Mappings as a Fundamental Instrument in Model Transformations

Zinovy Diskin[1]([✉]), Abel Gómez[2], and Jordi Cabot[2,3]

[1] McMaster University, Hamilton, Canada
`diskinz@mcmaster.ca`
[2] IN3, Universitat Oberta de Catalunya, Barcelona, Spain
`agomezlla@uoc.edu, jordi.cabot@icrea.cat`
[3] ICREA, Barcelona, Spain

Abstract. Technological importance of traceability mappings for model transformations is well-known, but they have often been considered as an auxiliary element generated during the transformation execution and providing accessory information. This paper argues that traceability mappings should instead be regarded as a core aspect of the transformation definition, and a key instrument in the transformation management.

We will show how a transformation can be represented as the result of execution of a metamodel mapping, which acts as a special encoding of the transformation definition. Since mappings enjoy Boolean operations (as *sets* of links) and sequential composition (as sets of *directed* links), encoding transformations by mappings makes it possible to define these operations for transformations as well, which can be useful for model transformation reuse, compositional design, and chaining.

1 Introduction

Translating models from one to another metamodel (also known as model-to-model transformation, MMT) is ubiquitous in software engineering. The technological importance of traceability for MMT is well recognized in the MMT community. Such widely used transformation languages as ATL [11,16] and ETL [12,17] automatically create traceability links during the transformation execution in order to resolve dependencies between the rules, and perhaps for debugging and maintenance. Moreover, a traceability mapping (i.e., a set of links) between the metamodels can be used as an MMT definition, which may be immediately executed [7,13,14], or used for automatic transformation code generation [4].

Here, we present a theoretical framework, in which traceability aspects of MMT are precisely discussed: we specify execution of metatraceability mappings as an abstract mathematical operation, show the importance of several concepts, which are underestimated or missing from the literature, and derive some practical recommendations on MMT management, including transformation chaining.

In Sect. 2, we show that semantics of MMTs without traceability mappings is essentially incomplete: we present an example of two different transformations indistinguishable in the traceability-free setting. We then demonstrate that

© Springer-Verlag GmbH Germany 2017
M. Huisman and J. Rubin (Eds.): FASE 2017, LNCS 10202, pp. 247–263, 2017.
DOI: 10.1007/978-3-662-54494-5_14

traceability links between the source and the target models work in concert with the respective links between the source and the target metamodels, which means commutativity of the respective diagrams. Moreover, execution of a metamodel mapping for a given source model can be specified as an algebraic operation (called *pullback* in category theory), for which commutativity is central.

However, simple traceability mappings considered in Sect. 2, which relate two metamodels with similar structures, do not cover many practically interesting cases of structurally different metamodels. To address the problem of executing metamodel mappings relating metamodels with different structures, several complex approaches have been developed [7, 19]. We propose a simpler solution, in which we first augment the source metamodel with derived elements that make its structure similar to the target metamodel, and then relate the two by a simple mapping. The derived elements actually encode operations/queries against the source metamodel, which can be executed for any model instantiating it. Hence, a complex metamodel mapping is executed in two steps: first the query is executed, then the mapping as such is executed. The approach is discussed in Sect. 3, and in Sect. 5 we show how it can be implemented with ATL.

Thus, even complex MMTs are encoded in a unified and transparent way as mappings relating metamodels with, perhaps, derived elements/queries involved. An important consequence of this encoding is that we can employ well studied algebraic operations over mappings for manipulating MMTs as black-boxed objects. Specifically, being *sets* of links, mappings enjoy intersections and union operations over them, which can be employed for reuse. Being sets of *directed* links, mappings can be sequentially composed, and the respective transformations chained (which is considered to be a challenging task). Particularly, chaining can be employed for incremental compositional design of MMTs. Algebra of MMTs is considered in Sects. 4, and 5 we show how it can be applied for manipulating ATL transformations. Finally, we observe related work in Sect. 6, and conclude in Sect. 7.

2   Analysing Traceability Mappings

We show the semantic necessity of traceability mappings in Sect. 2.1, consider their properties and representation in Sect. 2.2, and execution in Sect. 2.3.

2.1   The Semantic Necessity of Traceability Mapping

Semantics of a model-to-model transformation $\mathbf{T}$ is commonly considered to be a function $[\![\mathbf{T}]\!]\colon [\![M]\!] \to [\![N]\!]$, where $[\![M]\!]$ and $[\![N]\!]$ are model spaces defined by, resp., the source, M, and the target, N, metamodels. However, in this section we present two different transformations generating the same model space mapping, and then call traceability mappings to the rescue.

Figure 1(a) presents a toy transformation example. The source metamodel M specifies two classes, Car and Boat, and the target metamodel N specifies their possible roles as Commuting and Leisure Vehicles, connected by association same

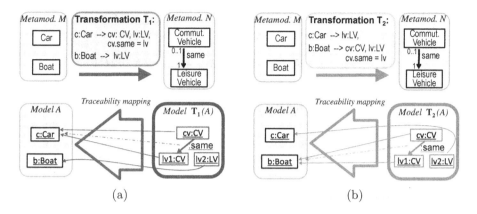

Fig. 1. Two sample transformations. (Color figure online)

if two roles are played by the same physical vehicle; e.g., such a transformation may be needed for an insurance company. The transformation T_1 consists of two rules specified in Fig. 1(a) in some pseudo MT language. The first rule says that a car produces a commuting vehicle and a leisure vehicle connected by a same-link. The second rule says that a boat generates a leisure vehicle. An example of executing this transformation for a model A consisting of a car and a boat is shown in the lower half of Fig. 1(a), where $T_1(A)$ denotes the target model produced by the transformation; ignore the mapping from $T_1(A)$ to A for the moment. Here we write $T(A)$ for $[\![T]\!](A)$. We will often abuse such a notation and use the same symbol for a syntactic construct and its intended semantics.

Figure 1(b) presents a different transformation T_2. Now a boat gives rise to a commuting and a leisure vehicle, whereas a car only produces a leisure vehicle (think about people living on an island). Clearly, being executed for the same source model A, transformation T_2 produces the same target model consisting of three objects and a same-link. More accurately, models $T_1(A)$ and $T_2(A)$ are isomorphic rather than equal, but the same transformation T executed twice for the same model A would also produce isomorphic rather than equal models as MMTs are normally defined up to OIDs. We will always understand equality of models up to OID isomorphism, and thus can write $T_1(A) = T_2(A)$. It is easy to see that such an equality will hold for any source model containing equal numbers of cars and boats. If wesuppose that the metamodel M includes a constraint requiring the numbers of cars and boats to be equal (e.g., has an association between classes Car and Boat with multiplicity 1..1 at both ends), then any instance X of M would necessarily consist of equal numbers of cars and boats. Hence, $T_1(X) = T_2(X)$ holds for *any* source instance $X \in [\![M]\!]$.

Thus, the common semantics of a model transformation as a model space mapping $[\![T]\!]: [\![M]\!] \to [\![N]\!]$ is too poor and should be enriched. Comparison of the two transformations in Fig. 1(a, b), now with traceability mappings, shows what should be done: we need to include traceability mappings into the semantics of MMTs, and define it as a function $[\![T]\!]: [\![M]\!] \to [\![N]\!] \times Map([\![N]\!],[\![M]\!])$, where

$Map(\llbracket N \rrbracket, \llbracket M \rrbracket)$ denotes the set of all mappings from N-models (elements of $\llbracket N \rrbracket$) to M-models (in $\llbracket M \rrbracket$). It is convenient to split semantics into two functions:

$$\llbracket \mathbf{T} \rrbracket^{\bullet}: \llbracket M \rrbracket \rightarrow \llbracket N \rrbracket \text{ and } \llbracket \mathbf{T} \rrbracket^{\blacktriangleleft}: \llbracket M \rrbracket \rightarrow Map(\llbracket N \rrbracket, \llbracket M \rrbracket)$$

such that for any source model A, mapping $\llbracket \mathbf{T} \rrbracket^{\blacktriangleleft}(A)$ is directed from model $\llbracket \mathbf{T} \rrbracket^{\bullet}(A)$ to A (as suggested by the tringle superindex). Thus, what is missing in the common MMT-semantics is the mapping-valued function $\llbracket \mathbf{T} \rrbracket^{\blacktriangleleft}$. Including this function into semantics has several important consequences discussed below. Below we will use a simplified notation with semantic double-brackets omitted.

2.2 Traceability Under the Microscope

We discuss properties of traceability mappings: structure preservation, commuting with typing, and their span representation. As an example, we use transformation $\mathbf{T}_1$ from Fig. 1(a), but denote it by $\mathbf{T}$ to avoid excessive indexing.

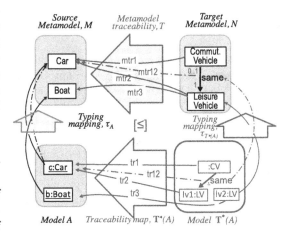

2.2.1 Structure Preservation

A mapping is a collection of directed links that is compatible with models' structure. If models are graphs, then their graph structure, i.e., the incidence

Fig. 2. Meta-traceability (Color figure online)

of nodes and edges, should be respected. Consider, e.g., the lower mapping $\mathbf{T}^{\blacktriangleleft}(A)$ in Fig. 2, which reproduces the respective traceability mapping in Fig. 1(a). The dashed link from edge same to node c:Car in this mapping actually denotes a link targeted at the *identity* loop of the node c, which relates c to itself. Such loops can be added to every graph node, and when we draw a link from an arrow to a node, it is just a syntactic sugar to specify a link targeted at the node's identity loop. With this reservation, it is seen that both traceability mappings in Fig. 1 are correct graph morphisms, which map nodes to nodes and edges to edges so that the incidence between nodes and edges is preserved.

2.2.2 Meta-Traceability and Commutativity

Another important condition to be respected is compatibility of links between model elements with relationships between metamodel elements established by the transformation definition. To explicate the latter, we need *meta-traceability* links between metamodels as shown in the upper half of Fig. 2. The mapping T

consists of four links mtr_i ($i = 1, 12, 2, 3$) "tracing" the origin of the target meta-model elements according to the (green) transformation definition in Fig. 1(a): commuting vehicles appear from cars (rule 1) and only from cars (neither of the other rules produce commuting vehicles), and leisure vehicles appear either from cars (rule 1) or boats (rule 2). The dashed link to Car again denotes a formal link from edge same to not-shown identity loop link from Car to Car, and encodes the clause in rule 1 that a same-link appears when a car generates both a commuting and leisure vehicle. Thus, the upper three meta-links in mapping T "trace" rule 1 in transformation $\mathbf{T}$, and the lower link "traces" rule 2.

Now recall that a model A is actually a pair (D_A, τ_A) with D_A the model's datagraph, and $\tau_A \colon D_A \to M$ a *typing* mapping. By a common abuse of notation, we denote the datagraph by the same letter A as the entire model. In Fig. 2, two typing mappings (two vertical block-arrows) and two traceability mappings (two horizontal block-arrows) form a square, and this square is *semi-commutative* in the sense that the following two conditions hold. First, each of the four paths from $\mathbf{T}^\bullet(A)$ to A (via traceability links tr_i) to M (via A's type links) can be matched by a same-source-same-target path from $\mathbf{T}^\bullet(A)$ to N (via type links) to M (via meta-traceability links mtr_i). Second, there is an upper path without match, namely, the path from object $lv1 \in \mathbf{T}^\bullet(A)$ to class LeisureVehicle to class Boat (hence the $\leq$ symbol denoting this property of the square diagram). As commutativity rather than semi-commutativity is an important ingredient of the mapping machinery, we need to fix the commutativity violation. The next sections shows how to do it.

2.2.3   Traceability Mappings via Spans

As traceability links are fundamental, we reify them as model elements, and collect these elements in model $|T|$ in the upper part of Fig. 3. Three nodes in this model reify links $mtr_{1,2,3}$ between nodes in the metamodels (see Fig. 2), and the arrow in $|T|$ reifies the (dashed) link tr_{12} between arrows in the metamodels (recall that the actual target of this link is the identity loop of the targte node). In this way we build a metamodel $|T|$ consisting of three classes and one association. The special nature of $|T|$'s elements (which are, in fact, links) is encoded by mapping each element to its ends in metamodels M and N. These secondary links form totally-defined single-valued mappings $T_M \colon M \leftarrow |T|$ and $T_N \colon |T| \to N$ so that we replaced a many-to-many mapping T by a pair of single-valued (many-to-one) mappings. Working with single-valued mappings is usually much simpler technically, and below we will see that it allows us to fix commutativity.

The triple $T = (T_M, |T|, T_N)$ is called a *span* with the *head* $|T|$, and *legs* T_M and T_N. We will call the first leg in the triple the *source* leg, and the second one the *target* leg. Thus, span T in Fig. 3 encodes mapping T in Fig. 2 (and they are thus denoted by the same letter). We will also use the same letter for the head of the span to reduce the number of symbols in our formulas. Note that the head of the span is a graph (because mapping T is a graph mapping), and its legs are correct graph morphisms. This is an accurate formalization of the structure preservation property discussed in Sect. 2.2.1.

The reification procedure applied to mapping $\mathbf{T}^{\blacktriangleleft}(A)$ (Fig. 2) provides the span shown in the lower part of Fig. 3. We denote its head by $T_M^{\bullet}(A)$ rather than by $\mathbf{T}^{\blacktriangleleft}(A)$, as in the next subsection we will show how this model (and mapping $\mathbf{T}_M^{\blacktriangleleft}$) can be computed from the left half of the upper span and model A, and by the same reason, these elements are blank (and blue with a color display) rather than shaded (and black)—ignore these details for a moment. We also omitted all vertical links constituting typong mappings (shown by vertical block arrows).

Since in contrast to mapping T, mapping $\mathbf{T}^{\blacktriangleleft}(A)$ in Fig. 2 is many-to-one, the right leg of the span is an isomorphism (of graphs), which we show as a block-rectangle rather than a block-arrow (actually we could identify the two models). Now it is easy to check commutativity of the two square diagrams, which is recorded by markers [=] at their centers. Commuting makes it possible to type elements in model $|\mathbf{T}^{\blacktriangleleft}(A)|$ (i.e., traceability links) by elements in model $|T|$ (i.e., meta-traceability links), and ensures that typing is a correct graph morphism. We have thus obtained an accurate formal specification of mutually consistent traceability mappings.

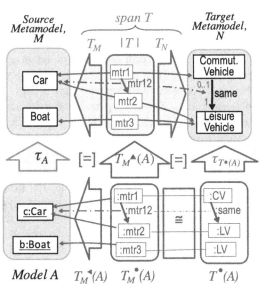

Fig. 3. Meta-traceability via spans (Color figure online)

Span T (the upper half of Fig. 3) is presented in Fig. 4 in a MOF-like way via metamodeling. In these terms, meta-traceability links are classifiers for model traceability links, and commutativity conditions in Fig. 3 provide consistency of traceability links' classification with model elements' classification.

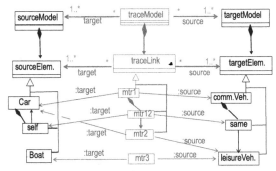

Fig. 4. Trace-links metamodel

2.3   Meta-Traceability Links Can Be Executed!

A somewhat surprising observation we can make now is that the meta-traceability mapping can actually replace the transformation definition $\mathbf{T}$: by applying two standard categorical operations to the span T and the typing mapping of model A, we can produce model $\mathbf{T}^{\bullet}(A)$ (together with its typing) and the traceability mapping $\mathbf{T}^{\blacktriangleleft}(A)$ in a fully mechanized way.

The first operation is called (in categorical jargon) *pull-back (PB)*. Its takes as its input two graph mappings with a common target, T_M and τ_A (such configuration is called a *cospan*), and outputs a span of graph mapping shown in Fig. 3 blank and blue (to recall the mechanic nature of the operation) so that the entire square diagram is commutative. The PB works as follows. For any pair of elements $a \in A$ and $n \in N$ such that there is an element $m \in M$ together with a pair of links (ℓ_1, ℓ_2) targeted at it, $\ell_1 \colon a \to m$ in mapping τ_A and $\ell_2 \colon m \leftarrow n$ in mapping T_M, an object (a, n) is created together with *projection* links to a and n. All such pairs (a, n) together with projection links to N make a model $T_M^{\bullet}(A)$ (whose typing mapping is denoted by $T_M^{\blacktriangle}(A)$ – note the tringle pointing upward), and projection links to A constitute its traceability mapping $T_M^{\blacktriangleleft}(A)$. The entire operation can be seen as $p$ulling the model A together with its typing mapping $b$ack along mapping T_M, hence, the name PB. Note that commutativity of the left square now becomes the very essence of the transformation: we build model $T_M^{\bullet}(A)$ and its traceability mapping in such a way that commutativity holds. Moreover, we make this model the maximal model that respect commutativity by collecting in $T_M^{\bullet}(A)$ *all* pairs (a, n) that respect commutativity. For example, if model A would have three cars and boats, model $T_M^{\bullet}(A)$ would have three commuting and five leisure vehicles with three same-links.

The second operation is fairly easy: we sequentially compose mappings $T_M^{\blacktriangle}(A)$ and T_N by composing their links, and obtain a mapping $T_M^{\bullet}(A) \to N$ that provides graph $T_M^{\bullet}(A)$ with typing over N. We will denote the model whose datagraph is $T_M^{\bullet}(A)$ (or its isomorphic copy up to OIDs) and typing map is composition $T_M^{\blacktriangle}(A); T_N$ by $T^{\bullet}(A)$. The right square in Fig. 3 illustrates this specification. It is now seen that PB followed by composition produce exactly the same model as rule-based definition $\mathbf{T}_1$ in Fig. 1(a), and the span with head $T_M^{\bullet}(A)$ is exactly the reified traceability mapping $\mathbf{T}_1^{\blacktriangleleft}(A)$ from Fig. 1(a).

3   Transformations via Mappings and Queries

Pulling a source model A back along a meta-traceability mapping T as described above covers a useful but not too wide class of transformations; more complex transformations need a more expressive mechanism. In [5,10], it was proposed to separate an MT into two parts: first, a complex computation over the source model is encoded by a query against the source metamodel, and then the result is relabeled (with, perhaps, multiplication) by the target metamodel according to the meta-traceability mapping.

We will illustrate how the machinery works by encoding the same transformation $\mathbf{T}$ by a different type of meta-traceability mapping employing queries against the source metamodel as shown in Fig. 5. The first basic idea of the transformation—creation of commuting vehicles by cars only—is encoded by direct linking class Commut.Vehicle to class Car as we did before. The second idea—creation of leisure vehicles by both cars and boats—is now encoded in two steps. First, we augment the source metamodel M with a derived class Car + Boat computed by applying the operation (query) of taking the disjoint union of two classes; we denote the augmented metamodel by $Q(M)$ with Q referring to the query (or a set of queries) used for augmentation. Second, we link class LeisureVehicle to the derived class Car + Boat, and association same in metamodel N is linked to its counterpart in metamodel $Q(M)$, as shown in Fig. 5.

All links have a clear semantic meaning: given a link $qmtr$ from an element n of N to an element m on $Q(M)$, we declare that n is to be instantiated exactly as m is instantiated, that is, for any model A, every element instantiating m in A or $Q(A)$ (see below), generates an element instantiating n in $T_1{}^\bullet(A)$. Note also that the mapping is of one-to-one type: two classes responsible for LeisureVehiclegeneration now contribute to a single query, and two respective links ($mtr2$ and $mtr3$ in Fig. 2) are replaced by one link $qmtr2$ into the query.

Execution of the transformation for a model A also goes in two steps. First, the query used in the mapping definition is executed for the model. In our example, we take the disjoint union of Car and Boat instantiations in A, i.e., the set $\{c', b'\}$. A reasonable implementation would add a new type Car + Boat to the same object c rather than creating a new object c', but the pair (c, Car) is still different from pair $(c, \text{Car} + \text{Boat})$. Thus, it may happen that $c' = c$ and $b' = b$, but this is just a special

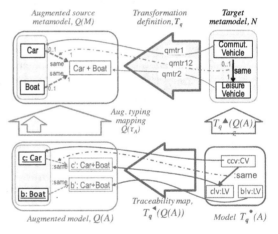

Fig. 5. Meta-traceability via queries

case of a general pattern presented in Fig. 5. Second, objects c, c', b' are retyped according to the respective meta-traceability links $qmtr_1$ (for c) and $qmtr_2$ (for c' and b'). The link cc' is also retyped along the link $qmtr12$.

Thus, a model transformation definition is divided into two parts: finding a query (or a set of queries) Q against the source metamodel M, which captures the computationally non-trivial part of the transformation, and then mapping the target metamodel into the augmentation $Q(M)$, which shows how the results of the computation are to be retyped into the target metamodel. The second part can capture some simple computations like multiplication of objects (which often appears in MMT), but not more. In contrast, with a broad understanding of queries as general operations, the first part is Turing complete with the

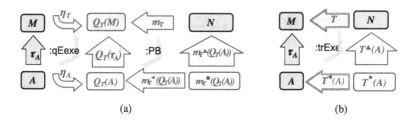

(a)   (b)

Fig. 6. Execution of meta-traceability mappings. Derived elements are blank.

only reservation that all result of the computation must have new types (which distinguishes queries from updates).

A formal abstraction of the example is described in Fig. 6(a). A model transformation is considered to be a pair $T = (Q_T, m_T)$ with Q_T a query against the source metamodel M and $m_T \colon Q_T(M) \leftarrow N$ a mapping from the target metamodel N to model M augmented with derived elements specified by the query. Formally, we have an inclusion $\eta_T \colon M \hookrightarrow Q_T(M)$. Note that construct Q_T is a query *definition*, which can be executed for any data conforming to schema M, i.e., for any model properly typed over the metamodel M. Execution is modeled by an operation qExe, which for a given query Q_T and model A produces an augmented model $Q_T(A)$[1] properly typed over the augmented metamodel by an augmented typing mapping $Q_T(\tau_A)$. To complete the transformation, the result of the query is retyped according to the mapping m_T (retyping is given by pulling back the augmented typing mapping as discussed above). In Fig. 6(b), an abstract view of Fig. 6(a) is presented, in which the upper double arrow encodes the sequential composition of the two upper arrows in diagram (a), and operation trExe of *transformation execution* is a composition of two operations in diagram (a). Paper [6] presents an accurate categorical formalization of this construction by modeling the query language as a *monad* and the transformation definition mapping T as a *Kleisli mapping* over this monad. We do not need formal details in this paper, but we will use the term Kleisli mapping to refer to mappings such as $m_T \colon Q_T(M) \leftarrow N$. By an abuse of notation, we will often use the same symbol T for both transformation T and its mapping m_T.

4   An Algebra for Model Transformations

Mappings have a dual nature. As *sets* of links, mappings are amenable to Boolean operations (union, intersection, difference). As sets of *directed* link, mappings can be sequentially composed in the associative way. Hence, representing a model transformation by a mapping allows us to build an algebra of useful operations over model transformations. For example, Boolean operations allow for

---

[1] We should write $[\![Q_T]\!](A)$ but we again use the same symbol for both syntactic and semantic constructs.

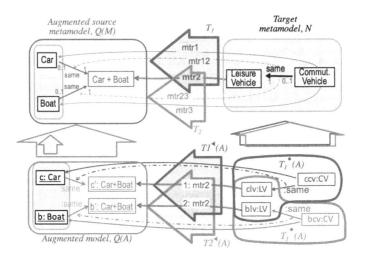

Fig. 7. BA for traceability mappings (Color figure online)

reuse, and sequential composition establishes a mathematical approach to model transformation chaining. In this section, we briefly and informally consider, first, Boolean operations, and then sequential composition.

4.1 Boolean Operations for Model Transformations

Consider our two transformations, $\mathbf{T}_1$ and $\mathbf{T}_2$, each consisting of two rules, described in Fig. 1(a, b). Although rules are related, they are all different, and, formally speaking, for model transformation understood as sets of rules, we have $\mathbf{T}_1 \cap \mathbf{T}_2 = \varnothing$. Hence, specifying commonalities and differences between transformations needs going inside the rules and working on a finer granularity level, which may be not easy for complex rules. In contrast, encoding transformation definitions by mappings, i.e., sets of (meta) links, makes them well amenable to the variability analysis.

Mappings $T_{1,2}$ encoding transformations $\mathbf{T}_{1,2}$ resp. are shown in Fig. 7 (colored green and resp. orange with a color display). Each mapping consists of three links, and one link (double-lined and brown) is shared. This link constitutes the intersection mapping, whose domain consists of the only class LeisureVehicle (in the categorical jargon, this mapping is called the *equalizer* of T_1 and T_2). Thus, $T_{1 \wedge 2} = T_1 \cap T_2 = \{mtr2\}$. We can also merge T_1 and T_2 into mapping $T_{1 \vee 2} = T_1 \cup T_2$ consisting of five links. It is easy to see that for our example, execution of mappings via pullbacks is compatible with these operations so that $T_{1\wedge2}^{\blacktriangleleft}(A) = T_1^{\blacktriangleleft}(A) \cap T_2^{\blacktriangleleft}(A)$ and $T_{1\vee2}^{\blacktriangleleft}(A) = T_1^{\blacktriangleleft}(A) \cup T_2^{\blacktriangleleft}(A)$; particularly $T_{1\wedge2}^{\bullet}(A) = T_1^{\bullet}(A) \cap T_2^{\bullet}(A)$ and $T_{1\vee2}^{\bullet}(A) = T_1^{\bullet}(A) \cup T_2^{\bullet}(A)$ (note the boot-like shapes of $T_i^{\bullet}(A)$ ($i = 1, 2$) and their intersection consisting of two objects).

The simple and appealing algebraic picture described above does not hold if transformations are seen as sets of rules as described in Fig. 1: then, as mentioned, $\mathbf{T}_1 \cap \mathbf{T}_2 = \varnothing$, and transformation $\mathbf{T}_1 \cup \mathbf{T}_2$ would translate model A into a model consisting of six rather than four objects (consider disjoint union of model $\mathbf{T}_1(A)$ and $\mathbf{T}_2(A)$ presented in Fig. 1(a, b)), which seems not well matching the intuition of how the merged transformation should work. Indeed, the two transformations differ in how commuting vehicles are generated, but agree on leisure vehicles. This agreement is exactly captured by shared link $mtr2$ in mappings $T_{1,2}$, but is not taken into account in $\mathbf{T}_1 \cup \mathbf{T}_2$.

Nevertheless, suppose we still want to merge the two transformations in a disjoint way so that the merged transformation would produce a six element model from model A. We can do it with the mapping representation as well by defining a new mapping T_{1+2} via disjoint union $T_1 + T_2$, in which link $mtr2$ is repeated twice: imagine a version of Fig. 7, in which one copy of link $mtr2$ belongs to mapping T_1, and the other copy belongs to T_2. It is easy to check that PB applied to mappings $Q(\tau_A)$ and T_{1+2} would result in the disjoint union of models $\mathbf{T}_1^\bullet(A)$ and $\mathbf{T}_2^\bullet(A)$ with the respective disjoint union of their traceability mappings (see Fig. 1) as required. Thus, $(T_1 + T_2)^\bullet(A) = T_1^\bullet(A) + T_1^\bullet(A)$ and $(T_1 + T_2)^\blacktriangleleft(A) = T_1^\blacktriangleleft(A) + T_1^\blacktriangleleft(A)$, and our traceability execution procedure is compatible with disjoint union as well.

4.2   Sequential Composition of Model Transformations

Suppose that transformation $\mathbf{T}_1$ is followed by a transformation $\mathbf{T}_3$ from metamodel N to metamodel O consisting of the only class Vehicle (Fig. 8). This transformation is defined by two rules: every object of class Commut.Vehicle generates a Vehicle-object, and every LeisureVehicle-object generates a Vehicle-object too. Mapping T_3 encoding this transformation would consist of the only link mapping class Vehicle to the disjoint union of Commut.Vehicle and LeisureVehicle. To chain the transformations, we need to compose mappings T_3 and T_1 but they are not composable: mapping T_1 is not defined for the target class of mapping T_3.

The problem can be fixed if we apply the query Q_3 to the augmented metamodel $Q_1(M)$ by replacing arguments of Q_3 (classes Commut.Vehicle and LeisureVehicle) by their images in $Q_1(M)$ along mapping T_1 as shown in the figure. In this way, mapping T_1 can be homomorphically extended to mapping $Q_3(T_1)$, and now mappings T_3 and $Q_3(T_1)$ can be composed. The lower part of Fig. 8 is a "link-full" demonstration that the consecutive composition of two executions is equal to the execution of the composed mapping:

$$T_3^\bullet(T_1^\bullet(A)) = (T_3 \circ T_1)^\bullet(A) \text{ and } T_3^\blacktriangleleft(T_1^\bullet(A)) = (T_3 \circ T_1)^\blacktriangleleft(A),$$

where $\circ$ denotes sequential mapping composition. In fact, the case is nothing but an instance of the well known construction of query substitution and view compositionality: a view of a view is a view of the very first source.

5   From Rule-Based MMT to Kleisli Mappings (and Back)

General Landscape. Rule-based programs such as in ATL or ETL are good for effective execution of MMTs, but their analysis and manipulation may be

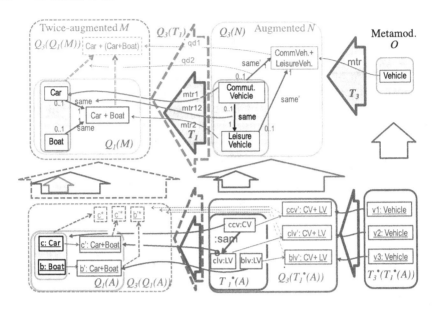

Fig. 8. Model chaining via mapping composition

difficult. For example, it is not easy to say whether the result of transformation always satisfies the constraints of the target metamodel, and chaining rule-based transformations is difficult too. The Kleisli mapping encoding of MMTs can help by providing a more abstract view that may be better amenable for some analyses and operations. For instance, it was shown in [9] the Kleisli mapping encoding converts the target metamodel conformance into to a well-known logical problem of whether a formula is entailed by a theory, for which a standard theorem prover or a model checker could be applied. To perform such logical analyses, we need a translating procedure tl2km: TL → KM$_{QL}$, where TL denotes the set of programs written in the rule-based language at hand, and KM$_{QL}$ denotes the set of Kleisli mappings over some query language QL. Below we will omit the subindex QL.

To employ the KM approach for operations over rule-based transformations, we also need an inverse translation km2tl: TL ← KM. Suppose that $\mathbf{T}_1: M \to N$ is a rule-based transformation that maps instances of metamodel M to instances of metamodel N, and $\mathbf{T}_3: N \to O$ is another transformation that we want to chain with $\mathbf{T}_1$. To do this, we translate both transformations to the respective Kleisli mappings T_1, T_3, then perform their sequential composition and obtain mapping $TT = T_3 \circ T_1$ as it was explained in Sect. 4, and then translate the result back to TL obtaining a rule-based transformation $\mathbf{T} = \text{km2tl}(TT)$, which is semantically equivalent to sequential composition of $\mathbf{T}_1$ and $\mathbf{T}_3$. In a similar way, we can perform Boolean operations over rule-based parallel transformations $\mathbf{T}_i: M \to N$, $i = 1, 2$ (see Sect. 4) and employ them, e.g., for reuse.

Example. Suppose we want to chain two ATL transformations: $\mathbf{T}_1: M \to N$ and $\mathbf{T}_3: N \to O$ specified in Listings 1.1 and 1.2 resp. The first one is an ATL encoding of transformation $\mathbf{T}_1$ in Fig. 1, and the second transformation, in fact,

Listing 1.1. T_1 expressed in ATL

```
1  module T1;
2  create OUT : N from IN : M;
3  rule car2vehicle {
4    from  c  : M!Car
5    to    cv : N!CommutVehicle
6              (same <- lv),
7          lv : N!LeisureVehicle
8  }
9  rule boat2vehicle {
10   from b  : M!Boat
11   to   lv : N!LeisureVehicle
12 }
```

Listing 1.2. T_3 expressed in ATL

```
1  module T3;
2  create OUT : O from IN : N;
3  rule commutVehicle2vehicle {
4    from  cv : N!CommutVehicle
5    to    v  : O!Vehicle
6  }
7  rule leisureVehicle2vehicle {
8    from lv : N!LeisureVehicle
9    to   v  : O!Vehicle
10 }
```

merges two classes in N into class Vehicle in O. To chain these transformations, we first encode them as Kleisli mappings as shown in Fig. 8. Then we compose them using query substitution as explained in Sect. 4.2, and let the resulting mapping be $m_{TT} \colon QQ(M) \leftarrow O$, where $QQ(M) = Q_3(Q_1(M))$ is the composed query against metamodel M, which augments it with derived class Car + Car + Boat (see Fig. 8). Now we need to translate Kleisli mapping $TT = (QQ, m_{TT})$ into an ATL transformation.

We do the inverse translation in two separate steps. First, we translate query QQ into an ATL module QQ as shown in Listing 1.3. Then we translate the mapping $m_{TT} \colon QQ(M) \leftarrow O$ into an ATL module mTT as shown in Listing 1.4. The structure of these modules makes their chaining quite straightforward (in contrast to chaining the initial two transformation), and the result is shown in Listing 1.5. Of course, in our trivial example, chaining the initial modules is also easy, but even in moderately more complex cases, chaining ATL modules is difficult, whereas with the Kleisli mapping approach, all the complexity is managed via query substitution, while the final chaining of the query module QQ and the mapping module mTT remains simple (see Fig. 8).

Listing 1.3. Query QQ in ATL

```
1  module QQ;
2  create OUT : QQM from IN : M;
3  rule car2carcarboat {
4    from  c  : M!Car
5    to    qqc : QQM!Car
6               (same <- qqccb1),
7               (same <- qqccb2),
8      qqccb1 : QQM!CarCarBoat
9      qqccb2 : QQM!CarCarBoat
10 }
11 rule boat2carcarboat {
12   from  b  : M!Boat
13   to    qqb  : QQM!Boat
14               (same <- qqccb),
15     qqccb : QQM!CarCarBoat
16 }
```

Listing 1.4. Mapping m_{TT} in ATL

```
1  module mTT;
2  create OUT : O from IN : QQM;
3  rule carcarboat2vehicle {
4    from ccb : QQM!CarCarBoat
5    to    v  : O!Vehicle
6  }
```

Listing 1.5. TT as an ATL transformation

```
1  module TT;
2  create OUT : O from IN : M;
3  rule boat2vehicle {
4    from  b : M!Boat
5    to    v : N!Vehicle
6  }
7  rule car2vehicle {
8    from c  : M!Car
9    to   v1 : O!Vehicle
10        v2 : O!Vehicle
11 }
```

Automatic Translations TL ↔ KM and ATL. Finding general algorithms for automatization of both translations is a very non-trivial task because of the conceptual and technical differences between the two views of MMTs. Particularly, the TL view is *elementwise*, i.e., based on model elements, while the KM— view is *setwise* as queries are typically formulated as operations over sets (cf. SQL). Bridging the gap is a challenge, and we have began to work in this direction for the case of ATL as a rule-based language. Below we argue why, we think, ATL should be sufficiently well-amenable for the TL ↔ KM translations.

In rule-based transformation languages, rules applied to different parts of the model may interact in complex ways. However, in ATL, inter-rule communication is specially constrained by specific properties of the language (cf. [3]), which make it suitable to express declarative metamodel mappings. Such properties are: ① *forbidden target navigation*, ② *locality*, ③ *non-recursive rule application*, and ④ *single assignment on target properties*.

Owing these properties, a direct correspondence between a metamodel mapping and the ATL constructs can be defined as follows. A *meta-traceability mapping* can be completely described using a *module* in which every independent *matched rule* represents a *meta-traceability link* between two *entities* (e.g. classes) of the source and the target metamodels ①. This is possible due to the fact that a *matched rule* is the only responsible of the computation of the elements it creates ②, and model elements that are produced by ATL rules are not subject to further matches ③. In such a *matched rule*, the *source* of the link is represented using the *to* block, and the *target* of the link is represented using the *from* block. On the other hand, in the case of *meta-traceability links* between two properties of the source and the target metamodel, the *source* of the link is represented by the property being initialised, and the *target* of the link is represented by the property on the source metamodel. This assignment is possible because ATL allows assigning the default target model element of another rule. In this case, *meta-traceability links* between two properties can only be defined in the rule that maps the owner of the property, since that rule is the only responsible of the initialisation of the attributes of the owner ②, and the assignment of a single-valued property in a target model element happens only once in the transformation execution ④.

6   Related Work

Traceability understood broadly is an enormous area [1,15], but in the present paper we consider its special sub-area connected with MMT, and especially using traceability mappings as transformation definitions.

Atlas Model Weaver was proposed in [4] as a means to facilitate transformation design. *Weaving models (WMs)* represent different kinds of relationships between model elements, and are comparable to the metamodel mappings considered in our paper. WMs are executed with higher-order transformations, which build an ATL transformation from a WM. However, WMs aim to manage MMT's complexity in a single step. Hence, as WMs cannot cope with all the semantics provided by general purpose transformation languages, they may produce incomplete ATL transformations that must be manually reviewed.

To provide a more structured framework to define executable mappings between metamodels, Wimmer et al. [19] propose a set of *kernel* operators, from which *composite mapping operators* are built. The building process is performed by connecting input and output ports. Executability of the composite complex mappings is achieved by extending the framework proposed in [4].

Since meta-traceability links provide limited semantics compared to generic MMT, and building rich mappings may imply complex meta-traceability links, a generic transformation algorithm is proposed in [7] to execute mapping models. This proposal uses simple mapping models to execute MMT putting the hard work in the execution of the algorithm. Any ambiguity caused by the semantic gap between mapping models and MMT is solved by using a "smart" algorithm that analyses the target metamodel. Since the philosophy of this proposal is to provide a result *as good as possible*, it does not guarantee that ambiguities are always correctly resolved (and may even require users' interaction).

Paper [18] provides an in-depth discussion of traceability in the context of QVT-rules execution, and hence executability of meta-traceability links. The machinery employed is described informally, but seems close to our use of pullback. The overall picture is broader than ours and includes mapping refinement, dynamic dispatch, and concurrency. A formalization of these constructs in terms of our framework would be a useful application; we leave it for future work.

In papers [2,8,9], the authors translate the source and the target metamodels to Alloy and specify the transformation rules as relations. In terms of our paper, both queries and mappings are encoded as logical theories, whose execution is provided by Alloy instance finder. Separating queries and mappings is discussed in [10], but the expressiveness of pullback seems underestimated; particularly, the many-to-many traceability mappings are not considered. A precise formalization of traceability mappings with queries in categorical terms as Kleisli mappings is provided in [6], sequential composition then follows from Kleisli mapping composition. However, the general context for paper [6] is general inter-model relationships (which corresponds to a broad view of traceability as correspondence emphasized in [1]), while in the present paper we consider traceability in the MMT context and are focused on mapping execution. In neither of the works mentioned above, operations over transformations are considered, and we are not aware of their explicit introduction and discussion in the literature.

7 Conclusion

Technological importance of traceability mappings for model transformations is well-known, but they have often been considered as an auxiliary element generated during the transformation execution and providing accessory information. This paper argues that traceability mappings should instead be regarded as a core aspect of the transformation definition, and a key instrument in the transformation management. We have shown that MMT semantics is essentially incomplete without traceability links between models, which should be typed by the respective metalinks between metamodels. Metalinks taken together constitute a traceability mapping between metamodels, which can be executed and thus appears as a transformation definition. We considered two cases of such definitions: simple mappings whose execution can be specified by an operation called pullback, and complex (Kleisli) mappings involving queries against the source metamodel, whose execution consists of the query execution followed by pullback. An important consequence of defining transformations via mappings is that algebraic operations over mappings can be translated into operations over transformations specified in conventional transformation languages. We argue that ATL should be well amenable to such translation, and presented a simple example illustrating these ideas. Of course, a real application of our algebraic framework requires an automatic translation from ATL to Kleisli mappings and back. This challenging task is an important future work.

References

1. Aizenbud-Reshef, N., Nolan, B.T., Rubin, J., Shaham-Gafni, Y.: Model traceability. IBM Syst. J. **45**(3), 515–526 (2006)
2. Anastasakis, K., Bordbar, B., Küster, J.M.: Analysis of model transformations via alloy. In: Proceedings of the 4th MoDeVVa workshop Model-Driven Engineering, Verification and Validation, pp. 47–56 (2007)
3. Benelallam, A., Gómez, A., Tisi, M., Cabot, J.: Distributed model-to-model transformation with ATL on mapreduce. In: Proceedings of the 2015 ACM SIGPLAN International Conference on Software Language Engineering, SLE 2015, pp. 37–48. ACM, New York (2015)
4. Didonet Del Fabro, M., Valduriez, P.: Towards the efficient development of model transformations using model weaving and matching transformations. Softw. Syst. Model. **8**(3), 305–324 (2009)
5. Diskin, Z.: Model synchronization: mappings, tiles, and categories. In: Fernandes, J.M., Lämmel, R., Visser, J., Saraiva, J. (eds.) GTTSE 2009. LNCS, vol. 6491, pp. 92–165. Springer, Heidelberg (2011). doi:10.1007/978-3-642-18023-1_3
6. Diskin, Z., Maibaum, T., Czarnecki, K.: Intermodeling, queries, and kleisli categories. In: Lara, J., Zisman, A. (eds.) FASE 2012. LNCS, vol. 7212, pp. 163–177. Springer, Heidelberg (2012). doi:10.1007/978-3-642-28872-2_12
7. Freund, M., Braune, A.: A generic transformation algorithm to simplify the development of mapping models. In: Proceedings of the ACM/IEEE 19th International Conference on Model Driven Engineering Languages and Systems, MODELS 2016, pp. 284–294. ACM, New York (2016)
8. Gammaitoni, L., Kelsen, P.: F-alloy: an alloy based model transformation language. In: Kolovos, D., Wimmer, M. (eds.) ICMT 2015. LNCS, vol. 9152, pp. 166–180. Springer, Cham (2015). doi:10.1007/978-3-319-21155-8_13
9. Gholizadeh, H., Diskin, Z., Kokaly, S., Maibaum, T.: Analysis of source-to-target model transformations in quest. In: Dingel, J., Kokaly, S., Lucio, L., Salay, R., Vangheluwe, H. (eds.) Proceedings of the 4th Workshop on the Analysis of Model Transformations co-located with the 18th International Conference on Model Driven Engineering Languages and Systems (MODELS 2015), Ottawa, Canada, 28 September 2015, vol. 1500, CEUR Workshop Proceedings, pp. 46–55 (2015). CEUR-WS.org

10. Gholizadeh, H., Diskin, Z., Maibaum, T.: A query structured approach for model transformation. In: Dingel, J., de Lara, J., Lucio, L., Vangheluwe, H. (eds.) Proceedings of the Workshop on Analysis of Model Transformations co-located with ACM/IEEE 17th International Conference on Model Driven Engineering Languages & Systems (MoDELS 2014), CEUR Workshop Proceedings Valencia, Spain, September 29, 2014, vol. 1277, pp. 54–63. CEUR-WS.org (2014)
11. Jouault, F., Allilaire, F., Bézivin, J., Kurtev, I.: ATL: a model transformation tool. Sci. Comput. Program. **72**(1–2), 31–39 (2008)
12. Kolovos, D.S., Paige, R.F., Polack, F.A.C.: The epsilon transformation language. In: Vallecillo, A., Gray, J., Pierantonio, A. (eds.) ICMT 2008. LNCS, vol. 5063, pp. 46–60. Springer, Heidelberg (2008). doi:10.1007/978-3-540-69927-9_4
13. Lopes, D., Hammoudi, S., Bézivin, J., Jouault, F.: Mapping specification in MDA: from theory to practice. In: Konstantas, D., Bourriéres, J.-P., Léonard, M., Boudjlida, N. (eds.) Interoperability of Enterprise Software and Applications, pp. 253–264. Springer, London (2006)
14. Marschall, F., Braun, P.: Model transformations for the MDA with BOTL. In: Proceedings of the Workshop on Model Driven Architecture: Foundations and Applications, pp. 25–36 (2003)
15. Paige, R.F., Drivalos, N., Kolovos, D.S., Fernandes, K.J., Power, C., Olsen, G.K., Zschaler, S.: Rigorous identification and encoding of trace-links in model-driven engineering. Softw. Syst. Model. **10**(4), 469–487 (2011)
16. The Eclipse Foundation: ATL, October 2016. url:http://www.eclipse.org/atl/
17. The Eclipse Foundation: Epsilon October 2016. url:http://www.eclipse.org/epsilon/
18. Willink, E., Matragkas, N.: QVT traceability: what does it really mean? In: Analysis of Model Transformations, AMT 2015, 4th Workshop Models 2015 (2015)
19. Wimmer, M., Kappel, G., Kusel, A., Retschitzegger, W., Schoenboeck, J., Schwinger, W.: Surviving the heterogeneity jungle with composite mapping operators. In: Tratt, L., Gogolla, M. (eds.) ICMT 2010. LNCS, vol. 6142, pp. 260–275. Springer, Heidelberg (2010). doi:10.1007/978-3-642-13688-7_18

Reusing Model Transformations Through Typing Requirements Models

Juan de Lara[1], Juri Di Rocco[2(✉)], Davide Di Ruscio[2], Esther Guerra[1],
Ludovico Iovino[3], Alfonso Pierantonio[2], and Jesús Sánchez Cuadrado[1]

[1] Universidad Autónoma de Madrid, Madrid, Spain
[2] University of L'Aquila, L'Aquila, Italy
juri.dirocco@univaq.it
[3] Gran Sasso Science Institute, L'Aquila, Italy

Abstract. Model transformations are key elements of Model-Driven Engineering (MDE), where they are used to automate the manipulation of models. However, they are typed with respect to concrete source and target meta-models and hence their reuse for other (even similar) meta-models becomes challenging.

In this paper, we describe a method to extract a *typing requirements model* (TRM) from an ATL model-to-model transformation. A TRM describes the requirements that the transformation needs from the source and target meta-models in order to obtain a transformation with a syntactically correct typing. A TRM is made of three parts, two of them describing the requirements for the source and target meta-models, and the last expressing dependencies between both. We define a notion of conformance of meta-model pairs with respect to TRMs. This way, the transformation can be used with any meta-model conforming to the TRM. We present tool support and an experimental validation of correctness and completeness using meta-model mutation techniques, obtaining promising results.

1 Introduction

Model-Driven Engineering [19] (MDE) employs models as first-class assets during the software development life cycle. Models are typically constructed using Domain-Specific Languages (DSLs), specially tailored to a particular domain. In MDE, the abstract syntax of a DSL is described through a meta-model, which describes the structure of the models considered valid. Therefore, it does not come as a surprise that meta-models proliferate in MDE as a means of formalising application domains [23]. Sometimes, these meta-models are variants of known languages like state-machines or workflow languages [17], for which services, like model transformations, already exist.

Model transformations are key to MDE, because they can leverage automation in model manipulation and management. Model transformations are typed with respect to the involved (source and target) meta-models. Therefore, reusing transformations is difficult, because they are not immediately applicable to other

© Springer-Verlag GmbH Germany 2017
M. Huisman and J. Rubin (Eds.): FASE 2017, LNCS 10202, pp. 264–282, 2017.
DOI: 10.1007/978-3-662-54494-5_15

meta-models, different from the ones they were initially conceived for. Hence, techniques to enhance transformation reusability are needed [1,15] since developing (non-trivial) transformations from scratch is typically a complex and time-consuming task.

Some works propose transformation reuse based on *concepts* [9] to express meta-model requirements, and bindings from those concepts into concrete meta-models. The binding induces an adaptation of the transformation, which becomes applicable to the concrete meta-models. However, concepts have limitations: they have to be manually created, and they present limited expressiveness, as for instance when variability must be described (e.g., when a feature can be typed according to a set of allowed types). Other approaches extract *effective meta-models* [20] by pruning unused typing information of the source/target domains according to the syntactical requirements in the transformation. Similarly to concept-based techniques, they also present limited expressiveness, although the procedure can be partly automated.

In this paper, we propose using a transformation *typing requirements model* (TRM) to express the syntactical needs of a transformation with respect to its source and target domains. TRMs support variability regarding, e.g., the concrete types of attributes, the inheritance relations between classes, the allowed targets for references, or the existence of classes with certain features but for which the class name is unknown or irrelevant. We propose an algorithm to automatically infer a TRM from an ATL model-to-model transformation, as ATL is one of the most widely used transformation languages nowadays [14]. Moreover, as ATL transformations consider several meta-models (typically source and target), dependencies between the allowed feature types in the source and target meta-models are required. This way, the transformation can be reused *as-is* with any pair of meta-models conforming to the extracted TRM.

The main advantages of TRMs with respect to existing techniques are: *(i)* TRM extraction is automatic; *(ii)* source and target meta-models are not needed to extract the TRMs; *(iii)* TRMs permit more expressive requirements (e.g., variability) that lead to improved reuse possibilities; and *(iv)* dependencies cross-linking requirements over source and target meta-models can be given in terms of feature models.

A preliminary evaluation is provided by means of a prototype tool. For this purpose, TRMs of third-party transformations have been extracted and variants of source and target meta-models have been defined by means of mutation techniques. The correctness and completeness of the method is empirically assessed by measuring the degree in which the transformation is correctly typed with meta-models conformant to the TRM, and incorrectly with meta-models not conformant to the TRM. Correctness of typing is checked with the ANATLYZER tool as oracle [6]. The evaluation shows promising results, encouraging further investigation of transformation reuse based on TRMs.

Paper Organization. Section 2 discusses applicability scenarios. Section 3 introduces TRMs, and a notion of conformance. Section 4 explains how to extract TRMs from ATL transformations. Section 5 validates the approach over a set of transformations developed by third parties. Section 6 compares with related work and Sect. 7 concludes the paper.

2 Motivating Scenarios and Running Example

Figure 1 describes our approach for model transformation reuse. Model transformations are typed with respect to source and target meta-models. However, these meta-models might not be available (e.g., for transformations found in code repositories like GitHub or BitBucket), or we might want to reuse the transformation with other meta-models, different from the ones the transformation was designed for. Therefore, given an existing transformation, we extract its typing requirements model (TRM, see label ①) that consists of three parts: the requirements for the source and target meta-models, and a compatibility model specifying the dependencies between them. The TRM can be used in different ways. For example, to query an existing meta-model repository in order to find conforming meta-model pairs (see ②a). In particular, such queries are OCL expressions [16], generated from the TRM. Any meta-model pair $\langle MM_s, MM_t \rangle$ conforming to the TRM can be used as source/target meta-models of the transformation. The TRM can also be used to generate suitable meta-model pairs (see ②b), so that the transformation can be executed on instances of them (see ③).

We illustrate our proposal using ATL since it is one of the most widely accepted transformation languages. However, the approach can be adapted to most of the existing model-to-model transformation languages. ATL [14] provides a mixture of declarative and imperative constructs to develop model-to-model transformations. Listing 1 shows our running example, partially taken

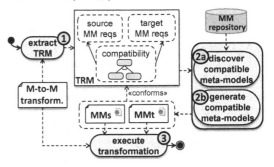

Fig. 1. Overview of our approach

from the ATL Zoo[1]. The transformation creates a table with the number of times each method in a piece of Java code is called within any declared method. The transformation is defined by a module specification consisting of a header section (lines 1–2), helpers (lines 4–7) and transformation rules (lines 9–23). The header specifies the source and target models of the transformation together with their corresponding meta-models. This way, the JavaSource2Table module is a one-to-one transformation, which generates a target model conforming to a Table meta-model from a source JavaSource model (see line 2).

---

[1] http://www.eclipse.org/atl/atlTransformations/#Java2Table.

```
1 module JavaSource2Table;
2 create OUT : Table from IN : JavaSource;
3
4 helper context JavaSource!MethodDefinition
5       def : computeContent(col : JavaSource!MethodDefinition) : String =
6            self.invocations->select(i | i.method.name = col.name
7            and i.method.class.name = col.class.name)->size().toString();
8
9 rule Table {
10     from s : JavaSource!ClassDeclaration
11     to t : Table!Table ( rows <- s.methods  )
12 }
13 rule MethodDefinition {
14     from m : JavaSource!MethodDefinition
15     to    row : Table!Row (
16        cells <- Sequence{JavaSource!MethodDefinition.allInstances()
17                ->collect(md | thisModule.DataCells(md, m))}
18     )
19 }
20 lazy rule DataCells {
21     from md: JavaSource!MethodDefinition, m: JavaSource!MethodDefinition
22     to    cell: Table!Cell ( content <- m.computeContent(md) )
23 }
```

Listing 1. Fragment of a sample ATL transformation

Helpers and rules are the main ATL constructs to specify the transformation behaviour. The source pattern of rules (e.g., line 10) consists of types from the source meta-model. Thus, a rule gets applied for any instance of the given source types that satisfies the optional OCL rule guard. Rules also specify a target pattern (e.g., line 11) indicating the target objects created by the rule application, and a set of bindings to initialize their features (attributes and references). For example, the binding rows ← s.methods (line 11) initializes the rows feature of the target type Table with the elements created by the rules applied on the input elements referred by s.methods.

Rule MethodDefinition (lines 13–19) creates a target Row from each source MethodDefinition. The binding in this rule assigns to the reference cells a sequence of elements created by an OCL expression, which selects all the source Method-Definition objects and apply on them the lazy rule DataCells. Differently from *matched* rules (like rules Table and MethodDefinition), lazy rules are executed only when explicitly called and use the passed parameters. The DataCell rule takes two MethodDefinition objects as input and generates a target Cell containing a number calculated by the helper of lines 4–7. Helpers are auxiliary operations that permit defining complex model queries using OCL. In particular, the helper computeContent returns a string with the number of occurrences of the received MethodDefinition object.

Our goal is to extract, from this transformation, a description (a TRM) of the features needed in source and target meta-models for the transformation to work. This way, the transformation can be reused with any meta-model satisfying the TRM, and not just with the ones used for its definition. Details about the TRM are given in Sect. 3, whereas the algorithm able to extract TRMs from ATL transformations is detailed in Sect. 4.

3   Representing Transformation Typing Requirements

This section explains how we describe transformation typing requirements through TRMs. TRMs contain three parts, two describing the typing requirements from source and target meta-models (Sect. 3.1), and a compatibility model relating both (Sect. 3.2).

3.1   Describing Single Meta-Model Requirements

Domain Typing Requirements. We use the meta-model in Fig. 2 to represent structural requirements for single meta-models. Its instances, called *domain typing requirements models* (DRMs), resemble meta-models but where some decisions can be left open if they are irrelevant for the problem at hand, like class names, the type of attributes, the target of references, or the cardinality of features. This way, a potentially infinite set of meta-models may conform to a DRM.

We consider two kinds of classes: named and anonymous. While the former have a name, in the latter the name is irrelevant as the class can have any name. Classes can be flagged as abstract, for which we use a three-valued enum type UBoolean which allows us to require the class to be abstract, concrete or any. A class defines a collection of features. The flag mandatoryAllowed permits a class to have more mandatory fields than those indicated in collection feats, while there is no constraint concerning the number of extra non-mandatory fields. A class may defer the conformance checking to all its concrete subclasses, which is indicated by the subsAllowed flag. A class may be required to inherit (directly or indirectly) from another class, and this is specified through relation ancs. Conversely, a class is forbidden to inherit from those in relation antiancs. More precisely, if B ∈ A.antiancs, then we reject meta-models in which B is an ancestor of A, or both share a common subclass.

Features have minimum and maximum cardinality, which can be a number, many, or we might allow any cardinality. If the maximum is many, it can also be

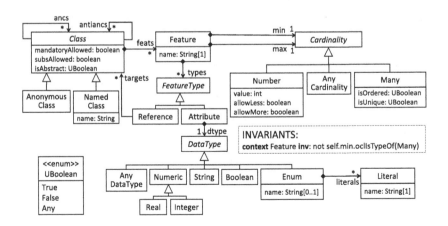

Fig. 2. Domain typing requirements meta-model (excerpt)

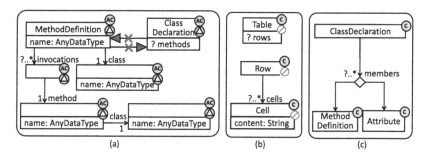

Fig. 3. DRM examples: (a) Source DRM of Listing 1. (b) Target DRM of Listing 1. (c) Multiple compatible reference targets.

specified whether the feature should be ordered or unique using UBoolean values. For the case of a number, we can define whether the cardinality is allowed to be lower (allowLess) or upper (allowMore) than this number. Features always have a name, and optionally, they may have a type which can be Reference, Attribute or both. References can indicate the admissible compatible target types, some of which can be anonymous classes. Attributes can specify their data type, or it can be left open using the AnyDataType class.

Example. Figure 3 shows three DRM examples. A specific concrete syntax has been adopted to denote additional characteristics. In particular, in the upper-right corner of a class is specified whether *(a)* it can be either abstract or concrete ((AC)), only abstract ((A)), or only concrete ((C)); *(b)* it can defer the conformance checking to its subclasses (encircled inheritance-like triangle); and finally *(c)* it forbids extra mandatory features (crossed-out circle). In addition, the anti-ancestor relation is shown as a crossed-out red inheritance relation.

DRM (a) has been extracted from the source domain of the transformation in Listing 1. The extraction procedure is described in Sect. 4. The DRM requires two classes named ClassDeclaration and MethodDefinition, which cannot inherit from each other otherwise the transformation would raise a runtime error due to multiple matches on the same element, that is not allowed in ATL. The latter class should have an attribute name whose type can be any, and two references named class and invocations to anonymous classes (i.e., their name is unimportant). The lower bound of invocations is open. In its turn, ClassDeclaration requires a feature methods which can be an attribute or a reference (we use a "?" prefix to denote this). The DRM also demands four anonymous classes for which only certain features are required. These classes could be matched by the same or different classes in concrete meta-models, or even by the same classes conforming to the named classes.

DRM (b) has been extracted from the target domain of Listing 1. It requires three named concrete classes. Class Table requires a feature rows which can be an attribute or a reference. As shown in Sect. 3.2, the transformation requires the types of Table.rows and ClassDeclaration.methods in DRM (a) to be correlated, for which we will introduce a compatibility model. None of the classes are allowed to have extra mandatory features (which is represented with a crossed-out circle).

Finally, DRM (c) shows that a reference can be required to be compatible with several target types. In a concrete meta-model, this could be realized by reference members targeting a (possibly indirect) common superclass of Method-Definition and Attribute.

Meta-Model Conformance. Next, the notion of conformance of a meta-model with respect to a DRM is introduced. For this purpose we define predicate $conf_{MM}$ which applies to a requirements model RM and a meta-model MM, and checks if for every Class in RM, there is a conforming class in MM.

$$conf_{MM}(RM, MM) \triangleq \forall RC \in RM \; \exists C \in MM \; \bullet \; conf_C(RC, C) \quad (1)$$

where RC is a Class in RM, C is a class in MM, and we use the predicate $conf_C$ to check conformance of the latter with respect to the former. As defined in Eq. (2), this accounts to assessing conformance of names ($conf_{name}$), abstractness ($conf_{abs}$), features ($conf_{feat}$) and ancestors ($conf_{ancs}$). In the case of abstract meta-model classes, compatibility may also come from the compatibility of all their concrete subclasses ($conf_{subs}$). Instead, for concrete meta-model classes, there is no need to check the compatibility of their subclasses because if a class is conformant, so will be its subclasses as they inherit the class features and ancestors. In the following equations, we use $isTypeOf$ to check if the type of an object is compatible with the given type parameter. Moreover, given a class $C \in MM$, $C.feats^*$ yields its owned and inherited features, $C.ancs^*$ yields its direct and indirect superclasses, and $C.subs^*$ yields the set of its direct and indirect subclasses including C.

$$conf_C(RC, C) \triangleq conf_{name}(RC, C) \; \wedge$$
$$(\; (conf_{abs}(RC, C) \; \wedge conf_{feat}(RC, C) \; \wedge conf_{ancs}(RC, C)) \; \vee \quad (2)$$
$$conf_{subs}(RC, C) \;)$$

$$conf_{name}(RC, C) \triangleq RC.isTypeOf(AnonymousClass) \vee RC.name = C.name \quad (3)$$

$$conf_{abs}(RC, C) \triangleq (RC.isAbstract = true \implies C.isAbstract = true) \; \wedge \quad (4)$$
$$(RC.isAbstract = false \implies C.isAbstract = false)$$

$$conf_{feat}(RC, C) \triangleq \forall rf \in RC.feats \; \exists f \in C.feats^* \; \bullet \; conf_F(rf, f) \; \wedge$$
$$\neg RC.mandatoryAllowed \implies \quad (5)$$
$$|\{fm \mid fm \in C.feats^* \wedge fm.isMand\}|$$
$$= \quad |\{fm \mid fm \in RC.feats \; \wedge fm.isMand\}|$$

$$conf_{ancs}(RC, C) \triangleq \forall RC_A \in RC.ancs, \; \exists C_A \in C.ancs^* \; \bullet \; conf_C(RC_A, C_A) \; \wedge$$
$$\forall RC_A \in RC.antiancs, \forall \; C' \in MM \; \bullet \; conf_C(RC_A, C') \implies \quad (6)$$
$$C' \notin C.ancs^* \wedge \nexists C'' \in MM \; \bullet \; \{C, C'\} \subseteq C''.ancs^*$$

$$conf_{subs}(RC, C) \triangleq RC.subsAllowed \land RC.isAbstract \in \{any, true\} \land$$
$$C.isAbstract = true \land$$
$$\forall C' \in C.subs^* \bullet C'.isAbstract = false \implies \quad (7)$$
$$(conf_{feat}(RC, C') \land conf_{ancs}(RC, C'))$$

In particular, predicate $conf_{name}$ (Eq. (3)) requires classes to have the same name, or if RC is an AnonymousClass, no name checking is performed. Predicate $conf_{abs}$ (Eq. (4)) checks compatibility of the isAbstract flag, which may have value true, false or any. Equation (5) checks that every feature of RC is matched by some owned or inherited feature in C. If RC forbids additional mandatory features (i.e., mandatoryAllowed is false), then the set of mandatory features of C should be exactly that required by RC^2. We use $f.isMand$ to check if feature f is mandatory. Equation (6) checks that the ancestor set of C includes classes matching those in $RC.ancs$, and none from $RC.antiancs$. Finally, $conf_{subs}$ checks conformance when RC allows abstractness and subsAllowed is true. In that case, if C is abstract, then the conformance relation is required for all its concrete subclasses. Typically, subsAllowed will be true on classes of the input transformation domain, whenever no isTypeOf OCL operator is used on them.

For features, the $conf_F$ predicate in Eq. (8) checks the conformance of their names (which are always known), cardinalities (using predicates $conf_{min}$ and $conf_{max}$), and types (either there is no type requirement, in which case any reference and attribute would match, or some allowed type in types should match as reference or as attribute).

$$conf_F(rf, f) \triangleq rf.name = f.name \land conf_{min}(rf, f) \land conf_{max}(rf, f) \land$$
$$(\ rf.types = nil \lor \exists t \in rf.types \bullet$$
$$(t.isTypeOf(Reference) \land conf_{ref}(t, f)) \lor \quad (8)$$
$$(t.isTypeOf(Attribute) \land conf_{att}(t, f)))$$

A reference $f \in MM$ matches $t \in RM$ if, in addition to the conditions in Eq. (8), both have compatible target types. This is so if t.targets is empty as any target type would be valid, or if every target in t.targets is matched by the target class of f or a subclass. Predicate $conf_{ref}$ in Eq. (9) checks this compatibility condition. Similarly, predicate $conf_{att}$ (omitted) checks the compatibility of attribute types. Hence, this predicate holds if no specific attribute type is required, if it is AnyDataType, or if the type of f is compatible with that of rf.

$$conf_{ref}(t, f) \triangleq \forall RC \in t.targets \bullet \exists D \in f.target.subs^* \bullet conf_C(RC, D) \quad (9)$$

We omit the formulation of predicates $conf_{min}(rf, f)$ and $conf_{max}(rf, f)$ for space constraints. The former holds when the required minimum cardinality of a feature is AnyCardinality, or when the minimum cardinalities of f and rf are the same (or less or more if allowed). The latter predicate is similar but for the

---

[2] For simplicity, this formalization ignores opposite references. In practice, we exclude from this set the mandatory features which are opposite of already matched references.

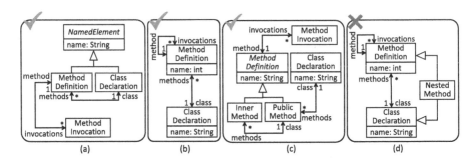

Fig. 4. Conformance examples with respect to DRM (a) in Fig. 3.

maximum cardinality of features. Moreover, in this case, rf can also be Many (a collection), for which (non-)uniqueness and (non-)ordered is checked if required.

Example. Figure 4 shows conforming (a, b, c) and non-conforming (d) meta-models with respect to DRM (a) in Fig. 3. Meta-model (a) conforms to the DRM because both MethodDefinition and ClassDeclaration inherit a name attribute from NamedElement. Moreover, MethodInvocation conforms to one of the anonymous classes in the DRM, MethodDefinition conforms to another anonymous class, and ClassDeclaration to two of them. The feature methods in the DRM, which can be either a reference or an attribute, has been matched by the meta-model reference ClassDeclaration.methods.

Meta-model (b) also conforms to the DRM. In this case, the name attribute is directly owned by the classes and has different types. In addition, there is no class MethodInvocation, whose role is played by MethodDefinition. This way, the four anonymous classes in the DRM are matched by the two meta-model classes. Meta-model (c) is conforming because all concrete subclasses of the abstract class MethodDefinition structurally conform to MethodDefinition in the DRM. Finally, meta-model (d) does not conform because NestedMethod inherits from both MethodDefinition and ClassDeclaration, which is forbidden by the antiancs relations in the DRM. With reference to the transformation in Listing 1, some instances of this meta-model could cause a runtime error as NestedMethod objects would be matched by rules Table and MethodDefinition.

In essence, the proposed conformance relation performs a structural comparison of classes, as required features can be owned or inherited by meta-model classes. However, it does not rely on an explicit mapping between classes and features of RM and MM. While several classes in a meta-model may conform to an anonymous class in RM, our conformity just checks that any such class exists. An explicit definition of the mapping, allowing adaptation (e.g., class renamings) through adapters [4], is left for future work.

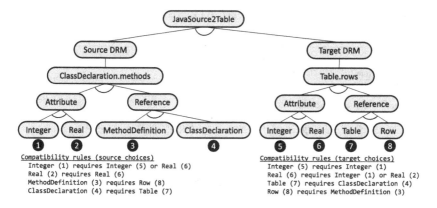

Fig. 5. Excerpt of the compatibility model for the running example.

3.2 Expressing Compatibility Requirements

The DRM implicitly describes possible choices for a concrete meta-model to satisfy the conformance relationship introduced above. However, a given choice for an open element of the source (or target) DRM may forbid some choices of the target (or source) DRM in case such choices break the syntactic correctness of the transformation. For instance, in Listing 1, the binding rows ← s.methods constrains the possible types of the rows and methods features to those that yield a non-faulty execution.

Hence, we gather the inter-dependencies between the source and target DRMs in a *compatibility model* which makes explicit how the choices for one DRM restrict the choices in the other DRM. We represent this compatibility model as a feature model where the different choices are depicted as nodes and the compatibility requirements are shown as dependencies between child nodes, so that the occurrence of a child node forces the presence of the dependent nodes.

Figure 5 shows an excerpt of the compatibility model for the running example, which focuses on the admissible types for attributes (i.e., data types) and references (i.e., target classes). Feature ClassDeclaration.methods can be either an attribute or a reference, as it is only used in line 11 as part of a binding. If it is an attribute, then it can have any data type (the figure only shows Integer and Real). However, the particular selection restricts the choices for feature Table.rows in the target DRM to keep the transformation syntactically correct. Similarly, if methods is a reference with type MethodDefinition, then the type of Table.rows must be Row because, otherwise, the binding will assign an incorrect target value. These dependencies also work from target to source.

4 Extracting Typing Requirements from ATL Transformations

This section explains the procedure for extracting TRMs out of existing ATL transformations. To this end, we rely on the Attribute Grammar formalism,

Table 1. Fragment of the developed ATL attribute grammar (AG_{ATL})

#	Productions	Computation Rules
p1	$\langle$matchedRule$\rangle$::= **rule** ID { $\langle$inPattern$\rangle$ $\langle$outPattern$\rangle$* }	
p2	$\langle$inPattern$\rangle$::= **from** $\langle$inPatternElement$\rangle$*	
p3	$\langle$InPatternElement$\rangle$::= ID:$\langle$oclModelElement$\rangle$	$type(\langle$InPatternElement$\rangle) \leftarrow$ $addClassToSourceDRM(type(\langle$oclModelElement$\rangle))$
p4	$\langle$outPattern$\rangle$::= **to** $\langle$outPatternElement$\rangle$	
p5	$\langle$OutPatternElement$\rangle$::= ID:$\langle$oclModelElement$\rangle$ ($\langle$binding$\rangle$*)	$type(\langle$OutPatternElement$\rangle) \leftarrow$ $addClassToTargetDRM(type(\langle$oclModelElement$\rangle))$
p6	$\langle$binding$\rangle$::= ID '<-' $\langle$oclExpression$\rangle$;	$leftType \leftarrow createFeature(name(\text{ID}), type(\langle$oclExpression$\rangle))$ $rightType \leftarrow type(\langle$oclExpression$\rangle)$ $type(\langle$bindings$\rangle) \leftarrow addClassToTargetDRM(owner(leftType))$ $analyseCompatibilityNodes(leftType, rightType)$
p7	$\langle$oclModelElement$\rangle$::= ID$_1$!ID$_2$	$type(\langle$oclModelElement$\rangle) \leftarrow createClass(name(\text{ID}_2))$
p8	$\langle$oclExpression$\rangle$::= $\langle$navigationOrAttributeCallExp$\rangle$	 $\langle$oclModelElement$\rangle$	...	

p9	$\langle$navigationOrAttributeCallExp$\rangle$::=
	 $\langle$oclExpression$\rangle$.ID;
		$type(\langle$oclExpression$\rangle) \leftarrow$
		 if $(isNavigationOrAttributeCallExp(\langle$oclExpression$\rangle)$ **then**
		    $createReference(type(\langle$oclExpression$\rangle),$ "AnonymousClass")
		 $type(\langle$navigationOrAttributeCallExp$\rangle) \leftarrow$
		 if $(isOperation(name(\text{ID})))$ **then**
		    $createFeatureByOperation($
		       $name(\text{ID}), getReferenceClass(\langle$oclExpression$\rangle))$
		 else
		    $createFeature(name(\text{ID}), getReferenceClass(\langle$oclExpression$\rangle))$)

which represents an elegant and powerful mechanism to describe computations over syntax trees [21].

Attribute grammars extend context-free grammars by associating *attributes* with the symbols of the underlying context-free grammar. The values of such attributes are computed by rules, which are executed while traversing the syntax trees as needed. More formally, let $G = (N, T, P, S)$ be a context-free grammar for a language L_G where N is the set of non-terminals, T is the set of terminals, P is the set of productions, and $S \in N$ is the start symbol. An *attribute grammar* AG is a triple (G, A, AR), where G is a context-free grammar, A associates each grammar symbol $X \in N \cup T$ with a set of attributes, and AR associates each production $R \in P$ with a set of attribute computation rules. While traversing syntax trees, values can be passed from a node to its parent (by means of *synthesized attributes*), or from the current node to a child (by means of *inherited attributes*). Attribute values can be assigned, modified, and checked at any node in the considered syntax tree.

Table 1 shows a fragment of the ATL attribute grammar (AG_{ATL}) we have developed to create TRMs while traversing the syntax tree of the considered ATL transformations. It is important to remark that the shown grammar is a simplification of the real one. The aim of such a simplification is to give a flavour of how the proposed extraction mechanism works, without compromising the readability of the explanation. However, the developed tool

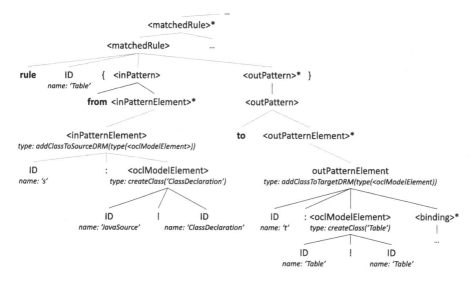

Fig. 6. A sample AG_{ATL} parse tree

available online[3] takes into account all the productions defined for the actual AG_{ATL} by implementing all the concepts presented in Sect. 3.

The first column of Table 1 contains ATL grammar productions. For each production, computation rules are given. The defined computations aim at inferring the value of the attribute *type* of the parsed elements and thus generating the DRMs as presented in Sect. 3.1. The attribute *type* behaves both as inherited and synthesized, thus it is initialized during a top-down phase, and it is updated during a bottom-up phase.

Figure 6 shows a fragment of the AG_{ATL} parse tree related to the rule Table of the transformation given in Listing 1. Each node of the tree is decorated with the corresponding computation rules according to the grammar given in Table 1. Such computation rules makes use of the auxiliary functions described below, developed to properly create and update elements in the TRM while traversing the syntax tree:

▷ *createClass(name: String):* it creates and returns a new class named *name*. The function is used in the production *p7* to manage the non-terminal ⟨oclModelElement⟩ like JavaSource!ClassDeclaration and Table!Table of the sample ATL transformation. The actual DRMs including the newly created classes are decided later in the process while traversing the tree bottom-up.

▷ *addClassToSourceDRM(c: Class)* and *addClassToTargetDRM(c: Class):* they add a new class of type *c* in the source and target DRM, respectively. They are used in the production *p3* to manage the non-terminal ⟨InPatternElement⟩ like the element s:JavaSource!ClassDeclaration, and in *p5* for managing ⟨OutPatternElement⟩

---

[3] http://github.com/totem-mde/totem.

like Table!Table. In both cases, the new classes previously generated by the function *createClass* (e.g., *ClassDeclaration* and *Table*) are added in the corresponding DRMs. The value of the mandatoryAllowed attribute for the created classes is specified as true (false) for those added in the source (target) DRMs. The value of the isAbstract attribute is specified as Any for the classes added in the source DRMs, and false otherwise. The antiancs relation is set between any non-anonymous classes of the source domain, which were created by the production *p2* applied on ⟨inPattern⟩ elements consisting of only one ⟨inPatternElement⟩.

▷ *isNavigationOrAttributeCallExp(o: OclExpression)*: since the non-terminal element ⟨oclExpression⟩ can be matched in several cases (see production *p8*), this function checks if the input OCL expression is a ⟨navigationOrAttributeCallExp⟩. Examples of ⟨navigationOrAttributeCallExp⟩ are i.method.name and s.methods, which use the infix "." operator to call properties and to navigate across association ends, respectively.

▷ *getReferenceClass(o: OclExpression)*: it returns the class of the DRM being generated related to the input OCL expression.

▷ *isOperation(c: String)*: it checks if the input string is the name of an OCL operation (e.g., *size*, *sum*, and *exists*) defined over OCL data types. The function is used in the production *p9* to check if the last part of the matched ⟨navigationOrAttributeCallExp⟩ is an operation. If it is not (e.g., name in the expression i.method.name) then a new feature is added in the class, which is being created because of the matched ⟨oclExpression⟩ element (e.g., i.method). If *isOperation* returns true then a new feature is created by means of the *createFeatureByOperation* function (see below).

▷ *createFeature(name: String, c: Class)*: it creates a new feature typed by the input class c. It is used in the productions *p6* and *p9*. The former is for managing the non-terminal ⟨binding⟩ like rows <- s.methods at line 11 of Listing 1, whereas the latter is for managing the non-terminal ⟨NavigationOrAttributeCallExp⟩ like i.method.name at line 6. In the case at line 11, a new feature named rows is added in the target DRM and its type is inferred from the type of the OCL expression s.methods. In the case at line 6, the production *p9* would match i.method with ⟨oclExpression⟩ and name with ID. Since name is not an operator, a new feature named name will be created in the class referred by the reference i.method. Concerning the cardinality of the created features, when a Number element is created, the corresponding attribute allowMore is true in the minimum cardinality of the source DRM, or in the maximum cardinality of the target DRM. The value of the attribute allowLess is true in the maximum cardinality of the source DRM, or in the minimum cardinality of the target DRM.

▷ *createFeatureByOperation(opName: String, c: Class)*: it creates a new feature and its cardinality is specified according to the operation name given as input. For instance, if the operation is *size*, then it means that the matched expression refers to a collection and, consequently, the max cardinality of the created feature has to be Many.

▷ *createReference(f: Feature):* given a previously created feature as input, it specializes it as a Reference element. It is used in *p9* in case the matched ⟨oclExpression⟩ is a ⟨navigationOrAttributeCallExp⟩. In such a case, the previously created feature has to be specialized to a reference typed with a new Anonymous-Class.

▷ *analyseCompatibilityNodes(left: Class, right: Class):* it is used in the production *p6* for adding elements in the compatibility model being generated. In particular, it does a case analysis between the left and right types of the matched ⟨binding⟩ element by checking compatibility issues like cardinality or problems regarding the types of resolving rules. Then, it creates the corresponding nodes of the feature model accordingly.

5   Implementation and Validation

The approach has been implemented as an Eclipse plugin called TOTEM. This is able extract a TRM from an ATL transformation, and check the conformance of meta-models with respect to the TRM. The tool, a screencast demonstration, and the evaluation results are available at http://github.com/totem-mde/totem.

Next, we evaluate the precision of our TRM extraction process and the flexibility of the conformance relationship. While a formal proof of correctness and completeness of the TRM extraction method would be desirable and will be tackled in future work, ATL is an unformalised language[4]. Therefore, we opted for an empirical evaluation using mutation-based testing. This has the advantage of validating the approach in practice, testing the specificities of real transformations and the particularities of the EMF framework (e.g., opposite references, compositions, etc.).

We use the following ATL transformations in our evaluation: JavaSource2Table (the original version of the running example), PetriNet2PNML (a translation from Petri nets to the PNML document format), KM32EMF (a conversion between OO formalisms), and HSM2FSM (a flattening of hierarchical state machines). The selection criterion was to choose transformations written by a third-party, with no errors or very easily fixable not to introduce a bias. In particular, the first three transformations belong to the ATL Zoo, while the latter is presented in [2].

For each transformation, we extract its TRM (i.e., source and target DRMs and compatibility model) using TOTEM. Then, we generate first-order mutants[5] of the original source and target meta-models (which are also available in the ATL Zoo together with the transformations) by systematically applying the meta-model modifications identified in [3]. Our aim is generating many slightly different variants of the original meta-models, so that some break the transformation, while others do not. Finally, we evaluate whether our algorithm correctly

---

[4] Some efforts exist to express the *execution* semantics of ATL by compilation into Maude [22]. However, formal typing rules for ATL, including OCL, are not available.

[5] First-order mutants are obtained by applying a mutation operator to the original artifact once.

classifies each mutant as conformant when the transformation can use it safely, and non-conformant otherwise. To determine if the classification is correct, we use the ANATLYZER [6] ATL static type checker as an oracle of the typing relationship between the mutated meta-model and the transformation.

For each meta-model mutant, we may obtain one of the following results: our conformance method correctly categorizes the mutant as conformant (*true positive, TP*) or non-conformant (*true negative, TN*), or it incorrectly categorizes the mutant as conformant (*false positive, FP*) or non-conformant (*false negative, FN*). Then, we compute *precision* (an indicator of correctness) as $\frac{\#TP}{\#TP+\#FP}$, and *recall* (an indicator of completeness) as $\frac{\#TP}{\#TP+\#FN}$. The transformations, meta-models and scripts to run the experiment, as well as the evaluation results, are available in the tool website.

Table 2 summarizes the obtained results. There are no false negatives, and thus recall is 100%, signifying that our method classifies correctly non-conforming meta-models as such. There are some false positives though, meaning that some non-conformant meta-models get incorrectly classified as conformant, and the transformation may raise runtime errors if executed with them. Nev-

Table 2. Evaluation results.

	JavaSource2Table	HSM2FSM	PetriNet2PNML	KM32EMF
Mutants	141	316	325	2,515
True positives	70	150	185	1,785
True negatives	64	154	131	695
False positives	7	12	9	35
False negatives	0	0	0	0
Precision	91%	93%	95%	98%
Recall	100%	100%	100%	100%
Conforming	70	150	185	1,785
Non-conforming	62	141	113	684
Incompatible	2	13	18	11

ertheless, the overall precision is still high. An example of false positive occurs in the expression i.method.name of the running example (line 6). In the original meta-model, the name attribute is compulsory, but one meta-model mutant relaxes this cardinality to 0..1. The extracted DRM is not precise enough to put any restriction about the cardinality, however ANATLYZER does signal this typing problem, and thus it is reported as a false positive. We have observed that false positives occur due to limitations in the extraction process. To solve these cases, we plan to combine our TRM extraction mechanism with information from ANATLYZER's static analysis. However, this is only possible if the source and target meta-models are available.

To analyse the effects of the mutations, the second and third last rows of the table show the number of conforming and non-conforming generated meta-model mutants. The numbers are comparable in the first three transformations. Notably, there is a high number of conforming meta-models correctly classified by our algorithm, which means that we can reuse the transformations with many meta-models (more than 2,000) different from the ones used to develop the transformations. The last row of the table shows how many meta-models individually conform to the DRMs but do not satisfy the compatibility model. This shows the usefulness of this model.

We have manually revised the extracted DRMs and some mutants to analyse whether the evaluation demanded a flexible typing from our conformance relationship. We found several interesting cases. For instance, PNML2PetriNet exercised the subsAllowed flag (illustrated in Fig. 4(c) for the running example), since some features of an abstract class Arc were located in all subclasses. Mutations like *pull meta-property*, *push meta-property*, *inline meta-class* and *flatten hierarchy* generate variants which require structural typing to enable conformance. All these cases were correctly handled by our conformance algorithm.

Threats to Validity. A few aspects may threat the internal validity of the experiment. The number of transformations in the evaluation is low, and it will be expanded in future evaluations. However, our first results are promising and encourage us to follow this line of research. In any case, the number of generated meta-model mutants is relatively high (around 3,300). Still, the set of considered meta-model mutation operators might be not complete, potentially preventing exercising all features of our conformance relationship. Finally, we use ANATLYZER as oracle to well-typedness. Although ANATLYZER has been reported to have high precision and recall [6–8], it is not infallible. However, we have manually revised the dubious cases and have not find any incorrect result.

6   Related Work

The closest related work is by Zschaler [24], who uses logic to express meta-model requirements extracted from toy in-place transformations. Instead, we use a model to represent requirements. The advantage is that we can process those models to, e.g., generate OCL queries, check meta-model conformance, or synthesize meta-models. Our TRM includes abstractions to express common model-to-model transformation requirements (e.g., that a class may have extra mandatory features), and includes a compatibility model, which is novel. Finally, extracting the requirements from ATL transformations is more challenging as we need to deal with OCL expressions, mechanisms like automated binding resolution, and dependencies between meta-models.

In the previous work of some of the authors [4,5], we developed the notion of *concepts* to enable transformation reuse. Concepts are meta-models representing the transformation interface, which need to be bound to meta-models. Instead, in this work we propose using TRMs, which provide further flexibility to express meta-model requirements, like (dis-)allowing extra mandatory features in classes, or declaring features which can be references or attributes. While bindings may encode some of these requirements, the TRMs make explicit constraints that bindings ought to obey. Moreover, concepts lack the notion of compatibility model. On the other hand, bindings permit bridging heterogeneities between concepts and concrete meta-models, while resolving heterogeneities between TRMs and meta-models is future work.

Other approaches to reusability [10,12] are based on establishing a subtyping relationship or binding between the transformation meta-model and other meta-model. However, these approaches still describe the transformation interface in terms of meta-models, while TRMs are more expressive.

Several works analyse the model transformations to obtain their footprint [6,13]. This is the part of the input and output meta-models accessed by the transformation, which is itself a meta-model. While these works rely on the actual transformation meta-models, our analysis is done without them. Moreover, we produce a TRM, which is more general as it allows using the transformation with different meta-models.

Transformation *intents* [18] describe semantical properties that ensure a correct transformation reuse according to the designer expectations. In our case, we aim at ensuring syntactical correctness, but it would be interesting to incorporate such intents into our framework in the future.

Finally, Famelis et al. [11] propose a meta-model independent approach to express uncertainty in models, which is applicable to meta-models. We use a DRM meta-model as it allows expressing domain-specific aspects in a more natural way, like the possibility of features to be both attributes and references, the semantics of flags mandatoryAllowed and subsAllowed, or defining transformation-specific compatibility constraints.

7   Conclusions and Future Work

In this paper, we have presented a new approach, based on TRMs, for model transformation reusability. TRMs are automatically extracted from model transformations, and contain a compatibility model constraining the possible options in the source and target meta-models. We have implemented prototype tool support and presented an experiment, based on meta-model mutation, showing promising results.

In the future, we would like to add the notion of *binding* into our conformance relationship in order to improve reusability. Such bindings may resolve heterogeneities (e.g., class renamings) between the TRMs and the meta-models, inducing a transformation adaptation like in [4]. We plan to explore heuristics for automatic meta-model generation from TRMs. As our checks are syntactical, we would like to incorporate the notion of *transformation intent*. Finally, we are working on building a graphical modelling tool to visualize and bind TRMs, and on formal proofs of correctness of the TRM extraction procedure.

Acknowledgements. Work supported by the Spanish Ministry of Economy and Competitivity, grants TIN2014-52129-R and TIN2015-73968-JIN (AEI/FEDER, UE), and the Madrid Region (S2013/ICE-3006).

References

1. Basciani, F., Di Ruscio, D., Iovino, L., Pierantonio, A.: Automated chaining of model transformations with incompatible metamodels. In: Dingel, J., Schulte, W., Ramos, I., Abrahão, S., Insfran, E. (eds.) MODELS 2014. LNCS, vol. 8767, pp. 602–618. Springer, Cham (2014). doi:10.1007/978-3-319-11653-2_37

2. Cheng, Z., Monahan, R., Power, J.F.: Formalised EMFTVM bytecode language for sound verification of model transformations. Softw. Syst. Model. 1–29 (2016, in press)
3. Cicchetti, A., Di Ruscio, D., Eramo, R., Pierantonio, A.: Automating co-evolution in model-driven engineering. In: 12th International IEEE Enterprise Distributed Object Computing Conference, EDOC 2008, pp. 222–231. IEEE Computer Society (2008)
4. Cuadrado, J.S., Guerra, E., de Lara, J.: A component model for model transformations. IEEE Trans. Softw. Eng. **40**(11), 1042–1060 (2014)
5. Cuadrado, J.S., Guerra, E., de Lara, J.: Reverse engineering of model transformations for reusability. In: Ruscio, D., Varró, D. (eds.) ICMT 2014. LNCS, vol. 8568, pp. 186–201. Springer, Cham (2014). doi:10.1007/978-3-319-08789-4_14
6. Cuadrado, J.S., Guerra, E., de Lara, J.: Uncovering errors in ATL model transformations using static analysis and constraint solving. In: 25th IEEE International Symposium on Software Reliability Engineering, ISSRE, pp. 34–44. IEEE Computer Society (2014)
7. Cuadrado, J.S., Guerra, E., de Lara, J.: Quick fixing ATL transformations with speculative analysis. Softw. Syst. Model. 1–32 (2016, in press). Springer
8. Cuadrado, J.S., Guerra, E., de Lara, J.: Static analysis of model transformations. IEEE Trans. Softw. Eng. 1–32 (2017, in press)
9. de Lara, J., Guerra, E.: From types to type requirements: genericity for model-driven engineering. Softw. Syst. Model. **12**(3), 453–474 (2011)
10. de Lara, J., Guerra, E., Cuadrado, J.S.: A-posteriori typing for model-driven engineering. In: 18th ACM/IEEE International Conference on Model Driven Engineering Languages and Systems, MoDELS 2015, pp. 156–165. IEEE (2015)
11. Famelis, M., Salay, R., Chechik, M.: Partial models: towards modeling and reasoning with uncertainty. In: 34th International Conference on Software Engineering, ICSE 2012, 2–9 June 2012, Zurich, Switzerland, pp. 573–583. IEEE Computer Society (2012)
12. Guy, C., Combemale, B., Derrien, S., Steel, J.R.H., Jézéquel, J.-M.: On model subtyping. In: Vallecillo, A., Tolvanen, J.-P., Kindler, E., Störrle, H., Kolovos, D. (eds.) ECMFA 2012. LNCS, vol. 7349, pp. 400–415. Springer, Heidelberg (2012). doi:10.1007/978-3-642-31491-9_30
13. Jeanneret, C., Glinz, M., Baudry, B.: Estimating footprints of model operations. In: Proceedings of the 33rd International Conference on Software Engineering, ICSE 2011, Waikiki, Honolulu, HI, USA, 21–28 May 2011, pp. 601–610. ACM (2011)
14. Jouault, F., Allilaire, F., Bézivin, J., Kurtev, I.: ATL: a model transformation tool. Sci. Comput. Program. **72**(1–2), 31–39 (2008)
15. Kusel, A., Schönböck, J., Wimmer, M., Kappel, G., Retschitzegger, W., Schwinger, W.: Reuse in model-to-model transformation languages: are we there yet? Softw. Syst. Model. **14**(2), 537–572 (2015)
16. Object Management Group. UML 2.0 OCL Specification. http://www.omg.org/docs/ptc/03-10-14.pdf
17. Pescador, A., Garmendia, A., Guerra, E., Cuadrado, J.S., de Lara, J.: Pattern-based development of domain-specific modelling languages. In: MODELS, pp. 166–175. IEEE (2015)
18. Salay, R., Zschaler, S., Chechik, M.: Correct reuse of transformations is hard to guarantee. In: Van Gorp, P., Engels, G. (eds.) ICMT 2016. LNCS, vol. 9765, pp. 107–122. Springer, Cham (2016). doi:10.1007/978-3-319-42064-6_8
19. Schmidt, D.C.: Guest editor's introduction: model-driven engineering. Computer **39**(2), 25–31 (2006)

20. Sen, S., Moha, N., Baudry, B., Jézéquel, J.-M.: Meta-model pruning. In: Schürr, A., Selic, B. (eds.) MODELS 2009. LNCS, vol. 5795, pp. 32–46. Springer, Heidelberg (2009). doi:10.1007/978-3-642-04425-0_4
21. Slonneger, K., Kurtz, B.L.: Formal Syntax and Semantics of Programming Languages, vol. 340. Addison-Wesley, Reading (1995)
22. Troya, J., Vallecillo, A.: A rewriting logic semantics for ATL. J. Object Technol. **10**(5), 1–29 (2011)
23. van Deursen, A., Klint, P., Visser, J.: Domain-specific languages: an annotated bibliography. SIGPLAN Not. **35**(6), 26–36 (2000)
24. Zschaler, S.: Towards constraint-based model types: a generalised formal foundation for model genericity. In: VAO, pp. 11:11–11:18. ACM, New York (2014)

Change-Preserving Model Repair

Gabriele Taentzer[1(✉)], Manuel Ohrndorf[2], Yngve Lamo[3], and Adrian Rutle[3]

[1] Philipps-Universität Marburg, Marburg, Germany
taentzer@informatik.uni-marburg.de
[2] Universität Siegen, Siegen, Germany
mohrndorf@informatik.uni-siegen.de
[3] Western Norway University of Applied Sciences, Bergen, Norway
{Yngve.Lamo,Adrian.Rutle}@hvl.no

Abstract. During modeling activities, inconsistencies can easily occur due to misunderstandings, lack of information or simply mistakes. In this paper, we focus on model inconsistencies that occur due to model editing and cause violation of the meta-model conformance. Although temporarily accepting inconsistencies helps to keep progress, inconsistencies have to be resolved finally. One form of resolution is model repair. Assuming that model changes are state-based, (potentially) performed edit operations can be automatically identified from state differences and further analyzed. As a result, inconsistent changes may be identified causing a need to repair the model. There may exist an overwhelming number of possible repair actions that restore consistency. The edit history may help to identify the relevant repairs. Model inconsistencies are repaired by computing and applying complement edit operations that are needed to re-establish the overall model consistency. In this paper, we clarify under which conditions this kind of model repair can be applied. The soundness of this approach is shown by formalizing it based on the theory of graph transformation. A prototype tool based on the Eclipse Modeling Framework and Henshin is used to conduct an initial evaluation.

Keywords: Model-based engineering · Model repair · Graph transformation

1 Introduction

Model-based engineering has gained increasing popularity in various disciplines, especially in software development. This means that modeling plays a primary role throughout the engineering process and thus, it has to be well supported. While models are edited, they may get inconsistent for various reasons as, e.g., misunderstandings, lack of information, incomplete modeling actions or simply mistakes. Another source of inconsistency may be different interpretations of requirements especially where models are developed collaboratively [1]. In this paper, we focus on model inconsistencies related to the violation of conformance to the underlying meta-model, especially as they occur during editing processes.

© Springer-Verlag GmbH Germany 2017
M. Huisman and J. Rubin (Eds.): FASE 2017, LNCS 10202, pp. 283–299, 2017.
DOI: 10.1007/978-3-662-54494-5_16

Prior to model repair, model inconsistencies have to be detected. Currently many approaches are available that detect inconsistencies fast and correctly, e.g. [2–4]. This may be performed in a check-only mode or integrated with model repair as done in various rule-based approaches such as [5–9].

While it is important to allow inconsistencies during modeling processes [10], they must be resolved eventually. One way of inconsistency resolution is model repair. There are various approaches to repair models which capture this problem in different ways. An overview is given in [11], also stating a common problem in model repair: "One of the main challenges of model repair is that for any given set of inconsistencies, there (possibly) exists an overwhelming number of repair updates that restore the consistency. Yet, since the selection of the most suitable repair is ultimately a choice of the developer, approaches to model repair must balance the automation level of the technique and the need for user guidance in the generation of the repairs." Roughly, we distinguish between the following approaches to model repair: Given an inconsistent model, search-based approaches return a repaired model which is consistent, such as [12–15]. Syntactic and rule-based approaches return a (partially ordered) set of possible repair actions instead (see e.g. repair plans in [8]). Badger [16] is the only model repair approach so far that uses the change history: It uses the date of model revisions to select repair plans but does not consider the performed edit operations to select repair actions.

So far, model repair approaches have not taken the history of user actions into account, hence they miss an important information source for repair generation. By the performed edit operations, users state how they want to evolve the model. Guiding the repair process by the change history can help to identify promising repair possibilities from the overwhelming number of possible ones.

Model changes are either recorded in a state-based manner where just pre- and post-states are stored, or in a delta-based manner where information about the performed user actions is stored. Delta-based approaches have the advantage of keeping the history of the model evolution. If model changes are given state-based, all interesting information about a possible sequence of user actions is not immediately available but can be automatically determined assuming that all the possible user actions have been specified before [17]. Specifications of edit operations can be computed to a large extent as shown in [18]. Hence, independent of the approach that is applied to record changes, we will assume that the delta information can be automatically computed when needed.

Our approach is *rule-based* in the sense that an *edit operation* (EO) is specified by one or more rules depending on its complexity. We assume that a repair action is also specified by a rule, called *repair operation* (RO), such that the composition of an edit operation with a suitable repair operation leads to a *consistency-preserving operation* (CPO), i.e., a rule that – being applied to a consistent model – yields a consistent model again (see Fig. 1). Hence, ROs are complementing preceding

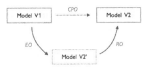

Fig. 1. Change-preserving model repair

EOs and therefore, preserve already performed model changes. In general, there may be several possible ROs for one EO.

This repair approach is *interactive* since the user may select among several applicable repair actions to repair a model step-by-step. Moreover, it is *consistency improving* with each application of a repair action. We will show as a main result that, if all the repair operations are causally independent from the subsequent edit operations, all inconsistencies can be resolved without side-effects in the sense that no new inconsistencies are introduced while repairing the model, i.e., the repair is *fully consistent* in that case. In addition, if an edit operation does not cause any inconsistency, there is not any repair action to be performed, hence, our approach is *stable*. Our model repairs are not necessarily *least change*, i.e., repaired models are not necessarily as close as possible to the original model, since this is dependent on the specified CPOs.

Typical application scenarios are the following ones: If a model consists of several viewpoints as, e.g., UML models which consist of several diagrams, edit operations in one viewpoint may have to be complemented by actions in other diagrams. If one or several of these complements are forgotten in the original editing process, they may be easily repaired by our approach. Although this complementation might sound a bit mechanical, it cannot be automated in general since often necessary information is lacking. When, e.g., a new method call is inserted in a sequence diagram, it has to be complemented with the definition of a corresponding method in the class model. While the method name may already be fixed by the call, its return type as well as its parameters (with name and type) still have to be specified.

Considering a scenario with just one viewpoint, our approach may also be useful to easily complete more complex edit activities that are not available as separate edit operations. For example, changes of interfaces have to be repeated on implementing classes or attribute changes have to be repeated on their getter and setter methods. Another motivation may be fast editing where just key information is given which can be automatically completed to a bigger extent.

The main contributions of this paper are:

1. A new process for repairing model inconsistencies taking the history of edit operations into account.
2. A formalization of this process using algebraic graph transformation (see e.g. [19]), i.e., a precise formulation of each of its tasks. The main theorem shows that all repair processes of our approach are consistency-improving.
3. A prototypical implementation in Henshin [20], a model transformation language based on the Eclipse Modeling Framework and graph transformation concepts. The prototype is used to conduct a case study where edit processes in the bCMS (Barbados Crash Management System) [21] are considered.

The rest of this paper is organized as follows: The running example is presented in Sect. 2. Section 3 introduces our model repair process. The formalization of our approach follows in Sect. 4. Tool support and an initial evaluation are presented in Sect. 5. Finally, we compare with related work and conclude in Sects. 6 and 7.

2   Running Example

Let us consider an example: A simple class model of an online shop focusing on the customer's viewpoint covers (at least) orders and a shopping cart collecting these orders (see Fig. 2).

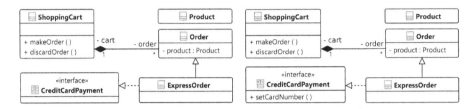

Fig. 2. Class model of an online shop - Versions 0 and 1

The model declares ExpressOrders as a special kind of orders. This class shall implement the interface class CreditCardPayment. The interface is extended by a method called setCard-Number() as shown in Fig. 2. The modeler has introduced an inconsistency here since the class ExpressOrder does not implement this method; the model has to be repaired. A suitable model repair that takes the performed model

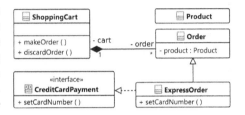

Fig. 3. Class model of an online shop - Inconsistency repaired, Version V1-R

change into account is to execute the indicated completion, i.e., to add the method also to the class ExpressOrder as shown in Fig. 3.

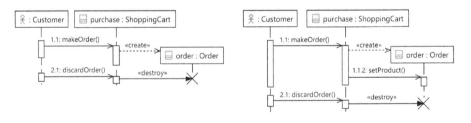

Fig. 4. A sequence diagram for ordering a product - Versions 1 and 2

Building on our example, we will now specify the behavior related to the main use case which is ordering of a product. It is modeled by a simple sequence diagram as shown on the left of Fig. 4 which – together with the class model in Fig. 3 – constitutes a consistent view on the system model in the sense that all object types and messages used are defined in the class model. (Note that attribute values and links are not visible in sequence diagrams.) On the right of Fig. 4 the sequence diagram has been further developed by inserting a new method call of setProduct on the object of type Order. This method is not defined in the current class model; hence, this view of the system model is inconsistent and has to be repaired.

In principle, there are many different repair actions possible, e.g., adding a method setProduct to class Order, removing the message from the sequence diagram while keeping the lifeline of type Order, or removing also this structure. Since the modeler added the message, its removal is a possible repair action. If the modeler selects it, our approach is not specifically helpful for this repair but could

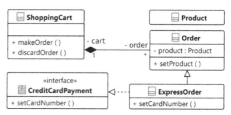

Fig. 5. A class model of an online shop - Inconsistency repaired, version V2-R

be used to identify repairs that are still missing thereafter. But if the modeler wants to keep the added message, our repair approach would immediately propose the missing complement operation which is the addition of the method to the class model; this is shown in Fig. 5.

3   Model Repair Approach

In the following, we informally present our approach to change-preserving model repair. The approach relies on edit operations (EOs), consistency-preserving operations (CPOs) and repair operations (ROs); EOs and CPOs have to be defined first by the language designer. Thereafter, modelers can repair their inconsistent models.

3.1   Preparing Change-Preserving Model Repair

Before being able to perform change-preserving model repair, the necessary operations for the modeling language and its model editor have to be specified. An overview on the preparation tasks is given in Fig. 6.

For a given modeling language which is specified by a meta-model MM, a set of CPOs w.r.t. the MM has to be defined. These CPOs are usually defined by language designers in cooperation with domain experts. For identifying reasonable edit operations (EOs), we do not consider the original language meta-model but an *effective meta-model* being the original one in a relaxed form, i.e., without (most of the) OCL constraints and with relaxed multiplicities. The effective meta-model defines the language of all possible

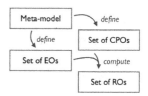

Fig. 6.   Preparation   for change-preserving   model repair

inputs to a model editor (which may cause inconsistencies w.r.t. the original meta-model). In [18], an automated approach for deriving EOs from effective meta-models is presented and evaluated at several modelling languages and editors.

For each CPO, one need to identify sub-operations that are reasonable edit operations in the modeling language, e.g. EOs for inserting, deleting, and moving model parts as well as for changing their attributes [18,22]. An EO is completed to a CPO by a repair operation (RO); i.e., applying an EO followed by an RO to a model, yields the same result as applying the corresponding CPO. In this way, an EO can be seen as a sub-operation of a CPO. It may also happen that an EO is not a sub-operation of any CPO or of several CPOs; in the former case the application of an EO may lead to irreparable inconsistencies while in the latter case, the complement ROs w.r.t. each containing CPO are computed. We stick to the case where each EO is complemented by at most one RO to each of its CPOs. A more general case would be EOs being complemented by sequences of ROs, e.g. adding an interface operation is complemented with adding an operation in each realizing class. In the special case that an EO is already a CPO, model repair is obviously not needed.

3.2   Change-Preserving Model Repair

A change-preserving model repair takes the preceding applications of EOs, i.e., *edit steps*, into account; edit steps that may cause inconsistencies are followed by applications of ROs, called *repair steps*, that re-establish consistency (see Fig. 1). To find out which ROs shall be applied, the edit steps since the last consistent model version are needed. If edit steps are not already provided by the model editor, they can be automatically computed as follows: Given two model versions M_1 and M_2 and a set of EOs, we are looking for a sequence of edit steps from M_1 to M_2. The algorithm presented in [17] yields an *edit script*, i.e., a set of EOs with actual arguments being partially ordered along their sequential dependencies. This algorithm is fast in the sense that it does not need backtracking. It has been implemented for EMF models and applied in several case studies.

Next, the reported edit steps can be analyzed w.r.t. inconsistencies. Each edit step which causes inconsistencies will lead to one of the following two cases:

1. There exists one or more CPOs that have the applied EO as a sub-operation. The modeler chooses one of them and thereby determines the complement RO that has to be performed to re-establish consistency w.r.t. the considered edit step. In Sect. 2 we presented two inconsistent edit steps which are repaired by complements.
2. The edit step introduces a model for which there does not exist any CPO that has the applied EO as a sub-operation. In this case the model change cannot be preserved. It has to be rolled back, at least partly. An example for such an EO (in the context of class models) is the insertion of a generalization relation between two classes such that the overall generalization structure becomes cyclic. The model editor usually allows such an EO.

If all edit steps can be repaired (if needed) and each of the repair steps is causally independent of all the edit steps following the edit step it repairs, we can guarantee the overall consistency of the final model after all repairs (see Theorem 1 below).

The independence of steps can be checked automatically based on the critical pair analysis implemented in Henshin (for more details see Sect. 4.4 below).

4   Formalization

The formalization of the described model repair approach is a means to clarify the assumptions and outcomes of each involved task. Since models can be basically considered as graphs, we rely on the theory of algebraic graph transformation as presented in [19]. In the following, we first recall all basic concepts needed to precisely define models, model changes and modeling languages. We define CPOs as graph transformation rules whose applications preserve the model consistency. Thereafter, change-preserving model repair is formally defined.

4.1   Defining Modeling Languages

When formalizing meta-modeling, graphs occur at two levels: the type level (representing meta-models) and the instance level (given by all valid instance models). This idea is described by the concept of *typed graphs*, where a fixed *type graph* TG together with a set C of constraints serves as an abstract representation of the meta-model. Types are usually structured by an inheritance relation. Multiplicities and other annotations are expressed by additional constraints as well as additional well-formedness rules. The constraints could be defined by means of graph constraints, OCL, first order logic, etc., however the proposed approach is not limited to any particular constraint language. Instances of the type graph are *typed graphs* being equipped with a structure-preserving mapping to the type graph, i.e., a mapping that preserves the source and target functions for edges.

Definition 1 (Meta-model and modeling language). *A meta-model $MM = (TG, C)$ consists of a type graph TG and a set C of constraints typed over TG. All well-typed graphs w.r.t. TG form the set $L(TG)$. All graphs in $L(TG)$ satisfying all the constraints in C form the set $L(MM)$, i.e., the modeling language specified by MM.*

Example 1 (UML meta-model excerpt). Looking behind the scenes of our initial example, the example meta-model presented in Fig. 7 is a small and simplified excerpt of the UML meta-model.

It focuses on classifiers with their properties and operations being core ingredients of class models on the one hand and lifelines sending messages as core concepts of sequence diagrams on the other hand. To make the *Realization* relationship between interfaces and classes more precise, we require the following

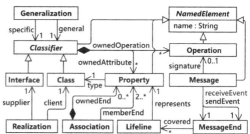

Fig. 7. Small and simplified excerpt of the UML meta-model

constraint: *Each class has to provide all operations which are defined by implemented interfaces.* Another constraint which is used in the running example is
this: *Each message has to refer to an operation with the same signature belonging
to a class the receiving lifeline is typed over.*

4.2 Model Changes and Their Consistency

Model changes may be formalized by *graph transformation*, i.e. the rule-based
modification of graphs. A rule r is defined by two graphs (L, R) and a left
application condition AC. L is the left-hand side (LHS) of the rule representing
a pattern that has to be found to apply the rule. In addition, this pattern has
to fulfill the condition AC before rule application. After the rule application,
a pattern equal to R, the right-hand side (RHS), has to occur in the resulting
graph. The intersection $L \cap R$, i.e. the graph part that is not changed, and the
union $L \cup R$ have to form a graph each. The graph part that is to be deleted is
defined by $L \setminus (L \cap R)$, and $R \setminus (L \cap R)$ defines the graph part to be created.

A *graph transformation step* $G \xRightarrow{r,m} H$ between two instance graphs G and H
is defined by first finding a match m of the left-hand side L of rule r in the current
instance graph G such that m is structure-preserving and type-compatible (i.e.,
m is a typed graph morphism) and second by constructing H in two passes:
(1) building $D := G \setminus m(L \setminus (L \cap R))$, i.e., erasing all the graph items that are to
be deleted, and (2) constructing $H := D \cup (R \setminus (L \cap R))$, i.e., adding all the graph
items that are to be created. Note that m has to fulfill the *dangling condition*,
i.e., all adjacent graph edges of a graph node to be deleted have to be deleted
as well, such that D becomes a graph.

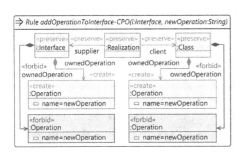

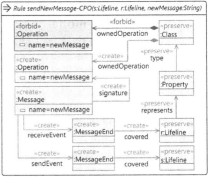

Fig. 8. Rules for adding an operation to an interface class (left) and for sending a new
message (right)

Example 1 (Transformation rules). To specify the consistency-preserving operations (CPOs) in our running example, we rely on two rules that preserve the
consistency of the simplified UML meta-model. On the left of Fig. 8 the rule for

synchronously adding a new operation to an interface and a realizing class is shown. The rule is denoted in a compact form where all elements denoted with preserve are in the LHS, all elements denoted with preserve or create are in the RHS, and all elements denoted with preserve and forbid form a negative application condition. All forbidden elements must not occur in the graph. Note that this rule would have to be extended if there are more than one realizing class for the same interface. Actually a new operation has to be inserted in all the realizing classes. It could also be accomplished with the complement rule in Fig. 10 on the right. The rule on the right of Fig. 8 specifies the synchronous insertion of a message call between two lifelines and its operation into the corresponding class.

Given a UML model in abstract syntax, edit and model repair actions can be expressed by graph transformation steps. Consider, e.g., the graph in Fig. 9 which shows an excerpt of the abstract syntax of the class model on the right of Fig. 2 and the sequence diagram on the left of Fig. 4. Rule *addOperationToInterface* can be applied to the subgraph indicated by V0 and V1 and adds the object marked with V1-R. Applying rule *sendNewMessage* thereafter adds all elements marked with V2 and V2-R as well.

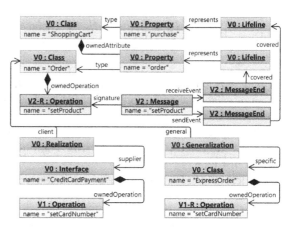

Fig. 9. Example object diagram showing an excerpt of the class model in Fig. 2 and the sequence diagram in Fig. 2 in abstract syntax evolving over time, different versions are indicated by colors and object names

For a given meta-model, all available CPOs can be specified by a graph transformation system.

Definition 2 (Graph transformation system). *Given a set $\mathcal{R}$ of rules, a graph transformation (sequence) $G \xrightarrow{\mathcal{R}} H$ consists of zero or more graph transformation steps applying rules of $\mathcal{R}$. A set $\mathcal{R}$ of graph rules, together with a type graph TG, are called a graph transformation system $GTS = (TG, \mathcal{R})$. A $GTS = (TG, \mathcal{R})$ is consistency-preserving w.r.t. MM if, for every graph G in $L(MM)$, all transformations $G \xrightarrow{\mathcal{R}} H$ yield a consistent graph, i.e., H is in $L(MM)$.*

A modeling language may also be formally defined by a graph grammar GG being a $GTS = (TG, \mathcal{R})$ together with a start graph G_0. It defines a modeling language by all graphs G resulting from transformation sequences starting at G_0, that is, $L(GG) = \{G \in L(TG) | G_0 \xrightarrow{\mathcal{R}^*} G\}$. A graph grammar conforms to meta-model MM if $L(GG) \subseteq L(MM)$.

4.3   Complement Construction

Our model repair approach is mainly based on the complement construction. Given an edit operation (EO), its complement w.r.t. some CPO can be computed. This complement forms the RO to be performed. If an edit operation is already consistency-preserving, it is also a CPO leading to an empty complement rule.

EOs are specified as sub-rules of corresponding CPOs. An EO has to be large enough in the sense that it does not delete nodes that are used as source or target for edges in the super-rule, i.e., it has to fulfill the dangling condition w.r.t. its rule embedding. Otherwise, a complete complement rule cannot be constructed.

Definition 3 (Sub-rule). *A rule* $r_s = ((L_s, R_s), AC_s)$ *is a sub-rule of rule* $r = ((L, R), AC)$ *if* $L_s \subseteq L$, $R_s \subseteq R$, *the inclusion of* r_s *in* r *fulfills the dangling condition, and* AC *can be decomposed into* AC_s *and a (possibly empty) rest application condition.*

Example 2 (Complement rules). A simple EO that just inserts a new operation into an interface has to be complemented by doing so in all realizing classes. This means that the computed RO has to be applied as often as possible to repair all the affected classes. The left rule in Fig. 10 shows the edit rule while the right one shows the corresponding repair rule computed as its complement w.r.t. the left rule in Fig. 8.

The left rule in Fig. 11 inserts a new message between two lifelines and ignores the existence of the corresponding operation in the class model. Since it does not delete anything, it trivially fulfills the dangling condition. The right rule in Fig. 11 shows its complement rule w.r.t. to the overall rule shown on the right of Fig. 8. It inserts the missing operation and its relation to the message call.

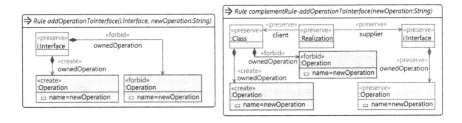

Fig. 10. Adding an operation to an interface: sub-rule (left) and complement rule (right)

Theorem 4.4 in [23] shows that, given a rule r with a sub-rule r_s, there is a canonical way to construct a rule $\bar{r}_s$ with an overlap graph E such that the sequential composition $r_s *_E \bar{r}_s = r$. Such a constructed rule $\bar{r}_s$ is called *complement rule* of r_s w.r.t. r. Furthermore, Fact 4.8 in [23] states that any transformation step $G \xRightarrow{r,m} H$ can be decomposed into two steps $G \xRightarrow{r_s,m_s} \bar{G}$ and $\bar{G} \xRightarrow{\bar{r}_s,\bar{m}_s} H$ of edit step and complement step such that m is an extension of m_s and $\bar{r}_s$ is the complement rule of r_s w.r.t. r.

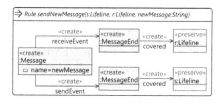

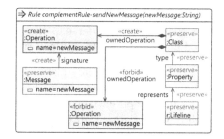

Fig. 11. Sending a message: sub-rule (left) and complement rule (right)

To apply this result to model repair we have to do the following check: Given $G \overset{r_s,m_s}{\Longrightarrow} \bar{G}$ we compute the difference of pre-conditions w.r.t. some $G \overset{r,m}{\Longrightarrow} H$. This means that the match m has to complete the match m_s for $L \setminus L_s$ and all $AC \setminus AC_s$ have to be fulfilled.

If an edit rule is already consistency-preserving, it is a CPO as well. In this case, the complement transformation would apply the empty rule, i.e., $\bar{G} = H$. Hence, our approach is stable in the sense of [11].

4.4 Sequential Independence and Confluence of Transformations

Since the application of complement rules is meant to repair previous edit steps, they usually depend on their edit operations and cannot be applied before the edit step is performed. For example, a graph node has to be created first to further connect it with other model parts. However, the application of a complement rule may be independent of all subsequent edit steps. In that case, a model repair step is called *side effect-free*, and may be exchanged with subsequent edit steps. This means that repairing steps may be performed flexibly throughout the editing process, i.e., immediately after an inconsistent edit step or later – allowing temporary inconsistencies.

Definition 4 (Sequential independence). *Given two transformation steps $t_1 : G_1 \overset{r_1,m_1}{\Longrightarrow} \bar{G}_2$ and $t_2 : \bar{G}_2 \overset{r_2,\bar{m}_2}{\Longrightarrow} G_3$, the execution of $t_1;t_2$ is sequentially independent if match m_2 does not need any element of $\bar{G}_2$ newly created by applying r_1 and does not use any attribute changed in t_1, i.e., t_2 does not need the preceding application of r_1. Furthermore, match m_1 is not destroyed by t_2. The rules r_1 and r_2 are sequentially independent if all sequences $t_1;t_2$ applying first rule r_1 and then r_2 are sequentially independent.*

Example 3 (Independent steps). Considering the edit steps applying first the left rule in Fig. 10 and then the left one in Fig. 11, these two steps are sequentially independent of each other since they do not overlap. Actually, any two applications of these rules are sequentially independent of each other since they act on different viewpoints, i.e., they can never overlap. An execution consisting of an edit step and its repair step by applying the complement rule is usually sequentially dependent. Consider e.g. the rules in Fig. 11 where the message is first inserted and then used to add a corresponding operation.

Checking the sequential independence of rules by hand is tedious. Fortunately this is not necessary since the critical pair analysis (CPA) is a well-known technique to analyze potential conflicts and dependencies of transformation systems. The CPA was originally introduced for term rewriting and later generalized to graph transformation [24]. Henshin contains tool support for the CPA. If there does not exist any critical pair for two given rules r_1 and r_2, all transformation pairs $t_1 : G \overset{r_1,m_1}{\Longrightarrow} H_1$ and $t_2 : G \overset{r_2,m_2}{\Longrightarrow} H_2$ applying these two rules are independent of each other. In this case, the Local-Church-Rosser Property [19] holds ensuring that two independent transformation steps may be executed in any order yielding the same result, i.e., they are also sequentially independent and confluent.

4.5   Change-Preserving Model Repair

The main result in this paper is the following: Given a model change history by a sequence of transformation steps where each rule has at least one complement, each step can be complemented such that a consistent graph can be reached finally. The following result ensures that our approach is fully consistent. To show it we have to ensure that the repair steps are sequentially independent from all edit steps following the edit step it repairs. In that case, repair steps can be arbitrarily interleaved with these edit steps. Several repair steps, however, may dependent on each other such as, for a method call in an interface class, creating first the corresponding interface method and then all corresponding methods in implementing classes.

Theorem 1 (Change-preserving model repair). *Let be given a meta-model MM, a graph transformation system $GTS = (TG, \mathcal{R})$ with a set $\mathcal{R}_s \subseteq \mathcal{R}$ of subrules and $\overline{\mathcal{R}}_s$ of all complement rules of $\mathcal{R}_s$, a graph G in $L(MM)$, and a transformation sequence $G \overset{\mathcal{R}_s}{\Longrightarrow} G_{0n}$. If all rule pairs $(r_{s_i}, \bar{r}_{s_j})$ in $\mathcal{R}_s \times \overline{\mathcal{R}}_s$ for $i > j$ are sequentially independent then there exists a repairing transformation sequence, i.e., a transformation sequence $G_{0n} \overset{\overline{\mathcal{R}}_s}{\Longrightarrow} H$ such that graph H is in $L(MM)$.*

This theorem tells us that a repair is easier if not too many edit steps have to be considered. Its proof can be found in [25]. The main proof idea is to split each CPO into an EO and an RO which can be shifted after all EOs due to the local Church-Rosser property.

Example 4 (Change-preserving model repair). The two subsequent edit steps in our initial example lead both to inconsistencies (of different kinds). Each edit rule is sequentially independent of its opposite repair rule (i.e., the repair rule of the other edit rule) since it just inserts elements that are not needed by the opposite repair rule.

5   Tool Support and Initial Evaluation

Tool support. A first prototype implementation of change-preserving model repair is available at [26]. It is based on the Eclipse Modeling Framework (EMF), Papyrus, and Henshin and supports the following activities: (1) comparison of model versions, (2) recognition of performed edit operations, and (3) provision of concrete repair steps.

Initially the historic version V_1 and the potentially inconsistent version V_2 of a model have to be *compared*. The modeler can choose between different comparison algorithms, e.g. ID-based, signature-based, or similarity-based [27]. Having the set of common model elements available, the tool derives the elementary changes of versions V_1 and V_2, on the level of model elements, references and attributes. We call this kind of change description the technical difference of V_1 and V_2.

For recognizing performed edit operations, the algorithm requires a rule set containing all available EOs for a given model editor. Each edit operation produces a pattern of changes in the technical difference. There is an algorithm presented in [28] which describes how to transform a graph transformation-based rule into a graph pattern which recognizes the corresponding set of changes in the technical difference. In this way, we can recognize all performed EOs. By hiding all those EOs that are already CPOs, only true sub-operations remain in the technical difference showing some inconsistencies. Now the remaining EOs are recognized on the remaining changes using the same algorithm. This even works with incomplete sets of EOs, i.e. elementary changes which cannot be recognized as EOs are ignored.

For each recognized EO we have to *calculate all possible embeddings into corresponding CPOs* (Sect. 4.3). For each pair of CPO and EO rules, a corresponding complement rule RO can be created, by removing all already executed changes of the EO from the CPO.

Next, the *available repair steps are determined*, i.e. the complement rules still have to be provided with parameters for the remaining changes. This means that we have to find all complete matches of the LHS of an RO in the actual model V_2. Usually, a part of the match is already determined by the corresponding EO. Each completed match is reported as a repair to the user. The tool can visualize a selected repair by highlighting the parts in the model diagrams that will be changed. The user can also test a repair by applying and, if necessary, reverting it. The underlying graph transformation logic of the presented approach is transparent to the tool user.

Initial evaluation. For an initial performance estimation, we applied our prototype to the class, sequence and state machine diagrams of the bCMS (Barbados Crash Management System) [21] case study. The UML model V_1 contains approx. 2600 model elements and 22.000 references. The difference to a model V_2 has been computed in ≈ 2 s and contains approx. 600 model elements and 1900 reference changes. 12 inconsistencies were introduced in this edit sequence. Including the EOs of our running example, there are 15 CPOs and 12 EOs. The additional operations consider changes in state machines, e.g. dangling transitions after deleting a state. The EO detection took ≈ 500 ms and filters already

500 consistent changes of 50 steps. (Approx. 2000 changes are ignored since they are not covered by the EOs provided.) The subsequent EO recognition took ≈100 ms; it detects 60 changes performed by 12 steps. After the calculation of the $EO \times CPO$ embeddings in ≈500 ms, a total of 33 concrete repairs were found. The initial performance estimation already allows some conclusions to be made. The performance of the model difference calculation depends on the size of models. The time for the repair calculation, however, mainly depends on the size of the calculated difference and the number of inconsistencies.

To support larger rule sets efficiently, we intend to store rule embeddings in a database. Furthermore, an incremental difference calculation and CPO detection would be interesting for an *online* editing scenario, i.e. suggesting repairs during the user edits the model.

6   Related Work

Most of the existing model repair techniques can be categorized into syntactic, rule- and search-based approaches [11]. In this section, we will compare our approach to existing techniques of those categories.

Syntactic and rule-based approaches. A syntactic repair generator derives repair plans by analyzing the consistency rules at specification time. In rule-based approaches a repair tool is configured with a set of repair rules for frequently occurring inconsistencies. Repair rules or plans are suggested and instantiated at modeling time when inconsistencies occur.

Our approach is closely related to triple graph grammars (TGGs) [29] in the sense that the consistency between two kinds of graphs is specified by rules, called triple rules. Those rules can be used to evolve both related graphs simultaneously in a consistent manner. If the source graph is changed independently by source rules, the corresponding forward rules can be used to synchronize the target graph. A corresponding result is shown in [30]. In this paper, we consider a more general setting where graphs do not have to be sub-structured, edit operations may contain add and delete actions, an edit rule may have several (or no) repair rules (and CPOs), and complex application conditions may be used.

In a wider context, syntactic and rule-based approaches as presented in e.g. [5–9,31] are interactive and incremental since each inconsistency is repaired separately. While providing full control over the repair process, it may happen, however, that the repair of existing inconsistencies leads to new ones. Criteria for side-effect-free repair are usually not considered. Moreover, the change history is not taken into account to restrict the usually overwhelming number of possible repair rules.

Search-based approaches. Search-based approaches such as [14–16] take the inconsistent model as input and search for a consistent one which is usually related to the original one by least changes. This problem is mostly solved by using a constraint solver. Supporting tools may be parameterizable through the definition of valid edit operations giving the user the possibility to find favored solutions. Current approaches, however, are somewhat restricted to handle small models only; otherwise the search space has to be restricted to user-defined upper bounds w.r.t. instance size, back-tracking or time.

A search-based tool which considers the model history is Badger [16]. The regression planning algorithm can take a variety of parameters to guide the search process. One of them is to prioritize model elements by their version in the model history, e.g., repairs should change preferably newer model elements and keep the older ones. Therefore, the algorithm respects the temporal dimension of the history but does not necessarily preserve the edit operations that have taken place.

7 Conclusion

To handle model inconsistencies, there are often many possible repair actions to consider. In this paper, we have proposed a change-preserving model repair approach to tackle this challenge. Based on the edit operations already performed, model repairs are proposed building on the assumption that the latest change of the model is the most significant. To use this approach, we have to do the following: For a given modeling language we specify a set of consistency-preserving operations. For a given model editor we identify the set of allowed edit operations. The basic idea is to identify the history of performed edit operations since the last consistent model state, and to analyze these operations for identifying those causing inconsistencies. If an inconsistent edit operation turns out to be a sub-rule of a consistency-preserving operation, the complement operation is constructed which is able to repair this inconsistency. The soundness of our approach is shown based on the theory of graph transformation. A prototypical implementation illustrates its practical applicability.

Our approach may be combined with other rule-based approaches: Since rule-based approaches usually allow to choose among a large number of repair operations, their selection needs more guidance. Preserving already performed changes seems to be a reasonable criterion. Our approach supports to find out if a repair operation is a complement of an edit operation such that their sequential combination leads to a consistency-preserving operation. Furthermore, a change-preserving model repair process is side-effect-free if each edit operation is independent of all repair operations of later applied edit operations. It is up to future work to further investigate relations between existing rule-based approaches in different editing scenarios and thereby, integrate change-preservation with other important aspects of model repair.

References

1. Easterbrook, S., Nuseibeh, B.: Using viewpoints for inconsistency management. Softw. Eng. J. **11**(1), 31–43 (1996)
2. Grundy, J.C., Hosking, J.G., Mugridge, W.B.: Inconsistency management for multiple-view software development environments. IEEE Trans. Softw. Eng. **24**(11), 960–981 (1998)

3. Egyed, A.: Instant consistency checking for the UML. In: 28th International Conference on Software Engineering (ICSE), pp. 381–390. ACM (2006)
4. Blanc, X., Mounier, I., Mougenot, A., Mens, T.: Detecting model inconsistency through operation-based model construction. In: 30th International Conference on Software Engineering (ICSE), pp. 511–520. ACM (2008)
5. Enders, B., Heverhagen, T., Goedicke, M., Tröpfner, P., Tracht, R.: Towards an integration of different specification methods by using the viewpoint framework. Trans. SDPS 6(2), 1–23 (2002)
6. Amelunxen, C., Legros, E., Schürr, A., Stürmer, I.: Checking and enforcement of modeling guidelines with graph transformations. In: Schürr, A., Nagl, M., Zündorf, A. (eds.) AGTIVE 2007. LNCS, vol. 5088, pp. 313–328. Springer, Heidelberg (2008). doi:10.1007/978-3-540-89020-1_22
7. Königs, A., Schürr, A.: MDI: a rule-based multi-document and tool integration approach. Softw. Syst. Model. 5(4), 349–368 (2006)
8. Reder, A., Egyed, A.: Computing repair trees for resolving inconsistencies in design models. In: International Conference on Automated Software Engineering, pp. 220–229. ACM (2012)
9. Straeten, R.V.D., D'Hondt, M.: Model refactorings through rule-based inconsistency resolution. In: Proceedings of the ACM Symposium on Applied Computing (SAC), pp. 1210–1217. ACM (2006)
10. Balzer, R.: Tolerating inconsistency. In: Proceedings of the 13th International Conference on Software Engineering, pp. 158–165. IEEE Computer Society/ACM Press (1991)
11. Macedo, N., Tiago, J., Cunha, A.: A feature-based classification of model repair approaches. CoRR, vol. abs/1504.03947 (2015)
12. Straeten, R.V.D., Mens, T., Simmonds, J., Jonckers, V.: Using description logic to maintain consistency between UML models. In: Stevens, P., Whittle, J., Booch, G. (eds.) UML 2003. LNCS, vol. 2863, pp. 326–340. Springer, Heidelberg (2003). doi:10.1007/978-3-540-45221-8_28
13. Straeten, R.V.D., Puissant, J.P., Mens, T.: Assessing the kodkod model finder for resolving model inconsistencies. In: France, R.B., Kuester, J.M., Bordbar, B., Paige, R.F. (eds.) ECMFA 2011. LNCS, vol. 6698, pp. 69–84. Springer, Heidelberg (2011). doi:10.1007/978-3-642-21470-7_6
14. Sen, S., Baudry, B., Precup, D.: Partial model completion in model driven engineering using constraint logic programming. In: 17th International Conference on Applications of Declarative Programming and Knowledge Management (INAP 2007) and 21st Workshop on (Constraint) (2007)
15. Macedo, N., Guimarães, T., Cunha, A.: Model repair and transformation with echo. In: 28th International Conference on Automated Software Engineering, ASE 2013, pp. 694–697. IEEE (2013)
16. Puissant, J.P., Straeten, R.V.D., Mens, T.: Resolving model inconsistencies using automated regression planning. Softw. Syst. Model. 14(1), 461–481 (2015)
17. Kehrer, T., Kelter, U., Taentzer, G.: Consistency-preserving edit scripts in model versioning. In: 28th IEEE/ACM International Conference on Automated Software Engineering (ASE), pp. 191–201. IEEE (2013)
18. Kehrer, T., Taentzer, G., Rindt, M., Kelter, U.: Automatically deriving the specification of model editing operations from meta-models. In: Van Gorp, P., Engels, G. (eds.) ICMT 2016. LNCS, vol. 9765, pp. 173–188. Springer, Cham (2016). doi:10.1007/978-3-319-42064-6_12

19. Ehrig, H., Ehrig, K., Prange, U., Taentzer, G.: Fundamentals of Algebraic Graph Transformation. Monographs in Theoretical Computer Science. An EATCS Series. Springer, Heidelberg (2006)
20. Arendt, T., Biermann, E., Jurack, S., Krause, C., Taentzer, G.: Henshin: advanced concepts and tools for in-place EMF model transformations. In: Petriu, D.C., Rouquette, N., Haugen, Ø. (eds.) MODELS 2010. LNCS, vol. 6394, pp. 121–135. Springer, Heidelberg (2010). doi:10.1007/978-3-642-16145-2_9
21. Capozucca, A., Cheng, B., Guelfi, N., Istoan, P.: Oo-spl modelling of the focused case study. In: Comparing Modeling Approaches (CMA) International Workshop affiliated with ACM/IEEE 14th International Conference on Model Driven Engineering Languages and Systems (CMA@ MODELS2011) (2011)
22. Rindt, M., Kehrer, T., Kelter, U.: Automatic generation of consistency-preserving edit operations for MDE tools. In: Demonstrations Track of the ACM/IEEE 17th International Conference on Model Driven Engineering Languages and Systems (MoDELS). CEUR Workshop Proceedings, vol. 1255 (2014)
23. Golas, U., Habel, A., Ehrig, H.: Multi-amalgamation of rules with application conditions in M-adhesive categories. Math. Struct. Comput. Sci. **24**(4), 68 (2014)
24. Plump, D.: Critical pairs in term graph rewriting. In: Prívara, I., Rovan, B., Ružička, P. (eds.) MFCS 1994. LNCS, vol. 841, pp. 556–566. Springer, Heidelberg (1994). doi:10.1007/3-540-58338-6_102
25. Taentzer, G., Ohrndorf, M., Lamo, Y., Rutle, A.: Change-preserving model repair: extended version. Philipps-Universität Marburg, Technical report (2017). www.uni-marburg.de/fb12/swt/research/publications
26. Taentzer, G., Ohrndorf, M., Lamo, Y., Rutle, A.: Change-preserving model repair - tool support and initial evaluation. pi.informatik.uni-siegen.de/projects/SiLift/fase2017/
27. Kehrer, T., Kelter, U., Pietsch, P., Schmidt, M.: Adaptability of model comparison tools. In: IEEE/ACM International Conference on Automated Software Engineering (ASE), Essen, Germany, pp. 306–309. ACM (2012)
28. Kehrer, T., Kelter, U., Taentzer, G.: A rule-based approach to the semantic lifting of model differences in the context of model versioning. In: 26th IEEE/ACM International Conference on Automated Software Engineering (ASE), Lawrence, KS, USA, pp. 163–172. IEEE (2011)
29. Schürr, A.: Specification of graph translators with triple graph grammars. In: Mayr, E.W., Schmidt, G., Tinhofer, G. (eds.) WG 1994. LNCS, vol. 903, pp. 151–163. Springer, Heidelberg (1995). doi:10.1007/3-540-59071-4_45
30. Ehrig, H., Ehrig, K., Ermel, C., Hermann, F., Taentzer, G.: Information preserving bidirectional model transformations. In: Dwyer, M.B., Lopes, A. (eds.) FASE 2007. LNCS, vol. 4422, pp. 72–86. Springer, Heidelberg (2007). doi:10.1007/978-3-540-71289-3_7
31. Mens, T., Straeten, R.V.D., D'Hondt, M.: Detecting and resolving model inconsistencies using transformation dependency analysis. In: Nierstrasz, O., Whittle, J., Harel, D., Reggio, G. (eds.) MODELS 2006. LNCS, vol. 4199, pp. 200–214. Springer, Heidelberg (2006). doi:10.1007/11880240_15

A Deductive Approach for Fault Localization in ATL Model Transformations

Zheng Cheng[✉] and Massimo Tisi

AtlanMod Team (Inria, IMT Atlantique, LS2N), Nantes, France
{zheng.cheng,massimo.tisi}@inria.fr

Abstract. In model-driven engineering, correct model transformation is essential for reliably producing the artifacts that drive software development. While the correctness of a model transformation can be specified and checked via contracts, debugging unverified contracts imposes a heavy cognitive load on transformation developers. To improve this situation, we present an automatic fault localization approach, based on natural deduction, for the ATL model transformation language. We start by designing sound natural deduction rules for the ATL language. Then, we propose an automated proof strategy that applies the designed deduction rules on the postconditions of the model transformation to generate sub-goals: successfully proving the sub-goals implies the satisfaction of the postconditions. When a sub-goal is not verified, we present the user with sliced ATL model transformation and predicates deduced from the postcondition as debugging clues. We provide an automated tool that implements this process. We evaluate its practical applicability using mutation analysis, and identify its limitations.

1 Introduction

Model-driven engineering (MDE), i.e. software engineering centered on software models and their transformation, is widely recognized as an effective way to manage the complexity of software development. One of the most widely used languages for model transformation (MT) is the AtlanMod Transformation Language (ATL) [18]. Like several other MT languages, ATL has a relational nature, i.e. its core aspect is a set of so-called matched rules, that describe the mappings between the elements in the source and target model.

With the increasing complexity of ATL MTs (e.g., in automotive industry [25], medical data processing [29], aviation [6]), it is urgent to develop techniques and tools that prevent incorrect MTs from generating faulty models. The effects of such faulty models could be unpredictably propagated into subsequent MDE steps, e.g. code generation. Therefore, the correctness of ATL is our major concern in this research. Typically *correctness* is specified by MT developers using contracts [9–13,19,21,23]. Contracts are pre/postconditions that express under which condition the MT is considered to be correct. In the context of MDE, contracts are usually expressed in OCL [22] for its declarative and logical nature.

© Springer-Verlag GmbH Germany 2017
M. Huisman and J. Rubin (Eds.): FASE 2017, LNCS 10202, pp. 300–317, 2017.
DOI: 10.1007/978-3-662-54494-5_17

In [12], Cheng et al. developed the *VeriATL* verification system to deductively verify the correctness of ATL transformations w.r.t. given contracts. VeriATL automatically generates the axiomatic semantics of a given ATL transformation in the Boogie intermediate verification language [5], combined with a formal encoding of EMF metamodels [26] and OCL contracts. The Z3 automatic theorem prover [20] is used by Boogie to verify the correctness of the ATL transformation.

However, when a contract on the MT is not verified, current verification systems like VeriATL do not report useful feedback to help the transformation developers fix the fault. Consequently, manually examining the full MT and its contracts and reasoning on the implicit rule interactions become a time-consuming routine to debug MTs.

Because of the advancement in computer science in the last couple of decades (e.g. in the performance of satisfiability modulo theory - SMT - solvers), many researchers are interested in developing techniques that can partially or fully automate the localization of faults in software (we refer the reader to [24,31] for an overview).

In this work, we argue that the characteristics of the considered programming language have a significant impact on the precision and automation of the fault localization. More precisely, we think that in MT languages like ATL, automated fault localization can be more precise because of the available static trace information, i.e. inferred information among types of generated target elements and the rules that potentially generate these types. This idea has recently been introduced in [8] using a conservative and syntactical approach. However, we believe that a deductive approach can fully exploit its potential.

Our deductive approach is based on a set of sound natural deduction rules. It includes 4 rules for the ATL language based on the concept of static trace information, and 16 ordinary natural deduction rules for propositional and predicate logic [16]. Then, we propose an automated proof strategy that applies these deduction rules on the input OCL postcondition to generate sub-goals. Each sub-goal contains a list of hypotheses deduced from the input postcondition, and a sub-case of the input postcondition to be verified. Successfully proving the sub-goals soundly implies the satisfaction of the input OCL postcondition. When a sub-goal is not verified, we exploit its hypotheses in two ways to help the user pinpoint the fault: (a) slicing the ATL MT into a simpler transformation context; (b) providing debugging clues, deduced from the input postcondition to alleviate the cognitive load for dealing with unverified sub-cases. Our fault localization approach has been implemented and integrated with VeriATL. We evaluate our approach with mutation analysis. The result shows that: (a) the guilty constructs are presented in the slice; (b) deduced clues assist developers in various debugging tasks (e.g. the elaboration of a counter-example); (c) the number of sub-goals that need to be examined to pinpoint a fault is usually small.

Paper Organization. We motivate our work by a sample problem in Sect. 2. Section 3 illustrates our fault localization approach in detail. Evaluation is presented in Sect. 4, followed by discussion of the limitations identified in our approach. Section 5 compares our work with related research, and Sect. 6 draws conclusions and lines for future work.

2   Motivating Example

As our running example we use the *HSM2FSM* MT. *HSM2FSM* transforms
hierarchical state machine (*HSM*) models to flattened state machine (*FSM*)
models. Both models conform to the same metamodel (Fig. 1). However, classifiers in the two metamodels are distinguished by the *HSM* and *FSM* prefix.
Specifically, a named *StateMachine* contains a set of labelled *Transitions* and
named *AbstractStates*. Each *AbstractState* has a concrete type, which is either
RegularState, *InitialState* or *CompositeState*. A *Transition* links a *source* to a
target AbstractState. Moreover, *CompositeStates* are only allowed in the models
of HSM, and optionally contain a set of *AbstractStates*.

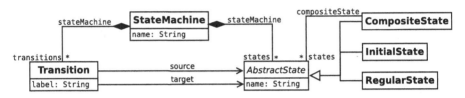

Fig. 1. The hierarchical and flattened state machine metamodel

2.1   Specifying OCL Contracts

We consider a contract-based development scenario where the developer first
specifies correctness conditions for the to-be-developed ATL transformation by
using OCL contracts. Let us first consider the contracts shown in Listing 1.1.
The precondition *Pre1* specifies that in the input model, each *Transition* has at
least one *source*. The postcondition *Post1* specifies that in the output model,
each *Transition* has at least one *source*.

```
1  context HSM!Transition inv Pre1:
2    HSM!Transition.allInstances()−>forAll(t | not t.source.oclIsUndefined())
3  − − − − − − − − − − − − − − − − − − − − − − − − − − − − − − − −
4  context FSM!Transition inv Post1:
5    FSM!Transition.allInstances()−>forAll(t | not t.source.oclIsUndefined())
```

Listing 1.1. The OCL contracts for HSM and FSM

2.2   Developing the ATL Transformation

Then, the developer implements the ATL transformation *HSM2FSM* (a snippet
is shown in Listing 1.2[1]). The transformation is defined via a list of ATL matched
rules in a mapping style. The first rule maps each *StateMachine* element to the
output model (*SM2SM*). Then, we have two rules to transform *AbstractStates*:
regular states are preserved (*RS2RS*), initial states are transformed into regular
states when they are within a composite state (*IS2RS*). Notice here that initial

---

[1] Our HSM2FSM transformation is adapted from [9]. The full version can be accessed
at: https://goo.gl/MbwiJC.

```
1  module HSM2FSM;
2  create OUT : FSM from IN : HSM;
3
4  rule SM2SM { from sm1 : HSM!StateMachine to sm2 : FSM!StateMachine ( name <−
       sm1.name ) }
5
6  rule RS2RS { from rs1 : HSM!RegularState
7              to rs2  : FSM!RegularState ( stateMachine <− rs1.stateMachine, name <−
                  rs1.name ) }
8
9  rule IS2RS { from is1 : HSM!InitialState (not is1.compositeState.oclIsUndefined())
10             to   rs2  : FSM!RegularState ( stateMachine <− is1.stateMachine, name <−
                  is1.name ) }
11
12  −− mapping each transition, that between two noncomposite states, of the source model
        into the target model.
13  rule T2TA { ... }
14
15  −− mapping each transition, whose source is a composite state, of the source model into
        the target model.
16  rule T2TB { ... }
17
18  rule T2TC {
19     from t1 : HSM!Transition, src : HSM!AbstractState, trg : HSM!CompositeState, c :
            HSM!InitialState
20     ( t1.source = src and t1.target = trg and c.compositeState = trg
21       and not src.oclIsTypeOf(HSM!CompositeState) )
22     to   t2 : FSM!Transition
23     ( label <− t1.label, stateMachine <− t1.stateMachine, source <− src, target <− c }
```

Listing 1.2. Snippet of the HSM2FSM model transformation in ATL

states are deliberately transformed partially to demonstrate our problem, i.e. we miss a rule that specifies how to transform initial states when they are **not** within a composite state. The remaining three rules are responsible for mapping the *Transitions* of the input state machine.

Each ATL matched rule has a *from* section where the source pattern to be matched in the source model is specified. An optional OCL constraint may be added as the guard, and a rule is applicable only if the guard evaluates to true on the source pattern. Each rule also has a *to* section which specifies the elements to be created in the target model. The rule initializes the attributes/associations of a generated target element via the binding operator (<-). An important feature of ATL is the use of an implicit *resolution* algorithm during the target property initialization. Here we illustrate the algorithm by an example: (1) considering the binding *stateMachine <- rs1.stateMachine* in the *RS2RS* rule (line 7 of Listing 1.2), its right-hand side is evaluated to be a source element of type *HSM!StateMachine*; (2) the resolution algorithm then resolves such source element to its corresponding target element of type *FSM!StateMachine* (generated by the *SM2SM* rule); (3) the resolved result is assigned to the left-hand side of the binding. While not strictly needed for understanding this paper, we refer the reader to [18] for a full description of the ATL language.

2.3   Formally Verifying the ATL Transformation

The source and target EMF metamodels and OCL contracts combined with the developed ATL transformation form a Hoare triple which can be used to verify

```
1  context HSM!Transition inv Pre1: ...
2
3  rule RS2RS { ... }
4  rule IS2RS { ... }
5  rule T2TC { ... }
6
7  context FSM!Transition inv Post1_sub:
8  *hypothesis* var t0
9  *hypothesis* FSM!Transition.allInstances()->includes(t0)
10 *hypothesis* genBy(t0,T2TC)
11 *hypothesis* t0.source.oclIsUndefined()
12 *hypothesis* not (genBy(t0.source,RS2RS) or genBy(t0.source,IS2RS))
13 *goal* false
```

Listing 1.3. The problematic transformation scenario of the *HSM2FSM* transformation w.r.t. *Post1*

the correctness of the ATL transformation, i.e. MM, Pre, Exec ⊢ Post. The Hoare triple semantically means that, assuming the axiomatic semantics of the involved EMF metamodels (*MM*) and OCL preconditions (*Pre*), by executing the developed ATL transformation (*Exec*), the specified OCL postcondition has to hold (*Post*).

In previous work, Cheng et al. have developed the VeriATL verification system that allows such Hoare triples to be soundly verified [12]. Specifically, the VeriATL system describes in Boogie what correctness means for the ATL language in terms of structural Hoare triples. Then, VeriATL delegates the task of interacting with Z3 for proving these Hoare triples to Boogie. The axiomatic semantics of EMF metamodels and the OCL language are encoded as Boogie libraries in VeriATL. These libraries can be reused in the verifier designs of MT languages other than ATL.

In our example, VeriATL successfully reports that the OCL postcondition *Post1* is not verified by the MT in Listing 1.2. This means that the transformation does not guarantee that each *Transition* has at least one *source* in the output model. Without any capability of fault localization, the developer then needs to manually inspect the full transformation and contracts to understand that the transformation is incorrect because of the absence of an ATL rule to transform *InitialStates* that are not within a *CompositeState*.

2.4   Our Goal: Localizing the Fault

In our running example, our proposed fault localization approach presents the user with two problematic transformation scenarios. One of them is shown in Listing 1.3. The scenario consists of the input preconditions (abbreviated at line 1), a slice of the transformation (abbreviated at lines 3–5), and a sub-goal derived from the input postcondition. The sub-goal contains a list of hypotheses (lines 7–12) with a conclusion (line 13).

The scenario in Listing 1.3 contains the following information, that we believe to be valuable in identifying and fixing the fault:

– *Transformation slicing.* The only relevant rules for the fault captured by this problematic transformation scenario are *RS2RS*, *IS2RS* and *T2TC* (lines 3–5).

– *Debugging clues.* The error occurs when a transition *t0* is generated by the rule *T2TC* (lines 8–10), and when the *source* state of the transition is not generated (line 11). In addition, the absence of the *source* for *t0* is due to the fact that none of the *RS2RS* and *IS2RS* rules is invoked to generate it (line 12).

From this information, the user could find a counter-example in the source models that falsifies *Post1* (shown in the top of Fig. 2): a transition t_c between an initial state i_c (which is not within a composite state) and a composite state c_c, where c_c composites another initial state i_c'. This counter-example matches the source pattern of the *T2TC* rule (as shown in the bottom of Fig. 2). However, when the *T2TC* rule tries to initialize the *source* of the generated transition *t2* (line 23 in Listing 1.2), i_c cannot be resolved because there is no rule to match it. In this case, i_c (of type *HSM!InitialState*) is directly used to initialize the *source* of *t2* (*t2.source* is expected to be a sub-type of *FSM!AbstractState*). This causes an exception of type mismatch, thus falsifying *Post1*. The other problematic transformation scenario pinpoints the same fault, showing that *Post1* is not verified by the MT also when *t0* is generated by *T2TA*.

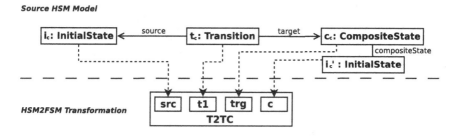

Fig. 2. Counter-example derived from Listing 1.3 that falsify *Post1*

In the next section, we describe how we automatically generate problematic transformation scenarios like the one shown in Listing 1.3.

3   Overview of Fault Localization for ATL by Natural Deduction and Program Slicing

The flowchart in Fig. 3 shows a bird's eye view of our approach to enable fault localization for VeriATL. The process takes the involved metamodels, all the OCL preconditions, the ATL transformation and one of the OCL postconditions as inputs. We require all inputs to be syntactically correct. If VeriATL successfully verifies the input ATL transformation, we directly report a confirmation message to indicate its correctness (w.r.t. the given postcondition) and the process ends. Otherwise, we generate a set of problematic transformation scenarios (as the one shown in Listing 1.3), and a proof tree to the transformation developer.

To generate problematic transformation scenarios, we first perform a systematic approach to generate sub-goals for the input OCL postcondition. Our approach is based on a set of sound natural deduction rules. The set contains 16 rules for propositional and predicate logic such as introduction/elimination rules for ∧ and ∨ [16], but also 4 rules specifically designed for ATL expressions (e.g. rewriting single-valued navigation expression).

Then, we design an automated proof strategy that applies the designed natural deduction rules on the input OCL postcondition. Executing our proof strategy generates a proof tree. The non-leaf nodes are intermediate results of deduction rule applications. The leafs in the tree are the sub-goals to prove. Each sub-goal consists of a list of hypotheses and a conclusion to be verified. The aim of our automated proof strategy is to simplify the original postcondition as much as possible to obtain a set of sub-conclusions to prove. As a by-product, we also deduce new hypotheses from the input postcondition and the transformation as debugging clues.

Next, we use the trace information in the hypotheses of each sub-goal to slice the input MT into simpler transformation contexts. We then form a new Hoare triple for each sub-goal consisting of the semantics of metamodels, input OCL preconditions, sliced transformation context, its hypotheses and its conclusion.

We send these new Hoare triples to the VeriATL verification system to check. Notice that successfully proving these new Hoare triples implies the satisfaction of the input OCL postcondition. If any of these new Hoare triples is not verified by VeriATL, the input OCL preconditions, the corresponding sliced transformation context, hypotheses and conclusion of the Hoare triple are presented to the user as a problematic transformation scenario for fault localization. The Hoare triples that were automatically proved by VeriATL are pruned away, and are not presented to the transformation developer. This deductive verification step by VeriATL makes the whole process practical, since the user is presented with a limited number of meaningful scenarios.

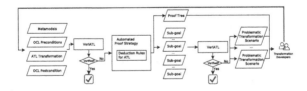

Fig. 3. Overview of providing fault localization for VeriATL

Then, the transformation developer consults the generated problematic transformation scenarios and the proof tree to debug the ATL transformation. If modifications are made on the inputs to fix the bug, the generation of sub-goals needs to start over. The whole process keeps iterating until the input ATL transformation is correct w.r.t. the input OCL postcondition.

3.1   Natural Deduction Rules for ATL

Our approach relies on 20 natural deduction rules (7 introduction rules and 13 elimination rules). The 4 elimination rules (abbreviated by X_e) that specifically involve ATL are shown in Fig. 4. The other rules are common natural deduction rules for propositional and predicate logic [16]. Regarding the notations in our natural deduction rules:

– Each rule has a list of hypotheses and a conclusion, separated by a line. We use standard notation for typing (:) and set operations.
– Some special notations in the rules are T for a type, MM_T for the target metamodel, R_n for a rule n in the input ATL transformation, $x.a$ for a navigation expression, and i for a fresh variable / model element. In addition, we introduce the following auxiliary functions: cl returns the classifier types of the given metamodel, $trace$ returns the ATL rules that generate the input type (i.e. the static trace information)[2], $genBy(i,R)$ is a predicate to indicate that a model element i is generated by the rule R, $unDef(i)$ abbreviates $i.oclIsUndefined()$, and $All(T)$ abbreviates $T.allInstances()$.

$$\frac{x.a : T \qquad T \in cl(MM_T)}{x.a \in All(T) \vee unDef(x.a)} \; \text{TP}_{e1} \qquad\qquad \frac{x.a : Seq\ T \qquad T \in cl(MM_T)}{(|x.a| > 0 \quad i \cdot (i \in x.a \Rightarrow i \in All(T) \vee unDef(i))) \vee |x.a| = 0} \; \text{TP}_{e2}$$

$$\frac{T \in cl(MM_T) \quad trace(T) = \{R_1, ..., R_n\} \quad i \in All(T)}{genBy(i, R_1) \vee ... \vee genBy(i, R_n)} \; \text{TR}_{e1} \qquad \frac{T \in cl(MM_T) \quad trace(T) = \{R_1, ..., R_n\} \quad i : T \quad unDef(i)}{\neg(genBy(i, R_1) \vee ... \vee genBy(i, R_n))} \; \text{TR}_{e2}$$

Fig. 4. Natural deduction rules that specific to ATL

Some explanation is in order for the natural deduction rules that are specific to ATL:

– First, we have two type elimination rules (TP_{e1}, TP_{e2}). TP_{e1} states that every single-valued navigation expression of the type T in the target metamodel is either a member of all generated instances of type T or undefined. TP_{e2} states that the cardinality of every multi-valued navigation expression of the type T in the target metamodel is either greater to zero (and every element i in the multi-valued navigation expression is either a member of all generated instances of type T or undefined) or equal to zero.
– Second, we have 2 elimination rules for trace (TR_{e1}, TR_{e2}). These rules state that, given that the rules $R_1,...,R_n$ in the input ATL transformation are responsible to create model elements of type T in the target metamodel, we may rightfully conclude that:
  • (TR_{e1}): every created element i of type T is generated by one of the rules $R_1,...,R_n$.

---

[2] In practice, we fill in the *trace* function by examining the output element types of each ATL rule, i.e. the *to* section of each rule.

- (TR_{e2}): every undefined element i of type T is not generated by any of the rules $R_1,...,R_n$.

Soundness of Natural Deduction Rules. The soundness of our natural deduction rules is based on the operational semantics of the ATL language. Specifically, the soundness for type elimination rules TP_{e1} and TP_{e2} is straight-forward. We prove their soundness by enumerating the possible states of initialized navigation expressions for target elements. Specifically, assuming that the state of a navigation expression $x.a$ is initialized in the form $x.a$<-exp where $x.a$ is of a non-primitive type T:

- If exp is not a collection type and cannot be resolved (i.e. exp cannot match the source pattern of any ATL rules), then $x.a$ is *undefined*[3].
- If exp is not a collection type and can be resolved, then the generated target element of the ATL rule that matches exp is assigned to $x.a$. Consequently, $x.a$ could be either a member of *All(T)* (when the resolution result is of type T) or undefined (when it is not).
- If exp is of collection type, then all of the elements in exp are resolved individually, and the resolved results are put together into a pre-allocated collection *col*, and *col* is assigned to $x.a$.

The first two cases explain the two possible states of every single-valued navigation expressions (TP_{e1}). The third case explains the two possible states of every multi-valued navigation expressions (TP_{e2}).

The soundness of trace elimination rules TR_{e1} is based on the surjectivity between each ATL rule and the type of its created target elements [9]: elements in the target metamodel exist if they have been created by an ATL rule since standard ATL transformations are always executed on an initially empty target model. When a type can be generated by executing more than one rule, then a disjunction considering all these possibilities is made for every generated elements of this type.

About the soundness of the TR_{e2} rule, we observe that if a target element of type T is undefined, then clearly it does not belong to *All(T)*. In addition, the operational semantics for the ATL language specifies that if a rule R is specified to generate elements of type T, then every target elements of type T generated by that rule belong to *All(T)* (i.e. $R \in trace(T) \Rightarrow \forall i \cdot (genBy(i, R) \Rightarrow i \in All(T)))$) [12]. Thus, TR_{e2} is sound as a logical consequence of the operational semantics for the ATL language (i.e. $R \in trace(T) \Rightarrow \forall i \cdot (i \notin All(T) \Rightarrow \neg genBy(i, R)))$).

3.2   Automated Proof Strategy

A proof strategy is a sequence of proof steps. Each step defines the consequences of applying a natural deduction rule on a proof tree. A proof tree consists of a set

---

[3] In fact, the value of exp is assigned to $x.a$ because of resolution failure. This causes a type mismatch exception and results in the value of $x.a$ becoming undefined (we consider ATL transformations in non-refinement mode where the source and target metamodels are different).

of nodes. Each node is constructed by a set of OCL expressions as hypotheses, an OCL expression as the conclusion, and another node as its parents node.

Next, we illustrate a proof strategy (Algorithm 1) that automatically applies our natural deduction rules on the input OCL postcondition. The goal is to automate the derivation of information from the postcondition as hypotheses, and simplify the postcondition as much as possible.

Algorithm 1. An automated proof strategy for VeriATL

1: Tree ← {createNode({}, Post, null)}
2: **do**
3:     leafs ← size(getLeafs(Tree))
4:     **for** each node *leaf* ∈ getLeafs(Tree) **do**
5:         Tree ← intro(leaf) ∪ Tree
6:     **end for**
7: **while** leafs ≠ size(getLeafs(Tree))
8: **do**
9:     leafs ← size(getLeafs(Tree))
10:     **for** each node *leaf* ∈ getLeafs(Tree) **do**
11:         Tree ← elimin(leaf) ∪ Tree
12:     **end for**
13: **while** leafs ≠ size(getLeafs(Tree))

Our proof strategy takes one argument which is one of the input postconditions. Then, it initializes the proof tree by constructing a new root node of the input postcondition as conclusion and no hypotheses and no parent node (line 1). Next, our proof strategy takes two sequences of proof steps. The first sequence applies the *introduction* rules on the leaf nodes of the proof tree to generate new leafs (lines 2–7). It terminates when no new leafs are yield (line 7). The second sequence of steps applies the *elimination* rules on the leaf nodes of the proof tree (lines 8–13). We only apply type elimination rules on a leaf when: (a) a free variable is in its hypotheses, and (b) a navigation expression of the free variable is referred by its hypotheses. Furthermore, to ensure termination, we enforce that if applying a rule on a node does not yield new descendants (i.e. whose hypotheses or conclusion are different from their parent), then we do not attach new nodes to the proof tree.

3.3   Transformation Slicing

Executing our proof strategy generates a proof tree. The leafs in the tree are the sub-goals to prove by VeriATL. Next, we use the rules referred by the *genBy* predicates in the hypotheses of each sub-goal to slice the input MT into a simpler transformation context. We then form a new Hoare triple for each sub-goal consisting of the axiomatic semantics of metamodels, input OCL preconditions, sliced transformation context ($Exec_{sliced}$), its hypotheses and its conclusion, i.e. MM, Pre, $Exec_{sliced}$, Hypotheses ⊢ Conclusion.

If any of these new Hoare triples is not verified by VeriATL, the input OCL preconditions, the corresponding sliced transformation context, hypotheses and conclusion of the Hoare triple are constructed as a problematic transformation scenario to report back to the user for fault localization (as shown in Listing 1.3).

Our transformation slicing is based on the independence among ATL rules [28]: each ATL rule is exclusively responsible for the generation of its output elements. Hence, when a sub-goal specifies a condition that a set of target elements should satisfy, the rules that do not generate these elements have no effects on the sub-goal. These rules can hence be safely sliced away.

4   Evaluation

In this section, we evaluate the practical feasibility and performance of our fault localization approach for the ATL language. The section concludes with a discussion of the obtained results and lessons learnt.

4.1   Research Questions

We formulate two research questions to evaluate our fault localization approach:

(RQ1) Can our approach **correctly** pinpoint the faults in the given MT?
(RQ2) Can our approach **efficiently** pinpoint the faults in the given MT?

4.2   Evaluation Setup

Our evaluation uses the VeriATL verification system [12], which is based on the Boogie verifier (version 2.2) and Z3 (version 4.3). The evaluation is performed on an Intel 3 GHz machine with 8 GB of memory running the Windows operating system. VeriATL encodes the axiomatic semantics of the ATL language (version 3.7). The automated proof strategy and its corresponding natural deduction rules are currently implemented in Java.

To answer our research questions, we use the HSM2FSM transformation as our case study, and apply mutation analysis [17] to systematically inject faults. In particular, we specify 14 preconditions and 5 postconditions on the original HSM transformation from [9]. Then, we inject faults by applying a list of mutation operators defined in [8] on the transformation. We apply mutations only to the transformation because we focus on contract-based development, where the contract guides the development of the transformation. Our mutants are proved against the specified postconditions, and we apply our fault localization approach in case of unverified postconditions. We kindly refer to our online repository for the complete artifacts used in our evaluation [1].

4.3 Evaluation Results

Table 1 summarizes the evaluation results for our fault localization approach on the chosen case study. The first column lists the identity of the mutants[4]. The second and third columns record the unverified OCL postconditions and their corresponding verification time. The fourth, fifth, sixth and seventh columns record information of verifying sub-goals, i.e. the number of unverified sub-goals / total number of sub-goals (4th), average verification time of sub-goals (5th), the maximum verification time among sub-goals (6th), total verification of sub-goals (7th) respectively. The last column records whether the faulty lines (L_{faulty}, i.e. the lines that the mutation operators operated on) are presented in the problematic transformation scenarios (PTS) of unverified sub-goals.

Table 1. Evaluation metrics for the *HSM2FSM* case study

	Unveri. Post.		Sub-goals				$L_{faulty} \in PTS$
	ID	Veri. Time(ms)	Unveri. / Total	Avg. Time (ms)	Max Time (ms)	Total Time (ms)	
MT2	#5	3116	3 / 4	1616	1644	6464	True
DB1	#5	2934	1 / 1	1546	1546	1546	-
MB6	#4	3239	1 / 12	1764	2550	21168	True
AF2	#4	3409	2 / 12	1793	2552	21516	True
MF6	#2	3779	0 / 6	1777	2093	10662	N/A
	#4	3790	1 / 12	1774	2549	21288	True
DR1	#1	2161	3 / 6	1547	1589	9282	-
	#2	2230	3 / 6	1642	1780	9852	-
AR	#1	3890	1 / 8	1612	1812	12896	True
	#3	4057	6 / 16	1769	1920	28304	True

First, we confirm that there is no inconclusive verification results of the generated sub-goals, i.e. if VeriATL reports that the verification result of a sub-goal is unverified, then it presents a fault in the transformation. Our confirmation is based on the manual inspection of each unverified sub-goal to see whether there is a counter-example to falsify the sub-goal. This supports the correctness of our fault localization approach. We find that the deduced hypotheses of the sub-goals are useful for the elaboration of a counter-example (e.g. when they imply that the fault is caused by missing code as the case in Listing 1.3).

---

[4] The naming convention for mutants are mutation operator Add(A) / Del(D) / Modify(M), followed by the mutation operand Rule(R) / Filter(F) / TargetElement(T) / Binding(B), followed by the position of the operand in the original transformation setting. For example, *MB1* stands for the mutant which modifies the binding in the first rule.

Second, as we inject faults by mutation, identifying whether the faulty line is presented in the problematic transformation scenarios of unverified sub-goals is also a strong indication of the correctness of our approach. Shown by the last column, all cases satisfies the faulty lines inclusion criteria. 3 out 10 cases are special cases (dashed cells) where the faulty lines are deleted by the mutation operator (thus there are no faulty lines). In the case of *MF6#2*, there are no problematic transformation scenarios generated since all the sub-goals are verified. By inspection, we report that our approach improves the completeness of VeriATL. That is the postcondition (#2) is correct under *MF6* but unable to be verified by VeriATL, whereas all its generated sub-goals are verified.

Third, shown by the fourth column, in 5 out of 10 cases, the developer is presented with at most one problematic transformation scenario to pinpoint the fault. This positively supports the efficiency of our approach. The other 5 cases produce more sub-goals to examine. However, we find that in these cases each unverified sub-goal gives an unique phenomenon of the fault, which we believe is valuable to fix the bug. We also report that in rare cases more than one sub-goal could point to the same phenomenon of the fault. This is because the hypotheses of these sub-goals contain a semantically equivalent set of *genBy* predicates. Although they are easy to identify, we would like to investigate how to systematically filter these cases out in the future.

Fourth, from the third and fifth columns, we can see that each of the sub-goals is faster to verify than its corresponding postcondition by a factor of about 2. This is because we sent a simpler task than the input postcondition to verify, e.g. because of our transformation slicing, the Hoare triple for each sub-goal encodes a simpler interaction of transformation rules compared to the Hoare triple for its corresponding postcondition. From the third and sixth columns, we can further report that all sub-goals are verified in less time than their corresponding postcondition.

4.4   Limitations

Language Coverage. In this work we consider a core subset of the ATL and OCL languages: (a) We consider the declarative aspect of ATL (matched rules) in non-refining mode, many-to-one mappings of (possibly abstract) classifiers with the default resolution algorithm of ATL. Non-recursive ATL helpers can be easily supported by inlining, and many-to-many mappings can be supported by extending our Boogie code generator. We also plan to investigate other features of ATL (e.g. lazy rules) to make our approach more general. (b) We support first-order OCL contracts and we plan to study more complex contracts in future work.

Completeness of Proof Strategy. We define the completeness of a proof strategy meaning that every elements of target types referred by each sub-goal and every rule that may generate them are correctly identified after applying the proof strategy. If not detected, an incomplete proof strategy could cause our transformation slicing to erroneously slice away the rules that the sub-goal might depend on. By manual inspection, we confirm the completeness of our proof strategy in our case study. However, our proof strategy is in generally incomplete because: (a) we might lack deduction rules to continue the derivation of the proof tree; (b) our current proof strategy lacks of a backtracking mechanism when it chooses an unsuitable deduction rule to apply. Our current solution is detecting incomplete cases and reporting them to the user. In practice we check whether every elements of target types referred by each sub-goal are accompanied by a *genBy* predicate (this indicates full derivation). In future, we plan to improve the completeness of our approach by adding other natural deduction rules for ATL and smarter automated proof strategies.

Completeness of Verification. Although we confirmed that there are no inconclusive sub-goals in our evaluation, our approach could report inconclusive sub-goals in general due to the underlying SMT solver. We hope the simplicity offered by the sub-goals would facilitate the user in making the distinction between incorrect and inconclusive sub-goals. In addition, if an input postcondition is inconclusive, our approach can help users to eliminate verified sub-goals to find the source of its inconclusiveness.

Threats to Validity of Evaluation. We take a popular assumption in the fault localization community that multiple faults perform independently [31]. Thus, such assumption allows us to evaluate our fault localization approach in a one-postcondition-at-a-time manner. However, we cannot guarantee that this is the case for realistic and industrial MTs. We think classifying contracts into related groups could improve these situations.

Scalability. The main scalability issue of our approach is that a complex OCL postcondition (e.g. an OCL expression with deeply nested quantifiers) can potentially generate a big number of sub-goals and corresponding problematic transformation scenarios. Verifying and displaying all of them becomes impractical for transformation developers. Since sub-goals are meant to be manually examined by the user, a reasonable solution is allowing the user to specify a bound for the maximum number of unverified cases to generate. To improve scalability we are also investigating the possibility of verifying intermediate nodes in the proof tree, and stop applying deduction rules if they are verified.

Usability. Currently, our approach relies on the experience of transformation developer to interpret the deduced debugging clues. We think combining debugging clues with model finders would further help in debugging MT, e.g. by automatically generating the counter-examples [14].

5 Related Work

There is a large body of work on the topic of ensuring MT correctness [2]. To our knowledge our proposal is the first applying natural deduction with program slicing to increase the precision of fault localization in MT.

Büttner et al. use Z3 to verify a declarative subset of the ATL and OCL contracts [9]. Their result is novel for providing minimal axioms that can verify the given OCL contracts. To understand the root of the unverified contracts, they demonstrate the UML2Alloy tool that draws on the Alloy model finder to generate counter examples [10]. However, their tool does not guarantee that the newly generated counter example gives additional information than the previous ones. Oakes et al. statically verify ATL MTs by symbolic execution using DSLTrans [21]. This approach enumerates all the possible states of the ATL transformation. If a rule is the root of a fault, all the states that involve the rule are reported.

Sánchez Cuadrado et al. present a static approach to uncover various typing errors in ATL MTs [14], and use the USE constraint solver to compute an input model as a witness for each error. Compared to their work, we focus on contract errors, and provide the user with sliced MTs and modularized contracts to debug the incorrect MTs.

Researchers have proposed several techniques that can partially or fully automate the localization of faults in software [24,31]. Program slicing refers to detect a set of program statements which could affect the values of interest [27,30], which is used for fault localization of general programming languages. Few works have adapted this idea to localize faults in MTs. Aranega et al. define a framework to record the runtime traces between rules and the target elements these rules generated [4]. When a target element is generated with an unexpected value, the transformation slices generated from the runtime traces are used for fault localization. While Aranega et al. focus on dynamic slicing, our work focuses on static slicing which does not require test suites to exercise the transformation.

The most similar approach to ours is the work of Burgueño et al. on syntactically calculating the intersection constructs used by the rules and contracts [8]. W.r.t. their approach we aim at improving the localization precision by considering also semantic relations between rules and contracts. This allows us to produce smaller slices by semantically eliminating unrelated rules from each scenario. Moreover, we provide debugging clues to help the user better understand why the sliced transformation causing the fault. However, their work considers a larger set of ATL. We believe that the two approaches complement each other and integrating them is useful and necessary.

We implement our approach in Java. However, we believe that integrating our approach to interactive theorem provers/framework such as Coq [7] and Rodin [3] could be beneficial (e.g. drawing on recursive inductive reasoning). One of the easiest ways is through the Why3 language [15], which targets multiple theorem provers as its back-ends.

6   Conclusion and Future Work

In summary, in this work we confronted the fault localization problem for deductive verification of MT. We developed an automated proof strategy to apply a set of designed natural deduction rules on the input OCL postcondition to generate sub-goals. Each unverified sub-goal yields a sliced transformation context and debugging clues to help the transformation developer pinpoint the fault in the input MT. Our evaluation with mutation analysis positively supports the correctness and efficiency of our fault localization approach. The result showed that: (a) faulty constructs are presented in the sliced transformation, (b) deduced clues assist developers in various debugging tasks (e.g. generate counter-example), (c) the number of sub-goals that need to be examined to pinpoint a fault are usually small.

Our future work includes facing the limitations identified during the evaluation (Sect. 4.4). We also plan to investigate how our decomposition can help us in reusing proof efforts. Specifically, due to requirements evolution, the MT and contracts are under unpredictable changes during the development. These changes can invalidate all of the previous proof efforts and cause long proofs to be recomputed. We think that our decomposition of sub-goals would increase the chances of reusing verification results, i.e. sub-goals that are not affected by the changes.

References

1. A deductive approach for fault localization in ATL model transformations (2016). https://goo.gl/xssbpn
2. Ab. Rahim, L., Whittle, J.: A survey of approaches for verifying model transformations. Softw. Syst. Model. **14**(2), 1003–1028 (2015)
3. Abrial, J.R., Butler, M., Hallerstede, S., Hoang, T.S., Mehta, F., Voisin, L.: Rodin: An open toolset for modelling and reasoning in Event-B. Int. J. Softw. Tools Technol. Transf. **12**(6), 447–466 (2010)
4. Aranega, V., Mottu, J., Etien, A., Dekeyser, J.: Traceability mechanism for error localization in model transformation. In: 4th International Conference on Software and Data Technologies, Sofia, Bulgaria, pp. 66–73 (2009)
5. Barnett, M., Chang, B.-Y.E., DeLine, R., Jacobs, B., Leino, K.R.M.: Boogie: A modular reusable verifier for object-oriented programs. In: Boer, F.S., Bonsangue, M.M., Graf, S., Roever, W.-P. (eds.) FMCO 2005. LNCS, vol. 4111, pp. 364–387. Springer, Heidelberg (2006). doi:10.1007/11804192_17
6. Berry, G.: Synchronous design and verification of critical embedded systems using SCADE and esterel. In: Leue, S., Merino, P. (eds.) FMICS 2007. LNCS, vol. 4916, pp. 2–2. Springer, Heidelberg (2008). doi:10.1007/978-3-540-79707-4_2
7. Bertot, Y., Castéran, P.: Interactive Theorem Proving and Program Development: Coq'Art The Calculus of Inductive Constructions, 1st edn. Springer, Heidelberg (2010)
8. Burgueño, L., Troya, J., Wimmer, M., Vallecillo, A.: Static fault localization in model transformations. IEEE Trans. Softw. Eng. **41**(5), 490–506 (2015)
9. Büttner, F., Egea, M., Cabot, J.: On verifying ATL transformations using 'off-the-shelf' SMT solvers. In: France, R.B., Kazmeier, J., Breu, R., Atkinson, C. (eds.) MODELS 2012. LNCS, vol. 7590, pp. 432–448. Springer, Heidelberg (2012). doi:10.1007/978-3-642-33666-9_28
10. Büttner, F., Egea, M., Cabot, J., Gogolla, M.: Verification of ATL transformations using transformation models and model finders. In: Aoki, T., Taguchi, K. (eds.) ICFEM 2012. LNCS, vol. 7635, pp. 198–213. Springer, Heidelberg (2012). doi:10.1007/978-3-642-34281-3_16

11. Calegari, D., Luna, C., Szasz, N., Tasistro, Á.: A type-theoretic framework for certified model transformations. In: Davies, J., Silva, L., Simao, A. (eds.) SBMF 2010. LNCS, vol. 6527, pp. 112–127. Springer, Heidelberg (2011). doi:10.1007/978-3-642-19829-8_8

12. Cheng, Z., Monahan, R., Power, J.F.: A sound execution semantics for ATL via translation validation. In: Kolovos, D., Wimmer, M. (eds.) ICMT 2015. LNCS, vol. 9152, pp. 133–148. Springer, Cham (2015). doi:10.1007/978-3-319-21155-8_11

13. Combemale, B., Crégut, X., Garoche, P., Thirioux, X.: Essay on semantics definition in MDE - an instrumented approach for model verification. J. Softw. 4(9), 943–958 (2009)

14. Cuadrado, J.S., Guerra, E., de Lara, J.: Uncovering errors in ATL model transformations using static analysis and constraint solving. In: 25th IEEE International Symposium on Software Reliability Engineering, pp. 34–44. IEEE, Naples (2014)

15. Filliâtre, J.-C., Paskevich, A.: Why3 — Where programs meet provers. In: Felleisen, M., Gardner, P. (eds.) ESOP 2013. LNCS, vol. 7792, pp. 125–128. Springer, Heidelberg (2013). doi:10.1007/978-3-642-37036-6_8

16. Huth, M., Ryan, M.: Logic in Computer Science Modelling and Reasoning About Systems. Cambridge University Press, Cambridge (2004)

17. Jia, Y., Harman, M.: An analysis and survey of the development of mutation testing. IEEE Trans. Softw. Eng. 37(5), 649–678 (2011)

18. Jouault, F., Allilaire, F., Bézivin, J., Kurtev, I.: ATL: A model transformation tool. Sci. Comput. Program. 72(1–2), 31–39 (2008)

19. Lano, K., Clark, T., Kolahdouz-Rahimi, S.: A framework for model transformation verification. Formal Aspects Comput. 27(1), 193–235 (2014)

20. Moura, L., Bjørner, N.: Z3: An efficient SMT solver. In: Ramakrishnan, C.R., Rehof, J. (eds.) TACAS 2008. LNCS, vol. 4963, pp. 337–340. Springer, Heidelberg (2008). doi:10.1007/978-3-540-78800-3_24

21. Oakes, B.J., Troya, J., Lúcio, L., Wimmer, M.: Fully verifying transformation contracts for declarative ATL. In: 18th ACM/IEEE International Conference on Model Driven Engineering Languages and Systems, pp. 256–265. IEEE, Ottawa (2015)

22. Object Management Group: The Object Constraint Language Specification (ver. 2.0) (2006). http://www.omg.org/spec/OCL/2.0/

23. Poernomo, I., Terrell, J.: Correct-by-construction model transformations from partially ordered specifications in Coq. In: Dong, J.S., Zhu, H. (eds.) ICFEM 2010. LNCS, vol. 6447, pp. 56–73. Springer, Heidelberg (2010). doi:10.1007/978-3-642-16901-4_6

24. Roychoudhury, A., Chandra, S.: Formula-based software debugging. Commun. ACM 59(7), 68–77 (2016)

25. Selim, G.M.K., Wang, S., Cordy, J.R., Dingel, J.: Model transformations for migrating legacy models: an industrial case study. In: Vallecillo, A., Tolvanen, J.-P., Kindler, E., Störrle, H., Kolovos, D. (eds.) ECMFA 2012. LNCS, vol. 7349, pp. 90–101. Springer, Heidelberg (2012). doi:10.1007/978-3-642-31491-9_9

26. Steinberg, D., Budinsky, F., Merks, E., Paternostro, M.: EMF: Eclipse Modeling Framework, 2nd edn. Pearson Education, London (2008)

27. Tip, F.: A survey of program slicing techniques. Technical report, Centrum Wiskunde & Informatica (1994)

28. Tisi, M., Martínez, S., Choura, H.: Parallel execution of ATL transformation rules. In: Moreira, A., Schätz, B., Gray, J., Vallecillo, A., Clarke, P. (eds.) MODELS 2013. LNCS, vol. 8107, pp. 656–672. Springer, Heidelberg (2013). doi:10.1007/978-3-642-41533-3_40

29. Wagelaar, D.: Using ATL/EMFTVM for import/export of medical data. In: 2nd Software Development Automation Conference, Amsterdam, Netherlands (2014)
30. Weiser, M.: Program slicing. In: 5th International Conference on Software Engineering, pp. 439–449. IEEE, New Jersey (1981)
31. Wong, W.E., Gao, R., Li, Y., Abreu, R., Wotawa, F.: A survey on software fault localization. IEEE Trans. Softw. Eng. Pre-Print (99), 1–41 (2016)

Configuration and Synthesis

OpenSAW: Open Security Analysis Workbench

Noomene Ben Henda[1], Björn Johansson[1], Patrik Lantz[1], Karl Norrman[1(✉)],
Pasi Saarinen[1], and Oskar Segersvärd[2]

[1] Ericsson Research Security, Stockholm, Sweden
{noamen.ben.henda,bjorn.a.johansson,patrik.lantz,
karl.norrman,pasi.saarinen}@ericsson.com
[2] School of CSC, Royal Institute of Technology (KTH), Stockholm, Sweden
oskarseg@kth.se

Abstract. Software is today often composed of many sourced components, which potentially contain security vulnerabilities, and therefore require testing before being integrated. Tools for automated test case generation, for example, based on white-box fuzzing, are beneficial for this testing task. Such tools generally explore limitations of the specific underlying techniques for solving problems related to, for example, constraint solving, symbolic execution, search heuristics and execution trace extraction. In this article we describe the design of OPENSAW, a more flexible general-purpose white-box fuzzing framework intended to encourage research on new techniques identifying security problems. In addition, we have formalized two unaddressed technical aspects and devised new algorithms for these. The first relates to generalizing and combining different program exploration strategies, and the second relates to prioritizing execution traces. We have evaluated OPENSAW using both in-house and external programs and identified several bugs.

1 Introduction

Background. Dynamic test generation is a testing technique where the test inputs are automatically generated while running the System Under Test (SUT) in a continuous loop. In each iteration, the new test input is generated based on information collected during the execution of the SUT on previously generated input. When the SUT is an executable binary program, that for example reads an input file, the technique consists in performing the following procedure. First, the program is executed on an initial file obtaining a trace of executed instructions; second, the trace is used to generate a new input file; and finally, the previous two steps are iteratively applied using the new file as input. Such a procedure can continue running until a termination criterion is reached, for example a timeout or a user interruption. The process of input generation usually relies on symbolic execution and constraint solving, which we briefly explain as follows. A program trace consists of instructions executed by the processor. Among these instructions are conditional ones such as "jump if equal". Conditional instructions have two possible outcomes or branches. For each conditional instruction that occurs in a trace, one of the branches must have been taken. Given a trace

© Springer-Verlag GmbH Germany 2017
M. Huisman and J. Rubin (Eds.): FASE 2017, LNCS 10202, pp. 321–337, 2017.
DOI: 10.1007/978-3-662-54494-5_18

and a conditional instruction, we are interested in generating a new input that causes the program to take the other untaken branch of the instruction. For that, symbolic execution help us generate the constraint on the input that could potentially achieve this. Symbolic execution maps the input bytes to symbolic variables and then emulates the execution of the trace instruction while tracking these variables. During the simulation, the symbolic variables are assigned expressions reflecting the effect of the instructions. When a conditional instruction is reached, a constraint is generated by substituting, in the condition, the variables in scope by their corresponding expressions. Within a trace, the conjunction of all the branch instruction constraints defines what often is referred to as the *path condition*. For our goal, we only need to stop at the branch instruction of interest The constraint is then fed to a constraint solver, which delivers the desired input.

In academia the technique is sometimes referred to as white-box fuzzing [12]. Compared to black-box fuzzing, used by, for example, AFL [23] and Sulley [22] where the program input is randomly generated, the technique is guaranteed to achieve better code coverage and thus is more likely to find bugs. Think of a program that first tests if the input is equal to a certain value and just exits otherwise. With black-box fuzzing it is more likely that we never pass the test but with this technique we will be able to generate an input that passes the test after the first iteration. The drawback is that white-box fuzzing is slower. Nevertheless the technique will always benefit from the continuous increase in efficiency and speed of SAT solving [2] which is the underlying key procedure in constraint solving and symbolic execution. Currently, there are several academic [5,8] and industrial [11] frameworks implementing the technique and efficiently used to test industrial applications. In particular, for security testing the technique is used to detect vulnerabilities by generating input that can cause the program to crash, or that can allow for hijacking the execution, etc [7]. Other use-cases involve back-door detection and malware analysis for detecting unwanted functionality and behavior in binaries [13].

One of the challenges that we identified in this approach is the following. Given an execution trace, how to best select the branch instruction, i.e., the conditional instruction for which to trigger the other branch. The problem is that there is no well-defined generic technique for such selection strategies. Existing frameworks differ greatly in their implementations. A systematic approach that selects each branch in each encountered trace would work for small programs with small input domain. In such cases the technique could potentially cover all possible execution paths in a reasonable time. For real size applications like compilers, or document processors such an approach is inefficient. One would think of a strategy that spreads the search across the execution path and avoid exploring already covered portions of code. This would require some sort of code book-keeping. In some other cases one would possibly prefer a more focused selection strategy (in a Depth-first search manner) for traces containing portions of code for example from newly added or upgraded libraries.

One other challenge is the following. In parallel settings where several execution traces can be obtained simultaneously, how to best select the trace to consider first. One good measure for selection relies on how many new blocks are visited by the trace. In other terms, one can measure the amount of new program code in the trace compared to the previous traces processed earlier and use that as a ranking measure. There is no clear method on how to effectively implement such method. Obviously, one wants to avoid comparing each new trace with each of the old traces as this is extremely inefficient.

Related Work. In [16] a technique is described for keeping track of execution traces. The technique is based on recording an execution history for each trace. An execution history records all executed instructions and their occurrences. This is a standard data structure used for program slicing techniques. The choice of this structure is for handling symbolic execution rather than for branch (or path) selection strategy. For branch selection, [16] relies on a critical path oriented strategy which is mainly based on choosing instructions that follow the input data (tainted) propagation.

In [12] a technique called Generational search is proposed for branch selection. The technique is based on classifying the generated program inputs according to their generation level. The initial input has level 0. The inputs generated during the ith iteration of the framework have level $i + 1$. Given an execution trace obtained by running the program on an i level input, the branch conditions that are selected are the ones that appear in i^{th} position and upwards in the trace. MergePoint [3] is a system which utilizes this strategy by initiating the symbolic execution using a concrete input seed and explore paths using generational search. It adds an additional step in the symbolic execution denoted as path merging in order to reduce the number of explored paths.

Haller et al. introduce yet another search heuristic, denoted as Value Coverage Search (VCS) [13,14]. This strategy identifies potentially vulnerable code regions using static analysis, and then steer the symbolic execution along branches that are probable to lead to those regions. Code regions are deemed potentially vulnerable if they change pointer values. The authors argue that their strategy is superior to other traditional strategies, such as Depth-first search which can also be infeasible to use when the symbolic input size increases. In [14], the strategy is based on weights from a learning phase which are used to steer its symbolic execution toward new and interesting pointer dereferences. During the learning phase each branch is assigned a weight approximating the probability that the path following the direction contains new pointer dereferences.

In Driller [21], a guided fuzzer is described for vulnerability detection. Whenever the fuzzer is stuck and is unable to find new paths through a program, a concolic execution engine is invoked. The engine uses the traces from the fuzzing to identify new input that diverge into new code. When encountering conditional branches, the tool checks if negating the condition would result in execution of undiscovered code. A similar approach is also used in [10], named directed search. There is no mentioning of how to select branch instructions given a trace containing several instructions.

The technique closest to ours is described in [6] where a server is used in order to decide which branch instruction to select. The server uses a heuristic to pick the best instruction. One of the heuristic is based on picking the instruction that were executed the fewest number of times. It is also mentioned that the server can be configured for different heuristics. However there is no description on how this is implemented. A project which both builds and refines upon [6], is the symbolic execution tool KLEE [5]. When encountering branch conditions, KLEE forks a process for each possible path. Each process executes a single instruction within its context. For the case where there are multiple concurrent processes at the same instruction step, a process scheduling algorithm is used to decide which one to execute next.

S2E [8], a platform for selective symbolic execution, includes basic selection strategy such as random, Depth- and Breadth-first strategies and mentions that there is support for other strategies. However, these additional ones are not described. Other projects which support Depth- and/or Breadth-first strategies include [15, 19]. In [7, 18, 20] the focus is on performance of symbolic execution and applications for discovering vulnerabilities rather than selection strategies.

Compared to the other methods, ours is agnostic to the other steps of the testing framework, i.e., how the new inputs are generated or how the program is run. When it comes to trace prioritization, most of the related work does not address the issue, with some exceptions. In [6, 12], a code-coverage-block method is used for ranking the traces. In particular, in [12], this measure is used for giving scores to the generated program inputs. The rank of a trace (or the corresponding input) is based on the number of unexplored code blocks that appear in the trace compared to all other encountered traces. In [5] the process scheduling depends on interleaving two strategies, randomly selecting paths at branch conditions and selecting processes which are most likely to reach new code. The latter apply a combination of the minimum distance to uncovered instructions, and whether the process has recently discovered new code.

Contribution. We present OPENSAW, an open, flexible and scalable framework for dynamic test generation. The framework leverages already available tools like constraint solvers and trace extractors, and implements two new methods to solve the issue of branch selection and trace prioritization. More precisely, the framework provides a method that allows customization of the strategies in a flexible manner. The method keeps track of the generated execution traces by storing them in a special directed graph structure, *the trace graph*. In this graph, each node represents a portion of the program code ending in a (possibly conditional) jump instruction. Each edge represents a trace and the relative position of the target node in the trace. We generalize branch selection strategies to functions over trace graphs. Furthermore, the framework delivers a method for ranking of the traces, that is fully integrated with the trace graph updating procedure. The resulting rank value can be used to prioritize the execution traces for parallelization purposes.

Outline. The next section gives an overview of the framework. Section 3 describes in details the trace graph concept. Section 4 lists some of the features of OPEN-SAW. Section 5 presents some of our experiments with the framework. Finally, Sect. 6 concludes the article with some future work.

2   Overview of the Framework

2.1   Preliminaries

For a sequence s, we use $|s|$ to denote its length, and $s[i]$ to denote its ith element for all $1 \leq i \leq |s|$. We let $s[i]$ be $\bot$ for all $i > |s|$. Given two sequences s, s', we use $s \sqsubseteq s'$ to denote that s is a subsequence of s'. A program input is a sequence of bytes and a trace is a sequence of binary (or assembly) instructions corresponding to a run of the program on a particular input. We will be only working with finite inputs, and we assume that programs are deterministic and that they do always terminate. We let i and t range respectively over program inputs and traces. Given a program p, for an input i, we denote by $tr(p, i)$ the trace obtained by running p on i. We use $\mathcal{I}$ and $\mathcal{T}$ to denote respectively the set of all possible inputs and traces. For a trace t, we denote by $in(p, t) := \{i \in \mathcal{I} | tr(p, i) = t\}$, i.e. the set of all inputs on which p generates t. Sometimes we omit p, and write $tr(i)$ or $in(t)$ whenever the program is clear from the context.

In general a framework such as ours generates new inputs based on the conditional branch instructions in the program traces. For that, we adopt a less granular definition for traces and let a trace be a sequence of *instruction blocks* or *blocks* for short. Given a trace t, a block is a maximum length subsequence of consecutive instructions containing no branch instructions except maybe in the last position. Observe that this definition is similar to basic blocks in the context of Control Flow Graphs (CFG). The main difference being that blocks may have multiple entry points. As we are dealing with individual traces, it is not possible to know in advance how many entry points a block has. Following our definition, in a trace t, any conditional branch instruction will be at the end of a unique block from t. We will use $\mathcal{B}$ to denote the set of all possible blocks.

Let's fix a program p. Given an input i, the corresponding trace $t = tr(i)$ and a block of interest $b \in t$, the framework performs a series of operations in order to generate a new input that can potentially trigger the other branch of b. More precisely, the framework first performs symbolic execution on t up-to the instruction of interest in order to generate a *path condition*. A path condition is a conjunction of formulas on symbols corresponding to the bytes of $in(t)$. Each such formula represents the condition on the taken branch of one of the encountered conditional instructions in t up-to and including the one in b. Second, the framework generates a new path condition by negating the formula corresponding to the branch of interest. Afterwards, the framework queries a constraint solver for a possible solution. In case a solution is found, the framework uses it in order to finally construct a new input based on the previous input i. We will hide and collapse all theses steps into a single function $gen(t, b)$ whose co-domain is in $\mathcal{I} \cup \{\bot\}$.

2.2   Architecture

During the development of OPENSAW, the main focus was on flexibility and performance. For flexibility, the goal is that the framework should be as agnostic as possible to the underlying used tools such as for symbolic execution, constraint solving. For performance, the aim is that it should be able to distribute and parallelize the tasks so that it benefits as much as possible from the available computational resources. As a result, the framework architecture is as illustrated in Fig. 1 and its main procedure in Algorithm 1.

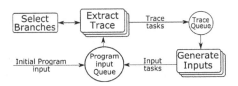

Fig. 1. OPENSAW's architecture

The framework relies on two procedures that can be run in parallel, namely the EXTRACTTRACE and the GENERATEINPUTS procedures defined in Algorithm 1. The modules feed each other with tasks through two different priority queues: an input queue and a *trace task* queue denoted respectively by $inpQ$ and trQ in Algorithm 1 (1.1). A trace task is a tuple (t, b) where t is a trace and b is a sequence of blocks from t.

The EXTRACTTRACE procedure (1.5–13) reads program inputs from an input queue. For each read input i, the procedure first generates the corresponding trace $tr(i)$. From the resulting trace, it then computes a priority $r \in \mathbb{N}$ and selects a number of blocks arranged in a sequence b. Finally, the resulting trace task (t, b) is pushed onto an output queue with priority r. The GENERATEINPUTS procedure (1.14–25) reads trace task from an input queue. For each obtained task of the form (t, b), the procedures loops through each element in the sequence $b[j]$ for $1 \leq j \leq |b|$ and attempts to generate an input i triggering the untaken branch, i.e., $i' = gen(t, b[j])$. The set iDB is used to keep track of produced inputs that are discarded whenever they are generated again. In case the input i' is both valid and new, it is pushed onto an output queue. For now, we assume that the returned values of the GETPRIORITY (1.9) and SELECTBRANCHES (1.10) functions are computed by an oracle.

For each task that is read, whether it is an input or a trace task, the processing steps can be in fact delegated to worker subprocesses. and hence the nesting representation in Fig. 1. Observe, that the priorities can be rendered useless in case there is no queue buildup. Nevertheless, one can think of a scheme where the priority computation is activated or deactivated depending on the queue size. This and similar implementation details are further discussed in Sect. 4.

Algorithm 1. OPENSAW's main algorithm

Input: A program p and an initial input i_0
1: $(iDB, inpQ, trQ) \leftarrow (\emptyset, \emptyset, \emptyset)$
2: push i_0 in $inpQ$
3: EXTRACTTRACE(p, $inpQ$, trQ)   ▷ Lines 3–4 are executed in parallel
4: GENERATEINPUTS(iDB, trQ, $inpQ$)
5: **procedure** EXTRACTTRACE(p: program, inQ, $outQ$: queue)
6:      **while** $true$ **do**
7:          pop inQ in i ▷ blocking
8:          $t \leftarrow tr(p, i)$
9:          $r \leftarrow$ GETPRIORITY(t)
10:         $b \leftarrow$ SELECTBRANCHES(t)
11:         push (t, b) in $outQ$ with priority r
12:     **end while**
13: **end procedure**
14: **procedure** GENERATEINPUTS(iDB: set, inQ, $outQ$: queue)
15:     **while** $true$ **do**
16:         pop inQ in (t, b) ▷ blocking
17:         **for** $j = 1 \ldots |b|$ **do**
18:             $i \leftarrow gen(t, b[j])$
19:             **if** $i \neq \bot \wedge i \notin iDB$ **then**
20:                 add i to iDB
21:                 push i in $outQ$
22:             **end if**
23:         **end for**
24:     **end while**
25: **end procedure**

---

3   Trace Graphs

3.1   Selection Strategies

One of the central features in such frameworks is the branch selection operation performed, in our case, by the SELECTBRANCHES function in Algorithm 1. The selection can be done randomly, or by a heuristic [6,12,14], or based on a graph search algorithm such as Breadth-first or Depth-first search. Furthermore, some kind of book-keeping must be performed, for example, in order to avoid repeatedly processing the branch instructions from the same trace. Overall, a strategy is needed. Obviously, the choice of the strategy has a direct impact on the performance of the framework.

In order to define strategies in general, two aspects are taken into consideration. On the one hand, a strategy itself should be easy to change and hence our choice to refactor it out and delegate to an abstract function with a specific interface (SELECTBRANCHES) unlike for example how it is handled in the SAGE framework. On the other hand, our framework must provide support for a class of strategies as large as possible or at least that subsumes all the ones used in similar frameworks including for example the generational search strategy used in SAGE. Observe that it is difficult to know what the most general and common prerequisites of a selection strategy are. Nevertheless, the current *history* during a run of the framework provides a good basis for a generic selection strategy.

3.2   Run Data

By history, we mean all the data generated during the run such as the program inputs, the computed priorities, the selected branches but most importantly the program traces. In fact, even for small applications, the number and length of the encountered traces may quickly grow into an unmanageable number. Therefore a new structure is needed to efficiently represent the set of generated traces.

Definition 1. *A trace graph G is a tuple (N, E, wit) where $N \subseteq \mathcal{B}$ is a set of nodes, $E \subseteq N \times N$ is a set of edges, and $wit : E \to \mathcal{T} \times \mathbb{N}$ is a function called the* witness *function mapping to each edge a pair consisting of a trace and a block index. In addition, the witness function wit is such that for each $e = (b, b') \in E$, $t \in \mathcal{T}$ and $j \in \mathbb{N}$ where $wit(e) = (t, j)$, it holds that $t[j-1] = b$ and $t[j] = b'$.*

Intuitively, a trace graph can be used to represent a set of execution traces obtained so far during a run, like a snapshot of the run. In this structure, each block is uniquely represented by a node. An edge is used as a *witness* (wit) of the trace and corresponding position where the block, represented by the edge target node, has occurred. More precisely, given a set of traces $T \subseteq \mathcal{T}$, a good representative trace graph must account for at least each block in T. This can be fulfilled by choosing the set of nodes to include the set of all blocks from the traces in T, and the set of edges to account for all pairs of blocks that occur consecutively in a trace from T. Observe that for the witness function there may be different traces that fulfill the condition of Definition 1, for example in case the traces overlap. Now the question is which trace to use in the function definition. To handle this, we assume that we are given a total order on the set T.

Definition 2. *For a set of traces $T \subseteq \mathcal{T}$ equipped with a total order $\preceq$, the induced trace graph of T with respect to $\preceq$ denoted by $G(T)$ is the trace graph (N, E, wit) where:*

- $N := \{b \in \mathcal{B} | \exists t \in T : b \in t\}$,
- $E := \{(b, b') \in \mathcal{B} \times \mathcal{B} | \exists t \in T : bb' \sqsubseteq t\}$, *and*
- $\forall e = (b, b') \in E$, $wit(e) := (t, j)$ *where* $t := \min\{t' \in T | bb' \sqsubseteq t'\}$ *(w.r.t. $\preceq$)* *and* $j := \min\{1 \le k < |t| \, | \, t[k] = b \wedge t[k+1] = b'\}$.

Think of a total order on a set of traces as a way of arranging the traces in a specific sequence so that the witness function can be uniquely defined in the induced trace graph. If the traces are rearranged, for example by changing the order in which the inputs are fed to the program, the set of nodes and edges in the induced graphs are not affected. The trace order change only affects the witness function. In particular, rearranging overlapping traces changes the witness function value for the edges in scope of that overlap. This is since by definition only the minimal trace, w.r.t. the global ordering, is used in the witness function definition a witness as captured in the following proposition.

This is relevant because it shows that the data structure captures the notion of *what* has happened, but is not bogged down by details about in which order they happened. Specifically, it allows strategies to be defined in terms of what has happened and what is possible, which seems more meaningful compared to in which order the information was collected. The following proposition formalizes the notion.

Proposition 1. *For a set of traces $T \subseteq \mathcal{T}$ and two total orders $\preceq_1$ and $\preceq_2$ on T, the induced graphs of T, G_1 and G_2 w.r.t. $\preceq_1$ and $\preceq_2$ are equal up-to an order automorphism.*

This property is useful for a distributed framework such ours, since regardless of which framework settings are used to analyze a program, the resulting trace graph is canonical in the sense of the previous proposition.

The order in our framework is that in which the traces are generated and we let $\preceq$ denote this order in the remainder of the section. Later on we will describe how graphs induced by this order can be used to define different selection strategies. What remains to do now is to devise an efficient method to construct such graphs incrementally so that it can be integrated in our framework.

3.3 Graph Construction

Assume a set of traces $T \subseteq \mathcal{T}$ and the induced trace graph $G(T) := (N, E, wit)$. Given a trace t, Algorithm 2 computes the graph induced by $T' := T \cup \{t\}$ where it is assumed that t is newly generated, i.e., t is a maximal element w.r.t. $\preceq$ in T'. The resulting trace graph is denoted by $G' := (N', E', wit')$.

Algorithm 2. Trace graph update algorithm

Input: A trace graph $G := (N, E, wit)$ induced by some set of traces $T \subseteq \mathcal{T}$ and a newly generated trace t
Output: The trace graph induced by $T \cup \{t\}$
1: $(n, N', E', wit') \leftarrow (\bot, N, E, wit)$
2: **for** $j = 1 \ldots |t|$ **do**
3:      **if** $t[j] \notin N'$ **then**
4:          add $t[j]$ to N'
5:      **end if**
6:      **if** $n \neq \bot \wedge (n, t[j]) \notin E'$ **then**
7:          add $e := (n, t[j])$ to E
8:          $wit'(e) \leftarrow (t, j)$
9:      **end if**
10:     $n \leftarrow t[j]$
11: **end for**
12: **return** $G' := (N', E', wit')$

Initially, G' is defined by copying the input graph G. The main loop of the algorithm iterates through the instruction blocks of the input trace t in their sequence order. The variable n, which is initially undefined, is used in the loop to keep track of the previous taint block in t. In each iteration j of the loop, first the block $t[j]$ is checked against the set N' and possibly added to it (1.3–5). Then, the edge $e := (n, t[j])$ is checked against the set E' and possibly added to it as well. In particular, when the edge e is added, then the function wit' is defined at e to be (t, j) (1.6–9). The algorithm has a linear time complexity in the length of the input trace $\mathcal{O}(|t|)$.

Proposition 2. *Given a set of traces $T \subseteq \mathcal{T}$, the induced $G(T)$, and a trace t such that t is the maximal element w.r.t. $\preceq$ of the set $T \cup \{t\}$, Algorithm 2 computes $G(T \cup t)$ w.r.t $\preceq$.*

3.4   Task Priorities

Another feature in the framework is the priority computation performed by the GETPRIORITY function in Algorithm 1. A common measure is usually based on the number of new instructions not encountered in previously processed traces. In our case, we adopt a similar approach based on the trace graph structure.

Given a set of traces $T \subseteq \mathcal{T}$ and a trace $t \in \mathcal{T}$, we define first two basic measures on t w.r.t. to T which we will later combine to define the main measure used in our framework. First, we define $nd(t, T)$ by:

$$nd(t, t') := |\{b \in t \mid \nexists t' \in T : b \in t'\}|.$$

Intuitively, nd counts the number of blocks occurring only in t. Second, we let $ed(t, T)$ denote the following:

$$ed(t, T) := |\{j \mid \exists t.t[j] \in T \land \forall t' \in T.t' \neq t : t'[j] \neq t[j]\}|.$$

This measure counts the number of new positions in which some of the blocks in the traces from T, occur in t. We are now ready to define the measure we used.

Definition 3. *Given a set of traces $T \subseteq \mathcal{T}$ and a trace t, the rank of t w.r.t. T denoted by $rk(t, T)$ is defined by*

$$rk(t, T) := nd(t, T) + ed(t, T).$$

Although, the computation of the rank can be fully integrated in the trace graph update algorithm, we choose to keep it separate in Algorithm 3 for clarity of the presentation. In this algorithm, the variables nd and ed are used to compute the measures $nd(t, T)$ and $ed(t, traces)$ respectively. The main loop iterates through the blocks of the input trace in their sequence order. The loop code block can be divided into two parts where in the first part (1.3–5) nd is updated and in the second one (1.6–15). Like in Algorithm 2, the variable n is used to keep track of the previous taint block in t.

Algorithm 3. Rank computation algorithm

Input: A trace graph $G := (N, E, wit)$ induced by some set of traces $T \subseteq \mathcal{T}$ and a
newly generated trace t

Output: The rank of t w.r.t. T

```
 1: (n, nd, ed) ← (⊥, 0, 0)
 2: for j = 1 . . . |t| do
 3:     if t[j] ∉ N then
 4:         nd ← nd + 1
 5:     end if
 6:     if n =⊥ ∨ (n, t[j]) ∉ E then
 7:         v ← 1
 8:         for e ∈ E where wit(e) := (t', k) do
 9:             if k = j ∧ t'[k] = t[j] then
10:                 v ← 0
11:                 break
12:             end if
13:         end for
14:         ed ← ed + v
15:     end if
16:     n ← t[j]
17: end for
18: return nd + ed
```

In each iteration j of the loop, first the taint block $t[j]$ is checked against the
set n and nd is updated accordingly. Then, each edge $e \in E$, where $wit := (t', k)$
for some trace $t' \in t$ and $k \in \mathbb{N}$, is considered in order to check whether the
current taint block $t[j]$ already occurs in the same position $(k = j)$ in some
other trace t' from T. In case it does not, then the increment variable v is not
reset and ed is updated accordingly.

Proposition 3. *Given a set of traces $T \subseteq \mathcal{T}$, the induced $G(T)$, and a trace
$t \in \mathcal{T}$, Algorithm 3 computes $rk(t, T)$.*

4   Framework Features

We highlight some of the main features of OPENSAW including the choice of
the underlying tools, the support for user-defined branch selection strategies,
and the progress visualization web interface. An implicit feature is the choice
of implementation language. OPENSAW is implemented in Python, a popular
programming language. Hopefully, this will make it easier for users to write their
own modules and extend the framework.

4.1   Choice of the Underlying Tools

OPENSAW uses a modular execution engine that is responsible for extracting
execution traces and generating new inputs. The interface between this engine

and OPENSAW itself is generic enough so that it is easy to plug-in other engines. The engine currently supported in OPENSAW uses Intel's PIN [17] in combination with BAP [4]. For symbolic execution OPENSAW relies on BAP's iltrans tool. For constraint solving STP [9] is used.

4.2   User-Defined Strategies

Strategies are central in OPENSAW. They allow the user to steer the exploration of the executable. Strategies could be generic and based on common graph search algorithms. They could also be program specific and based for example on instruction addresses. OPENSAW's strategies enable users to control both the order in which tasks are handled and which branches of a trace to examine.

OPENSAW comes with some built-in strategies and offers support for user-defined ones. The built-in strategies include basic operations. For example, operations for handling redundancies by skipping analyzed branches, trying to improve coverage by only analyzing branches if they have exits that have never been taken, and trying to avoid loops by only analyzing each branch once per trace are included. They also cover graph search based ones such as Depth-first, Breadth-first and Generational search. In addition, OPENSAW has two built-in meta strategies for sequential and parallel composition of strategies. A sequential strategy chains the effect of its operand strategies while a parallel strategy rotates among them. The command line interface allows the user to choose and compose freely the built-in strategies.

In general, all the strategies in OPENSAW are derived from an abstract superclass with several callback methods. This superclass defines the strategy interface in OPENSAW. The callbacks offer hooks in the framework that are useful during the run. Each callback method is bound to a particular event so that it is only called when the corresponding event takes place. For example, there is a callback method for the generation of a new input, the extraction of a new trace, the failure of the constraint solver on a particular branch, etc. Users can extend the framework with other strategies as long as they implement the interface.

4.3   Progress Visualization

OPENSAW is shipped with a web interface for progress visualization and shown in the figures below. Figure 2 corresponds to the trace graph view. This view is animated so that the user can see the effect of the trace graph updates during the framework run. Figure 3 shows the statistics view. Among the component in this view is the pie graph illustrating how much of the overall runtime each of the underlying tool accounts for. Other components in this view include the number and type of crashes and a chart illustrating the number of visited branches over time.

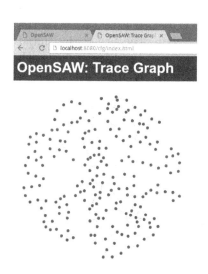

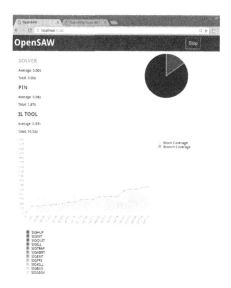

Fig. 2. OpenSAW features a trace graph view that visualizes the generation of the trace graph

Fig. 3. OpenSAW features a statistics view that, for example, contains a graph of visited branches over time

5   Experiments

We have tested OPENSAW on the binaries used in DARPAS Cyber Grand Challenge (CGC) Qualification round [1]. CGC was a challenge developed to test the ability of cyber reasoning systems to find, prove and patch vulnerabilities in programs. We chose this test set because the programs are complex, contain vulnerabilities based on real-world-bugs and are written by people with different background and skill. Additionally we have evaluated OpenSAW on a codec used in production. By comparison to the CGC tests, the codec is much larger, runs on a real Linux system and requires inputs of much larger size.

5.1   DARPA CGC

The DARPA CGC qualification round consisted of 131 vulnerable binaries. These binaries run on a system called DECREE (DARPA Experimental Cyber Research Evaluation Environment) This is a system built on Linux but with only seven different syscalls. These allow I/O, memory allocation, randomness and program termination. This limitation leads to a small and well defined environment, which allows developers of analysis tools to focus on the analysis and not on the internals and quirks of the complete set of Linux syscalls.

We were able to execute OPENSAW on 126 of the 131 CGC binaries. Five binaries were omitted because they use inter-process communication and currently OPENSAW can only analyze one binary at a time. We let OPENSAW execute with the generational search strategy for 30 min per binary. If OPENSAW had not exhaustively searched the input space of the binary within this time we aborted the search and continued with the next binary. For each binary the initial input consisted of the same 10 kB random data. The size of this initial input was chosen with the assumption that all binaries could be crashed with some input of this size.

The testing was done in a virtual machine running on a four core i7-4800 MQ CPU with 2.70 GHz and support for eight threads. The host machine only ran the virtual machine and assigned 15 GB of memory and four cores to it. Using this setup, OPENSAW found seven reproducible crashes that were not caused by the initial input.

5.2   Production Code

We also tested OpenSAW on a codec used in production. In contrast to the CGC binaries, the source code of the codec has 200 k lines. In addition it requires inputs of sizes between 0.5–120 kB to achieve high coverage of the code. The codec consists of two binaries: an encoder and a decoder. The initial input files for the encoder and the decoder were valid inputs of 46 kB and 120 kB in size respectively. It is worth noting that the codec had already been tested internally with AFL and presumably also by external users. As AFL was already in use internally we have compared OpenSAW with AFL. The tools are also similar as they both handle programs that use a single file as input and also in that neither requires any modification of the tested program or any additional wrapper code.

We ran two instances of OPENSAW simultaneously during 96 h, one on the encoder and the other one on the decoder on the same system setup as DARPA CGC. We also ran AFL on the codec for the same amount of time, on the same system setup, with multi-threaded AFL running for both the encoder and decoder. The result of these runs can be seen in Table 1.

The inputs generated by AFL did not identify any bugs. This is probably due to the fact that all the bugs revealed earlier by AFL have been already corrected in the version we were testing.

OPENSAW generated a bug finding input after 40 h. This bug was identified by executing the generated inputs on the codec with additional error detection in place. In comparison with AFL, OPENSAW also achieved better code coverage with fewer test cases.

Table 1. Results of running OPENSAW and AFL for 96 h each on the codec.

	Inputs	Bugs found	Function coverage in %	Line coverage in %
AFL	42 775	0	61.0	51.0
OpenSAW	464	1	66.5	53.3

6   Conclusion

Summary. We have presented OPENSAW, a new framework for white-box fuzzing. OPENSAWstrives to be open, flexible and agnostic to the underlying tools and techniques such as for symbolic execution, trace analysis and constraint solving. In fact, it could be used as a test platform for experimenting with such tools. We have addressed the issue of branch selection. For that purpose, we have defined the trace graph structure and generalized the concept of selection strategies to functions over trace graphs. This is one of the central features in OPENSAW which offers a large catalog of built-in strategies and support for user-defined ones. OPENSAW aims to be a flexible and efficient testing tool that can be scaled in or scaled out depending on the available computation power. In order to achieve this particular goal, we have addressed the issue of task priritization and devised an efficient trace ranking algorithm fully integrated with the trace graph update procedure. We have tested OPENSAW successfully on an external benchmark and on an internal production code. In particular, the analysis of the production code did discover a new bug not revealed earlier by the testing process in place.

Future Work. There is potential for many research directions with OPENSAW. In terms of use cases, it could be interesting to use strategies that steer the search towards specific parts of the program binary. This would be a useful feature for example for restricting the testing during upgrades. In relation to strategies, another interesting direction could be to use machine learning to define good strategies. This could be based on observing the program behavior during normal operations and then developing a strategy that focuses the search along less common paths. Another example could be based on analyzing a large data set of OPENSAW runs over similar types of programs in order to identify crash patterns. In terms of extensions, it could be worth looking into how to integrate static analysis in the framework to further tune the search. For example, what would be the benefit when starting from an approximate CFG provided by a static analyzer. If used properly, such information could potentially reduce the size of the trace graph and make the search converge faster.

Reflections. Our industry is extremely heterogeneous in terms of software and hardware platforms. OPENSAW will always benefit from advances in symbolic execution techniques addressing for example the support of multi-threading and floating point computation. OPENSAW is good for testing in some niches and has proven to be a useful complement to the testing process for at least one. Therefore, this will only drive forward our quest in promoting and developing such technology.

References

1. DARPA Cyber Grand Challenge Competitor Portal. http://archive.darpa.mil/CyberGrandChallenge_CompetitorSite/
2. The international SAT Competitions web page. http://www.satcompetition.org/
3. Avgerinos, T., Rebert, A., Cha, S.K., Brumley, D.: Enhancing symbolic execution with veritesting. In: Proceedings of the 36th International Conference on Software Engineering, ICSE 2014, pp. 1083–1094. ACM, New York (2014)
4. Brumley, D., Jager, I., Avgerinos, T., Schwartz, E.J.: BAP: A binary analysis platform. In: Gopalakrishnan, G., Qadeer, S. (eds.) CAV 2011. LNCS, vol. 6806, pp. 463–469. Springer, Heidelberg (2011). doi:10.1007/978-3-642-22110-1_37
5. Cadar, C., Dunbar, D., Engler, D.R.: KLEE: unassisted and automatic generation of high-coverage tests for complex systems programs. In: Draves, R., van Renesse, R. (eds.) OSDI, pp. 209–224. USENIX Association (2008)
6. Cadar, C., Ganesh, V., Pawlowski, P.M., Dill, D.L., Engler, D.R.: EXE: automatically generating inputs of death. In: Juels, A., Wright, R.N., di Vimercati, S.D.C. (eds.) Proceedings of the 13th ACM Conference on Computer and Communications Security, CCS 2006, October 30–November 3, 2006, pp. 322–335. ACM, Alexandria (2006)
7. Cha, S.K., Avgerinos, T., Rebert, A., Brumley, D.: Unleashing mayhem on binary code. In: IEEE Symposium on Security and Privacy, pp. 380–394. IEEE Computer Society (2012)
8. Chipounov, V., Kuznetsov, V., Candea, G.: S2E: A platform for in-vivo multi-path analysis of software systems. In: Proceedings of the Sixteenth International Conference on Architectural Support for Programming Languages and Operating Systems, ASPLOS XVI, pp. 265–278. ACM, New York (2011)
9. Ganesh, V., Dill, D.L.: A decision procedure for bit-vectors and arrays. In: Damm, W., Hermanns, H. (eds.) CAV 2007. LNCS, vol. 4590, pp. 519–531. Springer, Heidelberg (2007). doi:10.1007/978-3-540-73368-3_52
10. Godefroid, P., Klarlund, N., Sen, K.: Dart: Directed automated random testing. In: Proceedings of the 2005 ACM SIGPLAN Conference on Programming Language Design and Implementation, PLDI 2005, pp. 213–223. ACM, New York (2005)
11. Godefroid, P., Levin, M.Y., Molnar, D.: Sage: Whitebox fuzzing for security testing. Queue 10(1), 20:20–20:27 (2012)
12. Godefroid, P., Levin, M.Y., Molnar, D.A.: Automated whitebox fuzz testing. In: NDSS. The Internet Society (2008)
13. Haller, I., Slowinska, A., Neugschwandtner, M., Bos, H.: Dowser: A guided fuzzer for finding buffer overflow vulnerabilities. In: login: The USENIX Magazine. vol. 38(6), December 2013
14. Haller, I., Slowinska, A., Neugschwandtner, M., Bos, H.: Dowsing for overflows: A guided fuzzer to find buffer boundary violations. In: Proceedings of the 22nd USENIX Conference on Security, SEC 2013, Berkeley, CA, USA, pp. 49–64. USENIX Association (2013)
15. Khurshid, S., PǍsǍreanu, C.S., Visser, W.: Generalized symbolic execution for model checking and testing. In: Garavel, H., Hatcliff, J. (eds.) TACAS 2003. LNCS, vol. 2619, pp. 553–568. Springer, Heidelberg (2003). doi:10.1007/3-540-36577-X_40
16. Lanzi, A., Martignoni, L., Monga, M., Paleari, R.: A smart fuzzer for x86 executables. In: Proceedings of the Third International Workshop on Software Engineering for Secure Systems, SESS 2007, p. 7. IEEE Computer Society, Washington, DC (2007)

17. Luk, C.-K., Cohn, R., Muth, R., Patil, H., Klauser, A., Lowney, G., Wallace, S., Reddi, V.J., Hazelwood, K.: Pin: Building customized program analysis tools with dynamic instrumentation. In: Proceedings of the 2005 ACM SIGPLAN Conference on Programming Language Design and Implementation, PLDI 2005, pp. 190–200. ACM, New York (2005)

18. Ramos, D.A., Engler, D.: Under-constrained symbolic execution: Correctness checking for real code. In: Proceedings of the 24th USENIX Conference on Security Symposium, SEC 2015, pp. 49–64. USENIX Association, Berkeley (2015)

19. Sen, K., Marinov, D., Agha, G.: CUTE: A concolic unit testing engine for C. In: Proceedings of the 10th European Software Engineering Conference Held Jointly with 13th ACM SIGSOFT International Symposium on Foundations of Software Engineering, ESEC/FSE-13, pp. 263–272. ACM, New York (2005)

20. Shoshitaishvili, Y., Wang, R., Hauser, C., Kruegel, C., Vigna, G.: Firmalice- automatic detection of authentication bypass vulnerabilities in binary firmware (2015)

21. Stephens, N., Grosen, J., Salls, C., Dutcher, A., Wang, R., Corbetta, J., Shoshitaishvili, Y., Krugel, C., Vigna, G.: Driller: Augmenting fuzzing through selective symbolic execution. In: NDSS (2016)

22. Sutton, M., Greene, A., Amini, P.: Fuzzing Brute Force Vulnerability Discovery. Pearson Education, Upper Saddle River (2007)

23. Zalewski, M.: American fuzzy lop. http://lcamtuf.coredump.cx/afl/

Visual Configuration of Mobile Privacy Policies

Abdulbaki Aydin[1]([⊠]), David Piorkowski[2], Omer Tripp[2], Pietro Ferrara[2],
and Marco Pistoia[2]

[1] University of California, Santa Barbara, CA, USA
baki@cs.ucsb.edu
[2] IBM T.J. Watson Research Center, Yorktown Heights, NY, USA
pistoia@us.ibm.com

Abstract. Mobile applications often require access to private user information, such as the user or device ID, the location or the contact list. Usage of such data varies across different applications. A notable example is advertising. For contextual advertising, some applications release precise data, such as the user's exact address, while other applications release only the user's country. Another dimension is the user. Some users are more privacy demanding than others. Existing solutions for privacy enforcement are neither *app-* nor *user-* sensitive, instead performing general tracking of private data into release points like the Internet. The main contribution of this paper is in refining privacy enforcement by letting the user configure privacy preferences through a visual interface that captures the application's screens enriched with privacy-relevant information. We demonstrate the efficacy of our approach w.r.t. advertising and analytics, which are the main (third-party) consumers of private user information. We have implemented our approach for Android as the VISIDROID system. We demonstrate VISIDROID's efficacy via both quantitative and qualitative experiments involving top-popular Google Play apps. Our experiments include objective metrics, such as the average number of configuration actions per app, as well as a user study to validate the usability of VISIDROID.

1 Introduction

The mobile era is marked by contextual and user-sensitive functionality. Notable examples include location-aware apps and services (browsing, advertising, and more); social features (e.g. in gaming and navigation apps); as well as personalization capabilities (often based on analysis of text, audio or video content). These and other similar features are all based on access to, and use of, personal user information.

A. Aydin–The author performed the research leading to this paper while working at IBM Research as an intern.

O. Tripp–The author performed the research leading to this paper while at IBM Research, but is currently affiliated with Google, Inc.

P. Ferrara–The author performed the research leading to this paper while at IBM Research, but is currently affiliated with Julia, S.R.L.

© Springer-Verlag GmbH Germany 2017
M. Huisman and J. Rubin (Eds.): FASE 2017, LNCS 10202, pp. 338–355, 2017.
DOI: 10.1007/978-3-662-54494-5_19

In some cases the user is conscious of the privacy/functionality tradeoff, and can sometimes even disable (or refrain from enabling) privacy-threatening functionality. Unfortunately, there are also common cases wherein users, and sometimes even developers, are in the dark regarding the contexts where, and the extent to which, their private information is exploited.

This worrisome situation links back to the design of mobile platforms. The two major platforms, Android and iOS, both mediate access to private information via a permission model. Permissions govern access to designated resources, such as the contact list or GPS system. In Android, prior to API level 23 permissions were managed at install time. Now both Android and iOS either grant or deny a given permission by seeking user approval upon first access to the respective resource. In both cases, permissions apply globally across all contexts and usage scenarios, and so for example usage of the user's location for navigation cannot be distinguished from its usage for contextual advertising.

Scope and Threat Model. This paper is informed by the need to create a *usable* interface for *end users* to understand and configure how their private information is utilized. Within this general scope, we take a first step in targeting the release of private data related to contextual advertising, as well as UI/UX (aka usability) and navigational analytics. Advertising is the most popular Android monetization model. Analytics is the gateway to user experience. As such, these are the most prominent third-party consumers of private data.

In line with past research on user privacy [25], our assumed threat model concerns authentic (rather than malicious) mobile applications. Such applications, in contrast with malware, are aimed at executing their declared functionality. At the same time, extraneous behaviors, such as advertising and analytics, may access private information and share it with third parties without explicit authorization. Given our focus on these clients, we define release of private user information to remote advertising/analytics websites as a potential *privacy threat*, and concentrate on this category in particular.

Blocking such releases completely is not an acceptable solution. First, for advertising, this would disrupt the Android monetization model that currently allows users to download apps for free. Also, certain users actually take interest in ad content.[1] Analytics data is of immense value to customize and improve user experience. Hence, our goal is to create a method to configure, rather than blindly suppress, usage of private information by analytics/advertising engines.

One challenge, which we later illustrate, is that private data is seldom embedded into ad/analytics web messages in clear form. For security as well as performance reasons, such messages often carry encoded and sometimes even encrypted data. This obviates naive attempts to detect (and anonymize) sensitive data in ad/analytics messages (e.g. via a man-in-the-middle proxy).

Our Approach. We address the gap between user experience, which is typically far removed from notions like code-level permissions, and the need to tailor

---

[1] http://www.adweek.com/socialtimes/study-kenshoo-mobile-app-advertising-trends/617293.

privacy enforcement according to the preferences and sensitivities of the user at hand. We bridge this gap via a visual configuration interface. This critical aspect of the enforcement system is complementary to existing solutions, which typically enforce privacy via (user-insensitive) information-flow tracking [5, 9, 11, 25, 28], in specializing the system per the given user. In our approach, usages of private information are rendered onto the app UI, which resonates directly with user experience. The user can then visually configure privacy preferences atop the UI, which are subsequently enforced by instrumenting the app. This creates a separation of concerns: The user is provided with a visual interface to reason about — and express — privacy concerns, while the enforcement system benefits from a tight privacy policy, which contributes to both performance and accuracy.

In our concrete system, we instantiate the above workflow — as a first step — w.r.t. privacy threats due to contextual advertising and UI/UX analytics. The user is presented with annotated UI screenshots that reflect, atop advertising widgets and analytics-empowered screens, the private information. The user can then configure constraints on the context, which the system enforces by anonymizing respective private fields before these are sent to the remote server.

Contributions. This paper makes the following principal contributions:

1. Usable privacy enforcement: We take a first step toward a general solution to the challenge of usable configuration of privacy enforcement systems (Sects. 2.2 and 3.2). In our solution, which focuses on advertising and analytics, usage of private data is reported atop the app UI, enabling seamless configuration of privacy preferences.
2. System design: We describe and illustrate the architecture and algorithms underlying our solution (Sects. 3 and 4). These include offline analyses as well as per-user code rewriting, where — for portability and general applicability — we do not require a custom platform build.
3. Implementation and evaluation: We have implemented our solution as the VISIDROID system for Android. We report on quantitative measurements as well as a user study that we have conducted, which validate the viability of our approach and the usability of VISIDROID. Some of the experimental data is of wider applicability, characterizing which fields typically flow into advertising/analytics servers and how often (Sect. 5).

2   Overview

The VISIDROID workflow begins with offline analysis of the target application A; the user then performs interactive policy configuration; finally, an instrumented app that enforces the user privacy settings is emitted. We discuss these steps, which are visualized in Fig. 1, in more detail below with reference to Listings 1.1 and 1.2 that are based on the popular photo-blogging theCHIVE app (package name: `com.thechive`). theCHIVE is a highly popular Android photo-blogging app.[2] It utilizes the location and device ID for advertising, where

---

[2] https://play.google.com/store/apps/details?id=com.thechive.

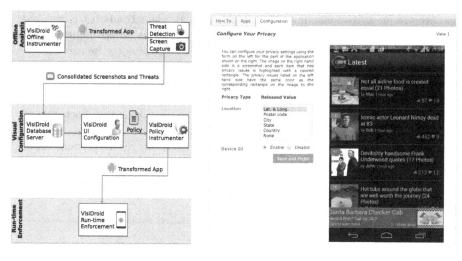

Fig. 1. VisiDroid architecture   **Fig. 2.** The VisiDroid configuration interface

the recommended practice to instead use a coarsening of the precise location and the Android ID [23].

Listing 1.1. Transformed code for offline analysis

```
1  adv = findViewById(id);
2  did = getSysService("phone")
       .getDeviceId();
3  LOGSOURCE(DEVICE_ID, did);
4  adv.setKeywords("User:"+did);
5  LOGSINK(adv);    //adv.loadAd();
6  // method declarations
7  LOGSINK(MoPubView adv) {
8    adReq = adv.getAdRequest();
9  LOG(adReq); CAPTURESCREEN();
10   adv.loadAd(); }
```

Listing 1.2. Transformed code for runtime enforcement

```
1  adv = findViewById(id);
2  did = getSysService("phone")
       .getDeviceId();
3  adv.setKeywords("User:"+did);
4  LOADAD(adv); //adv.loadAd();
5  // method declarations
6  LOADAD(MoPubView adv) {
7    Mdid = MOCK(DEVICE_ID, did);
8    adv.setKeywords("User:"+Mdid);
9    adv.loadAd();
10 }
```

2.1   Phase I: Offline Analysis

Offline analysis is conducted once per application A. It mines the contexts associated with UI objects in A. This is done in two steps. The first step is to track flow of private data starting at *privacy sources*, such as getDeviceId() and getLastKnownLocation(). The second step, if the data reaches an outgoing ad/analytics request, is to match the message against one or more UI objects.

For high accuracy, offline tracking is done dynamically. The app is instrumented to enable runtime tracking (lines 3, 5 in Listing 1.1). The instrumented version is then exercised (either manually or automatically) on a designated device that is set up with mock user information. In the case of theCHIVE, the location and device ID are tracked into their respective MoPubView setters.

Next, the request/response matching is established when `loadAd()` is invoked. Internally, this method serializes the `MoPubView` object as an ad request, sends the request, and renders the ad content received in response to the screen.

Another aspect of offline analysis is to persist programmatic and geometric information about the UI objects to enable specification and enforcement of privacy restrictions on the different screens/widgets across different runs. This is done via the *adb* library, which provides APIs to capture stateful screenshots with XML-structured data (line 9 in Listing 1.1).

Automated crawling is a challenging problem that has received considerable attention [4,12,18]. To simplify and focus the contributions of the current paper, we neither developed nor used any of the available solutions. Instead, we crawled the subject apps manually, which was neither difficult nor burdensome. We detail our methodology for manual crawling in Sect. 5.

2.2   Phase II: Visual Configuration

Offline analysis yields stateful app screenshots that visually link advertising/-analytics libraries to the private information they consume. These artifacts are uploaded to the VISIDROID server. A user can then perform visual configuration with the VISIDROID client application (i.e., website). The VISIDROID client application displays the screenshots from the server, as illustrated in Fig. 2. The user is presented with the different privacy threats visually, with the available configuration options on the left and a screenshot of the view under configuration on the right. The user can then choose the granularity of data release (or prevent release altogether using mock data; *Disable, None*) on a per-widget basis. For example, for the location data flowing into `MoPubView`, the user may permit state and city information but not their exact address.

2.3   Phase III: Enforcement

The third and final step is to rewrite the app per the customized policy, as configured by the user. This is done via code instrumentation, which imposes anonymized values on the private fields constrained by the user. We illustrate the transformation in Listing 1.2 (the `MOCK` call at line 7). The actual values are substituted with their anonymized counterparts at the very last point before the ad/analytics request is discharged. This is to ensure that there are no side effects w.r.t. other functionality that consumes the values, which is confirmed to be a problem in practice [11].

VISIDROID imposes the anonymized values on the outgoing request via built-in interface methods. In our running example, these are the setters defined by the respective widget object. The `loadAd()` method is called inside `LOADAD` at line 9 in Listing 1.2, such that prior to the original code, setter methods exposed by `MoPubView` are invoked with the anonymized location and device-ID fields.

2.4   Scope and Limitations

In its current form, VISIDROID is designed to address privacy threats in contextual advertising as well as UI/UX, or navigational, analytics. Linking privacy threats in other categories to user experience is our goal in future research.

VISIDROID exploits commonalities across different libraries for efficiency. An example of this, noted above, is the use of built-in setter APIs to overwrite private fields with their anonymized counterparts. Leveraging knowledge of the different ad/analytics servers simplifies the VISIDROID architecture, as well as optimizes its performance and accuracy. At the same time, new servers need to be welded into VISIDROID, which is a limitation of our design. Though this process is facilitated by a declarative interface exposed by VISIDROID, it still needs to be performed for every new server.

3   Offline Analysis

Offline analysis is performed once per (all users of an) app. It takes as input the app, and produces as its output — following a crawling session that explores different app views and states — a visual representation of advertising -/analytics-related privacy threats. For this, VISIDROID integrates between privacy-related information flows and screen captures, which is the focus of this section.

3.1   Detection of Privacy Threats

A common method to track flow of private information across a mobile system is via taint tracking [5]. Doing so via app instrumentation is highly nontrivial, and leads to prohibitive slowdown, and so a common solution is to customize the platform. This limits the portability and maintainability of the detection system. Instead, inspired by the BayesDroid system [25], VISIDROID performs *value-based* threat detection. Intuitively, the idea is to record private fields as they originate, and compare them — using similarity metrics — against values about to be released. If the level of similarity is significant, then a potential threat has been detected. Specifically, VISIDROID utilizes the Levenshtein metric to assess value similarity. Informally, $\text{lev}(|a|, |b|)$ is the minimum number of single-character edits — insertion, deletion or substitution — needed to transform string a into string b. The significance of using "fuzzy" similarity analysis, rather than precise matching, stems from cases where the value is reformatted by the app (e.g., accepting email address john.doe@gmail.com as input, then releasing john and doe separately as the first and last names). See the BayesDroid paper [25] for more discussion. Compared to statement-level information-flow (or taint) tracking, this approach is lightweight. It further enables characterization of the type and amount of information about to be released per the value at hand (e.g., if the value matches the street name out of the full address).

VISIDROID is equipped with a diversified set of privacy sources, including built-in platform APIs to obtain the user's location (e.g. the `getLastKnownLocation()` method in `LocationManager`), device identifiers (e.g. the `getSimSerialNumber()` method in `TelephonyManager`), etc.; APIs exposed by social apps (e.g. the Facebook graph interface); and user inputs received through the UI, which are obtained via platform APIs (e.g. `EditText.getText()`).

VISIDROID currently accounts for the five top-popular advertising libraries (in non-gaming apps),[3] as well as two of the most popular UI/UX analytics libraries.[4] These are Google AdMob, MoPub, Millenial Media, Amazon Ads and Ad Marvel, and Google Analytics and Adobe Analytics, respectively. Extending VISIDROID with additional libraries is straightforward via a declarative specification interface.

While informed by BayesDroid, the detection technique of VISIDROID is slightly different. First, rather than accounting for a single release flow, VISIDROID has to monitor — in the case of ad requests — the composition of (i) the outgoing flow from the app to the server (the sink being the request) and (ii) the incoming flow from the server back to the app (the sink being the widget). Treating both as a single composed flow — as in BayesDroid — is futile, as the ad content reaching the widget sink is rich media rather than text that can be searched for matches against the private field.

Instead, VISIDROID leverages a predefined specification of how different popular ad libraries load remote content. In the example in Listing 1.1, for instance, `loadAd` is the API provided by MoPub to send out the ad request and render the resulting content to the UI. Inspecting the values stored in the widget receiving the `loadAd` call as it is entered establishes which private fields (if any) are about to be released to the remote server. The widget is then annotated with these private fields, which accounts for the incoming flow.

An advantage of performing value similarity analysis against the (fields of the) widget object, rather than the HTTP request, is that at that point the values are still stored in clear form. Hashing, encryption and other transformations all take place downstream, as the widget's state is serialized into an HTTP message. This enables direct (and efficient) similarity analysis, without the need to account neither for standard nor for custom transformations (unlike BayesDroid).

Another important point is that our offline analysis detects threats at the subfield level, also accounting for transformations. If for instance the location is transformed into a street address, but only the city (sub)field is passed to the third-party library, then the analysis would report that subfield alone rather than the entire location/address.

To achieve this robustness, the VISIDROID analysis proactively computes for certain private fields, and in particular the user's location and date of birth, other common equivalent representations as well as derivative information. For birthday, these include the user's age as well as other date patterns including month/day, round trip, short time and long time. For the location, the corresponding address is computed. VISIDROID computes the transformations via

---

[3] http://www.appbrain.com/stats/libraries/ad.

[4] http://www.appbrain.com/stats/libraries/dev.

Algorithm 1. Geometric representation of ad widgets

1: **procedure** GEOMETRICREP(s : app screen)
2:     $ids \longleftarrow [\,]$, $A \longleftarrow$ GETFOCUSEDACTIVITY(s), $layout \longleftarrow$ GETLAYOUT(A)
3:     **for all** node $n \in layout$ **do**
4:         **if** n is an ad widget **then**
5:             $C \longleftarrow$ extract bounds, $ids \longleftarrow ids \cdot [n \mapsto (A, C)]$
6:     **return** ids

---

standard APIs (like the `Geocoder.getFromLocation` method for location/address transformation).

3.2   Screen Capturing

Interleaved into threat detection during the crawling process is the collection of UI screens. This is done via built-in *adb* utilities, and in particular the *screencap*, *dumpsys* and *uiautomator* shell commands.

At a given instant in the crawling process, the steps described in Algorithm 1 are executed. First, the current screen is captured and the XML layout of the screen, providing rich hierarchical information regarding the UI elements and their geometrical representation, is derived with the help of the *adb* utilities (line 2). Next, for each XML node n, representing a distinct UI element, we read its coordinates as the **bounds** attribute (line 5), and compute an identity for it as a pair (A, C) consisting of the the parent activity A and coordinates C (line 5). Figures 3 and 4 presents example screen capture from theCHIVE and its corresponding decomposition into UI elements, as given by the XML layout. Note in particular the precise boundaries surrounding the ad widget, which is disambiguated from the other content on the screen.

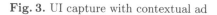

Fig. 3. UI capture with contextual ad   **Fig. 4.** UI structure of Fig. 3

The geometric representation of a UI object is sensitive to the display properties, varying across users and devices, which would seemingly pose a challenge to VISIDROID. Observe, however, that VISIDROID utilizes geometric information only for visual configuration. This is done atop offline screen captures, and not the user's device, which offsets the risk of distorting the bounds for a UI object.

Yet there is another aspect of bounds extraction that is subtle. Computing the boundaries of a UI element is straightforward as long as the element is known to occupy a fixed region on the screen. Sometimes, however, UI widgets — in particular ads and sometimes also views enriched with analytics — are embedded into scrolling banners. In such cases, we fix the boundaries of the widget to be those of a non-scrolling parent element.

4   Configuration and Enforcement

Configuration. Before installing an app A, the user performs visual configuration of the privacy policy for A via the VISIDROID client. The resulting policy is then sent to the server as input to the VISIDROID instrumentation agent, which transforms A accordingly, and makes the new version available for the user to download and install. We have chosen this design, rather than downloading all the artifacts to the device and performing the configuration locally, to lower network and (device) storage costs.

As illustrated in Fig. 2, the user is presented with the screen captures due to offline analysis one by one. For each screen, all elements linked to privacy threats are highlighted, such that the user can authorize which, if any, of the private fields to release. As discussed in Sect. 3.1, the user is shown the subfields that are actually released (e.g., city rather full address or location). This is crucial, as otherwise the user may form a wrong impression of the app's behavior and/or perform redundant configuration (e.g., constraining location release even though only the city is released).

Code Instrumentation. Upon completion of the policy configuration, the resultant constraints are discharged to the VISIDROID instrumentation agent (hosted on the VISIDROID server). The agent rewrites the app accordingly, as illustrated in Fig. 1. Code instrumentation aims to mock values only for third parties without any crashes and side effects.

We have found that the idealized assumption regarding app/library insulation often holds in practice. Advertising and analytics libraries often consume the context from the app, and then operate on their own as an independent third party in obtaining and acting upon the contextual content. Knowing that, VISIDROID synthesizes the mock value immediately before setting it on the library, as shown at line 9 in Listing 1.2. The original value is preserved and propagated beyond the setter call, such that the mock value only flows into the library. VISIDROID is equipped with specification of formatting and logical constraints on privacy related data. It synthesizes a mock data that is consistent with the original. Hence, there would not be any side effects due to enforcement beyond potential changes to ad content and/or analytics data.

VISIDROID ensures that no private field is released without user authorization. It (statically) scans through the entire app code base for occurrences of advertising/analytics APIs (like `loadAd()`). For any such call that has not already been handled, and also for private fields not configured by the user w.r.t. handled calls (since flow of such fields has not been observed during offline analysis), VISIDROID inserts instrumentation code immediately prior to the call to trigger a warning at runtime. This ensures that if an unhandled privacy-relevant call is made, then the user has the opportunity to either authorize or reject the communication with the respective library.

5 Experimental Evaluation

We demonstrate VISIDROID's efficacy via both quantitative and qualitative experiments involving top-popular Google Play apps. We explain how we designed our experiments in the following.

Benchmarks. Our benchmark selection methodology consisted of several steps. We started from the 60 top-popular apps in every Google Play category, except games (as we explain shortly), for a total of 25 categories and 1,462 apps. The ideal number of apps should have been 1,500, but we experienced some technical issues downloading certain apps.

We skipped the games category for two reasons: First, the monetization strategy of gaming apps is mostly in-app purchases, where ad content (if present) mostly refers to other games. Second, from a technical standpoint, gaming apps are often equipped with large media files. Since the games category has 18 subcategories, the download process would have become very heavy with the addition of 1,200 big apps. Gaming apps are left for future research.

We pruned the initial set of apps via a script that searches through the app code for usage of ad and analytics libraries (supported by VISIDROID), and in particular initialization code for the libraries. This resulted in 364 apps (25% of all apps), which we further filtered using a similar script that scans for contextual advertising (i.e. occurrence of setter APIs like `setAge(...)`, `setBirthday(...)`, etc.). 126 apps survived this filter.

Experimental methodology. To uncover UI screens and releases of private information, we exercised each of the 126 applications manually, spending approximately 5 min per app. For exhaustive crawling, as well as authentication via social apps, we created mock Facebook accounts and user profiles.

For unbiased and consistent overhead measurement, we automated — using the adb toolset — each of the manual interaction sequences. For statistical significance, we repeated overhead measurements 20 times per app. Running times, divided into user and system times, were derived from the device via built-in platform APIs.

Hardware setup. We executed all the apps on a Google Nexus 4 phone, running version 4.4.4 of the Android platform, with a Qualcomm Snapdragon S4 Pro 1.5 GHz processor and 2 GB of memory. We used a single physical device per all apps and all experiments.

Experimental Results. VISIDROID's offline analysis identifies 31 apps that release private data to either advertising parties or analytics engines or both. These are listed in Table 1, which also specifies the involved libraries (second column), the released private fields (third column), as well as the source(s) of the private fields (fourth column). The privacy threats identified by VISIDROID are distributed as follows: full location – 35%; postal code – 12%; other location fields – 25%; birthday and/or age – 9%; gender – 11%; and other threats – 9%. Of special interest is that theCHIVE releases the device ID, and Job Search the build serial. These identifiers are unique, enabling identification of the device and thus also the user, though utilizing such identifiers is considered a bad practice. These statistics, and the data underlying them in Table 1, shows that different apps release different private fields, and at different granularities, to third-party websites. This, combined with the fact that different users have different privacy concerns, emphasizes the need for a configurable privacy policy.

For unbiased measurement of configuration cost, we first fixed the privacy restrictions prior to the offline runs. We restrict location to city, personal info to only age and gender, and device info to only operator name. These restrictions reflect our own perspective, whereby it would be legitimate to use coarsened private information for advertising/analytics but not fully precise data. Equipped with the restrictions defined (i.e., policy), we configured each of the 31 applications from Table 1 via the VISIDROID client. We quantify the involved effort by counting (i) *configuration forms*, where each such form is linked to one or more ad widgets or view on some screen; (ii) *configuration items*, where we refer to the total number of selections that the user can potentially make across all screens and forms (there are e.g. 2 configuration items in the form in Fig. 2); and (iii) *configuration actions*, where an action is an actual selection we made guided by the restrictions. The results are summarized in the last 3 columns of Table 1. In total, across all apps, 6.61 configuration items need to be reviewed and 4.94 configuration actions are required on average. Aside from myHomework and MeetMe, which define 52 and 21 configuration items, respectively, all the rest of the apps require a total of 0–16 configuration item reviews and 0–16 configuration actions. The user performs these actions once (modulo changes to policy), and so we conclude that the user effort demanded by VISIDROID is tolerable if not low.

Although much of the VISIDROID workflow is automated, determining what privacy permissions to set requires users to interact with the web-application interface of VISIDROID. Prior work has already shown that mobile device users are aware of privacy concerns when installing mobile applications [7,8,10,14, 15,17,22]. Therefore, for the usability study, our goal was not to confirm users' concerns, but rather to validate that users can change privacy settings easily and correctly in the user-facing client application. To this end, we ran a usability study based on standard approaches.

Usability Study Design. The usability study consisted of 7 male and 3 female participants whose ages ranged from 30 to 69 and had 1 to 8 years of experience (mean: 3.0 years) using mobile devices. Each participant was randomly assigned

Table 1. Applications with privacy threats ('D'=device; 'inp'=user input; 'FB'=Facebook; 'UIE'=UI element; 'pcode'=postal code; 'GAn'=Google Analytics; 'GAds'=Google Ads; 'AA'=Adobe Analytics; 'MM'=Millennial Media)

Application	Ad libs	Private fields	Sources	Config. forms	Config. items	Action items
1Weather	GAn	main views, settings	UIE	10	10	10
AccuWeather	GAn	main views	UIE	4	4	4
AroundMe	MoPub	long/lat	D	1	1	1
Brightest Flashlight	MM	long/lat	D	1	1	1
Cars.com	GAds	city, sub state, pcode	D, inp	6	6	6
Checkout 51	GAn	login (+FB), browsing, account	UIE	8	8	8
com.idemfactor	MoPub	long/lat	D	1	1	1
Daily Workouts	MoPub	long/lat	D	3	3	3
Endomondo	GAds	long/lat, birthday, gender	D, inp, FB	8	16	16
Final Countdown	MoPub Amazon Ads	first/last name, gender	FB	2	4	2
FlightStats	GAds	country, mcc	D	2	4	0
Fox News	AA	browsing	UIE	6	7	7
GasBuddy	GAds	long/lat	D	2	2	2
GrubHub	GAn	main views	UIE	6	6	6
Horoscope	GAds	long/lat, birthday, gender	D, inp, FB	5	15	10
JackThreads	GAn	main views	UIE	5	5	5
KAYAK	GAds	long/lat	Dice	3	3	3
KBB	GAds	pcode	D	6	8	8
MeetMe	AdMarvel	long/lat, pcode, country, mcc, age, gender	D, inp, FB	7	21	7
myHomework	GAds Amazon Ads MM	long/lat, birthday, age, gender	D, inp, FB	13	52	26
Photobucket	AdMarvel	long/lat, pcode, gender	D, inp, FB	1	2	1
Radar Express	Amazon Ads	long/lat	D	1	1	1
Scanner Radio	MoPub MM	long/lat	D	1	1	1
Snagajob	GAds	long/lat, build serial	D	1	2	2
theCHIVE	MoPub MM	D ID, long/lat	D	2	4	4
theScore	MoPub	long/lat	D	5	5	5
Urbanspoon	GAds	long/lat	D	1	1	1
WeatherBug	AdMarvel GAn	long/lat, pcode, city, state, operator name, main view	D, UIE	4	5	5
Weather Kitty	GAds	long/lat	D	1	1	1
Whitepages	AdMarvel	long/lat, pcode, address #, city, sub state, state	D	5	5	5
Yelp	GAds	pcode, city, country	D	1	1	1

to three of five possible app configuration tasks. In each configuration task, they were asked to modify the privacy data released by the app such that it matched the permissions given to them with the task, such as the following example: *"Set the granularity of the location released by the advertising to None."* We gave participants the configuration instead to test all the possible granularities of configuration options.

Prior to each session, participants filled out a brief background questionnaire. Then, participants were asked to complete each of the three tasks until they stated that they were done. No instructions were given on how to complete the configuration task, but help was available within the client application if needed.

After the three tasks, each participant was asked to select and rank words that best represented their experience with VISIDROID. The words were taken from the Microsoft Desirability Toolkit [1]. After all, we asked the participant: "Could you provide additional details about why you selected <word>?".

We measured participants' ability to finish the task via three metrics. *Completeness* is the measure of how many participants were able to finish the task and generate any configuration. *Correctness* is a measure of how many participants were able to complete each task correctly. *Errors* occur each time a setting was misconfigured, the wrong application was selected, or an action unrelated to the task at hand was performed. A participant can recover from errors and still complete a given task correctly.

Usability Study Results. All 30 tasks were evaluated to be complete and correct, and 26 of those tasks were completed error-free. We observed six errors over four tasks. Participants 6 and 10 each made errors in their first task, where they configured the wrong app (and saved the configuration). Participant 6 did it three times. Participant 10 did it once. Participants 7 and 8 each had one error, wherein they clicked on an item that had a broken link. Despite these errors, all participants were able to return to the correct configuration page and successfully finish all the configuration tasks.

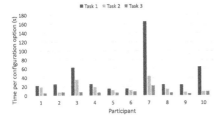
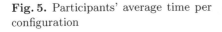

Fig. 5. Participants' average time per configuration

Fig. 6. Responses for the desirability evaluation

Efficiency. As participants became more familiar with the interface, they were able to complete their tasks more quickly. Figure 5 indicates, across all participants, that the average time to configure a single option decreased during Task 2 and yet again during Task 3. The mean time to configure one option decreased from 44.2 s in Task 1 to 8.1 s in Task 3, or approximately a five-fold improvement. This suggests that the learning curve for understanding the interface and how to configure privacy options was sufficiently low to qualify as practical and feasible in real life. Participants' statements from the interview corroborate this hypothesis:

- P5: '...Once a workflow pattern is established, it's the same for all screens.'
- P7: 'After doing a couple of pages of examples, I really didn't have to think much about what was going on there.'
- P9: 'Once I got into the task, especially after the first task, I found the experience to be very consistent.'

The outlier in Fig. 5 was Participant 7 for Task 1. Participant 7 spent time in the beginning of Task 1 switching back and forth between reading the instructions available within the application and experimenting with configurations options for other apps before reading the task and completing it. After Task 1, he did not return to the instructions and finished the tasks faster.

Table 2. Responses to the words selected from the desirability toolkit.

Selected words	Participant responses
Easy-to-use	P1: "It seemed to be fairly obvious what to select from the given tasks."
	P3: "It was very easily understandable what the controls meant and what it was that I was doing."
	P4: "There is no confusion about what's happening. It's pretty straightforward and easy to use."
	P6: "[It's] similar to the existing applications. So I don't need to think a lot."
Straightforward	P2: "There's just a small number of things that you can select over on the left."
	P4: "It's pretty clear that it's about the [privacy threats] coming out of the featured views."
	P6: "Because it's highly predictable, so I know what I'm doing."
Efficient	P1: "It seemed to be pretty quick to go in there an select them [the configuration options]."
	P3: "It was very obvious what I selecting and what I was revealing."
	P6: "I guess the setting options are not so many, so I can know what I'm doing so easily."
Predictable	P6: "After finishing the first task, I know what I was expecting for the others."
	P8: "I can predict what's going to happen on the next page. So I think the learning path is just very short."
	P9: "I knew what to expect when I was going into the different apps and how to use the different settings."

User Sentiment. We also collected participants' sentiments about configuring privacy via the desirability toolkit. The word cloud visualization in Fig. 6 depicts all the words that participants selected as part of their top-five words during that part of the usability study. The more participants that select a word, the larger it appears in the visualization. The most frequently selected words and the number of times they were selected were: Easy-to-use (6), Straightforward (5), Efficient (4) and Predictable (4). Table 2 provides excerpts from the participants' responses for selecting words in the visualization.

Along with the positive responses, Fig. 6 also shows that there is room for improvement. Participants 1 and 8 found VISIDROID *confusing*, expressing that they did not understand the relationship between the released data the the screenshots provided. Participants 8 and 9 selected *too technical*, referring to the instructions in the tool. Participants 9 and 10 found VISIDROID to be *rigid* because there was no way to set permissions once and apply the settings to multiple screens. Participant 4's selection of *overwhelming* referred to the large number of screens to configure for some applications. We shall address this feedback in a future revision.

Enforcement. Lastly, we discuss VISIDROID's runtime enforcement. We focus performance (or overhead) and correctness (i.e. no missed leaks and no side effects). First, for performance, we measured the overhead per the methodology given in Sect. 5. On average, VISIDROID is responsible for an increase of 2.16% in user time and 0.96% in system time. For 9 out of the 31 apps we recorded a modest decrease in user and/or system times following the enforcement transformation (i.e., negligible if any overhead). The app exhibiting the highest overhead is Car Buying - KBB, which uses an old version of Google Ads. Our support for this version is based heavily on reflective calls as well as serialization/deserialization of objects, which cause the high overhead.

Next, to validate absence of side effects, we executed the automated crawling sessions for each of the apps with and without enforcement. We monitored the sessions to validate that intermediate as well as final app states are the same across both runs (modulo ad content). This was indeed the case for all apps. As an illustration, we detail our experience with GasBuddy. This app utilizes the user's precise location to find nearby gas stations, but at the same time, it also sends the location to ad servers. VISIDROID only mocks the location in the latter scenario. Indeed, relevant gas stations are still displayed, and alongside them, ad content that is not immediately related to the given location.

Finally, to confirm that there are no misses, we created another instrumentation scheme that — beyond applying anonymization transformations — intercepts the internal state of ad widgets and analytics engines. This step, shared in common with offline instrumentation, is to check whether any of the fields classified as sensitive (according to Sect. 3.1) has unexpectedly reached the remote library. As expected, we were unable to find a single instance of sensitive data reaching a third-party library in its original form. As additional anecdotal evidence, we further interacted with approximately one third of the apps beyond the automated crawling scripts to check whether previously unseen advertising/analytics behaviors would be discovered. Encountering fresh behaviors would have resulted in a runtime warning by VisiDroid, as explained in Sect. 4. We could not, however, trigger any such warning.

6   Related Work

Tools like MockDroid [2] and LP-Guardian [6] replace actual user data with mock data at the cost of functionality degradation. VisiDroid does the same, though the user is provided with rich context to decide where and how to enable mocking. Also, unlike MockDroid and LP-Guardian, which rely on OS-level customizations, VisiDroid is portable.

Another approach is runtime privacy enforcement. Roesner, *et al.* [20] do so via *access control gadgets*, which are custom gadgets embedded into the app. TaintDroid [5], and other solutions built on top of it [13,21], perform runtime taint tracking. Additional solutions for online monitoring and control of release of private information are AppFence [11] and AppAudit [26], which are similar in spirit to TaintDroid; BayesDroid [25], which VisiDroid utilizes as its core tracking engine; Aurasium [27], which relies on sandboxing; as well as the approach of packet-padding-like mitigation [29] (cf. [3,24]). Unlike all of these solutions, which enforce a general privacy policy, VisiDroid allows privacy enforcement to be customized by the end user through a user-friendly visual interface.

Yet another category of tools is turned towards developers and analysts. The Aquifer framework [19] lets the developer define secrecy restrictions that protect the entire UI workflow defining a user task. AppIntent [28] outputs a sequence of GUI interactions that lead to transmission of sensitive data, thus helping an analyst determine whether that behavior was intended. VisiDroid targets end users rather than developers or analysts.

Finally, there are tools to derive privacy specifications. Lin, *et al.* [16] cluster privacy preferences into a small set of profiles to help users manage their private information. Their approach relies on static code analysis to determine why an app requests a given permission (e.g. advertising vs core functionality). Unlike Lin, *et al.*, VisiDroid provides a specification interface, and not inference capabilities, with the goal of serving the exact preferences of the specific user at hand.

7   Conclusion and Future Work

We have presented VisiDroid, a privacy enforcement system that allows the user to understand and manage usage of private information for advertising/analytics via a accessible interface. In the future, inspired by Lin, *et al.* [16], we intend to explore possibilities for crowd-sourced policies. We also plan to optimize runtime enforcement, e.g. by coarsening low-relevance privacy tags.

References

1. Benedek, J., Miner, T.: Measuring desirability: new methods for evaluating desirability in a usability lab setting. In: Proceedings of Usability Professionals Association 2003, pp. 8–12 (2002)
2. Beresford, A.R., Rice, A., Skehin, N., Sohan, R.: Mockdroid: trading privacy for application functionality on smartphones. In: HotMobile 2011 (2011)
3. Chen, S., Wang, R., Wang, X., Zhang, K.: Side-channel leaks in web applications: a reality today, a challenge tomorrow. In: S&P (2010)
4. Choi, W., Necula, G., Sen, K.: Guided gui testing of android apps with minimal restart and approximate learning. In: OOPSLA (2013)
5. Enck, W., Gilbert, P., Chun, B., Cox, L.P., Jung, J., McDaniel, P., Sheth, A.N.: TaintDroid: an information-flow tracking system for real-time privacy monitoring on smartphones. In: OSDI (2010)
6. Fawaz, K., Shin, K.G.: Location privacy protection for smartphone users. In: CCS (2014)
7. Felt, A.P., Egelman, S., Wagner, D.: I've got 99 problems, but vibration ain't one: a survey of smartphone users' concerns. In: Proceedings of the Second ACM Workshop on Security and Privacy in Smartphones and Mobile Devices, pp. 33–44. ACM (2012)
8. Felt, A.P., Ha, E., Egelman, S., Haney, A., Chin, E., Wagner, D.: Android permissions: user attention, comprehension, and behavior. In: Proceedings of the Eighth Symposium on Usable Privacy and Security, p. 3. ACM (2012)
9. Ferrara, P., Tripp, O., Pistoia, M.: MorphDroid: fine-grained Privacy Verification. In: ACSAC (2015)
10. Fu, B., Lin, J., Li, L., Faloutsos, C., Hong, J., Sadeh, N.: Why people hate your app: making sense of user feedback in a mobile app store. In: Proceedings of the 19th ACM SIGKDD International Conference on Knowledge Discovery and Data Mining, pp. 1276–1284. ACM (2013)
11. Hornyack, P., Han, S., Jung, J., Schechter, S.E., Wetherall, D.: These aren't the droids you're looking for: retrofitting android to protect data from imperious applications. In: CCS (2011)
12. Jensen, C., Prasad, M., A. Møller, A.: Automated testing with targeted event sequence generation. In: ISSTA (2013)
13. Jung, J., Han, S., Wetherall, D.: Short paper: enhancing mobile application permissions with run-time feedback and constraints. In: SPSM (2012)
14. Kelley, P.G., Cranor, L.F., Sadeh, N.: Privacy as part of the app decision-making process. In: Proceedings of the SIGCHI Conference on Human Factors in Computing Systems, pp. 3393–3402. ACM (2013)
15. Khalid, H., Shihab, E., Nagappan, M., Hassan, A.E.: What do mobile app users complain about? IEEE Softw. 32(3), 70–77 (2015)
16. Lin, J., Liu, B., Sadeh, N.M., Hong, J.I.: Modeling users' mobile app privacy preferences: restoring usability in a sea of permission settings. In: SOUPS (2014)
17. Lin, J., Amini, S., Hong, J.I., Sadeh, N., Lindqvist, J., Zhang, J.: Expectation and purpose: understanding users' mental models of mobile app privacy through crowdsourcing. In: Proceedings of the 2012 ACM Conference on Ubiquitous Computing, pp. 501–510. ACM (2012)
18. Machiry, A., Tahiliani, R., Naik, M.: Dynodroid: an input generation system for android apps. In: FSE (2013)

19. Nadkarni, A., Enck, W.: Preventing accidental data disclosure in modern operating systems. In: CCS (2013)
20. Roesner, F., Kohno, T., Moshchuk, A., Parno, B., Wang, H.J., Cowan, C.: User-driven access control: rethinking permission granting in modern operating systems. In: Proceedings of the 2012 IEEE Symposium on Security and Privacy, SP 2012, pp. 224–238 (2012)
21. Schreckling, D., Posegga, J., Köstler, J., Schaff, M.: Kynoid: real-time enforcement of fine-grained, user-defined, and data-centric security policies for android. In: Askoxylakis, I., Pöhls, H.C., Posegga, J. (eds.) WISTP 2012. LNCS, vol. 7322, pp. 208–223. Springer, Heidelberg (2012). doi:10.1007/978-3-642-30955-7_18
22. Shklovski, I., Mainwaring, S.D., Skúladóttir, H.H., Borgthorsson, H.: Leakiness and creepiness in app space: perceptions of privacy and mobile app use. In: Proceedings of the 32nd Annual ACM Conference on Human Factors in Computing Systems, pp. 2347–2356. ACM (2014)
23. Stevens, R., Gibler, C., Crussell, J., Erickson, J., Chen, H.: Investigating user privacy in android ad libraries. In: W2SP (2012)
24. Sun, Q., Simon, D.R., Wang, Y., Russell, W., Padmanabhan, V.N., Qiu, L.: Statistical identification of encrypted web browsing traffic. In: S&P (2002)
25. Tripp, O., Rubin, J.: A Bayesian approach to privacy enforcement in smartphones. In: USENIX Security (2014)
26. Xia, M., Gong, L., Lyu, Y., Qi, Z., Liu, X.: Effective real-time android application auditing. In: 2015 IEEE Symposium on Security and Privacy, SP 2015, San Jose, CA, USA, 17–21 May 2015, pp. 899–914 (2015)
27. Xu, R., Saïdi, H., Anderson, R.: Aurasium: practical policy enforcement for android applications. In: USENIX Security (2012)
28. Yang, Z., Yang, M., Zhang, Y., Gu, G., Ning, P., Wang, X.S.: AppIntent: analyzing sensitive data transmission in android for privacy leakage detection. In: CCS (2013)
29. Zhou, X., Demetriou, S., He, D., Naveed, M., Pan, X., Wang, X., Gunter, C.A., Nahrstedt, K.: Identity, location, disease and more: inferring your secrets from android public resources. In: CCS (2013)

Automated Workarounds from Java Program Specifications Based on SAT Solving

Marcelo Uva[1]([✉]), Pablo Ponzio[1,3], Germán Regis[1], Nazareno Aguirre[1,3], and Marcelo F. Frias[2,3]

[1] Universidad Nacional de Río Cuarto, Río Cuarto, Argentina
{uva,pponzio,gregis,naguirre}@dc.exa.unrc.edu.ar
[2] Instituto Tecnológico de Buenos Aires (ITBA), Buenos Aires, Argentina
mfrias@itba.edu.ar
[3] Consejo Nacional de Investigaciones Científicas y Técnicas (CONICET), Buenos Aires, Argentina

Abstract. The failures that bugs in software lead to can sometimes be bypassed by the so called *workarounds*: when a (faulty) routine fails, alternative routines that the system offers can be used in place of the failing one, to circumvent the failure. Previous works have exploited this workarounds notion to automatically recover from runtime failures in some application domains. However, existing approaches that compute workarounds automatically either require the user to manually build an abstract model of the software under consideration, or to provide equivalent sequences of operations from which workarounds are computed, diminishing the automation of workaround-based system recovery.

In this paper, we present two techniques that automatically compute workarounds from Java code equipped with formal specifications, avoiding abstract software models and user provided equivalences. These techniques employ SAT solving to compute workarounds on concrete program state characterizations. The first employs SAT solving to compute *traditional* workarounds, while the second directly exploits SAT solving to circumvent a failing method, building a state that mimics the (correct) behaviour of this failing routine. Our experiments, based on case studies involving implementations of collections and a library for date arithmetic, enable us to show that the techniques can effectively compute workarounds from complex contracts in an important number of cases, in time that makes them feasible to be used for run time repairs.

1 Introduction

Even in software systems that are built with high quality standards using rigorous software development techniques, bugs still make it through to deployment. Various issues contribute to this situation: the intrinsic complexity of software, the constant adaptation and extension that software systems undergo during maintenance, and the increasing pressure to shorter time to market, among other factors. These circumstances, combined with demands for availability on software, make techniques that help systems tolerate bug-related failures highly

© Springer-Verlag GmbH Germany 2017
M. Huisman and J. Rubin (Eds.): FASE 2017, LNCS 10202, pp. 356–373, 2017.
DOI: 10.1007/978-3-662-54494-5_20

relevant. A mechanism that has been useful for bypassing failures led to by program bugs is the so called *workaround*: when a call to a (faulty) routine leads to a failure, alternative routines or combinations of routines that the software system offers can be used in place of the failing one, to circumvent the failure. Previous works have exploited the workaround notion to automatically recover from runtime failures in some application domains, notably web applications [5]. However, while existing approaches compute workarounds automatically, they do so from an abstract, state machine like model of the software being considered [4,5], that needs to be manually provided, or require the user to provide equivalent alternative sequences of operations [7], from which workarounds are computed, diminishing the automation of workaround-based system recovery.

In this paper, we propose two techniques that, through the use of state-of-the-art SAT-based technology, can automatically compute workarounds directly from formal specifications accompanying Java source code in the form of JML *contracts*, thus avoiding the need for more abstract, manually built software models or user provided alternatives to system routines. These techniques have similar requirements for their application, but differ in the actual mechanism to compute, and provide, workarounds. The first technique employs SAT solving to compute *traditional* workarounds, in the sense that these exploit the intrinsic redundancy of the module holding the failing routine. The second technique directly exploits SAT solving to circumvent the failing method, automatically building a state that mimics the (correct) behaviour of this failing routine. This second technique is then closer to work on constraint-based repair, e.g., [26,30, 31], although it differs in the approaches used to improve scalability. In order to assess the applicability of the presented techniques, we develop a number of case studies based on contract-equipped collection classes and a Java library for date arithmetic, combined with randomly generated program state scenarios for these classes, where methods of these are assumed to fail, and workarounds for them, of the two kinds just described, are computed. These case studies show that the techniques can effectively compute workarounds from complex contracts in an important number of concrete state situations, in times that makes them feasible to be used for run time repairs.

2   Background

Workarounds and Run Time Repair. The concept of *workaround* was initially defined in the context of self-healing systems [4]. Intuitively, a workaround exploits the implicit redundancy present in system modules in order to overcome a fault in the module. Given an initial state S_i, a routine m (failing when invoked in state S_i), and a desired final state S_f, a *workaround* is a procedure P composed of a sequence of other routines in the module that contains m, that leads from S_i to S_f. If the intended behaviour of a given system module is captured through a finite state machine abstraction, then a method or routine failing in a specific state is represented by a particular transition from a source state (the initial state) to the desired target state. Workarounds composed of sequences of other routines can be systematically explored by traversing the state machine, from the initial state, attempting to reach the final state without traversing through transitions labeled with the failing routine. This is in fact the process employed for automated workaround computation presented in [4,6].

Other approaches employing workarounds (although not computing them automatically) have been developed in the context of self-healing systems. A distinguishing approach is that presented in [7], where an architecture for self healing systems, composed of a mechanism to monitor system execution and automatically recover via rollbacks and the application of (user provided) workarounds, is introduced. The concept of workaround has been successfully applied in real software systems through the above described approaches, with demonstrating case studies involving complex software systems such as Google Maps and Flickr [5]. Moreover, further experimental analyses have been performed, showing that the redundancy exploited by the workarounds mechanism is actually inherent to many component based systems [8].

The Alloy and DynAlloy Modeling Languages. In Alloy [18], datatypes are defined by *signatures*. For instance, assuming that we want to model the behaviour of linked lists, their structure can be defined through signatures Null, Node and List in Fig. 1(a). Int (integers) is the only predefined signature. Every signature defines a set of atoms, i.e., a domain. The modifier one forces the corresponding signatures to have exactly one element, i.e., to be singletons, which is useful to define constants to be used in specifications (in our case, Null is such a "constant"). Signatures can have fields. For instance, signature List has two fields, head and size. Field head is in fact a relation (more precisely, a function) from List atoms to Node atoms or Null.

Alloy also features *facts*, *predicates*, and *assertions*. Facts define properties assumed to be true of the models, and are written in relational logic (first-order logic with relational operators, including transitive and reflexive-transitive closures). For instance, if one would want to restrict analysis to *acyclic* lists, one may impose acyclicity via fact acyclicLists in Fig. 1(a). In this fact, dot (.) is relational composition (which can be intuitively seen as a navigational operator), * and ^ represent reflexive-transitive and transitive closures; so, the formula expresses that, for every list *l* and every node *n* reachable from the list's head, *n* cannot be reached from *n* navigating through (one or more) "next" links.

Predicates are formulas with potentially free variables, and can be used to express properties, and in particular to capture operations. For instance, predicate getFirst in Fig. 1(a) captures the "get first" operation on lists. Finally, assertions are *intended* properties, i.e., properties that should be implied by facts, but must be checked for. For instance, one may check that, when lists have size one, getFirst and getLast return the same value, expressed in assertion getFirstEqGetLast in Fig. 1(a). Both predicates and assertions can be subject to automated analysis using Alloy Analyzer, a tool that employs off-the-shelf SAT solvers to build satisfying instances of predicates or violating instances for assertions, under user provided scopes. Figure 1(a) shows some sample commands running Alloy Analyzer. These will use SAT solving to build

```
one sig Null { }

sig Node {
    elem: Int,
    next: Node+Null
}

sig List {
    head: Node+Null,
    size: Int
}

fact acyclicLists {
    all l: List | all n: Node | n in
l.head.*next => not (n in n.^next)
}

pred getFirst[l: List, result': Int] {
    l.head != Null and result' = l.head.elem
}

assert getFirstEqGetLast {
all l: List | all n1, n2: Int |
    l.size = 1 and getFirst[l,n1] and getLast[l,
n2] => n1 = n2
}

run getFirst for 5 but 1 List, 5 Int
check getFirstEqGetLast for 5 but 1 List, 5 Int
```

(a)

```
act removeAll[thiz: List,
            head: List -> one (Node+Null),
            size: List -> one Int] {
    pre { }

    post { head' = head ++ (thiz -> Null) and
size' = size ++ (thiz -> 0) }

}

program choose[l: List, result: Int] {
    local [chosen: Boolean, curr: Node+Null]
    chosen := false;
    curr := l.head;
    ( [curr!=Null]?;
    {
        (result:=curr.elem; chosen:=true)+(skip));
        curr:=curr.next
    )*;
    [chosen = true]?
}

assertCorrectness chooseIsCorrect[l: List,
result: Int]
{
    pre { l.size>0 and repOK[l] }
    program = choose[l, result]
    post { some e: l.head.*next.elem | e=result' }
}

run choose for 5 but 1 List, 5 Int, 5 lurs
check chooseIsCorrect for 5 but 1 List, 5 Int, 5
lurs
```

(b)

Fig. 1. Alloy and DynAlloy specifications for linked lists.

instances involving at most 1 list, 5 nodes and using integers with bit-width 5, that satisfy getFirst, and violate getFirstEqGetLast, respectively. In the first case it will serve as a sample execution of getFirst. In the second case, if a violation is found it exhibits a problem regarding a property that the user thought it would be valid; if on the other hand no counterexample is found, it helps gaining confidence on the correctness of the model and the validity of the property (although it is clearly not a proof of validity).

Alloy is a convenient, simple and expressive language for building *static* models of software. Dealing with *dynamic* models, i.e., models that capture system execution elements such as state change, is less straightforward. DynAlloy [12] is an extension of Alloy that incorporates convenient constructs to easily capture state change. DynAlloy's syntax and semantics is based on dynamic logic. The language extends Alloy with *basic actions*, *programs*, and *partial correctness assertions*. Basic actions are *defined* through pre and postconditions. For instance, an action that removes all elements of a list can be defined as removeAll in Fig. 1(b). This atomic action updates the head and size of the list, using relational overriding (++). A few things are worth noticing. First, action removeAll has List's fields head and size as explicit parameters, instead of being attributes of argument thiz. This is a necessary part of our mutable model of the heap (see [13] for details). Second, as opposed to Alloy predicates, which require parameters for post-state variables, these are implicit in DynAlloy's actions. Indeed, notice that the postcondition refers to primed variables head' and size', which are not listed explicitly as action arguments.

Moreover, when a primed variable is not mentioned in the postcondition, it is assumed to be left unchanged by the action; that is, variable `thiz` (the list object to which `removeAll` is applied) is not changed by this atomic action. DynAlloy programs are built using assignment (`:=`), skip, tests and atomic actions as base cases, combined using sequential composition (`;`), nondeterministic choice (`+`) and iteration (`*`). A sample program that nondeterministically returns some element of a linked list is program `choose` in Fig. 1(b). DynAlloy programs can be equipped with partial correctness assertions. For instance, one may specify the intended behaviour of the `choose` program as a partial correctness assertion, as illustrated in Fig. 1(b), where we assume `repOK` to be a provided Alloy predicate characterizing the representation invariant of lists (e.g., acyclicity). DynAlloy programs are subject to SAT-based analysis, via a translation into Alloy [12]. They can be run (i.e., producing instances that correspond to program executions), and when they are equipped with partial correctness assertions, they can be verified against their specifications. For instance, the first command in Fig. 1(b) produces an execution of `choose` on a list with at most 5 nodes with at most 5 iterations; the second command checks whether *every* terminating execution of at most 5 iterations of `choose`, on valid and non-empty lists with at most 5 nodes and integers of bit-width 5, returns an element of the list.

Alloy and DynAlloy are sufficiently expressive to capture Java programs and JML specifications, and have been used as intermediate languages for various analyses, including bounded verification and test generation of JML-annotated Java programs [2,14,15] (although the SAT-based analysis of Alloy/DynAlloy is intrinsically incomplete). Our translation is based on [14,15], and relies on symmetry breaking and *tight field bounds* as optimizations. More precisely, we use the symmetry breaking technique introduced in [14,15], which automatically builds predicates that force canonical orderings in heap allocated structures, allowing the analysis to remove structures which are isomorphic to others already considered. Tight field bounds, on the other hand, are used to reduce the number of variables and clauses in the propositional encodings of the memory heap, for Java program analysis [14,15]. They are automatically computed from *assumed* properties, such as preconditions and invariants, and are employed to restrict structures in states that are assumed to satisfy such properties. These optimizations are crucial to our analysis' efficiency, especially because we use the encoding for numerical datatypes originally introduced in [2] (extended to support some Alloy functions, notably cardinality), enabling us to support increased precision in numerical characterizations of Java basic datatypes. We refer the reader to [2,14,15] for further details.

3   Computing Workarounds from Program Specifications

Let us now turn our attention to our first technique for computing automated workarounds for Java program specifications, employing the SAT based automated analysis described in the previous section. The approach exploits the translation of JML contracts of Java programs into DynAlloy, and the bounded iteration ($*$) and non-deterministic choice ($+$) operators from this language, to build a partial correctness assertion involving a (nondeterministic) program, whose counterexamples correspond to workarounds.

The overall approach works as follows. Let C be a class, and $m_1, m_2, \ldots, m_k$ the public methods in C. Each method m_i is accompanied by its pre and post-condition in JML, say pre_{m_i} and $post_{m_i}$, respectively. Notice that, as explained in the previous section, from the JML formulas corresponding to the contract of m_i, we can obtain corresponding Alloy formulas, using the translation embedded in TACO [14]. This process leads to Alloy formulas $pre_{m_i}^A$ and $post_{m_i}^A$. According to DynAlloy's syntax, we can, with these formulas, define a DynAlloy atomic action a_i: act a_i {pre { $pre_{m_i}^A$ } post { $post_{m_i}^A$ }}. Notice that the behaviour of DynAlloy atomic action a_i is *defined* by its pre and post-condition, i.e., it is assumed that a_i behaves exactly as its specification prescribes. Now, given actions $a_1, a_2, \ldots, a_k$, corresponding to the translation of methods $m_1, m_2, \ldots, m_k$ into DynAlloy, we can build the DynAlloy program $(a_1 + a_2 + \cdots + a_k)*$. According to the semantics of nondeterministic choice and iteration, this program represents *all* sequential compositions of actions $a_1, a_2, \ldots, a_k$, and consequently, of methods $m_1, m_2, \ldots, m_k$.

Now, let us suppose that method m_i fails at run time, in a concrete program state s_i. Again, we can capture state s_i as an Alloy predicate s_i^A, as shown in the previous section. Thus, we have all the elements to construct the following partial correctness assertion:

$$\{ s_i^A \} \ (a_1 + a_2 + \cdots + a_{i-1} + a_{i+1} + \cdots + a_k) * \ \{ \neg post_{m_i}^A \}$$

which can be automatically analyzed using DynAlloy Analyzer. A counterexample of the above assertion would consist of a sequence of Alloy states $s_{A_0}, \ldots, s_{A_j}$ such that: *(i)* s_{A_0} is state s_i^A; *(ii)* there is a sequence $a_{p(1)}; a_{p(2)}; \ldots; a_{p(j)}$ of operations such that $\langle s_{A_i}, s_{A_{i+1}} \rangle$ are related by $a_{p(i)}$ transition relation; and *(iii)* s_{A_j} is a state s_f^A that does *not* satisfy $\neg post_{m_i}^A$, i.e., that satisfies $post_{m_i}^A$. Taking into account that s_i^A and $post_{m_i}^A$ are Alloy representations of state s_i and the postcondition of method m_i, respectively, such counterexample is indeed a workaround: it provides a sequence of actions, representing methods of class C, that take the system from state s_i to a state that satisfies $post_{m_i}$. Moreover, if DynAlloy Analyzer does not find a counterexample to the above assertion, within a provided scope, it is guaranteed that there are no workarounds in that scope (with workarounds understood as simple sequences of other methods, not more complex programs).

Dealing with Parameterized Methods. When looking for a workaround involving methods that receive parameters, we have an additional problem, namely how to choose appropriate values to pass as parameters so that these lead to workarounds. To do so, we define atomic actions that nondeterministically assign a value to a variable. For instance, for integer-typed variables such an action is defined as follows:

```
 1  act nonDetAssign[x: Int] {
 2      pre { }
 3      post { x' in Int }
 4  }
```

Then, if a method m(int i) is involved when attempting to build workarounds for another method, it will participate in the iteration of nondeteministic choice of methods, as program: nonDetAssign[i] ; m[i]. Notice that this nonde-terministic assignment is inside the iteration *, to allow for the possibility of using m[i] more than once, with different parameters. Also, in this example we are using Alloy's Int signature, for illustration purposes. In our case studies we use the custom-built signatures for Java precision integers defined in [2].

An Example. Consider a simple Java implementation of tuples, with methods setFirst(int value), setSecond(int value) and swap() (swaps first and second elements of a tuple). Suppose that method setFirst(3) fails on a tuple object t with values t.first: 4 and t.second: 3. Then, the DynAl-loy program that is built to produce workarounds from is the following:

```
 1  assertCorrectness computeWorkaround[ t: Tuple+Null, first: Tuple -> one Int,
 2          second: Tuple -> one Int ] {
 3      pre { t!=Null and t.first=4 and t.second=3 }
 4      program { local i: Int;
 5          ( t.swap() + (nonDetAssign[i] ; t.setSecond[i]) )*
 6      }
 7      post { !(t.first'=3 and t.second'=t.second)}
 8  }
```

For this program, the analysis would return, for instance, the fol-lowing workaround: swap(); nonDetAssign(i); setSecond(i), where nonDetAssign assigned 3 to variable i (these values can be recovered from the counterexample instance built by DynAlloy Analyzer). The minimum scope to provide to find such workaround is 2 loop unrolls, 1 tuple and 2 32-bit integers.

It is important to notice that in the above described approach to compute workarounds, methods are seen as *atomic*, i.e., we do not take into account the *code* of method implementations, only their specifications. This simplification is made for scalability reasons, since there is no technical limitation in translating methods as programs (rather than doing so as atomic actions, as in our case).

The technique that we introduce in the following section tackles the workaround computation problem in a different way, by resorting to the use of SAT solving to directly build a recovery program state, rather than a recovery sequence of methods.

4   Program State Repair Using SAT

The technique in the previous section computes standard workarounds, and dif-fers from other workaround approaches in that it applies to contract specifica-tions at the level of detail of source code, and it computes workarounds fully automatically. In this section we present a different approach, which attempts to repair the failing routine by directly producing the expected post state using the specification of the routine and SAT solving.

While this technique has in principle the same constraints as the previous one, i.e., that contracts must be available for the programs being subject to the analysis, it can be better explained (and exploited) through the use of *abstraction functions*. Data representations often attempt to capture more abstract models. For instance, binary search trees are often used as an implementation of sets of elements. The abstraction function is part of a data representation specification, that indicates how concrete data representation instances map to the corresponding abstract elements. Going back to our example of binary search trees, the abstraction function would indicate, for each binary search tree, which is the set is represents (i.e., it essentially returns the set of values held in the AVL). Contract languages such as JML [9] support the definition of model variables and abstraction functions; abstraction functions can also be captured directly in Java, as shown in [21]. In our case, to simplify the presentation, we will use Alloy to express abstraction functions. For instance, the abstraction function of binary search trees, we just referred to, is captured in Alloy (in this case, using a predicate) as follows:

```
pred absFunction[thiz: Tree, root: Tree -> one (Node+Null),
        left: Node -> one (Node+Null), right: Node -> one (Node+Null),
        key: Node -> one Int, result: set Int] {
    result = thiz.root.*(left+right).key
}
```

So, let us assume that, besides the pre and post-conditions for all class methods, and the class invariant, we have the Alloy specification of the abstraction function (this may be given in JML, and then translated to Alloy). Now, as in the previous technique, assume that method m_i breaks at run time in a concrete program state s_i. We would want to recover from this failure, reaching a state s_f that satisfies the postcondition $post_{m_i}(s_i, s_f)$ (notice that the postcondition in languages such as JML and DynAlloy is actually a postcondition *relation*, that indicates the relationship between precondition states and postcondition states). We can build a formula that characterizes these "recovery" states, as follows:

```
pred recoveryStates[s_f: State] {
    some x, y | alpha[s_i, x] and alpha[s_f, y] and post_m_i [x, y] and repOK[s_f]
}
```

where repOK is the class invariant translated to Alloy, post_m_i is the postcondition relation of method m_i, translated to Alloy from JML, and alpha is the abstraction function. Finding satisfying instances of this predicate will produce valid post-states, in the sense that they satisfy the class invariant, that mimic the execution of method m_i.

An Example. Consider a binary search tree representation of sets. Assume that the JML invariant for binary search trees and the JML postcondition of method remove have already been translated into Alloy predicates repOK and post_rem, respectively. These would look as follows:

```
ı  pred repOK[thiz: Tree, root: Tree -> one(Node+Null), left: Node -> one(Node+Null),
2        right: Node -> one (Node+Null), key: Node -> one Int] {
3    all n : Node | n in thiz.root.*(left + right) implies (n.key != null and
4    (no (((n.left).*(left+right) & (n.right).*(left+right)) -Null)) and
5    (n !in n.^(left+right)) and
6    (all m: Node | m in n.left.*(left+right) implies n.key>m.key)  and
7    (all m: Node | m in n.right.*(left+right) implies m.key>n.key) )
8  }
9  pred post_rem[elems, elems': set Int, elem: Int] {
10      elem in elems and elems' = elems - elem
11  }
```

Now, consider the left-hand side binary search tree in Fig. 2, and suppose that method `remove(x)` failed on this tree, for `x = 3`. By looking for models of the following Alloy predicate:

```
ı  pred recoveryStates [thiz: Tree, root,root': Tree -> one (Node+Null),
2        left,left': Node -> one (Node+Null), right,right': Node -> one(Node+Null),
3        key,key': Node -> one Int ] {
4    thiz = T0 and root = (T0->N0) and
5    left = (N0->N1)+(N1->N3)+(N2->Null)+ (N3->Null)+(N4->Null) and
6    right =...and...key =...and...
7    some x, y : set Int | absFunction[thiz,root,left,right,key,x] and
8    absFunction[thiz',root',left',right',key',y] and post_rem[x, y, 3]
9  }
```

we will be searching for a valid binary search tree that represents the set resulting from removing 3 from the left-hand side tree of Fig. 2. The right-hand side binary tree in Fig. 2 is an instance satisfying the predicate. Notice how this returned structure does not perform the expected change that a removal method, of a leaf in this case, would produce. But as far as the abstract datatype instance that the structure represents, this resulting structure is indeed a valid result of removing key 3.

Predicate `recoveryStates` above makes some simplifications, for presentation purposes. First, it uses Alloy `Int` signature, whereas in our experiments we use a Java precision integer specification. Second, notice the use of higher-order existential quantification (`some x, y: set Int`). Such quantifications are *skolemized* for analysis (a "one" signature declares x and y as `set Int` fields, which are then used directly in the `recoveryStates` predicate), a standard mechanism to deal with existential higher-order quantification in Alloy, since Alloy Analyzer does not directly support it (see [18] for more details). Finally, and more importantly, two elements are also part of `recoveryStates`, though not explicitly mentioned in the predicate. One is the addition of an automatically computed *symmetry breaking* predicate, as put forward in [14,15], which forces a canonical ordering in the structures and has a substantial impact in analysis. Second, we use *tight bounds* [14,15] computed from class invariants (these reduce propositional state representations by removing propositional variables that represent field values deemed infeasible by the invariants) to constrain post-condition states, since these states are assumed to satisfy the corresponding invariants, as shown in the above predicate.

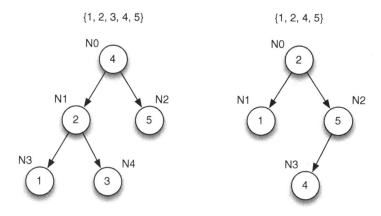

Fig. 2. Two binary search trees, and the sets they represent.

5 Evaluation

Our evaluation consists of an experimental assessment of the effectiveness of the two presented techniques for automatically computing workarounds, and repairing faulty states, respectively. The evaluation is based on the following benchmark of collection implementations (accompanied by their corresponding JML contracts including requires/ensures clauses, loop variant functions and class invariants): *(i)* two implementations of interface java.util.List, one based on singly linked lists, taken from [15], the other a circular double linked list taken from AbstractLinkedList in Apache Commons.Collections; *(ii)* three alternative implementations of java.util.Set, one based on binary search trees taken from [28], another based on AVL trees taken from [3], and the red-black trees implementation TreeSet from java.util; and *(iii)* one implementation of java.util.Map, based on red-black trees, taken from class TreeMap in java.util. This benchmark is complemented with the analysis of a Java library, namely library JodaTime for date arithmetic. All the experiments were run on a PC with 3.40 Ghz Intel(R) Core(TM) i5-4460 CPU, with 8 GB of RAM. We used GNU/Linux 3.2.0 as the OS. The workaround repair prototypes together with the specifications used for the experiments can be found in [1]. Experiments can be reproduced following the instructions provided therein. Also, further experimental data are presented in [1].

In order to assess our workaround techniques, we artificially built repair situations, i.e., situations in which it was assumed that a method *m* has failed. These situations were randomly and automatically constructed, using Randoop [22]. For each data structure interface, we ran Randoop for 1 h, producing 116000 list traces, 136000 set traces, and 138000 map traces, leading to the same number of instances of the corresponding data structure. We sampled one every 1000 structures (number 1000, number 2000, number 3000, etc., since Randoop tends to produce structures of increasing size due to its feedback driven generation policy based on randomly extending previously obtained sequences [22]), obtaining 116 lists, 136 sets and 138 maps. We proceeded in a similar way for class TimeOfDay of JodaTime, producing 50 scenarios. For each method m in the corresponding class, we assumed it failed on each of the structures, and attempted a workaround based repair using the remaining methods. So, for instance, for method removeLast from List, we attempted its workaround repair using the remaining 32 methods of the class, in 116 different repair situations. Notice that for the first technique, and since workarounds are computed at the interface level from method specifications (not implementations), we have one experiment per interface (e.g., AVL and TreeSet set implementations are equivalent from the specification point of view, so computing workarounds for one implementation also work for the others). For the second technique, on the other hand, each implementation leads to different experiments, since the technique depends on the structure implementation.

We summarize the experimental results of the evaluation of the first technique in columns Lists, Sets and Maps of Tables 1, 2 and 3. Tables report: *(i)* method being fixed (the fix is computed from the iteration of nondeterministic choice of remaining methods); *(ii)* total time, the time spent in fixing *all* 100 faulty situations; time is reported in h:mm:ss format; *(iii)* average repair time, i.e., the time that in average it took to repair *each* faulty situation; again, time is reported in h:mm:ss format; *(iv)* average workaround length, i.e., number of routines that the found workaround had, in average; and *(v)* number of timeouts, i.e., faulty situations that could not be repaired within 10 min. It is important to remark that, in the tables, we only count the repairs that actually ended within the timeout, to compute the total and average repair times. Also, each table reports, for the corresponding structure, the minimum, maximum and average size for the randomly generated structures (see table headings).

Regarding the second technique, we evaluated its performance on producing recovery structures on the same scenarios as the first technique. Recall that scenarios were produced using, for all implementations of the same data type, the same interface, so these are shared among different implementations of the same datatype. The timeout is set in 10 min. Results are reported in the remaining columns of Tables 1, 2 and 3. Notice that for this technique we do not report workaround size, since it "repairs" the failing method by directly building a suitable post-execution state. Regarding the results of both techniques on the JodaTime date arithmetic library, these are summarized in a single table (Table 4) due to space restrictions, for varying bitwidths in numeric datatypes.

Assessment. Notice that our first technique performed very well on the presented experiments. Many methods could be repaired within the timeout limit of 10 min (see the very small number of timeouts in the tables), and with small traces; in fact, the great majority could be repaired by workarounds of size 1 (i.e., by calling only one alternative method), and some with workarounds of size up to 3, confirming the observations in [8]. It is important to observe that some methods are difficult to repair. For instance, method clear, that removes all elements in the corresponding collection, cannot be solved alternatively by *short*

Table 1. Workaround computation for Lists.

Lists: 116 structs.; min. size: 6; max. size: 25; avg. size: 14.85
Singly Lkd Lists: 116 structs.; min. size: 6; max. size: 25; avg. size: 14.85
Abst. Lkd Lists: 116 structs.; min. size: 6; max. size: 25; avg. size: 14.85

Method to fix	Lists				Singly Lkd Lists			Abst. Lkd Lists		
	Total Time	Avg. Rep.Time	Avg wa.	# TOs	Total Time	Avg Rep.Time	# TOs	Total Time	Avg Rep.Time	# TOs
add	0:36:06	0:0:18	1	0	0:08:01	0:0:04	0	0:11:18	0:0:05	0
addfirst	0:36:05	0:0:18	1	0	0:08:09	0:0:04	0	0:11:20	0:0:05	0
clear	19:20:00	-	-	116	0:07:50	0:0:04	0	0:10:22	0:0:05	0
contains	0:36:16	0:0:18	1	0	0:07:44	0:0:04	0	0:10:36	0:0:05	0
get	0:36:25	0:0:18	1	0	0:07:42	0:0:04	0	0:11:19	0:0:05	0
getfirst	0:36:14	0:0:18	1	0	0:09:52	0:0:05	0	0:11:11	0:0:05	0
indexof	0:35:18	0:0:18	1	0	0:09:20	0:0:04	0	0:12:23	0:0:06	0
isempty	0:36:05	0:0:18	1	0	0:07:40	0:0:04	0	0:11:12	0:0:05	0
lastindexof	0:35:29	0:0:18	1	0	0:09:00	0:0:04	0	0:12:23	0:0:06	0
offer	0:36:18	0:0:18	1	0	0:08:16	0:0:04	0	0:11:17	0:0:05	0
peek	0:36:35	0:0:18	1	0	0:08:00	0:0:04	0	0:11:23	0:0:05	0
poll	0:36:14	0:0:18	1	0	0:08:32	0:0:04	0	0:11:31	0:0:05	0
pop	0:36:07	0:0:18	1	0	0:08:24	0:0:04	0	0:10:28	0:0:05	0
push	0:36:25	0:0:18	1	0	0:08:33	0:0:04	0	0:11:26	0:0:05	0
remove	0:36:05	0:0:18	1	0	0:08:40	0:0:04	0	0:10:58	0:0:05	0
removem	1:34:34	0:0:48	1,732	0	0:11:18	0:0:06	0	0:11:12	0:0:05	0
setelement	1:48:38	0:0:56	1,948	0	0:07:54	0:0:04	0	0:10:42	0:0:05	0
size	0:36:24	0:0:18	1	0	0:08:04	0:0:04	0	0:10:39	0:0:05	0

Table 2. Workaround computation for Sets and Trees.

Sets: 136 structs.; min. size: 11; max. size: 22; avg. size: 13.17
TreeSet: 136 structs.; min. size: 11; max. size: 22; avg. size: 13.17
AVL Tree: 136 structs.; min. size: 11; max. size: 22; avg. size: 13.17
Search Tree: 136 structs.; min. size: 11; max. size: 22; avg. size: 13.17

Method to fix	Sets				TreeSet			AVL Tree			Search Tree		
	Total Time	Avg. Rep.T.	Avg. wa.	# TOs	Total Time	Avg Rep.T.	# TOs	Total Time	Avg Rep.T.	# TOs	Total Time	Avg Rep.T.	# TOs
add	3:03:48	0:1:21	2	0	2:30:13	0:1:02	1	1:18:07	0:0:30	1	0:49:11	0:0:17	1
ceiling	1:00:11	0:0:26	1	0	0:19:15	0:0:08	0	0:19:27	0:0:08	0	0:18:48	0:0:08	0
clear	22:40:00	0:0:00	-	136	0:10:19	0:0:04	0	0:11:33	0:0:05	0	0:10:48	0:0:04	0
contains	22:40:00	0:0:00	-	136	0:10:33	0:0:04	0	0:11:44	0:0:05	0	0:10:51	0:0:04	0
first	1:04:50	0:0:28	1	0	1:33:50	0:0:37	1	0:57:40	0:0:21	1	0:49:26	0:0:13	2
floor	1:05:06	0:0:28	1	0	2:01:34	0:0:49	1	1:00:19	0:0:22	1	0:27:46	0:0:12	0
higher	0:51:24	0:0:22	1	0	1:55:17	0:0:42	2	0:58:13	0:0:21	1	1:10:47	0:0:27	1
isEmpty	1:13:01	0:0:22	1	2	1:42:16	0:0:41	1	1:00:26	0:0:22	1	1:14:17	0:0:24	2
last	1:09:14	0:0:30	1	0	1:19:27	0:0:30	1	0:53:02	0:0:19	1	0:35:47	0:0:15	0
lower	0:52:03	0:0:22	1	0	1:29:02	0:0:35	1	0:57:28	0:0:21	1	1:11:47	0:0:18	3
pollFirst	1:09:52	0:0:30	1	0	1:23:57	0:0:37	0	0:51:05	0:0:22	0	0:47:43	0:0:12	2
remove	1:00:29	0:0:26	1	0	1:41:19	0:0:40	1	0:51:38	0:0:22	0	0:34:28	0:0:15	0

workarounds. In fact, this method requires performing as many element removals as the structure holds, which went beyond the 10-minute timeout in all cases. This technique also performed well on our arithmetic-intensive case study. Notice that, as bit-width is increased, analysis becomes slightly more expensive, but more workarounds arise (since some workarounds are infeasible with smaller bit-widths). Our second technique features even more impressive experimental results. Most of the repair situations that we built with Randoop were repaired using this technique. This included repairing methods that, from many program states, could not be repaired by the first technique.

Table 3. Workaround computation for Maps.

	Maps				Tree Maps		
Method to fix	Total Time	Avg. Rep.Time	Avg wa.	# TOs	Total Time	Avg Rep.Time	# TOs
ceilingkey	0:48:38	0:0:21	1	0	0:34:38	0:0:15	0
clear	23:00:00	-	-	138	0:29:53	0:0:12	0
containsvalue	0:47:01	0:0:20	1	0	0:30:45	0:0:13	0
firstentry	0:51:09	0:0:22	1	0	0:31:29	0:0:13	0
get	23:00:00	-	-	138	0:29:37	0:0:12	0
higherentry	1:17:04	0:0:33	1	0	0:32:44	0:0:14	0
isempty	1:20:19	0:0:34	1	0	0:27:16	0:0:11	0
lastkey	1:20:10	0:0:34	1	0	0:30:02	0:0:13	0
lowerentry	1:17:03	0:0:33	1	0	0:32:57	0:0:14	0
polllastentry	7:26:46	0:3:14	1	0	7:54:33	0:2:55	10
put	23:00:00	-	-	138	16:36:33	0:5:55	44
remove	23:00:00	-	-	138	9:27:27	0:3:03	21

Table 4. Workaround Computation for JodaTime.

	Technique 1						Technique 2					
	Int.16 bits			Int.32 bits			Int.16 bits			Int.32 bits		
Method to fix	# wa.	Total Time	Avg. Rep.	# wa.	Total Time	Avg. Rep.	# wa.	Total Time	Avg. Rep.	# wa.	Total Time	Avg. Rep.
minusHours	48	0:08:23	0:00:10	48	0:13:12	0:00:16	48	0:01:18	0:00:01	48	0:02:32	0:00:03
minusMillis	1	7:50:09	0:00:09	48	1:21:53	0:01:42	1	0:01:46	0:00:02	48	0:05:27	0:00:06
minusMinutes	9	6:31:30	0:00:10	46	1:00:00	0:00:52	9	0:01:30	0:00:01	48	0:05:37	0:00:07
minusPeriodHours	48	0:08:41	0:00:01	48	0:13:12	0:00:16	48	0:01:18	0:00:01	48	0:02:31	0:00:03
minusPeriodMillis	1	7:50:09	0:00:09	45	1:48:05	0:01:44	1	0:01:45	0:00:02	48	0:05:26	0:00:06
minusPeriodMinutes	9	6:31:32	0:00:10	46	1:01:53	0:00:54	9	0:01:34	0:00:01	48	0:04:38	0:00:05
plusHours	48	0:08:57	0:00:11	48	0:12:38	0:00:15	48	0:01:18	0:00:01	48	0:02:32	0:00:03
plusMillis	1	7:50:12	0:00:12	47	1:12:01	0:01:19	1	0:01:39	0:00:02	48	0:04:55	0:00:06
plusMinutes	29	3:13:21	0:00:09	48	0:13:00	0:00:16	29	0:01:30	0:00:01	48	0:02:51	0:00:03
plusPeriodHours	48	0:08:45	0:00:01	48	0:12:50	0:00:16	48	0:01:17	0:00:01	48	0:02:31	0:00:03
plusPeriodMillis	1	7:50:12	0:00:12	47	1:06:41	0:01:12	1	0:01:44	0:00:02	48	0:05:01	0:00:06
plusPeriodMinutes	29	3:14:41	0:00:09	48	0:12:42	0:00:15	29	0:01:31	0:00:01	48	0:02:53	0:00:03
withHourOfDay	48	0:09:21	0:00:11	48	0:13:18	0:00:16	48	0:01:07	0:00:01	48	0:02:22	0:00:02
getHourOfDay	0	8:00:00	-	0	8:00:00	-	48	0:01:07	0:00:01	48	0:02:41	0:00:03
getMillisOfSecond	0	8:00:00	-	0	8:00:00	-	48	0:01:06	0:00:01	48	0:02:39	0:00:03

These techniques scaled for the evaluated classes beyond some SAT based analysis techniques, e.g., for test generation or bounded verification [2,14]. The reason for this increased scalability might at first sight seem obvious, since the analysis starts from a concrete program state. However, the nondeterminism of the (DynAlloy) program used in the computation of the workarounds, formed by an iteration of a nondeterministic choice of actions (representing methods), makes the analysis challenging and the obtained results relatively surprising. A technical detail that makes the results interesting is the fact that the translation from Java into Alloy and Dynalloy that we use encodes numerical datatypes with Java's precision. That is, integers are encoded as 32-bit integers (in the case of JodaTime, where arithmetic is heavily used, we assessed our techniques with different bit-widths), as opposed to other works that use Alloy integers (very limited numerical ranges). The approach is that presented in [2], extended to make some Alloy functions, notably cardinality (#), work on these numerical characterization of Java basic datatypes.

Threats to Validity. Our experimental evaluation involved implementations accompanied by corresponding abstract datatypes. When available, these were taken from previous work, that used them in a benchmark for automated analysis. We did not formally verify that these implementations and specifications are correct, and they may contain errors that affect our results. We manually checked that the obtained workarounds were correct, confirming that, as far as our techniques required, the specifications were correct. Our experiments involved randomly generated scenarios (program states), from which workaround computations were launched. Different randomly picked scenarios may of course lead to different results. We attempted to build a sufficiently varied set of such program states, while at the same time keeping the size of the sample maneagable. In all cases we performed workaround computations, for each method under analysis, on more than 100 scenarios. These were selected following an even distribution, and taking into account how Randoop (the random testing tool used to produce the scenarios) performed the generation, reporting our results as an average. We took as many measures as possible to ensure that the selection of the cases did not particularly favor our techniques. Our workaround computation tools make use of optimizations, such as tight bounds [14,15]. These may introduce errors, e.g., making the exploration for workarounds not bounded exhaustive. We experimentally checked consistency of our prototypes with/without these optimizations, to ensure these did not affect the outcomes.

6   Related Work

Existing approaches to workaround computation are among the closest work related to our first technique. We identify two lines, one that concentrates in *computing* workarounds, as in [4,6], and another that focuses on *applying* workarounds [7]. Our work is closer to the former. As opposed to [4,6], requiring a state transition system abstraction, our workarounds are computed directly from source code contracts. Workarounds of the kind used in [7] are alternative equivalent programs to that being repaired. Thus, workarounds can be thought of as automated program repair strategies. In this sense, the work is related to the works on automated program repair, e.g., [10,20,29]. The workarounds that we compute can repair a program *in a specific state*, i.e., they are workarounds as in the original works [4,6], that do not constitute "permanent" program repairs, but "transient" ones, i.e., that only work on specific situations. Program repair techniques often use tests as specifications and thus can lead to spurious fixes (see [23,27] for detailed analyses of this problem).

Our second technique for workarounds directly manipulates program states, as opposed to trying to produce these indirectly via method calls. This technique is closely related to constraint-based and contract-based structure repair approaches, e.g. [11,17,19], in particular the approach of Khurshid and collaborators to repair complex structures, reported in [30,31]. While Khurshid et al.

compute a kind of structure "frame" (the part of the structure that the failing program modified), and then try to repair structures by only modifying the frame, we allow modifications on the whole structure. Also, in [30,31], Alloy integers are used, instead of integers with Java precision. Thus, a greater scalability can be observed in their work (in that work the authors can deal with bigger structures, compared to our approach), whereas in our case the program state characterization is closer to the actual Java program states. Moreover, our technique can repair structures that the approach in [31] cannot. A thorough comparison cannot be carried out, because the tool and experiments from [31] are not available. Nevertheless, we have followed that paper's procedure, and attempted to repair some of the randomly produced structures of our experiments. For instance, in cases where a rotation is missing (in a balanced tree), the approach in [31] cannot produce repairs, since the fields that are allowed to change are restricted to those visited by the program, and since the rotation is mistakenly prevented, the technique cannot modify fields that are essential for the repair. If, instead, we allow the approach in [31] to modify the whole structure, then the approach is similar to ours without the use of tight bounds and symmetry breaking, which we already discussed in the previous section. The approaches are however complementary, in the sense that we may restrict modifiable fields as proposed in [31], and they could exploit symmetry breaking predicates and tight bounds, as in our case. Our work uses tight field bounds to improve analysis. Tight bounds have been exploited in previous work, to improve SAT-based automated bug finding and test input generation, e.g., in [2,14,15,24], and in symbolic execution based model checking, to prune parts of the symbolic execution search tree constraining nondeterministic options, in [16,25].

7   Conclusions and Future Work

The intrinsic complexity of software, the constant adaptation/extension that software undergoes and other factors, make it very difficult to produce software systems maintaining high quality throughout their whole lifetime. This fact makes techniques that help systems tolerate bug-related failures highly relevant. In this paper, we have presented two techniques that contribute to tolerate runtime bug related failures. These techniques propose the use of SAT-based automated analysis to automatically compute workarounds, i.e., alternative mechanisms offered by failing modules to achieve a desired task, and automated program state repair. These techniques apply directly to formal specifications at the level of detail of program contracts, which are exploited for workaround and state repair computations. Our program state characterizations are closer to the actual concrete program states than some related approaches, and can automatically deal with program specifications at the level of detail of source code, as opposed to alternatives that require the engineer to manually produce high level state machine program abstractions. We have performed an experimental evaluation that involved various contract-equipped implementations (including arithmetic-intensive ones), and showed that our techniques can circumvent run time failures by automatically computing workarounds/state repairs from complex program specifications, in a number of randomly produced execution scenarios.

As future work, we plan to evaluate the techniques' performance in software other than our case studies, as well as to develop more sophisticated optimization techniques, e.g., by further exploiting tight bounds. Moreover, while the repairs produced by workarounds are in principle "transient", many of the computed workarounds are instances of "permanent" workarounds; we plan to study ways to automatically produce "permanent" workarounds from "transient" candidates, as a proposal of a program repair technique.

References

1. Replication package for Automated Workarounds from Java Program Specifications based on SAT Solving. http://dc.exa.unrc.edu.ar/staff/naguirre/sat-workarounds/
2. Abad, P., Aguirre, N., Bengolea, V., Ciolek, D., Frias, M., Galeotti, J., Maibaum, T., Moscato, M., Rosner, N., Vissani, I.: Improving test generation under rich contracts by tight bounds and incremental SAT solving. In: Proceedings of 6th IEEE International Conference on Software Testing, Verification and Validation, ICST 2013, Luxembourg City, Luxembourg. IEEE (2013)
3. Belt, J., Robby, Deng, X.: Sireum/Topi LDP: a lightweight semi-decision procedure for optimizing symbolic execution-based analyses. In: Proceedings of the 7th Joint Meeting of the European Software Engineering Conference and The ACM SIGSOFT International Symposium on Foundations of Software Engineering ESEC/FSE 2009. ACM (2009)
4. Carzaniga, A., Gorla, A., Pezzè, M.: Self-healing by means of automatic workarounds. In: Proceedings of 2008 ICSE Workshop on Software Engineering for Adaptive and Self-Managing Systems, SEAMS 2008, Leipzig, Germany, 12–13 May. ACM (2008)
5. Carzaniga, A., Gorla, A., Perino, N., Pezzè, M.: Automatic workarounds for web applications. In: Proceedings of the 18th ACM SIGSOFT International Symposium on Foundations of Software Engineering, FSE 2010, Santa Fe (NM), USA. ACM (2010)
6. Carzaniga, A., Gorla, A., Perino, N., Pezzè, M.: RAW: runtime automatic workarounds. In: Proceedings of the 32nd ACM/IEEE International Conference on Software Engineering, ICSE 2010. ACM, New York (2010)
7. Carzaniga, A., Gorla, A., Mattavelli, A., Perino, N., Pezzè, M.: Automatic recovery from runtime failures. In: Proceedings of the 35th International Conference on Software Engineering ICSE 2013. IEEE/ACM, San Francisco (2013)
8. Carzaniga, A., Gorla, A., Perino, N., Pezzè, M.: Automatic workarounds: exploiting the intrinsic redundancy of web applications. ACM Trans. Softw. Eng. Methodol. 24(3) (2015). ACM
9. Chalin, P., Kiniry, J.R., Leavens, G.T., Poll, E.: Beyond assertions: advanced specification and verification with JML and ESC/Java2. In: Boer, F.S., Bonsangue, M.M., Graf, S., Roever, W.-P. (eds.) FMCO 2005. LNCS, vol. 4111, pp. 342–363. Springer, Heidelberg (2006). doi:10.1007/11804192_16
10. Debroy, V., Wong, W.E.: Using mutation to automatically suggest fixes to faulty programs. In: ICST 2010, pp. 65–74 (2010)

11. Demsky, B., Rinard, M.: Static specification analysis for termination of specification-based data structure repair. In: Proceedings of the 2003 ACM SIGPLAN Conference on Object-Oriented Programming Systems, Languages and Applications, OOPSLA 2003. ACM (2003)

12. Frias, M., Galeotti, J., López Pombo, C., Aguirre, N.: DynAlloy: upgrading alloy with actions. In: Proceedings of International Conference on Software Engineering, ICSE 2005, St. Louis, Missouri, USA. ACM (2005)

13. Galeotti, J.P., Frias, M.F.: DynAlloy as a formal method for the analysis of Java programs. In: Sacha, K. (ed.) Software Engineering Techniques: Design for Quality. IFIP, vol. 227, pp. 249–260. Springer, Boston (2006). doi:10.1007/978-0-387-39388-9_24

14. Galeotti, J.P., Rosner, N., López Pombo, C., Frias, M.: Analysis of invariants for efficient bounded verification. In: Proceedings of the Nineteenth International Symposium on Software Testing and Analysis, ISSTA 2010, Trento, Italy, 12–16 July. ACM (2010)

15. Galeotti, J.P., Rosner, N., López Pombo, C., Frias, M.: TACO: efficient SAT-based bounded verification using symmetry breaking and tight bounds. IEEE Trans. Softw. Eng. **39**(9), 1283–1307 (2013). IEEE

16. Geldenhuys, J., Aguirre, N., Frias, M.F., Visser, W.: Bounded lazy initialization. In: Brat, G., Rungta, N., Venet, A. (eds.) NFM 2013. LNCS, vol. 7871, pp. 229–243. Springer, Heidelberg (2013). doi:10.1007/978-3-642-38088-4_16

17. Hussain, I., Csallner, C.: Dynamic symbolic data structure repair. In: Proceedings of the 32nd ACM/IEEE International Conference on Software Engineering, ICSE 2010. ACM (2010)

18. Jackson, D.: Software Abstractions: Logic, Language, and Analysis. The MIT Press, Cambridge (2006)

19. Khurshid, S., García, I., Suen, Y.L.: Repairing structurally complex data. In: Godefroid, P. (ed.) SPIN 2005. LNCS, vol. 3639, pp. 123–138. Springer, Heidelberg (2005). doi:10.1007/11537328_12

20. Kim, D., Nam, J., Song, J., Kim, S.: Automatic patch generation learned from human-written patches. In: ICSE 2013, pp. 802–811 (2013)

21. Liskov, B., Guttag, J.: Program Development in Java: Abstraction, Specification and Object-Oriented Design. Addison-Wesley, Boston (2000)

22. Pacheco, C., Lahiri, S.K., Ernst, M.D., Ball, T.: Feedback-directed random test generation. In: Proceedings of International Conference on Software Engineering, ICSE 2007. IEEE (2007)

23. Qi, Z., Long, F., Achour, S., Rinard, M.C.: An analysis of patch plausibility and correctness for generate-and-validate patch generation systems. In: Proceedings of the 2015 International Symposium on Software Testing and Analysis, ISSTA 2015, Baltimore, MD, USA, 12–17 July 2015, pp. 24–36 (2015)

24. Rosner, N., Bengolea, V., Ponzio, P., Khalek, S., Aguirre, N., Frias, M., Khurshid, S.: Bounded Exhaustive test input generation from hybrid invariants. In: Proceedings of the ACM International Conference on Object Oriented Programming Systems Languages & Applications, OOPSLA 2014. ACM (2014)

25. Rosner, N., Geldenhuys, J., Aguirre, N., Visser, W., Frias, M.: BLISS: improved symbolic execution by bounded lazy initialization with SAT support. IEEE Trans. Softw. Eng. **41**(7), 639–660 (2015). IEEE

26. Samimi, H., Aung, E.D., Millstein, T.: Falling back on executable specifications. In: D'Hondt, T. (ed.) ECOOP 2010. LNCS, vol. 6183, pp. 552–576. Springer, Heidelberg (2010). doi:10.1007/978-3-642-14107-2_26

27. Smith, E.K., Barr, E., Le Goues, C., Brun, Y.: Is the cure worse than the disease? overfitting in automated program repair. In: Symposium on the Foundations of Software Engineering (FSE) (2015)

28. Visser, W., Pasareanu, C., Pelánek, R.: Test input generation for java containers using state matching. In: Proceedings of the ACM/SIGSOFT International Symposium on Software Testing and Analysis, ISSTA 2006. ACM (2006)

29. Weimer, W., Nguyen, T., Le Goues, C., Forrest, S.: Automatically finding patches using genetic programming. In: ICSE 2009, pp. 364–374 (2009)

30. Nokhbeh Zaeem, R., Khurshid, S.: Contract-based data structure repair using alloy. In: D'Hondt, T. (ed.) ECOOP 2010. LNCS, vol. 6183, pp. 577–598. Springer, Heidelberg (2010). doi:10.1007/978-3-642-14107-2_27

31. Nokhbeh Zaeem, R., Gopinath, D., Khurshid, S., McKinley, K.S.: History-aware data structure repair using SAT. In: Flanagan, C., König, B. (eds.) TACAS 2012. LNCS, vol. 7214, pp. 2–17. Springer, Heidelberg (2012). doi:10.1007/978-3-642-28756-5_2

Slicing from Formal Semantics: Chisel

Adrián Riesco[1]([⊠]), Irina Mǎriuca Asǎvoae[2], and Mihail Asǎvoae[2]

[1] Universidad Complutense de Madrid, Madrid, Spain
ariesco@fdi.ucm.es
[2] Inria Paris, Paris, France
{irina-mariuca.asavoae,mihail.asavoae}@inria.fr

Abstract. We describe Chisel—a tool that synthesizes a program slicer directly from a given algebraic specification of a programming language operational semantics. This semantics is assumed to be a rewriting logic specification, given in Maude, while the program is a ground term of this specification. We present the tool on two types of language paradigms: high-level, imperative and low-level assembly languages. We conduct experiments with standard benchmarking used in avionics.

1 Introduction

Lately we observe an increased interest in defining programming languages semantics as rewriting systems. This desideratum is stated in *the rewriting logic semantics project* [5], where the languages semantics are defined as rewriting systems using Maude [3], and it is followed by the 𝕂 framework [8]. Our work complements the rewriting logic semantics project by developing static analysis methods, e.g., slicing, for programs written in languages with semantics already defined in Maude. Here we present Chisel—a Maude tool for *generic* slicing.

Slicing is an analysis method employed for program debugging, testing, code parallelization, compiler tuning, etc. In essence, a slicing method evaluates data flow equations over the control flow graph of the program. Tip gives in [9] a comprehensive survey on the standard program slicing techniques applied over different programming language concepts. All these techniques are built using different models that represent augmentations of the control flow graph. Hence, the translation of the programs into these models has to be automatized and this has to be produced at the level of the programming language under consideration.

Chisel aims to advance the generic synthesis of program models from any programming language, provided the algebraic semantics of the language is given as a rewriting system. Namely, from a programming language semantics, given as a Maude specification, Chisel extracts pieces of interest for slicing, and uses these pieces to augment the program term and to produce the model, which is then sliced. We use for experiments two semantics: one for an imperative

Research partially supported by MINECO Spanish projects *StrongSoft* (TIN2012-39391-C04-04) and *TRACES* (TIN2015-67522-C3-3-R), and Comunidad de Madrid project N-Greens Software-CM (S2013/ICE-2731).

M. Huisman and J. Rubin (Eds.): FASE 2017, LNCS 10202, pp. 374–378, 2017.
DOI: 10.1007/978-3-662-54494-5_21

programming language with functions, WhileFun, and another for the MIPS assembly language. Chisel analyzes these semantics and extracts key information for slicing (e.g. side-effect constructs and their data flow direction) that are used when traversing the program term in order to obtain the program slice.

With Chisel we target sequential imperative code generated from synchronous designs—a class of applications used in real-time systems, e.g., avionics. Note that Chisel is not yet able to handle pointers, but the synchronous programs do not contain pointers either. For the evaluation of Chisel on industrial benchmarks, the pointers are transformed into function calls.

Related Work: An early work on generic slicing is presented in [4] where the tool compiles a program into a self slicer. Generic slicing is also the focus of the ORBS [2] tool which proposes observation-based slicing, a statement deletion technique for dynamic slicing. In rewriting logic [1] implements dynamic slicing for execution traces of the Maude model checker. In comparison with these tools, Chisel proposes a static approach to generating slicers for programming languages starting from their formal semantics. Given its static base, Chisel computes slices for programs and not for (model checker) runs. In [7] we refer to more technical details of the approach. Nevertheless, the developing platform of Chisel—Maude allows us to approach other types of slicing, e.g., dynamic or amorphous. Note that while dynamic slicing methods (either the classic or deletion-based) let us preserve genericity, determining generic statements equivalence for amorphous slicing might prove difficult. For the later case, we envision heuristics that start with our data dependence inference and compute some form of transitive closure.

The rest of the paper is organized as follows: Sect. 2 gives an overview of the tool, Sect. 3 describes the experimental results obtained, while Sect. 4 concludes and outlines some lines of future work. The complete code of the tool and examples are available at https://github.com/ariesco/chisel.

2   Chisel Design

In this section we describe the ideas underlying the tool. The main observation we use for Chisel is the fact that side-effects induce an update in the memory afferent to the program. Hence, Chisel first detects the operators used by the semantics to produce memory updates. Then, the usage of the memory update operators is traced through semantics up to the language constructs. Any language construct that may produce a memory update is classified as producing side-effects. Moreover, following the direction of the memory updates, we infer also the data flow details for each side-effect language construct. Finally, the information gathered by Chisel about language constructs is used to traverse the term representing the program and to extract the subterms representing the slice.

In Fig. 1 we depict the structure of Chisel by components and their input-output relation. We present next details about each of Chisel's components that work with $\mathcal{S}$—the Maude specification of the programming language semantics.

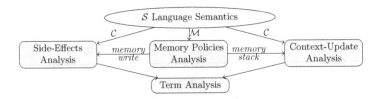

Fig. 1. Chisel components: the formal language semantics and the analyses.

Memory Policies Semantics Analysis: Let us define $\mathcal{M}$ as the part of $\mathcal{S}$ that defines some (abstract) form of the memory used during program execution. Our assumption about the structure of the memory is that it connects the variables in the program with their values possibly via a chain of intermediate addresses. We define a *memory policy* as a particular type of operators specified using $\mathcal{M}$. For example, a *memory-read* is the set of operators in $\mathcal{M}$ that contain in their arity the sort for variables and for memory, and in their co-arity the sort for values. A *memory-write* operator contains in the arity the memory, the variable, and a value, in the co-arity the memory, and the rules defining this operator change the memory variable by updating the value.

Side-Effect Semantics Analysis: Let us denote as $\mathcal{C}$ the part of $\mathcal{S}$ that defines the operators representing the programming language constructs, i.e., language instructions. We name *side-effect constructs* those operators in $\mathcal{C}$ that may produce a memory-write over some of its variable component. The side-effect analysis starts with the rules with $\mathcal{C}$ operators in the left-hand side and constructs a *hyper-tree* $\mathcal{T}$ whose nodes are sets of rewrite rules and edges are unification-based dependencies between these rules. The paths $\mathcal{P}$ in $\mathcal{T}$ with leaves that contain rules classified by the memory policy phase as memory-writes are signalling the side-effect constructs. Next, by trickling-up the paths in $\mathcal{P}$, Chisel determines the data flow (source-destination) produced by the side-effect constructs.

Context-Update Semantics Analysis: We see the program p as a term $t \in \mathcal{S}$ that can be flattened into a list $\mathcal{L}$ of elements from $\mathcal{C}$ by a preorder traversal of the tree associated to t. We define as *context-update constructs* those operators in $\mathcal{C}$ that, during p execution using $\mathcal{S}$, produce changes to $\mathcal{L}$. For example, function calls and gotos are context-updates. The inference of a set of constructs that may produce context-updates filters the paths in $\mathcal{T}$ by using a *stack memory policy* at the leaves level. This analysis is work in progress, which we only brief here. Currently, we provide these constructs for each $\mathcal{S}$.

Term Augmentation and Traversal: The algorithm for slicing a program takes as input a *slicing criterion* S consisting in a set of program variables. In this step, Chisel takes the list $\mathcal{L}$ of $\mathcal{C}$ subterms obtained from the program term and traverses it repeatedly until the set S stabilizes. While traversing the list $\mathcal{L}$, whenever a side-effect construct is encountered, if the destination of this construct is from S then all the source variables are added to S. Moreover, whenever a context-update construct is encountered, the traversal of $\mathcal{L}$ is redirected towards the element of $\mathcal{L}$ matching a particular subterm in the context-update construct.

3 Chisel Experiments

We run Chisel on a standard benchmark for real-time systems called PapaBench [6], a code snapshot extracted from an actual real-time system designed for Unmanned Aerial Vehicle. We report the results of Chisel for the core functionalities (rows 1, 2), and the complete PapaBench benchmark (rows 3, 4). For both WhileFun and MIPS variants of the benchmarks, we quantify the number of functions and function calls (columns #Funs and respectively #Calls), the code size (LOC), and the slicing reduction factor, red(%). The reduction factor captures the slicing performance w.r.t. the original code on both WhileFun and MIPS variants (Fig. 2).

No	Name	# Funs	# Calls	LOC (WhileFun)	red (%) (WhileFun)	LOC (MIPS)	red (%) (MIPS)
1	scheduler_fbw	14	18	103	72.8 %	396	44.4 %
2	periodic_auto	21	80	225	73.3 %	779	36.3 %
3	fly_by_wire	41	110	638	91.1 %	1913	41 %
4	autopilot	95	214	1384	92 %	5639	41.5 %

Fig. 2. Chisel performance on PapaBench benchmark

The lower percentages obtained for the MIPS code appear because of the current limitation of Chisel in handling memory addresses. Moreover, any function call in a small sized function involves setting the function stack with registers global and stack pointer, which dominate the code size yielding longer slices.

4 Conclusions

In this paper we have presented Chisel, a Maude tool that, given the semantics of a programming language written as a rewriting specification in Maude, can (both intra- and interprocedural) slice programs written in that language. We tested Chisel with different semantics: WhileFun (imperative) and MIPS (assembly), both with different variations (e.g. different memory models and data flow styles). In future work, we plan to extend the language with pointers, hence supporting more complex memory policies, based on more refined memory models.

References

1. Alpuente, M., Ballis, D., Frechina, F., Sapiña, J.: Combining runtime checking and slicing to improve Maude error diagnosis. In: Martí-Oliet, N., Ölveczky, P.C., Talcott, C. (eds.) Logic, Rewriting, and Concurrency. LNCS, vol. 9200, pp. 72–96. Springer, Cham (2015). doi:10.1007/978-3-319-23165-5_3

2. Binkley, D., Gold, N., Harman, M., Islam, S., Krinke, J., Yoo, S.: ORBS: language-independent program slicing. In: SIGSOFT FSE 2014, pp. 109–120. ACM (2014)
3. Clavel, M., Durán, F., Eker, S., Lincoln, P., Martí-Oliet, N., Meseguer, J., Talcott, C.: All About Maude - A High-Performance Logical Framework. LNCS, vol. 4350. Springer, Heidelberg (2007). doi:10.1007/978-3-540-71999-1
4. Danicic, S., Harman, M.: Espresso: a slicer generator. In: SAC 2000, pp. 831–839. ACM (2000)
5. Meseguer, J., Roşu, G.: The rewriting logic semantics project. Theoret. Comput. Sci. **373**(3), 213–237 (2007)
6. Nemer, F., Cassé, H., Sainrat, P., Bahsoun, J.P., Michiel, M.D.: PapaBench: a free real-time benchmark. In: WCET 2006. IBFI, Schloss Dagstuhl (2006)
7. Riesco, A., Asavoae, I.M., Asavoae, M.: Memory policy analysis for semantics specifications in Maude. In: Falaschi, M. (ed.) LOPSTR 2015. LNCS, vol. 9527, pp. 293–310. Springer, Cham (2015). doi:10.1007/978-3-319-27436-2_18
8. Roşu, G., Şerbănuţă, T.F.: An overview of the K semantic framework. J. Logic Algebraic Program. **79**(6), 397–434 (2010)
9. Tip, F.: A survey of program slicing techniques. JPL **3**(3), 121–189 (1995)

EASYINTERFACE: A Toolkit for Rapid Development of GUIs for Research Prototype Tools

Jesús Doménech[1], Samir Genaim[1(✉)], Einar Broch Johnsen[2],
and Rudolf Schlatte[2]

[1] Complutense University of Madrid, Madrid, Spain
genaim@gmail.com
[2] University of Oslo, Oslo, Norway

Abstract. EASYINTERFACE is an open-source toolkit to develop web-based graphical user interfaces (GUIs) for research prototype tools. This toolkit enables researchers to make their tool prototypes available to the community and integrating them in a common environment, rapidly and without being familiar with web programming or GUI libraries.

1 Introduction

During the lifetime of a research project, research prototype tools are often developed which share many common aspects. For example, in the Envisage [2] project, we developed various tools for processing ABS programs: static analyzers, compilers, simulators, etc. Both as individual researchers and as groups, we often develop several related tools over time to pursue a specific line of research.

Providing the community with easy access to research prototype tools is crucial to promote the research, get feedback, and increase the tools' lifetime beyond the duration of a specific project. This can be achieved by building GUIs that facilitate trying tools; in particular, tools with *web-interfaces* can be tried without the overhead of first downloading and installing the tools.

In practice, we typically avoid developing GUIs until tools are fairly stable. Since prototype tools change continuously, in particular during a research project, they will often not be available to the community during early development. Both programming plug-ins for sophisticated frameworks such as Eclipse Scout and building simpler GUIs from scratch are tedious tasks, in particular for web-interfaces. It typically gets low priority when developing a research prototype. Often we opt for copying the GUI of one tool and modifying it to fit the needs of a new related tool. Apart from code duplication, these tools will "live" separately, although we might benefit from having them in a common GUI.

EASYINTERFACE is a toolkit that aims at simplifying the process of building and maintaining GUIs for (but not limited to) research prototype tools.

This work was partially funded by the EU project FP7-ICT-610582 ENVISAGE: Engineering Virtualized Services, the Spanish MINECO projects TIN2012-38137 and TIN2015-69175-C4-2-R, and the CM project S2013/ICE-3006.

M. Huisman and J. Rubin (Eds.): FASE 2017, LNCS 10202, pp. 379–383, 2017.
DOI: 10.1007/978-3-662-54494-5_22

Avoiding complex programming, it provides an easy, declarative way to make existing (command-line) tools available via different environments such as a web-interface, within Eclipse, etc. It also defines a text-based output language that can be used to improve the way results are presented to the user without requiring any particular knowledge of GUI/Web programming; e.g., if the output of a tool is (a structured version of) *"highlight line number 10 of file ex.c"* and *"when the user clicks on line 10, open a dialog box with the text ..."*, the web-interface will interpret this and convert it to corresponding visual effects. An advantage of using such an output language is that it will be understood by all the front-end environments of EASYINTERFACE, e.g., the web-interface and the Eclipse plug-in (which is still under development). EASYINTERFACE is open source and available at http://github.com/abstools/easyinterface. Detailed description of EASYINTERFACE, including a step by step example on how to integrate tools and discussion of related work, is available in the user manual [1].

2   General Overview

The overall architecture of EASYINTERFACE is depicted in Fig. 1. Its two main components are (*i*) *server side*: a machine with several tools (the circles Tool1, etc.) executable from the command-line, and with output going to the standard output. These are the tools that we want to make available for the outside world; and (*ii*) *client side*: several clients that communicate with the server to execute

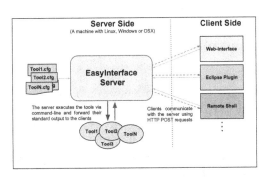

Fig. 1. EASYINTERFACE architecture.

a tool. Tools may run on the server machine or on other machines; e.g., the web-interface can be installed as a web-page on the server, and accessed from anywhere with a web browser. Clients can connect to several servers simultaneously.

The server side addresses the problem of *providing a uniform way to remotely execute locally installed tools*. This problem is solved by the server, which consists of PHP programs (on top of an HTTP server). The server supports *declarative specifications* of how local tools can be executed and which parameters they take, using simple configuration files. For example, the XML snippet to the right is a configuration file for a tool

```
<app id="myapp" visible="true">
...
 <execinfo method="cmdline">
  <cmdlineapp>
   /path-to/myapp _ei_parameters
  </cmdlineapp>
 </execinfo>
 <parameters prefix = "-" check="false">
  ...
  <selectone name="c">
   <option value="1" />
   <option value="2" />
  </selectone>
 </parameters>
</app>
```

called `myapp`. The `cmdlineapp` tag is a template describing how to execute the tool from the command-line. The template parameter `_ei_parameters` is replaced by an appropriate value before execution. The server also supports template parameters for, e.g., passing files, temporal working directories, session identifiers, etc. The `parameters` tag includes a list of parameters accepted by the tool. For example, the parameter "c" above takes one of the values 1 or 2.

Once the configuration file is installed on the server, we can access the tool using an HTTP POST request that includes JSON-formatted data like the one on the right. When receiving such a request, the server generates a shell command according to the specification in the configuration file (e.g., "/path-to/myapp -c 1"), executes it and redirects the standard output to the client. The

```
{
  command: "execute",
  app_id: "myapp",
  parameters: {
    c: ["1"],
    ...
  },
  ...
}
```

server also supports (*i*) tools that generate output in the background, we let clients fetch output (partially) when it is ready; and (*ii*) tools that generate files, we let clients download them later when needed. In all cases, the server can *restrict the resources* available to a tool (e.g., the processing time), and *guarantees the safety* of the generated command; i.e., clients cannot manipulate the server to execute other programs installed on the server. In addition to tools, the server can include example files, so users can easily try the tools.

EASYINTERFACE not only makes the server side execution of a tool easy, it provides client side GUIs that (1) connect to the server and ask for available tools; (2) let users select the tool to execute, set its parameters and provide a source program; (3) generate and send a request to the server; and (4) display the returned output. EASYINTERFACE provides three generic clients: a *web-interface* similar to an IDE; an Eclipse IDE plug-in; and a remote command-line shell. The last two clients are under development, so we focus here on the web-interface.

The web-interface, shown in Fig. 2, is designed like an IDE where users can edit programs, etc. Next to the **Run** button there is a drop-down menu with all available tools obtained from the associated servers. In the settings window, the user can select values for the different parameters of each tool. These parameters are specified in the corresponding configuration files on the server side, and automatically converted to combo-boxes, etc., by the web-interface. When the user clicks the **Run** button, the web-interface sends a request to the associated server to execute the selected tool and prints the received output back in the console area of the web-interface.

Since the web-interface and Eclipse plug-in are GUI based clients, EASY-INTERFACE allows tools to generate output with some graphical effects, such as opening dialog-boxes, highlighting code lines, adding markers, etc.

```
<highlightlines dest="/path-to/sum.c">
  <lines> <line from="5" to="10"/> </lines>
</highlightlines>
...
<oncodelineclick dest="/path-to/sum.c" outclass="info">
  <lines><line from="17" /></lines>
  <eicommands>
    <dialogbox boxtitle="Hey!">
      <content format="text"> some message </content>
    </dialogbox>
  </eicommands>
</oncodelineclick>
```

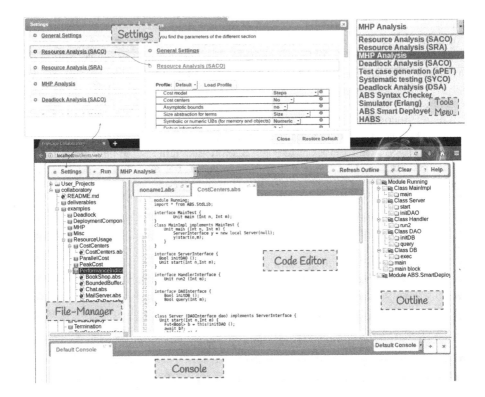

Fig. 2. EASYINTERFACE web-interface client

To use this feature, tools must support the EASYINTERFACE output language, shown in the XML snippet to the right. The tag `highlightlines` indicates that Lines 5–10 of file `/path-to/sum.c` should be highlighted. The tag `oncodelineclick` indicates that when clicking on Line 17, a dialog-box with a corresponding message should be opened. Note that a tool is only modified once to produce such output, with similar effect in all EASYINTERFACE clients (including future ones).

3   Concluding Remarks

EASYINTERFACE is a toolkit for the rapid development of GUIs for command-line research prototype tools. The toolkit has been successfully used in the Envisage project to integrate the tools from the different partners in a common web-based environment, including parsers, type-checkers, compilers, simulators, deadlock and worst-case cost analyzers, and a systematic testing framework (see http://abs-models.org). Our experience suggests that the methodology implied by EASYINTERFACE for building GUIs is adequate for research prototype tools; as such tools change continuously, the corresponding GUIs can be modified immediately and with negligible effort. Future work includes plans to develop more clients, and libraries for different programming languages to facilitate generation of the output commands/actions instead of printing these directly.

References

1. Easyinterface User Manual. http://costa.ls.fi.upm.es/papers/costa/eiusermanual.pdf
2. Envisage: Engineering Virtualized Services. http://www.envisage-project.eu

Software Product Lines

Family-Based Model Checking with mCRL2

Maurice H. ter Beek[1]([✉]), Erik P. de Vink[2], and Tim A.C. Willemse[2]

[1] ISTI–CNR, Pisa, Italy
maurice.terbeek@isti.cnr.it
[2] TU/e, Eindhoven, The Netherlands

Abstract. Family-based model checking targets the simultaneous verification of multiple system variants, a technique to handle feature-based variability that is intrinsic to software product lines (SPLs). We present an approach for family-based verification based on the feature μ-calculus μL_f, which combines modalities with feature expressions. This logic is interpreted over featured transition systems, a well-accepted model of SPLs, which allows one to reason over the collective behavior of a number of variants (a family of products). Via an embedding into the modal μ-calculus with data, underpinned by the general-purpose mCRL2 toolset, off-the-shelf tool support for μL_f becomes readily available. We illustrate the feasibility of our approach on an SPL benchmark model and show the runtime improvement that family-based model checking with mCRL2 offers with respect to model checking the benchmark product-by-product.

1 Introduction

Many software systems are configurable systems whose variants differ by the *features* they provide, i.e. the functionality that is relevant for an end-user, and are therefore referred to as software product lines (SPLs) or *product families*. SPLs challenge existing formal methods and analysis tools by the potentially high number of different products, each giving rise to a large behavioral state space in general. SPLs are popular in the embedded and critical systems domain. Therefore, analysis techniques for proving the correctness of SPL models are widely studied (cf. [1] for a survey).

Because for larger SPL models enumerative product-by-product approaches become unfeasible, dedicated *family-based* techniques have been developed, exploiting variability in product families in terms of features (cf., e.g., [2–8]). In this paper, we contribute to the field of *family-based model checking*. Over the past decades, model checking has seen significant progress [9]. However, state-space explosion remains an issue, amplified for SPL models by the accumulation of possible variants and configurations. To mitigate these problems, family-based model checking was proposed as a means to simultaneously verify multiple variants in a single run (cf. [1]). To make SPL models amenable to family-based reasoning, feature-based variability was introduced in many behavioral models, e.g. based on process calculi [2,10–12] and labeled transition systems (LTSs) [3,13–15].

© Springer-Verlag GmbH Germany 2017
M. Huisman and J. Rubin (Eds.): FASE 2017, LNCS 10202, pp. 387–405, 2017.
DOI: 10.1007/978-3-662-54494-5_23

Arguably the most widely used behavioral SPL models are *featured transition systems* (FTSs) [13]. An FTS compactly represents multiple behaviors in a single transition system by exploiting transitions guarded by *feature expressions*. A transition of a given product can be taken if the product fulfills the feature expression associated with the transition. Thus, an FTS incorporates the behavior of all eligible products, while individual behavior can be extracted as LTSs. Properties of such models can be verified with dedicated SPL model checkers [16–18] or, to a certain degree, with single system model checkers [7,12,14].

As far as we know, none of the existing tools can verify modal μ-calculus properties over FTSs in a family-based manner. However, there have been earlier proposals for using the μ-calculus to analyze SPLs (cf., e.g., [2,10,12,19,20]). In [19], for instance, mCRL2 and its toolset [21,22] were used for *product-based* model checking. The flexibility of mCRL2's data language allowed to model and select valid product configurations and to model and check the behavior of individually generated products. While the SPL models of [19] have an FTS-like semantics, to actually perform family-based model checking also the supporting logic must be able to handle the specificity of FTSs, viz. transitions labeled with feature expressions. In [20], we generalized the approach that led to the feature-oriented variants fLTL [13] and fCTL [14] of LTL and CTL to the modal μ-calculus by defining μL_f, a *feature-oriented* variant of μL with an FTS semantics obtained by incorporating feature expressions. While μL_f paves the way for family-based model checking, so far the logic was without tool support, and it remained unclear whether it could be used effectively to model check FTSs.

Contributions. In this paper, we show how to effectively perform family-based model checking for μL_f by exploiting the mCRL2 toolset *as-is*, i.e. avoiding the implementation of a dedicated SPL-oriented verifier. We first show how to solve the family-based model-checking problem via an embedding of μL_f into mCRL2's modal μ-calculus with data. Then we define a partitioning procedure for μL_f that allows us to apply our results from [20]. Next, we evaluate our approach by verifying a number of representative properties over an mCRL2 specification of the minepump SPL benchmark model [8,13,23–25]. We verify typical linear-time and branching-time properties. We also verify properties involving more than one feature modality in a single formula, which is a novelty that allows to check different behavior for different variants *at once*. Finally, we discuss the improvement in runtime that results from using mCRL2 for family-based model checking as opposed to product-based model checking.

Further Related Work. There is a growing body of research on customizing model-checking techniques for SPLs. Like our FTS-based proposals [19,20], the CCS-based proposals PL-CCS [2,10] and DeltaCCS [12] are grounded in the μ-calculus. In [26], PL-CCS was proven to be less expressive (in terms of the sets of definable products) than FTSs, while DeltaCCS allows only limited family-based model checking (viz. verifying family-wide invariants for entire SPLs). DeltaCCS does provide efficient *incremental* model checking, a technique that improves product-based model checking by partially reusing verification results obtained for previously considered products. The state-of-the-art by the end of 2013 is summarized in [1], which also discusses type checking, static analysis, and theorem proving tailored for SPLs, as well as *software* model checking.

In a broader perspective, also *probabilistic* model checking was applied to SPLs recently, e.g. on feature-oriented (parametric) Markov chains [27–29] or Markov decision processes [30], and via a feature-oriented extension of the input language of the probabilistic model checker Prism [31], making the tool amenable to (family-based) SPL model checking [32]. Most recently, also *statistical* model checking was applied to SPLs [33,34], based on a probabilistic extension of the feature-oriented process calculus of [11].

2   A Feature μ-Calculus μL_f over FTSs

The μ-calculus is an extension of modal logic with fixpoint operators whose formulas are interpreted over LTSs (cf. [35]). We fix a set of actions $\mathcal{A}$, ranged over by $a, b, \ldots$, and a set of variables $\mathcal{X}$, ranged over by $X, Y, \ldots$.

Definition 1. *The μ-calculus μL over $\mathcal{A}$ and $\mathcal{X}$ is given by*

$$\varphi ::= \bot \mid \top \mid \neg\varphi \mid \varphi \vee \psi \mid \varphi \wedge \psi \mid \langle a \rangle \varphi \mid [a]\varphi \mid X \mid \mu X.\varphi \mid \nu X.\varphi$$

where for $\mu X.\varphi$ and $\nu X.\varphi$ all free occurrences of X in φ are in the scope of an even number of negations (to guarantee well-definedness of the fixpoint semantics). □

Next to the Boolean constants falsum and verum, μL contains the connectives $\neg$, $\vee$ and $\wedge$ of propositional logic and the diamond and box operators $\langle \rangle$ and $[]$ of modal logic. The least and greatest fixpoint operators μ and ν provide recursion used for 'finite' and 'infinite' looping, respectively.

Definition 2. *An LTS over $\mathcal{A}$ is a triple $L = (S, \rightarrow, s_*)$, with states from S, transition relation $\rightarrow \subseteq S \times \mathcal{A} \times S$, and initial state $s_* \in S$.* □

Definition 3. *Let L be an LTS with set of states S. Let $sSet = 2^S$ be the set of state sets with typical element U and $sEnv = \mathcal{X} \rightarrow sSet$ the set of state-based environments. The semantics $[\![\cdot]\!]_L : \mu L \rightarrow sEnv \rightarrow sSet$ is given by*

$$[\![\bot]\!]_L(\varepsilon) = \varnothing$$
$$[\![\top]\!]_L(\varepsilon) = S$$
$$[\![\neg\varphi]\!]_L(\varepsilon) = S \setminus [\![\varphi]\!]_L(\varepsilon)$$
$$[\![(\varphi \vee \psi)]\!]_L(\varepsilon) = [\![\varphi]\!]_L(\varepsilon) \cup [\![\psi]\!]_L(\varepsilon)$$
$$[\![(\varphi \wedge \psi)]\!]_L(\varepsilon) = [\![\varphi]\!]_L(\varepsilon) \cap [\![\psi]\!]_L(\varepsilon)$$

$$[\![\langle a \rangle\varphi]\!]_L(\varepsilon) = \{\, s \mid \exists t \colon s \xrightarrow{a} t \wedge t \in [\![\varphi]\!]_L(\varepsilon) \,\}$$
$$[\![[a]\varphi]\!]_L(\varepsilon) = \{\, s \mid \forall t \colon s \xrightarrow{a} t \Rightarrow t \in [\![\varphi]\!]_L(\varepsilon) \,\}$$
$$[\![X]\!]_L(\varepsilon) = \varepsilon(X)$$
$$[\![\mu X.\varphi]\!]_L(\varepsilon) = \mathit{lfp}(\lambda U.[\![\varphi]\!]_L(\varepsilon[U/X]))$$
$$[\![\nu X.\varphi]\!]_L(\varepsilon) = \mathit{gfp}(\lambda U.[\![\varphi]\!]_L(\varepsilon[U/X]))$$

where $\varepsilon[U/X]$, for $\varepsilon \in sEnv$, denotes the environment which yields $\varepsilon(Y)$ for variables Y different from the variable X and the set $U \in sSet$ for X itself. □

As typical for model checking, we only consider closed μL-formulas whose interpretation is independent of the environment. In such case we write $[\![\varphi]\!]_L$ for the interpretation of φ. Given a state s of an LTS L, we set $s \models_L \varphi$ iff $s \in [\![\varphi]\!]_L$.

We next fix a finite non-empty set $\mathcal{F}$ of features, with f as typical element. Let $\mathbb{B}[\mathcal{F}]$ denote the set of Boolean expressions over $\mathcal{F}$. Elements χ and γ of $\mathbb{B}[\mathcal{F}]$ are referred to as feature expressions. A product is a set of features, and $\mathcal{P}$ szdenotes the set of products, thus $\mathcal{P} \subseteq 2^{\mathcal{F}}$, with $p, q, \ldots$ ranging over $\mathcal{P}$. A subset $P \subseteq \mathcal{P}$ is referred to as a family of products. A feature expression γ, as Boolean expression over $\mathcal{F}$, can be interpreted as a set of products Q_γ, viz. the products p for which the induced truth assignment (**true** for $f \in p$, **false** for $f \notin p$) validates γ. Reversely, for each family $P \subseteq \mathcal{P}$ we fix a feature expression γ_P to represent it. The constant $\top$ denotes the feature expression that is always true. We now recall FTSs from [13] as a model for SPLs, using the notation of [20].

Definition 4. *An FTS over $\mathcal{A}$ and $\mathcal{F}$ is a triple $F=(S,\theta,s_*)$, with states from S, transition constraint function $\theta \colon S \times \mathcal{A} \times S \to \mathbb{B}[\mathcal{F}]$, and initial state $s_* \in S$.* □

For states $s, t \in S$, we write $s \xrightarrow{a|\gamma}_F t$ if $\theta(s, a, t) = \gamma$ and $\gamma \not\equiv \bot$. The projection of an FTS $F = (S, \theta, s_*)$ onto a product $p \in \mathcal{P}$ is the LTS $F|p = (S, \to_{F|p}, s_*)$ over $\mathcal{A}$ with $s \xrightarrow{a}_{F|p} t$ iff $p \in Q_\gamma$ for a transition $s \xrightarrow{a|\gamma}_F t$ of F.

Example 1. Let P be a product line of (four) coffee machines, with independent features $\{\$, \in\}$ representing the presence of a coin slot accepting dollars or euros.

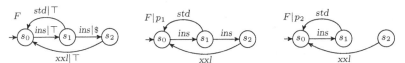

FTS F models its family behavior, with actions to insert coins (*ins*) and to pour standard (*std*) or extra large (*xxl*) coffee. Each coffee machine accepts either dollars or euros. Extra large coffee is exclusively available for two dollars. LTSs $F|p_1$ and $F|p_2$ model the behavior of products $p_1 = \{\$\}$ and $p_2 = \{\in\}$. Note that $F|p_2$ lacks the transition from s_1 to s_2 that requires feature $\$$. □

In [20], we introduced μL_f, an extension with features of the μ-calculus μL, interpreted over FTSs rather than LTSs.

Definition 5. *The feature μ-calculus μL_f over $\mathcal{A}$, $\mathcal{F}$ and X, is given by*

$$\varphi_f ::= \bot \mid \top \mid \neg\varphi_f \mid \varphi_f \vee \psi_f \mid \varphi_f \wedge \psi_f \mid \langle a|\chi\rangle\varphi_f \mid [a|\chi]\varphi_f \mid X \mid \mu X.\varphi_f \mid \nu X.\varphi_f$$

where for $\mu X.\varphi_f$ and $\nu X.\varphi_f$ all free occurrences of X in φ_f are in the scope of an even number of negations. □

Also for μL_f we mainly consider closed formulas. The logic μL_f replaces the binary operators $\langle a\rangle\varphi$ and $[a]\varphi$ of μL by ternary operators $\langle a|\chi\rangle\varphi_f$ and $[a|\chi]\varphi_f$, respectively, where χ is a feature expression.

A Product-Based Semantics. In [20], we gave a semantics $(\!(\varphi_f)\!)_F$ for closed μL_f-formulas φ_f with subsets of $S \times \mathcal{P}$ as denotations. We showed that this product-based semantics can be characterized as follows

$$(\!(\varphi_f)\!)_F = \{\, (s,p) \in S \times \mathcal{P} \mid s \in [\![\, \mathrm{pr}(\varphi_f, p)\,]\!]_{F|p}\,\}$$

where the projection function $\mathrm{pr} \colon \mu L_f \times \mathcal{P} \to \mu L$ is given by

$$\mathrm{pr}(\bot, p) = \bot \qquad \mathrm{pr}(\top, p) = \top \qquad \mathrm{pr}(X, p) = X \qquad \mathrm{pr}(\neg \varphi_f, p) = \neg \mathrm{pr}(\varphi_f, p)$$
$$\mathrm{pr}(\varphi_f \vee \psi_f, p) = \mathrm{pr}(\varphi_f, p) \vee \mathrm{pr}(\psi_f, p) \qquad \mathrm{pr}(\mu X.\varphi_f, p) = \mu X.\mathrm{pr}(\varphi_f, p)$$
$$\mathrm{pr}(\varphi_f \wedge \psi_f, p) = \mathrm{pr}(\varphi_f, p) \wedge \mathrm{pr}(\psi_f, p) \qquad \mathrm{pr}(\nu X.\varphi_f, p) = \nu X.\mathrm{pr}(\varphi_f, p)$$
$$\mathrm{pr}(\langle a|\chi \rangle \varphi_f, p) = \textbf{if } p \in Q_\chi \textbf{ then } \langle a \rangle \mathrm{pr}(\varphi_f, p) \textbf{ else } \bot \textbf{ end}$$
$$\mathrm{pr}([a|\chi]\varphi_f, p) = \textbf{if } p \in Q_\chi \textbf{ then } [a]\mathrm{pr}(\varphi_f, p) \textbf{ else } \top \textbf{ end}$$

Thus, for a formula $\varphi_f \in \mu L_f$ and a product $p \in \mathcal{P}$, a μL-formula $\mathrm{pr}(\varphi_f, p)$ is obtained from φ_f, by replacing subformulas $\langle a|\chi \rangle \psi_f$ by $\bot$ and $[a|\chi]\psi_f$ by $\top$, respectively, in case $p \notin Q_\chi$, while omitting χ otherwise. Formulas of μL_f permit reasoning about the behavior of products, as illustrated below.

Example 2. Formulas of μL_f for Example 1 include the following.

(a) $\varphi_f = \langle ins|\top \rangle ([ins|\epsilon]\bot \wedge \langle std|\top \rangle \top)$ characterizes the family of products P that can execute *ins*, after which *ins* cannot be executed by products satisfying ϵ, while *std* can be executed by all products of P.
(b) $\psi_f = \nu X.\mu Y.(([ins|\epsilon]Y \wedge [xxl|\epsilon]Y) \wedge [std|\epsilon]X)$ characterizes the (sub)family of products which, when having feature ϵ, action *std* occurs infinitely often on all infinite runs over *ins*, *xxl*, and *std*. □

In practice, we are often interested in deciding whether a family of products P satisfies a formula φ_f. The semantics of μL_f, however, does not allow for doing so in a family-based manner as it is product-oriented. For that reason, we introduced in [20] a second semantics $[\![\cdot]\!]_F$ for μL_f (cf. Definition 6 below) providing a stronger interpretation for the modalities to enable family-based reasoning. We stress that this second, family-based interpretation was designed to specifically support efficient model checking; the product-oriented $(\!(\cdot)\!)_F$ remains the semantic reference. The correspondence between the two interpretations was studied in detail in [20]. We next summarize the most important results.

A Family-Based Semantics. In our family-based interpretation, the ternary operator $\langle a|\chi \rangle \varphi_f$ holds for a family P with respect to an FTS F in a state s, if all products in P satisfy the feature expression χ and there is an a-transition, *shared among all products in P*, that leads to a state where φ_f holds for P (i.e. the products in P can collectively execute a). The $[a|\chi]\varphi_f$ modality holds in a state of F for a set of products P, if for each subset P' of P for which an a-transition is possible, φ_f holds for P' in the target state of that a-transition. While under the product-based interpretation $(\!(\cdot)\!)_F$ of μL_f, the two modalities in μL_f are, like in μL, each other's dual, this is no longer the case under the family-based interpretation $[\![\cdot]\!]_F$ below.

Definition 6. *Let* $F = (S, \theta, s_*)$ *be an FTS. Let* $sPSet = 2^{S \times 2^{\mathcal{P}}}$ *be the set of state-family pairs with typical element* W *and* $sPEnv = \mathcal{X} \rightarrow sPSet$ *the set of state-family environments. The semantics* $[\![\cdot]\!]_F : \mu L_f \rightarrow sPEnv \rightarrow sPSet$ *is given by*

$$
\begin{aligned}
&[\![\bot]\!]_F(\zeta) = \varnothing &&[\![\top]\!]_F(\zeta) = S \times 2^{\mathcal{P}} \\
&[\![\neg\varphi_f]\!]_F(\zeta) = (S \times 2^{\mathcal{P}}) \setminus [\![\varphi_f]\!]_F(\zeta) &&[\![X]\!]_F(\zeta) = \zeta(X) \\
&[\![(\varphi_f \vee \psi_f)]\!]_F(\zeta) = [\![\varphi_f]\!]_F(\zeta) \cup [\![\psi_f]\!]_F(\zeta) &&[\![\mu X.\varphi_f]\!]_F(\zeta) = \mathrm{lfp}(\lambda W.[\![\varphi_f]\!]_F(\zeta[W/X])) \\
&[\![(\varphi_f \wedge \psi_f)]\!]_F(\zeta) = [\![\varphi_f]\!]_F(\zeta) \cap [\![\psi_f]\!]_F(\zeta) &&[\![\nu X.\varphi_f]\!]_F(\zeta) = \mathrm{gfp}(\lambda W.[\![\varphi_f]\!]_F(\zeta[W/X]))
\end{aligned}
$$

$$[\![\langle a|\chi\rangle\varphi_f]\!]_F(\zeta) = \{\, (s, P) \mid P \subseteq Q_\chi \wedge \exists \gamma, t : s \xrightarrow{a|\gamma}_F t \wedge P \subseteq Q_\gamma \wedge (t, P \cap Q_\chi \cap Q_\gamma) \in [\![\varphi_f]\!]_F(\zeta) \,\}$$

$$[\![[a|\chi]\varphi_f]\!]_F(\zeta) = \{\, (s, P) \mid \forall \gamma, t : s \xrightarrow{a|\gamma}_F t \wedge P \cap Q_\chi \cap Q_\gamma \neq \varnothing \Rightarrow (t, P \cap Q_\chi \cap Q_\gamma) \in [\![\varphi_f]\!]_F(\zeta) \,\}$$

where $\zeta[W/X]$, *for* $\zeta \in sPEnv$, *denotes the environment which yields* $\zeta(Y)$ *for variables* Y *different from* X *and the set* $W \in sPSet$ *for* X. □

The interpretation of a closed μL_f formula φ_f is independent of the environment and we therefore again simply write $[\![\varphi_f]\!]_F$. Given a state s of an FTS F, and a set of products $P \subseteq \mathcal{P}$, we write $s, P \models_F \varphi_f$ iff $(s, P) \in [\![\varphi_f]\!]_F$.

The theorem below summarizes the main results of [20], relating the family-based interpretation of μL_f to the LTS semantics of μL (and by extension, μL_f's product-based interpretation).

Theorem 1. *Let* F *be an FTS, and let* $\mathcal{P}$ *be a set of products.*

(a) *For each formula* $\varphi_f \in \mu L_f$, *state* $s \in S$, *and individual product* $p \in \mathcal{P}$:
$$s, \{p\} \models_F \varphi_f \iff s \models_{F|p} \mathrm{pr}(\varphi_f, p).$$
(b) *For negation-free formula* $\varphi_f \in \mu L_f$, *state* $s \in S$, *and product family* $P \subseteq \mathcal{P}$:
$$s, P \models_F \varphi_f \implies \forall p \in P : s \models_{F|p} \mathrm{pr}(\varphi_f, p)$$ □

Note that in general, $s, P \not\models_F \varphi_f$ does not imply $s \not\models_{F|p} \mathrm{pr}(\varphi_f, p)$ for *all* products in the family P. In the next section, we discuss how the above results can be exploited for family-based model checking of μL_f-formulas.

3   Family-Based Model Checking with mCRL2

In this section, we show how to obtain a decision procedure for $s_*, P \models_F \varphi_f$ via a mapping into the first-order μ-calculus μL_{FO} and solving the corresponding model-checking problem. Our approach consists of two steps: (i) translation of the μL_f-formula at hand; (ii) translation of the FTS describing the family behavior into an LTS with parametrized actions. Since μL_{FO} is a fragment of the logic from [36,37], we can use off-the-shelf tools such as the mCRL2 toolset [21,22] to perform family-based model checking of properties expressed in μL_f. We first review μL_{FO} before we proceed to describe the above translations.

3.1   The First-Order μ-Calculus μL_{FO}

The first-order μ-calculus with data of [36,37] is given in the context of a data signature $\Sigma = (S, O)$, with set of sorts S and set of operations O, and of a set of 'sorted' actions $\mathcal{A}$. μL_{FO} is essentially a fragment of the logic of [36,37] in which S is the single sort FExp, with typical elements β, χ, γ, representing Boolean expressions over features and data variables taken from a set $\mathcal{V}$, with typical element v. In toolsets such as mCRL2, FExp can be formalized as an abstract data type defining BDDs ranging over features (cf. [38]). We fix a set of recursion variables $\tilde{X}$. Formulas $\varphi \in \mu L_{FO}$ are then given by

$$\varphi ::= \bot \mid \top \mid \neg\varphi \mid \varphi \lor \psi \mid \varphi \land \psi \mid \gamma_1 \Rrightarrow \gamma_2 \mid \exists v.\varphi \mid \forall v.\varphi \mid$$
$$\langle a(v) \rangle \varphi \mid [a(v)]\varphi \mid \tilde{X}(\gamma) \mid \mu\tilde{X}(v_{\tilde{X}} := \gamma).\varphi \mid \nu\tilde{X}(v_{\tilde{X}} := \gamma).\varphi$$

where for $\mu\tilde{X}(v_{\tilde{X}} := \gamma).\varphi$ and $\nu\tilde{X}(v_{\tilde{X}} := \gamma).\varphi$ all free occurrences of $\tilde{X}$ in φ are in the scope of an even number of negations, and each variable $\tilde{X}$ is bound at most once. To each recursion variable $\tilde{X}$ a unique data variable $v_{\tilde{X}}$ is associated, but we often suppress this association and simply write $\mu\tilde{X}(v := \gamma).\varphi$ and $\nu\tilde{X}(v := \gamma).\varphi$ instead. The language construct $\gamma_1 \Rrightarrow \gamma_2$ is used to express that the set of products characterized by γ_1 is a subset of those characterized by γ_2.

We interpret μL_{FO} over LTSs whose actions carry closed feature expressions.

Definition 7. *A parametrized LTS over $\mathcal{A}$ and $\mathcal{F}$ is a triple $(S, \rightarrow, s_*)$ with states from S, transition relation $\rightarrow \subseteq S \times \mathcal{A}[\mathcal{F}] \times S$ where $\mathcal{A}[\mathcal{F}] = \{ a(\gamma) \mid a \in \mathcal{A}, \gamma \in \mathbb{B}[\mathcal{F}] \}$, and initial state $s_* \in S$.*   □

In the presence of variables ranging over feature expressions, we distinguish two sets of environments, viz. data environments $\theta \in VEnv = \mathcal{V} \to 2^{\mathcal{P}}$ and recursion variable environments $\xi \in XEnv = \tilde{X} \to 2^{\mathcal{P}} \to 2^S$. The semantics $[\![\cdot]\!]_{FO}$ is then of type $\mu L_{FO} \to XEnv \to VEnv \to 2^S$. To comprehend our translation of μL_f into μL_{FO}, we address the semantics for the non-trivial constructs of μL_{FO}. The full semantics can be found in [36,37].

$$[\![\exists v.\varphi]\!]_{FO}(\xi)(\theta) = \bigcup \{ [\![\varphi]\!]_{FO}(\xi)(\theta[Q/v]) \mid Q \subseteq \mathcal{P} \}$$
$$[\![\langle a(v) \rangle \varphi]\!]_{FO}(\xi)(\theta) = \{ s \mid \exists \gamma, t \colon s \xrightarrow{a(\gamma)} t \land \theta(v) = Q_\gamma \land t \in [\![\varphi]\!]_{FO}(\xi)(\theta) \}$$
$$[\![\mu\tilde{X}(v := \gamma).\varphi]\!]_{FO}(\xi)(\theta) = \Big(\mathrm{lfp}(\lambda\pi{:}2^{\mathcal{P}} \to 2^S.\lambda Q.[\![\varphi]\!]_{FO}(\xi[\pi/\tilde{X}])(\theta[Q/v])) \Big)(\theta(\gamma))$$

For existential quantification, the data environment $\theta[Q/v]$ assigns a family of products Q to the data variable v; the set of states that satisfy $\exists v.\varphi$ is then the set of states satisfying φ for any possible assignment to data variable v.

For the diamond modality, a state s is included in its semantics, if in the parametrized LTS, state s admits a transition with parametrized action $a(\gamma)$ to a state t such that the set of products $\theta(v)$ is exactly the set of products Q_γ associated with the feature expression γ of the transition, while the target state t satisfies φ. Note that the set of products Q_γ can be established independently from the environment θ since γ is closed, i.e. variable-free.

The least fixpoint construction is more involved compared to the corresponding construct of μL_f because of the parametrization. Here the semantics of the least fixpoint is taken for the functional that fixes both the recursion variable $\tilde{X}$ and the data variable v, with π and Q, respectively. Next, application to the value of the initializing feature expression γ yields a set of states.

With respect to a parametrized LTS L, we put $s \models_L \varphi$, for $s \in S$ and $\varphi \in \mu L_{\mathsf{FO}}$ closed, if $s \in [\![\varphi]\!]_{FO}(\xi_0)(\theta_0)$ for some $\xi_0 \in XEnv$ and $\theta_0 \in VEnv$.

3.2   Translating the Family-Based Interpretation of μL_f to μL_{FO}

To model check a μL_f-formula against an FTS, we effectively verify its corresponding μL_{FO}-formula against the parametrized LTS that is obtained as follows.

Definition 8. *Let* $F = (S, \theta, s_*)$ *be an FTS over* $\mathcal{A}$ *and* $\mathcal{F}$. *Take* $\mathcal{A}[\mathcal{F}] = \{ a(\gamma) \mid a \in \mathcal{A}, \gamma \in \mathbb{B}[\mathcal{F}] \}$. *Define the parametrized LTS* $L(F)$ *for* F *by* $L(F) = (S, \rightarrow, s_*)$ *where* $\rightarrow$ *is defined by* $s \xrightarrow{a(\gamma)} t$ *iff* $\theta(s, a, t) = \gamma$ *and* $\gamma \not\equiv \bot$. $\qquad\square$

Thus, we use the parameter of an action as placeholder for the feature expression that guards a transition, writing $s \xrightarrow{a(\gamma)} t$.

Next, we define a translation tr that yields for a set of products P, represented by a closed feature expression γ_P of sort FExp, and a μL_f-formula φ_f, a μL_{FO}-formula $tr(\gamma_P, \varphi_f)$. We provide an explanation of this transformation, guided by the family-based semantics of μL_f, afterwards (cf. Definition 6).

Definition 9. *The translation function* $tr : \mathsf{FExp} \times \mu L_f \rightarrow \mu L_{FO}$ *is given by*

$$tr(\gamma, \bot) = \bot \qquad\qquad tr(\gamma, \top) = \top$$
$$tr(\gamma, \neg\varphi_f) = \neg tr(\gamma, \varphi_f) \qquad\qquad tr(\gamma, X) = \tilde{X}(\gamma)$$
$$tr(\gamma, \varphi_f \vee \psi_f) = tr(\gamma, \varphi_f) \vee tr(\gamma, \psi_f) \qquad tr(\gamma, \mu X.\varphi_f) = \mu\tilde{X}(v{:=}\gamma).tr(v, \varphi_f)$$
$$tr(\gamma, \varphi_f \wedge \psi_f) = tr(\gamma, \varphi_f) \wedge tr(\gamma, \psi_f) \qquad tr(\gamma, \nu X.\varphi_f) = \nu\tilde{X}(v{:=}\gamma).tr(v, \varphi_f)$$
$$tr(\gamma, \langle a|\chi\rangle\varphi_f) = (\gamma \Rightarrow \chi) \wedge \exists v.\langle a(v)\rangle((\gamma \Rightarrow v) \wedge tr(\gamma\wedge\chi\wedge v, \varphi_f))$$
$$tr(\gamma, [a|\chi]\varphi_f) = \forall v.[a(v)]((\gamma\wedge\chi\wedge v \Rightarrow \bot) \vee tr(\gamma\wedge\chi\wedge v, \varphi_f)) \qquad\square$$

Logical constants and propositional connectives are translated as expected. The feature expression γ in our translation symbolically represents the set of products that collectively can reach a given state in our parametrized LTS. Note that this expression is 'updated' only in our translation of the modal operators and passed on otherwise. For the $\langle\cdot|\cdot\rangle$-operator, the existence of a feature expression β in Definition 6 with an $a|\beta$-transition is captured by the existentially quantified data variable v: a state s in a parametrized LTS satisfies $\exists v.\langle a(v)\rangle((\gamma \Rightarrow v) \wedge tr(\gamma\wedge\chi\wedge v, \varphi_f))$ only when a transition from s exists labeled with a parametrized action $a(\beta)$ such that for v matching β, also $\gamma \Rightarrow v$ and $tr(\gamma\wedge\chi\wedge v, \varphi_f)$ hold. Likewise, for the $[\cdot|\cdot]$-operator, the universal quantification over feature expressions guarding transitions is captured by a universally quantified data variable v that is passed as a parameter to the action a. The formula $(\gamma\wedge\chi\wedge v \Rightarrow \bot)$ expresses that the corresponding product families are disjoint.

We utilize the data variables associated to recursion variables in $tr(\gamma, X)$ to pass the feature expression γ to the recursion variable $\tilde{X}$. A similar mechanism applies to the fixpoint constructions. Thus, we assign γ to the data variable v associated with $\tilde{X}$, signified by the bindings $\mu\tilde{X}(v:=\gamma)$ and $\nu\tilde{X}(v:=\gamma)$, and use the data variable in the translation of the remaining subformula, i.e. $tr(v, \varphi_f)$.

Next, we state the correctness of the translation.

Theorem 2. *Let F be an FTS and let $\mathcal{P}$ be a set of products. For each μL_f-formula φ_f, state $s \in S$ and product family $P \subseteq \mathcal{P}$, it holds that*

$$s, P \models_F \varphi_f \iff s \models_{L(F)} tr(\gamma_P, \varphi_f)$$

Proof. (Sketch) The proof relies on the claim that, for state s, product family P, data environment θ, and feature expression γ such that $\theta(\gamma) = P$, we have

$$(s, P) \in [\![\varphi_f]\!]_F(\zeta) \iff s \in [\![tr(\gamma, \varphi_f)]\!]_{FO}(\xi)(\theta)$$

for environments $\zeta \in sPEnv$, and $\xi \in XEnv$ such that $(s, P) \in \zeta(X)$ iff $s \in \xi(\tilde{X})(P)$ for all $X \in \mathcal{X}$. The claim is shown by structural induction, exploiting iteration for the fixpoint constructions. From the claim the theorem follows directly. □

As a consequence of the above theorem we can model check a μL_f-formula over an FTS by model checking the corresponding μL_{FO}-formula over the corresponding parametrized LTS.

Example 3. From Examples 1 and 2, recall FTS F of family P and μL_f-formula ψ_f stating that for products with ϵ, action *std* occurs infinitely often on all infinite runs over $\{ins, xxl, std\}$. Take the corresponding parametrized LTS $L(F)$. Clearly, ψ_f holds in state s_0 for all products without

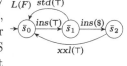

both features ϵ and $\$$. mCRL2 can verify this, as deciding $s_0, P' \models_F \psi_f$ for the family $P' = \{\varnothing, \{\epsilon\}, \{\$\}\}$ translates to model checking $\bar{s}_0 \models_{L(F)} tr(\gamma_P, \psi_f)$, where $tr(\gamma_P, \psi_f)$ is the μL_{FO}-formula

$$\nu\tilde{X}(v_x:=\gamma_P).\mu\tilde{Y}(v_y:=v_x).\big(\,\forall v.[ins(v)]\big((v_y \wedge \epsilon \wedge v \Rightarrow \bot) \vee \tilde{Y}(v_y \wedge \epsilon \wedge v)\big) \wedge$$
$$\forall v.[xxl(v)]\big((v_y \wedge \epsilon \wedge v \Rightarrow \bot) \vee \tilde{Y}(v_y \wedge \epsilon \wedge v)\big) \wedge$$
$$\forall v.[std(v)]\big((v_y \wedge \epsilon \wedge v \Rightarrow \bot) \vee \tilde{X}(v_y \wedge \epsilon \wedge v)\big)\big)$$

Note the passing of γ_P via the respective assignments $v_x:=\gamma_P$ and $v_y:=v_x$. □

4   Family-Based Partitioning for μL_f

With Theorem 2 in place we are in a position where family-based model-checking a system can be performed using a standard μ-calculus model checker. The final issue we face is to find, given a formula $\varphi_f \in \mu L_f$ and a family of products P, the subfamily of P whose products satisfy φ_f, as well as the subfamily whose products do not satisfy φ_f. Thus, given a negation-free formula φ_f and a family of products P, we are interested in computing a partitioning $(P_\oplus, P_\ominus)$ of P such that

$$\forall p \in P_\oplus \colon s_*, p \models_{F|p} \mathrm{pr}(\varphi_f, p) \quad \text{and} \quad \forall p \in P_\ominus \colon s_*, p \not\models_{F|p} \mathrm{pr}(\varphi_f, p) \qquad (1)$$

Rather than establishing this product-by-product, we are after a procedure that decides Property (1) in a family-based manner.

The previous section provides a sound decision procedure for $s_*, P \models_F \varphi_f$. If the procedure returns **true** for the family P, we are done: Theorem 1 guarantees that the property holds for all products of P, i.e. $s_* \models_{F|p} \mathrm{pr}(\varphi_f, p)$ for all $p \in P$. If, on the other hand, the decision procedure for $s_*, P \models_F \varphi_f$ returns **false** and P is not a singleton family, we cannot draw a conclusion for any of the products. However, in view of Lemma 1 below, we can run the decision procedure to decide $s_*, P \models_F \varphi_f^c$, where φ_f^c is the *complement* of φ_f. Formally, for negation-free μL_f-formula φ_f, the formula φ_f^c is defined inductively by

$$\bot^c = \top \qquad (\varphi_f \vee \psi_f)^c = \varphi_f^c \wedge \psi_f^c \qquad (\mu X.\varphi_f)^c = \nu X.\varphi_f^c$$
$$\top^c = \bot \qquad (\varphi_f \wedge \psi_f)^c = \varphi_f^c \vee \psi_f^c \qquad (\nu X.\varphi_f)^c = \mu X.\varphi_f^c$$
$$X^c = X \qquad (\langle a|\chi\rangle \varphi_f)^c = [a|\chi]\varphi_f^c \qquad ([a|\chi]\varphi_f)^c = \langle a|\chi\rangle \varphi_f^c$$

We have the following result.

Lemma 1. *For each negation-free formula φ_f and set of products P, it holds that $s_*, P \models_F \varphi_f^c$ implies $s_* \not\models_{F|p} \mathrm{pr}(\varphi_f, p)$ for all $p \in P$.*

Proof. Let $\varphi_f \in \mu L_f$ be closed and negation-free, and let P be a family of products. For closed and negation-free $\psi_f \in \mu L_f$, state s, and product p,

$$s \models_{F|p} \mathrm{pr}(\psi_f^c, p) \iff s \models_{F|p} \neg\mathrm{pr}(\psi_f, p) \qquad (2)$$

a fact readily proven by induction on ψ_f. Assume $s_*, P \models_F \varphi_f^c$. Observe, if φ_f is negation-free then so is φ_f^c. Hence, by Theorem 1, $s_* \models_{F|p} \mathrm{pr}(\varphi_f^c, p)$ for every $p \in P$. By Equivalence (2) we find $s_* \not\models_{F|p} \mathrm{pr}(\varphi_f, p)$ for all $p \in P$.   □

On the lemma we base the straightforward partition procedure $\mathrm{FBP}(P, \varphi_f)$ of Algorithm 1 for computing $(P_\oplus, P_\ominus)$ for a product family P such that each product in $P_\oplus$ satisfies the μL_f-formula φ_f, while each product in $P_\ominus$ fails φ_f.

Algorithm 1. Family-Based Partitioning

```
1: function FBP(P, φ_f)
2:     if s_*, P ⊨_F φ_f then return (P, ∅)
3:     else
4:         if s_*, P ⊨_F φ_f^c then return (∅, P)
5:         else partition P into (P_1, P_2)
6:             (P_1^+, P_1^-) ← FBP(P_1, φ_f)
7:             (P_2^+, P_2^-) ← FBP(P_2, φ_f)
8:             return (P_1^+ ∪ P_2^+, P_1^- ∪ P_2^-)
9:         end if
10:    end if
11: end function
```

Theorem 3. *For closed and negation-free φ_f, procedure* FBP(P, φ_f) *terminates and returns a partitioning* $(P_\oplus, P_\ominus)$ *of P satisfying Property (1).*

Proof. Observe that the algorithm can be called at most $2^{|P|}$ times as each call is performed on a strictly smaller subset of P. Therefore, the algorithm terminates iff the procedure for deciding $s_*, P \models_F \varphi_f$ terminates. The correctness of the resulting partitioning $(P_\oplus, P_\ominus)$ follows by a straightforward induction, using Theorem 1 and Lemma 1. □

Example 4. Applying the algorithm to the FTS of Example 1 and the formula ψ_f of Example 2, running FBP$(\top, \psi_f)$, we find $s_0, \top \not\models_F \psi_f$ and $s_0, \top \not\models_F \psi_f^c$. Splitting the family in sets $\in \wedge \$$ and $\neg(\in \wedge \$)$ and recursively running FBP$(\in \wedge \$, \psi_f)$, returns the partition $(\bot, \in \wedge \$)$, since we have $s_0, \in \wedge \$ \models_F \psi_f^c$, and subsequently running FBP$(\neg(\in \wedge \$), \psi_f)$ returns $(\neg(\in \wedge \$), \bot)$ since $s_0, \neg(\in \wedge \$) \models_F \psi_f$. Therefore FBP$(\top, \psi_f)$ returns the partition $(\neg(\in \wedge \$), \in \wedge \$)$. □

Clearly, repeatedly splitting families into subfamilies may lead to an exponential blow-up, in the worst case ultimately yielding a product-based analysis. Examples can be synthesized achieving this. However, in the SPL setting, an obvious strategy to partition a family P is to split along a feature f, i.e. in the algorithm set $P_1 = \{ p \in P \mid f \in p \}$ and $P_2 = \{ p \in P \mid f \notin p \}$. In general, the order of subsequent features f will influence the number of split-ups needed. Fortunately, candidate features for splitting along may be distilled from the structure of the system and from specific domain knowledge. The experiments reported in the next section confirm this. As we will see, with an appropriate decomposition a low number of splittings will do.

5   Case Study

In this section, we report on our experiments to use the mCRL2 toolset to perform product-based and family-based model checking of an SPL model of the minepump from [39], making use of the logics and translations discussed above.

The SPL minepump model was first introduced in [4] as a reformulation of the configurable software system controlling a pump for mine drainage. The purpose of the minepump is to pump water out of a mine shaft, for which a controller operates a pump that may not start nor continue running in the presence of a dangerously high level of methane gas. Therefore, it communicates with a number of sensors measuring the water and methane levels. Here, we consider the model as used in [13] that consists of 7 independent optional features for a total of $2^7 = 128$ variants. These features concern command types, methane detection, and water levels, abbreviated as Ct, Cp, Ma, Mq, $L\ell$, Ln, and Lh.

The minepump model of [13] is distributed with the ProVeLines SPL toolset [18] (http://projects.info.unamur.be/fts/provelines/). We first manually translated the fPROMELA model to a parametrized LTS encoded in mCRL2.[1] For our model checking we considered twelve properties expressed in μL_f. The first six are μ-calculus versions of LTL properties of [13] (four of which are analyzed also in [8]). The others are CTL-like properties. Following the approach described in this paper, the formulas were translated into μL_{FO} and model checked over the mCRL2 model representing a parametrized LTS. The properties, results, and runtimes are summarized in Table 1. All our experiments were run on a standard Macbook Pro using revision 14493 of the mCRL2 toolset.

Family-Based Model Checking. For each of the twelve properties, we provide its intuitive meaning, its specification in μL_f, and the result of model checking the property (indicating also the number of products for which the result holds). This concerns the first three columns of Table 1.[2, 3] In the remaining columns, we report the runtimes (in seconds) needed to verify the properties with mCRL2, both product-based (*one-by-one*, abbreviated to 'one') and family-based (*all-in-one*, abbreviated to 'all'). We report the internal time as measured by the tools. We immediately notice that family-based model checking with mCRL2 compares rather favorably to product-based model checking.

Next we discuss the verification of the properties listed in Table 1. Absence of deadlock turns out to be one of the more involved formulas to check family-wise for the case of the minepump. This is because in search for the truth value of the formula, all reachable states need to be visited. The μL-formula $[\mathtt{true}^*]\langle\mathtt{true}\rangle\top$, translates to the μL_f-formula $[\mathtt{true}^*|\top]\langle\mathtt{true}|\top\rangle\top$. The main complication arises from the fact that for each non-empty set of products P that can reach a state s in the FTS, the family-based semantics of $\langle\mathtt{true}|\top\rangle\top$ requires that there is a transition from s shared among all P. A partitioning of the set of all products that is too coarse leads to a trace indicating a violation of the μL_f-formula. Next, the trace can be analyzed with the mCRL2 toolset to identify a suitable decomposition into subfamilies.

---

[1] The mCRL2 code is distributed with the mCRL2 toolset (svn revision 14493).

[2] For a compact presentation of formulas in Table 1 we allow regular expressions in the modalities as syntactic sugar, as done in [22,37].

[3] Standard μ-calculus formulas in μL can be seen as μL_f-formulas by adjoining the feature expression $\top$ to every modality, i.e. replacing each 'diamond' modality $\langle a\rangle$ by $\langle a|\top\rangle$ and each 'box' modality $[a]$ by $[a|\top]$.

Table 1. Minepump properties and results (**true/false**) and runtimes (in seconds) of both product-based (*one-by-one*) and family-based (*all-in-one*) verification with mCRL2

Φ	property in μL_f	result	one	all
φ_1	*Absence of deadlock* $[\text{true}^*]\langle\text{true}\rangle\top$	128/0	10.02	2.07
φ_2	*The controller cannot infinitely often receive water level readings* $\mu X.[(\neg levelMsg)^*.levelMsg]X$	0/128	10.18	0.16
φ_3	*The controller cannot fairly receive each of the three message types* $\mu X.([\text{true}^*.commandMsg]X \vee [\text{true}^*.alarmMsg]X \vee [\text{true}^*.levelMsg]X)$	0/128	24.33	0.25
φ_4	*The pump cannot be switched on infinitely often* $(\mu X.\nu Y.([pumpStart.(\neg pumpStop)^*.pumpStop]X \wedge [\neg pumpStart]Y))$ $\wedge ([\text{true}^*.pumpStart]\mu Z.[\neg pumpStop]Z)$	96/32	21.09	0.89

φ_5	*The system cannot be in a situation in which the pump runs indefinitely in the*
	  presence of methane
	$[\text{true}^*](([pumpStart.(\neg pumpStop)^*.methaneRise]\mu X.[R]X)$
	  $\wedge ([methaneRise.(\neg methaneLower)^*.pumpStart]\mu X.[R]X))$
	for $R = \neg(pumpStop + methaneLower)$
		96/32	17.26	0.86

φ_6	*Assuming fairness (φ_3), the system cannot be in a situation in which the pump*
	  runs indefinitely in the presence of methane (φ_5)
	$[\text{true}^*](([pumpStart.(\neg pumpStop)^*.methaneRise]\Psi)$
	  $\wedge ([methaneRise.(\neg methaneLower)^*.pumpStart]\Psi))$
	for $\Psi = \mu X.([R^*.commandMsg]X \vee [R^*.alarmMsg]X \vee [R^*.levelMsg]X)$
	and $R = \neg(pumpStop + methaneLower)$
		112/16	27.32	3.67

φ_7	*The controller can always eventually receive/read a message, i.e. it can return* *to its initial state from any state* $[\text{true}^*]\langle\text{true}^*.receiveMsg\rangle\top$	128/0	18.36	2.40
φ_8	*Invariantly the pump is not started when the low water level signal fires* $[\text{true}^*.lowLevel.(\neg(normalLevel + highLevel))^*.pumpStart.]\bot$	128/0	5.67	3.05
φ_9	*Invariantly, when the level of methane rises, it inevitably decreases* $[\text{true}^*.methaneRise]\mu X.[\neg methaneLower]X \wedge \langle\text{true}\rangle\top$	0/128	20.47	0.21
φ_{10}	*Products with feature Ct can switch on the pump* $\langle\text{true}^*.pumpStart \mid Ct\rangle\top$	32/96	6.49	0.31
φ_{11}	*Products with feature Ct can always switch on the pump* $[\text{true}^* \mid Ct]\langle\text{true}^*.pumpStart \mid Ct\rangle\top$	28/100	21.11	2.32
φ_{12}	*Products with features Ct, Ma, and Lh can start the pump upon a high water* *level, but products without feature Lh cannot* $[\text{true}^* \mid \top](([highLevel \mid Ct \wedge Ma \wedge Lh]\langle\text{true}^*.pumpStart \mid \top\rangle\top) \wedge [pumpStart \mid \neg Lh]\bot)$	128/0	13.35	3.36

For the minepump we identified 12 subfamilies, whose sets of trajectories are pairwise independent (i.e. for any two distinct subfamilies there exists a complete path possible for all products in one family, but not for all products in the other, and vice versa). These are the product sets characterized by the feature expressions $Ct \wedge \tilde{C}p \wedge \tilde{M}a \wedge \tilde{M}q$, where $\tilde{f} = f, \neg f$, yielding eight families, and four further families yielded by the product sets given by $\neg Ct \wedge \tilde{C}p \wedge \tilde{M}a$. As we shall see below, the combinations of features mentioned turn up in the analysis of other properties as well, which shows that the analysis of deadlock freedom (property φ_1) is a fruitful investigation.

Since no specific feature setting is involved in performing *levelMsg* infinitely often (for a stable and acceptable water level), property φ_2 can be refuted for the complete family of products at once by proving its complement. Also property φ_3, seemingly more complex, can be refuted via its complement, requiring a decomposition in subfamilies given by the four Boolean combinations of Cp and Ma.

The properties discussed so far cover general system aspects: absence of dead-lock, future execution of an action, and fairness between subsystems. In contrast, property φ_4 is specific to the minepump model. The property, modeled as a fluent [40], states that every computation involving *pumpStart* has, after a while, a finite number of alternations of starting and subsequent stopping the pump (fluent *pumpStart.(¬pumpStop)*.pumpStop*), after which it is never again started, and after starting the pump (fluent **true****.pumpStart*) it is inevitably switched off. This property does not hold for all eligible products. However, a decomposition into a subfamily of 96 products given by $\neg(Ct \wedge Lh)$, i.e. products missing Ct or Lh, and in two subfamilies $Ct \wedge Mq \wedge Lh$ and $Ct \wedge \neg Mq \wedge Lh$, of 32 products in total, does the job. The products in the first family satisfy φ_4, whereas products in the second and third family do not.

More involved system properties are φ_5 and φ_6, mixing starting and stop-ping of the pump with the rising and dropping of the methane level. Property φ_5 considers the rising of methane after the pump started but did not stop (fluent *pumpStart.(¬pumpStop)*.methaneRise*) and, symmetrically, starting the pump after the methane level rose (fluent *methaneRise.(¬methaneLower)*.pumpStart*). Formula φ_6 is a refinement of formula φ_5, restricting it to fair computations. For property φ_5, family-based model checking is achieved using the same decomposi-tion of the product space, with the same outcome, as for property φ_4. For prop-erty φ_6, because of the fairness requirement, the number of satisfying products increases from 96 to 112. This can be checked for all 112 products at once. To identify the violating products, we consider φ_6's complement φ_6^c which is proven to hold for the family $Ct \wedge \neg Ma \wedge Lh$ of 16 products as a whole.

An important liveness property for circuit design, the so-called reset property *AG EF reset*, is expressible in CTL, but not in LTL (cf., e.g., [41]). For our case study, φ_7 is such a reset property. It states that from any state the controller can, possibly after a finite number of steps, receive a message. Thus, it can always return to the initial state. The μL-formula $[\textbf{true}^*] \langle \textbf{true}^*.receiveMsg \rangle \top$ can be verified using the same split-up in subfamilies that was used before for absence of deadlock (φ_1). A typical safety property is property φ_8, expressing that the pump is not started as long as water levels are low. It holds for all products, which can be verified for all product families at once. The third CTL-type property φ_9 states that when the level of methane rises, it inevitably drops again. It holds for no products. Refuting φ_9 can also be done for all product families at once.

Finally, we have verified feature-rich μL_f-formulas. Properties φ_{10} and φ_{11} focus on the family of products featuring Ct by means of the modalities $[\textbf{true}^* \mid Ct]$ and $\langle \textbf{true}^*.pumpStart \mid Ct \rangle$. However, by definition of pr, for prod-ucts without feature Ct, property φ_{10} translates into $\bot$ of μL. Since a formula $[R^*|\chi]\varphi$ is to be read as $\nu X.[R|\chi]X \wedge \varphi$, we have that property φ_{11}, for prod-ucts without Ct, coincides with $\nu X.[\textbf{true}|Ct] \wedge \bot$. Apparently, comparing φ_{10} and φ_{11}, four more products with Ct (viz. those without any Cp, $L\ell$, or Ma) fail to meet the stronger φ_{11}. Finally, property φ_{12} holds for all products. Note that the first conjunct $[\textit{highLevel} \mid Ct \wedge Ma \wedge Lh] \langle \textbf{true}^*.pumpStart \mid \top \rangle \top$ is trivially true for products without any Ct, Ma, or Lh due to the box modality, while the second conjunct $[\,pumpStart\,|\,\neg Lh\,]\,\bot$ holds trivially for products that include Lh. Model checking this property requires a decomposition into two subfamilies, viz. the set of products with the feature Mq and the set of products without.

Family-Based Partitioning. The results from the case study underline that family-based model checking has the potential to outperform product-based model checking. Next, we explore the requirements for a successful implementation of family-based partitioning using off-the-shelf technology.

Figure 1 (left) shows the runtimes (in seconds) associated with the model-checking problems of lines 2 and 4 of Algorithm 1 for deadlock freedom (property φ_1). The total time needed to run this algorithm, given the refinement strategy indicated in Fig. 1, is 27.9 s. Observe that checking all leaves takes 8.4 s.[4] We see similar figures for other properties we verified.

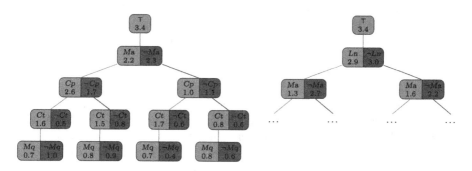

Fig. 1. Execution of Algorithm 1 for deadlock freedom (property φ_1) and the initial product family $\top$, using an optimal partitioning strategy (depicted on the left) vs. using an 'unproductive' refinement strategy, splitting Ln and $\neg Ln$ and following the optimal strategy afterwards (excerpt depicted on the right). The characterized family described at each node is the conjunction of the features along the path from the root to that node. Total computation time for the optimal strategy: 27.9 s; total computation time for the 12 leaves (i.e. all Mq, $\neg Mq$, and $\neg Ct$ nodes): 8.4 s. Total computation time for partitioning using the 'unproductive' strategy: 45.0 s.

We draw two further conclusions from our experiments. First, as expected, refining a family of products with respect to non-relevant features can have a negative effect on runtime. For instance, partitioning with respect to a single non-essential feature Ln at an early stage, cf. Fig. 1 (right), while following an optimal splitting otherwise, increases the runtime to 45 s; i.e. an additional 60%. Second, as illustrated by Fig. 1 (left), even for 'productive' refinements, model checking a property for a large family of products can consume a disproportionate amount of time. For instance, the three top nodes together account for almost 8 s, a quarter of the time spent on all model-checking problems combined.

---

[4] The additional overhead of approximately 6 s compared to the 2.07 s we reported in Table 1 is due to the fact that there we could inspect the model *once* for all possible families, whereas here we must inspect the model once *per* family.

We conclude that the performance of SPL verification using a general-purpose model checker for family-based partitioning crucially depends on the initial partitioning of products and the 'quality' of the refinements of families of products in the algorithm. This suggests that one must invest in: (i) determining heuristics for finding a good initial partitioning of a family of products, (ii) extracting information from the failed model-checking problems that facilitates an informed/productive split-up of the family of products in line 5 of Algorithm 1. In particular for the μ-calculus, the second challenge may be difficult, since easily-interpretable feedback from its model checkers is generally missing so far.

6   Concluding Remarks and Future Work

We have showed how the feature μ-calculus μL_f can be embedded in μL_{FO}, a logic accepted by toolsets such as mCRL2. Through this embedding, we obtain a family-based model-checking procedure for verifying μ-calculus properties of SPLs, and similar systems with variability, using off-the-shelf verifiers. Moreover, as our experiments indicate, the resulting family-based model-checking approach trumps the product-based model-checking approach of [19].

The efficiency of *computing* a partitioning of a product family from which we can read which products satisfy which formula, strongly depends on the adopted strategy for splitting product families and may constitute a bottleneck in practice. We leave it for future research to find heuristics to guide this splitting. One possibility may be to deduce an effective strategy from the lattice of product families that can be obtained by exploring the FTS model and keeping track of (the largest) product families that are capable of reaching states. This lattice may even allow for determining a proper partitioning *a priori*. Another potentially promising direction is to split product families using information that is obtained from counterexamples. Indeed, in our product-based and family-based model-checking experiments we used counterexamples to find suitable subfamilies of products by splitting with respect to feature expressions on transitions that led to the violations. We must note, however, that this was largely a manual activity which required a fair share of tool experience. More generally, we note that constructing and interpreting counterexamples for the modal μ-calculus is notoriously difficult, as such counterexamples are not necessarily linear.

Finally, we believe that for particular properties specific insight regarding the model under study is required to quickly identify a successful split-up. We liken this to the approach taken in [8], where the theory of Galois connections is used to establish suitable abstractions of the minepump model prior to model checking with SPIN; we quote "Given sufficient knowledge of the system and the property, we can easily tailor an abstraction for analyzing the system more effectively". It is indeed common in SPL engineering to assume substantial understanding of the SPL under scrutiny, in particular of its commonalities and variability as documented in variability models like feature diagrams.

Acknowledgements. Maurice ter Beek was supported by the EU FP7 project QUANTICOL (600708). The authors are grateful to Franco Mazzanti for his help with the minepump model. Finally, we thank the anonymous referees for their suggestions, which helped improve the presentation of this paper.

References

1. Thüm, T., et al.: A classification and survey of analysis strategies for software product lines. ACM Comput. Surv. **47**(1), 1–45 (2014)
2. Gruler, A., Leucker, M., Scheidemann, K.: Modeling and model checking software product lines. In: Barthe, G., Boer, F.S. (eds.) FMOODS 2008. LNCS, vol. 5051, pp. 113–131. Springer, Heidelberg (2008). doi:10.1007/978-3-540-68863-1_8
3. Lauenroth, K., Pohl, K., Töhning, S.: Model checking of domain artifacts in product line engineering. In: ASE, pp. 269–280. IEEE (2009)
4. Classen, A., et al.: Model checking lots of systems: efficient verification of temporal properties in software product lines. In: ICSE, pp. 335–344. ACM (2010)
5. Damiani, F., Schaefer, I.: Family-based analysis of type safety for delta-oriented software product lines. In: Margaria, T., Steffen, B. (eds.) ISoLA 2012. LNCS, vol. 7609, pp. 193–207. Springer, Heidelberg (2012). doi:10.1007/978-3-642-34026-0_15
6. Thüm, T., Schaefer, I., Hentschel, M., Apel, S.: Family-based deductive verification of software product lines. In: GPCE, pp. 11–20. ACM (2012)
7. ter Beek, M.H., Fantechi, A., Gnesi, S., Mazzanti, F.: Using FMC for family-based analysis of software product lines. In: SPLC, pp. 432–439. ACM (2015)
8. Dimovski, A.S., Al-Sibahi, A.S., Brabrand, C., Wąsowski, A.: Family-based model checking without a family-based model checker. In: Fischer, B., Geldenhuys, J. (eds.) SPIN 2015. LNCS, vol. 9232, pp. 282–299. Springer, Cham (2015). doi:10.1007/978-3-319-23404-5_18
9. Clarke, E.M., Emerson, E.A., Sifakis, J.: Model checking: algorithmic verification and debugging. C. ACM **52**(11), 74–84 (2009)
10. Gruler, A., Leucker, M., Scheidemann, K.: Calculating and modeling common parts of software product lines. In: SPLC, pp. 203–212. IEEE (2008)
11. ter Beek, M.H., Lluch Lafuente, A., Petrocchi, M.: Combining declarative and procedural views in the specification and analysis of product families. In: SPLC, vol. 2, pp. 10–17. ACM (2013)
12. Lochau, M., Mennicke, S., Baller, H., Ribbeck, L.: Incremental model checking delta-oriented software product lines. J. Log. Algebr. Meth. Program. **85**(1), 245–267 (2016)
13. Classen, A., et al.: Featured transition systems: foundations for verifying variability-intensive systems and their application to LTL model checking. IEEE Trans. Softw. Eng. **39**(8), 1069–1089 (2013)
14. Classen, A., et al.: Formal semantics, modular specification, and symbolic verification of product-line behaviour. Sci. Comput. Program. **80**(B), 416–439 (2014)
15. ter Beek, M.H., Fantechi, A., Gnesi, S., Mazzanti, F.: Modelling and analysing variability in product families: model checking of modal transition systems with variability constraints. J. Log. Algebr. Meth. Program. **85**(2), 287–315 (2016)
16. ter Beek, M.H., Mazzanti, F., Sulova, A.: VMC: a tool for product variability analysis. In: Giannakopoulou, D., Méry, D. (eds.) FM 2012. LNCS, vol. 7436, pp. 450–454. Springer, Heidelberg (2012). doi:10.1007/978-3-642-32759-9_36
17. Classen, A., et al.: Model checking software product lines with SNIP. Int. J. Softw. Tools Technol. Transf. **14**(5), 589–612 (2012)

18. Cordy, A., et al.: ProVeLines: a product line of verifiers for software product lines. In: SPLC, vol. 2, pp. 141–146. ACM (2013)
19. ter Beek, M.H., de Vink, E.P.: Using mCRL2 for the analysis of software product lines. In: FormaliSE, pp. 31–37. IEEE (2014)
20. ter Beek, M.H., de Vink, E.P., Willemse, T.A.C.: Towards a feature mu-calculus targeting SPL verification. In: FMSPLE, EPTCS, vol. 206, pp. 61–75 (2016)
21. Cranen, S., Groote, J.F., Keiren, J.J.A., Stappers, F.P.M., de Vink, E.P., Wesselink, W., Willemse, T.A.C.: An overview of the mCRL2 toolset and its recent advances. In: Piterman, N., Smolka, S.A. (eds.) TACAS 2013. LNCS, vol. 7795, pp. 199–213. Springer, Heidelberg (2013). doi:10.1007/978-3-642-36742-7_15
22. Groote, J.F., Mousavi, M.R.: Modeling and Analysis of Communicating Systems. MIT Press, Cambridge (2014)
23. Kim, C.H.P., et al.: SPLat: lightweight dynamic analysis for reducing combinatorics in testing configurable systems. In: ESEC/FSE, pp. 257–267. ACM (2013)
24. Bürdek, J., Lochau, M., Bauregger, S., Holzer, A., von Rhein, A., Apel, S., Beyer, D.: Facilitating reuse in multi-goal test-suite generation for software product lines. In: Egyed, A., Schaefer, I. (eds.) FASE 2015. LNCS, vol. 9033, pp. 84–99. Springer, Heidelberg (2015). doi:10.1007/978-3-662-46675-9_6
25. Lity, S., Morbach, T., Thüm, T., Schaefer, I.: Applying incremental model slicing to product-line regression testing. In: Kapitsaki, G.M., Santana de Almeida, E. (eds.) ICSR 2016. LNCS, vol. 9679, pp. 3–19. Springer, Cham (2016). doi:10.1007/978-3-319-35122-3_1
26. Beohar, H., Varshosaz, M., Mousavi, M.R.: Basic behavioral models for software product lines: expressiveness and testing pre-orders. Sci. Comput. Program. **123**, 42–60 (2016)
27. Ghezzi, C., Sharifloo, A.: Model-based verification of quantitative non-functional properties for software product lines. Inform. Softw. Technol. **55**(3), 508–524 (2013)
28. Varshosaz, M., Khosravi, R.: Discrete time markov chain families: modeling and verification of probabilistic software product lines. In: SPLC, vol. 2, pp. 34–41. ACM (2013)
29. Rodrigues, G.N., et al.: Modeling and verification for probabilistic properties in software product lines. In: HASE, pp. 173–180. IEEE (2015)
30. Dubslaff, C., Baier, C., Klüppelholz, S.: Probabilistic model checking for feature-oriented systems. In: Chiba, S., Tanter, É., Ernst, E., Hirschfeld, R. (eds.) Transactions on Aspect-Oriented Software Development XII. LNCS, vol. 8989, pp. 180–220. Springer, Heidelberg (2015). doi:10.1007/978-3-662-46734-3_5
31. Kwiatkowska, M., Norman, G., Parker, D.: PRISM 4.0: verification of probabilistic real-time systems. In: Gopalakrishnan, G., Qadeer, S. (eds.) CAV 2011. LNCS, vol. 6806, pp. 585–591. Springer, Heidelberg (2011). doi:10.1007/978-3-642-22110-1_47
32. Chrszon, P., Dubslaff, C., Klüppelholz, S., Baier, C.: Family-based modeling and analysis for probabilistic systems – featuring PROFEAT. In: Stevens, P., Wąsowski, A. (eds.) FASE 2016. LNCS, vol. 9633, pp. 287–304. Springer, Heidelberg (2016). doi:10.1007/978-3-662-49665-7_17
33. ter Beek, M.H., Legay, A., Lluch Lafuente, A., Vandin, A.: Statistical analysis of probabilistic models of software product lines with quantitative constraints. In: SPLC, pp. 11–15. ACM (2015)
34. ter Beek, M.H., Legay, A., Lluch Lafuente, A., Vandin, A.: Statistical model checking for product lines. In: Margaria, T., Steffen, B. (eds.) ISoLA 2016. LNCS, vol. 9952, pp. 114–133. Springer, Cham (2016). doi:10.1007/978-3-319-47166-2_8
35. Bradfield, J.C., Stirling, C.: Modal logics and μ-calculi: an introduction. In: Handbook of Process Algebra, Chap. 4, pp. 293–330. Elsevier (2001)

36. Groote, J.F., Mateescu, R.: Verification of temporal properties of processes in a setting with data. In: Haeberer, A.M. (ed.) AMAST 1999. LNCS, vol. 1548, pp. 74–90. Springer, Heidelberg (1998). doi:10.1007/3-540-49253-4_8

37. Groote, J.F., Willemse, T.A.C.: Model-checking processes with data. Sci. Comput. Program. **56**(3), 251–273 (2005)

38. Zantema, H., van de Pol, J.C.: A rewriting approach to binary decision diagrams. J. Log. Algebr. Program. **49**(1–2), 61–86 (2001)

39. Kramer, J., Magee, J., Sloman, M., Lister, A.: CONIC: an integrated approach to distributed computer control systems. IEE Proc. E **130**(1), 1–10 (1983)

40. Giannakopoulou, D., Magee, J.: Fluent model checking for event-based systems. In: ESEC/FSE, pp. 257–266. ACM (2003)

41. Clarke, E.M., Grumberg, O., Peled, D.A.: Model Checking. MIT Press, Cambridge (1999)

Variability-Specific Abstraction Refinement for Family-Based Model Checking

Aleksandar S. Dimovski$^{(\boxtimes)}$ and Andrzej Wąsowski

Computer Science, IT University of Copenhagen, Copenhagen S, Denmark
adim@itu.dk

Abstract. Variational systems are ubiquitous in many application areas today. They use features to control presence and absence of system functionality. One challenge in the development of variational systems is their formal analysis and verification. Researchers have addressed this problem by designing aggregate so-called family-based verification algorithms. Family-based model checking allows simultaneous verification of all variants of a system family (variational system) in a single run by exploiting the commonalities between the variants. Yet, the computational cost of family-based model checking still greatly depends on the number of variants. In order to make it computationally cheaper, we can use variability abstractions for deriving abstract family-based model checking, where the variational model of a system family is replaced with an abstract (smaller) version of it which preserves the satisfaction of LTL properties. The variability abstractions can be combined with different partitionings of the set of variants to infer various verification scenarios for the variational model. However, manually finding an optimal verification scenario is hard since it requires a good knowledge of the family and property, while the number of possible scenarios is very large.

In this work, we present an automatic iterative abstraction refinement procedure for family-based model checking. We use Craig interpolation to refine abstract variational models based on the obtained spurious counterexamples (traces). The refinement procedure works until a genuine counterexample is found or the property satisfaction is shown for all variants in the family. We illustrate the practicality of this approach for several variational benchmark models.

1 Introduction

Software Product Line Engineering (SPLE) [9] is a popular methodology for building a family of related systems. A large number of related systems (*variants*) are developed by systematically reusing common parts. Each variant is specified in terms of *features* (statically configured options) selected for that particular variant. Due to the popularity of SPLs in embedded and critical system domain (e.g. cars, phones, avionics), they require rigourous verification and analysis.

Partially supported by The Danish Council for Independent Research under a Sapere Aude project, VARIETE.

© Springer-Verlag GmbH Germany 2017
M. Huisman and J. Rubin (Eds.): FASE 2017, LNCS 10202, pp. 406–423, 2017.
DOI: 10.1007/978-3-662-54494-5_24

Model checking is a well-known technique for automatic verification of systems against properties expressed in temporal logic [1]. Model checking families of systems is more difficult than model checking single systems, since the number of possible variants is exponential in the number of features. Hence, the simplest enumerative variant-by-variant approach, that applies single-system model checking to each individual variant of a system family, is very inefficient. Indeed, a given execution behaviour is checked as many times as the number of variants that are able to execute it. In order to address this problem, new dedicated family-based model checking algorithms have been introduced [7,8,10]. They rely on using compact mathematical structures (so called variational models or featured transition systems) for modelling variational systems, which take the commonality within the family into account, and on which specialized family-based (variability-aware) model checking algorithms can be applied. Each execution behaviour in a variational model is associated with the exact set of variants able to produce it. Therefore, the family-based algorithms check an execution behaviour only once, regardless of how many variants can produce it. In this way, they are able to model check all variants of a family simultaneously in a single step and pinpoint those variants that violate properties. In order to further speed-up family-based model checking, a range of variability abstractions can be introduced [13,14]. They give rise to abstract family-based model checking. The abstractions are applied at the variability level and aim to reduce the exponential blowup of the number of configurations (variants) to something more tractable by manipulating the configuration space of the family. Abstractions can be combined with partitionings of the set of all variants to generate various verification scenarios. Still, suitable verification scenarios are currently chosen manually from a large set of possible combinations. This often requires a user to have a considerable knowledge of a variational system and property. In order for this approach to be used more widely in industry, automatic techniques are needed for generating verification scenarios.

Abstraction refinement [4,5,10] has proved to be one of the most effective techniques for automatic verification of systems with very large state spaces. In this paper, we introduce a purely variability-specific (state-independent) approach to abstraction refinement, which is used for automatic verification of LTL properties over variational models. In general, each variability abstraction computes an over-approximation of the original model, in a such a way that if some property holds for the smaller abstract model then it will hold for the original one. However, if the property does not hold in the abstract model, the found counterexample may be the result of some behaviour in the over-approximation which is not present in the original model. In this case, it is necessary to refine the abstraction so that the behaviour which caused the spurious counterexample is eliminated. The verification procedure starts with the coarsest variability abstraction, and then the obtained abstract model is fed to a model checker. If no counterexample is found, then all variants satisfy the given property. Otherwise, the counterexamples are analysed and classified as either *genuine*, which correspond to execution behaviours of some variants in the original model, or *spurious*, which are introduced due to the abstraction. If a genuine counterexample exist, the corresponding variants do not satisfy the given property; otherwise a spurious counterexample is used to refine the abstract models. The procedure is then repeated on the refined abstract variational model only for variants for which no conclusive results have been found. We use Craig interpolation [18,27] to extract from a spurious counterexample (i.e. the unsatisfiable feature expression associated with it) the relevant information which needs to be known in order to show the unsatisfiability of the associated feature expression. This information is used to compute refined abstract models for the next iteration. The main contribution of this paper is an efficient automatic abstraction refinement procedure for family-based model checking, which uses variability-aware information obtained from spurious counterexamples to guide the verification process. When the employed variability abstractions give rise to abstract models verifiable by a single-system model checker, we obtain a completely automatic alternative to a dedicated family-based model checker. The experiments show that the proposed abstraction refinement procedure combined with the single-system model checker SPIN achieves performance gains compared to the family-based model checker $\overline{\text{SNIP}}$ when applied to several benchmark variational systems for some interesting properties.

2   Abstract Family-Based Model Checking

We now introduce featured transition systems (FTSs) [8] for modelling variational systems, fLTL temporal formulae [8] for specifying properties of variational systems, and variability abstractions [13,14] for defining abstract FTSs.

2.1   Featured Transition Systems

Let $\mathbb{F} = \{A_1, \ldots, A_n\}$ be a finite set of Boolean variables representing the features available in a variational system. A specific subset of features, $k \subseteq \mathbb{F}$, known as *configuration*, specifies a *variant* (valid product) of a variational system. The *set of all valid configurations* (variants) is defined as: $\mathbb{K} \subseteq 2^{\mathbb{F}}$. An alternative representation of configurations is based upon propositional formulae. Each configuration $k \in \mathbb{K}$ can be represented by a formula: $k(A_1) \wedge \ldots \wedge k(A_n)$, where $k(A_i) = A_i$ if $A_i \in k$, and $k(A_i) = \neg A_i$ if $A_i \notin k$ for $1 \leq i \leq n$. We will use both representations interchangeably. The set of valid configurations is typically described by a feature model [22], but in this work we disregard syntactic representations of the set $\mathbb{K}$.

The behaviour of individual variants is given with transition systems.

Definition 1. *A transition system (TS) is a tuple $\mathcal{T} = (S, Act, trans, I, AP, L)$, where S is a set of states; Act is a set of actions; $trans \subseteq S \times Act \times S$ is a transition relation[1]; $I \subseteq S$ is a set of initial states; AP is a set of atomic propositions; and $L : S \rightarrow 2^{AP}$ is a labelling function.*

---

[1] We often write $s_1 \xrightarrow{\lambda} s_2$ when $(s_1, \lambda, s_2) \in trans$.

– *An* execution *(behaviour) of $\mathcal{T}$ is a nonempty, infinite sequence $\rho = s_0\lambda_1s_1\lambda_2\ldots$ with $s_0 \in I$ such that $s_i \xrightarrow{\lambda_{i+1}} s_{i+1}$ for all $i \geq 0$. The* semantics *of the TS $\mathcal{T}$, denoted as $[\![\mathcal{T}]\!]_{TS}$, is the set of its executions.*

The combined behaviour of a whole system family is compactly represented with *featured transition systems* [8]. They are TSs where transitions are also labelled with feature expressions, $FeatExp(\mathbb{F})$, which represent propositional logic formulae defined over $\mathbb{F}$ as: $\psi ::= true \mid A \in \mathbb{F} \mid \neg\psi \mid \psi_1 \wedge \psi_2$. The feature expression $\psi \in FeatExp(\mathbb{F})$ indicates for which variants the corresponding transition is enabled.

Definition 2. *An featured transition system (FTS) represents a tuple $\mathcal{F} = (S, Act, trans, I, AP, L, \mathbb{F}, \mathbb{K}, \delta)$, where $S, Act, trans, I, AP,$ and L are defined as in TS; $\mathbb{F}$ is the set of available features; $\mathbb{K}$ is a set of valid configurations; and $\delta : trans \rightarrow FeatExp(\mathbb{F})$ is a total function labelling transitions with feature expressions. We write $[\![\delta(t)]\!]$ to denote the set of variants that satisfy $\delta(t)$, i.e. $k \in [\![\delta(t)]\!]$ iff $k \models \delta(t)$. Moreover:*

– *The* projection *of an FTS $\mathcal{F}$ to a variant $k \in \mathbb{K}$, denoted as $\pi_k(\mathcal{F})$, is the TS $(S, Act, trans', I, AP, L)$, where $trans' = \{t \in trans \mid k \models \delta(t)\}$.*
– *The* projection *of an FTS $\mathcal{F}$ to a set of variants $\mathbb{K}' \subseteq \mathbb{K}$, denoted as $\pi_{\mathbb{K}'}(\mathcal{F})$, is the FTS $(S, Act, trans', I, AP, L, \mathbb{F}, \mathbb{K}', \delta)$, where $trans' = \{t \in trans \mid \exists k \in \mathbb{K}'.k \models \delta(t)\}$.*
– *The* semantics *of an FTS $\mathcal{F}$, denoted as $[\![\mathcal{F}]\!]_{FTS}$, is the union of behaviours of the projections on all variants $k \in \mathbb{K}$, i.e. $[\![\mathcal{F}]\!]_{FTS} = \cup_{k \in \mathbb{K}}[\![\pi_k(\mathcal{F})]\!]_{TS}$.*
– *The* size *of an FTS $\mathcal{F}$ is defined as [8]: $|\mathcal{F}| = |S| + |trans| + |expr| + |\mathbb{K}|$, where $|expr|$ is the size of all feature expressions bounded by $O(2^{|\mathbb{F}|} \cdot |trans|)$.*

Example 1. Throughout this paper, we will use a beverage vending machine as a running example [8]. The VENDINGMACHINE family has five features: VendingMachine (denoted by v) for purchasing a drink which is a mandatory root feature enabled in all products; Tea (denoted by t) for serving tea; Soda (denoted by s) for serving soda; CancelPurchase (denoted by c) for canceling a purchase after a coin is entered; and FreeDrinks (denoted by f) for offering free drinks. The FTS of VENDINGMACHINE is shown in Fig. 1a. The feature expression label of a transition is shown next to its label action, separated by a slash. The transitions enabled by the same feature are colored in the same way. For example, the transition ③ $\xrightarrow{soda/s}$ ⑤ is enabled for variants that contain the feature s. By combining various features, a number of variants of this VENDING-MACHINE can be obtained. In Fig. 1b is shown the basic version of VENDINGMA-CHINE that only serves soda, which is described by the configuration: $\{v, s\}$ (or, as formula $v \wedge s \wedge \neg t \wedge \neg c \wedge \neg f$). It takes a coin, returns change, serves soda, opens a compartment so that the customer can take the soda, before closing it again. We can obtain the basic vending machine in Fig. 1b by projecting the FTS in Fig. 1a to the configuration $\{v, s\}$. The set of all valid configurations of VENDINGMACHINE can be obtained by combining the above features. For example, we can have $\mathbb{K} = \{\{v, s\}, \{v, s, t, c, f\}, \{v, s, c\}, \{v, s, c, f\}\}$. □

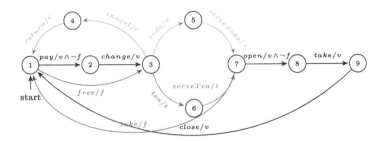

(a) The FTS for VENDINGMACHINE.

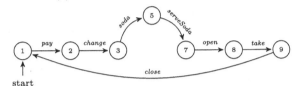

start
(b) A variant of VENDINGMACHINE for configuration $\{v, s\}$.

Fig. 1. The VENDINGMACHINE variational system.

2.2   fLTL Properties

The model checking problem consists of determining whether a model satisfies a given property expressed as LTL (linear time logic) temporal formula [1].

Definition 3. *An LTL formula ϕ is defined as: $\phi ::= true \mid a \in AP \mid \neg\phi \mid \phi_1 \wedge \phi_2 \mid \bigcirc\phi \mid \phi_1 U \phi_2$.*

– *Satisfaction of a formula ϕ for an infinite execution $\rho = s_0\lambda_1 s_1\lambda_2 \ldots$ (we write $\rho_i = s_i\lambda_{i+1}s_{i+1}\ldots$ for the i-th suffix of ρ) is defined as:*

$$\rho \models true, \qquad \rho \models a \quad iff \quad a \in L(s_0),$$
$$\rho \models \neg\phi \quad iff \quad \rho \not\models \phi, \qquad \rho \models \phi_1 \wedge \phi_2 \quad iff \quad \rho \models \phi_1 \ and \ \rho \models \phi_2,$$
$$\rho \models \bigcirc\phi \quad iff \quad \rho_1 \models \phi$$
$$\rho \models \phi_1 U \phi_2 \quad iff \quad \exists k \geq 0. \rho_k \models \phi_2 \ and \ \forall j \in \{0, \ldots, k-1\}. \rho_j \models \phi_1$$

– *A TS $\mathcal{T}$ satisfies a formula ϕ, denoted as $\mathcal{T} \models \phi$, iff $\forall \rho \in [\![\mathcal{T}]\!]_{TS}. \rho \models \phi$.*

Note that other temporal operators can be defined as well: $\Diamond\phi = true\, U\phi$ (eventually) and $\Box\phi = \neg\Diamond\neg\phi$ (always). When we consider variational systems, we sometimes want to define properties with a modality that specifies the set of variants for which they hold.

Definition 4.

– *An feature LTL (fLTL) formula is defined as: $[\chi]\phi$, where ϕ is an LTL formula and $\chi \in FeatExp(\mathbb{F})$ is a feature expression.*

– An FTS $\mathcal{F}$ satisfies an fLTL formula $[\chi]\phi$, denoted as $\mathcal{F} \models [\chi]\phi$, iff $\forall k \in \mathbb{K} \cap [\![\chi]\!].\, \pi_k(\mathcal{F}) \models \phi$. An FTS $\mathcal{F}$ satisfies an LTL formula ϕ iff $\mathcal{F} \models [true]\phi$.

Note that $\mathcal{F} \models [\chi]\phi$ iff $\pi_{[\![\chi]\!]}(\mathcal{F}) \models \phi$. Therefore, for simplicity in the following we focus on verifying only LTL properties ϕ.

Example 2. Consider the FTS VENDINGMACHINE in Fig. 1a. Suppose that states ⑤ and ⑥ are labelled with the proposition `selected`, and the state ⑧ with the proposition `open`. An example property ϕ is: $\Box(\texttt{selected} \implies \Diamond\texttt{open})$, which states that after selecting a beverage, the machine will eventually `open` the compartment to allow the customer to take his drink. The basic vending machine satisfies this property: $\pi_{\{v,s\}}(\text{VENDINGMACHINE}) \models \phi$, but the entire variational system does not satisfy it: VENDINGMACHINE $\not\models \phi$. For example, if the feature f (`FreeDrinks`) is enabled, a counter-example where the state ⑧ is never reached is: ① $\to$ ③ $\to$ ⑤ $\to$ ⑦ $\to$ ① $\to \ldots$. The set of violating products is $\{\{v, s, t, c, f\}, \{v, s, c, f\}\} \subseteq \mathbb{K}$. However, we have that VENDINGMACHINE $\models [\neg f]\phi$. Therefore, we can conclude that the feature f is responsible for violation of the property ϕ. □

2.3   Variability Abstractions

We now define variability abstractions [13,14] for decreasing the sizes of FTSs, in particular for reducing the number of features, the configuration space, and the size of feature expressions. The goal of variability abstractions is to weaken feature expressions, in order to make transitions in FTSs available to more variants. We define variability abstractions as Galois connections for reducing the Boolean complete lattice of propositional formulae over $\mathbb{F}$: $(FeatExp(\mathbb{F})_{/\equiv}, \models$, $\vee, \wedge, true, false)$. Elements of $FeatExp(\mathbb{F})_{/\equiv}$ are equivalence classes of propositional formulae $\psi \in FeatExp(\mathbb{F})$ obtained by quotienting by the semantic equivalence $\equiv$. The pre-order relation $\models$ is defined as the satisfaction relation from propositional logic, whereas the least upper bound operator is $\vee$ and the greatest lower bound operator is $\wedge$. Furthermore, the least element is $false$, and the greatest element is $true$. Subsequently, we will lift the definition of variability abstractions to FTSs.

The *join abstraction*, α^{join}, confounds the control-flow of all variants, obtaining a single variant that includes all executions occurring in any variant. The information about which transitions are associated with which variants is lost. Each feature expression ψ defined over $\mathbb{F}$ is replaced with $true$ if there exists at least one configuration from $\mathbb{K}$ that satisfies ψ. The new abstract set of features is empty: $\alpha^{\text{join}}(\mathbb{F}) = \emptyset$, and the abstract set of valid configurations is a singleton: $\alpha^{\text{join}}(\mathbb{K}) = \{true\}$ if $\mathbb{K} \neq \emptyset$. The abstraction $\alpha^{\text{join}} : FeatExp(\mathbb{F}) \to FeatExp(\emptyset)$ and concretization functions $\gamma^{\text{join}} : FeatExp(\emptyset) \to FeatExp(\mathbb{F})$ are:

$$\alpha^{\text{join}}(\psi) = \begin{cases} true & \text{if } \exists k \in \mathbb{K}.k \models \psi \\ false & \text{otherwise} \end{cases} \qquad \begin{aligned} &\gamma^{\text{join}}(true) = true \\ &\gamma^{\text{join}}(false) = \bigvee\nolimits_{k \in 2^{\mathbb{F}} \setminus \mathbb{K}} k \end{aligned}$$

The proposed abstraction-concretization pair is a Galois connection[2] [13,14].

The *feature ignore abstraction*, $\alpha_A^{\text{fignore}}$, ignores a single feature $A \in \mathbb{F}$ by confounding the control flow paths that only differ with regard to A, but keeps the precision with respect to control flow paths that do not depend on A. Let ψ be a formula into negation normal form (NNF). We write $\psi[l_A \mapsto true]$ to denote the formula ψ where the literal of A, that is A or $\neg A$, is replaced with *true*. The abstract sets of features and configurations are: $\alpha_A^{\text{fignore}}(\mathbb{F}) = \mathbb{F} \setminus \{A\}$, and $\alpha_A^{\text{fignore}}(\mathbb{K}) = \{k[l_A \mapsto true] \mid k \in \mathbb{K}\}$. The abstraction and concretization functions between $FeatExp(\mathbb{F})$ and $FeatExp(\alpha_A^{\text{fignore}}(\mathbb{F}))$, which form a Galois connection [13,14], are defined as:

$$\alpha_A^{\text{fignore}}(\psi) = \psi[l_A \mapsto true] \qquad \gamma_A^{\text{fignore}}(\psi') = (\psi' \wedge A) \vee (\psi' \wedge \neg A)$$

where ψ and ψ' are in NNF.

The sequential composition $\alpha_2 \circ \alpha_1$ runs two abstractions α_1 and α_2 in sequence (see [13,14] for precise definition). In the following, we will simply write (α, γ) for any Galois connection $\langle FeatExp(\mathbb{F})/_\equiv, \models \rangle \xrightarrow[\alpha]{\gamma} \langle FeatExp(\alpha(\mathbb{F}))/_\equiv, \models \rangle$ constructed using the operators presented in this section.

Given a Galois connection (α, γ) defined on the level of feature expressions, we now induce a notion of abstraction between FTSs.

Definition 5. *Let* $\mathcal{F} = (S, Act, trans, I, AP, L, \mathbb{F}, \mathbb{K}, \delta)$ *be an FTS, and* (α, γ) *be a Galois connection. We define* $\alpha(\mathcal{F}) = (S, Act, trans, I, AP, L, \alpha(\mathbb{F}), \alpha(\mathbb{K}), \alpha(\delta))$, *where* $\alpha(\delta) : trans \to FeatExp(\alpha(\mathbb{F}))$ *is defined as:* $\alpha(\delta)(t) = \alpha(\delta(t))$.

Example 3. Consider the FTS $\mathcal{F} = \text{VENDINGMACHINE}$ in Fig. 1a with the set of valid configurations $\mathbb{K} = \{\{v, s\}, \{v, s, t, c, f\}, \{v, s, c\}, \{v, s, c, f\}\}$. We show $\alpha^{\text{join}}(\pi_{[\![f]\!]}(\mathcal{F}))$ and $\alpha^{\text{join}}(\pi_{[\![\neg f]\!]}(\mathcal{F}))$ in Fig. 2. We do not show transitions labelled with the feature expression *false* and unreachable states. Also note that both $\alpha^{\text{join}}(\pi_{[\![f]\!]}(\mathcal{F}))$ and $\alpha^{\text{join}}(\pi_{[\![\neg f]\!]}(\mathcal{F}))$ are ordinary TSs, since all transitions are labeled with the feature expression *true*.

For $\alpha^{\text{join}}(\pi_{[\![f]\!]}(\mathcal{F}))$ in Fig. 2a, note that $\mathbb{K} \cap [\![f]\!] = \{\{v, s, t, c, f\}, \{v, s, c, f\}\}$. So, transitions annotated with $\neg f$ are not present in $\alpha^{\text{join}}(\pi_{[\![f]\!]}(\mathcal{F}))$.

For $\alpha^{\text{join}}(\pi_{[\![\neg f]\!]}(\mathcal{F}))$ in Fig. 2b, note that $\mathbb{K} \cap [\![\neg f]\!] = \{\{v, s\}, \{v, s, c\}\}$, and so transitions annotated with the features t and f (Tea and FreeDrinks) are not present in $\alpha^{\text{join}}(\pi_{[\![\neg f]\!]}(\mathcal{F}))$. □

Abstract FTSs have interesting preservation properties [13,14].

Theorem 1 (Soundness). *Let* (α, γ) *be a Galois connection and* $\mathcal{F}$ *be an FTS. If* $\alpha(\mathcal{F}) \models \phi$, *then* $\mathcal{F} \models \phi$.

---

[2] $\langle L, \leq_L \rangle \xrightarrow[\alpha]{\gamma} \langle M, \leq_M \rangle$ is a *Galois connection* between complete lattices L and M iff α and γ are total functions that satisfy: $\alpha(l) \leq_M m \iff l \leq_L \gamma(m)$ for all $l \in L, m \in M$. Here $\leq_L$ and $\leq_M$ are the pre-order relations for L and M, respectively.

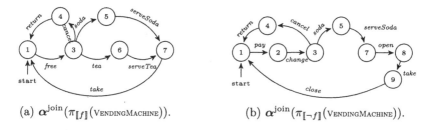

(a) $\alpha^{\text{join}}(\pi_{[\![f]\!]}(\text{VENDINGMACHINE}))$. (b) $\alpha^{\text{join}}(\pi_{[\![\neg f]\!]}(\text{VENDINGMACHINE}))$.

Fig. 2. Various abstractions of VENDINGMACHINE.

The family-based model checking problem given in Definition 4 can be reduced to a number of smaller problems by partitioning the set of variants.

Proposition 1. *Let the subsets* $\mathbb{K}_1, \mathbb{K}_2, \ldots, \mathbb{K}_n$ *form a partition of the set* $\mathbb{K}$. *Then:* $\mathcal{F} \models \phi$, *if and only if,* $\pi_{\mathbb{K}_1}(\mathcal{F}) \models \phi, \ldots, \pi_{\mathbb{K}_n}(\mathcal{F}) \models \phi$.

Corollary 1. *Let* $\mathbb{K}_1, \mathbb{K}_2, \ldots, \mathbb{K}_n$ *form a* partition *of* $\mathbb{K}$, *and* $(\alpha_1, \gamma_1), \ldots, (\alpha_n, \gamma_n)$ *be Galois connections. If* $\alpha_1(\pi_{\mathbb{K}_1}(\mathcal{F})) \models \phi, \ldots, \alpha_n(\pi_{\mathbb{K}_n}(\mathcal{F})) \models \phi$, *Then* $\mathcal{F} \models \phi$.

In other words, correctness of abstract FTSs implies correctness of the concrete FTS. Note that verification of abstract FTSs can be drastically (even exponentially) faster. However, if abstract FTSs invalidate a property then the concrete FTS may still satisfy the property, i.e. the found counterexample in abstract FTSs may be spurious. In this case, we need to refine the abstract FTSs in order to eliminate the spurious counterexample.

Example 4. Recall the formula $\phi = \Box(\texttt{selected} \implies \Diamond \texttt{open})$ from Example 2, and $\alpha^{\text{join}}(\pi_{[\![f]\!]}(\text{VENDINGMACHINE}))$ and $\alpha^{\text{join}}(\pi_{[\![\neg f]\!]}(\text{VENDINGMACHINE}))$ shown in Fig. 2. First, we can successfully verify that $\alpha^{\text{join}}(\pi_{[\![\neg f]\!]}(\text{VENDINGMACHINE})) \models \phi$, which implies that all valid variants from $\mathbb{K}$ that do not contain the feature f (those are $\{v, s\}$ and $\{v, s, c\}$) satisfy the property ϕ. On the other hand, we have $\alpha^{\text{join}}(\pi_{[\![f]\!]}(\text{VENDINGMACHINE}))\,not \models \phi$ with the counterexample: ① $\rightarrow$ ③ $\rightarrow$ ⑤ $\rightarrow$ ⑦ $\rightarrow$ ① $\rightarrow$ …. This counterexample is genuine for the variants from $\mathbb{K}$ that contain the feature f (those are $\{v, s, t, c, f\}$ and $\{v, s, c, f\}$). In this way, the problem of verifying the FTS VENDINGMACH. against ϕ can be reduced to verifying whether two TSs, $\alpha^{\text{join}}(\pi_{[\![\neg f]\!]}(\text{VENDINGMACH.}))$ and $\alpha^{\text{join}}(\pi_{[\![f]\!]}(\text{VENDINGMACH.}))$, satisfy ϕ. $\quad\Box$

3   Abstraction Refinement

We now describe the abstraction refinement procedure (ARP), which uses spurious counterexamples to iteratively refine abstract variational models until either a genuine counterexample is found or the property satisfaction is shown for each variant in the family. Thus, the ARP determines for each variant whether or not it satisfies a property, and provides a counterexample for each variant that do not satisfy the given property.

The ARP for checking $\mathcal{F} \models \phi$, where $\mathcal{F} = (S, Act, trans, I, AP, L, \mathbb{F}, \mathbb{K}, \delta)$, is illustrated in Fig. 3. We apply an initial abstraction α, thus obtaining an initial abstract variational model $\alpha(\mathcal{F})$. If the initial abstract model satisfies the given property, then all variants satisfy it and we stop. Otherwise, the model checker returns a counterexample. Let ψ be the feature expression computed by conjoining feature expressions labelling all transitions that belong to this counterexample in $\mathcal{F}$. There are two cases to consider.

The ARP checks $\mathcal{F} \models \phi$, where $\mathcal{F} = (S, Act, trans, I, AP, L, \mathbb{F}, \mathbb{K}, \delta)$.

1 Let α be the initial abstraction used to build $\alpha(\mathcal{F})$. Check $\alpha(\mathcal{F}) \models \phi$?

2 If the property is satisfied, then return that ϕ is satisfied for all variants in $\mathbb{K}$.

3 Otherwise, if a genuine (feasible) counterexample is found, let ψ be the feature expression obtained by conjoining the guards $\delta(t)$ over all transitions t appearing in the execution of this counterexample in $\mathcal{F}$. Since the execution is feasible, it follows that ψ is satisfiable. Report that the property is violated for variants in $\mathbb{K} \cap \llbracket \psi \rrbracket$. We generate $\mathcal{F}' = \pi_{\llbracket \neg \psi \rrbracket}(\mathcal{F})$, and call the ARP to check $\mathcal{F}' \models \phi$ for variants in $\mathbb{K}' = \mathbb{K} \cap \llbracket \neg \psi \rrbracket$.

4 Otherwise, if a spurious (infeasible) counterexample is found, let ψ be the feature expression obtained by conjoining the guards $\delta(t)$ over all transitions t appearing in the execution of this counterexample in $\mathcal{F}$. Since the execution is infeasible, it follows that $\psi \wedge (\bigvee_{k \in \mathbb{K}} k)$ is unsatisfiable. Find $\psi' = \texttt{CraigInterpolation}(\psi, \mathbb{K})$. We generate $\mathcal{F}_1 = \pi_{\llbracket \psi' \rrbracket}(\mathcal{F})$ and $\mathcal{F}_2 = \pi_{\llbracket \neg \psi' \rrbracket}(\mathcal{F})$, and call the ARP two times to check $\mathcal{F}_1 \models \phi$ for variants in $\mathbb{K}_1 = \mathbb{K} \cap \llbracket \psi' \rrbracket$ and $\mathcal{F}_2 \models \phi$ for variants in $\mathbb{K}_2 = \mathbb{K} \cap \llbracket \neg \psi' \rrbracket$. By construction, both $\mathcal{F}_1$ and $\mathcal{F}_2$ do not contain this spurious counterexample.

Fig. 3. The abstraction refinement procedure (ARP)

First, if ψ is satisfiable and $\mathbb{K} \cap \llbracket \psi \rrbracket \neq \emptyset$, then the found counterexample is *genuine* for variants in $\mathbb{K} \cap \llbracket \psi \rrbracket$. For the other variants from $\mathbb{K} \cap \llbracket \neg \psi \rrbracket$, the found counterexample cannot be executed (i.e. the counterexample is spurious for $\mathbb{K} \cap \llbracket \neg \psi \rrbracket$). Therefore, we call the ARP again to verify $\pi_{\llbracket \neg \psi \rrbracket}(\mathcal{F})$ with updated set of valid configurations $\mathbb{K} \cap \llbracket \neg \psi \rrbracket$.

Second, if $\psi \wedge (\bigvee_{k \in \mathbb{K}} k)$ is unsatisfiable (i.e. $\mathbb{K} \cap \llbracket \psi \rrbracket = \emptyset$), then the found counterexample is *spurious* for all variants in $\mathbb{K}$ (due to incompatible feature expressions). Now, we describe how a feature expression ψ' used for constructing refined abstract models is determined by means of Craig interpolation [27] from ψ and $\mathbb{K}$. First, we find the minimal unsatisfiable core ψ^c of $\psi \wedge (\bigvee_{k \in \mathbb{K}} k)$, which contains a subset of conjuncts in $\psi \wedge (\bigvee_{k \in \mathbb{K}} k)$, such that ψ^c is still unsatisfiable and if we drop any single conjunct in ψ^c then the result becomes satisfiable. We group conjuncts in ψ^c in two groups X and Y such that $\psi^c = X \wedge Y = false$. Then, the interpolant ψ' is such that: (1) $X \implies \psi'$, (2) $\psi' \wedge Y = false$, (3) ψ' refers only to common variables of X and Y. Intuitively, we can think of the interpolant ψ' as a way of filtering out irrelevant information from X.

In particular, ψ' summarizes and translates why X is inconsistent with Y in their shared language. Once the interpolant ψ' is computed, we call the ARP to check $\pi_{[\![\psi']\!]}(\mathcal{F}) \models \phi$ for variants in $\mathbb{K} \cap [\![\psi']\!]$, and $\pi_{[\![\neg\psi']\!]}(\mathcal{F}) \models \phi$ for variants in $\mathbb{K} \cap [\![\neg\psi']\!]$. By construction, we guarantee that the found spurious counterexample does not occur neither in $\pi_{[\![\psi']\!]}(\mathcal{F})$ nor in $\pi_{[\![\neg\psi']\!]}(\mathcal{F})$.

Note that, in Step **1**, the initial abstraction can be chosen arbitrarily. This choice does not affect correctness and termination of the ARP, but it allows experimentation with different heuristics in concrete implementations. For example, if we use the initial abstraction α^{join}, then as an abstract model we obtain an ordinary TS where all feature expressions associated with transitions of $\mathcal{F}$ occurring in some valid variant are replaced with *true*. Therefore, the verification step can be performed using a single-system model checker (e.g. SPIN). Also note that we call the ARP until there are no more counterexamples or the updated set of valid configurations $\mathbb{K}$ becomes empty.

Example 5. Let $\mathcal{F}$ be VENDINGMACHINE of Fig. 1a with configurations $\mathbb{K} = \{\{v, s\}, \{v, s, t, c, f\}, \{v, s, c\}, \{v, s, c, f\}\}$. Let α^{join} be the initial abstraction.

We check $\mathcal{F} \models \phi$, where $\phi = \Box(\texttt{selected} \implies \Diamond \texttt{open})$ using the ARP. We first check $\alpha^{\text{join}}(\mathcal{F}) \models \phi$? The following spurious counterexample is reported: ① $\xrightarrow{pay}$ ② $\xrightarrow{change}$ ③ $\xrightarrow{tea}$ ⑥ $\xrightarrow{serveTea}$ ⑦ $\xrightarrow{take}$ ① . . .. The associated feature expression in $\mathcal{F}$ is: $(v \wedge \neg f) \wedge v \wedge t \wedge f$. The minimal unsatisfiable core is: $(v \wedge \neg f) \wedge f$, and the found interpolant is $\neg f$. In this way, we have found that the feature f is responsible for the spuriousness of the given counterexample. Thus, in the next iteration we check $\alpha^{\text{join}}(\pi_{[\![\neg f]\!]}(\mathcal{F})) \models \phi$ and $\alpha^{\text{join}}(\pi_{[\![f]\!]}(\mathcal{F})) \models \phi$, which give conclusive results for all variants from $\mathbb{K}$ as explained in Example 4.

Consider the property $\phi' = \Box\Diamond \texttt{open}$. The following counterexample is found in $\alpha^{\text{join}}(\mathcal{F})$: ① $\xrightarrow{pay}$ ② $\xrightarrow{change}$ ③ $\xrightarrow{cancel}$ ④ $\xrightarrow{return}$ ① . . .. The associated feature expression in $\mathcal{F}$ is: $v \wedge \neg f \wedge c$, so this is a genuine counterexample for the variant $\{v, s, c\} \in \mathbb{K}$. In the next iteration, we check $\alpha^{\text{join}}(\pi_{[\![\neg(v \wedge \neg f \wedge c)]\!]}(\mathcal{F})) \models \phi'$ for variants $\mathbb{K} \backslash \{v, s, c\}$. We obtain the counterexample: ① $\xrightarrow{free}$ ③ $\xrightarrow{cancel}$ ④ $\xrightarrow{return}$ ① . . ., with associated feature expression $f \wedge c$, realizable for variants $\{v, s, t, c, f\}$ and $\{v, s, c, f\}$). In the final iteration, we check $\alpha^{\text{join}}(\pi_{[\![\neg(f \wedge c)]\!]}(\pi_{[\![\neg(v \wedge \neg f \wedge c)]\!]}(\mathcal{F}))) \models \phi'$ for the variant $\{v, s\}$. The property holds, so ϕ' is satisfied by $\{v, s\}$.   □

Theorem 2. *The ARP terminates and is correct.*

Proof. At the end of an iteration, the ARP either terminates with answer 'yes', or finds a genuine counterexample and updates $\mathbb{K}$ into $\mathbb{K}'$, or finds a spurious counterexample and updates $\mathbb{K}$ into $\mathbb{K}_1$ and $\mathbb{K}_2$. Given that $\mathbb{K}' \subset \mathbb{K}$ (the counterexample is genuine for some non-empty subset of $\mathbb{K}$), and $\mathbb{K}_1 \subset \mathbb{K}$, $\mathbb{K}_2 \subset \mathbb{K}$ (by def. $\mathbb{K}_1 \neq \emptyset$, $\mathbb{K}_2 \neq \emptyset$, $\mathbb{K}_1 \cup \mathbb{K}_2 = \mathbb{K}$), the number of possible updates and calls to the ARP are finite. Therefore, the number of iterations is also finite.

If the ARP terminates with answer that a property is satisfied (resp., property is not satisfied) by a variant, then the answer is correct by Theorem 1, since any abstraction constructs an over-approximated model for a given set of variants. □

4   Evaluation

In this section, we describe our implementation of the ARP, and present the results of experiments carried out on several variational models. We use experiments to evaluate in which cases and to what extent our ARP technique outperforms the family-based model checking algorithms of FTS [7,8] implemented in $\overline{\text{SNIP}}^3$.

Implementation. It is difficult to use FTSs directly to model large variational systems. Therefore, $\overline{\text{SNIP}}$ uses the high-level languages fPROMELA and *TVL* for modeling variational systems and their configuration sets, respectively. fPROMELA is an extension of PROMELA, the language of the SPIN model checker [19], adding *feature variables*, $\mathbb{F}$, and a new *guarded-by-features statement*, "gd". The "gd" is a non-deterministic statement similar to PROMELA's "if", except that only feature expressions can be used as guards. Actually, this is the only place where features may be used. Thus, "gd" plays the same role in fPROMELA as "#ifdef" in the C Preprocessor [24]. *TVL* [6] is a textual modelling language for describing the set of valid configurations, $\mathbb{K}$, for an fPROMELA model along with all available features, $\mathbb{F}$. It has been shown in [13,14] that variability abstractions and projections can be implemented as syntactic source-to-source transformations of fPROMELA and *TVL* models, which enable an effective computation of abstract models syntactically from high-level modelling languages. More precisely, let M and T be fPROMELA and *TVL* models, and let $[\![M]\!]_T$ represent the FTS obtained by their compilation. Since variability abstractions affect only variability-specific aspects of a system, for any abstraction α we can define $\alpha(M)$ and $\alpha(T)$ as syntactic transformations such that $\alpha([\![M]\!]_T) = [\![\alpha(M)]\!]_{\alpha(T)}$. That is, the abstract model obtained by applying α on the FTS $[\![M]\!]_T$ coincides with the FTS obtained by compiling $\alpha(M)$ and $\alpha(T)$. The same applies for projections $\pi_{[\![\psi]\!]}$. The fPROMELA RECONFIGURATOR tool [13,14] syntactically calculates the transformations corresponding to abstractions and projections. This is important for two reasons. First, it allows to easily implement our technique based on abstractions and projections. Second, we avoid the need for intermediate storage in memory of the concrete full-blown FTSs. In our implementation of the ARP, we use α^{join} as the initial abstraction. Hence, after applying α^{join} on fPROMELA and *TVL* models M and T, we obtain an ordinary PROMELA model and we call SPIN to check $[\![\alpha(M)]\!]_{\alpha(T)} \models \phi$? If a counterexample trace is returned, we inspect the error trace in detail by using SPIN's simulation mode. We replay the error trace through $\alpha(M)$ and M simultaneously, and we find the feature expression ψ that characterizes this trace in M. In order to do this, we use the fact that $\alpha(M)$ and M have the same control structures (same number of lines and statements), except that "gd" statements in M are replaced with "if" statements in $\alpha(M)$ by the corresponding transformations that affect only their guards.

---

[3] The project on development of the $\overline{\text{SNIP}}$ tool (https://projects.info.unamur.be/fts/) is independent of SPIN. $\overline{\text{SNIP}}$ has been implemented from scratch. We put a line over $\overline{\text{SNIP}}$ to make the distinction from SPIN clearer.

Experimental setup. For our experiments, we use: a warm-up example to demonstrate specific characteristics of our ARP, and the MINEPUMP [25] variational system whose *f*PROMELA model was created as part of the $\overline{\text{SNIP}}$ project. We verify a range of properties by using (1) the ARP with α^{join} as the initial abstraction and SPIN as the verification tool (denoted ARP+SPIN), and by using (2) plain family-based model checking with $\overline{\text{SNIP}}$. The reported performance numbers constitute the average runtime of five independent executions. For each experiment, we measure: TIME which is the time to verify in seconds; and SPACE which is the number of explored states plus the number of re-explored states (this is equivalent to the number of transitions fired). For the ARP, along with the total time the ARP takes to complete we also report in parentheses the time taken by SPIN to perform the actual model checking tasks. The rest of the total time the ARP uses to calculate abstractions, projections, analyze error traces, etc. We only measure the times to generate a process analyser (pan) for SPIN and to execute it. We do not count the time for compiling pan, as it is due to a design decision in SPIN rather than its verification algorithm. All experiments were executed on a LUbunutuVM 64-bit Intel®Core^{TM} i7-4600U CPU running at 2.10 GHz with 4 GB memory. The implementation, benchmarks, and all results obtained from our experiments are available from: http://www.itu.dk/people/ adim/arp.html.

Warm-up example. Consider the *f*PROMELA model $\mathcal{F}$ given in Fig. 4a. After declaring feature variables, A1 . . . An, the process foo() is defined. The first gd statement specifies that i++ is available for variants that contain the feature A1, and skip for variants with ¬A1. The following gd statements are similar, except that their guards are the features from A2 to An. We want to check the assertion, $i \geq k$, where k is a meta-variable that can be replaced with different values: 0, 1, ..., n. The corresponding *TVL* model specifies that all features are optional and unconstrained, which means that all possible 2^n configurations are valid. We use two approaches to check the above assertions: ARP+SPIN and the family-based model checker $\overline{\text{SNIP}}$. The initial abstract model $\alpha^{\text{join}}(\mathcal{F})$ used in the ARP is shown in Fig. 4b. Since there are valid variants where Aj is enabled

```
typedef features {
  bool A1; bool A2; ...bool An}
features f
active proctype foo() {
  int i = 0;
  gd :: f.A1 ⇒ i++ :: else ⇒ skip dg;
  gd :: f.A2 ⇒ i++ :: else ⇒ skip dg;
    ......
  gd :: f.An ⇒ i++ :: else ⇒ skip dg;
  assert(i ≥ k) }
```
(a) An *f*PROMELA model $\mathcal{F}$.

```
typedef features {
  bool A1; bool A2; ...bool An}
features f
active proctype foo() {
  int i = 0;
  if :: true ⇒ i++ :: true ⇒ skip fi;
  if :: true ⇒ i++ :: true ⇒ skip fi;
    ......
  if :: true ⇒ i++ :: true ⇒ skip fi;
  assert(i ≥ k) }
```
(b) A PROMELA model $\alpha^{\text{join}}(\mathcal{F})$

Fig. 4. An *f*PROMELA model and the corresponding α^{join} abstract model.

and valid variants where A_j is disabled (for any $j \in \{1,\ldots,n\}$), we have that both statements i++ and skip become available in $\alpha^{\mathrm{join}}(\mathcal{F})$ for all "gd" statements.

When $k = 0$, the assertion i ≥ 0 is satisfied by all variants. The ARP terminates in one iteration with only one call to SPIN, which reports that $\alpha^{\mathrm{join}}(\mathcal{F})$ satisfies the assertion. When $k = 1$, the ARP needs two iterations to find a (genuine) counterexample which corresponds to a single configuration where all features are disabled, and to certify that all other variants satisfy the assertion. When $k = 2$, the ARP runs in $\mathbf{n}+1$ iterations producing $\mathbf{n}+1$ erroneous variants: one variant where all features are disabled, and $\mathbf{n}$ variants where exactly one feature is enabled and all others are disabled. When $k = \mathbf{n}$, the ARP will need $\mathbf{n}+1$ iterations to terminate reporting that there is only one variant, where all features are enabled, that satisfies the assertion i $\geq \mathbf{n}$. All other variants are erroneous. This represents the worst case for our ARP, since all possible variants will be generated explicitly and checked by SPIN in a brute-force fashion. In addition, we have the overhead of generating all intermediate projections and abstractions as well as their verification with SPIN, for which spurious counterexamples are obtained. The performance results are shown in Fig. 5. We say that a task is *infeasible* when it is taking more time than the given timeout threshold, which we set on 1 h. Notice that $\overline{\mathrm{SNIP}}$ reports the correct results in only one iteration for all cases. Yet, as shown in Fig. 5, for $\mathbf{n} = 25$ (for which $|\mathbb{K}| = 2^{25} = 33,554,432$ variants) $\overline{\mathrm{SNIP}}$ timeouts after visiting 150 M states. On the other hand, our ARP based approach is feasible even for very large values of $\mathbf{n}$ when k is smaller (see Fig. 5). In general, the ARP aims to partition the configuration space into subspaces that satisfy and violate the property at hand. When k is higher, that split becomes more irregular and the ARP needs to perform more iterations and calls to SPIN to find it automatically. Therefore, in those cases it takes more time to complete.

MINEPUMP. The MINEPUMP variational system is given by an fPROMELA model with 200 LOC and a *TVL* model that contains 7 independent optional features: Start, Stop, MethaneAlarm, MethaneQuery, Low, Normal, and High, thus yielding $2^7 = 128$ variants. The FTS of MINEPUMP has 21,177 states. It consists of 5 processes: a controller, a pump, a watersensor, a methanesensor,

	$k = 0$				$k = 1$			
	ARP + SPIN		SNIP		ARP+SPIN		SNIP	
n	TIME	SPACE	TIME	SPACE	TIME	SPACE	TIME	SPACE
2	0.35 (0.02)	13	0.34	14	1.16 (0.15)	26	0.34	13
5	0.63 (0.06)	52	0.35	126	2.26 (0.26)	245	0.35	125
10	0.68 (0.06)	177	0.61	4,094	4.29 (0.47)	1,690	0.61	4,093
24	0.71 (0.07)	926	1262.7	67,108,862	8.63 (0.86)	21,696	1318.1	67,108,861
25	0.75 (0.07)	1002	– infeasible –		8.81 (0.88)	24,475	– infeasible –	
100	0.77 (0.08)	15,252	– infeasible –		39.54 (3.81)	1,515,400	– infeasible –	

Fig. 5. Verification of the warm-up example. TIME in seconds.

prop-erty	ARP + SPIN		SNIP	
	TIME	SPACE	TIME	SPACE
φ_1	0.79 (0.11) s	36,725	1.96 s	250,770
φ_2	0.91 (0.21) s	266,601	3.76 s	441,063
φ_3	0.85 (0.12) s	36,725	2.64 s	326,064
φ_4	8.15 (1.91) s	57,065	8.95 s	398,167
φ_5	7.82 (1.89) s	32,532	7.89 s	218,552

Fig. 6. Verification of MINEPUMP properties.

and a user. When activated, the controller should switch on the pump when the water level in the mine is high, but only if there is no methane within it.

For evaluation, we consider five interesting properties of MINEPUMP (taken from [8]). First, we consider three properties, φ_1, φ_2 and φ_3, that are intended to be satisfied by all variants. The property φ_1 is the absence of deadlock; the property φ_2 is that under a *fairness assumption* (the system will infinity often read messages of various types) the pump is never indefinitely off when the water level is high and there is no methane; whereas the property φ_3 is that if the pump is switched on then the controller state is running. For all three properties, the ARP terminates after one iteration reporting that the properties are satisfied by all variants. Then, we have two properties, φ_4 and φ_5, which are satisfied by some variants and violated by others, such that there are different counterexamples corresponding to violating variants. The property φ_4 (when the water is high and there is no methane, the pump will not be switched on at all eventually) is violated by variants that satisfy Start ∧ High (32 variants in total). The property φ_5 (when the water is low, then the pump will be off) is also violated by variants satisfying Start ∧ High. For both properties, our ARP runs in seven iterations, producing 12 different counterexamples for φ_4 and 13 different counterexamples for φ_5. Figure 6 shows the performance results of verifying properties, φ_1 to φ_5, using our ARP with SPIN approach and the SNIP. The ARP achieves improvements in both TIME and SPACE in most cases, especially for properties φ_1 to φ_3 satisfied by all variants which are verified in only one iteration. Of course, the performances of the ARP will start to decline for properties for which the ARP needs higher number of iterations and calls to SPIN in order to complete. However, we can see that for both φ_4 and φ_5 the actual verification time taken by SPIN (given in parentheses) in our ARP is still considerable smaller than the time taken by SNIP. Still, in these cases we obtain very long counterexamples (around thousand steps) so the ARP will need some additional time to process them.

Discussion. In conclusion, the ARP achieves the best results when the property to be checked is either satisfied by all variants or only a few erroneous variants exist. In those cases, the ARP will report conclusive results in few iterations. The worst case is when every variant triggers a different counterexample, so our ARP ends up in verifying all variants one by one in a brute-force fashion (plus the overhead for generating and verifying all intermediate abstract models). Variability abstractions weaken feature expressions used in FTSs, thus increasing the commonality between the behaviours of variants. In the case of α^{join} this enables the use of (single-system) SPIN model checker. SPIN is a highly-optimized industrial-strength tool which is much faster than the $\overline{\mathrm{SNIP}}$ research prototype. SPIN contains many optimisation algorithms, which are result of more than three decades research on advanced computer aided verification. For example, partial order reduction, data-flow analysis and statement merging are not implemented in $\overline{\mathrm{SNIP}}$ yet. Note that we can also implement the ARP to work with $\overline{\mathrm{SNIP}}$ by using $\alpha^{\mathrm{fignore}}$ instead of α^{join} as the initial abstraction. The ARP will work correctly for any choice of features to be ignored by $\alpha^{\mathrm{fignore}}$. However, in order the ARP to terminate faster and achieve some speedups, the ignored features should be chosen carefully by exploiting the knowledge of the variational system and property at hand.

5   Related Work

Family-based (lifted) analyses and verification techniques have been a topic of considerable research recently (see [30] for a survey). Some successful examples are lifted syntax checking [17,24], lifted type checking [23], lifted static data-flow analysis [3,15,16,28], lifted verification [20,21,29], etc.

In the context of family-based model checking, one of the earliest attempts for modelling variational systems is by using modal transition systems (MTSs) [2,26]. Following this, Classen et al. present FTSs in [7,8] and show how specifically designed family-based model checking algorithms (implemented in $\overline{\mathrm{SNIP}}$) can be used for verifying FTSs against fLTL properties. An FTS-specific verification procedure based on counterexample guided abstraction refinement has been proposed in [10]. Abstractions on FTSs are introduced by using existential F-abstraction functions (as opposed to Galois connections here), and simulation relation is used to relate different abstraction levels. There are other important differences between the approach in [10] and our ARP. Refinement of feature abstractions in [10] is defined by simply replacing the abstract (weakened) feature expressions occurring in transitions of the spurious counterexample by their concrete feature expressions. In contrast, we use Craig interpolation as well as suitable combinations of variability abstractions and projections to generate refined abstract models. The abstractions in [10] are applied on feature program graphs (an intermediate structure between high-level fPROMELA models and FTSs) in $\overline{\mathrm{SNIP}}$. In contrast, we apply variability abstractions as preprocessor transformations directly on high-level fPROMELA models thus avoiding to generate any intermediate concrete semantic model in the memory. In the case of α^{join}, this leads to generating PROMELA models and using SPIN for the ARP. The work [12] presents an approach for family-based software model checking of #ifdef-based second-order program families using symbolic game semantics models [11].

6   Conclusion

In this work we have proposed an automatic abstraction refinement procedure for family-based model checking of variational systems. Automatic refinement gives us an adaptive divide-and-conquer strategy for the configuration space. The obtained tool represents a completely automatic alternative to the family-based model checker $\overline{\text{SNIP}}$, which is simpler, easier to maintain, and more efficient for some interesting properties than $\overline{\text{SNIP}}$. It automatically benefits from all optimizations of SPIN. The overall design principle is general and can be applied to lifting of other automatic verification tools to variational systems.

References

1. Baier, C., Katoen, J.: Principles of Model Checking. MIT Press, Cambridge (2008)
2. ter Beek, M.H., Fantechi, A., Gnesi, S., Mazzanti, F.: Modelling and analysing variability in product families: model checking of modal transition systems with variability constraints. J. Log. Algebr. Meth. Program. **85**(2), 287–315 (2016). http://dx.doi.org/10.1016/j.jlamp.2015.09.004
3. Bodden, E., Tolêdo, T., Ribeiro, M., Brabrand, C., Borba, P., Mezini, M.: SPL^{LIFT}: statically analyzing software product lines in minutes instead of years. In: ACM SIGPLAN Conference on PLDI 2013, pp. 355–364 (2013)
4. Clarke, E., Grumberg, O., Jha, S., Lu, Y., Veith, H.: Counterexample-guided abstraction refinement. In: Emerson, E.A., Sistla, A.P. (eds.) CAV 2000. LNCS, vol. 1855, pp. 154–169. Springer, Heidelberg (2000). doi:10.1007/10722167_15
5. Clarke, E.M., Kroening, D., Sharygina, N., Yorav, K.: Predicate abstraction of ANSI-C programs using SAT. Formal Meth. Syst. Des. **25**(2–3), 105–127 (2004). http://dx.doi.org/10.1023/B:FORM.0000040025.89719.f3
6. Classen, A., Boucher, Q., Heymans, P.: A text-based approach to feature modelling: syntax and semantics of TVL. Sci. Comput. Program. **76**(12), 1130–1143 (2011). http://dx.doi.org/10.1016/j.scico.2010.10.005
7. Classen, A., Cordy, M., Heymans, P., Legay, A., Schobbens, P.: Model checking software product lines with SNIP. STTT **14**(5), 589–612 (2012). http://dx.doi.org/10.1007/s10009-012-0234-1
8. Classen, A., Cordy, M., Schobbens, P., Heymans, P., Legay, A., Raskin, J.: Featured transition systems: foundations for verifying variability-intensive systems and their application to LTL model checking. IEEE Trans. Softw. Eng. **39**(8), 1069–1089 (2013). http://doi.ieeecomputersociety.org/10.1109/TSE.2012.86
9. Clements, P., Northrop, L.: Software Product Lines: Practices and Patterns. Addison-Wesley, Reading (2001)
10. Cordy, M., Heymans, P., Legay, A., Schobbens, P., Dawagne, B., Leucker, M.: Counterexample guided abstraction refinement of product-line behavioural models. In: Cheung, S., Orso, A., Storey, M.D. (eds.) Proceedings of the 22nd ACM SIGSOFT International Symposium on Foundations of Software Engineering (FSE-22), pp. 190–201. ACM (2014). http://doi.acm.org/10.1145/2635868.2635919
11. Dimovski, A.S.: Program verification using symbolic game semantics. Theor. Comput. Sci. **560**, 364–379 (2014). http://dx.doi.org/10.1016/j.tcs.2014.01.016
12. Dimovski, A.S.: Symbolic game semantics for model checking program families. In: Bošnački, D., Wijs, A. (eds.) SPIN 2016. LNCS, vol. 9641, pp. 19–37. Springer, Heidelberg (2016). doi:10.1007/978-3-319-32582-8_2

13. Dimovski, A.S., Al-Sibahi, A.S., Brabrand, C., Wąsowski, A.: Family-based model checking without a family-based model checker. In: Fischer, B., Geldenhuys, J. (eds.) SPIN 2015. LNCS, vol. 9232, pp. 282–299. Springer, Heidelberg (2015). doi:10.1007/978-3-319-23404-5_18

14. Dimovski, A.S., Al-Sibahi, A.S., Brabrand, C., Wasowski, A.: Efficient family-based model checking via variability abstractions. STTT 1–19 (2016). doi:10.1007/s10009-016-0425-2

15. Dimovski, A.S., Brabrand, C., Wasowski, A.: Variability abstractions: trading precision for speed in family-based analyses. In: 29th European Conference on Object-Oriented Programming, ECOOP 2015. LIPIcs, vol. 37, pp. 247–270. Schloss Dagstuhl - Leibniz-Zentrum fuer Informatik (2015). http://dx.doi.org/10.4230/LIPIcs.ECOOP.2015.247

16. Dimovski, A.S., Brabrand, C., Wąsowski, A.: Finding suitable variability abstractions for family-based analysis. In: Fitzgerald, J., Heitmeyer, C., Gnesi, S., Philippou, A. (eds.) FM 2016. LNCS, vol. 9995, pp. 217–234. Springer, Heidelberg (2016). doi:10.1007/978-3-319-48989-6_14

17. Gazzillo, P., Grimm, R.: Superc: parsing all of C by taming the preprocessor. In: Vitek, J., Lin, H., Tip, F. (eds.) ACM SIGPLAN Conference on Programming Language Design and Implementation, PLDI 2012, Beijing, China, 11–16 June 2012, pp. 323–334. ACM (2012). http://doi.acm.org/10.1145/2254064.2254103

18. Henzinger, T.A., Jhala, R., Majumdar, R., McMillan, K.L.: Abstractions from proofs. In: Proceedings of the 31st ACM SIGPLAN-SIGACT Symposium on Principles of Programming Languages, POPL 2004, pp. 232–244. ACM (2004). http://doi.acm.org/10.1145/964001.964021

19. Holzmann, G.J.: The SPIN Model Checker - Primer and Reference Manual. Addison-Wesley, Reading (2004)

20. Iosif-Lazar, A.F., Al-Sibahi, A.S., Dimovski, A.S., Savolainen, J.E., Sierszecki, K., Wasowski, A.: Experiences from designing and validating a software modernization transformation (E). In: 30th IEEE/ACM International Conference on Automated Software Engineering, ASE 2015, pp. 597–607 (2015). http://dx.doi.org/10.1109/ASE.2015.84

21. Iosif-Lazar, A.F., Melo, J., Dimovski, A.S., Brabrand, C., Wasowski, A.: Effective analysis of c programs by rewriting variability. In: The Art, Science, and Engineering of Programming, Programming 2017 (2017)

22. Kang, K.C., Cohen, S.G., Hess, J.A., Novak, W.E., Peterson, A.S.: Feature-oriented domain analysis (FODA) feasibility study. Technical report, Carnegie-Mellon University Software Engineering Institute, November 1990

23. Kästner, C., Apel, S., Thüm, T., Saake, G.: Type checking annotation-based product lines. ACM Trans. Softw. Eng. Methodol. 21(3), 14 (2012)

24. Kästner, C., Giarrusso, P.G., Rendel, T., Erdweg, S., Ostermann, K., Berger, T.: Variability-aware parsing in the presence of lexical macros and conditional compilation. In: Proceedings of the 26th Annual ACM SIGPLAN Conference on Object-Oriented Programming, Systems, Languages, and Applications, OOPSLA 2011, pp. 805–824 (2011). http://doi.acm.org/10.1145/2048066.2048128

25. Kramer, J., Magee, J., Sloman, M., Lister, A.: Conic: an integrated approach to distributed computer control systems. IEE Proc. 130(1), 1–10 (1983)

26. Larsen, K.G., Nyman, U., Wąsowski, A.: Modal I/O automata for interface and product line theories. In: Nicola, R. (ed.) ESOP 2007. LNCS, vol. 4421, pp. 64–79. Springer, Heidelberg (2007). doi:10.1007/978-3-540-71316-6_6

27. McMillan, K.L.: Applications of craig interpolants in model checking. In: Halbwachs, N., Zuck, L.D. (eds.) TACAS 2005. LNCS, vol. 3440, pp. 1–12. Springer, Heidelberg (2005). doi:10.1007/978-3-540-31980-1_1

28. Midtgaard, J., Dimovski, A.S., Brabrand, C., Wasowski, A.: Systematic derivation of correct variability-aware program analyses. Sci. Comput. Program. **105**, 145–170 (2015). http://dx.doi.org/10.1016/j.scico.2015.04.005

29. von Rhein, A., Thüm, T., Schaefer, I., Liebig, J., Apel, S.: Variability encoding: from compile-time to load-time variability. J. Log. Algebr. Meth. Program. **85**(1), 125–145 (2016). http://dx.doi.org/10.1016/j.jlamp.2015.06.007

30. Thüm, T., Apel, S., Kästner, C., Schaefer, I., Saake, G.: A classification and survey of analysis strategies for software product lines. ACM Comput. Surv. **47**(1), 6 (2014). http://doi.acm.org/10.1145/2580950

A Unified and Formal Programming Model for Deltas and Traits

Ferruccio Damiani[1]([✉]), Reiner Hähnle[1,2], Eduard Kamburjan[2], and Michael Lienhardt[1]

[1] University of Torino, Torino, Italy
{ferruccio.damiani,michael.lienhardt}@unito.it
[2] Technical University Darmstadt, Darmstadt, Germany
{haehnle,kamburjan}@cs.tu-darmstadt.de

Abstract. This paper presents a unified model for two complementary approaches of code reuse: Traits and Delta-Oriented Programming (DOP). Traits are used to modularly construct classes, while DOP is a modular approach to construct Software Product Lines. In this paper, we identify the common structure of these two approaches, present a core calculus that combine Traits and DOP in a unified framework, provide an implementation for the ABS modelling language, and illustrate its application in an industrial modeling scenario.

1 Introduction

Systematic and successful code reuse in software construction remains a challenge and constitutes an important research problem in programming language design. The drive to digitalization, together with the fundamental changes of deployment platforms in recent years (cloud, multi-core), implies that modern software must be able to evolve and it must also support variability [33]. The standard reuse mechanism of mainstream object-oriented languages—class based inheritance— is insufficient to deal adequately with software evolution and reuse [14,24] and provides no support for implementing software variability.

Traits are a mechanism for fine-grained reuse aimed at overcoming the limitations of class-based inheritance (see [9,14,25] for discussions and examples). Traits are sets of methods, defined independently of a class hierarchy, that can be composed in various ways to build other traits or classes. They were originally proposed and implemented in a SMALTALK-like, dynamically typed setting [14,34]. Subsequently, various formulations of traits in a JAVA-like, statically typed setting were proposed [3,6,22,26,28,29,36].

Delta-oriented programming (DOP) [1, Sect. 6.6.1], [31] is a flexible and modular approach to implement Software Product Lines (SPL) [27]. Its core element

This work has been partially supported by: EU Horizon 2020 project HyVar (www.hyvar-project.eu), GA No. 644298; ICT COST Action IC1402 ARVI (www.cost-arvi.eu); Ateneo/CSP D16D15000360005 project RunVar (runvar-project.di.unito.it); project FormbaR (formbar.raillab.de), Innovationsallianz TU Darmstadt–Deutsche Bahn Netz AG.

© Springer-Verlag GmbH Germany 2017
M. Huisman and J. Rubin (Eds.): FASE 2017, LNCS 10202, pp. 424–441, 2017.
DOI: 10.1007/978-3-662-54494-5_25

is the *delta*, an explicit, structured construct for characterizing the difference between two program variants: DOP realizes SPL by associating deltas with product features (not necessarily one-to-one), which allows for a flexible and modular construction of program variants [32]. DOP is an extension of *Feature-Oriented Programming* (FOP) [1, Sect. 6.1], [2], a previously proposed approach to implement SPLs, where deltas are associated one-to-one with product features and have limited expressive power: like in DOP they can add and modify program elements (e.g., classes and attributes[1]), however, they cannot remove them. The explicit, flexible link between features and source code as realized in DOP is key to keep design-oriented and implementation-oriented views in sync. DOP was implemented on top of JAVA [21] and in the concurrent modeling language ABS [10], where it has been successfully used in industry [16,18].

In this paper, we observe (and justify in Sect. 3.1) that, while deltas are ideal to realize *inter-product* reuse, they are unsuitable to achieve *intra-product* reuse. It is, therefore, natural to combine deltas and traits into a single language that ideally supports flexible inter- as well as flexible intra-product reuse. Moreover, we also observe (and justify in Sect. 3.2) that most delta and trait operations are nearly identical from an abstract point of view: they add attributes to an existing declaration, they remove attributes, and they modify existing attributes. It is, therefore, natural to unify the operations provided by deltas and traits. Such a unification simplifies the language and makes it easier to learn (it has a smaller number of concepts). Based on these observations, we design (in Sect. 3.3) a minimal language with a completely *uniform* integration of traits and deltas. Moreover, we implement our design in the concurrent modelling language ABS [10] and illustrate its application in an industrial modeling scenario. Indeed, ABS represents an ideal platform for our investigation as it supports DOP, but it so far lacks a construct for intra-product reuse: evaluations of ABS against industrial requirements repeatedly identified intra-product reuse mechanisms [15,30] as an important factor to improve usability.

Paper Organization. In Sect. 2 we introduce the FABS and FDABS languages which formalize a minimal fragment of core ABS [20] and its extension with deltas [10], respectively. In Sect. 3 we introduce the FDTABS language which formalizes our proposal by adding traits on top of FDABS. We explain and motivate our design decisions systematically with the help of an instructive example. In Sect. 4 we provide a formal semantics in the form of a rule system that eliminates traits and deltas by "flattening" [26]. In Sect. 5 we present the implementation of our ABS extension. In Sect. 6 we illustrate how it is applied in an industrial modeling scenario. In Sect. 7 we discuss related work and conclude.

---

[1] As usual in the OOP literature, with *attribute* we mean any declaration element, i.e., a field or a method, in contrast to the usage in the UML community, where attribute means only field.

2   FDABS: A Minimal Language for ABS with Deltas

We first present (in Sect. 2.1) FABS, a minimal fragment of core ABS [20], and then (in Sect. 2.2) recall—as previously shown for ABS in [10]—how deltas add the possibility to construct SPLs by factoring out the code that is common to different products in the SPL.

2.1   FABS: Featherweight ABS

The syntax of FABS is given by the grammar in Fig. 1. The non-terminal P represents programs, ID interface declarations, CD class declarations, AD attribute declarations, FD field declarations, HD header declarations, MD method declarations, e expressions, and s statements.[2] As usual, $\overline{X}$ denotes a finite sequence with zero or more occurrences of a syntax element of type X. Our development is independent of the exact expression and statement syntax, so we leave it unspecified. Our examples use standard operators and statements whose syntax and semantics is obvious.

The code snippet in Fig. 2 illustrates the FABS syntax. It is a fragment of an application that manages bank accounts. Withdrawals that would result in a negative balance are not carried out.

2.2   FDABS: Adding Deltas to FABS

Delta-Oriented Programming implements SPLs by adding three elements to the base language: a *feature model* which encodes the variability available in the SPL;

$$
\begin{array}{ll}
P & ::= \overline{ID}\ \overline{CD} \\
ID & ::= \texttt{interface I [extends } \overline{\texttt{I}}]\ \{\ \overline{HD}\ \} \\
CD & ::= \texttt{class C [implements } \overline{\texttt{I}}]\ \{\ \overline{AD}\ \} \\
AD & ::= FD\ \mid\ MD
\end{array}
\qquad
\begin{array}{ll}
FD & ::= \texttt{I f} \\
HD & ::= \texttt{I m(}\overline{\texttt{I x}}) \\
MD & ::= HD\ \{\ \overline{s}\ \texttt{return } e;\ \}
\end{array}
$$

Fig. 1. FABS syntax

```
interface IAccount {
  Int withdraw(Int amount);
}
class Account() implements IAccount {
  Int withdraw(Int amount) {
    if (balance-amount >= 0) { balance = balance-amount; }
    return balance;
  }
}
```

Fig. 2. Bank account example in FABS

---

[2] ABS includes other features, like datatypes and concurrency, that we do not include in FABS as they are orthogonal to the delta and trait composition mechanisms.

a set of *deltas* that implement the variability expressed in the feature model; and *configuration knowledge* which links the feature model to the deltas.

The grammar resulting from the addition of DOP to FABS is shown in Fig. 3. An SPL L consists of a feature model $\mathcal{M}$, configuration knowledge $\mathcal{K}$, a (possibly empty) list of deltas $\overline{\Delta}$, and a (possibly empty or incomplete) base program P, defined as in Fig. 1. We leave the precise definition of the feature model and configuration knowledge unspecified, as it is not the focus of this work and invite the interested reader to look at [10] for a possible syntax for these elements. Deltas have a name d and a list of operations IO on interfaces and operations CO on classes. These operations can add or remove interfaces and classes, or modify their content by adding or removing attributes. Moreover, these operations can also change the set of interfaces implemented by a class or extended by an interface by means of an optional `implements` or `extends` clause in the `modifies` operation, respectively. Finally, it is also possible to *modify* the declaration of a method, with the `modifies` operation: in this operation, the new code can refer to a call of the original implementation of the method with the keyword `original`.

$$
\begin{array}{rcl}
L & ::= & \mathcal{M}\ \mathcal{K}\ \overline{\Delta}\ P \\
\Delta & ::= & \texttt{delta d}\ \{\overline{IO}\ \overline{CO}\ \} \\
IO & ::= & \texttt{adds}\ ID\ \mid\ \texttt{removes I}\ \mid\ \texttt{modifies I}\ [\texttt{extends}\ \overline{\texttt{I}}]\ \{\ \overline{HO}\ \} \\
HO & ::= & \texttt{adds}\ HD\ \mid\ \texttt{removes m} \\
CO & ::= & \texttt{adds}\ CD\ \mid\ \texttt{removes C}\ \mid\ \texttt{modifies C}\ [\texttt{implements}\ \overline{\texttt{I}}]\ \{\ \overline{AO}\ \} \\
AO & ::= & \texttt{adds}\ FD\ \mid\ \texttt{removes f}\ \mid\ \texttt{adds}\ MD\ \mid\ \texttt{removes m}\ \mid\ \texttt{modifies}\ MD
\end{array}
$$

Fig. 3. FDABS syntax: productions to be added to Fig. 1

We illustrate this extension of FABS by declaring an SPL over the example in Fig. 2. We add two variants to the original code: one that enables interest payment, identified by the feature "Saving" and parameterized by the interest rate, and one that permits a negative balance, identified by the feature "Overdraft" and parameterized by the overdraft limit. A visual representation of the corresponding feature model is shown in Fig. 4.

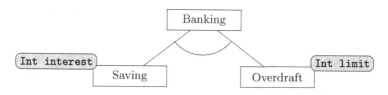

Fig. 4. Visual representation of the feature model of the bank account example

We exemplify delta operations with delta dOverdraft shown in Fig. 5 which implements the feature "Overdraft". The parameter of "Overdraft" is encoded by the field limit.[3] Moreover, dOverdraft adds a setter method for that field, and it modifies withdraw to take the limit into account.

```
delta dOverdraft {
  modifies Account {
    adds Int limit;
    adds Unit setLimit(Int value) { limit = value; }
    modifies Int withdraw(Int amount) {
      if (balance-amount+limit >= 0) { balance = balance-amount; }
      return balance;
    }
  }
}
```

Fig. 5. The dOverdraft delta in FDABS

3   FDTABS: Adding Traits to FDABS

To motivate the design of the FDTABS language, we first demonstrate (in Sect. 3.1) that deltas cannot be used for intra-product code reuse. Then (in Sect. 3.2) we argue—as previously shown in [14]—that traits are a nice fit instead. Finally (in Sect. 3.3), we show how deltas and traits can be used in collaboration to smoothly integrate intra- as well as inter-product code reuse.

3.1   Motivating Traits

In the previous subsection we used deltas to construct three variants of the Account class: the base product, one with a feature that allows saving with interest, and one with a feature allowing overdraft. One can also imagine that a bank wants to have all these variants available at the same time to satisfy different client needs. The result would be three very similar classes Account, AccountSaving and AccountOverdraft: in this case, intra-product code reuse would be highly useful to avoid the duplication of the common parts of the three classes.

Deltas, however, cannot implement intra-product code reuse: by design, they associate each delta operation to one class, and it is thus impossible to use them to add the same code to different classes. Instead, traits, discussed in Sect. 3.2, are a well-known and very flexible approach for factoring out code shared by several classes. Moreover, in Sect. 3.3, we will illustrate our novel approach for combing deltas and traits, which exploits traits also for *inter-delta* code reuse (i.e., code reuse across different deltas and the base program).

---

[3] ABS uses *parameterized deltas* to manage feature parameters, which we do not include in our language to keep it as simple as possible.

3.2   FTABS: Adding Traits to FABS

Historically, traits and deltas were developed independently from each other in different communities (traits in the OOP community, deltas in the context of SPL). Accordingly, they are usually presented in quite different styles with different notational conventions. Perhaps for these reasons, the surprisingly close analogies between traits and deltas have so far not been pointed out.

Traits are structurally simpler than deltas, because (i) they are declared independently of classes and interfaces and (ii) they satisfy the so called *flattening* principle [26], which states that each trait declaration just introduces a name for a set of methods and using a trait in a class declaration is the same as declaring the associated methods in the body of the class. Traits can be composed using operators[4] (where the first argument is always a trait) such as: (i) disjoint sum (taking as second argument a trait having method names disjoint with those of the first argument, resulting in a new trait that is their union); (ii) override (similar, but the methods in the second argument override those in the first); (iii) method exclusion (the second argument is a method name that is removed from the resulting trait); (iv) method alias (which duplicates a given method by supplying a new name).

The crucial observation is that these composition operators, except method aliasing, are present in the class-modify operation of deltas as well (where they have as implicit first argument the set of methods in the modified class): disjoint sum (with a singleton set of methods as second argument) corresponds to `adds`, overriding to `modifies` (without `original`),[5] method exclusion to `removes`.

We show in Fig. 6 our extension of FABS with traits. A program with traits *PT* is a finite number of trait declarations *TD* with an FABS program *P* using these traits. A trait is declared with the keyword `trait`, given a name `t`, and defined by a trait expression *TE*. A trait expression defines a set of methods by either declaring the methods directly, referencing other traits `t`, or applying a trait operation *TO* to a trait expression. The trait operations are the same as those of deltas, with the exception that `adds` and `modifies` manipulate a set of methods (described by a trait expression *TE*) instead of a single method. Moreover, our `modifies` trait operation is actually an extension of the trait override operation: each overriding method may contain occurrences of the keyword `original` to refer to the implementation of the overridden methods (in the same way as in deltas). In previous proposals of traits in a JAVA-like setting (see [3] for a brief overview) the attributes found in a trait (i.e., fields and methods accessed with `this` in method bodies) are listed in a separate declaration as requirements to classes that will use the trait. Here we adopt the convention from deltas to let requirements implicitly contain all undefined attributes invoked on `this`.

The last production in Fig. 6 overrides the production for attribute declarations in Fig. 1 by extending it with the possibility to import a trait into a class

---

[4] We mention those proposed in the original formulation of traits [14].

[5] To the best of our knowledge, the `original` concept is not present in any formulation of traits in the literature. It can be encoded in traits with aliasing.

and thus make use of it. This latter extension is the *only* change that is necessary in the syntax of FABS classes for them to use traits.

$$
\begin{aligned}
PT &::= \overline{TD}\ P \\
TD &::= \textbf{trait t} \ = \ TE \\
TE &::= \{\ \overline{MD}\ \} \ | \ \textbf{t} \ | \ TE\ TO \\
TO &::= \textbf{adds}\ TE \ | \ \textbf{removes m} \ | \ \textbf{modifies}\ TE \\
AD &::= FD \ | \ MD \ \boxed{| \ \textbf{uses}\ TE}
\end{aligned}
$$

Fig. 6. FTABS syntax: productions to be added to Fig. 1—the last production overrides the production in the last line of Fig. 1 (the differences are highlighted in gray)

In Fig. 7 we illustrate traits in FTABS with a new implementation of the `Account` class that uses a trait `tUpdate` that can be shared by classes `AccountSaving` and `AccountOverdraft`. The trait defines an `update` method which performs an unconditional update of the account's balance. The trait `tUpdate` is then re-used by the three different classes to define their `withdraw` method.

```
trait tUpdate = {
  Int update(Int amount) {
    // this assignment is in reality a complex database transaction:
    balance = balance+amount;
  }
}
class Account() implements IAccount {
  uses tUpdate
  Int withdraw(Int amount) {
    if (balance-amount >= 0) update(-amount);
    return balance;
  }
}
```

Fig. 7. The `tUpdate` trait and the refactored `Account` class in FTABS

3.3   FDTABS: Combining Traits and Deltas

Our chosen style of declaration for traits makes it extremely simple to combine traits and deltas without the need to introduce further keywords and with merely one change in one syntax rule. The key observation is that the production rule for trait operations TO in Fig. 6 and the one for delta operations on methods in Fig. 3 (final three slots in rule for AO) are identical, with the small exception that the `adds` and `modifies` trait operations work on a set of methods (described by a trait expression TE) instead of a single method. Hence, we can unify trait and delta operations by simply replacing delta operations on methods by trait operations. We present the full grammar of the resulting language in Fig. 8.

The desired effect of extending attribute operations to include trait operations is that we can now use traits and trait operations for the declaration of *deltas*, thereby supporting also intra- and inter-*delta* code reuse. It is worth to observe that trait declarations are not part of the base program, i.e., traits are not provided by the base language (the language in which each variant is written)—therefore, deltas are not able to modify trait declarations and **uses** clauses in classes. Our design decision is to provide traits as a construct to enabling code reuse in FDABS in the base program *as well as* in deltas. The alternative design choice of adding deltas to a base language that provides traits [13] is briefly discussed below in Sect. 7.

$$
\begin{array}{ll}
L & ::= \mathcal{M} \, \mathcal{K} \; \boxed{TD} \; \overline{\Delta} \; P \\
P & ::= \overline{ID} \; \overline{CD} \\
ID & ::= \texttt{interface I } [\texttt{extends } \overline{\texttt{I}}] \; \{ \; \overline{HD} \; \} \\
CD & ::= \texttt{class C } [\texttt{implements } \overline{\texttt{I}}] \; \{ \; \overline{AD} \; \}
\end{array}
$$

$$
\begin{array}{ll}
AD & ::= FD \; | \; MD \; | \; \texttt{uses } TE \\
FD & ::= \texttt{I f} \\
HD & ::= \texttt{I m}(\overline{\texttt{I x}}) \\
MD & ::= HD \; \{ \; \overline{s} \; \texttt{return } e; \; \}
\end{array}
$$

$$
\begin{array}{ll}
TD & ::= \texttt{trait t } = \; TE \\
TE & ::= \{ \; \overline{MD} \; \} \; | \; \texttt{t} \; | \; TE \; TO \\
TO & ::= \texttt{adds } TE \; | \; \texttt{removes m} \; | \; \texttt{modifies } TE
\end{array}
$$

$$
\begin{array}{ll}
\Delta & ::= \texttt{delta d } \{ \overline{IO} \; \overline{CO} \; \} \\
IO & ::= \texttt{adds } ID \; | \; \texttt{removes I} \; | \; \texttt{modifies I } [\texttt{extends } \overline{\texttt{I}}] \; \{ \; \overline{HO} \; \} \\
HO & ::= \texttt{adds } HD \; | \; \texttt{removes m} \\
CO & ::= \texttt{adds } CD \; | \; \texttt{removes C} \; | \; \texttt{modifies C } [\texttt{implements } \overline{\texttt{I}}] \; \{ \; \overline{AO} \; \} \\
AO & ::= \texttt{adds } FD \; | \; \texttt{removes f} \; | \; TO
\end{array}
$$

Fig. 8. FDTABS syntax (differences to FDABS syntax in Fig. 3 are highlighted)

We illustrate the capabilities of the FDTABS language with the refactored dOverdraft delta in Fig. 9. Observe that dOverdraft does not have to add the trait tUpdate, because it was already used in the base product as shown in Fig. 7. We achieved the maximal possible degree of reuse, because the method header of withdraw and the changed guard in its body must be repeated in any case.

The capability to use traits inside deltas is a powerful tool to describe cross-cutting feature implementations in a succinct manner. Assume we want to add a logging feature as illustrated in the feature diagram on the right (ABS permits multi-feature diagrams, i.e., orthogonal feature hierarchies). To implement logging we create a delta that adds a suitable method call to update. Since the latter is defined as a trait, we can use trait composition. First we declare a trait tUpdateLog that uses trait tUpdate, adds a logger and suitably modifies the original update method, see Fig. 10. Please observe that the **original** keyword (which, to the best of our knowledge, is not present in other formulation

```
delta dOverdraft {
  modifies Account {
    adds Int limit;
    adds Unit setLimit(Int value) { limit = value; }
    modifies Int withdraw(Int amount) {
      if (balance-amount+limit >= 0) update(-amount);
      return balance;
    }
  }
}
```

Fig. 9. Refactored dOverdraft delta

```
trait tUpdateLog = tUpdate
  adds { Unit log(Int value) { ... } } // logging facility
  modifies { Int update(Int amount) {
               original(amount);
               log(amount);
             }
           }
delta dLogging {
  modifies Account {
    removes update
    adds tUpdateLog
  }
}
```

Fig. 10. Using traits inside deltas

of traits) can be used in the same manner within traits as within deltas to refer to the most recent implementation. The delta that realizes logging now simply removes the old version of the obsolete update method and adds the new trait. This has to be done for each class, where the new trait is to be used, but that is intentional: for example, logging might not be desired to take place in each call of update throughout the whole product. This is in line with the general design philosophy of ABS-based languages that code changes should be specified extensionally (in contrast to aspect-oriented programming, for example) to facilitate code comprehension and analysis.

4 Semantics

We present the formal semantics of the FDTABS language. The *artifact base* *AB* of an SPL consists of its traits, deltas and base program. Given a specific product to generate, the semantics eliminates from the artifact base all traits and deltas to produce an FABS program corresponding to the specified product (in particular, first eliminating all traits produces an FDABS program). For simplicity, we suppose in our presentation that all the deltas that do not take part in the generation of the chosen product have already been removed from the artifact base and that all the remaining deltas have been sorted following the partial order in the configuration knowledge $\mathcal{K}$. This initial step is standard in DOP [4] and allows us to focus on the semantics of traits and delta operations.

4.1   Semantics of Traits

We structure the semantics of traits, shown in Fig. 11, into two rule sets. The first set formalizes the intuitive semantics of trait operations. This semantics uses the *name* function which retrieves the name of a method. We extend that notation and, given a sequence of field and method declarations $\overline{AD}$, also use $name(\overline{AD})$ to obtain the names of the fields and methods declared in $\overline{AD}$. Rule (T:ADDS) states that the `adds` operation combines two sets of methods that have no name in common. Rule (T:REMS) removes a method only if it exists in the given set of methods. Finally, rule (T:MODS) implements the modification of a set of methods. It replaces existing methods MD_i with new implementations MD'_i. The latter, however, may refer to the most recent implementation with references to `original` which our semantics inlines.

$$
\text{T:ADDS} \quad \frac{name(\overline{MD}) \cap name(\overline{MD'}) = \emptyset}{\{\ \overline{MD}\ \}\ \texttt{adds}\ \{\ \overline{MD'}\ \}\ \triangleright\ \{\ \overline{MD}\ \overline{MD'}\ \}}
$$

$$
\text{T:REMS} \quad \frac{name(MD) = \texttt{m}}{\{\ MD\ \overline{MD}\ \}\ \texttt{removes}\ \texttt{m}\ \triangleright\ \{\ \overline{MD}\ \}}
$$

$$
\text{T:MODS} \quad \frac{\forall 1 \le i \le n,\ (MD_i = \texttt{I}\ \texttt{m}_i(\overline{\texttt{I}\ \texttt{x}})\ \{\ \texttt{return}\ e_i;\ \})\ \wedge\ (name(MD'_i) = \texttt{m}_i)}{\{\ MD_1\ \ldots\ MD_n\ \overline{MD}\ \}\ \texttt{modifies}\ \{\ MD'_1\ \ldots\ MD'_n\ \}\ \triangleright\ \{\ MD'_1[^{e_1}/\texttt{original}_{(\overline{x})}]\ \cdots\ MD'_n[^{e_n}/\texttt{original}_{(\overline{x})}]\ \overline{MD}\ \}}
$$

$$
\text{T:TRAIT} \quad (\texttt{trait}\ \texttt{t} = TE\ AB)\ \triangleright\ AB[^{TE}/_{\texttt{t}}]
$$

$$
\text{T:CLASS} \quad \frac{name(\overline{AD}) \cap name(\overline{MD}) = \emptyset}{\texttt{class}\ \texttt{c}\ \texttt{implements}\ \overline{\texttt{I}}\ \{\ \overline{AD}\ \texttt{uses}\ \{\overline{MD}\}\ \}\ \triangleright\ \texttt{class}\ \texttt{c}\ \texttt{implements}\ \overline{\texttt{I}}\ \{\ \overline{AD}\ \overline{MD}\ \}}
$$

Fig. 11. Semantics of traits

The second set of rules enforces the flattening principle (cf. Sect. 3.2). Rule (T:TRAIT) eliminates a trait declaration from a program by replacing occurrences of its name by its definition. Finally, rule (T:CLASS) is applicable after the traits operations inside a class have been eliminated and puts the resulting set of method declarations inside the body of the class, provided that there is no name clash.

4.2   Semantics of Deltas

Due to the large number of operations a delta may contain, we split the set or reduction rules in three parts. The first part, in Fig. 12, presents the simplest elements of the semantics of deltas, which applies in sequence all the operations contained in a delta. Rule (D:EMPTY) is applicable when a delta does not contain any operation to execute: the delta is simply deleted. Rules (D:INTER)/(D:CLASS) extract the first interface/class operation from the delta and apply it to the full artifact base (denoted $AB \bullet IO/AB \bullet CO$).

$$\text{D:EMPTY} \atop \textbf{delta } d \ \{\ \} \ AB \rhd AB$$

D:INTER
$$\frac{AB = (\textbf{delta } d \ \{\ IO \ \overline{IO} \ \overline{CO} \ \} \ AB'}{AB \rhd (\textbf{delta } d \ \{\ \overline{IO} \ \overline{CO} \ \} \ AB') \bullet IO}$$

D:CLASS
$$\frac{AB = (\textbf{delta } d \ \{\ CO \ \overline{CO} \ \} \ AB')}{AB \rhd (\textbf{delta } d \ \{\ \overline{CO} \ \} \ AB') \bullet CO}$$

D:ADDSI
$$\frac{name(ID) \notin name(AB)}{AB \bullet (\textbf{adds } ID) \rhd ID \ AB}$$

D:REMSI
$$\frac{name(ID) = \text{I}}{(ID \ AB) \bullet (\textbf{removes } \text{I}) \rhd AB}$$

D:ADDSC
$$\frac{name(CD) \notin name(AB)}{AB \bullet (\textbf{adds } CD) \rhd CD \ AB}$$

D:REMSC
$$\frac{name(CD) = \text{C}}{(CD \ AB) \bullet (\textbf{removes } \text{C}) \rhd AB}$$

Fig. 12. Semantics of deltas: top-level

In case when the interface operation is the addition of an interface (rule (D:ADDSI)), the specified interface is added to the artifact base AB, provided that it was not already declared. In case the interface operation is the removal of an interface I, the interface with that name is extracted from the artifact base and deleted (rule (D:REMSI)). The addition and removal of classes is similar.

The rules for modifying interfaces and classes are shown in Figs. 13 & 14. The structure of these rules is similar to the ones for deltas, in the sense that they apply in order all the operations contained in the modification. Rule

D:I:EMPTY
$$(\textbf{interface } \text{I } \textbf{extends } \overline{\text{I}} \ \{\ \overline{HD} \ \} \ AB) \bullet (\textbf{modifies } \text{I } \{\ \})$$
$$\rhd \textbf{interface } \text{I } \textbf{extends } \overline{\text{I}} \ \{\ \overline{HD} \ \} \ AB$$

D:I:ADDS
$$\frac{name(HD) \notin name(\overline{HD})}{(\textbf{interface } \text{I } \textbf{extends } \overline{\text{I}} \ \{\ \overline{HD} \ \} \ AB) \bullet (\textbf{modifies } \text{I } \{\ (\textbf{adds } HD) \ \overline{HO} \ \})}$$
$$\rhd (\textbf{interface } \text{I } \textbf{extends } \overline{\text{I}} \ \{\ HD \ \overline{HD} \ \} \ AB) \bullet (\textbf{modifies } \text{I } \{\ \overline{HO} \ \})$$

D:I:REMS
$$\frac{name(HD) = \text{m}}{(\textbf{interface } \text{I } \textbf{extends } \overline{\text{I}} \ \{\ HD \ \overline{HD} \ \} \ AB) \bullet (\textbf{modifies } \text{I } \{\ (\textbf{removes } \text{m}) \ \overline{HO} \ \})}$$
$$\rhd (\textbf{interface } \text{I } \textbf{extends } \overline{\text{I}} \ \{\ \overline{HD} \ \} \ AB) \bullet (\textbf{modifies } \text{I } \{\ \overline{HO} \ \})$$

D:I:EXTENDS
$$(\textbf{interface } \text{I } \textbf{extends } \overline{\text{I}} \ \{\ \overline{HD} \ \} \ AB) \bullet (\textbf{modifies } \text{I } \textbf{extends } \overline{\text{I}}' \ \{\ \overline{HO} \ \})$$
$$\rhd (\textbf{interface } \text{I } \textbf{extends } \overline{\text{I}}' \ \{\ \overline{HD} \ \} \ AB) \bullet (\textbf{modifies } \text{I } \{\ \overline{HO} \ \})$$

Fig. 13. Semantics of deltas: interface modification

D:C:Empty
$$(\texttt{class}\ \texttt{C}\ \texttt{implements}\ \overline{\texttt{I}}\ \{\ \overline{AD}\ \}\ AB)\bullet(\texttt{modifies}\ \texttt{C}\ \{\ \})$$
$$\rhd\ \texttt{class}\ \texttt{C}\ \texttt{implements}\ \overline{\texttt{I}}\ \{\ \overline{AD}\ \}\ AB$$

D:C:AddsF
$$\frac{name(FD)\not\in name(\overline{AD})}{(\texttt{class}\ \texttt{C}\ \texttt{implements}\ \overline{\texttt{I}}\ \{\ \overline{AD}\ \}\ AB)\bullet(\texttt{modifies}\ \texttt{C}\ \{\ (\texttt{adds}\ FD)\ \overline{AO}\ \})}$$
$$\rhd\ (\texttt{class}\ \texttt{C}\ \texttt{implements}\ \overline{\texttt{I}}\ \{\ FD\ \overline{AD}\ \}\ AB)\bullet(\texttt{modifies}\ \texttt{C}\ \{\ \overline{AO}\ \})$$

D:C:RemsF
$$\frac{name(FD)=\texttt{f}}{(\texttt{class}\ \texttt{C}\ \texttt{implements}\ \overline{\texttt{I}}\ \{\ FD\ \overline{AD}\ \}\ AB)\bullet(\texttt{modifies}\ \texttt{C}\ \{\ (\texttt{removes}\ \texttt{f})\ \overline{AO}\ \})}$$
$$\rhd\ (\texttt{class}\ \texttt{C}\ \texttt{implements}\ \overline{\texttt{I}}\ \{\ \overline{AD}\ \}\ AB)\bullet(\texttt{modifies}\ \texttt{C}\ \{\ \overline{AO}\ \})$$

D:C:Trait
$$(\texttt{class}\ \texttt{C}\ \texttt{implements}\ \overline{\texttt{I}}\ \{\ \overline{FD}\ \overline{MD}\ \}\ AB)\bullet(\texttt{modifies}\ \texttt{C}\ \{\ TO\ \overline{AO}\ \})$$
$$\rhd\ (\texttt{class}\ \texttt{C}\ \texttt{implements}\ \overline{\texttt{I}}\ \{\ \overline{FD}\ (\texttt{adds}\ \{\ \overline{MD}\ \}\ TO)\ \}\ AB)\bullet(\texttt{modifies}\ \texttt{C}\ \{\ \overline{AO}\ \})$$

D:C:Extends
$$(\texttt{class}\ \texttt{C}\ \texttt{implements}\ \overline{\texttt{I}}\ \{\ \overline{AD}\ \}\ AB)\bullet(\texttt{modifies}\ \texttt{C}\ \texttt{implements}\ \overline{\texttt{I}'}\ \{\ \overline{AO}\ \})$$
$$\rhd\ (\texttt{class}\ \texttt{C}\ \texttt{implements}\ \overline{\texttt{I}'}\ \{\ \overline{AD}\ \}\ AB)\bullet(\texttt{modifies}\ \texttt{C}\ \{\ \overline{AO}\ \})$$

Fig. 14. Semantics of deltas: class modification

(D:I:Empty) is applicable when no further modification is requested on the given interface, so that the result is the interface itself. Rule (D:I:Adds) adds the specified method header to the interface (provided that no header with this name is already present in the interface). Rule (D:I:Rems) removes an existing method header from the interface. Finally, rule (D:I:Extends) is applicable when a modification of the **extends** clause is requested, in which case that clause is entirely replaced with the set specified in the modification.

The rules for class modification in Fig. 14 are very similar to the ones for interfaces, with two exceptions: first, manipulation (**adds** and **removes**) of method headers is replaced by manipulation of fields (rules (D:C:AddsF) and (D:C:RemsF)); second, class operations also include trait operations to modify their method set. Rule (D:C:Trait) applies a trait operation contained in a delta to the given class simply by applying it to its set of methods.

5 Integration into the ABS Tool Chain

We implemented our approach as a part of the ABS compiler tool chain, as illustrated in Fig. 15. The tool chain is structured as a pipeline of three components. The *parser* takes as its input an ABS program composed of a set of ABS files, and produces an extended Abstract Syntax Tree (AST) corresponding to that program. The *rewriter* is the component responsible for generating the variant corresponding to the selected features. This is done by applying in order the various deltas required by the selected features: the result is a *core* AST which does not contain any deltas. The core AST can then be analyzed by different tools developed for the ABS language [8]. It can also be executed using one of the ABS code generation backends [7,19,35].

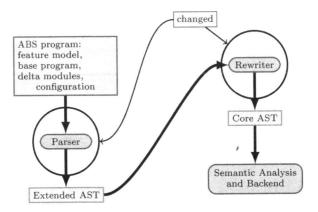

Fig. 15. Structure of the ABS compiler tool chain

The integration of traits and deltas, motivated and discussed in the previous sections, was implemented in the ABS compiler tool chain by modifying the parser and the rewriter components. We stress that, unlike in the previous sections, the implementation is based not merely on FABS, but on the complete core ABS language [20]. The parser was extended with the new syntax for traits, and with the new elements in the delta and class syntax (deltas may use trait operations, classes can use traits). The changes in the rewriter mostly concern the semantics of deltas that now include trait operations. Moreover, the extended rewriter eliminates traits in classes and deltas (as in Sect. 4.1): the rewriter now first eliminates all the traits declared in a program, then it applies the activated deltas to generate a core AST as before.

The trait extension of ABS is designed to be syntactically and semantically conservative, i.e., it is backward compatible: legacy ABS code produces the same result as before with the extended parser and rewriter. Moreover, as the rewriter still generates a core AST, none of the existing analysis tools and code generation backends for ABS need to be updated. They can correctly analyse and execute any ABS program with traits.

Our implementation performs some checks on the input program to make sure that traits and deltas are well-formed. First, it ensures that any call to `original` is performed inside a `modifies` trait operation. Second, it controls the validity of the `removes` operation, i.e., an error is raised if "`removes m`" is performed on a set of methods or a class that does not contain `m`. Third, it controls that traits do not contain circular definitions. The remaining well-formedness checks for traits and deltas are delegated to the ABS type system. For instance, if a method is added twice, or if method is called that is not part of the class after all deltas and traits have been applied, then standard ABS type checking will detect that during semantic analysis of the generated core AST.

6 Using Deltas and Traits in an Industrial Case Study

We adapted the FORMBAR [16] case study modelling railway operations[6] to use traits. Among other aspects, FORMBAR models components and rules of operation of a railway infrastructure in a precise and comprehensive manner. It is to date the largest ABS model with currently ca. 2600 LoC. Deltas contribute 830 LoC and are used to model different scenarios for simulation.

Due to the large number of different track elements and model ranges for these infrastructure elements, deltas are used for *variability management* [17]: Deltas are able to describe different types of track components which then can be added to a scenario. Traits, on the other hand, are used to encapsulate aspects or behavior of track elements shared by the core railway operations model. The following trait, for example, encapsulates that a track element transmits no information to the rear end of a train:

```
trait NoRear =
 { Info triggerRear(TrainId train, Edge e){ return NoInfo; } }
```

We use traits in two situations: as ABS does not have class-based inheritance, we declare at least one trait for each interface that is implemented multiple times and use it in the implementing classes. The trait in Fig. 16 is used in three different classes (only one of which is shown) that implement different components of a signal: the methods declared in the trait encapsulate the inner signal state. The NoRear trait is used in a different scenario: It does not accompany an interface and, hence, is not used in all classes implementing an interface, but only in a subset that shares behavior, but is not distinguished by type.

```
trait Sig = {
  [Atomic] Unit setSignal(Signal sig){ this.s = sig; }
  SignalState getState() { return this.state; }
  Unit setState (SignalState nState, Time t){ this.state = nState;}
}
interface TrackElement { ... }
interface MainSignal extends TrackElement { ... }
class MainSignalImpl implements MainSignal {
  uses Sig;
  ...
}
```

Fig. 16. Usage of traits in the railway case study

In one variant of the railway SPL it is modeled that a signal shows a defect with a certain probability after the main signal is set. The delta in Fig. 17 modifies only one of the classes where trait Sig is used and merely describes the additional behavior, while calling the original method afterwards.

---

[6] The model is available under formbar.raillab.de.

```
delta RandomDefect;
  modifies class TrackElements.MainSignalImpl {
    modifies Unit setState(SignalState nState, Time t) {
      if (random(100) > 95) this.s!defect(t);
      original(nState, t);
  }
}
```

Fig. 17. Usage of a delta with implicit trait in the railway case study

Table 1. Usage statistics of traits in the FORMBAR model

Trait	# methods in trait	# classes where used
Sig	3	3
NoSig	1	5
Block	2	2
NoRear	1	10
NoFront	2	3

The case study is an SPL with 7 features, 7 deltas and 9 products. Table 1 gives statistics on the current usage of traits in the railway study. The ABS model uses five traits with one to three methods each (only one of the traits is currently an extension of another trait and requires trait operations). In the module with 12 classes describing track elements, where 4 of the traits are used, the number of LoC shrinks from 262 to 203 (−22%). Using traits appears to be natural and straightforward for the modeler. It makes the railway model considerably easier to read and to maintain.

7   Related Work and Conclusions

We proposed a combination of traits and deltas in a uniform language framework that stresses the similarities between the composition operators. We have formalized it by means of the minimal language FDTABS, implemented it in the full language as part of the ABS tool chain, and illustrated its applicability in an industrial modeling scenario. The resulting language is a *conservative extension* (syntactically and semantically) of the ABS language.

The commonality between delta and trait operations had not been formally worked out and put to use in the literature so far. Relevant papers on deltas and traits have already been discussed above. In addition we mention some work on using traits to implement software variability and on adding deltas on top of trait-based languages.

Bettini et al. [5] propose to use traits to implement software variability. It is noted in [13] that this way to model variability is less structured that traits, i.e., traits are less suitable than deltas for the purpose. Lopez-Herrejon et al. [23]

evaluate five technologies for implementing software variability, including the "trait" construct of SCALA, which is in fact a mixin (see [14] for a detailed discussion about the differences between trait and mixins).

Damiani et al. [13] address the problem of defining deltas on top of *pure trait-based languages* (languages, where class inheritance is *replaced* by trait composition). The proposal does not permit using traits for inter-delta code reuse. Moreover, it does not exploit the commonalities between deltas and traits. Therefore, it results in a quite complex language, containing a disjoint union of (the operations provided by) deltas and traits. No formal description of the semantics and no implementation are provided.

The flattening semantics given in Sect. 4 allows to smoothly integrate traits into the ABS tool chain (cf. Sect. 5). We plan to improve the integration further by a type checking phase that identifies type errors before flattening traits (building on existing type checking approaches for deltas [4,11,12] and traits [5]).

In our proposal traits are not assumed to be part of the base language: they extend DOP by enabling code reuse in the base program as well as in deltas (see Sect. 3.3). Our proposal to extend DOP with traits can be straightforwardly added on top of languages that, like JAVA, support class-based inheritance: the flattening principle [26] provides a straightforward semantics for using traits in combination with class-based inheritance. In future work we would like to extend DOP for JAVA along these lines and evaluate, by means of case studies, its benefits with respect to the current implementation of DOP for JAVA [21,37].

Acknowledgments. We thank the anonymous reviewers for comments and suggestions for improving the presentation.

References

1. Apel, S., Batory, D.S., Kästner, C., Saake, G.: Feature-Oriented Software Product Lines: Concepts and Implementation. Springer, Heidelberg (2013)
2. Batory, D., Sarvela, J., Rauschmayer, A.: Scaling step-wise refinement. IEEE TSE **30**(6), 355–371 (2004)
3. Bettini, L., Damiani, F.: Generic traits for the Java platform. In: PPPJ, pp. 5–16. ACM (2014)
4. Bettini, L., Damiani, F., Schaefer, I.: Compositional type checking of delta-oriented software product lines. Acta Informatica **50**(2), 77–122 (2013)
5. Bettini, L., Damiani, F., Schaefer, I.: Implementing type-safe software product lines using parametric traits. Sci. Comput. Program. **97**, 282–308 (2015). Part 3
6. Bettini, L., Damiani, F., Schaefer, I., Strocco, F.: TraitRecordJ: a programming language with traits and records. Sci. Comput. Program. **78**(5), 521–541 (2013)
7. Bezirgiannis, N., de Boer, F.: ABS: a high-level modeling language for cloud-aware programming. In: Freivalds, R.M., Engels, G., Catania, B. (eds.) SOFSEM 2016. LNCS, vol. 9587, pp. 433–444. Springer, Heidelberg (2016). doi:10.1007/978-3-662-49192-8_35
8. Bubel, R., Flores Montoya, A., Hähnle, R.: Analysis of executable software models. In: Bernardo, M., Damiani, F., Hähnle, R., Johnsen, E.B., Schaefer, I. (eds.) SFM 2014. LNCS, vol. 8483, pp. 1–25. Springer, Cham (2014). doi:10.1007/978-3-319-07317-0_1

9. Cassou, D., Ducasse, S., Wuyts, R.: Traits at work: the design of a new trait-based stream library. Comput. Lang. Syst. Struct. **35**(1), 2–20 (2009)

10. Clarke, D., Diakov, N., Hähnle, R., Johnsen, E.B., Schaefer, I., Schäfer, J., Schlatte, R., Wong, P.Y.H.: Modeling spatial and temporal variability with the HATS abstract behavioral modeling language. In: Bernardo, M., Issarny, V. (eds.) SFM 2011. LNCS, vol. 6659, pp. 417–457. Springer, Heidelberg (2011). doi:10.1007/978-3-642-21455-4_13

11. Damiani, F., Lienhardt, M.: On type checking delta-oriented product lines. In: Ábrahám, E., Huisman, M. (eds.) IFM 2016. LNCS, vol. 9681, pp. 47–62. Springer, Cham (2016). doi:10.1007/978-3-319-33693-0_4

12. Damiani, F., Schaefer, I.: Family-based analysis of type safety for delta-oriented software product lines. In: Margaria, T., Steffen, B. (eds.) ISoLA 2012. LNCS, vol. 7609, pp. 193–207. Springer, Heidelberg (2012). doi:10.1007/978-3-642-34026-0_15

13. Damiani, F., Schaefer, I., Schuster, S., Winkelmann, T.: Delta-trait programming of software product lines. In: Margaria, T., Steffen, B. (eds.) ISoLA 2014. LNCS, vol. 8802, pp. 289–303. Springer, Heidelberg (2014). doi:10.1007/978-3-662-45234-9_21

14. Ducasse, S., Nierstrasz, O., Schärli, N., Wuyts, R., Black, A.P.: Traits: a mechanism for fine-grained reuse. ACM Trans. Program. Lang. Syst. **28**(2), 331–388 (2006)

15. Evaluation of Core Framework. Deliverable 5.2 of project FP7-231620 (HATS), August 2010. http://www.hats-project.eu

16. Kamburjan, E., Hähnle, R.: Uniform modeling of railway operations. In: Artho, C., Ölveczky, P. (eds.) FTSCS 2016. CCIS, vol. 694, pp. 55–71. Springer, Cham (2016). doi:10.1007/978-3-319-53946-1_4

17. Hähnle, R., Muschevici, R.: Towards incremental validation of railway systems. In: Margaria, T., Steffen, B. (eds.) ISoLA 2016. LNCS, vol. 9953, pp. 433–446. Springer, Cham (2016). doi:10.1007/978-3-319-47169-3_36

18. Helvensteijn, M., Muschevici, R., Wong, P.: Delta modeling in practice, a Fredhopper case study. In: 6th International Workshop on Variability Modelling of Software-intensive Systems, Leipzig, Germany. ACM (2012)

19. Henrio, L., Rochas, J.: From modelling to systematic deployment of distributed active objects. In: Lluch Lafuente, A., Proença, J. (eds.) COORDINATION 2016. LNCS, vol. 9686, pp. 208–226. Springer, Cham (2016). doi:10.1007/978-3-319-39519-7_13

20. Johnsen, E.B., Hähnle, R., Schäfer, J., Schlatte, R., Steffen, M.: ABS: a core language for abstract behavioral specification. In: Aichernig, B.K., Boer, F.S., Bonsangue, M.M. (eds.) FMCO 2010. LNCS, vol. 6957, pp. 142–164. Springer, Heidelberg (2011). doi:10.1007/978-3-642-25271-6_8

21. Koscielny, J., Holthusen, S., Schaefer, I., Schulze, S., Bettini, L., Damiani, F.: DeltaJ 1.5: delta-oriented programming for Java 1.5. In: PPPJ, pp. 63–74. ACM (2014)

22. Liquori, L., Spiwack, A.: Feathertrait: a modest extension of featherweight java. ACM Trans. Program. Lang. Syst. **30**(2), 11:1–11:32 (2008)

23. Lopez-Herrejon, R.E., Batory, D., Cook, W.: Evaluating support for features in advanced modularization technologies. In: Black, A.P. (ed.) ECOOP 2005. LNCS, vol. 3586, pp. 169–194. Springer, Heidelberg (2005). doi:10.1007/11531142_8

24. Mikhajlov, L., Sekerinski, E.: A study of the fragile base class problem. In: Jul, E. (ed.) ECOOP 1998. LNCS, vol. 1445, pp. 355–382. Springer, Heidelberg (1998). doi:10.1007/BFb0054099

25. Murphy-Hill, E.R., Quitslund, P.J., Black, A.P.: Removing duplication from java.io: a case study using traits. In: Companion 20th ACM SIGPLAN Conference on Object-Oriented Programming, Systems, Languages, and Applications, OOPSLA, pp. 282–291. ACM (2005)

26. Nierstrasz, O., Ducasse, S., Schärli, N.: Flattening traits. J. Object Technol. **5**(4), 129–148 (2006)

27. Pohl, K., Böckle, G., Van Der Linden, F.: Software Product Line Engineering: Foundations, Principles, and Techniques. Springer, Heidelberg (2005)

28. Quitslund, P.J., Murphy-Hill, R., Black, A.P.: Supporting java traits in eclipse. In: OOPSLA Workshop on Eclipse Technology eXchange, ETX, pp. 37–41. ACM (2004)

29. Reppy, J., Turon, A.: Metaprogramming with traits. In: Ernst, E. (ed.) ECOOP 2007. LNCS, vol. 4609, pp. 373–398. Springer, Heidelberg (2007). doi:10.1007/978-3-540-73589-2_18

30. Resource-aware Modeling of the ENG Case Study. Deliverable 4.4.2 of project FP7-610582 (Envisage), July 2015. http://www.envisage-project.eu

31. Schaefer, I., Bettini, L., Bono, V., Damiani, F., Tanzarella, N.: Delta-oriented programming of software product lines. In: Bosch, J., Lee, J. (eds.) SPLC 2010. LNCS, vol. 6287, pp. 77–91. Springer, Heidelberg (2010). doi:10.1007/978-3-642-15579-6_6

32. Schaefer, I., Damiani, F.: Pure delta-oriented programming. In: Proceedings of the 2nd International Workshop on Feature-Oriented Software Development, FOSD, pp. 49–56. ACM (2010)

33. Schaefer, I., Rabiser, R., Clarke, D., Bettini, L., Benavides, D., Botterweck, G., Pathak, A., Trujillo, S., Villela, K.: Software diversity: state of the art and perspectives. J. Softw. Tools Technol. Transf. **14**(5), 477–495 (2012)

34. Schärli, N., Ducasse, S., Nierstrasz, O., Black, A.P.: Traits: composable units of behaviour. In: Cardelli, L. (ed.) ECOOP 2003. LNCS, vol. 2743, pp. 248–274. Springer, Heidelberg (2003). doi:10.1007/978-3-540-45070-2_12

35. Serbanescu, V., Azadbakht, K., de Boer, F.S., Nagarajagowda, C., Nobakht, B.: A design pattern for optimizations in data intensive applications using ABS and Java 8. Concurrency Comput. Pract. Experience **28**(2), 374–385 (2016)

36. Smith, C., Drossopoulou, S.: *Chai*: traits for java-like languages. In: Black, A.P. (ed.) ECOOP 2005. LNCS, vol. 3586, pp. 453–478. Springer, Heidelberg (2005). doi:10.1007/11531142_20

37. Winkelmann, T., Koscielny, J., Seidl, C., Schuster, S., Damiani, F., Schaefer, I.: Parametric DeltaJ 1.5: propagating feature attributes into implementation artifacts. In: Workshops Software Engineering. CEUR Workshop Proceedings, vol. 1559, pp. 40–54. CEUR-WS.org (2016)

Author Index

Printed in the United States
By Bookmasters